Courtship, Marriage, and the Family

THIRD EDITION

ROBERT K. KELLEY

FULLERTON COLLEGE

Courtship, Marriage, and the Family

THIRD EDITION

Harcourt Brace Jovanovich, Inc.
NEW YORK SAN DIEGO CHICAGO SAN FRANCISCO ATLANTA

Cover art by Anna Kopczynski

ISBN: 0-15-515338-2

Library of Congress Catalog Card Number: 78-78166

Printed in the United States of America

Picture credits appear on page 639, which constitutes a continuation of the copyright page.

Preface

The third edition of *Courtship, Marriage, and the Family* marks another step forward in our evaluation of the emerging trends in American society and in marriage and family life in particular. In order to understand the process of change in our society, we need to recognize how it affects us as individuals, as members of families, and as members of the world community.

To this end, the third edition compares traditional family patterns with the new options available to men and women, both as individuals and as partners. It focuses on the changing roles of men and women within and outside of marriage, the challenge of the two-career family, and the search for the family's place as an integral part of society. A new chapter on family crises examines the different stresses that can threaten the solidarity of the family unit and offers guidance on how to deal with these problems. Research data on marriage, alternatives to marriage, the two-career family, birth control methods, divorce, and other aspects of family life have been updated throughout the text.

Young adults who are seriously considering their present relationships and their own status as potential marriage partners must consider several basic questions. First, "Who am I? How can I know myself and define my own values?" Second, "What lifestyle should I choose for myself? Can I be satisfied with a stable, conventional lifestyle, one similar to my parents'? Or should I strike out on my own, be independent, find new norms, ideals, values, and ways of living?" Third, "If I do decide to marry or to enter a long-term relationship with one particular person, how can I evaluate that partnership?" And finally, "If I do marry—either my present partner or some other—what may I reasonably expect married life to be like?"

There are no simple answers to these questions. My own teaching and counseling experience with hundreds of students is that each person must finally discover his or her own answers. Some sociologists might even suggest that it is wiser to sidestep questions involving future lifestyles and values to concentrate only on what has happened in the past and what seems to be happening today. But it has always been my conviction that the study of marriage and the family should be a functional one, that it should help young adults to prepare for marriage and family life as they will know it. We cannot guarantee the course that our society will take, but we must at least attempt to consider what life will be like in the coming decades. Our old prejudices and misconceptions need to be discarded; they will not serve the new generation. This is not to say that all our problems are new or that all the old answers should be forgotten. But it does mean that we must attend to new problems and alternatives as well as to the old—that we must reexamine traditional values as we consider new ones.

My continuing interaction with college students in the five years since the last edition of *Courtship, Marriage, and the Family* is reflected in this new edition. Student discussion groups, research projects, conferences, and counseling have helped me to understand young people's concerns about interpersonal relationships and the hopes and expectations they have for marriage and the family. Student input and the comments and criticisms of colleagues and reviewers have been invaluable. In particular, I would like to thank L. G. Budd, C. L. Englund, and K. L. Zuengler, all of the University of Minnesota, Twin Cities; Thelma Dunn Hansen, Michigan State University; and Dennis K. Orthner, University of North Carolina.

Along with the first and second editions, the third edition has profited from the wise counsel and assistance of the College Department of Harcourt Brace Jovanovich. Everett M. Sims, friend, colleague, and mentor, has kept the goals for this revision in focus throughout the months of preparation and writing. Paula F. Lewis's editing and thought-provoking questions helped to make the final work clear, concise, and well organized. Tina S. Barland has been a patient and accurate copy editor. Designer Anna Kopczynski, art editors Helen Faye and Elaine Bernstein, and production manager Tracy Cabanis all made excellent contributions to the book.

A book about marriage and the family is, in a very real sense, a family production. Certainly this edition continues to reflect the many rewarding family experiences of my own early years, and especially the life I share with my wife Delores and my teenage daughters Faye and Robbin. They continue to be my most stimulating teachers.

ROBERT K. KELLEY

Contents

Part II Patterns in Courtship

Part III The Decision to Marry

Part V The Developing Family

Courtship, Marriage, and the Family

THIRD EDITION

Part I
The Individual and Society

1 The Quest for Identity

- How can I find myself in today's society?
- How can I measure my growth and self-development?
- Will marriage help or hinder me in my quest for identity?
- What does it mean to be a self-actualized person?
- What is American society like today?
- Do my personal goals have any relationship to the society I live in?
- What are the priority values of my society?
- How can I establish my own system of values?

The Individual and the Family

A central concern in the study of marriage and the family in America is the nuclear family—husband, wife, and children. This is a natural starting point, although we will certainly want to broaden our study to include the extended family, and to examine the many alternative lifestyles that exist in today's society. But first, it is in the circle of our immediate family that we can discover most about ourselves and about the kind of person we are and will become in the years ahead.

As infants, we are the most helpless of all animals. We must be fed and clothed and protected from danger and the elements. We are "naked apes," without even the warmth of our own fur to protect us. In most cases, children in our society spend the first two years of their lives with their parents, or at least with a single parent. Our early lives are thus strongly influenced by our parents and other significant people who are a part of our everyday environment. There may be brothers and sisters, grandparents, aunts and un-

cles, and cousins. There may be baby sitters, nursery-school or day-care center teachers, or other substitute parents who spend a great deal of time supervising our growth and development. These people are all part of "family" as we know it through our childish viewpoint. All have a part in shaping what we are and will become.

A particular family and a particular environment, however, do not guarantee an exact pattern in our own lives. Two sisters, three years apart in age, may respond very differently to the same family setting. Even identical twins develop special traits and characteristics of their own. This is what makes our own individual "quest for identity" so exciting, although it certainly isn't easy to find oneself in modern society. As adults, we live in an automated, depersonalized world that emphasizes the sameness of things as good. We eat the same foods, listen to the same music on the radio, watch the same TV programs, and glance through the same magazines as many other people. We ride the same subway or drive on the same freeway to the office, college, or plant. Sometimes we feel reduced to a statistic by the IBM number on a college registration card or the ever present Social Security number that traces us down when income taxes are due. No one really seems to care about us as individuals.

One can go on for only so long living in a depersonalized world. Each person has to find some way of asserting his or her identity and of discovering a personal niche in the scheme of things. Because it is extremely difficult to "make a name for yourself" in the larger world, many people emphasize their personal and social lives, building their own circles of friends and their own personal preferences for what to eat, what to wear, and how to spend their leisure time. If a person cannot make much of a dent in the organizations that dominate most of life—big business, big government, big churches, big schools, the mass media—then that person must try to find satisfaction through personal achievement in order not to feel lost. But every person has limits—we cannot all walk on the moon!

Marriage as a Quest for Identity

Is marriage the clearest and simplest solution to the problem of finding one's place in the world? Do two live better than one? Is a relationship with another person the logical alternative to our feeling of alienation in a mass society? By seeking a partner to love and share life with, we establish a realistic goal. We become important to at least one other person. We reach out for such a relationship—almost blindly at times—because it seems such an obvious solution to all our problems. Have you been daydreaming lately about finding the perfect partner in the next year or so, so that you can drop out of college or stop worrying about getting a better job and just settle down into your own private world? Or are you already engaged or married and counting on life to unfold in conformity to your expectations? Don't be too complacent and don't trust that marriage will solve your problems and give you a secure future. Take a careful look at the present, and especially at your own selfhood, before you oversell the future. What kind of person are you, realistically? What kind of background did you come from, and where are you going? If you understand your own quest for identity, your motivations, your social and sexual patterns, and your goals and aspirations, you can make more realistic choices in the realm of courtship, marriage, and family living.

Should you decide to marry, and approach this important decision wisely and thoughtfully, the life you will share with your partner and companion will offer you a genuine chance to enhance your own sense of self-worth and value. We all know that the problems of alienation and depersonalization will not quickly fade away. Marriage is not a magic solution.

Everyone needs to find satisfying and direct ways of expressing personal identity, and such expression is unique for each person. Some students become involved in good works projects. Others prefer to socialize rather than to study. Nonconformism may take one form in the teenage years and another in the twenties. Nonconformism is a part of American history. The earliest settlers were religious nonconformists. Each new generation that headed toward the western frontier was spearheaded by those who did not find conventional society to their liking. The millions of immigrants who

came to this continent to begin a new life were not from the ranks of smug and satisfied society. Many of our greatest inventors, scientists, and intellectuals were nonconformists. The great social movements, such as women's suffrage, trade unionism, and, most recently, civil rights, were led by people that society considered nonconformists.

There are many ways for a person to express individuality and carry forward the quest for self-identity. But one thing is common to all theories of human personality: The development of a strong and mature personality is not a chance occurrence; it is the result of a number of contributing factors that influence a person over a considerable period of time. And development is usually not linear, for human growth often comes in spurts. One factor may be of crucial importance at one stage of development and another a prime influence at a later time; each plays its part in the total picture.

The Influence of Inheritance and Environment

Each man or woman is a unique individual. That individuality has been developed through inheritance and physical and social environments. We all inherit certain basic physical structures from our parents. The widening study of biological inheritance has made it possible for us to identify physical traits that come to us through one parental line or the other and also to recognize congenital diseases and injuries that occur during the prenatal period. Our total inheritance, which is divided approximately evenly between characteristics coming from the mother and those coming from the father, is a major and ever present factor in individual development.

We cannot attempt an exhaustive treatment of biological inheritance here. If you have not had a sound course in biology, psychology, or child development, there are excellent textbooks, covering the subjects in detail, that you can study on your own.[1] In later chapters we will touch on biological inheritance in relation to reproduction.

Any careful study of our biological makeup impresses us immediately with the complexity and distinctiveness of each human being. The sperm of the father and the ovum of the mother each have twenty-three chromosomes, which are merged when conception takes place and life begins. Each of the forty-six chromosomes in the newly formed zygote (fertilized ovum) contains a number of genes. It is almost impossible for two parents ever to pass the same genetic inheritance on to more than one child, since it has been estimated that a single man or woman can produce as many as eight million different genetic combinations. The odds against two identical sperm fertilizing two identical ova are astronomical. The only circumstance that normally produces persons with the same genetic makeup is the development of identical twins (or other multiple births), which happens when a single zygote divides. Although twins occur once in about every eighty-six births in the United States, most of them are fraternal twins—the result of two separate fertilized ova.

Another way to emphasize our biological differences is to reflect that each human organism is composed of trillions of individual cells arranged in countless different combinations. For example, the brain contains some ten billion neurons, and, thus, the possible combinations of thought and response in our gray matter are infinite. A computer wired to make similar responses and store similar material could not compare with our compact and efficient human thinking machine.

Experiences that are a part of our own personal life history also contribute heavily to our individuality. Most Americans move frequently; many college students have lived in from five to twenty homes before entering college. The hometown boy or girl who attends neighborhood schools from kindergarten through high school and then goes to college in the same town is a rarity today. And even within such a fixed pattern there are many alternative environmental factors. There are countless play groups and peer groups, competing church and civic groups, school activities, and family schedules. There are differing contacts and directions from father and mother, grandparents, siblings, and friends. Even identical twins will usually find themselves moving into widely varying patterns of experience as they grow up.

Trying to categorize yourself by simple stereotypes is not the way to dis-

[1]See Ernest R. Hilgard, Richard C. Atkinson, and Rita L. Atkinson, *Introduction to Psychology*, 6th ed. (New York: Harcourt Brace Jovanovich, 1977); Gary Parker et al., *Heredity*, 2nd ed. (Chicago: Educational Methods, 1977); Donald Helms and Jeffrey Turner, *Exploring Child Behavior* (Philadelphia: W. B. Saunders, 1976).

cover who you are. You are not merely an introvert or an extrovert, an aggressive or submissive person, an optimist or a pessimist. You may exhibit some of those traits or tendencies, but the unique way in which you function and react in different situations reflects the many complex inherited and learned patterns that have affected your life from the moment of conception.

Self-Growth: A Continuing Process

You can look at yourself in two basic ways. You may focus your attention on yourself as a distinct, permanently defined individual moving about in a changing world. Some psychologists describe this concept of one's personality as one's self-image. You think of your personality as a static thing and don't really expect any major changes to occur. A second kind of self-image is more flexible. You may see yourself moving forward through life step by step, realizing that you are changing a little with each step and that in twenty years you may be quite different from what you are today. This approach is advocated by a psychologist, the late Gordon W. Allport. In his book *Becoming*, he takes issue with the theories of many modern psychologists that see personality as the stable repository of general characteristics rather than as a constantly changing montage of particulars.

> Personality is less a finished product than a transitive process. While it has some stable features, it is at the same time continually undergoing change. It is this course of change, of becoming, of individuation that is now our special concern.
>
> The first fact that strikes us is . . . the uniqueness of both the process and the product. Each person is an idiom unto himself, an apparent violation of the syntax of the species. An idiom develops in its own peculiar context, and this context must be understood in order to comprehend the idiom. Yet at the same time, idioms are not entirely lawless and arbitrary; indeed they can be known for what they are only by comparing them with the syntax of the species.[2]

Allport calls this conflict between personality as a stable self-image and personality as a process the "dilemma of uniqueness." Psychologists are ready to classify people according to their separate properties—the syntax of the species—but they do not see the person as a whole—the idiom in context. To describe the idiom, Allport coins a new word, the *proprium*, de-

[2]Gordon W. Allport, *Becoming: Basic Considerations for a Psychology of Personality* (New Haven, Conn.: Yale Univ. Press, 1950), p. 19.

fined as "all aspects of personality that make for inward unity." This is our *self,* or *ego.* In it is found the core of personal identity and self-knowledge. Allport sees the proprium as developing in time, and a person's innate or potential disposition to develop in that way as closely linked to experiences of learning and socialization.

Allport's work provides a stimulating insight into the nature of our developing individuality. Reading of personality as process, we might consider ourselves as mere twigs in the stream of life, being swept along by unknown forces with no chance of affecting our course and destination. But is it not more reasonable to conclude that we are *involved* in this crucial process and can have a voice in choosing our own future?

Raymond never knew who his father was, and his mother died when he was three years old. He was placed in a state foster home for care and education. When he became old enough to work, he took a paper route and worked in a market to supplement the small income of his foster family. At age fifteen he was a school dropout and at eighteen he enlisted in the army for four years.

After completing his years in the service, Ray went back to night school to get his high school diploma. He also followed up his interest in athletics, inspired by participation on service teams with excellent coaching and competition. The next spring he developed his first really serious romance—with a young teacher who had moved to a new state to begin her teaching career and who appreciated his interest, his honesty and frankness, and his vibrant masculinity.

That summer Ray realized that new possibilities in life were opening up for him. He wasn't ready for marriage, and his girlfriend had decided to move back to her home state, but he could enter a state college and begin preparing for his own career. An athletic scholarship might pay half or more of his expenses. New voices were beckoning. He had met one wonderful young woman—would there be another? There was the coach who was sure he could make the team and hold his scholarship for four years. There was the teacher who spurred him on to master basic skills that had eluded him through the years. There were the friends who kidded him and challenged him to make the grade. Ray discovered that he could have a voice in charting his own course. He had new confidence in what he would become.[3]

[3]Student report.

Patterns of Self-Growth

The concept of self-development through a succession of stages was one of Sigmund Freud's theories. Freud suggested a psychosexual development from infancy through the adult period, with emphasis on particular crisis periods.[4] Numerous other scholars recognize that we are not the same at every stage in our growth toward maturity.[5]

Because college students and young adults focus so sharply on their own experiences and problems, they may miss the significance of their developmental pattern as a whole. To a certain degree, all college students are and should be strongly egocentric. They need definite ideas of what they hope to attain in the future and how they expect to reach those goals. They need to be independent of family and peers in order to assume full responsibility for their own actions and future life pattern. But it would be foolish for them to ignore all the circumstances that have shaped them and those that will continue to do so. Freedom from parents' control, or even antagonism toward their influence, should not prevent students from realizing that there was a period in their early life when their parents' training and control were at the very center of their growth and development. When they can recognize the way they moved from that early stage of dependence to relative independence, they will be much more capable of following the course they choose for the future.

The recognition of a pattern in the growth of one's personality, then, is important. Instead of thinking primarily in terms of personal interest, a person must learn to think of others to whom he is linked in the family, in the community, or in the wider society of the nation or the world. Only as he builds on a knowledgeable foundation of his past growth and development can he move with confidence toward maturity.

Becoming a Self-Actualizing Person

Contemporary humanistic psychology has focused on our quest for identity in terms of self-actualization, that is, the full development of one's abilities. Abraham Maslow, one of the founders of the Association of Humanistic Psychology, is a leading exponent of this view of people. Maslow postulates a hierarchy of human needs, with *basic physiological needs* as the starting point. We need to maintain our bodies to survive, and much of human existence must be lived on that level. People who are deprived of food or water will

[4]For a good brief summary of Freud's psychoanalytic theory, see Elton B. McNeil and Zick Rubin, *The Psychology of Being Human* (San Francisco: Canfield Press, 1977), pp. 422–29.

[5]For example, Erik H. Erikson, *Childhood and Society*, rev. ed. (New York: Norton, 1964); Robert J. Havighurst, *Developmental Tasks and Education*, 3rd ed. (New York: McKay, 1972); and Bärbel Inhelder and Jean Piaget, *The Growth of Logical Thinking from Childhood to Adolescence*, trans. Anne Parsons and Stanley Milgram (New York: Basic Books, 1958).

be unable to focus their attention on other things until those basic needs are satisfied. This is the lowest level of human existence.

Once the basic physiological needs are taken care of, another set of needs emerges—the *safety needs.* Fear is real and present to the child; he sees a great many things to be afraid of. The child wants his world to be well ordered and predictable. When his desire is met, he can turn his attention to his *belongingness and love needs* (other psychologists have termed this the *need for affiliation*). The interest in sensitivity groups and communal living certainly illustrates the power of these needs.

A higher level of human need is reached with the recognition of *esteem needs.* A person wants to feel well able to meet the challenges in life. He also seeks recognition and status. These needs are most fully met on a realistic level, when a person earns the respect of others and reveals to the world a picture of his true self, rather than on an idealized or false level involving a romanticized self-image.

But the highest need is the *need for self-actualization.* A person must find himself. He must express his inner powers creatively. Of self-actualization, Maslow writes:

> It refers to man's desire for self-fulfillment, namely, to the tendency for him to become actualized in what he is potentially. This tendency might be phrased as the desire to become more and more what one idiosyncratically is, to become everything that one is capable of becoming.[6]

According to Maslow, there are a number of admirable and important traits that characterize self-actualizing people. Such people are realistic in their outlook and accept life with spontaneity and simplicity. They face problems squarely. They do not become so absorbed in their relationships with others that they cannot enjoy privacy and their own autonomous interests. They can appreciate the peak experiences in life that seem to transcend everyday occurrences and reach a mystic level. They are creative, democratic in outlook, able to link their lives with the lives of others, and able to form their own ethical and cultural standards without being overwhelmed by the opinions of others.[7]

Maslow's development of the concept of self-actualization is built on a fascinating study of some of the greatest individuals of our own and past generations. He examined the lives of Abraham Lincoln, Thomas Jefferson, Albert Einstein, Eleanor Roosevelt, Jane Addams, Albert Schweitzer, John Keats, Henry Wadsworth Longfellow, and many others who were prominent achievers in many fields. Maslow believes that scientists have studied ab-

[6]Abraham H. Maslow, *Motivation and Personality,* 2nd ed. (New York: Harper & Row, 1970), p. 46.
[7]Maslow, pp. 153–75.

normal and unsuccessful people too often and consequently have neglected those people who are strong and healthy. They are the ones who will lead us to the course of self-actualization.

> *Self-actualization is intrinsic growth of what is already in the organism, or more accurately of what *is* the organism itself. Just as our tree needs food, sun, water from the environment, so does the person need safety, love, and respect from the social environment. But as in the first case, so also in the second, this is just where real development, i.e., of individuality begins. All trees need sunlight and all human beings need love, and yet, once satiated with these elementary necessities, each tree and each human being proceeds to develop in his own style, uniquely, using these universal necessities to his own private purposes. In a word, development then proceeds from within rather than from without, and paradoxically the highest motive is to be unmotivated and nonstriving, i.e., to behave purely expressively . . . self-actualization is growth-motivated rather than deficiency-motivated. It is a "second naivete," a wise innocence, an "Easy State."[8]

Honest Acceptance of Yourself and Others

*An important way of building your sense of personal identity is to accept yourself and others honestly. This concept is not new, but it has been restated and emphasized by Carl R. Rogers. His nondirective approach to counseling is used by many school counselors, by psychologists in private practice, by members of the clergy, and many others.[9]

Rogers has written a book that is closely related to the theme of this chapter, *On Becoming a Person.* There he indicates the approach he uses in counseling to enable the client to make significant changes in his life pattern. Rogers points out that the counselor first has to look within himself, listen to himself, and come to accept his deepest hidden feelings and thoughts.[10] When he has done this, he is ready to communicate with people and approach them in the same way he approaches himself. He accepts the worth and value of the person who comes to be his client. He tries to understand what the person is like and makes every effort to love and accept him. In that way he not only helps the other person but enriches his own experience.

Rogers has an optimistic view of life: "The facts are friendly." His philosophy and his approach to the important work of counseling have been among the most influential in the field in the last thirty years. His kind of

[8]Maslow, pp. 134–35.

[9]Carl R. Rogers, *Client-Centered Therapy* (Boston: Houghton Mifflin, 1951).

[10]Carl R. Rogers, *On Becoming a Person* (Boston: Houghton Mifflin, 1961), pp. 16–27.

honesty has helped many people who have lost purpose and direction in life to rediscover themselves. It is utilized in the most modern institutions for the rehabilitation of criminals, alcoholics, and drug addicts. In group therapy sessions men and women learn to "take off their masks" and reveal their inner selves. The more normal person will also discover that these two steps, accepting oneself and accepting others, are dynamic and effective in individual development.

There are, however, limitations to the Rogerian method. Not all people are strong enough to respond quickly to a positive, accepting approach. A neurotic person, or one with severe psychotic problems, may not have enough ego strength to respond to words of kindness, encouragement, and help. But for most of us, honest acceptance of ourselves and of others is a doorway to greater personal development and a more adequate self-structure.

Goals to Achieve

Identifying goals and purposes for which to strive also contributes to self-growth. Knowing where we are going and actively seeking to get there has a positive effect on our self-development.

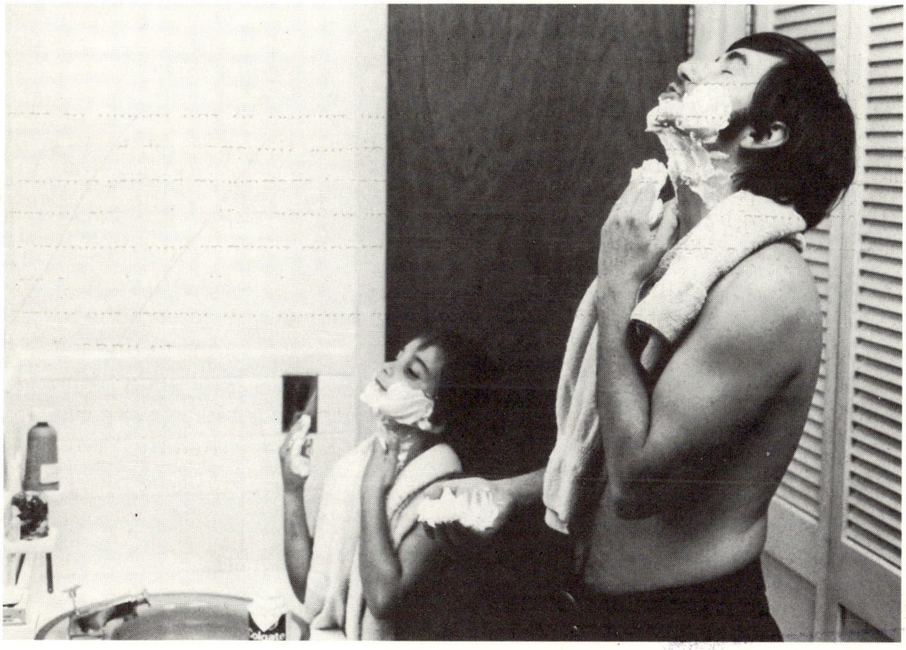

Very early in life we begin to identify with our parents, our siblings, our teachers, and others around us. The normal child passes through a number of stages. Very young children try to emulate what they see their parents doing. Little boys most often imitate their fathers, while little girls copy their mothers. Identification helps us as we grow into maturity; certain aspects of our parents' idealized personalities rub off on us.

In adolescence and young adulthood, we go outside our families, and our hopes for personal achievement direct and motivate us. We want to think and act for ourselves. A young man will set his sights on managing a store or working his way up in a corporation or starting a business of his own. A young woman will seek similar achievements—ones that may have been denied her mother.

In the early years of marriage, the same motivation for achievement is seen in the way we strive to acquire better houses, automobiles, and furniture, or even to make a special mark in the counterculture. Although the accomplishments of many of us are in the end remarkably similar to those of other people in our mass society, our individual sense of worth and uniqueness is still strengthened by the fact that we have thrust ourselves into the struggle and have in some measure reached higher levels of status and achievement.[11]

Finding a Sense of Adequacy

Do we have the resources to meet life's demands? Can we really become growing, sharing, caring, and self-actualizing men and women?

Two American psychologists, Arthur W. Combs and Donald Snygg, interpret the need we have for achievement as the goal of maintaining and making more adequate our phenomenal self, which is defined as "not only a person's physical self but everything he experiences as 'me' at that instant."[12] Other writers have called this the ego, the self-image, the person, or simply the self. Combs and Snygg go on to say:

> From birth to death the maintenance of the phenomenal self is the most pressing, the most crucial, if not the only task of existence. To maintain this personal organization of the self in the universe in which he lives, however, requires of a human being much more than mere survival. Man lives in a changing world . . . [which] requires changes in the organization of the self if it is to be maintained. . . . Because we are aware of the future and must maintain ourselves, in the future as well as in the

[11]See David C. McClelland et al., *The Achievement Motive* (New York: Appleton-Century-Crofts, 1953).

[12]Arthur W. Combs and Donald Snygg, *Individual Behavior—A Perceptual Approach to Behavior* (New York: Harper & Row, 1959), p. 44.

> present, it is necessary to enhance the self against the exigencies of tomorrow. . . . And since the future is uncertain and unknown, no enhancement of the individual's experience of personal value, no degree of self-actualization, is ever enough. Human beings are, by nature, insatiable.
>
> Thus, man seeks not merely the maintenance of a self by the development of an *adequate self*—a self capable of dealing effectively and efficiently with the exigencies of life, both now and in the future.
>
> Though the maintenance and enhancement of the self are two different words, this does not mean that man has two different needs. We express maintenance and enhancement as two different words, but both relate to exactly the same function—the production of a more adequate self.[13]

Our society is vastly different from those of Europe, the Middle East, Polynesia, or South America. To maintain ourselves and our loved ones is not enough. We must be going somewhere! We must become more adequate, more self-confident, and more successful in the eyes of our peers.

The state of the phenomenal self is also crucial to success or failure in marriage. It is not enough to have a fine courtship, a lovely wedding, a cozy little apartment, and a new baby in the family. This is the introduction, but it is not the whole story.

Stuart was a college freshman when he first met Sonya. He had completed most of his first year at a state university; she was a high school senior. They dated steadily through the summer, and in the fall he entered a well-known private college on a scholarship he won through his intellectual and athletic ability. He continued to see Sonya during his sophomore year. She was working as a receptionist and doing part-time film and TV work. The following fall she had an opportunity to appear in some theatrical productions in a large city some distance from home, which was within commuting distance of Stuart's college. She moved to the city, sharing an apartment with two other aspiring young actresses.

At Christmas time Stuart, then twenty, and Sonya, then nineteen, were engaged. When they decided to marry early in March, Stuart gave up his scholarship and had to drop school for the balance of the year in order to support himself and his wife. They moved back to their home town, where Stuart entered a new and speculative business in order to make enough money quickly to reenter school.

[13]Combs and Snygg, p. 45.

One year after marriage their son was born, and Sonya had to give up her career in order to care for the child. She still did some modeling and part-time TV work when her mother was able to babysit. But she never got the most promising opportunities, and her income was limited. Nor did Stuart fare much better. His business was curtailed sharply in a brief recession period, and he saw his hopes of further education growing slimmer and slimmer with increasing family responsibilities. Two years after marriage they separated, and ten months later they were divorced.

These young people had few serious problems maintaining their health, youth, vitality, and self-structure. They were in many ways a "normal" American couple. Stuart was a clean-cut, virile, friendly young man; Sonya was extremely attractive, vivacious, and charming. They were very much "in love." What soured them so quickly on their marriage? They were not going anywhere; they were not advancing themselves. It is encouraging to win a scholarship to a leading college or to be chosen to star in a play. It is frustrating to realize that you have once had those opportunities and that they have slipped away because of home and family responsibilities. Marriage can be wonderful, but it cannot be substituted for goals that have a higher priority to you.

Personal Growth Through Religion

A person can develop a strong sense of self-identity through religious faith and development. Many college students may find this strange because to them religion seems to restrain and deny self-identity rather than encourage it. Religious institutions and teachings are associated with parental control, rigid morality and social structures, and resistance to change. Such a religious framework threatens to destroy, rather than to enhance, their fullest and most creative growth and development.

This negative conclusion is not always valid. Prophetic religion has always struggled against the kind of formalism and legalism that stifles and destroys the human spirit. An Amos or a Jeremiah always found his task more difficult because of the resistance of those whose religion was more outward than inward. Jesus clashed sharply with the religious leaders of his day. The Reformation and Counter-Reformation remind us of a similar conflict in sixteenth-century Europe. Religion seems to be a constant in every human culture. Ninian Smart notes:

> Throughout history and beyond in the dark recesses of men's earliest cultures, religion has been a vital and pervasive feature of human life.

> To understand human history and human life it is necessary to understand religion, and in the contemporary world one must understand other nations' ideologies and faiths in order to grasp the meaning of life as seen from perspectives often very different from our own.
>
> . . .
>
> Altogether, the story of man's religious experience is a rich, strange, sometimes better, often noble one. In his religious life, and in his rejections of religion, man has expressed his deepest attitudes to the universe about him. Through religion, man has worked out these attitudes in a pattern of daily living and dying. Whether he feels himself surrounded by spirits, or guided by God, or striving towards nirvana, the religious man has tried to see beyond his senses. Is it just imagination, or is it a holy power that has enabled him to do so?[14]

Religious experience is often the stimulus to varied means of developing one's sense of personal worth. A vital religious experience can give one a sense of ultimate value and a feeling of relationship to that which he counts most important in the universe. A mature person, as Gordon Allport has suggested, should be open to religious truth and seek to discover his own pathway to spiritual meaning.[15]

A Society of Change

We all need to know something of ourselves. Through self-knowledge and understanding we begin to develop habits, patterns, and goals that set the stage for much of our day-by-day living. Without that self-awareness, and its consequent sense of purpose and direction, our lives may become frustrating and self-defeating.

We must also acknowledge, however, that human existence is essentially social in nature, that our development and achievement as individuals is largely dependent on the stimulus and stability of a satisfying home and social environment. We live in community with others. We must have a realistic understanding of the social context in order to assess individual behavior and motivation accurately. Most young Americans will find their primary orientation somewhere within American society, and they will find too that this is a society with a wide range of options.

Our social environment may also be considered in terms of a number of different nations, races, colors, and cultures. The world is caught up in a

[14]Ninian Smart, *The Religious Experience of Mankind* (New York: Charles Scribner's Sons, 1969), pp. 3, 537.

[15]Gordon W. Allport, *The Individual and His Religion* (New York: Macmillan, 1950).

century of rapid growth and change, revolution and upheaval, space exploration and nuclear confrontation; a century of both hope and fear, of promise and despair, of expanding freedom and opportunity contrasted with alienation and apathy. Every reasonable expectation tells us that even more dramatic changes will occur in the next ten to twenty years. Patterns that seem appropriate today will obviously need to be revised in the future. An upward rise in social status, which occurs particularly among college graduates, engenders different lifestyles.

Contemporary life is also marked by greater individual mobility, particularly for young adults. Heading in the direction of the frontier, Americans of past generations moved from east to west. Beginning in the mid-nineteenth century, they usually moved from the country to the city. Today in this country, people move in all directions: from a Southern city to a sparkling new suburb in the North, from a small Western town to an apartment in the center of a great Eastern metropolis, or from a new development in the Midwest to an older community in New England, where the company has decided to open a new branch office. For college-educated men and women, frequent moves are often an indication of upward social and economic mobility.

Our society is moving in several different directions at once. On the one hand there is a flood of electronic marvels: communication by satellite, solar heating, microwave ovens, the increasing complexity of computer operated factories and offices. At the same time, we are slowly learning that the depletion of natural resources may make it impossible to support our ever increasing population. We are discovering that some of our technological advances are actually threats to the continued prosperity of our natural environment. And, lurking in the background, is the possibility of a thermonuclear war that could destroy us all.

In the words of Alvin Toffler, "future shock is upon us." We are not ready for the changes that swiftly overtake our day-by-day living:

> In the three short decades between now and the twenty-first century, millions of ordinary, psychologically normal people will face an abrupt collision with the future. Citizens of the world's richest and most technologically advanced nations, many of them will find it increasingly painful to keep up with the incessant demand for change that characterizes our time. For them, the future will have arrived too soon.
>
> By changing our relationship to the resources that surround us, by violently expanding the scope of change, and, most crucially, by accelerating its pace, we have broken irretrievably with the past. . . . We have set the stage for a completely new society and we are now racing toward it . . . it is this that calls into question man's capacity for adap-

> tation—how will he fare in this new society? Can he adapt to its imperatives? And if not, can he alter these imperatives?[16]

Change is particularly threatening to our family life. We expect change in work or politics, but change in our family life is more difficult for us to accept. Since many of the conservative elements in our society are linked to the traditional family structure, change in this structure can be the most unsettling of all.

An Uncertain Future

Change results in another characteristic of our generation: uncertainty. What will the future be like? Will personal freedom continue to be an attainable goal in the last two decades of the twentieth century? Or will we surrender ourselves to big government, big industry, and big labor? Will our opportunities for self-growth and self-advancement expand in the years ahead, or will we see the end of independence and opportunity?

> To what extent does our present understanding of social change permit us to predict the future? We are able to do so within limits, particularly for those societies that have not yet reached our level of industrial development. Our society and other advanced industrial societies such as the Soviet Union provide the mirror in which developing societies can see the outlines of their own futures. . . . But when we look to our own future we have no example to guide us. We can, however, make fairly confident predictions about specific areas of society. We can anticipate the likely effect of population growth and we can project the future trends in urbanization, for example. When it comes to predicting the overall form of our society in the future, however, we are in real difficulty.[17]

It is always easier to look backward, and see how things actually happened, than to look forward and try to envision what the future holds. In a pluralistic society we don't all share the same education, the same language, the same ethnic background, the same religion, or the same goals. We're clearly not all headed in the same direction. And this affects our family experiences too.

> Dad and Mom were married before he had finished his education. All during the first few years he was plagued with guilt feelings because he

[16]Alvin Toffler, *Future Shock* (New York: Random House, 1970), pp. 11, 19.
[17]Ian Robertson, *Sociology* (New York: Worth, 1977), p. 555.

was not established and making a steady income for his growing family.

The first fall semester was spent at Junior College. Then in the spring he attended a small unaccredited school, during which time their second child was born. In the summer, desperately in need of financial stability for his growing family, Dad bought an old Ford for fifty-five dollars and took the family to Muncie, Indiana, where he was promised a well-paying roofing job. The job did not materialize, so the car was sold and the family headed west by bus to California. But that didn't really work out well at all, and soon the family had grown to five. Then we headed east again for another round of job and school and job and school again.

The history of my parents' migration during the first eight years of their marriage has always astounded me. I have always thought it remarkable that they were able to travel so many miles and produce four children, each in a different state, in this short a time. . . . When we finally settled down in a new community, Dad and Mom tried to establish the stable pattern that had been missing before.[18]

There is no easy way out of this dilemma. Each person and each family must find their own way of facing life's uncertainties. This seems to be a constant factor in our contemporary environment. We face an uncertain future.

[18]Student report.

Urbanization

A characteristic feature of our society today is urbanization. Three great metropolitan complexes have developed in America: one on the East Coast stretching from Boston to Washington, one in the Midwest centering on Chicago, and one on the West Coast extending from Santa Barbara to the Mexican border. In practically every state, the vast majority of people are concentrated in cities. Urbanization has left its mark on all of us. We protest the overcrowding, the smog, the pollution, the crime and violence, and our inability to put down roots, but the tremendous pull to the big city is still there. Our chances of locating in some beautiful wilderness area in the state of Oregon, in a lovely New England village nestled against the mountains, or in a sleepy Midwestern college town are very slight. Career opportunities, educational advantages, recreational facilities, and all the other accompaniments of our modern culture are concentrated in or near our large cities. Some planned decentralization has taken place, but not much.

A college sophomore who was soon to be married stopped to talk to me one day after I had lectured on this subject. She protested that she was marrying the son of a farming family in the Midwest, that she and her fiancé loved the rural way of life and were contradicting the very trend that I had suggested. I asked her how large a family her fiancé had. She said that he had eight brothers and sisters. I asked how many were going to stay on the farm and make it their permanent home. "Only he and I will still live there," she replied. "The rest have moved into town." It will be a pleasant and prosperous life for them on a well-run, modern dairy farm, but the family trend will still run in the opposite direction—from farm to city.

A strong influence on the life we live in the cities is the mass media. The clothes we wear are illustrated in identical advertisements in a dozen national magazines. A new washday detergent, breakfast food, or gasoline is advertised simultaneously on several hundred television stations. Political candidates speak on network television newscasts and special programs, while campaign managers spend hundreds of thousands of dollars for nationwide advertisements trying to put their candidates' "image" across to the voter. We often ridicule or try to ignore this torrent of propaganda and persuasion, but the influence is still there. Our culture is the first truly mass culture in history.

DEPERSONALIZATION

This leads, inevitably, to a depersonalization of life. The quest for identity and individuality may be a desperate one for this very reason. We seem to be more easily recognized as numbers than as individuals with thoughts and feelings and personal values. Much of our society, it might be noted, is affected by individuals or groups who are in rebellion against the impersonal and unconcerned structure of contemporary society. We do not want to be thought of as "teenagers" or "students" or "blacks" or "Japanese-Americans" or "farmers" or "white-collar workers." We want to be recognized as individuals.

The increasing complexity of our civilization has had a tremendous effect on family life, its structure and its functions. The change has been characterized by Ernest W. Burgess and Harvey J. Locke as the transition "from institution to companionship," in which the family finds its chief value and function in the realm of the intimate and the personal.[19] The affectional function that is carried out in the family is a crucial one. Paul Horton writes:

> Whatever else people need, they need intimate human response. Psychiatric opinion holds that probably the greatest single cause of emotional

[19]Ernest W. Burgess and Harvey J. Locke, *The Family from Institution to Companionship* (New York: American, 1963), p. 631.

> difficulties, behavior problems, and even of physical illness, is *lack of love*, that is, lack of a warm, affectionate relationship with a small circle of intimate associates. . . . A mountain of data shows that the serious delinquent is typically a child whom nobody cares much about. . . . The evidence is overwhelming that our need for companionship and intimate, affectionate human response is vitally important to us. . . .[20]

The answer to this need may lie in what we call the "companionship family." Within the circle of the immediate family one can find the closeness and emotional warmth that is so generally missing in the larger society. This is one of the factors that makes our interest in family life so crucial.

Discovering Our Value Structure

What is our American value system today? This is not an easy question to answer. The things that are important to us, and that we value most highly, seem to change with each new generation. We are coming to recognize that our value structure can have an important effect on the way we live our lives, and especially the emphasis we put on our marriage and family life. Norman Feather sees our value system as including both *terminal* and *instrumental* values. Terminal values can be measured. They are goals in themselves; often the "big things" we are working for, values such as wisdom, equality, inner harmony, salvation, social recognition, self-respect, peace, freedom, and mature love. Instrumental values are the means by which we reach our major goals. They include honesty, obedience, independence, responsibility, cheerfulness, forgiveness, imagination, and self-control.[21] No one of us orders our values in exactly the same way. But for each individual, the process of self-evaluation and self-direction in our complex society is a worthwhile goal.

A significant attempt to assess the direction of our modern industrial and technological society has been made by Riesman, Glazer, and Denney. They believe that: "Social character is the product of social forms; in that sense, man is made by his society. Yet we know that social forms change; sometimes men change them; and character changes with them."[22] The authors observe three types of social character: the *tradition-directed*, the *inner-directed*, and the *other-directed*.

[20]Paul B. Horton and Chester Hunt, *Sociology*, 4th ed. (New York: McGraw-Hill, 1976), p. 198.
[21]Norman T. Feather, *Values in Education and Society* (New York: Free Press, 1975), pp. 45–46.
[22]David Riesman, Nathan Glazer, and Reuel Denney, *The Lonely Crowd* (New Haven: Yale Univ. Press, 1950), p. 3.

Tradition-Directed Society

*The tradition-directed society, as the term implies, is guided by the past. It is most characteristic of countries like India, Egypt and other countries of the African continent. Usually the economy is agricultural. Birth and death rates are high. Life is a struggle for survival, and those who do survive deal with life by adaptation, not innovation. People often find the same solutions to the same problems, year after year, generation after generation.

The Middle Ages in Europe can be thought of as a tradition-directed period. The feudal system honored tradition very highly. Any society in which son follows father in a natural succession of duties and role functions illustrates tradition direction.

One may observe many vestiges of tradition direction in modern American society: in rural life; in metropolitan areas where European, Oriental, and Latin American culture patterns are still important; in many Jewish and Roman Catholic families; and also in families in which parents raise their children in accord with the traditional concepts of obedience, goodness, and virtue. Many of these traditions are strong and ennobling to the human spirit. But, as Riesman and his coauthors point out, this is not the most common pattern in twentieth-century America.

Inner-Directed Society

*In the inner-directed society the standard for action is within the individual; it is what he chooses as the right thing to do. Many of the values held by the traditionalists may be honored, but the individual must learn to choose them for himself. In preparing to become a lawyer, for example, the carpenter's son may need to learn new patterns of living in accord with his new career and status. However, his choice is not as free as it seems. To a large extent, "the source of direction for the individual is 'inner' in the sense that it is implanted early in life by the elders and directed toward generalized but nonetheless inescapably destined goals."[23] By the time the carpenter's son reaches adolescence, this inner direction is pushing him toward his goals. Riesman and his colleagues call it a "psychological gyroscope."

There are many reflections of the inner-directed character in American life. It is seen clearly in the daughter of a working-class family who completes high school and begins her college career. She pursues her lifelong dream of medicine, teaching, or government service. She is not turned aside by promises of higher salary or higher social status in a less demanding career. Her inner drive propels her forward toward the goal. Her parents have encouraged her to find where her interests and abilities lie and to enter that field of endeavor which is her highest choice.

[23]Riesman, Glazer, and Denney, p. 15.

The pattern of inner direction has certain religious meanings as well. The person with inner character and strength is supposed to stand fast against an outward storm of opposition, ridicule, or temptation. The young adult should pick a course of study and hard work in spite of the difficulties environment and circumstances may bring to him. On the negative side, the inner-directed person may be seen as a tool of forces beyond his control—molded by parents, teachers, and elders into an energetic, hard-working, but somewhat compulsive individual—pushing relentlessly forward to the goals shaped for him earlier by others.

Other-Directed Society

Riesman sees the third social type, the other-directed character, as more and more evident in our large cities, particularly among the upper middle class. It might be said that he is focusing on America's college graduates. Is this the wave of the future?

> My analysis of the other-directed character is at once an analysis of the American and of contemporary man. Much of the time I find it hard or impossible to say where one ends and the other begins. Tentatively, I am inclined to think that the other-directed type does find itself most at home in America, due to certain constant elements in American society, such as its recruitment from Europe and its lack of any seriously feudal past. As against this, I am also inclined to put more weight on capitalism, industrialism, and urbanization—these being international tendencies—than on any character-forming peculiarities of the American scene.[24]

A new control is at work in the other-directed character. Tradition in parental example and guidance are not enough; nor does any inexorable moral law or high and holy God direct it. Rather:

> What is common to all other-directeds is that their contemporaries are the source of direction for the individual—either those known to him or those with whom he is indirectly acquainted, through friends and through the mass media. This source is of course "internalized" in the sense that dependence on it for guidance in life is implanted early.[25]

Not every student of American life and culture would agree with the conclusions reached by Riesman et al. Theirs is not the final word on the direction in which our society will move. But their study is a thought-

[24]Riesman, Glazer, and Denney, p. 20.
[25]Riesman, Glazer, and Denney, p. 22.

provoking summary of what our culture has been and what it is today. Most of us will see many of the experiences of our families and our neighbors mirrored in this analysis. We feel the tremendous impact on us of the thoughts and opinions of others; we cannot ignore the "others" who have so much a part in shaping our lives. We have been cut loose from the traditional sources of authority of the past and taught to conform to the mores of contemporary life, and we no longer feel guilty because of having broken the divine or moral law. Rather we feel insecure because we do not know what our peers will think of us.

SUMMARY

Each one of us is engaged in the quest for personal identity. It is not enough to be a part of society or a family unit. We must first know and recognize ourselves. But we may be strengthened and encouraged in our quest by our families, our friends, and our marriage partners. Many factors are involved in the growth of self-identity; one of them is hereditary and the others are environmental. Identity should not be thought of as a completed state, but as a continuing process the individual experiences in stages from birth to adulthood.

Personal maturity involves the development of a strong sense of self-worth for each individual. It can be nurtured in a number of ways: A spirit of honesty and acceptance can help the individual to relate better to the people around him. Achievement also gives a person a feeling of self-worth; in a competitive culture, one's sense of himself is enhanced by his ability to meet the demands of daily life. And we all need room to grow; that means not only maintaining oneself but building a more adequate self through new and broader experiences. But the individual develops and matures within a society. Perhaps the most important influence on our society has been industrialization. It has changed it from a rural society, with stable traditional family systems, into a society of change. The future we look forward to is uncertain. We are not all going in the same direction. We must each choose our own way.

We live in an urbanized society that has a tremendous impact on us. One result is depersonalization; we lack intimate human relationships. In the critical view of David Riesman et al., we are other-directed rather than tradition-directed or inner-directed people. We take our cues from others, lest we be found to be out of step with our neighbors and contemporaries.

Where are we going? We cannot tell for certain. We do expect present-day patterns of marriage and family life to continue, with some modifications, for the next two or three generations. But how drastic the changes beyond that time will be, only the future generations will know.

SUGGESTED READINGS

Allport, Gordon W. *Becoming: Basic Considerations for a Psychology of Personality.* New Haven, Conn: Yale Univ. Press, 1950. An excellent brief and readable book which focuses attention on the individual process of becoming. Critique of mechanistic psychology.

Feather, Norman T. *Values in Education and Society.* New York: Free Press, 1975. Summary of the relationship of values to our contemporary educational system and society.

Fromm, Erich. *The Sane Society.* New York: Holt, Rinehart & Winston, 1955. German-born psychologist examines our society in the light of our experience of twentieth-century social insanity.

Hall, Calvin S., and Gardner Lindzey. *Theories of Personality.* 3rd ed. New York: Wiley, 1978. Sound treatment of the major contemporary psychological theories of personality.

Maslow, Abraham H. *Motivation and Personality.* 2nd ed. New York: Harper & Row, 1970. Major statement of leading humanistic psychologist. Explanation of major motive of self-actualization.

Nye, F. Ivan, and Felix Bernardo. *The Family: Its Structure and Function.* New York: Macmillan, 1973. Careful analysis of family behavior and structure by two leading sociologists.

Queen, S. A., and Robert W. Hagenstein. *The Family in Various Cultures.* Philadelphia: J. B. Lippincott, 1974. Introduction to family history and organization in cross-cultural perspective.

Riesman, David, Nathan Glazer, and Reuel Denney. *The Lonely Crowd.* New Haven: Yale Univ. Press, 1950. Perceptive evaluation of modern industrial society and its impact on the individual.

Robertson, Ian. *Sociology.* New York: Worth, 1977. Well-written contemporary textbook covering all basic aspects of sociology.

Smart, Ninian. *The Religious Experience of Mankind.* New York: Charles Scribner's Sons, 1969. Analysis of major world religions and the religious view of life.

2 Alternatives in Relationships

- What are the different options available in contemporary relationships? Why are there so many?
- Are all these options products of the "sexual revolution," or do we see some recurrent patterns from the past?
- What are the most common marriage patterns for contemporary American couples? How are they changing?
- What options in marriage and heterosexual relationships seem to have relevance for the future?
- How do these options help us to evaluate marriage and family life as we have known it in the past several generations?
- How do we choose between the alternatives?

Nonmarital Relationships

Our major interest in the study of marriage and the family is in the kind of nuclear family that most young adults will probably enter in the next five to ten years. But we recognize that there are changes in the way men and women develop their affectional relationships. These changes increase the kinds of relationships we may choose before—or in place of—settling down to a more conventional marriage and lifestyle.

What alternative patterns are being developed for men and women in their sexual relationships in contemporary society?*

Unstructured Relationships

No lasting Commitment

There have always been a certain number of men and women involved in unstructured sexual relationships, in which no lasting commitment of

*Homosexual relationships are discussed in Chapter 5.

any kind is made or expected. A highly mobile society enables many people to live their lives without much social restriction or control, even though the prevalent mores and ideals favor more permanent sexual relationships.

There is no question that the 1970s have seen an increase in unstructured relationships. The rapidly increasing incidence of venereal disease among teenagers, the more permissive sexual morality evidenced in literature, television, film, and the arts, and the removal of restrictions on dormitory life and cohabitation on many college campuses are all reflections of this fact. The impact of this increasing sexual freedom on the traditional nuclear family is not completely clear. Critics of unstructured relationships claim that they contribute to the spiraling divorce rate and are accelerating the destruction of the institution of marriage. But others say that such relationships raise our expectations for marriage and for sexual fulfillment within marriage, and that a much higher percentage of people are achieving their goals in marriage now than in previous generations. Let us keep an open mind on this controversy as we examine the options open to contemporary men and women.

Premarital Commitment

Many couples make a premarital commitment that includes a traditional standard restricting sexual intercourse to marriage. The relationship is stable, and assumed, in most cases, to be preparatory to marriage. The partners refrain from coitus until marriage because of personal, religious, family, or social reasons. In some instances, the partners are not committed to marriage in the near future, and want additional time for their relationship to develop. They accept the traditional social patterns and the advice of family members, counselors, or spiritual advisors.

What percentage of college students choose this kind of premarital commitment? Most studies note that the number of virgins at marriage is declining, that the level of sexual experience increases with age and college class, and that there are racial and ethnic differences involved.[1] Couples who make a premarital commitment tend to be more religiously active than sexually experienced men and women, come from more conservative families and communities, and more readily accept the tradition concerning premarital sexual relations. Certainly they are a minority of the present college population.

[1]See J. Richard Udry, Karl E. Bauman, and Naomi M. Morris, "Change in Premarital Coital Experience of Recent Decade-of-Birth Cohorts of Urban American Women," *Journal of Marriage and the Family*, 37, no. 4 (Nov. 1975), 783-87.

Premarital Sexual Understanding

A relationship that seems to be enlisting an increasing measure of support on the college campus is one that may be termed a "premarital sexual understanding." It represents a more serious involvement than the premarital commitment because the couples have an understanding which permits them to share sexual experience before marriage. There is evidently a wide range of behavior possible in this category. It includes some couples who engage in sexual intercourse only once or twice prior to marriage, perhaps at a time fairly close to the actual date of marriage. It also includes couples who have frequent sexual intercourse for a long period prior to marriage, but who do not establish a common residence. The relationship is described as an understanding because it is marked by the mutual loyalty of the partners.

This option is similar to what Ira L. Reiss and others have termed "permissiveness with affection."[2] The relationship is considered to be a fulfilling or love relationship, and it is implied that the woman accepts (or permits) a liberal standard of behavior because she perceives that such a stable, affectionate relationship is present. Her partner already had "permission" for sexual activity under the double standard. In most cases a premarital sexual understanding is developed during the time that a couple is going steady, engaged or about to be so, or maintaining a consistent pattern of dating. However, due to economic reasons or family disapproval of early marriage, couples in this category do not move immediately into marriage. Delay of marriage has an advantage for one or both partners, and they may remain at this stage in their relationship for a period of months or longer. Traditional patterns of "pinning" and engagement are included in this category. However, many couples with such a premarital sexual understanding reach some obstacle to their relationship, and do not eventually marry.

Experimental Cohabitation

One of most modern forms

The term experimental cohabitation is carefully chosen to describe a midpoint between an unstructured relationship and a living-together situation. The couple do take up residence together, at least for the majority of nights in a week, but they are not formally engaged and may have no commitment toward marriage, nor any definite idea of their future as a couple, when they enter the relationship.

Experimental cohabitation has been described briefly by Eleanor D.

[2]Ira L. Reiss, *The Social Context of Premarital Sexual Permissiveness* (New York: Holt, Rinehart & Winston, 1967).

Macklin in a pilot study of cohabitation at Cornell University. Macklin estimates that perhaps 40 percent of the undergraduates at Cornell experiment with cohabitation prior to graduation, although she bases her estimates on a small sample that may have been skewed due to the nature of the people and the subject matter involved. She found that many of the relationships described in her study conformed to the definition of experimental cohabitation.

> The initial commitment to the relationship varied greatly. Some saw it strictly as temporary (e.g., "while traveling," "he was planning to leave Ithaca," or "he was already committed to someone else") and a few, at the other extreme, definitely planned "marriage in the future when it was more convenient." But the vast majority entered it either with a "let's see" attitude (i.e., to test the relationship—to stay together as long as it was mutually satisfying), or—a somewhat more definite commitment—planned to do all they "could to develop a lasting relationship, but future marriage was not definite."
>
> This raises some question about the label "unmarried marrieds" which has often been applied in the popular literature to unmarried cohabitation. Most of the undergraduate couples did not consider themselves married in any sense of the word. Not only did they not consider themselves married, they rarely considered marriage as a viable alternative to their present cohabitation.[3]

Further studies have attempted to define cohabiting students more precisely. Lura Henze and John Hudson have collected data from a random sample of students at Arizona State University in an attempt to find out how common cohabitation was at this state university, and in order to develop profiles on both cohabiting and noncohabiting students. They found that 29 percent of the males and 18 percent of the females had cohabited at some time. Approximately three-fifths of the males and three-quarters of the females had had only a single cohabiting experience. Even those who had not had the experience were favorable toward trying it.[4]

A further study of cohabitation, drawing upon a sample obtained from Selective Service records of men born in the years from 1944 through 1954, showed that 82 percent (2,066 men) had never cohabited for six months or more, including 821 who had not married to the date of survey.[5] A total of

[3]Eleanor D. Macklin, "Heterosexual Cohabitation Among Unmarried College Students," *The Family Coordinator*, 21, no. 4 (1972), 467.

[4]Lura F. Henze and John W. Hudson, "Characteristics of Cohabiting and Noncohabiting College Students," *Journal of Marriage and the Family*, 36, no. 4 (Nov. 1974), 722–25.

[5]Richard R. Clayton and Harwin L. Voss, "Shacking Up: Cohabitation in the 1970s," *Journal of Marriage and the Family*, 39, no. 2 (May 1977), 273–83.

444 young men (18 percent) had cohabited for a six-month period or longer. A positive correlation was also found here between cohabitation and men who had been married two or more times. The study also reports on the incidence of cohabitation in relation to age, size of city of residence, social class, ethnicity, education, and church attendance.

The Clayton and Voss study has the advantage of moving beyond the typical college study that deals only with students who may come from a homogeneous background, but its disadvantage is that it deals only with men. We do not know from this study how the female partners of these cohabiting men compare in the same categories. Nor do we know what the results of these new heterosexual patterns will be in later stages in the life cycle. However, some conclusions are here:

> It would appear that neither cohabitation nor marriage has reached a peak . . . among the young men born in the years 1944 through 1954. A sizable proportion of the men are "at risk" to cohabit or marry. It is noteworthy that 21 percent of the men who formerly were married were cohabiting, whereas only 8 percent of the men who had never married were doing so. This suggests, but certainly does not demonstrate, that some of the men who are currently married may, if they experience marital disruption, establish a nonmarital heterosexual union . . . Cohabitation may be a prelude to marriage for some persons. For others, especially those who have experienced an unsatisfactory marriage, cohabitation may be a temporary or permanent alternative to matrimony.[6]

The number of studies dealing with student cohabitation is multiplying. One excellent source is the *Cohabitation Research Newsletter*, edited by Eleanor Macklin.[7] Students may be able to find research data done on their own campus, or in a metropolitan or statewide area, which will be helpful in understanding current trends here.

There are several advantages to experimental cohabitation. First, it permits the partners a high degree of freedom in their relationships with each other and with other persons. If one or both partners maintain two residences—for instance, an apartment and a college dormitory—it is easier to dissolve the relationship. The relationship also appears to offer a potentially high degree of sexual satisfaction and close companionship with a minimum of responsibility. Since the partners are not married and are free from any of the social obligations and expectations associated with marriage, the arrangement seems to promise much in return for little.

[6]Clayton and Voss, p. 283.
[7]Eleanor D. Macklin, *Cohabitation Research Newsletter*, no. 5 (April 1976). (Department of Psychology, State University College, Oswego, N.Y. 13126.)

Low expenses seem implicit in these unions. This may be only a matter of differential cost accounting if the expenses of one or both partners are being paid by parents or others. But the trend seems to be away from heavy capital expenditures (for apartment, furniture, and so forth), and toward pooling of incomes or resources in order to reduce individual living costs.

Another feature suggested in cohabitation is the ease of termination of the experiment if either or both partners become disenchanted. Even though divorce is now easy to obtain in many states, it is still rated as a marriage failure in the minds of most people: two people started out toward a common goal (that is, a happy marriage), and they failed. In experimental cohabitation, the goal is much more modest and easier to attain. There is a combination of enjoyment and expediency. It seems to be a natural and convenient thing to do. With this casual arrangement and low level of expectation, the threat of failure does not seem to loom so large. Termination is just one way (a fairly common way) of concluding the experiment. "We didn't fit." "It didn't work." "I'll try again."

Some problems and disadvantages are built into this sort of experimentation. Parents and other members of society may not approve of such arrangements. There is always pressure on people when their behavior is deviant from social norms. This pressure may have a greater or lesser effect on different couples, but it is always something to be considered. The effect of cohabitation on a future marital partnership, with the same person or with some other, is also open to question. (See Chapter 4, on premarital sexual relationships.) Will the experience of cohabitation help or hinder both man and woman in subsequent months and years?

Experimental cohabitation removes the woman from the pool of eligible partners in her college or community situation. She is paired and thus not an available partner for any other eligible man. Is that good or bad? If the experiment fails, she may reenter the field of eligibles. Can she do so as easily at age twenty-one as she did at age nineteen? Can she find as many eligible partners at age twenty-five as she did at age twenty-two? (Of course, the divorced or widowed woman faces the same problem.)

Similar considerations affect the man, although his bargaining position in the pool of eligibles does not seem to be as adversely affected as the woman's, since he is more likely to establish a relationship with a younger woman. Statistics show that divorced men and women have a higher rate of failure in subsequent marriages than those who are marrying for the first time (see Chapter 9). Is the same thing true of those who have been involved in one or more experimental premarital arrangements? We do not know, but the question ought to be explored.

We have little concrete evidence on whether or not couples involved in an experimental community (such as that envisioned in Robert H. Rimmer's *The Harrad Experiment*) develop into mature, open, responsible, loving, and committed marriage partners when they finally decide to try a monogamous marriage. No modern industrial nation has formed a whole generation of marriages on these principles. We will need to study carefully gathered evidence before we reach any conclusions.

One author has suggested that the majority of persons involved in cohabitation studies are 25 years of age or younger. The percentage of married persons rises steadily in each successive age grouping. How will these cohabitants evaluate their present experiences with one or more partners as students or young adults when they are 35, 45, or 55 years of age? The growing experimentation with cohabitation must be measured as one significant result of the more permissive and open sexual climate in which we live.

Trial Marriage

This may be summarized as those couples who are "living together." They are not simply experimenting, as are those in the previous grouping, but are trying things out with a definite look toward a future marriage relationship. The problems of money, or of college schedules and demands, or of single or mutual reluctance to rush into marriage make this stage a dry run for future marriage experience.

Like cohabitation, trial marriage does without the legality of a valid marriage ceremony or its binding responsibilities, but it differs from experimental cohabitation in that the couples involved have a greater commitment to the relationship and tend to imitate the patterns of monogamous marriage. In lower-class society, the common-law marriage, or "consensual union," has a long and practical history. Now we are observing this trial-marriage phenomenon on all social levels. Middle-class students and young adults are living together without being legally married, and the freedom and informality of this option may seem to have real advantages. Where no children are involved, the man and woman are able to continue their chosen lifestyles without the restrictions placed on traditional marriage partners, and without the economic and social responsibilities that come with children. Two incomes make possible a higher standard of living. There is time and money for recreation, travel, and leisure activities.

In previous generations, college women and women from middle-class families were hesitant to enter such informal marriages. It is a reflection of the greater freedom in today's society that women are now entering willingly into trial marriages, that there seems to be a mutual interest in such partnerships on the part of both men and women. The feminist movement, greater educational and employment opportunities for women, and a less restrictive social structure are all contributing to this change.

Our data regarding the outcome of these informal marriages for middle-class college men and women, as well as for those in other classes, are severely limited. Small studies of trial marriages on selected campuses have not included the end results of these arrangements five or ten years later. No statistics clearly show how many of these couples marry, and if they do how often they get divorced.[8]

One may decide that trial marriage should not be considered a real marriage at all if children are not expected or desired in the relationship. Then there will be no way to carry on the family's traditions into a new generation. Ira Reiss thinks we may be seeing here a different type of institution:

> It seems clear from the published reports of cohabiting couples that there is a very intense use of modern contraceptive methods (largely the pill) by such couples. In addition, there seems to be a widespread feeling that if pregnancy were to occur . . . abortion or marriage would be resorted to . . . if we apply our definition of the marital institution, there must be the key function of legitimization of offspring. This does not mean that one must have children but it does mean that one feels if children were born, they would be legitimatized by this relationship. Thus it ap-

[8]See, for example, Arno Karlen, "The Unmarried Marrieds on Campus," *New York Times Magazine* (Jan. 26, 1969), 29.

pears that the type of cohabitation we are discussing here is not an alternative to marriage, but rather is a new form of a more open sexual affair between people who are emotionally involved with each other.[9]

Long-Term Cohabitation

There is still another category of cohabitation that we need to include if we extend our consideration beyond the college or young adult level. This is "long-term cohabitation," where the partners are clearly settled into adult life and responsibilities, and choose to cohabit on a more or less permanent basis with no intent of legal marriage. We are seeing more of this type of relationship in American society at large, and it represents another change in the mores and customs of our contemporary life. Couples in their late twenties, thirties, forties, and fifties all need to be included if we recognize this further continuation of the collegiate trends we have previously discussed.

Contemporary Marriage Forms

Our attention now shifts to the categories of contemporary marriage. There are many ways of defining our current practices in married life. The nonmarital patterns we have summarized all have their special impact on married life. Without ignoring their impact, let us describe the three dominant patterns that probably include at least 90 percent of today's married couples—monogamous marriage, serial marriage, and open marriage.

Monogamous Marriage

The most common heterosexual relationship in our society is found in monogamous marriage. We will be considering aspects of monogamous marriage during the course of our study. Let us note briefly some characteristics that may contrast monogamous marriage with the other alternatives we have listed.

First, most American men and women enter one marriage and remain in it until the death of one spouse. Even though the American divorce rate has risen in the last decade, the majority of married couples still fulfill the traditional vow "till death do us part." And, in addition, this relationship is still the major goal of a majority of young married couples, even if the course of the relationship does eventually result in separation and divorce.

Second, monogamous marriage places central emphasis on love and fidel-

[9] Ira L. Reiss, *Family Systems in America,* 2nd ed. (Hinsdale, Ill.: Dryden, 1976), p. 88.

"We've had our ups and downs, Jeremy, but over-all it's been a good marriage."

Drawing by Martin. © 1973 The New Yorker Magazine, Inc.

ity.* These ideals are a basic part of the romantic element in our cultural heritage and are also reinforced by religious teaching. The ideals of love and fidelity have become more and more difficult to achieve under the stress and pressure of contemporary life, but they still seem to exert a powerful influence in most marriages and remain at the core of the lifestyle of many young couples.

Third, note the emphasis on permanence in the traditional monogamous marriage. Partners enter marriage with the expectation that the marriage will last and that divorce or separation is an undesirable end result of the union. This kind of commitment to a longer-term relationship is unquestionably a plus factor in enabling most of the couples in our society to remain in a first marriage. Although married couples do not always report themselves at the top of marital happiness scales, this may not be enough reason for them to change their status. Many of us find that life is not completely satisfying. We wish we could change jobs; we would like to live in another neighborhood; we are thinking of changing churches; we are dissatisfied with our political party. A change may not solve the problem. In the same way, despite the compromise of our original idealistic and romantic dreams, our commitment to a monogamous marriage often remains firm because of our original marriage vows, because of the children, because of our family's feelings, our religion, and other values important to us.

Fourth, monogamous marriage still has strong social sanction. Thus a person will receive broader social support for engaging in this type of relationship than for participating in any other type of relationship discussed in this chapter. You may wish to develop your own lifestyle and be a pace setter for new and innovative forms of family life. If so, you need to be able to create an above-average partnership of two unique individuals who both want to launch out into uncharted waters. But if you are not ready to make a break with tradition, monogamous marriage promises you social support and a place in the mainstream of the community.

Finally, we must remember that we have a greater degree of knowledge in discussing monogamous marriage because of the larger research base on which studies of such marriages are built. We are all aware of the many recent studies of communes, group marriage, swinging contract marriages, and so forth.[10] In almost every case, the samples taken are exceedingly small ones, and the length of time of the study varies from a few months to five or six years at the most. We are generally unable to make any systematic study of the families from which the innovators come, and in most cases we cannot yet make any study of what the effect of these new experimental forms of family living will be on these couples ten or twenty years from now, or what the effect on the children they may have will be. On the other hand, we have assembled a fair body of research (with limitations that we will need to consider seriously at many points during our study of contemporary marriage) that deals with monogamous marriage, including studies seeking correlations between two or three generations, counseling studies, and research dealing with the impact of patterns of married life on the couples involved and on their children, in many stages of the life cycle. We can thus make some useful predictions concerning marital life and adjustment in monogamous marriage (see Chapter 11).

Serial Marriage

A significant group of people is represented under the category of serial marriage. The individual may contract a number of marriages, one after the other, each having the outward appearance of a monogamous marriage. Very little research has been done on people involved in this type of marital relationship. The question can be raised whether or not those people involved in serial marriages consciously choose this kind of relationship. It would be hard to identify young husbands and wives who will eventually be involved in serial marriages. Somewhat later in the life cycle, we can identify people who have the opportunity, motivation, and financial resources necessary to enter a series of monogamous marriages should they choose to; the rising income level of middle- and upper-class families in America seems to make this option a more easily attainable one. But the only way to obtain data on couples actually involved in serial marriages is to examine the marriage pat-

[10]See, for example, Kathleen Kinkade, *A Walden Two Experiment: The First Five Years of Twin Oaks Community* (New York: Wm. Morrow, 1973).

terns of divorced persons after the sequence has begun. Today, most of us know of couples who are in their second, third, or fourth marriage and who retain their desire to be accepted as a conventional family unit. And in everyday life, we often hear expressions that reflect a tendency toward serial marriage. "If Leonard and I don't make a go of it, we'll just get a divorce. We're both young enough to start over." "I told Janette that I don't want any children now and I'm not even sure we ought to stay married when I go to medical school next August." "Larry and Carmen were such a swinging couple, but I understand they've separated now, and she's very much interested in that young accountant who used to live in their apartment building." Serial marriage may not be a consciously chosen relationship for people beginning married life, but it is clearly a significant one.

In the past, marriage was most often terminated by the death of one partner, usually the husband. But today many marriages end in divorce, so that there is a high incidence of remarriage among two previously married partners. While the marriage rate has remained almost constant in the past fifty years, the rate of divorce has more than tripled, and the rate of remarriage has increased by 47 percent from 1921 to 1975.[11] We can clearly identify serial marriage as a trend of the twentieth century.

Open Marriage

Nena and George O'Neill have popularized the concept of humanistic marriage in their book *Open Marriage.* The O'Neills state that their research on some four hundred couples leads them to conclude that a whole new form of marriage relationship is called for. Marriage has been too "closed" and confining. Men and women—particularly women—have felt trapped within its confines. The authors' goal is to blend freedom and relatedness. "We hope," they write, "that the concept of open marriage will help couples to realize that there *can* be both relatedness and freedom in marriage, and that freedom, with the growth and responsibility it entails, can be the basis for intimacy and love."[12]

The O'Neills paint a dismal picture of marriage as it existed in the past. According to them, the marriage contract was a passport to slavery. How could we ever have endured it for all those generations? They name six clauses of the traditional marriage contract that they think lead to problems: possession or ownership of the mate, denial of self, maintenance of the couple-front, rigid role behavior, absolute fidelity, and total exclusivity. These hidden clauses supposedly envelop all people who are involved in a traditional marriage. Unfortunately the O'Neills ignore the wealth of data

[11]See Frank D. Cox, *Human Intimacy* (St. Paul, Minn.: West Publishing, 1978), p. 372.
[12]Nena O'Neill and George O'Neill, *Open Marriage* (New York: M. Evans, 1972), p. 11.

that suggest these strictures are being modified in the majority of contemporary marriages (see Chapter 6).

The O'Neills suggest a new model for marriage involving new guidelines. The clauses proposed for the new marriage contract are: living for now and for realistic expectations, privacy, open and honest communication, flexibility in roles, open companionship, equality, identity, and trust.[13] Many of these guidelines seem to be characteristic of many contemporary American couples, particularly in the middle and upper classes. They are proposed, however, as a bold new concept.

The humanistic outlook is most clearly seen in the O'Neills' criticism of sexual fidelity. A traditional model for monogamous marriage is illustrated in the Hebrew statement of marriage in the Pentateuch: "Therefore a man leaves his father and his mother and cleaves to his wife, and they become one flesh."[14] In contrast, the O'Neills see sexual fidelity as a strong barrier to marital happiness, preventing couples from expressing true love and understanding.

> Sexual fidelity is the false god of closed marriage, a god to whom partners submit (or whom they defy) for all the wrong reasons and often at the cost of the very relationship which that god is supposed to protect. Sex in the closed marriage is envisioned in terms of fidelity, thus becoming the be-all and end-all of love, instead of being seen in its proper perspective as only one facet of the much larger reality of love. Fidelity in the closed marriage is the measure of *limited* love, *diminished* growth and *conditional* trust.
>
> . . .
>
> Love and sex should never be seen in terms of duty or obligation, as they are in closed marriage. They should be seen as experiences to be shared and enjoyed together, as they are in open marriage.[15]

In open marriage, as a result of this view, the partners need not be sexually faithful to each other. They should expect to openly have good friendships with people of the opposite sex, friendships that will help them to strengthen their marital partnership. Therefore:

> These outside relationships may, of course, include sex. That is completely up to the partners involved. If partners do have outside sexual relationships, it is on the basis of their own internal relationship. . . .
>
> We are not recommending outside sex, but we are not saying that it

[13]O'Neill and O'Neill, p. 76.
[14]Genesis 2:24.
[15]O'Neill and O'Neill, p. 256.

> should be avoided, either. The choice is entirely up to you. . . . When they [extramarital sexual relationships] are in the context of a meaningful relationship [they] may be rewarding and beneficial to an open marriage.[16]

The clause "open and honest communication" is the vital one in the couple's relationships with friends of the opposite sex. Open marriage allows extramarital sex, but not *secret* extramarital sex.

The open marriage model is based on a limited amount of research. The couples the O'Neills studied were not chosen at random, and we know very little about them as real people. The length of time it took to make the study (from 1967 to 1971) was a very short period in which to observe couples experimenting with change in a changing society. Whether the new guidelines will work any better than the antiquated older ones with which they are contrasted (or than the more contemporary role expectations that the O'Neills did not consider) is clearly open to question.

It is difficult to make any definitive assessment of the open marriage model because it has not been tested and carefully studied over an extended period of time in our culture. As Betty Cogswell points out, many of our experimental family forms have been widely observed only in the last decade. Cogswell discusses the nuclear family in terms of its mythology and our expectations from it. She suggests that we can only contrast this mythology with the variant forms that are "still extremely vague and ill defined."[17] This makes it difficult, of course, for the couple who want to make choices in their marriage, and set patterns for their life together in the here and now.

Innovative Marriage Forms

Let us now consider some innovative marriage forms that are making an impact on our understanding of the contemporary family. At this time, none of these forms involves enough individuals and couples to constitute even a sizable minority in the total population, but they often command an important place in terms of interest and discussion.

Contract Marriage

There is renewed interest in marriage contracts. Contract marriage is a marriage agreed on for a certain length of time, stated in a contract—much as a sports team agrees to employ a coach or a player. The contract is binding

[16]O'Neill and O'Neill, p. 257.

[17]Betty E. Cogswell, "Variant Family Forms and Life Styles: Rejection of the Traditional Nuclear Family," *The Family Coordinator*, 24, no. 4 (Oct. 1975), 391–406.

for the stated length of time and can be renewed at its termination if both parties are agreeable. Contract marriage rarely involves a legal document drawn up by a lawyer; rather it is a private agreement between the couple. But some people are suggesting that this approach to marriage should be legalized.

Personal marriage contracts seem to offer promising support for marriage in the future. If the preparation of a contract implies careful preparation for marriage, thoughtful consideration of the roles and responsibilities of both partners, and a willingness to modify and change their personal wishes to suit their partner, this is all to the good. One might project a legal situation, as well, where a premarital contract might be prepared by every couple applying for a marriage license, so that a trained counselor could discuss its implications with the couple *before* the wedding ceremony, rather than meet with them later on to attempt to patch up a bad marriage.

However, there is a negative side to contract marriage. J. Gipson Wells has taken a critical look at the personal marriage contract, and notes a number of criticisms of this proposal.[18] The legality of such a contract is questionable. Was it prepared by a lawyer? Will it stand up in court? Was the disposition of children or property adequately considered? Wells believes that actual areas of marital conflict cannot be realistically anticipated because people change after marriage. Unless the couple has already lived together, they will not know what they are getting into. The actual experience of being married may dictate a new approach to the couple's problems. The "antenuptial" agreement formerly required by the Roman Catholic Church is cited as an example of the difficulties in such conflict areas where the partners' views may change after marriage. The non-Catholic partner may have promised to raise children in the Catholic faith but then changed his or her mind. These contracts may also take away needed flexibility in the marriage. Under present laws, couples have great freedom to work out their own family life patterns, subject only to specific requirements dealing with aspects like marriage competence, basic human rights, and protection of family members in the case of broken marriages. Wells concludes that premarriage contracts may represent a pessimistic view of the marriage relationship.

Communal Living

A great deal of our interest in innovative marriage forms in the past two decades has focused on communal living, a group of people coming together to share a common life. The presence of communes in western European and

[18] J. Gipson Wells, "A Critical Look at Personal Marriage Contracts," *The Family Coordinator,* 25, no. 1 (Jan. 1976), 33–37.

American society is not new, but their sudden emergence as a part of the turbulent sixties was a real spur to the growth of interest in alternative life-styles.

Rosabeth Kanter, in a recent book *Communes—Creating and Managing the Collective Life*, sees much of the communal way of life reflected in Plato's *Republic.* The land was important to Plato, as it is to today's counterculture. Communal life is ascetic, and is best carried on in a small-sized community. Shared values, self-awareness, and self-knowledge were all elements of Plato's community, and are elements of communes today. The discipline and social stratification Plato envisioned also can be seen in some contemporary communes, especially those with a strong religious orientation.

The key concept is: communes are communities. The underlying theme that has been stressed from Plato to the present, despite variations in style or ideology, is wholeness or integration. Communes are social orders designed to counteract the fragmentation of human life in some kinds of society. They are seen as vehicles for bringing fragments to-

gether into unity, for making connections between people and parts of life, for developing the "whole person." Throughout this book we will see the various kinds of unity and integration communes have attempted to bring about . . . In the words of an Oneida song, "we all have one home and one family relation."[19]

A commune with a religious ideology, the Christ Commune, is described in *Psychology Today*. Although the Christ Commune was only two years old at the time the article was written, it promised to be fairly stable. A successful farming operation had been initiated, and the commune was participating in a number of government-aid programs. Although the members of the commune were politically inactive in a crucial election year, the authors of the article felt that the members made a positive contribution to society in other ways.

Many, for good reason, have applauded the Jesus movement for its success in changing attitudes and behavior concerning drugs, alcohol, sexual promiscuity, and other components of the counterculture. It is apparent that Christ Commune and other segments of the movement have built viable alternative life-styles, which many in our society still seek. The "new life" of the commune members deeply impressed all who worked on the project. Members had been transformed from purposeless, cynical, and self-destructive persons into loving, concerned, productive individuals with a sense of mission. The fellowship and sense of community that we encountered at Christ Commune is rare in today's world.[20]

The report by Bennett Berger, Bruce Hackett, and R. Mervyn Millar on their anthropological investigations of communes on the West Coast of the United States[21] distinguishes between two types of commune, creedal and noncreedal. The creedal commune espouses some systematic doctrine or creed that members are expected to accept if they become a permanent part of the group. This commune may have sacred books or writings and definite rituals and practices. Noncreedal communes have no such formal ideology, although there may be an unwritten body of assumptions that binds the group's members together.

Berger and his coauthors also make a further distinction between urban and rural communes. They see the rural commune as a purer type, since it

[19]Rosabeth Moss Kanter, *Communes—Creating and Managing the Collective Life* (New York: Harper & Row, 1973), pp. 1–5.

[20]Mary White Harder, James T. Richardson, and Robert B. Simmonds, "Jesus People," *Psychology Today*, 6, no. 7 (Dec. 1972), 45.

[21]Bennett Berger, Bruce Hackett, and R. Mervyn Millar, "The Communal Family," *The Family Coordinator*, 21, no. 4 (Oct. 1972), 419–27.

necessitates a greater sacrifice on the part of its members, who must usually leave careers and familiar surroundings (unless they remain in college) in order to accept the responsibilities of the new family. The rural commune is more clearly contracultural than others, as it represents a reaction against the dominant lifestyle in American life.

The exact total population of contemporary communes is not known. Their visibility and their unusual organization and group life make them a focal center of much student interest. The type of sexual relationship that is formed within them varies, but a high degree of sexual freedom and openness is characteristic of most nonreligious communes.

Group Marriage

James W. Ramey has defined group marriage as that in which "each of the three or more participants is pair-bonded with at least two others."[22] Pair-bonds are sexual links both between heterosexuals and between heterosexuals and homosexuals. Ramey states that he has found combinations of a couple and a single (two heterosexuals and one homosexual), two couples, two couples and a single, three couples, and three couples and a single. So defined, group marriage overlaps polygamy, including polygyny (several wives), polyandry (several husbands), and homosexual relationships.

> For some people the idea of being married to two or more individuals at once is overwhelming. But establishing a dyadic marriage involves a "growing together," not a spontaneous happening. The same is true for a group marriage which begins with a set of potentials that are developed fully only over time. To begin, all that is necessary is the assurance that everyone in the group can sustain multiple pair-bonding. This is why the definition specifies that each individual in the group have at least two pair-bonds before the group can be called a group marriage. Many groups that first appear to be group marriages do not meet this qualification. . . .
>
> The complexity of interaction that must be faced upon establishing a . . . group marriage is greater than that faced upon moving from pair-bond exclusivity to intimate friendship. The situation is further complicated by the fact that each group must work out its own ground rules.[23]

Ramey's focus has been on middle-class and upper-middle-class couples and singles, and his conception of group marriage seems to be largely founded on experience with an affluent, older, and more conventional seg-

[22]See James W. Ramey, "Emerging Patterns of Innovative Behavior in Marriage," *The Family Coordinator*, 21, no. 4 (Oct. 1972), 435–56.
[23]Ramey, p. 452.

ment of society. People over age thirty seem more successful at the complicated adjustments involved in group marriage than those under age thirty. Whether group marriage is a viable option for a younger person (such as a twenty-year-old college student) seems to be in question. However, it is pointed out that college students experimenting with communes, shared apartments, crash-pad arrangements, and other innovations may be preparing for this type of relationship.

Some overlap between group marriage and communal living is evident. It is conceivable that a group marriage could exist within a commune, with some commune members participating in the group marriage and others not. But no such arrangements have been detailed in current research. Ramey says that the number of group marriages today is small, but that their influence for the future will be significant.[24]

Swinging

A final category is that of swinging, or "spouse-swapping." Here two or more couples agree to exchange partners or to engage in group sex. Sometimes singles are included in swinging groups, but in other groups they are completely excluded. Duane Denfield and Michael Gordon have discovered that people who swing seem to be on a high socioeconomic and educational level and are often engaged in professional and white-collar occupations.[25] They seem also to be conservative, or "straight," in most ways, except for their sexual behavior. Denfield and Gordon believe that swinging couples regard monogamous marriage as their primary relationship. Evidence in support of their thesis includes the emphasis in swinging groups on couples rather than singles, the fact that wives frequently drop out of the group to achieve pregnancy with their husbands, the discretion used in discussing and publicizing participation in the group (even with the couple's own children), and the rigid rules followed by most groups, which define swinging as an adjunct to marriage. In such a context, swinging might be thought of as sexual freedom on a single (as opposed to double) standard, but in a socially acceptable format. (The double standard traditionally gave men the same freedom, also in a defined context that did not disrupt marriage.)

Another student of this phenomenon, Gilbert D. Bartell, stresses the middle-class orientation of swinging.[26] He finds swinging couples to be on the top side of the economic scale. Swinging couples are conventional in their outlook on many topics. Bartell notes that couples studied in 1968

[24]James W. Ramey, *Intimate Friendships* (Englewood Cliffs, N.J.: Prentice-Hall, 1976).

[25]Duane Denfield and Michael Gordon, "The Sociology of Mate Swapping: Or the Family That Swings Together Clings Together," *Journal of Sex Research*, 6, no. 2 (May 1970), 85–100.

[26]Gilbert D. Bartell, "Group Sex Among the Mid-Americans," *Journal of Sex Research*, 6, no. 2 (May 1970), 113–30.

seemed to be politically conservative and generally antiblack and antidrug in orientation. The median age for men was twenty-nine to thirty-four years of age, for women twenty-eight to thirty-one years of age. At the extremes the groups included people in their late teens and people over age sixty. Bartell's general conclusions regarding the movement seem pessimistic.

> In interviewing these respondents, we found that they have no outside activities or interests or hobbies. . . . These people do nothing other than swing and watch television. About 10 percent are regular nudists and attend some nudist camps in the area during the summer.
>
> . . .
>
> A striking contradiction is the fact that in their letters they list their interests as travel, sports, movies, dancing, going out to dinner, theater, etc. In reality they do none of these things. Therefore all conversational topics are related to swinging and swingers as well as television programs.[27]

Denfield has further expanded his research in this area with a questionnaire study of professional counselors in the American Association of Marriage and Family Counselors and the California Association of Marriage and Family Counselors. Four-hundred-seventy-three counselors had experience in counseling ex-swingers. There were many problems involved: guilt, threat to the marriage, outside emotional attachments, boredom, divorce and separation, and others. Denfield is cautious in seeing positive results of the practice. He writes:

> This report from marriage counselors does not allow a rejection of the optimistic view of swinging. It does, however, raise some questions as to the extent of positive outcomes and portrays some of the problems associated with the consensual exchange of marriage partners. . . .
>
> The delineation of problems may add some balance to the understanding of swinging. It is clear from the marriage counselors' reports that many couples left swinging hurt and psychologically damaged.[28]

Carl Rogers has explored other possible alternatives to marriage in a recent book entitled *Becoming Partners.* Rogers sees the present high divorce rate as a confirmation of the failure of marriage as we have known it.

> In my contacts with young people it has become clear to me, beyond the shadow of a doubt, that the contemporary young person tends to have

[27]Bartell, pp. 122, 123.
[28]Duane Denfield, "Dropouts from Swinging," *The Family Coordinator,* 23, no. 1 (Jan. 1974), 45–49.

> a distrust of marriage as an institution. He has seen too many flaws in it. He has often seen it fail in his own home. . . . He tends to regard the vows of complete permanence in marriage as clearly hypocritical.
>
> To me it seems that we are living in an important and uncertain age, and the institution of marriage is most assuredly in an uncertain state. If 50 to 75 percent of Ford or General Motors cars completely fell apart within the early part of their lifetimes as automobiles, drastic steps would be taken. We have no such well-organized way of dealing with our social institutions, so people are groping, more or less blindly, to find alternatives to marriage (which is certainly *less* than 50 percent successful). Living together without marriage, living in communes, extensive child-care centers, serial monogamy (with one divorce after another), the women's liberation movement to establish the woman as a person in her own right, new divorce laws which do away with the concept of guilt—these are all gropings toward some new form of man-woman relationship for the future. It would take a bolder man than I to predict what will emerge.[29]

Rogers makes a strong plea for greater freedom in developing experimental laboratories that will help us to find the right formula for the man-woman relationships of the future. There is much to be said for such an approach. But the unanswered question is whether most of us (or even a sizable minority) will profit from such experimentation. Every person will still have to decide what type of relationship is best and take the risks involved in making such an important decision. If one experiments and is unhappy with the results, one cannot simply turn the clock back two or three years and start over again.

Choosing from the Alternatives

The wide range of options now available to the young person seeking a meaningful relationship with another person may well seem overwhelming. What seems right and what seems wrong to us is no longer easy to determine. Future shock is upon us, and we see hundreds of diverse possibilities before us. We try to build wisely, but there is little cohesion. Alvin Toffler notes the fragmentation of our culture:

> Today we still create our life styles by forming a mosaic of components. But much has changed. Life style is no longer simply a manifestation of

[29]Carl R. Rogers, *Becoming Partners: Marriage and Its Alternatives* (New York: Delacorte Press, 1972), pp. 10–11.

> class position. Classes themselves are breaking up into smaller units. Economic factors are declining in importance. Thus today it is not so much one's class base as one's ties with a subculture that determine the individual's style of life. The working-class hippie and the hippie who dropped out of Exeter or Eton share a common style of life but no common class.[30]

The same fragmentation affects our choice of sexual relationship. In some manner a choice must be made; we cannot go a dozen different ways at once. Each person and each couple must find a way of plotting a course that they can follow with some measure of confidence.

Several elements in one's present and past experience will provide input for such important decisions. The influence of one's family experiences during childhood and adolescence is one such element. We all learn basic social and emotional responses within our parental family. If those experiences have been favorable, we will want to see them reproduced in some measure in later life. If disharmony, conflict, and tension have been common in our parental family, we will not want to see that reproduced in later relationships. (We will examine the influence of early family relationships again in Chapter 6.)

The influence of our peers and our experiences in school and in the community are also significant to our choice. Some writers have suggested that peer influence is the single most important determinant in our choice of a lifestyle. It is clear that many teenagers and young adults are highly other-directed in sexual behavior as well as in other aspects of life. But some people may find that peer influence is not as important in their decision-making process.

One's self-image is another crucial factor. Do you see yourself as a stable, independent individual, able to make your own decisions and have a part in shaping your own future? Or do you consider yourself dependent on other people and groups in order to maintain your sense of self-worth? Some researchers have attempted to correlate the preference for alternative lifestyles with personality characteristics. Certainly one's personality is an important influence in any decision-making.

The selection of one's attitudes and behavior patterns in a sexual relationship is also a reflection of one's basic philosophy of life. If a person in a relationship is willing to draw a high level of support and emotional satisfaction from his or her partner without investing anything in return, that tells us a good deal about this person's approach to life. In contrast, if a person in a relationship is self-giving and committed to his or her partner, that reflects a very different philosophy of life.

[30]Alvin Toffler, *Future Shock* (New York: Bantam, 1970), p. 306.

SUMMARY

Today's society includes many alternatives in heterosexual relationships, including nonmarital relationships, contemporary marriage patterns, and newer innovative forms of marriage. Probably none of us will follow all of these options, but they are all realities in contemporary society.

In unstructured relationships the partners desire complete freedom in their sexual relationships, with no ties to hold one to the other. A premarital commitment is a more stable and socially oriented pairing. For some college students, this relationship does not include sex. In a premarital sexual understanding, however, the couple do share sex before marriage.

In experimental cohabitation the partners share a residence as well as a sexual experience. But the cohabitation is considered an experiment, and the couple's commitment to each other may not be strong. In a trial marriage the couples see their relationship as a potentially permanent one. This more serious commitment is reflected in the terms commonly applied to informal marriage: common-law marriage and consensual union. The failure rate of informal marriage is high, but the number of couples choosing this alternative seems to be increasing nevertheless.

Long-term cohabitation is another nonmarital category, although it is linked with more mature adults. These couples have various practical and theoretical reasons for not marrying.

Monogamous marriage is still the norm for most contemporary couples; perhaps 75 percent or more of all married couples in America choose this traditional form of marriage. Monogamous marriage stresses love and fidelity, with stability in the marriage a major goal. Social support from family, religion, and community is strong in monogamous marriage. The bulk of the research conducted on the American family over the last forty years has dealt with this traditional marriage form.

Serial marriage is a twentieth-century innovation in contemporary marriage. Couples of all social classes, not merely the wealthy, are now able to dissolve one marriage and enter freely into another. Each subsequent marriage (second, third, and so on) has the outward appearance of a monogamous marriage. But since serial marriages are formed and broken quickly and easily, they do represent a marked departure from the traditional ideals of the monogamous marriage.

Open marriage is a widely discussed and debated contemporary marriage form that has been popularized by Nena and George O'Neill's *Open Marriage*. It proposes freedom and equality between marriage partners, including extramarital sexual freedom, based on open and honest communication between the couple.

Contract marriage is an innovative marriage form that sets a fixed time period for a marriage. The partnership may be renewed at the contract's termination date or ended without need for divorce. The legal simplicity of contract marriage might seem attractive, but handling the intimate interpersonal relationships involved and the feelings and development of the children of the marriage would seem complicated and difficult.

Communal living is another innovative marriage form. It is possible to distinguish between transcendent, utilitarian, and crash-pad communes, or creedal and noncreedal communes. The long-range success of a commune seems to be dependent on its ideology and on how much its members are willing to invest in it.

In group marriage, a small group of people live together and are pair-bonded—that is, each person has sexual ties with at least two others. Mature, affluent couples seem to be attracted to this particular innovative marriage form. On the other hand, swinging seems to be a more conventional innovation. Couples maintain separate residences and all the other outward appearances of monogamous marriage. They find extramarital sexual freedom in their swinging club, which they enter only if both husband and wife are willing to participate, but they consider their legal marriages their primary relationships.

How does one choose among these bewildering alternatives? Carl Rogers has proposed experimental laboratories to test them out, but this seems unrealistic for most couples. Take a second look at the basic view of life you have gained from your own family; evaluate the ideas and influences of your peers. Look honestly at yourself. The choices you make will determine the kind of person you will be in the future.

SUGGESTED READINGS

Constantine, Larry L., and Joan M. Constantine. *Group Marriage: A Study of Contemporary Multilateral Marriage*. New York: Macmillan, 1973. Sympathetic treatment of group marriages through interviews with many participants.

The Family Coordinator, 21, no. 4. October 1972. A special issue on alternative lifestyles. Reports from the Groves Conference.

The Family Coordinator, 24, no. 4. October 1975. Special issue on "The Second Experience: Variant Family Forms and Life Styles." Follow-up to 1972 special issue.

Francoeur, Anna K., and Robert T. Francoeur. *Hot & Cool Sex—Cultures in Conflict*. New York: Harcourt Brace Jovanovich, 1974. Former Roman Catholic priest and his wife propose a new sexual morality for our culture, free of old restrictions.

Kanter, Rosabeth Moss. *Commitment and Community: Communes and Utopias in Sociological Perspective*. Cambridge, Mass.: Harvard Univ. Press, 1972. Thorough analysis of nineteenth-century communes.

——. *Communes—Creating and Managing the Collective Life*. New York: Harper & Row, 1973. Broad collection of readings on contemporary communes.

Libby, Roger W., and Robert N. Whitehurst, eds. *Renovating Marriage*. Danville: Consensus Publishers, 1973. Critical view of contemporary marriage by a number of contributors.

Macklin, Eleanor D. *Cohabitation Research Newsletter*, no. 5. Oswego, N.Y.: State University Dept. of Psychology. April 1976. Brief review of research on cohabitation, including unpublished studies.

O'Neill, Nena, and George O'Neill. *Open Marriage.* New York: M. Evans, 1972. Popular book which sparked discussion in the 1970s on alternative marriage styles.

Ramey, James W. *Intimate Friendships.* Englewood Cliffs, N.J.: Prentice-Hall, 1976. Advocate of group marriages discusses advantages he sees in this new type of relationship.

Rimmer, Robert H. *The Harrad Experiment.* Los Angeles: Sherbourn Press, 1966. Novel by leading exponent of liberal sexual education for college students. Critical of monogamous marriage.

Part II
Patterns in Courtship

3 The Pairing System

- Can we find common pairing patterns among young people in the American culture?
- How do we define early marriage?
- What happens to young people when they assume early marriage responsibilities?
- What are the characteristics of the pairing system at the college and university level?
- What are some of the problems involved in developing mature relationships?
- How can we build satisfying interpersonal relationships with our partners?
- How will we know if we have found the right partner?

American Courtship

Every society must have some way of pairing off men and women so that new families may be established and new life created to perpetuate that society. In previous centuries, the choice of a marriage partner was often dictated by parents or some other authority so that the process of mating could proceed in an orderly way. Even in the twentieth century, there are still societies in which arranged marriage remains the norm.

In American society, however, the free choice system is dominant in mate selection. In some families, the process may be more or less left to chance. In other families, particularly in middle- and upper-class groupings, parents and various institutions in the community are very much involved in the entire structure of courtship. In many ways, the American culture has devised the most complex (and the most costly) prelude to marriage. Much of our courtship system is centered around our educational institutions. Today, most young Americans spend three or four years in high school, and millions more go on to college. Here they find a wide range of possible dating and marriage partners. Many of the stages of courtship that are common to our culture are made possible by the social interaction of students at the high school and college levels.

High School Pairing

Many young people begin to date in junior high school or intermediate school, and a large majority have had their first dating experiences by the time they finish high school (see Table 3–1). When they begin and the kind of dates they have are probably a result of several different factors: their parents' influence, their economic and social-class level, their personal feelings, the influence of their peers. Current dating patterns are also influenced by the media and by other cultural factors. Dating experiences that were possible only for young adults several generations ago are now widely imitated by high school students. Indeed, high school students often go on to full sexual involvement, and sometimes to marriage and parenthood. Thus we define the entire experience as "the pairing system."

The high school dating patterns of the parents of today's college students were summarized by E. E. Le Masters in his 1957 text *Modern Courtship and Marriage.*[1] Le Masters identified six stages: group dating, random dating, steady dating, pinning, engagement, and marriage. Although this was the pattern of dating after the Second World War, it has some influence on our contemporary experience. Several of the major characteristics that Le Masters summarized are still relevant today, such as the importance of the romantic element, and progressive commitement as individuals move through the various dating stages.

Today we can identify four stages in the high school dating system. These stages may be defined as initial dating, casual dating, steady dating, early engagement, and early marriage. These stages are important through high school. Students who move out to work or into college will be influenced by different dating and courtship patterns.

Initial Dating

Dating begins in the preteen years in many communities. There is some evidence that we have underestimated the importance of boy-girl activities during what some psychologists have called the latent period of the junior years (eight to eleven and a half). Carlfred Broderick suggests that there is a wide range of experiences and attitudes during these years and summarizes recent studies on preadolescents that indicate "between 40 and 50 percent of the boys and between 50 and 60 percent of the girls between ten and twelve years of age claim at some time that they are 'in love.' "[2] He also cites Kinsey's data, which reported males with a substantial incidence of sexual experience and behavior by age twelve.

[1]E. E. LeMasters, *Modern Courtship and Marriage* (New York: Macmillan, 1957), chaps. 4–8.
[2]Carlfred B. Broderick and Jessie Bernard, *The Individual, Sex, and Society* (Baltimore: Johns Hopkins Press, 1969), pp. 25–30.

We will limit our discussion, however, to the period beginning in junior high school, when most young people begin to date and when dating activities are more generally encouraged and sanctioned by the community.

The survey cited in Table 3–1 (page 62) shows that, in 1975, 58.6 percent of these community college students had had their first date during the seventh, eighth, or ninth grades. This percentage was almost identical with an earlier study in 1966. Thus early dating remains popular in an affluent society. Some parents try to increase the opportunities for their children to date (supplying money, clothes, a car) as a compensation for their lack of such experiences when they were teenagers themselves. There are a variety of patterns for initial dating experiences. Parents may invite a boyfriend or girlfriend of a daughter or son to share a trip to the lake or the mountains in order to make a family outing more attractive. A school friendship may develop into walk-home dates with a stop at the corner drugstore. Group activities such as roller skating, dancing, or bowling may provide the impetus for a first double date.

> I didn't date in the first year of high school, but one summer day it happened. My father had invited some old family friends to go water-skiing. My father drove the boat and my brother rode in the boat with him. So that left me to teach these friends how to water ski. Well, I did teach them to water ski—all but one. She would not let me teach her to ski. So I said, "OK—then don't have fun. Be a silly old female!"
>
> What I said made her angry. So she tried to ski, and she did well, too. That night we went to her parents' home for supper. We had supper on the patio. It was a cool evening, so I put my school jacket on her shoulders. She looked at me with a funny look on her face. I didn't pay any attention to that look, but finished eating supper. After supper we played ball and the jacket was forgotten.
>
> The next day I went to get my jacket back from her, but she wasn't home. Her mother told me she had gone to the beach. She asked me if I wanted to borrow a pair of trunks and a towel so I could go to the beach and find her. I said I would. I found my jacket at the beach—the jacket was attached to the girl I'd taught to water ski. Well, one thing led to another, and she became my first real date.[3]

Casual Dating

It is hard to pinpoint this second stage in the system. Dating should be fun. There is always some nervousness and fear when one first starts to date, but usually a boy or girl can overcome this. But this doesn't mean that the in-

[3]Student report.

dividual will fall into a rut, or do the same thing week after week. Now is the time to experiment. There is no uniformity among different schools, among different areas of the country, or among the various social classes. In some secondary schools the postwar emphasis on status, with its correlate, steady dating, is still very important. This is particularly true in suburban areas, where many families in the community are upwardly mobile and where parents want their sons and daughters to "have some of the things we couldn't have when we were growing up." In those situations the patterns that were dominant during the years immediately following the Second World War have continued to prevail.

At the other end of the scale is the situation in communities and schools that are in the midst of transition, where there is very little agreement as to what dating patterns and standards are most desirable. In a high school where there is a serious drug problem or a changing racial, ethnic, or social makeup of the student body, the changes may disrupt standardized patterns.

Table 3–1 Dating Experience of Community College Freshmen and Sophomores

Grade at time of first date	*1966 (n=443)*	*1975 (n=119)*
Seventh	19.6%	11.8%
Eighth	17.2	22.4
Ninth	22.4	24.4
Tenth	14.2	23.5
Eleventh	11.1	7.6
Twelfth	5.2	1.7
College	4.5	4.2
Have not dated, no answer	5.8	4.4
Grade when first went steady		
Jr. High	32.8%	37.0%
High School	31.8	53.0
College	10.1	7.5
Have not gone steady	25.3	2.5

SOURCE: Surveys taken at Fullerton College.

This is not an easy time for many teenagers. Many months, or even a year or two may go by, before a worthwhile steady may appear. One may not be the most popular girl in the class, and dates may be few and far between. Many young men, on the other hand, may spend most of their time in athletics, or fixing cars, or just "goofing around," because this frees them from the social pressure of finding the right date, and knowing the right things to say and do.

Steady Dating

The next stage for many high school students is steady dating. The majority of teenagers report having some steady dating experience, and the survey cited in Table 3–1 shows an increase in this experience in 1975 over the group surveyed in 1966. This doesn't mean, however, that all teenagers go steady at the same time; so many relationships are in flux that probably only a third or a quarter of any group of daters is going steady at any one time.

Often, partners who date steadily are also free to date others, and they do so from time to time in order to indicate that the relationship is not a completely exclusive one. This freedom is another indication of the more casual approach of the contemporary teen culture and reveals an adjustment of the steady dating system to some of the criticism leveled against it.

There have been several reasons advanced for the popularity of going steady. It assures the couple a date for regular social functions and places them in the mainstream of social activity. It gives the couple a sense of security and status with their peers. Many students find it is simpler to continue going steady, even with a person who doesn't live up to all their expectations, rather than make a change.

Steady partners may or may not remain a pair after high school, depending on their plans for the future. If they intend to go on to college, they will probably break up and look for new partners. If they plan no further education, the couple are more likely to continue their relationship into marriage since they will not meet as many potential partners when they enter the labor market. It is more natural for them to finalize their high school partnership in marriage, particularly if there are strong social, personal, and sexual interests holding them together.

What is important when one makes choices in dating? Fun is important, and everyone wants to have a good time. But there are other factors involved, and they will change in importance as one moves through the dating experience toward the serious choice of a mate. Table 3–2 shows the Rank-Order Choices given by some 354 high school students in a study completed in 1974 by Sally L. Hansen.[4] Both boys and girls are becoming more egalitarian.

Early Engagement and Early Marriage

A final stage in the dating pattern for some high school students involves early engagement and early marriage. This may be a natural outgrowth of the steady dating stage. Couples who become steady partners and spend a great deal of time together in high school are prime candidates to complete the process and move over into early marriage. Karen Winch Bartz and F. Ivan Nye have carefully studied the literature on early marriage and reached the following conclusions:

> Within a social class, the greater the heterosexual involvement at an early age the more likely early marriage will occur.
>
> . . .

[4] Sally L. Hansen, "Dating Choices of High School Students," *Family Coordinator*, 26, no. 2 (April 1977), 133–38.

Table 3–2 Rank-Order Choices on the Dating-Rating Checklist

Characteristics Important to Respondents' Peers	*Characteristics Important in a Date*	*Characteristics Important in a Mate*
1. Is pleasant and cheerful	1. Is pleasant and cheerful	1. Is pleasant and cheerful
2. Is neat in appearance	2. Is dependable	2. Is dependable
3. Has a sense of humor	3. Is considerate	3. Is considerate
4. Is dependable	4. Has a sense of humor	4. Is honest, straightforward
5. Is popular with the opposite sex	5. Is neat in appearance	5. Is affectionate
6. Is natural	6. Is honest, straightforward	6. Is natural
7. Is affectionate	7. Is natural	7. Is neat in appearance
8. Is considerate	8. Is affectionate	8. Has a sense of humor
9. Has a car or access to one	9. Has good sense, is intelligent	9. Has good sense, is intelligent
10. Knows how to dance	10. Thinks of things to do	10. Is a good listener
11. Is willing to neck on occasion	11. Is appropriately dressed	11. Is a good sport
12. Thinks of things to do	12. Is a good sport	12. Thinks of things to do
		13. Is appropriately dressed

SOURCE: Sally L. Hansen, "Dating Choices of High School Students," *Family Coordinator*, 26, no. 2 (April 1977), 135. Copyright 1977 by the National Council on Family Relations. Reprinted by permission.

The greater the positive discrepancy between satisfactions anticipated from marriage and satisfactions received from currently occupied roles, the more likely early marriage will occur.

. . .

The lower the social class, the more likely early marriage will occur.[5]

These conclusions seem to emphasize the major role of the cultural and social environment in influencing early mate selection and early marriage. Young people at the bottom end of the social scale have a less satisfactory situation at home than do those from more favored families and thus may move along more quickly toward marriage. Unfortunately, marriage does not usually provide a simple answer to their problems.

[5]Karen Winch Bartz and F. Ivan Nye, "Early Marriage: A Propositional Formulation," *Journal of Marriage and the Family*, 32, no. 2 (May 1970), 262–64.

REASONS FOR EARLY MARRIAGE

There are several reasons that help to account for the large number of early marriages. One is the desire for adult freedoms and status. The American social pattern sets teenagers apart as a subculture and establishes definite limits on their freedom. High school students can drive an automobile, can participate in public entertainment and recreation, can smoke and often drink in public, and can hold a part-time job. Yet they are expected to live at home, to meet standards for study and behavior suggested by their parents, and to limit relationships with the opposite sex to a casual or going-steady pattern. Consequently, marriage for a high school boy or girl, either with or without parental approval, represents a step up to adult status. The young married couple have the freedom to choose their own living quarters (although some may have to live with their families), and they are no longer dominated by parental rules and standards. The most common example of this newly gained status is the sense of achievement and satisfaction enjoyed by a teenage girl who marries and becomes a mother shortly thereafter. She feels she is an adult in every sense, and she has a husband and a child to prove it.

A desire for sexual satisfaction and freedom is another motivation for early marriage. There is no evidence of major changes in human biological makeup in the last fifty years, but there is much evidence of changes in our social patterns and overt behavior regarding sex. Dating begins earlier, and there are fewer restrictions on the partners. Adolescent boys and girls find it possible to satisfy their sexual curiosities and desires more easily. However, this mutual sexual satisfaction is fully recognized in our society only in marriage. It is not surprising that many high school marriages are forced marriages, since it has been estimated that premarital pregnancies may occur in as many as half of all young marriages.

Unfortunately, many teenagers who marry early do so to escape from an unpleasant or hostile home environment or to express reaction against society and its mores. If personality problems make the home a scene of constant bickering and tension, even a less-than-ideal marriage partner may seem to be a welcome change.

PROBLEMS IN EARLY MARRIAGE

There are a number of serious problems concerned with early marriage. A basic problem is one of immaturity. Marriage requires adjustment in many things, including routines, daily living, sex, finances, religion, relationships with in-laws, and so on. If the husband and wife are younger than average, the probabilities are that they are not mature enough to meet all of these new responsibilities. They may be overly dependent, defensive in relation to others at work or school, or unable to meet the crises thrust on them by heavy expenses, parenthood, and other new experiences.

Another major problem may center on the couple's lack of education. A couple married in their teens could continue their education at night school or a nearby community college. But certain practical obstacles often stand in the way. Their marriage will probably set them off in some degree from their old friends and classmates. In a desire to emphasize their new freedom and status, they may not wish to return immediately to the discipline and restriction of the classroom. Is there enough motivation to carry them through a part-time program that may require three to four times the length of time needed by their unmarried classmates to finish the same courses?

A third common problem is finances. Most occupations today require a minimum of twelve years of school, and many jobs are open only to those with one, two, or four years of college. If the couple marry early and do not complete their education, they will find it difficult to get and hold jobs that pay enough to support their family. When children are born, one partner usually stops working and the family must live on one minimum salary. Unfortunately, the present social and educational system does not always instruct people in consumer economics. Young couples are especially prey to unwise credit purchases, loan sharks, heavy installment payments, and impulse buying, which lead to more financial problems.

A fourth problem is associated with parenthood. A study of early motherhood by Lloyd Bacon emphasizes the fact that an accelerated role transition by young women is associated with a high incidence of marital dissolution, poverty, and truncated education.[6] The girl who became a mother at age 15 or less was typically faced with many more problems than women who became mothers after age twenty-two in a comparison group. It was difficult for these young mothers to finish high school, and almost impossible to enter college. In a word, the young mother had not finished growing up herself, and found it exceedingly difficult to take on the new roles of wife and mother. However, even if she handles this new responsibility capably, the problems of adjustment for her husband may be more serious. His ability to assume the new responsibilities of a father may not be equal to the challenge. If he has trouble asserting his own independence and has perhaps looked for a degree of mothering in his marriage, a new addition to the family may be threatening to his own self-image.

Early-marrying couples may find happiness and stability in their marriages if they are given time to adjust to each other and to their new relationships. Often early parenthood deprives them of this time, and the pres-

[6]Lloyd Bacon, "Early Motherhood, Accelerated Role Transition, and Social Pathologies," *Social Forces*, 52, no. 3 (March 1974), 333–41.

sures of the enlarged family push them apart instead of drawing them together.

Other disturbing problems may be found in these marriages. A strong sexual attraction may bring the couple together, but it may be too possessive, demanding, or selfish. They may enter into sexual intercourse early in their courtship and then discover after two or three years of marriage that they do not have the kind of mature love and respect for each other on which to build a permanent relationship. Relationships with one or both parental families may be strained, either because of the conditions of the marriage or because of tensions arising early in the couple's married life. Religious considerations, pushed aside during the adolescent period of rebellion, may gain importance once more when children arrive or when the new parents are ready to begin religious instruction for their child.

Vladimir de Lissovoy has reported a study of early marriage.[7] De Lissovoy's group of forty-eight couples in small towns and semirural areas of Pennsylvania included many teenagers who had been forced to drop out of high school; their social and economic circumstances tended to be unfavorable. The marriages seemed to have unusual staying power (only two couples were known to have been divorced over a three-year period), but that may have been the result of the influence of their communities and of the fact

[7]See Vladimir de Lissovoy, "High School Marriages: A Longitudinal Study," *Journal of Marriage and the Family*, 35, no. 2 (May 1973), 245–55.

that few other options were open to them. Social and economic pressures are undoubtedly heavier in urban areas and on higher socioeconomic levels.

All in all, one can feel a great deal of sympathy for many couples who find themselves thrust into marriage before high school graduation. Most advice is too little and comes too late. The American courtship system encourages young people to date early, to choose a partner early, and to spend a great deal of time alone together. Yet in many cases it denies them the sex education and the contraceptives that would enable them to avoid unwanted pregnancies and forced marriages. Only after the couples find themselves married do they feel the full force of the built-in problems that will surround them from that day forward.

The difficulty in high school marriages is closely related to the fact that the couple's freedom of choice to follow any other life pattern is limited by their early marriage. The marriage brings a gain in status, security, and emotional and sexual satisfaction to the partners. But in order to keep pace with their contemporaries, they usually enter the competition with other young couples by having children, trying to establish the most suitable living quarters, and purchasing automobiles, TV sets, furniture, and all the other varied products of the affluent society. In that kind of competition, handicapped by an inadequate education, they probably will fall behind and thus feel frustrated and disappointed.

High School Pairing: A Complex Situation

All in all, we cannot help but wonder at the complexity of pairing behavior in our society and the strength of the social pressures that affect it. In our culture, it is to the advantage of parents, the economic community, and the educational community to delay final pairing so that men and women will be educated and ready to play an adequate role in our industrial society when they are married. Society plays its role by setting up a system that many high schoolers can follow. It works best in a small community where parents "team up" to give their young people a push in the direction they would like them to follow. This often seems like an impossible task for parents in an urban area. But most courtship activities are controlled by young people themselves, and the peer group provides "other-direction." The way it was done a generation ago is summarized here:

> To begin with, there was a natural division between the students of the different courses—the academic on one side and the technical and commercial students on the other. I believe the academic students considered themselves, even though they did not openly admit it, superior to the others. . . .

As in the case of most high schools or within any group of that age-level, most of the students paired off. During the time that any two were dating each other, it was rare that they would think of going out with anyone else, whether any agreement of going steady had been reached or not. While a girl had a crush on a fellow, she usually would refuse to go out with any others if there was any possible chance that he might call her.

Also, many of the first dates were arranged by friends of each party. After it was revealed that Mary would like to go out with John, there was a chain reaction until John found out and made the date back through the same chain. It was almost as if everyone was making sure that fate brought these two, who were "just right for each other," together.

. . . Much of the dating took place at organized functions. Our sorority had dances, wiener roasts, and house parties quite regularly which were mixed with school affairs. At most of these it was the usual procedure to come with a date rather than waiting until you got there and seeing what was available. However, at many school dances some of the "dates" were arranged after the dance started.

As in most other high schools, much of the dating ended in "going steady." Although most of this was naturally of a temporary nature, several of the pairs have made it more permanent.[8]

Today's generation is much more informal. There is more spontaneity in dating, and there are more options open to the student who wants to find his or her own level of involvement and commitment. The important experiences may not come at a formal date or the senior prom. Young people are more natural and are interested in a variety of people they may meet in different situations.

I found out in July that we were going to move to Findley Park. I had just made songleader in the summer tryouts, and had to miss all that when we were moving. I was very disappointed. I didn't want to leave Lincoln High School.

Then we came to see our new house before we moved in, and I met this guy who was the son of the people we were buying the house from. He was very nice and said he didn't want to move from this house either. He came over a lot and began to show me different places around here. People say he came along with the house! We have been going steady now for two years, and are engaged to be married in August of this year. Isn't that the greatest![9]

[8]Quoted in Jessie Bernard, Helen E. Buchanan, and William M. Smith, Jr., *Dating, Mating, and Marriage Today* (New York: Arco, 1959), pp. 30–31.
[9]Student report.

College opens up a new social environment to millions of young men and women throughout America. It offers a fresh beginning in a new social setting and an opportunity for young people of many varying backgrounds to find a place for themselves in American life. Even if students commute to college, their new status brings important changes in their lives.

The most obvious change that college brings is freedom from parental control. But freedom also brings tensions. In a commuter situation (which is becoming more and more common), generational conflicts are most pronounced. Students must keep intact their roles as dutiful son or daughter at home, but their new collegiate identity cannot be denied either. They are absorbing new ideas and new insights and longing to test them out on everyone, including their families. Family politics, family religion, family moral standards, family social patterns—all are under attack. Whereas students away at school face these conflicts only on weekends or during vacations, commuting students are likely to have such conflicts at least once or twice a week.

Tensions between generations are a common part of American life. They were felt by each new group of immigrants who tried to raise their children in the old, familiar ways. They were felt when young men and women from the farms flocked to the industrialized cities and took on city ways far different from their parents' rural standards. Today's tensions are commonly found not so much in families in which living patterns have changed, but in families in which the children have significantly more education than their parents. The average level of education in the United States has risen steadily since 1946. In another generation it will have jumped again. This means that in a majority of homes, sons and daughters will probably continue to gain more education than either of their parents. The barrier between generations, therefore, is not merely old country versus new country or farm versus city, but the ever recurrent conflict between youth and age, with our modern educational system intensifying the separation.

College also brings changes in the dating system. There is a new note of seriousness. One's college partner may well develop into a permanent one. There is more motivation to experiment, and the range of possible partners is usually wider. Unless students are isolated from society in general at a campus remote from a major population center, there often is a variety of potential dating and marriage partners. A college man may date women at his own or neighboring campuses, women working in the business community, or high school girls. A college woman may date men on her own campus or others, men already working, or servicemen. Whereas most high schools are limited by geographical area (or, in some cases, by religious or ethnic group), colleges tend to be more inclusive and cosmopolitan. College students are more mature, and their interests are bound to expand throughout their college careers. They are bound to be more critical and selective in their dating as well. The competitive nature of the American system of courtship, evident at all levels, is more important than ever in college.

The college dating system can be described in terms of five stages: random dating, developing relationships, trial arrangements, engagement, and marriage or transition into single adulthood.

Random Dating

The term *random dating* may suggest a haphazard choice of partner, but this is not necessarily the case.

The dating partner may be an old friend, an inhabitant of a nearby dormitory, or a fellow student in an economics class. The dating is random, since no further commitment is involved and either partner may choose not to continue the relationship.

Some writers suggest that the random dating stage is more serious for the woman than the man. Previously she was considered more serious about her romantic interest, and about a permanent marriage partner than college and a career. But today a woman is thinking of preparing for her career, and desires flexibility in planning for the future. Still, for the man, random dating may serve the dual purpose of bringing him fun and recreation and female company, without tying him down to the more serious stages leading to marriage.

An interesting study of the functions of college dating for men during the 1960–1970 period is reported on by Rebecca S. Vreeland and Alan Austin (see Table 3–3). They find that to the Harvard men studied in 1964–1965 and in 1970, dating served more than simply a recreational function.

> It is quite clear that to some extent among the seniors of the sixties and both freshmen and seniors of 1970, learning about another's personality and securing one's identity is the most important function served by dating. To the current students, the most important dating motive is "finding a friend who is female." The most essential characteristic in a good date is her conversational ability and the primary dating activity is sitting around the room talking.[10]

Vreeland and Austin also find that sexual interests were much more significant in this study than in prior studies of college dating. They note:

> Sexual activities are the most important dating activities to more than a fifth of the Harvard men in all our samples. Sexual attractiveness ranks second in importance as a characteristic of a good date while "few inhibitions" ranks seventh among characteristics of a good date. "Sex" is the first or second ranking motive for dating to more than 40 percent of the Harvard men. Although it is possible the Harvard men date different girls for sex and companionship, it seems that both sexual intimacy and companionship are part of the function of dating.[11]

The random dating pattern is a unique and important one in the United States. It is only gradually making its presence felt in European countries and elsewhere. It represents freedom, a willingness to compete—even in interpersonal relationships—and a faith in our experimental learn-by-doing dating system. To gain the maximum benefit from the system, people need to be aware of the risks and benefits involved and to be willing to shape their behavior and feelings in order to fit the role imposed on them. One must strike a balance between too much involvement and too much romance (which may interfere with other aspects of personal development) and indifference or lack of interest in dating (which may retard social development and separate the student from the important peer group).

[10]Rebecca S. Vreeland and Alan Austin, "The Changing Functions of Dating: Dating Patterns of Harvard Men, 1960–1970." Paper presented to the American Sociological Association Annual Meeting, Aug. 1971, p. 15.

[11]Vreeland and Austin, pp. 15–16.

Table 3–3 Percentage of Harvard Men Endorsing Various Characteristics of Women as Essential in a Date

	Freshmen			*Sophomores*		*Juniors*		*Seniors*		
	1964	*1965*	*1970*	*1964*	*1965*	*1964*	*1965*	*1964*	*1965*	*1970*
Good conversationalist	59.7	57.0	48.7	53.5	60.0	57.4	44.0	53.7	47.0	39.8
Sexually attractive	24.0	57.0	48.7	53.5	60.0	57.4	44.0	53.7	47.0	39.8
Effervescent personality	19.6	16.2	11.5	12.0	13.0	12.2	12.4	13.6	13.0	11.2
Well dressed	16.1	19.0	14.2	20.8	20.0	14.2	16.3	14.7	16.2	5.1
Intellectually sophisticated	10.1	7.0	9.7	9.3	13.0	11.2	10.1	16.8	12.4	16.5
Good reputation	10.9	21.0	4.5	5.3	7.0	6.2	4.0	3.7	5.0	3.1
Few inhibitions[1]	12.0	10.2	11.6	4.4	10.0	6.6	6.0	3.7	7.0	11.3
Highly intelligent and shows it	8.0	6.2	4.5	6.3	10.0	4.6	5.1	10.0	6.2	11.3

[1]This characteristic was updated to read "sexually liberated" in the 1970 questionnaire.

SOURCE: Adapted from Rebecca S. Vreeland and Alan Austin, "The Changing Functions of Dating: Dating Patterns of Harvard Men, 1960–1970," Table II.

Developing a Relationship

Random dating represents a good starting point for college pairing patterns. It is also a good place to return to if things do not work out in a more involved and committed partnership. But most college students would be more accurately described as having arrived at a second stage—developing a relationship. They don't want to switch partners every week, even though random dating has been fun. They are reaching out to find the sort of person they enjoy being with, one who may become an important and central part of their lives in the future. The relationship may be one that blossoms very quickly because of mutual interests and attraction, or it may come slowly out of many shared experiences and feelings and even conflicts.

Some college students may continue steady dating patterns from high school. Others may spend more time in group activities, with less emphasis on couples. A group of students who share rides to campus may evolve into a dating triad or into two couples who enjoy spending a lot of time together. Some students describe this period as a time for "messing around." However, in the college situation a single dating partner is more and more the standard pattern. A dating survey taken at Fullerton College bears this out (see Table 3–4). There are still groups of nondaters and random daters, but they are clearly in the minority. More than half the students report concentrating on a single partner. Many of these relationships parallel the alternative patterns discussed in Chapter 2.

What are some of the characteristics of developing relationships on the college level, and what trends are emerging? Today's dating patterns stress equality between partners. Instead of waiting for a phone call from a man, the contemporary college woman is much more likely to make the phone call herself and arrange a date. She also may have a better car than he does, more gas in the tank, and more money to spend on the evening because of a more flexible budget or a better paying job than her partner.

Some of the changes in dating patterns over the last generation are revealed in a study at the University of Iowa (although the fraternity-sorority system is not as powerful or as exclusive as it once was). Krain, Cannon, and Bagford see the Greek organizations on that campus as being influenced more by prestige homogamy than a true "rating-dating" pattern. It is important for the girls from the "top" sororities to date men from high-ranking fraternities, but the influence of this factor is not overwhelming. There is considerable freedom in dating, but in the final analysis, perhaps it is safer and simpler to stay with someone who has a similar background and status to one's own.[12]

Table 3–4 Relationships of College Freshmen and Sophomores

Type of Relationship	*Percentage of Students Responding*
Unstructured Sexual Relationships	22.1
Premarital Commitment	36.9
Premarital Sexual Understanding	16.8
Experimental Cohabitation	3.3
Living Together	15.2
Other, no answer (or lack partner) (includes multiple answers to this question by some students)	21.7

SOURCE: Survey of 119 students at Fullerton College, 1975.

[12]Mark Krain, Drew Cannon, and Jeffrey Bagford, "Rating-Dating or Simple Prestige Homogamy? Data on Dating in the Greek System on a Midwestern Campus," *Journal of Marriage and the Family,* 39, no. 4 (Nov. 1977), 663–74.

Relationships with partners have certainly been influenced by the feminist movement. This means a move away from the older courtship patterns that forced a woman to take a passive role and wait for a man to take the initiative. Some men still resist these changes. They want to operate with the old rules, which put them more completely in charge. But as more women develop a sense of equality, fewer men will be successful in imposing the old order on potential partners. These men may even discover that their attitude causes them to lose potential partners.

A second trend is toward more freedom and responsibility for the couple developing a mature relationship. Parents suggest, threaten, and plead, but college students often go their own way regardless. A college student wants to show evidence of his newly acquired maturity and freedom. He wants to be more and more responsible for his own actions and for his own future. Naturally, he also wants to have greater freedom in choosing a partner for a serious understanding. If parents or friends object to the choice, the man or woman may feel doubly bound to prove, as a measure of his or her independence, that it is the right one.

Leonard, twenty years old, was a college junior living away from home at a state college for the first time in his college career. He had a small scholarship, but most of his expenses were provided for by his parents. He was a pharmacy major and hoped to finish his education before being called into the service. The oldest of four children, he knew that his family was very anxious to have him complete his education. For most of his life he had been dominated by his father, an automobile salesman with a high measure of drive and energy.

During the middle of the school year Leonard began dating Kathy, a sophomore girl he had met in his chemistry lab section. They soon became steady dating partners and began to talk seriously about engagement and marriage. Kathy was not averse to thinking about leaving school in order to work and help Len through college, if they should marry.

Leonard's parents were dismayed to hear him discussing this possibility seriously when he came home for spring vacation. His father threatened to withdraw financial support for his education, and his mother pleaded for him to forget all the hard work and sacrifice that his parents had invested in his future. After two or three emotional scenes, he returned to the campus early in order to escape this parental pressure.

Kathy and Leonard were worried by this antagonistic reaction on the part of his parents but determined to go ahead with their plans for the future. They became engaged in June and expected to marry the following Christmas vacation or midsemester break. For the entire semester, however, they had to face continuing indications of family disapproval and criticism.

In the third place, college partners developing a close and intimate relationship are much more likely to marry as a result of their pairing than high school steadies. Women are closer to the end of their formal schooling; and the marriages of friends, together with well-known attacks of senior panic or sophomore jitters, will intensify their interest in a permanent partnership. Also, women realize that they are reaching the mean age for marriage (about 20.9 years in 1971), and they don't want to waste time in dating patterns that will not necessarily lead to a successful marriage. College men recognize that their girlfriends are anticipating the achievement of marriage in the not-too-distant future, and they also know some of the suggested advantages of a college marriage for them. Although such a marriage poses some problems for the male college student, especially in the first two years of college, it is certainly an alternative worth considering.

> Stuart and I are good for each other, and he is especially good for me. He encourages me to keep striving for things I tend to take for granted. He builds up my ego, even though he does tend to lay it on pretty thick at times! He also expresses his opinion if I make decisions that seem unwise to him.
>
> He has high goals for himself and I have no doubt that he will make them. He loves college and works very hard at his studies . . . He has said to me on occasion that he wants a talented, intelligent, and beautiful wife. I'm sure, though, that he will take two out of three!
>
> I want to gain happiness and peace with myself. My marriage will be happy, I think. We won't be extremely rich, but will have the comforts of living. I'm very positive on just what I want out of marriage, because it's something that means a great deal to me.[13]

College relationships lead in several directions. Many couples continue their "pairing," become engaged, and marry. We can certainly hope that increased maturity and experience will give the couples a higher expectation of satisfying and stable future marriage partnerships. It may be hoped that partners have greater insight into their relationship and its potential for development or difficulty in the future. Courses in psychology, sociology, or marriage and the family introduce many students to some of the personal,

[13]Student report.

psychological, sociological, moral, and spiritual implications of the marriage relationship. We can hope that some of the college students' "book learning" will affect their courtship attitudes and relationships and make it possible for them to combine realistic expectations with romantic ones.

SOME EXCEPTIONS

There are many differences within American culture. We have been discussing primarily young adults and college students, who compose the majority of those studying in a course in marriage and family. They usually come from a middle-class family, or if not, they are put under a great deal of pressure in college to conform to middle-class mores and expectations. If we think primarily of a working-class couple, other factors come into play. Family traditions may be more influential, and parents may have a more assertive role to play in their son's or daughter's romantic relationships. There will be less emphasis on finishing a four-year college or entering a professional or technical career. There will be more discussion of the jobs the couples hold today, and perhaps less interest in where they will be ten or twenty years from now.

Another set of circumstances will be important if one or both partners come from a family at the bottom end of the social scale, or from a minority group that is excluded from the mainstream of American life because of race, color, religion, or ethnic background. Life can be pretty tough in some of

these circumstances, and the range of choices for a couple is narrowed considerably. There is less opportunity here to choose a partner with more than one option open, and more probability that the man, and especially the woman, may feel trapped into a dating and marital relationship that does not have too bright a chance for success.

ENDING THE RELATIONSHIP

In contrast to those students who marry in college, many couples resist this kind of commitment. The feminist movement certainly has something to do with this trend. A young woman planning to go on to graduate school or embark on a career may feel that she cannot be tied down by a marriage that would prevent completion of her college education. And a young man who also sees a long period of preparation for his career ahead or wants to spend some time traveling may also be glad to step aside from too serious a decision about marriage.

Other couples may find that their relationship has not developed as they would want it. They may spend too much time disagreeing with each other or may find that their mutual interest in jazz or some other recreational activity is not matched by similar ideas in regard to families, friends, politics, religion, or other vital subjects. One partner may prove to be more deeply involved and interested in the relationship than the other. There should be no social disapproval of such a parting of the ways; it is better to end an informal relationship than to let it lead to an unhappy marriage.

But breakups can be traumatic. Some college students exploit the freedom of random dating. Most women in college have standards that limit their sexual involvement to partners with whom they are in love. This standard has been termed permissiveness with affection. It is not too difficult for a college man to develop a line to match this expectation; even if he is honest about his unwillingness to marry, his affectionate behavior may lead his partner to think otherwise—especially if she does not want to accept the situation for what it is. (Women may also use this period for their own advantage—to maintain their social prestige or position, to get even with an old partner, or to pass the time until someone more attractive comes along.) When such a couple breaks up, emotional problems may result.

Trial Arrangements

Many college students are moving quickly beyond their high school pairing experiences into trial arrangements like the ones we discussed in Chapter 2. A couple may decide to live together or enter a commune rather than to simply go steady, become pinned or engaged, or meet some other social expectation of their parents or peers. Trial arrangements accelerate the pairing process in some ways, but they do not necessarily lead to an early marriage. In fact, most campuses now recognize that many of these experimenting couples are not candidates for marriage in the near future; rather they represent individuals who are part of a developing new society. These couples have left behind the restrictions of the old dating patterns, but it is not yet known where these new relationships will lead society.

Engagement

Traditionally, the final premarital stage in the pairing process has been engagement. It is difficult to give accurate figures as to how many married couples have a formal engagement before the wedding, and how many head for Las Vegas and skip the formalities. There are a large number of well-established social customs surrounding engagement that seem to have a great deal of durability and appeal even in our fast changing times: Parents may announce the engagement with parties and newspaper notices in keeping with the social background of the families. But even this stage of courtship does not follow an immutable pattern, since probably one-half to two-thirds of all engagements first contracted are broken and the couple go their separate ways to seek more suitable spouses.

Marriage or Single Adulthood

The majority of college seniors are married or well on the way toward taking the final step into matrimony. On many college campuses, particularly in urban areas, married students compose the majority of the enrollment. This seems to be a continuing norm in our society, since the proportion of the population over age eighteen who are married remains at an all-time high. In community colleges and other specialized training schools for young adults, the percentage of married students is consistently high. Thus marriage at the customary age—the early twenties—remains a primary goal for most young men and women.

However, there are alternatives to college marriage. The close of a college career may simply mean transferring one's primary interests to the young adult group, where differing interests, aims, philosophies, and lifestyles will predominate. Many college and university campuses are surrounded by a large community of young single adults, and the transition from the campus to that community is fairly simple. There tends to be a larger number of divorced people, a certain percentage of single women with responsibility for raising young children, some members of the gay community, some confirmed bachelors, some women strongly championing the liberation of women from social and sexual constraints, and many people who have simply chosen not to marry yet. An examination of the young adult community, whose number is on the increase, is beyond the scope of this work. But we should not forget that this alternative is a practical choice for many young men and women after they terminate their education.

We also need to keep in mind the large number of young adults who do not attend college and thus do not fit readily into most of the categories we have been discussing. The world of single people is one that has a constant interaction with the college world. The freshman girl may be steadily dating a young bus driver who has not yet finished high school, or an older man who is now the top salesman in "Urban Realty's" downtown office. A college man may be dating a secretary in a law office, or a former high school friend who is now employed by the County Public Works Department.

Individual Pairing Patterns

There are always exceptions, people who do not fit the descriptions even when we delineate stages in the pairing process in broad terms. In the first place, there are always a certain number of young men and young women who seem to have no interest in the opposite sex. Few social events at any college attract more than 10 or 20 percent of the students eligible to attend them. People mature at different rates. Some people don't consider serious relationships until they are through with their education. Some students complete four years of college without a single date. They may then turn around and meet a desirable partner and marry soon after leaving campus.

Others follow their own unique patterns. Examples include the young man engaged to two women in two different states and the young woman pinned to a navy pilot, a young engineer at home, and a fraternity man on her campus! Some students come to college without any prior dating experience and then quickly become engaged or share an apartment with a friendly partner in apparent contradiction of the way of life they knew at home. Some young men and women are hostile to parents and society and express their rebellion by divergence from the community norms in pairing as well as in other ways. Eventually more conventional patterns may replace adolescent rebellion and hostility. We are only beginning to appreciate some aspects of human diversity, and how to meet the differing social and heterosexual needs of many men and women.

A final exception includes people from particular ethnic groups or from the lower class. In some racial or ethnic groups, the pressures of family background, economics, religion, and traditions may be so strong that the young person is unable to follow the more generally accepted American norms. Similarly, at the lowest socioeconomic level we cannot expect to find men and women accepting the same value standards and following the same behavior patterns as those in the middle and upper classes. Such groups, who are economically, politically, and socially separated from middle-class society, have evolved their own dating customs, sexual mores, and family patterns. We cannot assume that the personal goals they seek are subject to the same influences that motivate the majority of people in our culture. Again, much more intensive and thoughtful investigation of these exceptions should be an important part of the study of American courtship and marriage patterns.

Problems in College Pairing

There are several recurrent problems in college pairing. The most basic is personality conflict between the two partners. The initial attraction between two people may be due to physical appearance, mutual friends, common interests, or classroom or extracurricular activities. But when they begin to see a great deal of each other, there will be a natural opening up of their total personalities. The first matching of a few interests may not develop into a deep mutual attraction. (The same thing may have been true of your impression of a college that you considered attending. A look at the catalog or a conversation with a student may have piqued your interest, but a visit to the campus or a close perusal of courses offered may have given you an entirely different impression.) Personality conflicts, of course, affect not only college couples but married couples as well. Marriage-counseling files are bulging with cases of couples who married too hastily on the basis of limited mutual attraction and discovered too late that their total personalities were almost hopelessly incompatible.

A second typical problem in college pairing is related to time. Most students in academic programs find their course work difficult and demanding. If they are also working their way through college, a job takes another huge chunk of time out of every week. There may be additional hours spent commuting between home and college or from home to school to job and back. Often there is not sufficient time left for dating. A steady couple may feel that they are being cheated out of time together because of the many other demands on them. In turn, they may try to spend most of their free time alone together and thus miss many valuable social occasions with other people that would give them a chance to evaluate their relationship more objectively.

Another major problem is that of family relationships. College students want to assert their independence from family domination. They are free to choose dating partners without parental supervision and often in clear opposition to parental wishes. Such rebellion is natural and in some ways beneficial, for normal adults do not rush home to their parents constantly for guidance. But rebellion per se does not make for objective judgment, and one of the best indications of future marital happiness is compatible family backgrounds. We all reflect family influences and family standards. If we court and marry a person very different from our family, we may be sadly disillusioned later on. When we reevaluate our outlook at that later time, we may return to a viewpoint much closer to that of our own family.

A fourth recurrent problem is money. Many college students are operating on a shoestring budget. Sometimes the family can pay tuition and living costs but nothing more, or scholarship aid may cover only tuition and books. Other students are working for half or more of their expenses. Thus there is frequently not enough money to go around for the extras that make dating attractive—special clothes, a car, or money for eating out. On residential campuses, social events are often held at the college, which may help to keep costs down. But for students on a large metropolitan campus, competing for commercial entertainment with working couples or wealthy teenagers, the financial side of courtship can be a real headache.

Another typical problem is sex. What limits to the expression of their physical desires should be set by the college couple? This is a question on which there is considerable disagreement. One segment of society favors strict controls over all dating behavior and cites high divorce rates, rising trends of illegitimacy and venereal disease, and frequent breakdown of the family as evidence of the failure of present liberal attitudes. Another segment, taking a different view, sees the gradual removal of arbitrary controls as a step toward a more stable, mature, and realistic set of attitudes in the future.

The establishment of a satisfactory level of sexual interaction is always a crucial problem for college couples. (We will deal with this subject in greater detail in Chapter 4.) New surveys and statistics on sexual standards are published in the journals and popular magazines practically every month. They usually note changes in behavior over the last five- or ten-year period and often give comparisons with earlier data. With such data at hand, however, a basic question remains. How useful is this information to you and to people you know? Should patterns begun in high school days be changed, extended, or thrown overboard entirely? What effect will your premarital sexual behavior have on the mature relationships of your adult life? It is not easy to gain a long-range perspective, and to predict our values and feelings in the future.

Preparedness for Pairing

College is a time to make choices. We choose a particular college and seek a course of study that will prepare us for a stimulating and satisfying career. It is sometimes assumed that every male or female college student is eager to be a part of the pairing process. That certain feeling is sure to come, we say, and when the thunderbolt strikes, we are sure to fall. However, the process is not so automatic. The way one behaves in dating and courtship, as in other situations in life, is closely related to one's experiences in childhood and adolescence. From the very beginning of existence, children are dependent on others. Their parents feed, clothe, and shelter them. Without parental protection, their lives would end. Then, as physical strength and ability grow, children broaden their contacts both with brothers and sisters and with friends outside the family circle. This process of socialization is a basic one, and without it we would be incapable of living in society as normal adults. But achieving maturity is not always easy. Many psychologists see our adult patterns reflecting attitudes we develop very early in life. Karen Horney has suggested that neurotic needs develop when the infant or child fails to feel secure.[14] This is his or her "basic anxiety." The child who feels insecure may strive for excessive affection or approval, try to dominate other people, or try to achieve perfect and impossible standards. For instance, some children (and some adults) move *toward* people, thus expressing their need for love and affection. The boy whose mother is too busy with older children to pay attention to him and who clings to her at every possible opportunity exemplifies this search for security. He lacks a basic sense of stability. Unfortunately, this anxiety often carries over into marriage, and two people discover too late that their common inadequacies tend to compound their problems.

A second kind of person reacting against insecurity moves *against* people. This is the hostile child (or adult) who tries to conquer people and dominate them in various ways. He or she may be involved in a lot of scraps as a child and then gradually shift to other avenues to satisfy his or her neurotic need as this person grows older. A boy may boss the neighborhood children, disrupt his math class, and push to the head of the cafeteria line. A girl may have the same need to conquer and dominate. She may play too aggressively in sports, dare a teacher to suspend her, or argue with her parents about curfew. Such people may be tragic figures in marriage. They can feel secure only with a partner who submits to their every wish and whim. If a spouse begins to develop any kind of independence, trouble results. Genuine teamwork and a truly happy marriage are virtually impossible.

A third possible result, Horney suggests, is that some children learn early in life to move *away* from people. Social contacts are unpleasant or difficult and are thus better avoided. Such a person may become shy and introverted. He may be so alone that he has no real friendships and finds it hard to enter into genuine interpersonal relations with others. He is self-made, perhaps, but made only for himself. His lack of love and security at home makes him insecure when he meets others outside the home, and he retreats from his normal social development.

[14]Karen Horney, *Our Inner Conflicts* (New York: Norton, 1943).

According to Horney's diagnosis, the normal mature person strikes a positive balance among these three patterns. He needs to move toward people in genuine love and respect, but not in such a way as to make himself completely dependent on them. It is also right for him to assert himself by moving against people, refusing to be a rubber stamp for the thoughts and opinions of others. But his assertiveness should not alienate him from others; it should enable him to enter into genuine and meaningful relationships with them. The individual must also strengthen his independence by moving away from people. Solitude and a chance for peace and quiet are important ingredients in living, ingredients that are often hard to find in metropolitan America. But they should not preclude contact with others. The truly mature person must learn to employ all three patterns in appropriate situations.

Maturity can also be described in terms of developing healthy "interpersonal relationships." At every stage in life, we gain confidence to meet new situations and new responsibilities with competence and success. The knowledge that our parents, siblings, and friends are close to us, and believe in us, is an immeasurable help in this process.[15]

A valuable analysis of human development in these terms is given by Erik Erikson. He has proposed a step-by-step theory of human development, suggesting that each stage has a typical crisis that must be resolved. Table 3–5 lists these eight stages of human growth and the central problem involved in each. Each crisis is related to our interaction with other people in our environment.

> Each successive stage and crisis has a special relation to one of the basic elements of society, and this for the simple reason that the human life cycle and man's institutions have evolved together. . . . We can do little more than mention, after the description of each stage, what basic element of social organization is related to it.[16]

A person brings to each new stage of development the skills and understanding he has gained in earlier years. In return, he receives further guidance and direction from the institutions of his society, such as education and government, that exist to help him meet these particular crises.[17]

Erikson's first stage is from birth to one year. Here trust is the key word. In early childhood, from two to three years, children begin to find them-

[15]See Harry S. Sullivan, *The Interpersonal Theory of Psychiatry* (New York: Norton, 1953), pp. 37–44.

[16]Erik H. Erikson, *Childhood and Society*, rev. ed. (New York: Norton, 1963), p. 250.

[17]This concept is utilized by Robert J. Havighurst in his treatment of what he calls the "developmental task." Robert J. Havighurst, *Human Development and Education* (New York: Longmans, Green, 1953).

Table 3–5 Stages of Human Growth

Age	*Crisis*
Infancy birth – ONe	Trust vs. mistrust
Early childhood 2 - 3	Autonomy vs. shame and doubt
Play age 4-5	Initiative vs. guilt
School age 6-11	Industry vs. inferiority
Puberty and adolescence teenage	Identity vs. role confusion
Young adulthood	Intimacy vs. isolation
Adulthood	Generativity vs. stagnation
Maturity	Ego integrity vs. despair

SOURCE: Adapted from *Childhood and Society*, 2nd ed., revised and enlarged, by Erik H. Erikson, pp. 247–74. By permission of W. W. Norton & Company, Inc. Copyright 1950, © 1963 by W.W. Norton & Company, Inc.

selves and develop autonomy. At four and five, the play age, their freedom expands. They prepare for school (ages 6–11), where they need support and encouragement for their new achievements. In the next stage, the teenage years, they must answer the question, "Who am I?" As young adults, they move into the crucial area of close involvements with others. In middle age, their concerns become broader: The needs of society are also important. Finally, in old age, individuals take stock of where they have been. Integrity is a product of a fulfilled life.

Horney, Sullivan, and Erikson give us important clues to the reason we choose particular partners as we move into serious college dating relationships. We may have been so firmly set in patterns of conflict, Horney mentions, that we are attracted to a partner who generates frequent tension with us. Or, as Sullivan notes, we may be so intent in our quest for security that we are uncritical of a person who represents stability and a secure relationship for us. Or, Erikson suggests, we may be forced to engage much of our energy in resolving a crisis that should have been faced earlier in life and are therefore not able to invest our normal attention in choosing our dating partner. It is helpful, then, to approach adult relationships with some insight into our earlier development.

Time to Choose

For many college students, the pairing process leads directly to the choice of a permanent marriage partner. It is natural to ask: "Is this person really the most desirable marriage partner for me?" or "Do I really love this person enough so that we can make a go of married life together?" There are no sure answers to these questions, but they are certainly worthy of investigation.

One question to ask is: "Should I marry a person similar to myself?" Most of the evidence seems to indicate that you should. The partners in most marriages, particularly if they are college students, are of similar ages. They tend to marry within their own social class, in spite of increasing mobility in our society. Other factors, which we will discuss in Chapter 9, tend to favor a homogamous marriage team.

Despite the preponderance of homogamous marriages, some observers have voiced support for greater heterogamy. This is evidenced in Robert Winch's theory of "complementary needs."[18] According to Winch's theory, we look for a marriage partner who will make up for some lack or weakness in our own self-structure. The weak and passive woman will marry a strong and aggressive man; the capable, mothering woman, a dependent husband; the shy and silent man, a talkative and sociable wife. There is some support for Winch's theory, but all in all it does not seem that the majority of couples build their relationship on that basis.

There are many logical elements involved in choosing a marriage partner. J. Richard Udry, in dealing with the same subject, has suggested that the final choice of a marriage partner is made through a series of "filters." A number of possible partners are physically near to us (on the same campus, in the same town, for example), but we are only attracted to certain individuals of the opposite sex. A "propinquity filter" and an "attractiveness filter" are both at work. During the dating relationship our partner must pass through other filters of social background, attitudes, values, and so forth. We have an "ideal mate" image we would like to see realized in our partner, and if he or she passes through the final filter, marriage is just around the corner.[19]

UTILIZING THE COMPUTER

It is natural that Americans, searching for ways to aid in the pairing process, should turn to the computer. The lonely hearts clubs of earlier generations have now been replaced by scientific matching techniques, which seek to utilize knowledge of personality characteristics and a number of other important factors in order to bring together men and women who might become suitable marriage partners.

One pioneer in the field was Karl M. Wallace, who organized a "personal

[18]Robert F. Winch, *The Modern Family*, 3rd ed. (New York: Holt, Rinehart & Winston, 1971), pp. 473–507.

[19]J. Richard Udry, *The Social Context of Marriage*, 2nd ed. (Philadelphia: Lippincott, 1971), pp. 212–16.

acquaintance service" in connection with his doctoral studies.[20] Wallace advertised for participants and then asked them to fill out questionnaires that categorized them on the basis of personality traits and socioeconomic level, among other things. The questionnaires were then sorted mechanically, and prospective partners were matched and introduced to each other by correspondence. There were 59,417 inquiries over a six-year period, with 6,023 persons being included in the final sample. A total of 320 couples were married as a result of the program. Wallace felt that the service met a definite need, particularly for those who did not have adequate opportunities to meet suitable dating partners.

The work of the earlier computer matching programs has been refined and is now marketed by a number of commercial firms nationwide. Computer dating companies are particularly visible in large metropolitan areas. Some charge fees of one thousand dollars or more, and provide videotaping, personality testing, personal interviews, and other related services. It would be most valuable if we had the results of a long-term study showing whether or not computer-matched couples have more stable and satisfying marriages. Unfortunately, no scientifically controlled study of this type has been conducted with a sufficiently large sample. There is no single recognized test that will predict how well a person will succeed in a pairing or marital relationship with one specific partner and no single company that can guarantee results from their services in this field. When we compare this deficiency with the help available in intelligence testing, we see that the social science of mate selection is still in its infancy.

Practical Advice on Pairing

The basic problem remains: How can you select the most suitable person with whom to pair in college—especially since the partner you select may well become your marriage partner? Is there any way to be assured that you are choosing wisely and well?

One suggestion seems appropriate: It is a good idea to take full advantage of the freedom and opportunity we have to choose our partners in the American system of courtship. It is wise to have the experience of regular or steady dating of several partners before you become engaged and marry. In this way, you have a chance to observe your feelings and reactions to several different kinds of personalities. The person who has not dated at all before choosing a permanent marriage partner or who has had very limited dating experience may find it difficult to make an objective and rational evaluation of a prospective spouse. A parallel can be seen in other important

[20]Karl Miles Wallace, "An Experiment in Scientific Matchmaking," *Marriage and Family Living*, 21, no. 4 (Nov. 1959), 342–48.

choices—for example, choosing a college or accepting your first full-time employment. If you were able to attend a number of colleges within a certain distance of your home, you would be foolish to choose the first school to send you a catalog. You would want to investigate further before making your final choice. Similarly, if five possible positions were available to you, it would be unwise to apply for only one of them. In the same way, there is danger in marrying the first eligible man or woman to whom you feel strongly attracted, without some basis of comparison.

Two other suggestions may be given to couples who are already paired. First, it is logical to make a careful evaluation of yourself, your partner, and your relationship before making a final commitment to marriage. There are several bases for such evaluation. One can attempt to match personality traits, backgrounds, and interests. The basic needs of each partner may be considered as balancing the needs and wishes of the other.[21] Although no single personality test is universally accepted for this purpose, it may be helpful to seek a counselor or testing service that offers a reliable and valid test program. Such tests are not foolproof, but they do offer sound indications of the ways in which two people compare in important personality variables and should be valuable in the analysis of the relationship between them.

Second, both partners should give careful consideration to the major elements making up successful marital adjustment. They include dating patterns, sexual attitudes, role expectations, cultural and family influences, the mature understanding of love, the function of the engagement period, the requirements of marriage while in college or under other special conditions, and the relationship of religious belief and affiliation to the success of the marriage.

Finally, it is important to keep a balance between an emotional and an intellectual appraisal of one's partner. Because strong personal and sexual feelings are involved in most dating relationships, one may think of future marriage primarily in terms of the continuation and reinforcement of those emotional feelings. But measuring a partner's suitability solely on a romantic and emotional level runs the risk of overlooking more significant factors in long-term adjustment. We all know couples who have had strong and deep feelings for each other during courtship but who are nevertheless totally unsuited for each other as marriage partners.

If it is axiomatic in twentieth-century America that none should marry without love, it should be just as basic that none should marry without a careful consideration of the other prime factors involved. Are man and woman compatible in regard to their outlook on life, their educational and social backgrounds, their family patterns, their economic level and attitude

[21]See Robert F. Winch, *Mate Selection* (New York: Harper & Row, 1958), p. 90.

toward money, their religious faith, their attitude toward children, and their leisure-time interests? One or several of these factors may prove to be crucial to the future marital adjustment of the partners. A couple should strive for a healthy balance between their feelings and their judgment of their prospects for future happiness and satisfaction. It is unwise to become overinvolved emotionally without first considering the ultimate result of the relationship.

SUMMARY The pairing system for men and women in our society is a very complex one. The pairing system of our parents' generation had reached something of an equilibrium. "Going steady" was a post–Second World War innovation, and random dating was another. In high schools today, however, we can identify four stages of pairing: initial dating, casual dating, steady dating, and early engagement and early marriage.

Initial dating usually starts in junior high school. Casual dating is the next step, and reflects a wide range of possibilities for the adolescent, particularly in middle-class communities. Steady dating has retained its popularity, although it rarely involves a majority of students. Early engagement and early marriage are still quite common, with pregnancy often accelerating such marriages. Some young men and women choose early marriage as a way to attain adult freedom and status, find sexual satisfaction, and move away from parental control.

Early marriages often pose serious problems for the couple, and often have a high failure rate. Immaturity, lack of education, and low income are some typical difficulties. In addition, couples may become parents soon after marriage and be unable to deal with the responsibilities of such a situation.

The college pairing system is important because it represents a testing ground for future marriage relationships. College relationships are more serious pairing relationships.

There are five stages in college pairing: random dating, developing a relationship, trial arrangements, engagement, and marriage or single adulthood. At the college level there is greater equality between the partners, and they both exercise greater freedom and greater responsibility. They are more likely to become permanent marriage partners. However, many differences between individuals and couples remain, such as personality conflict, social-class levels, family relationships, attitudes toward money, or inhibitions about sex.

Personal maturity is an important ingredient when considering pairing. It can be built on sound early learning experiences, primarily in one's own family and one's social environment.

Choosing a partner is also a crucial part of pairing. Finding a partner like oneself seems to be the most rational approach, although there are many factors to consider, since both intellect and emotion come into play.

Scientific pairing is now possible through computer matching, but this technique is in its infancy, not fully tested and proven. One should take advantage of the freedom and openness of the American pairing system. Evaluate yourself, your partner, and your growing relationship, before you reach the point of final choice. Mature preparation is needed—each couple must strike a delicate balance between romance and objective reality.

SUGGESTED READINGS

Bach, George R., and Robert M. Deutsch. *Pairing.* New York: Peter H. Wyden, Inc., 1974. Nontechnical treatment of the pairing process and the development of couple relationships.

Bacon, Lloyd. "Early Motherhood, Accelerated Role Transition, and Social Pathologies." *Social Forces,* 52, no. 3 (March 1974), 333–41. Good brief introduction to the problems of young mothers in our culture.

Bell, Robert R. *Marriage and Family Interaction.* 3rd ed. Homewood, Ill.: Dorsey Press, 1971. Chap. 4. Discussion of dating and sexual relationships with contemporary college student population.

Broderick, Carlfred B., and Jessie Bernard. *The Individual, Sex and Society.* Baltimore: Johns Hopkins Press, 1969. Good summary of material on heterosexual relationships, including childhood development.

Erikson, Erik H. *Childhood and Society.* 2nd ed. New York: W. W. Norton Co., 1963. Important basic work by noted developmental psychologist.

Huston, Ted L., ed. *Foundations of Interpersonal Attraction.* New York: Academic Press, 1974. Comprehensive treatment of development of interpersonal relationships, and their relation to types of social interaction.

Martinson, Floyd Mansfield. *Family in Society.* New York: Dodd, Mead, 1970. Chaps. 12, 13. Sociological development of family interaction. A positive view of the American family and its roots in our cultural history.

Murstein, Bernard, ed. *Theories of Attraction and Love.* New York: Springer, 1971. Collection of papers on attraction, love, and mate selection edited by theorist on interpersonal attraction.

Udry, J. Richard. *The Social Context of Marriage.* 3rd ed. Philadelphia: J. B. Lippincott, 1974. Basic study, with careful analysis of social and interpersonal factors in mate selection.

4 Premarital Sexual Relations

- What do we know about the development of sexuality in the early years of life? How is this development related to sex and gender?
- What is the attitude of today's college students toward premarital sexual relations?
- What are the most convincing arguments advanced in favor of premarital sexual intercourse? What arguments against premarital intercourse are most valid?
- What has been the attitude of American society concerning sex before marriage? Is this attitude changing?
- How does one establish norms for sexual behavior? Must a decision in this area be a personal one, or can it have significant social and moral implications?

Human Sexual Development

Sexual attitudes and behavior are important components of any personal relationship. Sexual attraction is a normal part of the beginning of most dating relationships. In a society that is moving toward more frank and open sexuality, the decision whether or not to share in premarital sexual intercourse will sooner or later be discussed by a couple.

Before we discuss the subject of premarital sexual relations in detail, we need to consider the course of human sexual development in the early years of life. It is difficult to evaluate the data we have on premarital sexual relationships unless we have a broad frame of reference in which to consider that data. In the last thirty years there has been growing interest in a more scientific study of human sexual development. The pioneering work of Alfred Kinsey and his associates, the studies of Masters and Johnson, the widespread interest in sex therapy and more realistic sex education for adults as well as young people, have all provided us with an ever-widening circle of knowledge of sexual matters. Today, a much wider range of possible sexual experience is available to both unmarried and married people. The study of human sexuality, originally considered appropriate only as a part of marriage or psychology courses, is now becoming a major subject in biology, health, and medical courses. The preliminary advances we have made in factual knowledge and the ability to deal objectively with our sexual feelings and behavior are significant. But we are just beginning to learn about human sexual development. How do we form sexual attitudes and behavior patterns? At what stage in life do they begin? Can we predict mature behavior by observing earlier sexual development?

Early Sexual Development

Sexual behavior reaches a turning point at puberty, but it does not begin there. It begins at birth and is a part of all of life's experiences. We learn our basic human sexuality as young children, and there are a number of interrelated factors involved. Obviously there are many biological differences between men and women, including differences in physical size and strength, intellectual aptitudes, and emotional and psychological characteristics. But to explain human sexual development and behavior solely in biological terms would be an oversimplification of a very complex aspect of human behavior. Amram Scheinfeld has pointed out that there are nonbiological factors in sexual development that are often difficult to isolate.

> Sex behavior and sexual behavior are perhaps the most complex of all traits and the hardest to analyze in terms of cause and effect. With the biological primary and secondary sex characteristics, heredity can be discerned as usually playing a major role, although environmental factors can be important as modifiers. But in sex and sexual behavior biology is so mixed up with psychology and sociology that the problem of sifting out hereditary factors may be . . . . most difficult.[1]

Our views of human sexuality have changed dramatically in the last century. It is hard for us to transport ourselves backward into the mind set of the nineteenth century. Herant Katchadourian and Donald Lunde write:

> Although evidence of infantile sexuality has been abundant in everyday life, formal recognition of it has come about relatively recently and over considerable opposition. Traditional views of human sexuality before this century assumed an orderly progression from childhood sexual innocence through awakening of sexual impulses in adolescence to their culmination in adult behavior. Although this theoretical sequence is ap-

[1]Amram Scheinfeld, *Your Heredity and Environment* (Philadelphia: Lippincott, 1965), pp. 517–18.

> plicable to the emergence of reproductive capacity, it is not a correct model for sexual development.
>
> . . . We also know that there are wide differences in the time at which sexual behavior emerges, and that only some but not all infants and children are sexually responsive at any given age.[2]

Recent research has shown that nonbiological influences may be of far greater importance in sexual development than was previously assumed. The social environment in which the child grows up is, then, every bit as important as the inherited sex characteristics that mark him or her as different from those of the opposite sex. These are almost never inherent differences; rather they are end products of specific home and cultural influences. In the earlier rural culture of our country, a child could easily recognize which basic functions within the family were carried out by the father and which by the mother, thereby gaining a fairly clear picture of masculine and feminine roles. In contemporary society, in which both parents may work outside the home, the child is likely to be strongly influenced by peer group and school environment. There may be no clear-cut masculine and feminine roles presented. Today we recognize that there are many variations in masculine and feminine roles. There are a large number of single-parent homes in American society and another sizable percentage of families in which a child lives with parent and stepparent or is in reality a part of two separate families, spending his or her childhood alternating between the two homes created by the divorced parents. Other families live in communes. In these situations, there are a number of role models before the child. A choice of one clear-cut model is then less likely to occur.

Contemporary civilization, then, has undoubtedly complicated our sexual development. We may have clear patterns for physical and intellectual development but confused models for sexual development.[3] It is easy to approach sex as psychiatrist David Reuben does—seek to accumulate a wide variety of facts, no matter how relevant or irrelevant they may be: "How big is the normal penis?" "Does ginseng really work?" "What kinds of things do girls insert into the vagina?" "Are nuns allowed to take birth control pills?"[4] But do such facts really answer the important questions of who we are sexually and how we should behave in regard to sex? Developing into a mature individual, intellectually and sexually, is difficult. It takes clear thinking and responsible decision-making as well as factual knowledge. Therefore let us consider premarital sexual behavior in a broader sociological, psychological, and ethical context.

[2]Herant A. Katchadourian and Donald T. Lunde, *Fundamentals of Human Sexuality,* 2nd ed. (New York: Holt, Rinehart & Winston, 1975), pp. 213–14.

[3]See Benjamin A. Kogan, *Human Sexual Expression* (New York: Harcourt Brace Jovanovich, 1973).

[4]David R. Reuben, *Everything You Always Wanted to Know About Sex* (New York: McKay, 1969).

Gender Identity

The development of gender identity is an important part of the sexual experience. Gender identity describes the psychological sense of self as male or female. A young child acquires a relatively fixed internal sense that he or she is either a boy or a girl. Obviously, this has a profound influence on future preferences and development. There is an interaction of biological and environmental factors that help to determine the way gender identity is shaped and formed. The biological factors are dominant in the prenatal period, and again in the dramatic changes at puberty. But, meanwhile, the environmental factors have their influence from birth until a person establishes a fairly consistent and workable gender identity upon beginning adult life.[5]

> *Gender identity* refers to the psychological state in which a person comes to believe "I am female" or "I am male." This is the first stage in gender development, and appears to be pretty well set by age three. In most instances, biological sex and gender identity correspond; that is, the child who is chromosomally female and has female genitals labels herself a girl, and the child who is chromosomally male and has male genitals labels himself a boy. However, there have been a number of cases of individuals whose gender identities do not match their genitals or chromosomes. . . . What is important . . . is that misassigned children appear to develop by age three a relatively stable gender identity, consistent with social labeling and not with biology.[6]

Our reactions to the opposite sex will reflect the strength and consistency of our gender identity. The wide range of individual differences in sexual interest, motivation, and experience means that we all look at the question of premarital sexual experience from different perspectives.

Premarital Sexual Behavior

One subject that has always been included in discussions of American marriage and family life is that of premarital sexual relations. The subject has been a vital one since the early research of Davis, Terman, and Burgess and Cottrell. The publication of the Kinsey reports on sexual behavior caused great controversy at the time (1948, 1953). There seems to be no end to the contemporary reports on the sexual revolution, which usually attempt to buttress their conclusions with new surveys or explanations of premarital

[5]John H. Gagnon, *Human Sexualities* (Glenview, Ill.: Scott, Foresman, 1977), pp. 59–66.
[6]Gagnon, p. 63.

sexual behavior. And no wonder, for the subject is of prime importance to young adults who are involved in making day-by-day decisions about the pattern of their premarital relationships.

Today, these studies on sexual behavior are a part of the increasing interest being given to human sexuality in its broader aspects, and to the relationship between the sexes before and during the marriage experience. The research studies available on premarital sexual relations indicate that sexual intercourse before marriage is more common today than it was fifty years ago. It is difficult to make comparisons with conditions one hundred years ago, because modern survey techniques were not widely used at that time. Also, today's studies are usually taken with college students or other middle-class groupings, and that segment of our population is much larger today than it was a century ago.[7] Our information on rural families and working-class families of previous generations is extremely limited.

The trends reported in studies by Terman,[8] Locke,[9] and Kinsey, together with a comparison of various other research studies of college students, show the ways that patterns are changing in our culture. In Terman's study of 792 couples, 49.4 percent of husbands born before 1890 reported premarital sexual experience, and 84.4 percent of husbands born after 1910. Fewer women reported premarital experience: only 13.5 percent of those born before 1890 and 68.3 percent of those born after 1910. The later generation, coming to their teens in the 1920s and 1930s, marked the real sexual revolution of the twentieth century. Locke's study reported the same trends, and Kinsey's data were similar. In his study *Sexual Behavior in the Human Male*,[10] Kinsey reported that 68 percent of the men had experienced premarital sex by age eighteen, 77 percent by age twenty-two, and 92 percent by age thirty-eight. Education was a significant factor here: men with at least a year of college education reported a much lower frequency.

Recent Studies

Contemporary studies have included both college and noncollege populations. Unfortunately, no research team in the 1970s has approached the question of sexual activity (particularly in the college situation) with the single-

[7]See Winston Ehrmann, "Marital and Nonmarital Sexual Behavior," *Handbook of Marriage and the Family* (Chicago: Rand McNally, 1964); Lester A. Kirkendall, *Premarital Intercourse and Interpersonal Relationships* (New York: Julian Press, 1961); Ira L. Reiss, *Premarital Sexual Standards in America* (New York: Free Press, 1960); Alfred C. Kinsey, Wardell B. Pomeroy, and Clyde E. Martin, *Sexual Behavior in the Human Male* (Philadelphia: Saunders, 1948); Alfred C. Kinsey and Paul H. Gebhard, *Sexual Behavior in the Human Female* (Philadelphia: Saunders, 1953); Vance Packard, *The Sexual Wilderness* (New York: McKay, 1968).

[8]Lewis M. Terman et al., *Psychological Factors in Marital Happiness* (New York: McGraw-Hill, 1938).

[9]Harvey J. Locke, *Predicting Adjustment in Marriage* (New York: Holt, Rinehart & Winston, 1951).

[10]Kinsey et al., *Sexual Behavior in the Human Male*, p. 550.

mindedness and dedication that Kinsey and his associates did in their pioneering work a generation ago. Samples are often not selected at random, or they are chosen from a limited college grouping, or they are chosen only from volunteers who may not be representative of others of a similar age, economic class level, ethnic or religious group. Yet there is a fairly wide range of studies to choose from. Let us examine, briefly, three reports on sexual behavior of teenagers and college students.

Vener and Stewart duplicated a survey of adolescent sexuality in a midwestern school system over a three-year period. They measured varying levels of sexual activity, comparing boys and girls in both 1970 and 1973. The results are shown in Table 4–1.

This study did not indicate that a major change in sexual behavior had occurred, but that there were moderate and significant changes during the three-year period studied. There were increases in the number of students who had intercourse, and in those who had more than one sexual partner. Also, the use of marijuana tripled, the use of hard drugs almost doubled, and there was increased consumption of beer, wine, and cigarettes. The authors do suggest that the changes in attitude which have been evidenced in our society in the past generation are now being reflected in youthful be-

Table 4–1 Heterosexual Activity in Community "B" by Sex: 1970–1973

	Percentage of Students Who Have Participated in an Activity At Least Once			
	Boys		*Girls*	
Levels of Sexual Activity	*1970 (989)*	*1973 (937)*	*1970 (924)*	*1973 (1035)*
I. Held hands	87.6	88.5	89.2	89.4
II. Held arm around or been held	80.5	81.7	84.6	86.5
III. Kissed or been kissed	76.6	79.7	81.6	81.2
IV. Necked (prolonged hugging and kissing)	63.3	63.7	67.8	64.1
V. Light petting (feeling above the waist)	57.3	59.0	49.7	51.4
VI. Heavy petting (feeling below the waist)	45.1	49.3	33.6	37.5
VII. Gone all the way (coitus)	27.8	33.4	16.1	22.4
VIII. Coitus with two or more partners	14.2	19.4	5.7	8.9

SOURCE: Arthur M. Vener and Cyrus S. Stewart, "Adolescent Sexual Behavior in Middle America Revisited: 1970–1973," *Journal of Marriage and the Family,* 36, no. 4 (Nov. 1974), 731. Copyright 1974 by the National Council on Family Relations. Reprinted by permission.

havior patterns, both sexually and in other areas such as drug use and school attitudes and study patterns.

A second study by Robert Sorensen also shows an increasing level of sexual behavior by teenagers in relation to earlier studies in the 1950s and 1960s.[11] His survey indicated a majority of teenagers of both sexes (52 percent) had experienced sexual intercourse (see Table 4–2). Several criticisms have been made of Sorensen's work because his respondents were volunteers and there was a lack of control over the sampling process. But the study does represent a serious attempt to investigate the range of sexual behavior among adolescents.

A third study that attempts to trace differences in sexual attitudes and behavior over a ten-year period is the work of King, Balswick, and Robinson. These authors surveyed students at a large southern university in 1965, 1970, and 1975. Their study reveals a continuing liberalization of sexual attitudes, with particular criticism of the double standard. Over the ten-year period, the number of male students reporting premarital intercourse has increased from 65.1 percent to 73.9 percent, and the number of female students from 28.7 percent to 57.1 percent. Liberalization was also indicated in an increase in the level of heavy petting behavior, again most noticeably among women students. King et al. conclude:

> The evidence suggests that society is approaching a single premarital sexual standard. . . . Indeed, if the liberalization of female and male sexual behavior and attitudes continues at the same rate of change in the late 1970s that it had in the early 1970s, an equalitarian premarital sexual standard may essentially replace the traditional double standard by 1980. This is not to say that more conservative behaviors and attitudes will disappear; rather, that as permissiveness increases, the equalitarian standard will take precedence over the double standard.[12]

There is always the question of whether or not college students represent a fair sample of behavior for the total American population. In some ways collegians are the pioneers in setting new trends in many areas of life. The antiwar movement in the 1960s certainly was one such case. In other ways, since college students represent "the establishment" either through their family connections or through their future careers and responsibilities, they may take a more thoughtful and sometimes a more conservative view on issues that affect their own future. This is undoubtedly the reason why we

[11]Robert C. Sorensen, *Adolescent Sexuality in Contemporary America* (New York: World, 1973).

[12]Karl King, Jack O. Balswick, and Ira E. Robinson, "The Continuing Premarital Sexual Revolution Among College Females," *Journal of Marriage and the Family*, 39, no. 3 (August 1977), 455–59.

Table 4–2 Adolescent Sexual Experience

Virgins (*All adolescents who have not had sexual intercourse*)	All Teenagers	By Sex: Boys	By Sex: Girls	By Age: 13–15	By Age: 16–19
Sexually inexperienced (Virgins with no beginning sexual activities)	22%	20%	25%	39%	9%
Sexual beginners (Virgins who have actively or passively experienced sexual petting)	17%	14%	19%	12%	21%
Unclassified virgins (Virgins who for whatever reason could not be classified in the above groups)	9%	7%	11%	12%	6%
Total	48%	41%	55%	63%	36%
Nonvirgins (*All adolescents who have had sexual intercourse one or more times*)					
Serial monogamists (Nonvirgins having a sexual relationship with one person)	21%	15%	28%	9%	31%
Sexual adventurers (Nonvirgins freely moving from one sexual-intercourse partner to another)	15%	24%	6%	10%	18%
Inactive nonvirgins (Nonvirgins who have not had sexual intercourse for more than one year)	12%	13%	10%	15%	10%
Unclassified nonvirgins (Nonvirgins who for whatever reason could not be classified in the above groups)	4%	7%	1%	3%	5%
Total	52%	59%	45%	37%	64%

SOURCE: After chart "American Adolescent—Sexual Behavior Groups" (p. 122) from *Adolescent Sexuality in Contemporary America* by Robert C. Sorensen (World Publishing Company). Copyright © 1973 by Robert C. Sorensen. Reprinted by permission of Harper & Row Publishers, Inc.

see a variation of opinion on different campuses and in different areas of the country.

These studies remind us that there is no dearth of research in this area. A good number of investigations have been made. We might then ask ourselves the question: Why don't individuals, couples, and sociologists agree on whether premarital sexual experience is desirable? There must be some legitimate differences of opinion—what are they? What are the motivating factors that lead many couples toward premarital sexual relations, and what are the factors that restrain others from the same experience? Are there any factors that are particularly important in the formation of a person's attitudes toward premarital sex? Let us look at the pros and cons of the question, recognizing that some individuals have a closed mind on the matter, and will not be willing to discuss it objectively.

Factors Encouraging Premarital Sexual Relations

There are a number of factors that motivate couples to engage in premarital sexual intercourse. The first and simplest reply to the question why a person might engage in premarital relations might be "Why not? What's wrong with it?" For many students, the discussion might stop at this point. "Why bother to talk about it?" "Among my close friends, or in the group that I run around with at school, or among my old high school friends here at state college, there isn't a single virgin." This kind of peer pressure is certainly powerful. The rising number of premaritally experienced students is putting increasing pressure on nonconformists to "go all the way." It is never easy to be in the minority, and especially when to do so seems to imply a personal failure to be popular, to be in with the latest trend. This factor cannot be underestimated.

A second motivation might be physical need. Our physical needs are a basic part of our makeup; we are frustrated if they are not met. The same principle may be applied from a Freudian point of view. We are said to have strong and basic *id* desires, many of which are sexual in nature. These desires reach out for satisfaction, and if they are repressed or otherwise thwarted, they will return to haunt us in another guise. Many people feel that it is natural to satisfy these physical and psychological needs through premarital sexual intercourse. (Under the double standard the almost universal presence of prostitution in past and contemporary societies can be explained as a concession to this motivation for men, allowing them to find satisfaction for the need outside the marriage relationship.)

Lester Kirkendall was a pioneer in the field of premarital sex research. He carefully interviewed a selected sample of male students with premarital experience. He then asked them to place their experience at certain levels of involvement. Many men reported intercourse with a prostitute (19 percent) or with a partner "picked up in some kind of casual circumstance (30 percent)."[13] Kirkendall sees this as clearly indicating physical satisfaction as a major sexual motivation for men. It is less common for typical middle-class or college women to enter into such casual relationships, since such activity

[13]Kirkendall, pp. 25, 57.

is frowned upon by society. But the number of women now engaging in sex for physical satisfaction is clearly increasing.

A third motivation for premarital sexual intercourse is the reasoning that premarital experience will help the couple to make a satisfactory sexual adjustment in marriage. A couple must learn to make many adjustments in order to build a strong mutual relationship. They must share common interests and common friendships. Such a relationship is built gradually, bit by bit, so it is proposed that they begin sexual adjustment early in order to prepare for their marriage. The premarital experience would also be a means of discovering a poor or unsuitable sexual partnership before the couple is fully committed to marriage. On most important questions in life, one is permitted evaluation and experience before making a major decision. In the same way, it is argued, one ought to be free to have premarital sex to be certain that one will have an adequate and satisfying relationship with a particular partner after marriage.

Kinsey's data are also cited in support of this position.[14] The women in his study who had the most frequent premarital sexual experience made more rapid adjustment in the beginning of their marital sexual relations. (The measure of adjustment was the ability to reach orgasm.) Those who failed to reach orgasm in premarital coitus also had a higher rate of failure to achieve orgasm in marital coitus. Kinsey's main argument is that more frequent early successes (using orgasm as the criterion) were correlated with the same pattern after marriage. We will reconsider this data when we discuss factors that restrain premarital sexual relationships.

[14]Kinsey and Gebhard, *Sexual Behavior in the Human Female*, pp. 328–30.

Premarital sexual experience is sometimes thought to help in overcoming inhibitions and frigidity in the marital relationship, particularly for the woman. There has been a great deal of criticism of the Victorian approach to sexual morality, because the severe restrictions it placed on sexual expression and sexual development stifled natural and wholesome impulses. Evidence of sexual curiosity in the young child was condemned, and any appearance of sexual interest before marriage was thought to be sinful. This kind of training often led to frigidity and lack of sexual satisfaction in marriage.

Although attitudes today are generally less rigid, psychiatrists still report that their patients often are unable to achieve normal sexual adjustment in marriage because they have been severely inhibited early in life. Cultural restrictions are still an important factor in restraining the premarital contacts of young women. These restrictions, however, may be a real hindrance when the same woman tries to become an enthusiastic sexual partner in marriage. If her sexual feelings have been turned off quite consistently, they may not turn on easily and rapidly in marriage. Those people in favor of greater premarital sexual freedom argue that it will counteract such negative training and enable the partners to enter more freely and naturally into their sexual relationship later on in marriage.

A further argument proposed in favor of premarital relations is that it is a natural expression of love. Two people have fallen in love, and that fact dominates their relationship with each other. They want to be together, to communicate together, to share together, to have sex together. They are of a reasonable age, let us assume; who can deny them this joyful experience?

A refinement of this motivation is the terminology proposed by Kirkendall. Will the choice to engage in premarital relations strengthen the interpersonal relationship between the partners? The morality of any sexual act depends on the answer to that question.

> Whenever a decision or a choice is to be made concerning behavior, the moral decision will be the one which works toward the creation of trust, confidence, and integrity in relationships. It should increase the capacity of individuals to cooperate, and enhance the sense of self-respect in the individual. Acts which create distrust, suspicion, and misunderstanding, which build barriers and destroy integrity, are immoral. They decrease the individual's sense of self-respect, and rather than producing a capacity to work together they separate people and break down the capacity for communication.[15]

Kirkendall proposes that this standard of behavior be applied to premarital

[15]Kirkendall, p. 6.

sexual relationships. If the coital act strengthens the relationship, it may be considered moral and helpful; but if it weakens the relationship, it is of negative value and immoral. Kirkendall's theory was developed and exemplified through interviews and counseling with a large number of college students, especially men.

It still seems more typical to hear a woman describe her attitude in regard to premarital sexual intercourse in emotional terms, viewing such a relationship as an expression of love: "It is right to engage in premarital sexual relations if there is genuine love and affection between the two partners." Ira L. Reiss terms this standard "permissiveness with affection."[16] Reiss believes that this code is becoming widely accepted, particularly on college campuses. If the relationship with the partner is a stable and meaningful one, and if the woman sees hope of future marriage with her partner, then she is willing to enter into intercourse. Love and sex are united.

Another motivation for premarital sex is one that has been most frequently advanced by men in many cultures. A man may claim the freedom to engage in premarital sexual relations because he thinks it will prove his manliness and maturity. Although this outlook is more common among lower-class men than in middle- or upper-class groups, there is still enough of the double standard present in the American culture to encourage premarital intercourse, even with prostitutes, for those men who accept this reasoning for their behavior. With this standard, a man has freedom in the choice of a sexual partner, and he is free to enter into intercourse with casual partners in order to satisfy his needs, prove his manliness, and gain the experience necessary to a satisfactory relationship with his wife at some future time.

There are a number of other motivations for premarital sex that might be cited. Loneliness is certainly one. In an impersonal, mechanized, hectic so-

[16]Ira L. Reiss, *Family Systems in America*, 2nd ed. (Hinsdale, Ill.: Dryden Press, 1976), pp. 149–54.

ciety, we all feel isolated and alone at times. Sexual intercourse promises us a note of intimacy, even if it is brief. One may find oneself just as frustrated and lonely after the experience, but nevertheless sexual contact does offer some satisfaction, even if it is only momentary. Curiosity is another possible motivation—perhaps a powerful one, especially for the adventurous. We are encouraged to explore the unknown, to gain more experience. "Have you traveled overseas?" "Have you considered working out-of-state next summer?" "Have you thought of taking your upper-division work at a different college?" We are invited to be curious. And in the same way, the argument runs, we should be curious enough to gain some premarital sexual experience. Rebellion is still another factor to be considered. How many young women, for example, have found premarital sex an ideal way to flaunt their rebellion against parents, school, or a boring job? If the experience leads to pregnancy, the encounter may have opened the door to a whole new way of life (which unfortunately may be fraught with more problems than the situation from which she escaped).

Most of the arguments favoring premarital intercourse have been developed culturally to favor the man. But the new trend toward a single standard of behavior in our culture means that now many women are using the same reasoning and seeking the same freedom of choice and behavior as men. And the increase of sexual intimacy between steady dating partners and engaged couples suggests that the motivation toward premarital intercourse, and the decision to engage in it, is probably more equally shared by both partners now than was the case under the double standard of behavior.

Factors Restraining Premarital Sexual Relations

Though many of the motivations for premarital sex seem sensible, and the experience is obviously attractive, a number of social scientists, as well as medical, educational, and religious leaders, would point out reasons for restraining premarital sexual relations. Many of their arguments contradict the favorable arguments that we have just considered. Let us examine premarital sex from this different point of view, utilizing additional research studies and comments made on the conclusions and the work of various social scientists.

In the first place, the argument for free and unregulated sex behavior is subject to serious question. Implicit in it is the assumption that a person's physical needs are paramount and must take precedence over intellectual, social, moral, and spiritual needs. But a major developmental task for the child at almost every stage of life is to learn to control and channel basic physical needs in realistic and socially acceptable ways. Children must learn to adjust to the requirements of formal schooling in order to gain the education necessary to survive as adults in modern society; their natural impulse to play rather than to study is subordinated to society's needs. In the same way we might expect sexual needs to be subject to social controls.

Kinsey's data showed a relationship between education and the occurrence of premarital intercourse.[17] His sample of 3,031 cases of men who reported premarital experience with companions and prostitutes by age twenty indicates that almost twice as many men with grade-school educations had premarital intercourse as did college men. And in the age period between sixteen and twenty, the grade-school group reported seven times as much premarital intercourse as the college group. Men more disciplined in their educational pursuits are also more disciplined in their sexual outlets. Or, in other words, there was a definite correlation between low educational attainment and frequent premarital sexual experience.

The answer to the "everyone is doing it" argument is obvious. Everyone isn't, just as everyone is not Republican, or in favor of gun control, or against abortion. Most serious discussions of our changing sexual mores in the sexual revolution stress the fact that our relationship to another person through sexual intercourse should be a very personal and meaningful one. We recognize the pressures of society around us, but we place a high value on the individual and on freedom of choice. In this very intimate side of life, every person should be true to himself or herself. When all the evidence is weighed, the choice must be a personal one.

The argument based upon physical and biological need is a common one. The Freudian view of psychology has been popular for half a century now, and we recognize the dangers of fear and repression. But modern psychology has also added to the insights of Freud, and we recognize other factors that strongly affect our decision-making processes. Learning theory is crucial in this regard. Do we learn to govern our daily life experiences strictly in accord with our personal desires and feelings (our *id* impulses), or do we learn the value of self-control, discipline, and even, at times, self-sacrifice? Which approach to life is most rewarding, over the long run? It is not hard to make a strong case in the direction of limiting premarital sexual experience upon a sound psychological basis.

How does premarital intercourse relate to satisfactory sexual adjustment in marriage? Changing cultural patterns are clearly significant here. If the experience of premarital sex is unsatisfactory, or if one or both partners have guilt feelings about their behavior, will it retard rather than enhance their later relationship? Some premarital sexual experience is hurried or carried on under conditions far less conducive to mutual trust and love than the conditions of marriage. The learning experience may well be negative rather than positive.

The Kinsey study of female sexual behavior is often cited at this point. Kinsey shows that those women who had the most premarital sexual expe-

[17]Kinsey et al., *Sexual Behavior in the Human Male,* p. 550.

rience were more likely to have successful orgasmic experiences during the first year of marriage.[18] Kinsey therefore concluded that premarital experience is a positive preparation for sexual adjustment and success in marriage. But premarital sexual experience also seemed to be correlated with extramarital sexual experience. Of the 2,480 married women who participated in Kinsey's study, nearly 50 percent had had sexual intercourse before marriage.[19] However, of the 514 women who reported that they had experienced extramarital sex, more than two-thirds had also had intercourse before marriage. Thus the sexually experienced women were twice as likely as the inexperienced women to look for sexual satisfaction outside marriage. A relaxed attitude toward sex before marriage seems to indicate a relaxed attitude toward sex after marriage.[20]

What can be said in answer to the problems of fear and inhibition? The potential damage to marital sexual adjustment is a real and serious one. It should be remembered, however, that premarital intercourse is only one way of dealing with such problems. Helen Colton suggests that competent sex counseling may be sought by married couples who have such problems.

> Today, many of us, because of the antisex recordings made on our nervous systems during our early years, find that we need at some point in our lives to seek sex counseling. A sex counselor who is a candid, unembarrassed, and warm human being serves the psychological purpose of reparenting. He or she helps to remove the effects of the repressive parents of long ago and gives approval to the counselees to enjoy their sexuality.
>
> . . .
>
> Our sexual patterns throughout life often repeat our earliest sexual experiences. . . .
>
> The goal of counseling is to free our personalities to enjoy the human being's most intense source of pleasure—our sexuality.[21]

Intercourse with a partner who does not really understand the nature of one's negative feelings and who may not be seriously concerned about one's real personhood—or who may have serious inhibitions of his or her own—may be traumatic. Again, we must view this solution with uncertainty as to its value.

The expression of sexual intercourse as the evidence for genuine love and affection also has both positive and negative components. We will consider love

[18]Kinsey and Gebhard, *Sexual Behavior in the Human Female,* pp. 328–30.
[19]Kinsey and Gebhard, *Sexual Behavior in the Human Female,* p. 286.
[20]Kinsey and Gebhard, *Sexual Behavior in the Human Female,* p. 427.
[21]Helen Colton, *Sex After the Sexual Revolution* (New York: Association Press, 1972), pp. 40–41.

in its myriad meanings in Chapter 7; it is sufficient to note here that the relationship of love to sex will depend on the meanings we attach to the word *love.* Giving, caring, knowing, sharing, responsibility—all those meanings are involved. Many young people who have doubts about the benefits of premarital sex prefer to express their commitment to their partners by refraining from intercourse until they are married. When such an attitude is based on mature and responsible thinking (rather than an exploitative attempt to gain a definite commitment from one's partner through sex teasing), it should be respected.

Kirkendall's classic study, which introduced the concept of interpersonal relationships in this area, should be clearly examined. The validity of this standard for a wide range of moral judgments has been questioned. There is no doubt that it is often a good thing to "enlarge the number of persons or groups with which we are able to cooperate."[22] Modern society is cold and impersonal, and we need to broaden our relationships with people. But can that be the sole criterion of what is moral and what is not? Most social situations are much more complex than that.

It is also interesting to note that Kirkendall's study, in analyzing the reactions of the men who had experienced premarital intercourse, found that few sexual experiences took place between engaged couples; many were with casual partners.[23] In total, the 200 men studied reported some 688 partners in their sexual relationships. Only 30 experiences, or 4.5 percent, were reported as having strengthened the interpersonal relationships between the partners. The vast majority of experiences were reported to have produced a negative result on the relationships. That shouldn't have been so, we think, but it was.

> Experience in intercourse did not facilitate communication, for the number of subjects who reported "no communication" following the beginning of intercourse was greater than the number who reported "no communication" prior to intercourse. . . .
>
> The data indicate that the men who were the subjects of this study were considerably more self-centered than partner-centered in their attitudes toward the persons with whom they were involved.[24]

Many other motivations for premarital sex are also subject to question. Does true maturity come through the superficial judgment that sexual experience equals manhood or womanhood, or does it come by a process of developing one's character over an extended period of time? Can the young men and women who are accepted by their peers because they have become sexually experienced translate this acceptance into a satisfying and mature adult sexuality without any further effort? Or will their development of a

[22]Kirkendall, p. 6.
[23]Kirkendall, p. 254.
[24]Kirkendall, pp. 295–96.

positive self-image depend on a number of factors, some of which are not primarily sexual?

Curiosity, loneliness, and rebellion may all be seen as negative motivations for premarital intercourse. Through the sexual encounter a person may be attempting to meet basic personality needs that should be fulfilled in more lasting and rational ways in the total life pattern. Undoubtedly this is one major reason why so many teenage marriages fail. Sexual attraction is strong and may reinforce a neurotic need the couple have for each other; but living together, within or without marriage, requires a much deeper kind of maturity than mere sexual experience.

Other considerations are involved. There is the problem of possible pregnancy. Theoretically, more effective contraceptives and a broader public knowledge of birth control should eliminate this possibility. But in practice it seems to be a continuing factor of major importance. The number of unwed mothers in our society is increasing. Kinsey indicated that only 19 percent of the women in his study having premarital pregnancies married the father.[25] Some studies of unwed mothers suggest that they consciously or unconsciously seek the pregnancy, either to force the man into marriage or to express their hostility against parental dominance.[26] A substantial number of high school marriages are forced because of pregnancy. The problem is still very much with us.

The relation of religious belief to one's attitude toward premarital and extramarital intercourse is another significant variable. There has been a strong religious emphasis on standards of sanctity and purity that stress the view of marriage as a sacred institution, with both human and divine implications. The key word here might be *consistency*. A person who seeks mature, integrated behavior patterns seeks to be consistent in his value judgments, his personal and social relationships, and his sexual behavior. If premarital intercourse is inconsistent with his moral and religious values, participation in it may be self-defeating.

Studies have shown consistently that premarital intercourse is less frequent among people who are strongly religious. Since there are many conflicting religious currents in our culture that pull people toward more liberal or more conservative religious stances, the future influence of this factor is not known for certain.

Another source of concern in premarital sex relations is the possibility of exploitation. In order to gratify himself, the man may seek to override the woman's objections and restraint by convincing her, untruthfully, that he is really committed to her. Or the woman may seek to obligate her partner beyond his own choice and intent through encouraging him to begin or con-

[25]Kinsey and Gebhard, *Sexual Behavior in the Human Female*, p. 57.
[26]Leontine R. Young, *Out of Wedlock*, rev. ed. (New York: McGraw-Hill, 1963).

tinue premarital sex. (Refusal of sexual relations can be used for the same purpose, however.) Such exploitation can lead to many unfortunate consequences.

The wide range of theoretical hypotheses regarding premarital intercourse among women has been summarized by Davidson and Leslie.[27] They tested twenty-two hypotheses among women associated with a major southern medical complex. Factors which they found to be significant included peer norms, permissive personal attitudes, affectional relationships, social class, religious orthodoxy, and later maturation. They point out that much of the work done in this field has lacked a consistent theoretical orientation. To the student first being introduced to this problem on the intellectual level, then, we must post a sign of caution, and continue to stress the necessity for individual evaluation and choice.

Premarital Sex: Sources of Conflict

Why is premarital sex so controversial? The position had been taken in an earlier generation that the very circumstances surrounding premarital sexual intercourse were a strong argument for abstinence. On the other hand, greater freedom and permissiveness in our culture are undoubtedly changing the setting of many premarital liaisons; these factors will probably be less significant in the future.

Today, however, three common conflicts over premarital sex may be recognized. One is the generational conflict: parents and the over-thirty generation are more conservative than adolescents and young adults. This has been true for many generations past—the generation gap was certainly not invented in the 1970s. The greatest trauma in the conflict undoubtedly comes when the young couple have mixed feelings about the values and behavior espoused by the parents. It is easier to be a thoroughgoing rebel and cut all ties with the older generation than to be a halfway one.

Another common conflict is a moral and religious one. If premarital sex conflicts with the couple's basic convictions, or with the convictions of one partner, then guilt feelings may result. These feelings may surface during courtship or perhaps after marriage, during disagreements over responsibilities, a forced marriage, infidelity, or other points of difference between the couple.

Another conflict may be seen as one of responsibility. Premarital sexual relations involve no final responsibility on the part of either partner. With the modern methods of birth control now available, fear of pregnancy is

[27] J. Kenneth Davidson, Sr., and Gerald R. Leslie, "Premarital Sexual Intercourse: An Application of Axiomatic Theory Construction," *Journal of Marriage and the Family*, 39, no. 1 (Feb. 1977), 15–25.

being minimized, although it is still present. Many couples initiate a premarital relationship rather than wait for marriage. A man may decide, for instance, that he is not ready for marriage, that he would prefer another partner, or that he doesn't want to surrender his independence; a premarital relationship is one he can always end in order to follow a new course. A woman may wish to change to a more promising partner, or she may have reservations about the stability of her marriage to her current partner; she can withdraw from the relationship without the complications and embarrassment of separation and divorce.

The concept of responsibility is a central one in modern society. We can no longer turn aside from the interests and needs of others, whether they are of our own race, religion, or nationality or of another. In the same sense, to enter into the intimate and personal life of another person through sexual intercourse and then to take no ultimate responsibility for that association seems to imply a course that is socially irresponsible.

Value Clarification

There is a basic need for value clarification in the area of premarital sex. What are our priorities? Human sexuality may be analyzed in terms of biological, psychological, and social factors.[28] But ultimately the ideal must be blended with the actual: we must consider how human beings should behave sexually as well as how they actually do behave. To remove sexual behavior from the ethical context is to oversimplify and dehumanize the individual. Man is an animal, but man is also more than an animal. Since the sex act usually involves other human beings, any thorough and meaningful examination of our sexuality must involve a recognition of our responsibility to our fellow man.

The discussion of premarital intercourse fifty years ago would have centered around three major issues. First, premarital coitus might result in an unwanted pregnancy, with consequent disgrace for the woman. This consequence would be public, and a just punishment for the woman's mistake. Second, both man and woman might contract venereal disease and suffer permanent damage from syphilis or gonorrhea. Here again, the consequence would be considered a punishment. Third, ethical and religious standards of purity and fidelity would be violated; the man and woman involved might have strong guilt feelings or feel separated from their religious community. However, their act would not necessarily have public consequences in the same sense as in the first two cases.

Today, the importance of the first two issues has been reduced by medical advances. Birth control methods have been refined and become widely

[28]Katchadourian and Lunde, chap. 1.

available in our society. Penicillin and other drugs have made it possible to treat venereal disease effectively. Unfortunately, both birth control and disease control are often ignored by couples participating in premarital sex (who are, to be fair, often hindered by parental, social, and legal restrictions), so the first two issues remain significant ones. However, most meaningful discussion is now on the ethical and religious level, or on the scientific level. We have already discussed the value system proposed by Kirkendall, which stresses the improvement of interpersonal relations as a goal. His conclusions call for adherence to that goal and "acceptance of the fact that the sexual impulse is essentially positive and life-giving in nature. Rather than fearing it, our task is learning how to direct and utilize it."[29] But what are the actual value standards existing in our society today?

Contemporary Sexual Standards

Ira L. Reiss, who has written extensively on sexual standards, suggests that there are four actual standards coexisting in our present society.[30] These four standards, all of which have certain inconsistencies in practice, are the double standard, abstinence, permissiveness with affection, and permissiveness without affection. Each has particular features that prevent its universal acceptance. The first two were the ones under which Western society operated prior to the twentieth century. The third, which we have already considered, is the more common of the two innovations developed in our contemporary culture. The fourth, the most liberal of all, is openly advocated by a vocal minority but is still not widely accepted.

We are in a period of accelerating change in our society. An important part of this change is certainly in the area of our sexual experience and standards. The more that a focus is put upon the immediate feelings of the individuals involved, in terms of their gratification at one particular point in time, the more difficult it becomes to maintain a perspective that encompasses the past and the future as well as the present. This is not a difference in standards of sexuality alone, it is a reflection of different value systems and different lifestyles in a pluralistic society.

WHAT DO STUDENTS THINK?

Can we discuss our attitudes toward premarital sex objectively? One can find support for each of the viewpoints for and against premarital sexual relations with surveys and case studies of college students. Students must realize that there are no easy answers to the question, and that their own views may

[29]Kirkendall, p. 252.
[30]Reiss, pp. 149–54.

change with further experience and maturity. The final choice must be made by the student.

It is unfortunate that when we take the scientific approach to such a question it becomes easy to leave out the personal element. We can quantify feelings and attitudes and standards and behaviors, but they may not really represent what sexual experience means to the individual man or woman. In some way, we have to consider the personal level and apply our new knowledge and insight to our own individual situation.

Women still bear the heaviest responsibility for determining the limits of premarital intimacy. Often they defer sexual experience on the basis of what they feel will be their husbands' attitudes toward it, or as an expression of their idealistic attitudes toward marriage.

> Though a person has an instinctive drive to have sex relations, love, that is, emotional love, should be most important. As young children we acquaint ourselves with certain facts through our sexual curiosity. As we mature physically and mentally, we learn of this beautiful miracle. We have the unspoken desire to partake of its joys and gratification.
>
> Our goal is sharing in marriage. What a marvelous thing to share this new experience with someone you love. If a person indulges in premarital coitus, some of the specialness is diminished. Learning to know your future partner is all-important. Empathy—sharing joy and sadness, illness and good health, and likes and dislikes, is all of help in establishing communication. Sexual communication is a necessary facet of marriage, but why not build first emotional communication? You are not only marrying a sex partner, but a "whole" person.[31]

Future Sexual Standards

It is difficult to predict future norms for premarital sexual behavior in our society. Several factors seem to be significant, and they will have a part in determining attitudes and behavior in the coming decades. One is the move toward a single standard. Logic, economics, social change, the feminist movement, and other considerations seem to bear this out. Women can no longer be regarded as second-class citizens, sexually or in any other way, and the double standard will gradually be eliminated.

Many sociologists are convinced that the present trends toward more permissive and free sexual expression will continue. "Permissiveness with affection" is perhaps the most popular standard with many college students. And the entire issue must be taken in perspective with other trends in our dating and courtship patterns. Bert Adams writes:

[31]Student report.

> Premarital sex is an element of heterosexual activity which is more widespread in the lower class than in the middle class, though that difference is lessening. In the middle class there are currently several competing value approaches to premarital sex, with humanistic liberalism, or "sex with affection," apparently predominating empirically. However, there are signs that premarital intercourse is becoming increasingly a matter of individual choice among middle-class young people, neither commanding the undue attention nor possessing the moral overtones that it still does among middle-class adults. One reason for this is that the phenomenon poses so little threat to the family system. . . . Whether these developments are viewed positively or negatively is as likely to be based on the biases of the writer as on empirical evidence that they are either good or bad for the individual himself.[32]

The youth culture has a strong impact on teenagers and young adults in our society.[33] Its present influence is certainly on the side of more liberal sexual attitudes, but not exclusively so.[34] It is possible that the trend may be toward what has been termed "enlightened asceticism" (no premarital sex) with a reaffirmation of the value of self-control and discipline as a preparation for stable and satisfying marriage. This standard is still very much alive, and it profits from a more positive attitude toward sex and the broader opportunities for discussion and education.

Finally, it is clear that premarital sexual behavior is closely related to other elements in society. What will the structure of the family be like ten or twenty years from now? Will smaller, better educated, more affluent families exercise more control over one or two sons and daughters than at present? Or will alternative lifestyles and trends toward a less confining family pattern

[32]Bert N. Adams, *The Family: A Sociological Interpretation* (Chicago: Rand McNally, 1975), p. 212.

[33]See discussion of Riesman's concept of the other-directed character, Chapter 1, pp. 25–28.

[34]See James J. Teevan, Jr., "Reference Groups and Premarital Sexual Behavior," *Journal of Marriage and the Family*, 34, no. 2 (May 1972), 283–91. See also Ira L. Reiss, "Premarital Sex as Deviant Behavior," *American Sociological Review*, 35, no. 1 (Feb. 1970), 78–87.

tilt the scale in the opposite direction? And what about ethnic groups? Will a resurgence of pride among blacks and Chicanos, for example, create a more liberal or conservative outlook on sex before marriage? And the same questions may be asked concerning politics, economics, and religion. We do not exist in a vacuum sexually.

Making the Choice

We have seen that there are many considerations that are of importance to college students and other young adults attempting to make their own personal decisions on premarital sexual relations. It is difficult to measure accurately the many complex personal and social factors that are involved. Each person is unique, and each one of us sees the factors involved from a personal point of view. Moreover, there is no way to tell ahead of time how a particular person's premarital sexual behavior will affect the marriage relationship.

We do know that marriage offers to most of us our greatest opportunity to be closely related to another human being, to share our deepest feelings and aspirations, hopes and fears. There are many ways that we express this feeling of closeness with husband or wife, but the sexual relationship is certainly one of the most significant, if not the dominant one. It is a natural and satisfying way of breaking down barriers that may separate husband from wife and wife from husband. The effect of premarital sexual intercourse on this intimate relationship is complex. Apparently, if the marriage is sound and the couple happily married, the remembrance of their behavior may not be disruptive. But if the couple have difficulty in their marriage, then their experience of premarital intercourse may create suspicion, and there is more likelihood that it will become an overt factor in their conflict.

Somehow, one wishes to find both experience and wisdom. We all look back on experiences that seem to have been meaningless and a waste of time to us. "Why did I bother?" "How could I have done that?" We want to live life to the full. There are peak experiences waiting ahead for us if we prepare ourselves for them, and give ourselves fully to them. In a unique way we realize that the treasures of our human sexuality contain the possibilities for some of life's highest and finest experiences. In seeking sexual experience thoughtfully, and even perhaps reverently, we can raise our interpersonal relationships to a new and richer plane.

SUMMARY

Sexual development is an important element in human growth. Heredity and environment both play a part in the normal development of sexuality. This growth is especially important in early years, which have a significant although not clearly understood influence on adult sexual relationships. Crucial to our sexual development is the development of gender identity, the sense of self as male or female.

A number of important studies have dealt with both premarital and marital sexual behavior. The Kinsey studies are the classic ones, but there have been numerous more recent and specialized studies, including many of college students. It is difficult, however, to be objective about this highly emotional and personal subject, which is so important to present and future life patterns.

Arguments in favor of premarital sexual relations include peer pressure from other students; the satisfaction of physical needs and desires; preparation for satisfactory sexual adjustment in marriage and overcoming inhibitions and frigidity; the expression of love, which strengthens interpersonal relationships; the desire to prove manliness or womanliness; as well as loneliness, curiosity, and rebellion.

Reasoning that tends to restrain premarital sexual relations is often based on the same evidence that is used to support premarital sexual experience. Free and unregulated sex behavior is open to question; every culture imposes some restrictions on sexual behavior. Even in our permissive society, many people, if not the majority, still choose to refrain from premarital sex. And the improvement of interpersonal relationships has been questioned as an adequate basis for determining moral behavior. Moreover, premarital sex experience may be considered a negative influence on marital adjustment, as indicated by Kinsey's data on extramarital affairs and divorce. Intercourse with an inconsiderate, thoughtless partner may also be damaging. And many other things need to be considered: pregnancy is still a problem; religion is another restraining factor; exploitation, curiosity, loneliness, and rebellion may all contribute to an unfulfilling experience in premarital intercourse. As a result many partners who are deeply in love prefer to express their commitment to each other by reserving sex for marriage.

Conflicts over premarital behavior are common. There is the generational conflict; the moral and religious dilemma; and the question of responsibility for the personhood of one's partner and for potential children of the union. There is a need for value clarification in which moral standards will be involved. We have all been influenced by the contemporary standard of permissiveness with affection. Student discussion of the subject reveals a wide range of attitudes, from an unrestrained liberal position to a more traditional support of premarital chastity. It is not easy to predict future norms for premarital sexual behavior, but a single standard for men and women seems to be becoming increasingly important. One must make his or her own decision about premarital sexual behavior. Our sexuality is a meaningful measure of our total life and personality.

SUGGESTED READINGS

Brecher, Edward M. *The Sex Researchers*. New York: Signet, 1971. Good introduction to the work of noted scholars in the field of human sexuality.

Davidson, J. Kenneth, Sr., and Gerald R. Leslie. "Premarital Sexual Intercourse: An Application of Axiomatic Theory Construction." *Journal of Marriage and the Family*, 39, no. 1 (Feb. 1977), 15–25. Careful and scholarly treatment of studies in the field with new summary of theory.

Gagnon, John H. *Human Sexualities*. Glenview, Ill.: Scott, Foresman, 1977. Recent statement of social learning view of sexual development.

Hettlinger, Richard. *Human Sexuality: A Psychosocial Perspective*. Belmont, Ca.: Wadsworth, 1975. Frank discussion of contemporary morality and views of sexuality directed toward college students.

Katchadourian, Herant A., and Donald T. Lunde. *Fundamentals of Human Sexuality*, 2nd ed. New York: Holt, Rinehart & Winston, 1975. Comprehensive treatment of the subject.

Kinsey, Alfred C., and Paul H. Gebhard. *Sexual Behavior in the Human Female*. Philadelphia: Saunders, 1953.

Kinsey, Alfred C., Wardell B. Pomeroy, and Clyde E. Martin. *Sexual Behavior in the Human Male*. Philadelphia: Saunders, 1948. Two basic works summarizing the Kinsey studies. Heavy use of statistical tables.

Kirkendall, Lester A. *Premarital Intercourse and Interpersonal Relationships*. New York: Julian Press, 1961. Study at Oregon State with reports of interviews with 200 male college students.

Reiss, Ira L. *The Social Context of Premarital Sexual Permissiveness*. New York: Holt, Rinehart & Winston, 1967. Systematic analysis of premarital behavior by leading family scholar.

Reuben, David. R. *Everything You Always Wanted to Know About Sex*. New York: McKay, 1969. Bestselling popular treatment of sexual questions. Good beginning for further discussion and study.

Sorensen, Robert C. *Adolescent Sexuality in Contemporary America*. New York: World, 1973. Report of national sample of adolescent sexual behavior. Helpful analysis within limits of volunteer sample.

5 Changing Role Expectations

- How do we define role and status?
- How are role and status related to our gender identity, and how do they affect our changing role expectations?
- What was the traditional definition of the masculine role?
- What was the traditional definition of the feminine role?
- How should we evaluate the feminist movement in terms of the changing role of women?
- What changes have been made in the masculine role in today's society, and how do these changes relate to the feminine role?
- We are seeing a reemphasis on the role of the single person. What steps should the single individual take toward maturity and self-actualization?
- Why do some men and women choose a homosexual orientation? How does their lifestyle differ from a heterosexual lifestyle?

Role Expectations

Very early in our dating and courtship experience we learn the importance of role expectations. The concept of roles is crucial to an understanding of marriage and the courtship process. We all have a certain position or status in society and are expected to carry out certain roles. In turn, we have similar expectations of other people, both in our families and in the larger society, and expect them to behave in certain ways because of the roles assigned to them.

We can define *status* as one's relative position or rank in a given group. It is closely related to prestige and depends on evaluations made by individuals. In our society, a banker has higher status than a deliveryman, a professor a higher standing than a college student, and an engineer a higher position than a machinist. These status rankings may change, as they are subject to shifts in a rapidly changing society, but they have a great influence on our judgment and expectation of any particular person.

Role can be defined as a set of expectations placed on one because of his or her status in a group. These role expectations tell us what kind of behavior to expect from an employer, a teacher, a husband or wife, or some other member of the community. Thus roles are descriptions of how persons in various categories will usually behave.

The average person belongs to several different groups in society—familial, occupational, and educational. In each group, he or she has a different role and a different set of role expectations. One set of roles is based on biological relationships. There are the sex roles of male and female; the kinship roles of mother, father, son, daughter, aunt, uncle, and so on; and the age roles of infant, child, adolescent, and adult. Another important set of roles in our society is based on occupation. The lawyer and the real estate salesperson, the carpenter and the electrical engineer, the teacher and the registered nurse—each has a specific occupational role. That role is carefully defined by society in terms of education, legal registration, employment contract, and other requirements. We do not expect the lawyer to repair a broken window in the courtroom or a registered nurse to sell insurance. There are other roles which require less training and preparation. One may be a host or hostess, a singer in a church choir, or a chaperone for a scouting overnight trip. Each role is derived from a certain status and meets certain expectations.

Role definitions, then, give the individual a basis for knowing what is expected of him and what he can expect of others. However, role definitions can also be a source of disturbance for the individual and for society. If, for example, a physician does not act like a doctor, a banker is not careful and well organized as people expect a banker to be, or a truck driver does not make his deliveries to the right locations, he may be in danger of losing his status. Such role inconsistency might result from the individual's rejection of the social norms that established the role in the first place; or it might occur because his role expectations differ greatly from those of others. In either case, his violation of group expectations is likely to provoke concern or even hostility and to bring him into conflict with the group.

In Chapter 4, we discussed the importance of gender identity in forming our role expectations. We think of ourselves as male or female, and this self-concept includes many factors such as physical characteristics, cultural acquisitions that help to match us with our society, and role behavior that helps us to fit the place we assume in our daily lifestyle. There are, of course, many deviations from a unified gender identity, including hermaphrodites, transsexuals, and transvestites.* However, in this chapter, we will be particularly concerned with the more general pattern of consistent male or female self-identity.

Everyone's behavior is affected by the number of roles he or she plays

Hermaphrodite: a biologically intersexed person, with some characteristics of both sexes including male and female gonads. *Transsexual:* an individual who believes he is trapped in the body of the wrong sex and wishes to change his sex through surgical and hormonal procedures. *Transvestite:* a person who has a tendency to dress in the clothing of the opposite sex.

because sometimes those roles conflict with one another. For example, a young woman might find that her role as class president requires her to spend the weekend at several recreational events, while her role as a student demands that she spend the weekend in the library. Because of such conflicts, and for other reasons, everyone at one time or another is frustrated and disappointed because he or she cannot live up to all the role expectations.

People often do not think about dating and marriage in terms of roles, yet these roles are extremely important. From the beginning of the courtship period, one anticipates a certain kind of dating and social partner. One's expectations will be influenced by family, peers, and personal experiences. If the young woman is not friendly and self-confident enough, or the young man not energetic or affectionate enough to measure up to those expectations, one may choose a different partner. We need to understand how role expectations are acquired and how people are prepared for the roles they are going to play in the relationships of courtship and marriage. If the ideal and actual role patterns are vastly different, then there may be serious trouble.

Courtship and marriage roles are strongly influenced by society. Ours is a stratified society, where those with money, education, and social, economic, and political power are at the top of the scale, and those without are at the bottom. (We will be examining the influence of socioeconomic class in more detail in Chapter 6.) Our families are a part of a specific class grouping in several significant ways, and from our families we derive our status and much of our role behavior. We absorb standards and status that come to us from our parents and then build from there. This family influence is still extremely important to us during our college years.

We might say that our role behavior is affected by our *set*, or readiness to respond in a certain way. If our childhood and family life have established certain stable patterns for us and we can carry them over into courtship and marriage, we are able to adopt new roles easily. But if we move up or down the social scale sharply and our new roles conflict with the old ones, our new roles may not be fulfilled so easily. For example, the habits and attitudes that are perfectly acceptable for the children of a middle-class family may be thought of as high-brow or foolish in a working-class family. In our present culture, in which people from widely different backgrounds may marry, it may be hard to match up one's expectations in marriage with the expectations and plans of one's spouse. Or, if backgrounds are similar, one partner may desire certain changes and innovations while the other would like to retain more traditional and comfortable patterns. Sudden economic and social changes in a couple's life may force them to adopt new roles they are not really enthusiastic about.

Wendell grew up in a rural family in central Georgia. He had seven brothers and sisters and remembered many days and weeks when the family was in a very poor economic position. The father worked for other farmers in the area but never managed well enough to buy and maintain a farm of his own. If the crops were poor or the labor market flooded, the father would be unemployed for weeks at a time. The family was run patriarchically. Father's word was law, although he failed to carry out many responsibilities. On payday he would often be home only for a quick meal and then go into town for a night-long bout in the local bar. At other times he would vent his frustrations on his unfortunate wife or on one of the children. Wendell remembered his father with an ambivalent feeling of love and fear.

Wendell married Elaine and the couple had two children. Elaine's father had been a warehouseman for a grocery chain in a suburban area, and the family lived in a lower-middle-class home. Her mother had worked part time. Elaine and her one brother shared in most of the household tasks; her father often cooked dinner, helped with the shopping, and ironed his shirts. When Wendell was out of work for six months Elaine found employment as a waitress on a swing-shift job; she continued working to help pay the bills and keep the family out of debt. The family was then theoretically run on a fifty-fifty basis. The wife was responsible for caring for the children in the morning and sending the oldest boy to kindergarten. In the afternoon, the children stayed at a neighbor's until the husband returned home from work. He served the children the evening meal and put them to bed. Family activities and recreation were concentrated on weekends and rotating days off.

The shifting of roles as a result of Wendell's unemployment made married life exceedingly difficult. After seven years of marriage, Wendell had been unable to adjust to a far different set of roles than existed in his parental family. The real problem for Wendell was in the assumption of what he considered feminine roles. He accepted the responsibilities of overseeing the children but balked strongly at dishwashing and scrubbing floors. His father had never done those things, he said, and it seemed an attack on his manliness to expect him to do them. He was especially touchy during the period when he was unemployed and a larger share of the household work fell on him.

There have been many changes in the institution of marriage in the last fifty years. Before we study the roles of individuals in our contemporary society, we should examine carefully the role expectations that have been accepted in the past.

Traditional Roles

The Masculine Role

The traditional masculine role that has strongly influenced our American society in the past has its roots in the patriarchal system, dating back to before the Greeks and Romans. This role remained fairly stable until the twentieth century. It reflected man's physical strength and his ability to protect his family against outside attack by other persons or by the elements. The influence of the traditional emphasis on the physical strength of the male can still be seen today. Most young American men seek the goal of physical strength and athletic skill and achievement.[1] Friendships with other boys and later popularity with the "fair sex" depended to a great degree on virility and athletic proficiency. His place on the first team or as a lowly substitute on the scrub squad was a clue to his standing among his friends. Later on as a young adult, husband, and father, his status was strengthened as he proved his manliness by keeping fit and perhaps competing in bowling, golf, or skiing.

The traditional masculine role also stressed masculine dominance in almost every important walk of life. Men ruled in the political world, in military affairs, in the economic sphere, in higher education, and in religion. This dominance was carried over into family life, in which wives and children were expected to be obedient and submissive to superior masculine experience and wisdom. Men also played the aggressive role in sexual relationships. The double standard, which was part of the traditional outlook, allowed them great sexual freedom, while women were limited and restricted. The wife was considered a passive partner in sexual intercourse and had to "endure" it to please her husband without finding any real enjoyment and satisfaction in it herself.

In this model, men were also expected to carry out the major economic role in the family as the chief wage earner. In earlier generations the self-made man was often praised and imitated as a masculine example. His story might have been one of success over great obstacles—the typical rags-to-riches tale. Irvin G. Wyllie analyzes the concept in this way:

[1]Note that this expectation was just as common in an earlier generation. See Talcott Parsons, "Age and Sex in the Social Structure," *American Sociological Review*, 7, no. 5 (Oct. 1942), 604–16.

> The legendary hero of America is the self-made man. He has been active in every field from politics to the arts, but nowhere has he been more active, or more acclaimed, than in business. To most Americans he is the office boy who has become the head of a great concern, making millions in the process. He represents our most cherished conceptions of success, and particularly our belief that any man can achieve fortune through the practice of industry, frugality, and sobriety.[2]

It is hard to separate fact from fiction in analyzing the marriage relationships of earlier generations. The ideas we gain from novels and historical accounts of families in the eighteenth and nineteenth centuries, for example, may not always be actually representative of the average middle-class or working-class family. In comparison with today's family patterns, however, we can certainly conclude that men were at that time less involved in the daily routine of homemaking and raising the children. Long working days of ten or twelve hours did not leave as much time for family activities and leisure.

The traditional masculine role also included certain expectations in the social realm, in the emotional and integrative phases of family life, and in the religious or philosophical orientation of the family. A man's status and position in the community was basic to the family's place socially, and his wife and children benefited if he had a high status because of his profession or his leadership in other community fields. His emotional-integrative role, through which he expressed love and affection and symbolized the family's unity, was not as important as that of his wife, but it still represented a given stable factor in the traditional pattern of family life. His status as husband and father was higher than it is today, and his influence was felt in a more rigid and less flexible way than it is now. Ideally, he wielded his authority in a benevolent and loving manner although, in reality, this might not have been the case. Similarly, the father was considered the head of the family's religious faith, and his wife and children were expected to follow his religion.

There should be no illusions about the extent to which American men actually lived up to this ideal characterization. The case for the traditional masculine role has undoubtedly been exaggerated. Women have always exerted a strong force in family and community life, and we would not have the records of outstanding women leaders in history if there were not countless other women of ability and influence whose names and accomplishments were not recorded. However, we cannot ignore the fact that men have clearly had a dominant influence; legally, politically, and in many other ways

[2]Irvin G. Wyllie, *The Self-Made Man in America* (New Brunswick, N.J.: Rutgers Univ. Press, 1954), p. 6.

women have been second-class citizens. And although there is more equality in modern American marriage, with many two-income families at every age level, men and women entering marriage today still retain much of the traditional masculine role expectation and often find it hard to change to a more egalitarian way of life.

The Feminine Role

The traditional feminine role was essentially the complement of the masculine role. Men were active, so women were passive and submissive. Men formed governments and made laws; women obeyed them. Men marched off to war; women kept the home and farm intact until the men returned. Women helped run the farm and worked in the factories, but all the important decisions were made by men. Mothers taught their children at home, but higher education belonged to men.

In the traditional culture woman found her greatest pride and accomplishment in the role of wife and mother. In the home a woman found fulfillment as a loving wife and companion to her husband and as the mother of his children. We can see this tradition exemplified clearly in our contem-

"One of you boys go help Mom with the groceries."

Drawing by Booth. © 1978 The New Yorker Magazine, Inc.

porary culture in families of recent European or Latin American or Asian origin. The wife and mother is honored for bringing children into the world, for her love and watchful care over the babies and small children, for her encouragement and guidance of husband and children in everyday living. She is the living symbol of the stability and strength of the home and of its continuity from generation to generation. Later on, as grandmother to her children's children, she passes on the family's tradition to yet another generation.

The focus of the feminine role in the traditional family was in the home and with the children, and that was a logical emphasis. Large families of eight to ten children involved a great deal of work and responsibility, and the wife's childbearing in such a family had to be spread over fifteen or twenty years. At the age of fifty or fifty-five, when the younger children came into their teens and older children left the home, the traditional wife and mother found it difficult to create any new role for herself. It was more natural and convenient to move immediately into the role of grandmother and matriarch of the enlarged family group.

When the traditional masculine role was prevalent, there was a tremendous amount of satisfaction in the traditional feminine role, which was reinforced by the pride of husband and children in the mother's contribution to the family's happiness and development. The beauty of home and furnishings and the atmosphere of religious festivals were largely created by her. In many ways she gave and they received; her feelings and wishes were secondary to the needs and desires of her family.

The woman's economic role can be analyzed in two different ways. In a rural economy, the daily work of the woman would be closely tied to the work and responsibility of her husband. She would have major responsibility for the home and children, with perhaps the added task of feeding and housing the hired hands who would assist with the farm work during the harvest seasons. In addition, she might care for small animals, plant and harvest vegetables for family use, or milk the family cow. In some cases, she would even join her husband in the heavier tasks of plowing and tilling the ground. No farmer would have an easy road to success without a wife who carried her share of the load in several significant ways.

In urban settings, the wife in the traditional middle-class feminine role would not always be expected to enter into productive work. The wife who worked in a factory (and children who may have worked there with her) was not thought to be in an enviable position. She would center her attention on housework and the care and guidance of the children; later in the twentieth century she would put increasing emphasis on their education and participation in community activities. She would not usually work outside the home, although she could take in work to do at home if necessary, such as washing and ironing, or supplement the family income by taking in boarders.

The common factor in these two different situations would be that in neither case was the wife expected or even allowed to earn and control a major part of the family's cash income. If a farmer received a good price for his wheat or corn crop, it would be largely his achievement and the money his to utilize, even if his wife had shared in the work. And the case of a woman in the city who earned even half the salary of her husband through employment would have been rare indeed.

The social role of the woman in the traditional pattern was also much more restricted than it is today.[3] Women rarely entered the business world, and most community activities were dominated by men. Women were not allowed to vote and were thus excluded from political life. Men were granted great opportunity to engage in social activities outside the home, while a wife was expected to be at home with her children. Only some activities included both husbands and wives, and a few, particularly in the smaller communities, the entire family. The remnants of this double standard in social participation can still be seen in rural communities and in industrial areas in the cities, where groups of men congregate for their own social life, apparently unconcerned about the participation of their wives.

As we have seen, the emotional-integrative roles played by women in the traditional feminine pattern were very important. A wife and mother was expected to supply most of the love and affection found in the home; her husband often neglected that function. She was the one to soften the rough edges of family life, nurse the hurts and bruises, and nurture the hopes and dreams of children for a happy life. In addition, she would generally take the lead in religious life, both in participation in the adult religious community and in the religious training of the children. If the husband was required to be away from home for long periods of time because of his occupation, she would bear the full responsibility of family life in his absence.

The traditional feminine role had many limitations and difficulties. Those difficulties are often minimized by people who look back to previous generations for idealized patterns of marriage. Women lived under personal and legal handicaps, and while many gladly accepted the traditional roles and tasks expected of them, others found achievement and satisfaction extremely difficult under such restrictions. If a man was a poor provider, he could make the life of his family miserable, and his wife was supposed to suffer in silence. She had no legal standing as a person, was not allowed to have any

[3]See Arthur W. Calhoun, *A Social History of the American Family* (New York: Barnes & Noble, 1945). Three volumes in one.

say in the financial affairs of the family, and in most cases could not get a divorce. The wife's place was in the home, and it was very hard for her to break out of her fixed social pattern, find outside employment, or make some other improvement in an unsatisfactory marital situation.

An interesting report of what one married woman's life was like in the nineteenth century is given in the autobiography of the founder of the women's suffrage movement, Elizabeth Cady Stanton:

> In the spring of 1847 we moved to Seneca Falls, New York. Here we spent sixteen years of our married life, and here our other children were born.
>
> . . . In Seneca Falls my life was comparatively solitary, and the change from Boston was somewhat depressing. There, all my immediate friends were reformers. I had near neighbors, a new home with all the modern conveniences, and well-trained servants.
>
> Here, our residence was on the outskirts of the town, roads were often very muddy and no sidewalks most of the way, Mr. Stanton was frequently away from home, I had poor servants, and an increasing number of children. To keep a house and grounds in good order, purchase every article for daily use, keep the wardrobes of half a dozen human beings in proper trim, take the children to dentists, shoemakers, and different schools, or find teachers at home, altogether made sufficient work to keep one brain busy, as well as all the hands I could impress into service.
>
> Then, too, the novelty of housekeeping had passed away, and much that was once attractive in domestic life was now irksome. I had so many cares that the company I needed for intellectual stimulation was a trial rather than a pleasure.
>
> . . . My duties were too numerous and varied, and none sufficiently exhilarating or intellectual to bring into play my higher faculties. I suffered with mental hunger, which, like an empty stomach, is very depressing. I had books, but no stimulating companionship.[4]

Support for a continuation of this traditional role for women is not absent from contemporary society. Alan Bayer, in reviewing a sample of 188,900 students entering college in 1972, found a substantial number of "sexist" students, both male and female. Approximately 23,700 students "strongly agreed" with the statement: "The activities of married women are best confined to the home and family." The profile of these students was summarized in this way:

[4]Elizabeth Cady Stanton, reprinted from her autobiography, *Eighty Years and More* (1898) in *Growing Up Female in America*, ed. Eve Merriam (Garden City, N.Y.: Doubleday, 1971), pp. 59–60.

> The sexist is more likely to be a male, although a substantial proportion of women also endorse traditional women's roles. . . . The sexist student is also somewhat more likely to be older than the college freshmen peer group, to come from lower socio-economic families, to be nonurban in origin, and to be less successful academically. Further, sexist students are more likely to have relatively low educational aspirations and to plan study in business, the health professions, or education.
>
> Students who endorse "traditional" women's roles are also more likely to subscribe to marrying soon and to raising a family as a primary life objective. They are also less likely than students-in-general to support equal opportunity in women's employment, to be more conservative in their politics, and to be more authoritarian in most of their attitudes and opinions.[5]

Changes in Traditional Roles

Some of the most dramatic changes affecting marriage and family life have been in role expectations and behavior. Because of the new opportunities for women in the working world, greater educational achievement, smaller family size, an increased life span, and the feminist movement, there is a radical change in what men and women expect in marriage and how they behave when they enter the marital relationship. The traditional role patterns have been changed and reshaped so dramatically that it is often difficult to know what role behavior is valid and consistent in particular family situations. This is most evident in the changing roles of women. Let us begin, then, by analyzing the emerging new feminine role.

The New Feminine Role

WORKING WOMEN

There has been a striking increase in the number of women in the working force. Table 5–1 shows the participation of women in the labor force during the last sixteen years. Note particularly the increase of working women in their twenties, when young children are often in the home. The projection for 1990 for these women shows that 75.1 percent of women aged twenty to twenty-four will be in the labor force. IMP

[5]Alan E. Bayer, "Sexist Students in American Colleges: A Descriptive Note," *Journal of Marriage and the Family*, 37, no.2 (May 1975), 391–98.

The growing number of women in the work force has important influences on our society. Business, industry, politics, and community are all affected by this increased feminine influence. Whether or not she has children, a woman has another life away from her family, and she must spread her energies in two directions. This will make a big difference in the role expectations of young women as they plan their high school and college studies in anticipation of the new roles opening up for them.

The increase in female employment does not mean that women are competing with men for jobs across a wide spectrum. Much employment is still "women's work." Van Dusen and Sheldon have shown that there is still a heavy demand for women in certain areas of the employment market.[6] They point out that women who are elementary school teachers and registered nurses accounted for 46 percent of all female professionals in 1970, while the principal employer of women today is the service industries and, more particularly, professional services (medical and health, education, and legal). Skilled and cheap labor is needed, where training has been completed before employment, and where women can transfer easily from one area and position to another.[7] Women have held these jobs for many decades, and the pattern has not yet changed. Thus we cannot project that women will attain full job equality with men in the near future.

Table 5–1 Female Labor Force, 1960 to 1976, with Projections to 1990, and Percentage of Age Group in Labor Force

Age	*1960*	*1970*	*1976*	*1990 Projected*
16–19	39.1	42.8	46.8	55.1
20–24	46.1	57.5	65.0	75.1
25–34	35.8	44.8	56.9	63.4
35–44	43.1	50.9	57.6	62.8
45–54	49.3	54.0	54.6	60.1
55–64	36.7	42.5	40.7	42.0
65 + over	10.5	9.1	7.8	7.2

SOURCE: U.S. Bureau of the Census, *Statistical Abstract of the United States, 1977* (Washington, D.C.: U.S. Government Printing Office, 1977), p. 387.

[6] Roxann A. Van Dusen and Eleanor Bernert Sheldon, "The Changing Status of American Women: A Life Cycle Perspective," *American Psychologist*, 31, no. 2 (Feb. 1976), 106–16.
[7] Van Dusen and Sheldon, p. 113.

EDUCATED WOMEN

Both black and white women have increased their educational level over a sixteen-year period. Table 5–2 shows this increase, with black women showing even larger gains than white women. In addition, women's educational levels are approaching parity with men's. At least the beginning of a college education is now a norm for American women, and we can expect this trend to continue. Part of the rise in the percentages is due to women who have married and begun their families and who are returning to colleges and universities for further education.

Education is the key to many significant changes in the roles women will play in the future. A college education prepares women for more remunerative employment and for more effective participation in the social, political, and religious community. The young married woman who has had some college training has the ability to play several roles later in life—career woman and community leader as well as wife and mother.

THE FEMINIST MOVEMENT

The thrust for equality generated by the feminist movement in the past two decades has encouraged women to break down the barriers that prevent them from participating fully in all areas of life. A study by Mason, Czajka, and Arber points out that this new freedom has resulted in major changes in the sex-role attitudes of American women. They conclude:

> There can be little question that women's sex-role attitudes have changed toward a more egalitarian stance over the past decade. These changes were not uniform across all attitude items but, on average, appear to have

Table 5–2 Median School Years Completed by Women (25 Years and Older), and Percentage Completing College Work

	1–3 Years College	*4 Years or More College*	*Median Years Education*
1960			
White females	9.5%	6.0%	11.2
Black females	4.1	3.3	8.6
1970			
White females	10.1	8.6	12.2
Black females	6.0	4.4	10.2
1976			
White females	12.8	11.6	12.4
Black females	8.6	6.8	11.4

SOURCE: U.S. Bureau of the Census, *Statistical Abstract of the United States, 1977* (Washington, D.C.: U.S. Government Printing Office, 1977), p. 136.

been as great for the items that refer to the family as for those referring to the work place. For some time the proportions of women endorsing equal rights in the labor market have been higher than those endorsing equality in the home, and this was still the case in 1974. However, although one might suppose that deciding to endorse equal job opportunities would be "easier" than giving up the belief that maternal employment harms preschool children, we find little evidence in these data that women were more likely to adopt one of these positions than the other with the passage of time.[8]

TECHNOLOGY

A further powerful influence on the feminine role comes from automation and mechanization. The amount of time and energy required for today's homemaker to carry out the basic tasks in the home has lessened tremendously. The invention of gas and electric appliances and the utilization of

[8]Karen Oppenheim Mason, John L. Czajka, and Sara Arber, "Change in U.S. Women's Sex-Role Attitudes, 1964–1974," *American Sociological Review*, 41, no. 4 (Aug. 1976), 585.

frozen and prepared foods in cooking has raised our standard of home living to the highest in history; there is less physical drudgery now than previous generations would have dreamed possible. Cooking, cleaning, washing and drying clothes, sewing, and other duties in the home can be done today in a quarter or less of the time previously required, and the result is a vast improvement in the woman's and the family's health and well-being.

Certainly the automobile should be considered part of the increased mechanization of our culture. Formerly the homemaker was tied to her home except when she could walk to a village store or travel with her husband; today she is able to move great distances by herself. Because she is able to go where she wants to go and can take her preschool childen with her if necessary, her whole range of contact with the community and society is broadened and expanded.

FREEDOM

Another key factor in the new role which women are assuming in our society is related to freedom. Yet freedom alone will not be sufficient for the modern woman. New positive roles must be found to give women a meaningful direction for their lives. The feminist movement must be given major credit for emphasizing such new role models for women in our society. As in every other social movement that brings about significant changes in society, there must be people who speak out and act as the agents of change. Customs and social patterns that have been accepted without question for centuries and even thousands of years are now subjected to close and critical examination. No social institution is exempt from this scrutiny. Although many people may protest against some positions or actions of these spokeswomen for a new society, they cannot ignore them.

Kate Millett is one voice of social change for women. In her book *Sexual Politics*, she traces the historical development of woman's subjection without the sentimentality with which such discussions have usually been veneered in the past.

> Our society, like all other historical civilizations, is a patriarchy. The fact is evident at once if one recalls that the military, industry, technology, universities, science, political office, and finance—in short, every avenue of power within the society, including the coercive force of the police, is entirely in male hands. As the essence of politics is power, such realization cannot fail to carry impact. What lingers of supernatural authority, the Deity, "His" ministry, together with the ethics and values, the philosophy and art of our culture—its very civilization—as T. S. Eliot once observed, is of male manufacture.

> . . . Patriarchy's chief institution is the family. It is both a mirror of and a connection with the larger society; a patriarchal unit within a patriarchal whole. Mediating between the individual and the social structure, the family effects control and conformity where political and other authorities are insufficient. As the fundamental instrument and the foundation unit of patriarchal society the family and its roles are prototypical. Serving as an agent of the larger society, the family not only encourages its own members to adjust and conform, but acts as a unit in the government of the patriarchal state which rules its citizens through its family heads. Even in patriarchal societies where they are granted legal citizenship, women tend to be ruled through the family alone and have little or no formal relation to the state.[9]

Similar conclusions are reached by Constantina Safilios-Rothschild. She points out that women are socialized into their sex roles early in life and that the feminine role is seen as clearly inferior to the masculine role. There is some possibility of taking over the man's role, but the woman usually comes out on the short end.[10] Such critiques cause us to reexamine the roles women are called on to play in our society and the ways in which they are forced to conform to them. Feminist leaders have suggested that we also need to rethink many of our basic sociological concepts, including the approach that is taken to family studies.

The National Organization for Women has set as a major goal the broadening of the freedom and opportunity afforded to women in our society. Their statement of purpose declares, in part:

> We, men and women who hereby constitute ourselves as the National Organization for Women, believe that the time has come for a new movement toward true equality for all women in America and toward a fully equal partnership of the sexes, as part of the worldwide revolution of human rights now taking place within and beyond our national borders.
>
> The purpose of NOW is to take action to bring women into full participation in the mainstream of American society now, exercising all the privileges and responsibilities thereof in truly equal partnership with men.
>
> . . . NOW is dedicated to the proposition that women, first and foremost, are human beings, who, like all other people in our society, must have the chance to develop their fullest human potential. We believe that

[9]Kate Millett, *Sexual Politics* (Garden City, N.Y.: Doubleday, 1970), pp. 25, 33.

[10]Constantina Safilios-Rothschild, *Toward a Society of Women* (Lexington, Mass.: Xerox, 1972), p. 32.

> women can achieve such equality only by accepting to the full the challenges and responsibilities they share with all other people in our society, as part of the decision-making mainstream of American political, economic, and social life.[11]

Perhaps the changes in woman's role are best summed up by noting the very complexity of the role played by women in our contemporary society. A woman no longer follows a systematic and orderly development of her feminine role in life. She may oscillate between one aspect of her role and another. Or she may play several roles at the same time—wife, mother, employee, community leader, political dissenter—whereas in earlier centuries she was clearly limited to the role of wife and mother. At eighteen she may enter into courtship, or she may decide to postpone serious courtship and devote herself to her studies. At twenty-eight she may concentrate on her role as mother, with two or three small children demanding most of her time and energy, or she may just be beginning to consider marriage after having proved herself in an exciting career. At thirty-eight, freed from the care of small children, she may enter more actively into community life—either the more traditional church and scouting activities or politics and women's rights; or she may go back to her career. At forty-eight or fifty-eight she may be planning an active retirement with her husband, with the necessity of relocating the family dwelling, choosing a retirement community, and maintaining close relationships with children and grandchildren. No one plays a single role consistently throughout life, but such a variety of roles is bound to create some problems. If the modern wife is unsure of which role she wants to choose, small wonder that her husband is bewildered as well! Margaret Mead and Frances Kaplan write:

> In the 1930s and early 1940s, the full-time homemaker was inclined to apologize and to describe her busy and exacting life as "doing nothing." In the next decade, with the glamorizing of "togetherness," early marriage, and the large family in the suburban home, the homemaker contended that hers was a wholly fulfilling life; in fact, she claimed to belong in the high-prestige category because she was doing what she chose and loved to do. Only a few years ago, a leading women's magazine published a symposium on women and marriage in which happy, frenetic young mothers reported on the crowding of their days with household tasks and told how they loved every overoccupied minute. [Later] when a compensating shift in the other direction was under way,

[11]Reprinted in Cynthia Fuchs Epstein and William J. Goode, eds., *The Other Half* (Englewood Cliffs, N.J.: Prentice-Hall, 1971), p. 193.

the same magazine published a special issue reporting on women's enjoyment of their freedom to get away from home into paid jobs and their willingness to pay for their gain by doing household chores far into the night.[12]

It is clear that changes in the woman's role have altered many of the basic relationships in marriage and family life that have long been widely and perhaps uncritically accepted in American society. The longer lifespan and the shorter period of time devoted to childbearing have made possible a new life cycle for women (see Table 5–3). A whole series of options that never existed for women before is opening up. It is staggering to think of the creative possibilities of so much free energy, which could be channeled into solving some of the crucial problems of our century.

Table 5–3 Changing Feminine Roles in the Life Cycle

Woman Born in 1900

	Age	*Birth*	*15*	*21*	*35*	*50*	*Death*
A.	*Stage*	Childhood	Youth	Young adulthood	Maturity	Old age	
	Role	Child and student	Daughter and worker	Wife and childbearer Childrearing	Wife and mother	Grandmother	

Woman Born in 1976

	Age	*Birth*	*20*	*43*	*65*	*Death*
B.	*Stage*	Childhood and youth	Young adulthood	Maturity		Old age
	Role	Child and student	Wife and mother Career woman Childrearing	Wife and career woman Grandmother		Retirement

NOTE: **A,** life expectancy (white female): 51 years. **B,** life expectancy (all females): 77.2 years.

SOURCE: **A,** U.S. Bureau of the Census, *Statistical Abstract of the United States, 1947* (Washington, D.C.: U.S. Government Printing Office, 1947), p. 81. **B,** U.S. Bureau of the Census, *Statistical Abstract of the United States, 1977* (Washington, D.C.: U.S. Government Printing Office, 1977), p. 58.

[12]Margaret Mead and Frances B. Kaplan, *American Women, The Report of the President's Commission* (New York: Charles Scribner's Sons, 1965), pp. 190–91.

The New Masculine Role

BRAWN VS. BRAINS

What is the emerging new masculine role in American life—sometimes overlooked in the shadow of the more dramatic shift in feminine role expectations? Although changes in the masculine role in our contemporary society have not been as pronounced as changes in the feminine role, they have nonetheless been significant. For example, a man's sheer physical strength and ability are of less and less importance today, while demands on his intelligence and education have increased enormously. The modern man can rarely earn a good salary solely because he is willing to do a hard day's work; he needs skills, brains, and training. IMP.

This change is illustrated by the drop in our farm population. We became an urban nation in the 1920 census, and the rural population has continued to decline ever since. But it is not always easy to make the shift from farm to city. Here is one clear illustration of the change from manual to mental labor, from man to machine.

Howard was the middle son in a large family. As a boy he was given regular tasks to do on the family farm, including running the two farm tractors, the harvesters, and the other farm equipment. Little stress was placed on education by his parents, and Howard left school after the ninth grade. He worked two more years on the farm and then went to a city some three hundred miles from home to seek employment.

After working at a variety of jobs, including truck driving and delivery work for a large dairy, Howard took a job as a private chauffeur. At twenty-three he married Trudy, a young woman he had met through relatives in the city. Three children were born to the couple in the next five years. Howard gained modest increases in pay but obtained no additional education and little contact with business outside his chauffeuring job.

Seven years after he and Trudy were married, Howard's employer moved to another city and no longer needed his services. He recommended Howard to three or four business associates, but no job materialized. Howard found it difficult to compete for jobs with so little education. The employment he could take was at a salary almost twenty-five dollars a week below his previous pay. It seemed impossible to meet family expenses on that limited income. The couple considered moving back to the farm, but Trudy had no farming experience, and neither she nor the children had any desire to leave the metropolitan area. Howard was strong and willing to work hard but unable to move easily into a new position in the competitive job market.

JOB SPECIALIZATION

A related trend in employment away from physical strength and skills is the increasing job specialization our present economic structure requires. Who can be a jack-of-all-trades today? One must find a specialty and do it well. Moreover, few men today can expect to learn a particular trade or vocation and then settle down to a lifetime of steady employment. The rapid changes brought about by automation, the invention of new products, and the demand for new and varied goods and services means that many men must change vocations once or more during their working careers. The security a man once gained from being a competent carpenter, farmer, or machinist, for example, no longer exists for many men. The plight of engineers in our society is another example of this problem. In one year large companies may be laying off engineers by the hundreds, and a qualified man may despair of ever landing a steady position. A few months later the newspapers may be full of advertisements, but all for engineers with specialized training available only to recent graduates of the engineering schools. In addition, a man has more competition in his daily work: from women who have entered the labor market; from younger men who are more adequately trained in specialized work; from men switching from other lines of work to his field.

EMOTIONAL FREEDOM

IMP. Another significant change in the masculine role has come about as husbands and fathers learn to take a more expressive and emotional role in family life. Much of our cultural tradition dictates that men should not cry, should not admit their mistakes, should not share their problems with women, should not reveal weakness in any way. To take a more direct part in the emotional side of life is difficult for most men. Warren T. Farrell espouses the cause of liberating men from stereotyped role behavior, which prevents them from utilizing the full strength of their expressive and emotional life. The movement for men's liberation has not enlisted as much support as the women's movement, but it is gaining in importance. Farrell writes:

> Getting beyond masculinity means getting beyond the concrete barriers to sharing roles, but it also means the achievement of new freedoms—freedom from proving oneself, from worrying about appearances—on the playing field or in the office, in earned degrees or job titles; in clothes, status, or swagger. It is getting beyond condescension and contempt for women, the need to be in control, to have an answer to all problems at all times, specializing past the point of diminishing returns, the need to become the expert, to be the sole breadwinner. It means learning how to listen to others rather than to dominate a conversation, to be personal as well as intellectual, to be vulnerable rather than to construct false facades of infallibility, to feel and show emotions rather than be emotionally constipated, to be dependent as well as independent, to value internal, human rewards as well as external rewards. It means recognizing the rap involved in treating women as sex objects. Going beyond masculinity, then, means overcoming the pressures that make us try to appear "masculine" rather than get in touch with our humanity.[13]

This is a difficult task. Many men find it very hard to give up the attitudes that have brought them "success" (in terms of income, education, prestige) in order to grow in the realm of their personal and emotional relationships.

[13]Warren T. Farrell, "Beyond Masculinity: Liberating Men and Their Relationships with Women," in Lucille Duberman, *Gender and Sex in Society* (New York: Praeger, 1975), pp. 245–46.

But, on the other hand, if women are broadening their roles in the "success" area, it is logical that there must be corresponding growth and development in the emotional areas for men. This is certainly more true for today's college men than it was for their fathers and grandfathers.

FAMILY ROLE

Man's traditional position of dominance in the family is also changing; no man can be certain that his position will be the same as that of his father. In fact, the chances are fairly high that it will not be—that he will marry a woman who wants to share more equally in family decision-making than his mother did. Moreover, the fragmentation of the family by many school, social, and community groups outside the home tends to minimize even more his traditionally secondary emotional-integrative role in the lives of his wife and children. And his wife is freer to question his behavior and to initiate new patterns herself. This carries over significantly into the sexual relationship itself, in which man's traditional concern only with his own prowess must now be tempered with a genuine concern for the response and satisfaction of his wife. The new role behavior of the wife has generally had a negative effect on the husband[14]—the more so if the husband was raised in a family with strong patriarchal dominance: any sharing of power seems to tarnish the man's self-image, to cause him to doubt his virility.

Some men have always seen women as a threat. Ashley Montagu goes so far as to speak of "the natural superiority of women":

> I am not the first to suggest, and I am sure I shall not be the last, that the male's drive in work and achievement may actually be the consequence of his recognition of his biological inferiority with respect to the female's creative capacity to conceive and create human beings. One of the ways in which the male may compensate for this biological inferiority is by work and by achievement. By keeping the means of making a livelihood almost exclusively a masculine prerogative, men have unconsciously, as well as consciously, been able to satisfy themselves that they are by nature the "breadwinners," the pillars of society, and the guarantors of the race. Hence, the great opposition to women when they begin to enter into "competition" with men in earning a living. Married men, in particular, frequently object to their wives' working; they consider it, somehow, a reflection upon themselves. They fear it will be said that they are unable to support their family. "My wife doesn't have to work. Why

[14]Helen M. Hacker, "The New Burdens of Masculinity," *Marriage and Family Living,* 19, no. 3 (Aug. 1957), 227–33.

should she?" The argument will be familiar to the reader, whether married or not.[15]

ASSUMPTION OF "FEMININE" ROLES

Another shock to the male ego comes when men are asked to assume roles that were once considered exclusively feminine. More and more they are being called on to do household tasks (cooking, washing dishes, cleaning, laundering, and so on), which involves both the acquisition of a minimum amount of skill and the psychological acceptance of doing "women's work." Men also take a much more active part in the education of their children than they did in former years. The shifts in economic life may also mean that many men are expected to show "feminine" traits of sympathy, understanding, and patience in their vocations; instead of driving ahead to complete a job by masculine strength and power, they must work harmoniously with other people, consider group interests and decisions, and play a moderating, conciliatory role. This may be threatening to men who have always held a more traditional view of the masculine role.

[15]Ashley Montagu, *The Natural Superiority of Women,* rev. ed. (New York: Macmillan, 1968), p. 39.

Will American men respond creatively to the changes in women's roles in our society? The answer is probably yes. We live in a society often dominated by large organizations, and the ability to become a self-made and self-directed man is becoming rarer. Thus, more and more men have discovered their families to be a major source of personal growth and satisfaction. They are becoming enthusiastic about taking on a more important emotional-integrative role at home. The closer they become emotionally to their families, and to their true inner selves, the less inclined they are to want to return to the pressure and strain of their old role as the all-powerful, all-knowing, but yet distant, patriarch.[16]

Role of the Single Person

IMP.

Must every man and woman fulfill his masculine or feminine role within marriage? Obviously the answer is no. The sex ratio is not identical in every community or area, and circumstances of race, occupation, and religion, as well as many other factors, enter into the matching of partners in marriage. Another factor limiting the number of possible partners for a given individual has been termed the mating gradient. This term refers to the fact that men tend to marry beneath themselves in social and economic status. Men also tend to marry younger women with less education. National marriage figures in the last fifty years have shown consistently that women marry several years younger than men. In addition, more men than women are college graduates, so it is probable that a man will have completed more education than his wife. The masculine ego is responsible for many of these tendencies, since a man in our culture wants to feel that he is superior to his wife in some ways and that she is looking up to him and partially dependent on him. He can achieve this superiority at the beginning of marriage if he stands a notch above her on the social scale, earns more money than she (or her family) has earned, has more education than she does, or has the added maturity of age.

Socioeconomic factors are particularly strong limitations. It is suggested that many men of minimum education at the bottom of the socioeconomic scale are poor marriage risks and either do not marry or are unsuccessful in marriage. Such men often cannot provide security for their wives and families and may try to escape their burdens through alcoholism or by deserting the home; they are then eliminated from the group of successfully married people. Women on the upper end of the scale, however, find the situation reversed. They are potentially excellent wives and mothers but may not find

[16]For another view of masculine development, see Daniel J. Levinson, "Growing Up with the Dream," *Psychology Today*, 11, no. 8 (Jan. 1978), 20–31, 89.

a man clearly above them socially, economically, or educationally. In competition with lower-status women, they may not even find a husband at their own level. Some of them may wish to reverse the normal gradient, and our society is flexible in accepting their freedom to make such a choice; but some women at the top of the social scale will never find marital happiness. This is not only their loss, but society's as well.

Why the Single Role?

Who are the men and women who remain single in a marriage-dominated society? They are men and women who have other patterns for their lives, and are often highly successful in following them. Although a majority of adults in our society marry, it is now increasingly recognized that the single life has many advantages too. One can fulfill a satisfying masculine or feminine role without entering into marriage. This achievement has always been easier for men, but it is now increasingly possible for women as well. A woman may fulfill her feminine role in the business world, in teaching, or in medicine without assuming the responsibilities of marriage. The feminist movement is helping single women to define their roles, and being single will probably be easier for the women of future generations as a result. The following excerpts from a taped conversation at a meeting of single women in Boston illustrate the effort single women are making to find new roles to replace the traditional married-woman role most of them were brought up to assume.

> *Judith:* When I felt there was a clear community of women that was autonomous, I think I stopped thinking about myself primarily as a "single" woman and started to think of myself more as a woman.
>
> . . .
>
> *Kathy:* I think there has been a growing respect for women who are more aggressive. A woman who is single is now given a certain amount of respect for having the strength to go out on her own.
>
> . . .
>
> *Deborah:* The women's movement opened up to me for the first time the option of not getting married. That's frightening, because it means that I have to create something new; there aren't the old forms of security. On the other hand, I feel better, since those old forms never really seemed quite so secure or didn't really give me the kind of happiness they were supposed to.[17]

[17] *Our Bodies, Ourselves: A Book By and For Women,* The Boston Women's Health Book Collective (New York: Simon and Schuster, 1973), p. 51.

Singlehood is a positive choice. Peter J. Stein has discussed the needs which single people have for group involvement and support to make their lifestyle more satisfying. To be single does not mean to be isolated. There are many ways of being closely involved with other people, and many social and interactional groups are growing up to meet the needs of single men and women, particularly in larger cities and in metropolitan areas. Stein's study of a small sample of single persons points to the future:

> The collective portrait that emerges is one of single persons who are trying to forge a meaningful life in a society that, though changing, continues to uphold marriage and the family as the model for interpersonal bonding. While the experience of being single is beset by problems and pressures created by restrictive social attitudes, singlehood as an alternative life style is in the process of cultural emergence.
>
> . . . The social credence of singlehood will grow as its supportive ideology develops, and, as our interviews suggest, it will then be recognized as an acceptable and viable choice.[18]

The new emphasis on self-identity, and on career satisfaction for both men and women, also focuses attention on the single individual. There is a positive correlation between higher education and occupational achievement and single status for women.[19] Women with higher incomes are less likely to marry. When a woman focuses a major amount of time, thought, and energy on her career, she spends less time and energy in preparing to get married. This is one way of explaining the fact that she is more likely to remain single when she attains her economic and career aspirations.

Advantages of the Single Life

Just as being single does not doom a person to an unfulfilling life, getting married does not guarantee a couple happiness. Maturity does not come effortlessly with the day of marriage; and a weak man does not become a strong and self-reliant one, or a selfish woman a gracious and unselfish one, simply through a wedding ceremony. There is no necessary correlation between marriage and maturity. In fact, every psychologist, minister, physician, or counselor who deals in family problems has met many couples who have married in haste only to repent at leisure. On the other hand, many single persons develop mature interests and build stable and satisfying interpersonal relationships.

[18]Peter J. Stein, "Singlehood: An Alternative to Marriage," *The Family Coordinator*, 24, no. 4 (Oct. 1975), 502.

[19]Charles W. Mueller and Blair G. Campbell, "Female Occupational Achievement and Marital Status: A Research Note," *Journal of Marriage and the Family*, 39, no. 3 (Aug. 1977), 587–93.

Nor is the achievement of satisfying roles in the business world necessarily advanced by marriage. Our present pattern of early courtship, marriage, and parenthood means that many men are forced to earn a living for themselves and their families without the advantage of as much technical or higher education as they would like to have. They find themselves doing routine jobs or filling unskilled laboring positions, taking what they can get without any real consideration of what they want to do. The job becomes a ceaseless round of futility for them, but because of their heavy family responsibilities they have little prospect of change. Such people may fall into what the psychologist Erich Fromm has called the work-and-pleasure syndrome.[20] Work is dull, unpleasant, frustrating, and carried on from necessity alone. So leisure hours, weekends, and vacations become a frantic search for pleasure to make up for the emptiness of the working life. A single person who is free to take a longer period of time for education and can move more freely in response to economic change may well be more satisfied in his or her job.

In other ways as well the single person may achieve more gratifying roles in the larger society than the married person. We must not ignore the contributions of unmarried men and women as illustrated by the work of many single Peace Corps volunteers, civil rights workers, and religious leaders from St. Paul and St. Augustine to the present. It would be revealing to most of us to discover how many achievements in the arts, politics, and the social services have been made by single persons. As childbearing becomes less and less important in an ecologically minded world, the contribution of the single person to society will continue to be better appreciated.

Problems of the Single Life

Problems may also occur for the single person in the fulfillment of sexual roles. A single person may find that expressional patterns that were satisfactory in his teens or early twenties are not adequate as he moves into his thirties or forties. In their teens and twenties single people have widely divergent sexual patterns; each individual feels free to adopt a particular pattern in accord with his moral values, his family standards, and the judgments of his peers. If a thirty- or forty-year-old single person wants to marry, however, he must reevaluate his premarital behavior and focus his attention solely on his relationship with his future spouse. This adjustment can sometimes be difficult, and as such it is a deterrent to marriage.

On the other hand, for the person who does not marry, the sexual role may be no more easily fulfilled. He has no central sexual relationship like that found in marriage. Behavior patterns that were entirely satisfactory in

[20]Erich Fromm, *The Sane Society* (New York: Holt, Rinehart & Winston, 1955), pp. 200–06.

relation to a large group of people in a high school or college community may be much more difficult for him to maintain as a single individual in a society in which most people are married. One reason young single adults tend to migrate to large cities is that there are larger groups of young adults there. But that is only a temporary solution to the problem. The highest status in our society still belongs, in most cases, to the man or woman who is successful both in the business world and in marriage. Thus the person who satisfies his sex needs in ways that are not completely acceptable socially may be rejected by society or develop guilt feelings because he is trying to function with a set of values that differs from his behavior patterns.

The traditional solution to the sexual problems of the single person is the sublimation of sex drives. Work and identification with the needs of others have often been thought to be wholesome alternative outlets for sexual feelings. But unless a person practicing celibacy has a sound awareness of his own feelings, a mature sense of value and proportion, and probably a healthy sense of humor, he will surely have periods of real frustration, anxiety, or depression. (Probably married people are more enthusiastic about this alternative for the single person than is the single person himself. But it should hardly need to be pointed out that it is incongruous for a person to recommend celibacy to others when he cannot accept it for himself.)

The single person's prospects for sexual fulfillment are improving with the advent of innovative lifestyles and greater sexual freedom. Society is now in the process of reevaluating the ways in which our sexuality can be expressed in meaningful relationships, both within and without marriage. With this reevaluation must certainly come a new recognition of the worth and value of every person as an individual.

Homosexual Relationships

A further change in role orientation has become evident in the last decade with the emergence of the "gay liberation" movement, which represents a new self-conscious effort on the part of homosexual persons to assert themselves and their individual and civil rights. The emergence of sizable homosexual communities in many large cities, and public discussion of the pros and cons of the homosexual lifestyle, have focused a high degree of interest on this subject.

Acceptance by Society

There are several arguments advanced in favor of "gay marriage" and increasing freedom for gay men and lesbian women. One argument stresses the fairly constant group of individuals in most societies who prefer this orientation. Kinsey's study of male homosexuality, for example, showed 37 percent of the total male sample reporting at least some overt homosexual experience to the point of orgasm between adolescence and old age.[21] Advocates of greater recognition for these individuals say that it is much better for them to affirm the innate or natural affection that they have for a partner of the same sex, than for it to remain hidden "in the closet."

Dr. Howard Brown has defended this viewpoint in presenting the personal story of his homosexual lifestyle in the book, *Familiar Faces, Hidden Lives.* A former Commissioner of Public Health in New York City, Brown feels that the story of homosexual men in America is one of increasing freedom and acceptance. He writes:

> The gay civil rights movement is gradually redefining society's view of homosexuals; even more importantly, it is helping us to see ourselves in a new light. As conditions change, we too, are changing.
>
> From the reactions of many straight people to my coming out publicly and from my meetings with young gay leaders from Maine to Hawaii ever since, I have good reason to believe that our future will be very different from the damaging past . . .
>
> I am aware that gays drawing together in groups are in a sense seceding from straight society. By emphasizing the need for young gays to join such groups I am, I can see, advocating gay separatism—for a time, at least . . .
>
> I believe it will take the rest of this century for society to rid itself of its prejudice against homosexuals. . . .[22]

Homosexual men and women also find support for their lifestyle in other areas of our society. A number of gay churches have been founded, with many joined together as the "Metropolitan Community Churches." There are gay newspapers, gay magazines, gay businesses, and gay cultural events.[23] A number of activist groups have been formed on college campuses, and in certain states, additional legal protection has been given to both men and women homosexuals.

Rejection by Society

The reaction to this increasing awareness of the views of the homosexual community and its desire for full social and legal rights in our society has been in many cases a strongly negative one. In several parts of the country,

[21] Alfred C. Kinsey, Wardell B. Pomeroy, and Clyde E. Martin, *Sexual Behavior in the Human Male* (Philadelphia: Saunders, 1948), p. 650.

[22] Howard Brown, *Familiar Faces, Hidden Lives* (New York: Harcourt Brace Jovanovich, 1976).

[23] See W. Dwight Oberholtzer, *Is Gay Good?* (Philadelphia: Westminster, 1971).

antihomosexual measures have been placed on the ballot. Some of these measures have been passed, depriving gay groups and individuals of their previous public and legal support. It is apparent that this will be an area of conflict during the next decade.

The arguments against increasing acceptance of the homosexual lifestyle are emotional. Homosexuality is said to be "unnatural," and has been condemned by some religious teaching. Although there is now some variation, the majority of Protestant, Catholic, and Jewish groups still are critical of the gay lifestyle, and exclude self-affirming homosexuals from full participation and leadership in their religious communities. Biblical traditions in both the Old Testament and New Testament are cited in support of this negative view.

Homosexual men and women are held to be poor models for heterosexual family life. It is said to be unwise to let them serve as school teachers, recreational and group leaders, and in other occupations where they might influence children and young people. Although much of the literature in the field is unclear as to what biological or environmental factors are most important in the development of homosexuality, almost all writers see some importance in the social influences upon the individual.[24]

There is also a tendency to make homosexuals convenient scapegoats for many of society's ills. It is difficult and often confusing to attempt a complete analysis of our culture and the complex factors that affect its change and development in both positive and negative ways. It is simpler to blame the politicians, or the school system, or the homosexuals.

One basic problem in assessing the place of homosexual men and women in our society is that most studies of homosexuals are based on adult samples. Attempts to understand the development of homosexual behavior are usually made by interpreting childhood experiences from an adult perspective. It would be considered an invasion of privacy to work with children and young teenagers to elicit similar information from them. Thus many of our hypotheses about what might have happened are untested by empirical evidence. The existence of a large minority of gay individuals is a reality, however, and the focus of attention will probably continue to be on society's relationship to the adult homosexual population.

SUMMARY

Role and status are important concepts in self-development. Role expectations are important to both the married and the unmarried at every stage of life. Certain role expectations provide us with satisfaction, and we try to

[24]See John H. Gagnon, *Human Sexualities* (Glenview, Ill.: Scott, Foresman, 1977), chap. 12.

meet them. If we are successful, we can achieve stable, mature, and fulfilling life patterns.

Many major role behaviors are associated with our gender. The traditional masculine role reflected man's physical strength and ability to defend his family. It was reinforced by masculine dominance in most parts of life outside the family: economics, education, religion, and politics. In contrast, women were expected to be passive and submissive. Life for them centered around the home, the family, and the children. A woman might assist her husband financially, but she could not become independent of him. There were limitations on a woman's social life too, and on her expression of her personal opinions. She learned to suffer in silence in the face of crisis or adversity rather than criticize her husband.

Changes in women's roles are most striking. There has been a dramatic increase in the number of employed women, causing a new focus of interest outside the home. A second change is the rise in education. A third change has come about through the feminist movement and the movement for full equality between the sexes. Technological advances have freed women from many tasks. Women are seeking full participation in the mainstream of American life. They want to achieve different roles at different stages in the life cycle.

There have also been many changes in the traditional masculine role. Sheer physical strength is not as important today as it once was. Rather, education and specialized training are a necessity for men today. As a result, many men feel threatened by the new roles being taken on by women. Husbands and fathers are also learning to take a more active expressive and emotional role. But it is not easy for all men to change to a different lifestyle with different role behavior.

Must every man and woman fulfill his role in life through marriage? Clearly, the answer is no. Our pairing system does not guarantee marriage to everyone. Many men and women fill mature and satisfying roles as single persons. In every avenue of life, a single person may make a very unique and worthwhile contribution. The new era of freedom and opportunity for all members of society holds promise for a satisfying life in the years ahead for those who do not marry.

There is a new self-conscious group of homosexual men and women in our society. Although a minority, they are nevertheless highly visible. Through the gay civil rights movement, they seek full social and civil equality. A large segment of society accepts the gay rights movement and what it stands for. However, there is also a vocal opposition to further public acceptance of the homosexual lifestyle. Some conservative groups want to redirect society toward a more critical view of homosexuality. Continuing debate on this issue seems inevitable.

SUGGESTED READINGS

Brenton, Myron. *The American Male.* Greenwich, Conn.: Fawcett, 1967. Focus on the masculine role in our society. Relation of men to the sexual revolution.

Brown, Howard. *Familiar Faces, Hidden Lives.* New York: Harcourt Brace Jovanovich, 1976. Experiences of a prominent male homosexual who became active in the gay liberation movement.

Calhoun, Arthur W. *A Social History of the American Family.* New York: Barnes & Noble, 1945, three volumes in one. Basic historical survey of the American family to early twentieth century.

Carden, Maren Lockwood. *The New Feminist Movement.* New York: Russell Sage Foundation, 1974. Careful analysis of feminism, including bibliography of survey of organizations.

David, Deborah S., and Robert Brannon, eds. *The Forty-Nine Percent Majority: The Male Sex Role.* Reading, Mass.: Addison-Wesley, 1976. Good selection of readings, with introduction and comments by editors.

Farrell, Warren T. *The Liberated Man: Beyond Masculinity: Freeing Men and Their Relationships with Women.* New York: Random House, 1974. Exponent of male liberation reports on his research and experience with male consciousness-raising groups.

Freeman, Jo, ed. *Women: A Feminist Perspective.* Palo Alto, Ca.: Mayfield, 1975. Good collection of contemporary materials, with several contributions by editor.

Friedan, Betty. *The Feminine Mystique.* New York: Norton, 1963. Challenging book which triggered growth of women's movement in the 1960s. Conflicting roles of women discussed.

Levinson, Daniel J. "Growing Up with the Dream." *Psychology Today,* 11, no. 8 (Jan. 1978), 20–31, 89. Interesting discussion of how successful men pattern their lives throughout the life cycle.

Lopata, Helena Z. *Occupation: Housewife.* New York: Oxford, 1971. Well-done study of housewives with young children in urban area by leading scholar.

Millett, Kate. *Sexual Politics.* Garden City, N.Y.: Doubleday, 1970. Strong critique of the patriarchal system that has long dominated male-female role relationships.

Montagu, Ashley. *The Natural Superiority of Women,* rev. ed. New York: Macmillan, 1968. Noted anthropologist lends his views to a revelation of the feminine role.

Petras, John W., ed. *Sex: Male. Gender: Masculine.* Port Washington, N.Y.: Alfred, 1975. Well-balanced collection of articles on development of masculine role.

Safilios-Rothschild, Constantina. *Toward a Sociology of Women.* Lexington, Mass.: Xerox College Publishing, 1972. Good balance of research, personal viewpoints, and predictions for the future.

Van Dusen, Roxann A., and Eleanor Bernert Sheldon. "The Changing Status of American Women: A Life Cycle Perspective." *American Psychologist,* 31, no. 2 (Feb. 1976), 106–16. Good survey of changes affecting contemporary women.

6 Exploring Our Marriage Expectations

- What do you expect from marriage?
- What models for marriage in our American culture seem most valid to you?
- What crises in our twentieth-century history have affected the family life of your parents and your grandparents?
- What do you know about your grandparents? Was their family life very different from what you have experienced?
- How has your family influenced your outlook on life and your expectations for the future? What have been the positive and negative factors?
- What values have you learned from your family? How have they shaped your own goals?
- Are there family values that you will reject instead of adopt as your own?
- How do you think your family will react to your choice of a marriage partner?

Traditional Patterns

Single people ask themselves many questions about marriage. What is marriage going to be like? Is it really going to be everything I expect? Will my marriage be very much like my parents' or my aunt and uncle's? Can I look forward to a marriage more ideal and more satisfying than other couples' because of the love my partner and I share? Or should I be fearful of dissension and failure in my marriage because so many marriages fail today? Should I think of my marriage as a lifetime partnership, taking seriously the vows to marry "until death do us part"? Or should my marriage be an experiment, to be put aside for some new relationship if it is unsuccessful?

Questions like these are not new. In earlier generations many people worried about what was happening to the family. A hundred years ago, a person writing on the future of the family saw the situation in this way:

> The sense of the sacredness of the marriage tie is unquestionably declining. The number of men and women who have separated from their wives and husbands is increasing and the discredit of such separations is diminishing; and we are assured that there is now to be found in some of the western states a large and increasing class of children . . . who, without having been formally and clandestinely abandoned by their parents, are nevertheless in a state of doubt as to who are their mothers.[1]

[1]In *The Nation,* New York, 1868, quoted in Arthur W. Calhoun, *A Social History of the American Family,* vol. 3 (New York: Barnes & Noble, 1960), pp. 255–56.

Each person forms his views and expectations of marriage according to his experiences, hopes, and ambitions. His expectations are also influenced by cultural traditions. In this chapter we will examine our marriage expectations, which have been influenced by our culture, the recent history of our country, our American social classes, and our own family experiences. All these influences affect our feelings for our potential and actual marriage partners. If we can get a clearer glimpse of the past and present factors that have had an effect on us, we will be able to see the future much more clearly.

American Courtship

Courtship in America has always been different from courtship in Europe. The migration from old and established cultures to the New World made differences in the economic, social, religious, and political life, and in marriage and family life as well. Often the most adventurous, unconventional, and restless members of a family would be the ones to come to America, and then pull up stakes and move west toward the frontier.

Ira Reiss points out that courtship customs usually fit into other aspects of the culture. This was true of one of the oldest forms of courting in early rural America—"bundling." He writes:

> Bundling affords an excellent illustration of how a courtship custom integrates with the basic type of social system in which it exists. Winters in New England were harsh and long, and the roads were few and difficult to travel in the winter. If a young man saw a woman who caught his eye in church, how could he get to see her during the winter months? He could with luck travel the few miles to her house on Saturday night. But to expect him to be able to return that same evening was too much. He could become lost or caught in a storm and, in any case, would arrive home quite late because no mechanical transportation was available then. Thus, if courtship was to be encouraged, some method of allowing the male to stay over at the female's house was needed.
>
> . . . The woman's parents wanted to leave the young couple alone to talk and get to know each other better, in the hope that matrimony might eventuate . . . there was a shortage of beds in most households, so that the man could not be offered his own bed for the night. Very often the man would have to share a bed, and since the object was to allow him time to talk to their daughter, the bed he shared would likely be hers. It was this sharing of a common bed during winter courtship in New England that came to be known as bundling.
>
> Bundling was supposed to operate on an honor system. There were to be no intimate embraces and certainly no sexual intercourse. . . . But

the high percentage of pregnant brides in New England at this time (the eighteenth century) testifies to the violation of the honor system. In Groton, Massachusetts, the Groton Church records examined by Arthur Calhoun show that of 200 weddings performed from 1761 through 1775, 66 involved confessions of fornication to the minister.[2]

The twentieth century finds our American culture in the midst of major changes in the way we look at our sexual life and our preparation for marriage. The casual approach to sex and marriage typified by "bundling" was replaced by the rigid Victorian attitude. Today, many young men and women seem to be swinging the pendulum back in the other direction.

read again

American Marriage

Floyd Martinson gives a classic analysis of the traditional American model for marriage patterned on the Judeo-Christian tradition. In this view, marriage is seen as a God-given order, one of God's good gifts to humans. Men and women expect to find their sexual needs fulfilled only in marriage. Sex is often seen negatively—"It is better to marry than to burn." In the Roman Catholic view, there is special emphasis on the importance of children and the family's role in their care and protection. Jewish and Protestant traditions emphasize the value of companionship in the marriage relationship.[3] Some scholars, like Gerald R. Leslie, have traced the course of family life in Western society from the ancient Hebrews.[4] We can thus isolate influences that come from the Greeks, the Romans, the early Christians, the Anglo-Saxons and the feudal society of the Middle Ages, the modern English, and the colonial Americans. Such an analysis is helpful, although it does treat separately many influences that have now been absorbed and coordinated by our society. Another approach is to study anthropological evidence in an attempt to discover what basic patterns may be common to all family life.[5]

Many high ideals of love and service and selflessness are stressed by the traditional model of marriage. The love a person shares with his marriage partner, the concern and care he expresses for his children, and the energy he expends in providing for his family should not prevent him from loving his neighbor, caring for the unfortunate, or willingly serving the religious

[2]Ira L. Reiss, *Family Systems in America*, 2nd ed. (Hinsdale, Ill.: Dryden, 1976), pp. 73–77.

[3]Floyd M. Martinson, *Marriage and the American Ideal* (New York: Dodd, Mead, 1960), pp. 37ff.

[4]Gerald R. Leslie, *The Family in Social Context*, 2nd ed. (New York: Oxford Univ. Press, 1971), chaps. 6 and 7.

[5]Panos D. Bardis, "Family Forms and Variations Historically Considered," *Handbook of Marriage and the Family*, ed. Harold T. Christensen (Chicago: Rand McNally, 1964), pp. 403–61. See also Rudy Ray Seward, "The Colonial Family in America: Toward a Socio-Historical Restoration of Its Structure," *Journal of Marriage and the Family*, 35, no. 1 (Feb. 1973), 50–70.

community. Rather, one's home and family are a small and intimate community that should reflect the heavenly love and grace of the larger religious fellowship.

The Romantic Tradition

There are many other aspects of our cultural tradition that have had a strong influence upon our expectations for marriage. There is a strong romantic element in our American tradition. The romantic attitude can be seen in poetry, literature, and drama and in the romantic cults of our own day. Love is not negative and sinful: "Rather it is a power that makes the evil good and by it the good becomes better."[6] But love is never to be taken for granted; the quest is always uncertain.

The romantic pattern puts heavy stress on the individual and his feelings. The interest is not in society and its preservation and stability, but in the

[6]Martinson, p. 37.

lovers and their personal needs and desires. The rites of courtship are more important and exciting than the routine and possibly boring responsibilities of the marriage partnership.

This model remains an influential one in America today. There is the enticing lure of the advertising media, which promise exciting romance with the purchase of an alluring perfume or whitening toothpaste. Americans worship the cult of physical attractiveness. A typical movie theme of the 1960s had Pulaski Tech out to do battle for the state football championship. Romantic love will help them to achieve their goal. Each game is preceded by and interspersed with a host of lovely coeds, marching, singing, cheering, and yelling for the stalwart heroes who will carry the red and black into the fray. Some people may remember the national intercollegiate championship basketball game in which the outcome hung in the balance until the attractive cheerleaders (including the superstar's beloved) arrived on the scene after a train delay. Then the extra lift was there and the victory was won!

Perhaps another bulwark of romantic thinking in our culture is our basically secular philosophy of life. Much of our life has no roots beyond the immediate and the material; we are thus anxious to exalt and glorify our present achievements. Those Americans who have little interest in the things of the mind and spirit cling all the more closely to romantic dreams and fancies. The fact that their dreams do not always materialize and that many of their romantic excursions turn out to be frustrating and heartbreaking does not shake their belief in romance.

Idealization of Women

Another aspect of our cultural tradition is the idealization of women. This is not a twentieth-century invention; it has roots much earlier in our history. Barbara Welter sees it as central to "the cult of true womanhood":

> The nineteenth-century American man was a busy builder of bridges and railroads, at work long hours in a materialistic society. The religious values of his forebears were neglected in practice if not in intent, and he occasionally felt some guilt that he had turned this new land, this temple of the chosen people, into one vast countinghouse. But he could salve his conscience by reflecting that he had left behind a hostage, not only to fortune, but to all the values which he held so dear and treated so lightly. Woman . . . was the hostage in the home. . . .
>
> The attributes of True Womanhood, by which a woman judged herself and was judged by her husband, her neighbors, and society could be divided into four cardinal virtues—piety, purity, submissiveness, and

domesticity. Put them all together and they spelled mother, daughter, sister, wife—woman. Without them, no matter whether there was fame, achievement, or wealth, all was ashes. With them she was promised happiness and power.[7]

European Heritage

A third significant influence on American marriage and family expectations, and one which is often overlooked, is the European influence. For more than two hundred years, since the establishment of the first colonies, the Anglo-Saxon influence was the predominant one on American families. In the past one hundred years, other European influences have had a strong impact on the United States. The peoples of continental Europe—German, Hungarian, Polish, Italian, Russian, Austrian, French, and others—have migrated to our shores, bringing with them their family traditions. They have been Roman Catholic or Jewish in faith, rather than Protestant. They have brought with them a patriarchal form of family organization. These ethnic groups have had a major influence on the American family in the twentieth century.

Rural Heritage

The rural nature of our country in the first three centuries of our history is a fourth influence on American family life. The gradual disappearance of the family farm may lead us to forget the rural heritage from which we have come. Yet in many families, there are links one, two, or three generations in the past with a small town, a ranch, or a farm where family traditions began.

The Changing Family

What has become of the American family as it has faced the twentieth century? Let us focus our attention particularly on two generations before us: that of our grandparents (marriages from 1925 to 1940)—the Depression generation, and that of our parents (marriages from 1945 to 1960), the postwar generation. In seeing how rapidly our family life has changed within the memories of those in our own family circle, we can see how our marriage expectations must also be changing rapidly as well.

[7]See Barbara Welter, "The Cult of True Womanhood: 1820–1860," in Michael Gordon, ed., *The American Family in Social-Historical Perspective,* 2nd ed. (New York: St. Martin's Press, 1978), p. 313.

Marriage: 1925–1940

Before 1920 most Americans lived on farms or in small rural towns. The 1920 census was the first census in which the urban population of the United States outnumbered the rural population: the rural population was estimated to be 49,973,000 in 1910 and 51,553,000 in 1920, while the urban population jumped from 41,990,000 in 1910 to 54,150,000 in 1920.[8] Since that time, the majority of our population has continued to grow up, marry, live, and work in cities and towns. The consequences of this change for family life have been tremendous. It is not that city life per se is a new development, for people have lived in great cities since the days of the Sumerians and the Egyptians. It is rather that the nature and relative importance of city and farm has changed. We no longer need the labor of large numbers of people to provide our basic food supply; this can be accomplished by a small number of people using modern farm machinery. The labor of those people living in the cities, however, produces a wider range of industrial and consumer goods than ever before imagined and provides innumerable services of all kinds.

Marriage for your grandparents was much more like the traditional American model than marriage of the 1970s. But most of the trends that are important now were being felt strongly then and were often bitterly criticized. Many men and women resented, for instance, the changes that were taking women away from the home and into the mainstream of political, economic, and social life. The view in 1927 of a noted sociologist, Dr. Ernest R. Groves, on the problems of the working mother illustrates the reaction against such social change.

> Many homes whose mothers are employed outside have conditions resembling those in the homes where death has removed the mother. A considerable part of the child's life, if supervised at all, is under the influence of someone else than the mother. Even when at home, the mother is likely to be too tired to deal wisely with her children or to give them a normal expression of mother-love; she may be so busy with the physical tasks of housekeeping that she cannot find time to pay them the necessary attention. . . . It is not uncommon for the children, especially the older ones, to act quite differently while the mother is at home than when they are under the control of her substitute. . . . The home life broken by the absence of the mother at work runs risk of injuring the school career of the child since he is liable to be kept at home to help with the household

[8] U.S. Bureau of the Census, *Statistical Abstract of the United States, 1966* (Washington, D.C.: U.S. Government Printing Office, 1966), p. 15.

> tasks; the amount of work put upon him during out of school hours may overtire him and prevent him from obtaining the necessary vitalizing recreation. As a consequence of absences or fatigue or little time for study, or apathy because of the dullness of life, he does not do as good work at school as his intellectual capacity warrants.[9]

Groves' theories about children whose mothers worked have clearly been disproved today.

How did husbands and wives relate to each other fifty years ago? An interesting study of American life by Robert and Helen Lynd gives us some insight into what primarily middle-class couples expected in their marriages. The Lynds' 1929 study of Middletown, a Midwestern town of from 25,000 to 50,000 people chosen as a city representative of American life, described married life in that period. The Lynds reported that the average family in the town shrank from 6.6 persons in 1890 to 4.2 in 1900 to 3.9 in 1910 to 3.8 in 1920. At the same time, the percentage of married persons over fifteen years of age rose. But old-fashioned European patterns of masculine and feminine behavior seemed to persist in Middletown in spite of the community's superficial modernization.

> In general, a high degree of companionship is not regarded as essential for marriage. There appears to be between Middletown husbands and wives of all classes when gathered together in informal leisure-time groups relatively little spontaneous community of interest. The men and women frequently either gravitate apart into separate groups to talk men's talk and women's talk, or the men do most of the talking and the women largely listen. Even since women have been allowed to vote with men some tendency persists for women of all classes to depend in such practical matters upon the opinions of their husbands. . . .
>
> This frequent lack of community interests, together with the ideas each sex entertains regarding the other, appears in many families in a lack of frankness between husband and wife, far-reaching in its emotional outcome. . . . With an increase, between 1890 and 1920, of 87 percent in the population of the county in which Middletown is located, the number of recorded divorces for the four years 1920–1924 has increased 622 percent over the number of divorces in the county in the four years 1889–1892.
>
> . . . The frequency of divorces and the speed with which they are rushed through have become commonplace in Middletown.[10]

[9]Ernest R. Groves, *Social Problems of the Family* (Philadelphia: Lippincott, 1927), pp. 165–86.
[10]Robert S. Lynd and Helen M. Lynd, *Middletown* (New York: Harcourt Brace Jovanovich, 1929), pp. 118–21.

As the Lynds point out, the generation of the 1920s was able to adjust to new technological advances more easily than to changes in interpersonal relationships.

In the 1920s, the future of America had never seemed brighter, but the quiet days of 1925–1928 were all too soon forgotten. The early years of your grandparents' marriages were dominated by the Great Depression. The stock market crash, the breadlines, Roosevelt and the new social legislation of the thirties overwhelmed our society more completely than an earthquake or a hurricane.

The testing experience of your grandparents' generation came with the Depression. Its impact affected deeply the course of American life. David Shannon, in chronicling the events of the period, describes it in this way:

> The Great Depression was a traumatic experience. It was all the more traumatic because the immediately preceding years had been quite comfortable ones on the whole and the American mood had been unusually optimistic. . . .
>
> And then came the crash of October, 1929. Optimism faded quickly. The spokesmen of the New Era issued reassuring public statements, but to most people the statements had a hollow tone. The Wall Street panic triggered a general economic collapse.[11]

We have known prosperity for so many years that it is hard to understand the real meaning of the Depression. Note, for example, the testimony of a Philadelphia official describing conditions there in 1932. He cited unemployment of 298,000 persons against a normal total of between 40,000 and 50,000. There were 55,000 families receiving relief.

> In December our . . . grant was $4.39 per week per family. It is now $4.23 per family. Of this $4.23 per family, about $3.93 is an allowance for food. This is about two-thirds of the amount needed to provide a health-maintaining diet. . . .
>
> We made an intensive study of 91 families to find out what happened when the food orders stopped.
>
> In a little less than 9 percent of these families there were pregnant mothers and in a little more than one-third of the families children of nursing age. . . .
>
> One woman said she borrowed 50 cents from a friend and bought stale bread for 3½ cents per loaf, and that is all they had for eleven days except for one or two meals.

[11]David A. Shannon, *The Great Depression* (Englewood Cliffs, N.J.: Prentice-Hall, 1960), pp. ix–x.

> With the last food order another woman received she bought dried vegetables and canned goods. With this she made a soup and whenever the members of the family felt hungry they just ate some of the soup. . . .
>
> One family had nothing the day the food order stopped until 9 o'clock at night. Then the mother went to a friend's house and begged for a loaf of bread. This woman finally got two days' work at 75 cents a day. She bought a little meat and made a stew from vegetables picked up which they cooked over again every day to prevent its spoiling. . . .
>
> [These cases] are typical. . . .[12]

This description gives some idea of what life was like during the years when your grandparents were growing up. Supporting a family was difficult; the time-honored virtues of thrift and hard work seemed especially important. Certainly your grandparents' plans for marriage and their expectations in raising their own families were directly influenced by the Depression.[13]

Typical of some of the courtship patterns of your grandparents' generation was the following excerpt from a woman's description of her own experiences.

> As young girls my sister and I were carefully supervised. Possibly because of the small town atmosphere, I always went to "mixed" parties, since the first one when I was a toddler. We children in town grew up together, our parents knew each other well, and it would have been a social blunder indeed to limit the festivities of a birthday or other special party to one sex. Early dating was a custom in our town. Although I did not "go out" with a boy until ninth grade, the adjustment was easy, for I had always known and associated with most of the boys in town through church or school activities.
>
> My first and only real "steady" was the man who is now my husband. "Going out" consisted of walking to church or the movies together, going to a party in a friend's home supervised by the parents, or attending a school function. Ten P.M. was curfew, and I had to be home by that hour. I was blissfully ignorant regarding accurate knowledge of sex, for my mother considered this topic taboo.
>
> There were a few families in town with whom we were not allowed to associate, and were bluntly told by our parents: "Because you are who you are, you do not go to so-and-so's house or have anything to do with

[12]Quoted in Shannon, pp. 45–46.

[13]See Evelyn M. Duvall, "American Families and NCFR—Since 1938," *Journal of Marriage and the Family*, 26, no. 1 (Feb. 1964), 10–19.

them. You are a lady and expected to behave accordingly." . . . It goes almost without saying that girls were forbidden to smoke or drink or use coarse language.[14]

There is a strong conservative trend in this generation, and the growing ranks of older Americans include many who reject outright the new patterns and lifestyles that have come out of the different historical setting that has produced the young adults of our day.

Marriage: 1945–1960

Today's college students are the children of the postwar generation. Although your parents may remember the Depression, their primary memories are of the Second World War and the postwar period. This has been an era of constant change, and most of our family histories reflect the tensions of this period.

[14]Student report.

The Second World War had a tremendous impact on American life. Even today, television programs and motion pictures are created to tell the story of this epic world conflict. The war had a great effect on courtship and marriage. Men were drafted and sent to training camps all over the country and overseas, where they frequently met and married women from different states, different ethnic and religious groups, even different countries. Naturally, wartime conditions affected behavior in courtship. There is no accurate national data on changes in premarital sexual behavior, for example; but the implication is that there was more sexual freedom during the war period. Courtship was often very brief; engagements were often omitted altogether. The traditional family and social restrictions on courtship were frequently forgotten.

Furthermore, husband and wife often began their marriage very much on their own, with no old friends, family, or familiar community associations to aid them in their initial adjustment. The peak divorce rate recorded in 1945 and 1946 demonstrated the instability of numerous wartime marriages; once the pressures of war and patriotism were removed, many poorly matched partners quickly sought freedom through divorce.

Still other changes came to this generation. The movement of women into the world outside the home, begun a generation or two before, was greatly accelerated. In the forties, millions of women were drawn into the labor force to replace men who had gone to war. When the war ended, many of them continued to work. Sociologists tended to frown on the working woman in this generation as well, though they did see advantages to her added salary in some circumstances. In 1949 sociologist Robert Harper suggested that a wife should not be employed early in marriage if her husband's income was ample, if she was in ill health or expecting children, or if her husband was strongly opposed to her working. He concluded:

> Providing no such conditions as those . . . exist for the couple, it is probably desirable for the wife to work until close to the time when the first child is planned. She thus has the opportunity to contribute to the earlier realization of such customary marital ambitions as the purchase of a home and the acquisition of other convenient material possessions and to the accumulation of savings to meet future expenses necessitated by children or a rainy day. Although some adjustments are necessary in departing from the traditional conception of the wife's serving the husband in the home, they are not too difficult for two relatively mature young people to make and are more than offset in many instances by the resulting economic security.[15]

[15]Robert A. Harper, *Marriage* (New York: Appleton-Century-Crofts, 1949), p. 106.

In a later chapter, Harper once more emphasized the fact that the added income would help to provide economic security for the family.[16] But the question of whether a woman should work after children were born or after they were grown and married did not seem to be a matter for serious consideration to Harper.

You can appreciate some of your parents' problems because you have been able to talk over their experiences with them and perhaps visit some of the places that were important to them during courtship and early marriage. Still, one never really feels the same about something when one hears it secondhand. The generation gap between parents and children is a very real one.

Many of the changes that affected your parents' generation were discussed in Chapter 5. Let us mention one or two other characteristics of your parents' generation.[17] They have been a very fertile generation. They married early, and produced a larger number of children than their parents did during the Depression. (The fertility rate peaked at 3.8 in 1957.) A high percentage of the total population married—Paul C. Glick estimates that less than 4 percent remained single by the time they ended their fifties. At the same time, there has been a rising incidence of divorce. This has had such a strong impact on the family that, in 1970, more than 30 percent of children of school age were not living with both their natural parents. Separation and divorce are especially high in black families, but the total picture for this generation is one in which family change, as evidenced by divorce and remarriage, is now a very common phenomenon.

Marriage Today: The Influence of Social Class

There are other important influences on our marriage expectations. We cannot ignore the social class in which we grow up. In most cases, we live within a single social-class environment, and expect this to continue in our own marriage. But even if our family moves up or down the class scale, or if we ourselves move into a new socioeconomic level, the influence of our original social class is still there.

In a sense, talk of social class goes against some deeply ingrained American traditions. America is the great melting pot, the land of freedom and opportunity, a democratic country with no titled aristocracy. When we examine this concept more closely, however, we see that a completely classless society is an almost impossible ideal. Incomes are different, education var-

[16]Harper, p. 178.
[17]See Paul C. Glick, "A Demographer Looks at American Families," *Journal of Marriage and the Family*, 37, no. 1 (Feb. 1975), 15–26.

ies, and differing occupations bring different prestige and rewards. Such distinctions are, in fact, an aspect of life in every community.

There is a large body of sociological literature dealing with social class. The work of W. Lloyd Warner and Paul S. Lunt has been basic.

> By class is meant two or more orders of people who are believed to be and are accordingly ranked by the members of the community, in socially superior and inferior positions. Members of a class tend to marry within their own order, but the values of the society permit marriage up and down. A class system also provides that children are born into the same status as their parents. A class society distributes rights and privileges, duties and obligations unequally among its inferior and superior grades.[18]

In the United States there have been many different estimates of the number of social classes and their composition. Since inflation is now bringing changes to our income levels each year, and the educational level of both men and women is rising, there must be a fairly constant reevaluation of the criteria for each class. Generally, at least five major divisions are recognized. These include the upper class, the upper-middle class, the lower-middle class, the working class (or upper-lower), and the lower class. Suggested breakdowns by percentage of population are summarized in Table 6–1.

In addition to the five major class levels, it is possible to identify ethnic

[18]W. Lloyd Warner and Paul S. Lunt, *The Social Life of a Modern Community* (New Haven: Yale Univ. Press, 1941), p. 82.

Table 6–1 Social Class in America

Upper class	1%–3%
Upper-middle class	10%–15%
Lower-middle class	30%–35%
Working class	40%–45%
Lower class	20%–25%

SOURCE: Daniel W. Rossides, *The American Class System,* p. 24. © 1976 by Houghton Mifflin Co. Reprinted by permission.

and racial subgroupings in our society. The Irish, Puerto Ricans, Chinese, Mexicans, Cubans, Italians, and other ethnic groups may retain many customs from their former homelands and be clearly distinguishable as separate social groups. Racial distinctions are also of major importance. The color system is perhaps more one of caste than of class: the class system provides for social mobility, but caste systems do not.

Before turning to an analysis of each of the class levels represented in most American communities, let us consider three preliminary questions that will help each of us to pinpoint our position in the American social structure and predict our future place in it.

1. Am I part of an ethnic group that can be clearly distinguished from the majority pattern in American life? Will I continue to live and work as a part of that group, or will education and social mobility lead me to identify with another group?
2. Do I belong to a distinct racial minority? Does that impose strict limitations on my personal and social development and mobility, or do I live in an area where it does not impose restrictions on me and my family? Will I move to a different area of the country because of such restrictions?
3. Will marriage or education change my social class in another three, four, or five years?

Class Levels in American Society

THE UPPER CLASS

The upper class stands at the top of the socioeconomic scale, and has wealth and influence far out of proportion to its size: It constitutes only 1 to 3 percent of the population. Ranking in the upper class is derived from high family income and acceptance by other upper-class families in the community. There are some self-made men in the upper class who have climbed to the top in business, politics, or the professions, but more frequently upper-class men have inherited the mantle of success from previous generations.[19] Their families form the core of "society," and their children attend the best private schools and colleges. Family traditions are strong and carry over from one generation to the next.

Ruth S. Cavan has given an excellent description of upper-class families in *The American Family*. She describes the Lowells as an example of famous upper-class families with long family histories.

> The Lowell family is a recognized upper-upper class family of Boston, best known at the present time for Abbot Lawrence Lowell, president of Harvard University from 1909 to 1933, and his poet-sister Amy Lowell; and in the past for James Russell Lowell. A family that provided outstanding leadership in public affairs, education, the courts, the church, and the cotton industry, it had its roots in this country in Percival Lowle, classified as a gentleman in England, who emigrated to America in 1639. The family required several generations to establish its prestige in America. Percival's great-great-grandson John set the family pattern, which still continues, of graduation of the men from Harvard and leadership in the professions and community affairs, supported (later) by wealth from the lucrative cotton manufacturing of New England. By 1800 the "high places of Boston were permeated with Lowell poets, manufacturers, diplomats, judges, historians, ministers, and educators," representing various branches of the family.[20]

THE UPPER-MIDDLE CLASS

The upper-middle class is another important part of our social structure. Here are the business managers, the professionals, the decision-makers in business and industry and government. Traditionally, upper-middle-class family life was built around the husband's career. But in the past generation we have begun to consider the wife's career also and the possibility that both husband and wife together, as doctors or university professors, for example, might each make a contribution to the family's standing in the community. Typically, the couple nurture and reinforce each other's ambitions. They establish a home that is an asset to their careers, and they encourage each other to move ahead to meet their expanding needs and wants. In addition, both partners recognize the pressures involved in building a career, and consequently try not to be overdemanding of each other's energies.

[19]See Suzanne Keller, *Beyond the Ruling Class: Strategic Elites in Modern Society* (New York: Random House, 1963).

[20]Ruth S. Cavan, *The American Family*, 4th ed. (New York: Thomas Y. Crowell, 1969).

THE LOWER-MIDDLE CLASS

The lower-middle class represents a large and ever-increasing part of the mainstream of American life. They are the people who keep industry and business in motion. They are the solid, stable center of the community. In many communities some higher education is a requisite to remain within this class. Their children will probably have greater opportunities than they had. In addition, there are many blue-collar workers whose skills and responsibilities fit them into this bracket—foremen, skilled craftsmen, and some industrial workers.

Respectability is important for the lower-middle-class family because it indicates that it is a cut above working-class families. They put great value on education, and send their children to college, even though it may involve sacrifice. Lower-middle-class families are more often regular churchgoers and strongly support the traditional pattern of morality.

IMP.

THE WORKING CLASS

Rossides sees the working class as the largest single grouping in our country, approximately 40 to 45 percent of the population. Their work is not the challenge to them that it is to career people, and their lack of education and opportunity for advancement makes them disdainful of attempts to enter the middle-class world. Their children may climb the ladder that they cannot, but they themselves are locked into their position and see no way out of it. Frequently working-class jobs are repetitious, and the only compensation comes in high pay, good fringe benefits, and a retirement plan. One accepts unpleasantness for the gain involved. Kahl describes this class as exemplified by automobile workers.

IMP

> The men did not like assembly-line work, and they remembered their previous jobs as having been more interesting. Why, then, did they come to the automobile plant? For the high pay it offered and the relative steadiness of its employment. In other words, a working-class job is something that one has to do in order to earn a living, and one accepts unpleasantness in order to bring home a good pay check. One does not expect to enjoy it, to be particularly interested in it, to have it mean anything to him in and of itself. This characteristic attitude, plus the fact of high movement from one job to another, alienates men from work. Such alienation is the exact opposite of a "career" orientation.[21]

The working class does not have as clearly defined a place in the future

[21]Joseph A. Kahl, *The American Class Structure* (New York: Irvington Publishers, 1957), pp. 205–06.

of America as the middle classes. Joseph Bensman and Arthur Vidich have suggested that they are cut off from the mainstream of society. Bensman and Vidich see the group as a disadvantaged one, a class that can achieve real pride only when a child moves up to middle-class status.[22] Perhaps this pessimistic evaluation of the working class is most justified in the old urban centers; in the South and the West and in the smaller population centers, the avenues of opportunity and change are more open to working-class families.

The working-class mother is a key person in the development of her children. She is the one who becomes involved in the children's school and sports activities. If she or her parents have been part of a higher class, or if she has a white-collar job, she may push her children toward higher education and a chance for upward social movement. The absence of the mother may result in a child's downward movement.

THE LOWER CLASS

The lower class has the most difficult role to play in our society. Many Americans seem to accept the fact that these families do not have adequate income, housing, education, health care, and opportunity to share in the good things of the American way of life. And there is no widely accepted solution to the problems that are generated in the slum areas of our cities and in the migrant camps of the rural poor.

In earlier generations, the ranks of lower-class families were continually replenished by new immigrants from Europe. Since this flood of immigration has slowed to a trickle, the focus has been on other groups. In present-day America, the lower-class sections of the cities are populated largely by racial minority groups and families who come from rural areas. Blacks, Puerto Ricans, Mexican-Americans, and other minority groups feel the impact of many restrictions and limitations on their advancement. And they have found these restrictions tighter and more difficult to overcome than did European minority groups in earlier generations—probably, as we have said, because of caste, rather than class, distinctions.

The plight of lower-class migrant families has been one of the best kept secrets of American society. The lives of these people have been carefully described by Robert Coles in the second volume of his series *Children of Crisis.*

> One migrant mother described her own feelings of helplessness and eventually indifference in the face of such circumstances: "My children, they suffer, I know. They hurts, and I can't stop it. I just have to pray

[22]Joseph Bensman and Arthur Vidich, *The New American Society* (Chicago: Quadrangle Books, 1971), pp. 151–53.

Table 6–2 Personal Income Before Taxes Compared to National Personal Income, by Income Bracket

	Percentage of National Personal Income Income Bracket			
Year	Highest 10 percent	Fourth highest 10 percent	Seventh highest 10 percent	Lowest 10 percent
1910	34%	9%	6%	3%
1929	39	9	6	2
1948	31	10	6	1
1956	31	11	6	1
1964	30	11	6	1

SOURCE: Adapted from Randall Collins, "Social Stratification," *Introduction to Sociology,* ed. Jack D. Douglas (New York: The Free Press, 1973), p. 364. Copyright © 1973 by The Free Press, a division of Macmillan Publishing Co., Inc.

that they'll stay alive, somehow. They gets the colic, and I don't know what to do. One of them, he can't breathe right and his chest, it's in trouble. I can hear the noise inside when he takes his breaths. The worst thing, if you ask me, is the bites they get. It makes them real unhappy. They itches and scratches and bleeds, and oh, it's the worst. They must want to tear all their skin off, but you can't do that. . . . But I say to myself it's life, the way living is, and there's not much to do but accept what happens. Do you have a choice, but to accept? . . ."[23]

Marriage Expectations and Social Class

Does it make any difference to our expectations of marriage if we come from one social class or another? Many powerful influences on marriage and family life spring from the existence of these clearly identifiable social classes. The roles we play as students, employees, spouses, and community members are often shaped by our social class. In addition, we all recognize the fact that we may spend our entire lives at our original social level or, in accord with the circumstances we encounter, move up or down the scale. We are usually motivated by the behavior patterns of those higher on the

[23]Robert Coles, *Children of Crisis: Migrants, Sharecroppers, Mountaineers* (Boston: Little, Brown, 1972), p. 52.

social scale and are perhaps skeptical of or hostile toward the mores of those below us.

There is limited information on the effects of marriage between people of different social classes. Some research indicates, for example, that marital adjustment is most satisfactory if both partners are of the same social class or if the woman marries a man somewhat higher on the social scale. One may accept the challenge of living on a more restricted income than that to which one is accustomed, but the patterns established in one's parental family are not easily broken. It would be interesting to discover whether the actual success or failure of interclass marriages is strongly influenced by wide differences in social class and lifestyle. (One study that attempted to measure class differences in marriage on a statistical basis did not find such a correlation.[24])

Measuring Social Class

INCOME

Some aspects of social class can be clearly measured. Families at the top of the social scale have many times the income of people at the bottom (see Table 6–3). Not only do upper-class people have a higher annual income, but they also own most of the nation's wealth. One report shows that the richest fifth of consumer units (families and single individuals) owns 76 percent of the nation's wealth, while the lowest fifth owns only 0.2 percent and the second fifth owns only 2.1 percent.[25]

Consider your own home town, where one group of families may earn eight times more than another group. There is certain to be a great many differences in the lifestyles of these people. In analyzing what effects poverty has on American families, Catherine Chilman sees the problems of lower-class families as a major and unsolved crisis in our society. She writes:

> A large proportion of the nation's families continue to live in poverty. This proportion varies from about 12 to 22 percent of the population, depending on what income levels are used as "poverty lines." A disproportionate number of children and youth, aged, minority group members, and female-headed families are poor. Factors associated with poverty include: unemployment and under-employment, age, education, family breakdown, region of residence, lack of income from sources other than wages, poor physical and mental health, and family size. Despite efforts made during the "war on poverty" during the 1960's, these factors,

[24]See Zick Rubin, "Do American Women Marry Up?" *American Sociological Review*, 33, no. 5 (Oct. 1968), 750–60.

[25]Ian Robertson, *Sociology* (New York: Worth, 1977), p. 238.

Table 6–3 Percent Distribution of Aggregate Income—1974

Top 5 percent	15.3
Highest fifth	41.0
Fourth fifth	24.1
Middle fifth	17.6
Second fifth	12.0
Lowest fifth	5.4

SOURCE: U.S. Bureau of the Census, *Statistical Abstract of the United States, 1975* (Washington, D.C.: U.S. Government Printing Office, 1975), Table 636.

as well as the pattern of income distribution, remain substantially unchanged.[26]

COMMUNITY

Obviously, where you stand economically will have a strong influence on your lifestyle and therefore on your attitudes toward courtship, marriage, and the family. Social-class standing also influences a family's relationships with the larger community. Middle-class parents are typically more active in social groups, PTA's, volunteer organizations, and religious groups than working-class parents. And Irving Tallman and Ramona Morgner have shown that working-class couples living in urban areas are less likely to know their neighbors, the kind of work they do, and their community interests or to visit with them than are people living in the suburbs.[27]

IMP

MENTAL HEALTH

The mental and emotional health of family members is also apparently related to social class status. Mental hospitals show a far higher rate of admission for persons from lower-class families than for persons of other classes. Why is that so? A recent article by Melvin Kohn concluded:

> My formulation suggests that the constricted conditions of life experienced by people of lower social-class position foster conceptions of social

[26]Catherine S. Chilman, "Families in Poverty in the Early 1970's: Rates, Associated Factors, Some Implications," *Journal of Marriage and the Family*, 37, no. 1 (Feb. 1975), 50.

[27]Irving Tallman and Ramona Morgner, "Life-Style Differences Among Urban and Suburban Blue-Collar Families," *Social Forces*, 48, no. 3 (March 1970), 334–48.

> reality so limited and so rigid as to impair people's ability to deal resourcefully with the problematic and the stressful. Such impairment would be unfortunate for all who suffer it, but would not in itself result in schizophrenia. In conjunction with a genetic vulnerability to schizophrenia and the experience of great stress, though, such impairment could well be disabling.[28]

Our mental health is affected by our total life situation. When many aspects are negative, we often break under the combined pressure upon us.

CHILDREARING

Another crucial aspect of social class influence is the way parents raise their children. According to Everett K. Wilson, within a given class grouping, there are common ways of disciplining children, of socializing them into various important roles, or encouraging them in their education. It is as though a social class is a large group of families who are about equal to each other and guide their children in a certain direction.[29] Upper-class families are high in prestige, but family life is more demanding in many ways. The upper class stresses family traditions: there are high expectations for the children.

Upper-middle-class families are not as firmly rooted in one geographical area as upper-class families. They exercise less strict control over their children socially, but dating and eventual marriage are still generally within the same class level. Members of this class are leaders in society and are active in community life. Their children are expected to follow suit.

The influence exerted by the upper-middle class on lower-middle-class and working-class families is potent. When a lower-middle-class family encourages its children to succeed in their schoolwork, they might in essence be saying: "You can go out and conquer the world in a way that your parents never could. You can be a lawyer, a doctor, or a professor; you can run your own business or succeed in industry or politics. It takes brains—which you seem to have—and persistence and luck and plenty of good, hard work. We might have done it if we had had the chance, but we never did. We'll make any sacrifice to give you that chance." Thomas Lasswell points out that middle-class children are taught a deferred-gratification pattern so that they will be willing to work hard for their future status in society. Otherwise they might fall back into a lower-class position.[30]

[28]Melvin L. Kohn, "Class, Family, and Schizophrenia: A Reformulation," *Social Forces*, 50, no. 3 (March 1972), 295–304.

[29]Everett K. Wilson, *Sociology—Rules, Roles, and Relationships* (Homewood, Ill.: Dorsey, 1971), pp. 252–62.

[30]Thomas E. Lasswell, *Class and Stratum* (Boston: Houghton Mifflin, 1965), pp. 283–86.

In the working class more immediate satisfaction is sought. Children in this class tend to marry young because less is expected of them in the way of achievement. They are not encouraged to remain dependent on their parents, and they do not defer sexual gratification as do middle-class children.

Middle- and working-class families are of most direct concern to us. Lower-middle-class families exhibit the folkways and habit patterns with which a majority of students are familiar—and also the kind of parental domination that many students rebel against. If respectability is the goal at home, it may be a spur to the promising career that is possible if the son or daughter can gain an education and climb upward on the class scale. The lower-middle-class son and daughter may adopt such parental goals and patterns without too much question or imitate those goals as they have seen them in other parts of their environment—school, church, club, or community group. However, they may also rebel against their parents' way of life, not so much because they disapprove of it as because they want to find an identity of their own.

Working-class students are faced with a greater dilemma. Their own background and family training fit them best for blue-collar or semiskilled work, and they will probably have already had a number of part-time jobs. The sooner they begin to work, the sooner they will have the money nec-

essary to buy the cars and clothes and other basics that will enable them to "enjoy life." Our culture, however, does not allow them to slip effortlessly into adult life. They read in newspaper and magazine articles about the importance of a college education. They note some of their neighbors, or their own parents, displaced on the assembly line or forced into new work or chronically unemployed because of the rapid changes in the economy and the swift pace of automation. High school counselors may have informed them that they have high potential in one field or another. If they have been admitted to a college or university, they have already stepped clearly ahead of their parents' rank and education. But competition may be so tough or finances so tight that it seems easier and more realistic to leave college and go to work. And most important, they may lack the kind of parental support for their efforts to improve themselves that middle-class students take for granted.

Lower-class families are of interest to us for several reasons. They have a higher birth rate than the classes above them on the social scale; thus they will always more than reproduce themselves. But social mobility enables many of them to move up and out of their class—some by marriage and some by steady employment or education.

The lower-class people who are unable to move up through education or hard work are important to us also because of the social problems and conflicts in their communities. Here are the uneducated, the unemployed, the unfortunate, and the underprivileged. Any realistic appraisal of our society must recognize the circumstances of this class and the urgency of its problems and frustrations.

Finally, we need to recognize the influence of social class on our goals and values. How important is money? What do we think of divorce? Do we become involved in local and national politics? Is religious affiliation worthwhile? What is our philosophy of life? We all learn a value structure from our place in the class system, and this has a profound effect on us when we marry and establish a new home. For instance, Melvin L. Kohn and Carmi Schooler, as a part of their cross-cultural study of values, have shown that men in higher social classes value self-direction a great deal, while those in lower social classes value conformity to higher authority.[31]

Marriage Expectations and Family Influence

A major influence on our marriage expectations comes from our families. Dating and mate selection may often take place at some distance from home—in a resident college community, for example. It may seem that fam-

[31]Melvin L. Kohn and Carmi Schooler, "Class, Occupation, and Orientation," *American Sociological Review*, 34, no. 5 (Oct. 1969), 659–78.

ily background is not important in such a setting, but that is not actually so. There are many ways that our parents influence us in courtship, even if we are not living with them.

The family serves several basic social functions. It gives us our initial place in society. It gives us the love and affection we need and socializes us. It brings new life into the world to continue the chain of life from one generation to another. Our primary interest is the influence the family has on our personality and how it prepares us for our role in marriage. The family's chief task, as Evelyn Duvall points out, is "producing persons" rather than making things. Children should gain from their families a sense of worth and direction and such protection, guidance, and encouragement that will allow them to be the best kind of persons they are capable of becoming. "Children learn how to live in families."[32] Let us consider some of the major areas where our families influence our marriage expectations.

Personality Development

What we want and expect in marriage is intimately associated with the kind of persons we are. The first years of life are crucial for human development. If a child is deprived of normal love and affection or is raised in an atmosphere of tension and hostility, he or she may bear the lifetime impression of that experience. Such early personality problems must be considered a factor in marital adjustment. On the positive side, if a child is brought up in a loving and accepting home in which his or her contributions are valued and approved, this child will probably build positive attitudes and responses that will be a solid asset in marriage.

Ellen grew up in a typical working-class neighborhood in an Eastern industrial city. Her father was in the service in the Second World War and was discharged in 1946. Of the four children in the family, Ellen was the oldest. Her mother was not employed while the children were in elementary school.

When Ellen was seven years old, conflict between her parents came into the open and intensified for several years. The father would come home late at night after heavy drinking and abuse the mother and older children. Until this time, father and daughter had had a good relationship. However, many of Ellen's sympathies were then directed toward her mother, who seemed powerless to change the situation.

When Ellen was fourteen her parents were divorced, and shortly thereafter her mother married again. That marriage was only moderately suc-

[32]See Evelyn M. Duvall, *Faith in Families* (Chicago: Rand McNally, 1970), chap. 2.

cessful, and Ellen was often in conflict with her stepfather. She saw her real father infrequently, although she still had a strong emotional attachment to him and he called her his favorite daughter.

Ellen is now twenty-two and seriously considering engagement to her steady boyfriend. "If only I could be certain we would be happy, I'd get married tomorrow," Ellen insists. "In the back of my mind, though, is the feeling that everything will go wrong for me, even as it seemed to do for my mother."

Throughout life each of us faces a series of "developmental tasks," to use Robert Havighurst's term, and the adolescent's task is "achieving emotional independence of parents and other adults."[33] The achievement of such independence involves a certain amount of sparring back and forth, the parents feeling they should retain some influence and control over their offspring and the children moving toward independent thinking and behavior. Ideally, this psychological weaning comes about step by step, from year to year, without the parents disowning their children or the son or daughter leaving home in anger or resentment. But it must be accomplished in order for a person to become a normal adult.

> Adults who have failed in this task are dependent people, often still tied to their parents, unable to make up their minds on important matters, unable to move about freely in our adult society because they are still children, emotionally. Failure in this task tends to be associated with failure in the task of establishing adult relations with age-mates. Marriage is often a difficult matter for such people, and successful only when a person finds a father-figure or a mother-figure for a mate. The great majority of boys and girls accomplish this task successfully, though seldom without a good deal of friction with their parents. They are able to establish new families of their own, and to take their rightful places in the adult society.[34]

Attitudes and Values

What is the world like outside our home and how will we react to it? Should it be cherished and imitated, or should it be viewed critically and perhaps even rejected? Most of our attitudes and values are strongly shaped by our

[33]Robert J. Havighurst, *Developmental Tasks and Education* (New York: Longmans, Green, 1952), p. 42.
[34]Havighurst, p. 43.

family experiences. Family attitudes and values differ tremendously; therefore one's family background deserves serious thought. Is the family atmosphere authoritarian or permissive? Are the children in the family expected to follow traditional patterns, or are they given freedom and allowed self-expression? Is the family open in its affection or reticent and reserved? Is there any democratic give-and-take between parents and children, or are all decisions in the hands of the parents? How does the atmosphere in the parental family compare to that in the family of a prospective partner? The answers to these questions will tell much about future marital and family interaction.

Many factors contribute to the differences in psychological atmosphere from one family to another. Some of them are ethnic, reflecting the heritage of Europe, Africa, the Near East, Asia, or Latin America. Some are a reflection of the particular temperaments of father, mother, or other family members. In many cases these differences in emotional life are not visible in day-to-day living and may surface only at a time of particular tension. But they are still of special relevance to the future marital and family relationships of the children.

We can also observe the role of the family in a child's sex education and his development of sexual roles. Although adequate and intelligent sex education is provided by some parents, there is a wide range of attitudes toward sex from family to family. Family influence will also be significant as the requirements of masculine and feminine roles change during the family life cycle.

The family also helps us to build basic value patterns. Are the primary family values economic, social, spiritual, or personal? It is interesting to see how often young adults adopt their parents' value structure, even though they may have rebelled against it in college.

As we observe the way our parents live, we gain impressions of how adults order their lives, and whether or not there is rhyme or reason in what they do. We store up memories of family life that will help us later to build our own. One older student writes:

> My father was a pediatrician, and his practice had many effects on our lives. Dad would get many telephone calls from concerned parents when he was at home. He also would make house calls in the evening when it was necessary. He never saw any patients at our home because he did not want to have any ill children around my brother and me. Apparently once he made an exception when I was a toddler and after examining the child's throat for trench mouth he very carefully wrapped up the tongue dispenser and put it in the trash. I must have been observing all of this very carefully because when they were not watching me I got the tongue

> dispenser and put it in my mouth! Luckily I did not get trench mouth, but my father never saw another patient in our home again. . . .[35]

Achievement

One of the major difficulties with our contemporary public school systems is related to student achievement. Many special programs to improve achievement fail to reach their objectives because there is not enough family support for the student. Family influence on achievement is crucial.

There are other elements within the family's structure that affect the child. Geoffrey Hawthorn has pointed out that family size is a significant factor in the achievement of children as reported in British sociological studies. He states that the IQ of children consistently decreased as the family size became larger. In one study of middle- and working-class mothers this was partially explained by the fact that the mother's interest in and attitudes toward her children suffered as the family size increased.[36]

A cross-cultural study by Glen Elder, Jr., found that parents who were democratic and equalitarian in their family decision-making patterns had the most positive influence on their children's education.

> In all nations except Italy, adults who report equalitarian relations between their parents and democratic parent-youth relations are indeed most likely to have reached secondary school. And in all five nations (U.S.A., Great Britain, West Germany, Italy, and Mexico) the likelihood of reaching secondary school is consistently low among persons with authoritarian parents.[37]

Parental support is the key. This will be a vital factor in deciding whether the boy or girl will be able to complete the desired schooling. Eva E. Sandis' research has shown that high school students whose mothers wanted them to attend college were planning to achieve that goal. Sandis considered parental influence highly significant. If a family prepares a child adequately for initial learning experiences in school and continues to motivate and encourage him or her throughout the school career, it will have contributed much to achievement of maturity and to later marital stability and success.[38] In turn, the individual's marriage expectations will be shaped and molded strongly by what he or she achieves in other areas. The young person who

[35]Student report.

[36]See Geoffrey Hawthorn, "A Sociological Portrait: Family Background," *New Society* (Nov. 4, 1971), 876–80.

[37]Glen H. Elder, Jr., "Family Structure and Educational Attainment," in *Life Cycle and Achievement in America*, ed. Rose L. Coser (New York: Harper Torchbooks, 1969), pp. 73–74.

[38]See Eva E. Sandis, "The Transmission of Mothers' Educational Ambitions, as Related to Specific Socialization Techniques," *Journal of Marriage and the Family*, 32, no. 2 (May 1970), 204–11.

is able to do well in school, to relate well to others, to find a rewarding and stimulating occupation, will also want to reach a high level in his or her marriage expectations.

Turning Expectations into Reality

Will your marriage expectations become a reality? There is no ninety-day guarantee or insurance policy that they will. But we can recognize clearly those influences that shape our expectations, and try to have some freedom in choosing a partner who most nearly combines that which we want to carry on from the past with the different hopes and dreams we have for the future.

There are countless factors that influence us in choosing a marriage partner. Perhaps they are part of a filtering process that prevents us from seriously considering certain people as potential partners. Programmed inside our compact yet marvelous computer, the human brain, are myriad signals from our culture, our social class, and our family. It seems true that most people tend to marry on their own social level. Opposites do attract, as Robert Winch maintains in his theory of complementary needs,[39] but when we look at the total picture, we note that people of the same social class tend to live in the same neighborhoods, attend the same schools, have contacts with each other in their employment, meet socially, and eventually fall in love and get married. The same is true of religious and ethnic groups. Usually like marries like. There are exceptions, however, and they are becoming more and more frequent as geographical mobility and educational opportunities increase.

A couple looking forward to engagement and marriage should be as objective as possible about their family backgrounds, their present and future social classes, and their attitudes toward work, education, social life, religion, and the other important ingredients of family life. If they do not discover these things about each other before the wedding, they will undoubtedly learn them soon after. Because such behavior patterns influence so much of day-by-day living, a review of family socioeconomic background will be extremely practical and rewarding.

SUMMARY

What do we expect from marriage? Our marriage expectations have been influenced by our culture, our recent history, our social class, and our own families.

The American way of courtship and marriage is a unique one. In the eighteenth century, "bundling" was one popular custom. One hundred and

[39]See Chapter 3, p. 89.

fifty years later, the views on sex and courtship became much more restrictive. We have a strong romantic element in our culture, and women are idealized. Our culture was strongly influenced by successive waves of immigrants from Europe, as well as by the rural nature of the first three hundred years of our history.

The twentieth century has been a century of change for the family. Our grandparents, married during the period 1925–1940, lived in an era of change, dominated by the Depression. For our parents, brought up in that period, the postwar era of marriage, 1945–1960, was crucial. Our parents married early, had large families, and experienced a very high divorce rate.

Social class is a powerful influence on us. Marriage and family life are strongly influenced by the class structure of our society; this influence shows up in lifestyle, income, mental health, and attitudes and values. American society is divided into five classes: the upper class; the upper-middle class; the lower-middle class; the working class; and the lower class. In addition, society may be divided into ethnic and racial subgroups. Each social class has certain characteristics.

The upper class often consists of the old established wealthy families. The upper-middle class has a strong career orientation, while the lower-middle class is known for respectability and stable social and moral values. The working-class family is typified by more routine jobs and lack of higher education; it has little social mobility. The lower class finds it difficult to break free from the vicious cycle of poverty and prejudice it is trapped in.

The influence of one's own family cannot be underestimated; family background is very much evident in courtship. The psychological atmosphere of the home has a strong impact on couples. The family influences a person's education and achievement, values, and development of sexual roles.

There is a strong desire on the part of most young people to make the choice of a marital partner a personal affair. Yet we must recognize that even in this very personal decision each one of us is subject to the forces around us, particularly as they are mediated by culture, social class, and parental family.

SUGGESTED READINGS

Glick, Paul. "A Demographer Looks at American Families," *Journal of Marriage and the Family*, 37, no. 1 (Jan. 1975), 15–26. A summary of trends in marriage, divorce, fertility, living arrangements, and other family data by a veteran demographer at the Bureau of the Census.

Goode, William J. *World Revolution and Family Patterns.* New York: Free Press, 1963. A scholarly look at the effect of industrialization on world family patterns. Sets the American experience in a world perspective. Effects of equality in marriage roles, greater freedom for women, and changing sexual patterns.

Gordon, Michael, ed. *The American Family in Social-Historical Perspective,* 2nd ed. New York: St. Martin's Press, 1978. Contemporary readings in the family with a sound historical coverage.

Leslie, Gerald R. *The Family in Social Context,* 3rd ed. New York: Oxford Univ. Press, 1976, chaps. 3, 6. Solid treatment of some of the historical background of the American family. Explanation of family traditions coming from the Hebrews.

Lynd, Robert S., and Helen M. Lynd. *Middletown.* Harcourt Brace Jovanovich, 1929. Study of life of a small midwestern town in the 1920s, including some insight into its family life patterns.

Reiss, Ira L. *Family Systems in America,* 2nd ed. Hinsdale, Ill.: Dryden, 1976. Basic sociological analysis of the American family by a leading family scholar. Reflection of diverse elements in our pluralistic family life.

Rossides, Daniel W. *The American Class System.* Boston: Houghton Mifflin, 1976. Study of social class system in the United States, with explanations and descriptions of the various class levels.

Sussman, Marvin B. *Sourcebook in Marriage and the Family,* 4th ed. Boston: Houghton Mifflin, 1974. Good selection of readings. Especially helpful in areas of definitions, nontraditional marriage forms, and theory.

Part III
The Decision to Marry

7 Love: The Universal Ingredient

- Why is love such a difficult subject to study?
- What do you consider the most important element in love between a man and a woman?
- How does love begin? Is physical attraction the natural basis for true love?
- What do we give in exchange for love?
- Is love most clearly seen as a relationship?
- How does one create loving relationships?
- How can one learn the art of love?
- What dimensions of love can be quantified?
- What is maturity in love?
- Why does love cease?

The American Love Pattern

Everyone is interested in love. As a people, Americans are probably as much "in love with love" as any society could be. But despite our preoccupation with love, not all men and women in our culture can find love, nor do our romantic images of what love should be always fit the actual situation. For many men and women love never arrives, and for many of the rest, the course of true love does not run smoothly. In this chapter, we want to examine some of the many and varied aspects of love, and try to understand its real meaning.

Love is the universal ingredient in American courtship that motivates us to marry. The customs of other cultures usually place marriage first, with love and physical attraction following, but that is not the American pattern. No matter how much one may consider family background, social class, economic position, religious affiliation, and a dozen other important social and personality factors, all of those are meaningless without love, the basic ingredient. But love is not an easy subject to discuss. Love is perhaps the most overworked word in our language. We love a new record or Sally's floppy felt hat; we love to go to the movies on Friday nights; we love the taste of that new salad dressing. If Eric is in love with Lynn, we know from past experience that it is only a passing fancy: he has a new love every month. But Lynn is less fortunate; when she is in love she can hardly eat or sleep and wears her heart on her sleeve for months afterward.

When we examine our idea of love, we discover that there are several concepts involved. Heterosexual love exists at different levels and in different dimensions. There is a physical level at which man and woman have a strong sexual attraction for each other without necessarily caring for each other in any other way. In its simplest form it might be illustrated by the feeling of a man toward a prostitute or a woman toward a movie idol. But in most heterosexual relationships physical love is only the first of many attractions a couple feel for each other.

Heterosexual love is known typically at the interpersonal level. At this level the partners are very much aware of each other, and each may make serious efforts to mold his behavior to meet the needs and desires of the other. Physical attraction is involved, but it is not the only aspect of the relationship. Such interpersonal love is characteristic of most American courtship and is a major factor in the entire process from initial dating through engagement and marriage. When we say we are in love, we assume that we have found the *person* who responds to our affirmation of love, both physically and emotionally.

Yet for all our preoccupation with love, and despite its universal acceptance in our culture, we have tremendous difficulty in translating this feeling into stable long-term relationships. The perplexing problem remains: Why do so many couples fall in love, make formal declarations of their love in their wedding and marriage, and then fail to maintain their feeling for each other? What is needed in order to transform physical love and interpersonal love into a lasting reality? Can we ask that love be also an adventure, a way of life that grows and develops over the years?

Love's adventure is a part of the mystery of life. It helps us to grow beyond some of the missing elements in our childhood experiences.

> Each person can be thought of as growing up with deficiencies in terms of certain forms of developmental love. This contributes to the attraction to and choice of certain complementary or symmetrical lovers or mate choices in the late teens and early twenties. Thus, most marriages at this critical choice time are developmentally deficient choices. With increasing maturity, however, growth toward ability to encounter with risk and with ability to be warm, to be intimate and even to be angry occurs.[1]

This, then, is our aim: to chart the course of love. Let us find love in its simplest beginnings and define it in all its breadth and complexity. We will see how it can be measured and how to find the direction that leads to true growth and maturity.

[1]Everett B. Shostrom, in *Love Today*, ed. Herbert Otto (New York: Association Press, 1972), p. 195.

How does love begin? Can it begin in the mind and feelings of one partner and then be transmitted and light its fire in the heart of another? Or must it strike a spark simultaneously in the lives of both, so that they recognize and accept its gentle conquest? These and a dozen other questions come to mind when we are faced with the important personal question: "Am I really in love?"

There is no single answer to such questions of the heart. Love begins in a multitude of ways and finds its course through myriad streams flowing from many sources. Our primary concern is not with the way in which a love relationship begins but with the development of the relationship over a period of time and the extension of its influence into marriage and family life.

I love you
Not only for what you are,
But for what I am
When I am with you.

I love you,
Not only for what
You have made of yourself
But for what
You are making of me.

I love you
For the part of me
That you bring out;

I love you
For putting your hand
Into my heaped-up heart
And passing over
All the weak, foolish things
That you can't help
Dimly seeing there,
And for drawing out
Into the light
All the beautiful belongings
That no one else had looked
Quite far enough to find.[2]

Author unknown

[2]From James Dalton Morrison, ed., *Masterpieces of Religious Verse* (New York: Harper & Row, 1948), pp. 329–30.

Initial Attraction

Love begins with some initial spark of interest, curiosity, or attraction, created by a new face, a new voice on the telephone, a new neighbor in the apartment house, or a new coworker at the office. It may be stimulated by curiosity about the background and attitudes of a different and intriguing personality. We may be attracted by a friendly smile, a shared concern or task, a word of sympathy or comfort. That first spark tells us, in a casual or a dramatic way, that some new and exciting personality has entered our life and experience.

It is normally expected of any young couple that as a prerequisite to their engagement and marriage they will be attracted to each other and desire mutual sexual satisfaction. This physical attraction is important and rewarding to the couple. It seems to be a confirmation of a love that they hope will continue to develop. Finding such satisfaction, they feel a keener sense of self-worth and greater ease in relating to other persons in concerned and loving ways. However, our culture has been justly accused of an irrational and often neurotic preoccupation with sex. Because of this preoccupation, physical attraction can be both the beginning and the end of a relationship. This kind of attraction may prevent the couple from recognizing the real limitations and obstacles to finding mature love together; the physical aspects of their love seem all-important to them and blot out a realistic conception of life.

Every campus has many couples who experience this kind of immature love. They have eyes only for each other. We share their happiness and their excitement, but with some misgivings. They often fail to recognize that infatuation cannot last and that its aftermath may be disillusionment, boredom, or even hostility if they are not suited to each other in other ways. Such an attraction often promises more than it can bring and thus frequently leads to disappointment.

Arlene Skolnick suggests that love does not necessarily have a fixed meaning, but acquires a "label" because of our experience and that of others in our social environment. Our thought processes are involved as well as our emotions. We have a share in the forming of our emotional experiences. She writes:

> We are not passion's slaves, in the sense that emotions are not events that "happen" to us. Rather, we construct emotional experience on the basis of culture, learning, and bodily responses. Currently, the most influential explanation of emotions has been advanced by Stanley Schachter, a social psychologist. Schachter suggests that emotional experience consists of two parts: physiological arousal, as manifested in a pounding heart, breathlessness, weakness in the knees, and so on; and an interpretation or labeling of the experience. Various kinds of strong emotions—fear, anger, and love—are not clearly distinguished from one another physiologically.
>
> . . . our culture encourages the experience of love in many ways. It teaches that practically everyone will fall in love, and it leads people to apply the label "love" to a wide range of feelings.[3]

Freud: The Origin of Love

How does love begin? And how does sex relate to it? What motivates us to love one person and not another? Are sexual drives basic to all human love? How universal is the motivation behind heterosexual love? Much of our thinking on these questions has been influenced by the founder of psychoanalysis, Sigmund Freud. Let us look briefly at some of his psychoanalytic theory and its relation to love and marriage.

[3]Arlene Skolnick, *The Intimate Environment*, 2nd ed. (Boston: Little, Brown, 1978), pp. 202–03.

Love and sex are very closely related. The id and the libido are the parts of the human personality that represent human nature at its most basic and universal. These powerful drives or instincts within us are sexual in nature. Our sexual drives and energies begin at birth; sexuality does not start with puberty. During the first five years of life we pass through what Freud terms the oral, anal, and genital stages of development, which further shape our feelings about sex and love. Our sexual feelings are usually first directed toward our parents. "I want a girl just like the girl who married dear old Dad" is a Tin Pan Alley expression of the Oedipus complex: A boy falls in love with his mother, a girl with her father. These feelings are a normal part of our growing up.

Freud was a developmental psychologist. He emphasized the fact that we move through one stage to another, with our development in each stage being affected by our experiences in the stages that went before. One of Freud's greatest contributions was his emphasis on the unconscious. Freud tried to discover the determining forces in personality that are not directly observable. He felt that the unconscious was of tremendous importance and that if we had a better understanding of what went on beneath the surface of our consciousness, we would be much better able to know why people talk and act and think the way they do.[4]

This Freudian contribution helps us to understand our sexual feelings and their importance in love. And it has made an impact on almost every field of literary and historical study. We have always known that Shakespeare was a great dramatist, Rousseau a gifted essayist, and Einstein a mathematical genius; but now that is not enough. We must psychoanalyze them and try to find out what made them tick. And we do the same to our friends as well. We are much less apt to accept people at face value than were earlier generations. And we are much more likely to ask two people in love what basic and perhaps unconscious factors led them to love each other.

We might thus conclude that very often our sex drive controls our love. We don't realize why, but it does. Some hidden drive beneath the surface directs us toward Yvette or David but away from Lianne or Harry. Sex *is* a major human drive. We cannot ignore it and pretend it does not exist. Ego and superego—two conscious elements of the personality—may seek to channel basic id impulses, but the effect of the id is still strong.

However, Freud's theories are not universally accepted. His work did not describe love in its entirety. Love is more than the physical and the biological alone. Life is not simply emotion; it is built on reason as well. Love involves conscious drives, as we will see when we study several major definitions of love. And finally, love usually controls our sex lives rather than the other way around.

[4]Calvin S. Hall, *A Primer of Freudian Psychology* (New York: New American Library, 1954), pp. 51–52.

What Is Love?

There are many ways to describe love. Let us examine it from several different perspectives so that it may be more clearly seen in its development, its influence on the couple's total relationship, and its effect on their future happiness and satisfaction in marriage.

Love as an Exchange of Desirable Qualities

Psychologists have begun to discuss love in terms of *exchange theory*. How much can I offer to my partner in a love relationship? Does what I give balance out with what I receive? If things are too far out of balance, should I drop this partner and look for another one?

An interesting study by Glen Elder, Jr., attempts to trace the results in terms of marriage mobility for attractive women studied over a twenty-year period in terms of exchange theory. Attractive women, first observed in 1929, were found in 1950 to be married to higher-status men than less attractive women. It was hypothesized that attractive women had married high-status men lacking in physical attractiveness or personal appeal.

> Physical attractiveness and status aspiration were significantly related to mobility through marriage, with the former most predictive of marriage to a high-status man among women from the working class. Social ascent from the working class was also associated with a well-groomed appearance and with an avoidance of steady dating and sexual involvement.[5]

Education, of course, was another factor in aiding women in moving up the social scale.

The conception of love as an exchange gives us a number of possible insights into marriage relationships, and into possible reasons for divorce as well. Consider, for example, a beautiful and talented young woman who marries an older, wealthier man who is basically selfish and immature. The fact that she is from a poor family, perhaps, makes marriage to this man seem a wise move for her. She "exchanges" her youthful beauty and energy for the security offered by his income and status. The exchange at time of marriage is fairly even, and she feels a certain measure of love for him.

When ten years go by, however, the exchange may definitely be out of balance. Time has taken away a good bit of his money, and his age is obviously showing, in contrast to his still vibrant and more attractive thirty-year-old wife. In addition, she has completed some additional schooling, has

[5]Glen H. Elder, Jr., "Appearance and Education in Marriage Mobility," *American Sociological Review*, 34, no. 4 (Aug. 1969), 519–33.

two lovely children, and has begun to consider seriously picking up her career where she left it before marriage. With the exchange now tipping strongly in one direction, can love flourish? Although we talk about marriage as a 50/50 arrangement, or perhaps better yet 60/40, what will happen to love if it goes to 80/20, or even 90/10? Can love continue if the exchange of desirable qualities and behaviors is completely out of balance?

Love as a Relationship

Love can be analyzed in terms of its development within the emotional life of the individual. Because we have feelings of pleasure and security as children and receive love from parents and other significant persons early in life, we develop the ability to love within that favorable environment. An abundance of love in early childhood produces a secure person with positive feelings toward others, while the absence of love can mean emotional and mental retardation and even in extreme cases death. Nurturing love is just as essential to full development as food, clothing, and shelter.

Sociologically, love can be most clearly seen as a relationship. We love in relation to other significant individuals, and our love develops over a period of time. Ira Reiss sees love in its sociological context, as an expression of a maturing interaction between two individuals. He has proposed a four-step development of love in his study of the sociological meaning of love.[6]

The first step identified by Reiss is rapport. We cannot fall in love with

[6]See Ira L. Reiss, *Family Systems in America,* 2nd ed. (Hinsdale, Ill.: Dryden, 1976), pp. 93–97.

someone who is repugnant to us. There must be an attraction, a feeling of closeness and rapport that makes us enjoy another's company and want to explore and deepen the relationship.

A second step in the development of love is the process of self-revelation. When we feel at ease with another person and the number of opportunities for intimate sharing increases, we want to express more freely our inner feelings and thoughts. This is an answer to the problem of alienation in our times. The ability to reveal ourselves frankly and confidentially to another person gives life an entirely different complexion. We can see the changes wrought by such a relationship in the couple deeply absorbed in their conversation in the student union or strolling hand in hand across the park, so enraptured with each other that they are oblivious of time or place.

The next stage is mutual dependency. Because we find rapport and the possibility of self-revelation with so few people, the discovery and creation of such a love relationship inevitably means that we come to rely on our partner. We depend on him or her for understanding and support, for encouragement and sympathy. This stage is characteristic of happily married couples. The husband depends on his wife to encourage him and to give him that extra measure of support he needs. The wife also has a relationship of mutual dependency with her husband and counts on his love and counsel when life becomes too hectic.

A final phase in the development of love is personality need fulfillment. The basic needs that have drawn us to another person and given us the feeling of closeness and rapport with him or her are met most fully because they are expressed and answered naturally within the love relationship. Potentialities that might have lain dormant and untouched are opened for growth and fulfillment. If the relationship continues to grow, the wheel of love continues to turn—toward continued rapport, expanded self-revelation, further mutual dependency, and more complete personality need fulfillment.

Unfortunately, as Reiss points out, the progress of this primary relationship may be reversed and the partners pulled apart by conflicting forces and interests. Events or persons can weaken rapport and confidence; and dishonesty, selfishness, or cruelty can drive us away from the loved one. Self-revelation may turn out to be self-exposure, opening us up to possible hurt or shame. Mutual dependency may reveal our insecurity or the instability of our partner. Or the fulfillment of our own needs may take place at the expense of the loved one rather than as a truly mutual accomplishment of both partners.

Human love, then, is a relationship. We learn love through our relationships with our parents, brothers and sisters, friends, and teachers. We experience love as an infant, a child, and an adolescent, and our ability to love develops as we interact with significant persons in our lives. If we take each step toward maturity successfully, we have good expectations of falling in love with the kind of man or woman who will be an ideal marriage partner for us.

Support for the importance of relationships in courtship comes from the recent work of Huston and Levinger. They find that it is difficult to chart the growth of love on the basis of similarity or complementarity of needs, or of personality "fit." Therefore:

> Research examining *relationship* characteristics to predict courtship progress has been more successful than that which focuses on combinations of the psychological attributes of the partners. Relationship research suggests that partners who "understand" each other and who agree in their definition of their relationship are more apt to escalate their commitment; thus, persons whose partners see them the way they see themselves are more likely to report having moved closer to marriage when queried about their relationship several months later. Moreover, persons who report that they and their partner are equally involved in their relationship are less likely to break than those who report asymmetrical involvement.[7]

Sensual and Spiritual Love

There are many differing aspects of love. Sometimes one seems antithetical to the other. This is shown by the Greek words *eros* and *agape*. Eros was the Greek god of love (called Cupid by the Romans). Eros represents sensual love, the erotic side of our nature, with an emphasis on sexual need and satisfaction. The classical picture brings to mind the love affairs of the gods and the orgiastic rituals of the mystery religions. We might define eros as sensual desire that recognizes no limits of propriety or custom. It may be more destructive than constructive in the long run.[8]

It is wrong, however, to try to separate eros from the love that needs to be fulfilled in courtship and marriage. To do away with eros would be an attempt to repress a significant aspect of the whole person. Unless this basic desire is recognized, life will be warped and constricted.

Agape represents the selfless love that was emphasized in the early Christian era, when it was seen as a reflection of divine love. Agape gives and asks nothing in return, and it is strong enough to survive even in the face of hatred. Such a love is a necessity if two persons are to maintain a permanent and harmonious relationship. In this kind of love there is a willing-

[7]Ted L. Huston and George Levinger, "Interpersonal Attraction and Relationships," p. 48 of prepublication manuscript to appear in M. R. Rosenzweig and L. W. Porter, eds., *Annual Review of Psychology* (Palo Alto, Calif.: Annual Reviews, 1978).

[8]Frank Cox, *Human Intimacy: Marriage, the Family and Its Meaning* (St. Paul, Minn.: West, 1978), pp. 68–69.

ness to give when the loved one is not able to reciprocate, whether it be because of illness, failure, or simply an hour of weakness. It is a love that can repair bonds severed by unfaithfulness, indifference, or jealousy. This agape is the ingredient that makes marriage more than a fifty-fifty arrangement, but rather a sixty-sixty or seventy-seventy partnership—that is, a partnership in which both husband and wife go more than halfway in order to express their love and concern for each other. Such love does not do away with eros; instead it transforms it into its highest and finest fulfillment.

A man and a woman need to find both eros and agape if they are to move from acquaintance and friendship to a lasting love relationship that can culminate in a mature and satisfying marriage. Both elements will be present during their courtship, and neither can be excluded, either before or after the wedding day. If desire is ignored and sex degraded and repressed, the couple will be prevented from establishing a normal and healthy sexual relationship together, and their marriage will become a union that is not fully satisfying and fulfilling. If agape is ignored and the courtship built around physical attraction and sexual intimacy alone, the union will falter when faced with adversity and challenge. Only when both elements are present and kept in proper balance and perspective will the couple build a solid basis for an enduring and ever widening relationship.

Romantic and Conjugal Love

We can also differentiate between love that is romantic and love that is conjugal. Romantic love is emotional, exciting, stimulating, and sometimes incomprehensible. It absorbs our time, our thought, and our energy. Conjugal love, on the other hand, is the kind of love that keeps a marriage going—a stable, solid, socially oriented love that suits mature married couples. We talk about "giddy" teenagers being swept up in an emotional and romantic sort of feeling. However, we also recognize that by the age of marriage (approximately twenty to twenty-three years of age), the girl who has been swooning over rock and roll stars for the last six or eight years may be more realistic and level-headed than her fiancé, and will try to test her love on a conjugal dimension, since she now realizes she is making some very important choices about her future. Although the boy has come down out of the clouds and no longer fantasizes about Miss America, he tends to think more about his job than about his forthcoming marriage. Consequently it is the girl who is more realistic and practical in her approach to marriage.

Graham Spanier has probed the relationship between romanticism and marital adjustment. Using the Dean Romanticism Scale and the Locke-Wallace Marital Adjustment Scale, he found that a romantic attitude did not seem to hinder the marital adjustment of college couples in their mid-twen-

ties. Romantic love does not necessarily pose a barrier to conjugal love; rather it may serve a useful function in helping us to make a smooth adjustment from single to married status.[9]

Once more, we probably need to be careful of going overboard in one direction or the other. Both romance and practicality are basic to the continuing growth of the love relationship.

The Art of Love

Do we do justice to love when we try to analyze it scientifically? Or do we scrutinize it so closely that we miss the true essence of its nature and meaning? This may be so. We Americans are so enamored of technology and our abundance of material things that we may overlook what we really are searching for. This would be the view of Erich Fromm, who has written a stimulating book on love entitled *The Art of Loving.* In it he criticizes the shallow and immature conception of love that he sees as dominant in Western society.

[9]Graham B. Spanier, "Romanticism and Marital Adjustment," *Journal of Marriage and the Family,* 34, no. 3 (Aug. 1972), 481–87. For a further critical analysis of romantic love, see Albert Ellis, "Romantic Love," in *Reflections on Marriage,* ed. William N. Stephens (New York: Thomas Y. Crowell, 1968), pp. 63–83.

> Love is not a sentiment which can be easily indulged in by anyone, regardless of the level of maturity reached by him. . . . All [one's] attempts for love are bound to fail, unless [one] tries most actively to develop his total personality, so as to achieve a productive orientation. Satisfaction in individual love cannot be attained without the capacity to love one's neighbor, without true humility, courage, faith, and discipline. In a culture in which those qualities are rare, the attainment of the capacity to love must remain a rare achievement.[10]

The great difficulty in learning the art of love is that we are always thinking of *being loved.* We put a great deal of emphasis on being packaged attractively so that we will have the physical qualities most sought after in our society. We commercialize ourselves, Fromm feels, and try to put a price tag on personality in much the same way that we put a price tag on an automobile, a suit of clothes, or a loaf of bread.

Imagine how exciting it is for someone to come into a large sum of money so that he or she can buy any product on the market. In the realm of love, we can accomplish the same thing by *falling in love,* for thus we suddenly gain possession of the sought-after prize. But is life really that simple? Are we not in a much better position if we can think of *being in love* or *staying in love,* with the kind of permanence that both those phrases suggest?

Love is the best possible answer to the problem of alienation. We may find satisfaction for a time through work or creative achievements; there is a fleeting answer given to us in physical union; we may find some contact through conformity. But none of those answers alone is really satisfying.

> The full answer lies in the achievement of interpersonal union, of fusion with another person, in *love.* . . . This desire for interpersonal fusion is the most powerful striving in man. It is the most fundamental passion, it is the force which keeps the human race together.
>
> . . .
>
> Mature love is union under the condition of preserving one's integrity, one's individuality. Love is an active power in man; a power which breaks through the walls which separate man from his fellow men. . . . In love the paradox occurs that two beings become one and yet remain two.[11]

Such love is rare. Although it is common in the first flush of romantic love and the satisfying initial interchange of affection and attention, it does not always last. The kind of union of which Fromm speaks is truly an art and an infrequent achievement. The essence of true love is in giving. A per-

[10]Erich Fromm, *The Art of Loving* (New York: Harper & Row, 1956), p. xix.

[11]Fromm, pp. 18, 20.

son does not look for self-satisfaction and comfort if love is mature, but for ways to open his or her life to the needs of others so that separation from them may be overcome. If we use love as an excuse for seizing something for ourselves, we fail really to understand it.

There are four basic elements in unselfish love. First, unselfish love demands a genuine care and concern for those we love—a desire to see them grow and develop to the fullest possible extent, a wish for them to be free and creative. It requires a willingness to sacrifice or do something that is not pleasing in order to give to the one we love.

A second element is responsibility. This does not mean the kind of responsibility that is thrust on us by others. It stands rather for a voluntary responsibility, chosen because it is a loving response of one person to another. In love between adults, the responsibility is not primarily physical, represented by food and clothing and other basic necessities. It is rather a responsibility for psychological and emotional needs that are basic to our health and well-being. A responsible husband does not turn away from his wife simply because she is tired and discouraged and irritable. He has a responsibility to help her through her bad days as well as to share the good.

Such responsibility is closely linked with a third element: respect. We do not pronounce judgment from Olympus or stand apart in fear and awe. We learn to respect our loved one in an atmosphere free of exploitation; we are free to help our partner to grow and develop. We love not to reform and change the partner's way of life, but rather to live and love and share together.

A final element of mature love is knowledge. Without knowledge, there is no firm basis for respect and responsibility. We may think that we are acquainted with someone, with how he or she feels and thinks and reacts, only to discover that our knowledge is superficial. Similarly, we all tend to protect ourselves from unwelcome intrusions into our inner selves. But love cannot grow in such conditions. Love's full attainment must be built on knowledge. Communication must be free and natural and each partner eager to know and be known.

This is the theory of love. It must be matched by the practice of love—earnest discipline, concentration on the major task, and patience for its slow fulfillment. In short, we must have a supreme concern for the mastery of this high art.

Fromm relates his study of the art of loving to sexual experience. Sex should not be considered simply an adjunct of our personal lives; it is actually a reflection of the kind of people we are.

> Love is not the result of adequate sexual satisfaction, but sexual happiness—even the knowledge of the so-called sexual technique—is the result of love. If aside from everyday observation this thesis needed to be

> proved, such proof can be found in ample material of psychoanalytic data. The study of the most frequent sexual problems—frigidity in women, and the more or less severe forms of psychic impotence in men—shows that the cause does not lie in a lack of knowledge of the right technique, but in the inhibitions which make it impossible to love. Fear of or hatred for the other sex are at the bottom of those difficulties which prevent a person from giving himself completely, from acting spontaneously, from trusting the sexual partner in the immediacy and directness of physical closeness. If a sexually inhibited person can emerge from fear or hate, and hence become capable of loving, his or her sexual problems are solved. If not, no amount of knowledge about sexual techniques will help.[12]

Fromm's analysis gives us some insight into the kind of love that can realize some of the lofty dreams of the romanticist. Such love gives nerve and fiber to the bare skeleton of vague hopes and expectations. Such mature love will come not suddenly or easily, but only as men and women are willing to pay the price of self-discipline, self-examination, and self-giving.

Measuring Love

It would not be fair to say that it is impossible to make any valid measurement of love, but it is certainly a difficult task and one that should not be undertaken lightly. Dennis Hinkle and Michael J. Sporakowski have worked with the "Attitudes Toward Love" scale developed by David Knox and Sporakowski. There were 29 significant items out of the original 200 utilized. Some 234 undergraduate students were used as subjects, and a complex factor analysis was performed to test the validity of the scale. The report stated:

> In the initial principal components analysis, eight factors were extracted using the criterion eigenvalues greater than 1.0 as the cutoff for extraction of factors.
>
> . . . the scale does appear to be unidimensional based upon the loadings on the first factor or the principal component. The criterion used to come to this conclusion was a factor loading of .30416 or greater which is one-half of the maximum loading on the principal component. The exception was item five with a factor loading of .27143. This 29x8 factor matrix was rotated obliquely to determine if at this stage of the analysis a simple factor structure existed. No simple structure was evidenced.[13]

[12]Fromm, p. 89.

[13]David H. Knox and Michael J. Sporakowski, "College Students' Attitudes Toward Love," *Journal of Marriage and the Family*, 30, no. 4 (Nov. 1968), 638–42. Also, Dennis E. Hinkle and Michael J. Sporakowski, "Attitudes Toward Love: A Reexamination," *Journal of Marriage and the Family*, 37, no. 4 (Nov. 1975), 764–67.

"You say we track well together. Is that anything like love?"

Drawing by Donald Reilly
© 1973 The New Yorker Magazine, Inc.

Some of the complexity of reducing love to a computer analysis is clear when you try to master this kind of statistical summary.

Bernard I. Murstein has suggested that love can be measured with some precision if it is seen as a step-by-step development.[14] Murstein has proposed a sophisticated theory involving three stages of love related to marital choice: *stimulus, value,* and *role.* In the beginning, courtship involves a stimulus from the newly discovered partner. Here is premarital bargaining: one matches himself with the potential partner. Then comes the value stage, when the relationship is strengthened if the "fit" is good. Finally comes the role stage, when behavior is matched against the role expectations of the partners. We can then measure how closely loving behavior is matched with the verbal expression of love.

Zick Rubin has devised a Love Scale and a Liking Scale to measure love. (*Love* is defined as attachment and caring and *liking* as affection and respect.) Rubin asked couples recruited at random on a college campus to respond to statements on a rating scale from "disagree completely" to "agree completely." Both men and women loved and liked their partners in similar degree, but were shown to like their friends more than they loved them.[15]

Rubin followed up his study with a simple experiment in which the sub-

[14]See Bernard I. Murstein, "A Theory of Marital Choice," in *Theories of Attraction and Love,* ed. Bernard I. Murstein (New York: Springer, 1971), pp. 100–51.
[15]Zick Rubin, *Liking and Loving* (New York: Holt, Rinehart & Winston, 1973), p. 221.

jects' behavior was observed. Six months later, a follow-up questionnaire was mailed to each participant. The results seemed favorable; most couples reported their relationships had become "more intense."[16] Still, these findings seem sketchy at best. No in-depth interviews were held, and the haphazard selection of couples makes it difficult to draw any firm conclusions about the reliability of Rubin's test.

Everett L. Shostrom has devised a similar questionnaire to be used by couples, entitled "Caring Relationship Inventory" (see Figure 7–1). Shostrom's inventory measures love in five ways: affection, friendship, eros, empathy, and self-love. Shostrom defines each dimension as a basic component of the nature of love. Affection springs from a childlike giving and acceptance of the loved one, with deep caring and understanding. It is initially experienced in the first six years of life. Friendship springs from common interests and respect for the partner. Eros is defined as romantic love, with a strong desire for exclusive possession of the lover. Its initial development takes place during the adolescent years. The partner is originally conceived of as an ideal mate; then a transformation must take place so that the romantic feeling is retained while the actual personality of the partner is recognized. Empathy is love that is charitable and altruistic. It is a result of mature development on the part of both husband and wife. And self-love is the "ability to accept one's strengths as well as one's own weaknesses." The person who does not love himself cannot love others—either his neighbor or his wife.[17]

Each of these dimensions of love may be seen in both its manipulative and actualizing aspects. Manipulative love is exploitative and selfish; the other person becomes a means to an end, that end being our own satisfaction. Actualizing love is admiring and respectful; we love our partner for what he or she is and do not wish to change or mold him or her to our own preconceptions.

The "Caring Relationship Inventory" uses different forms for men and women.[18] Each question expresses a feeling or reaction toward the partner and is to be marked *true* (mostly true) or *false* (not usually true). Since 1966 the inventory has been used by many professionals in counseling successfully married, troubled, and divorced couples. The successfully married couples scored higher on each of five dimensions of love than the other two groups. (Scores were totaled by noting the number of *true* responses on se-

[16] Rubin, p. 233.

[17] Everett L. Shostrom, *Man, the Manipulator: The Inner Journey from Manipulation to Actualization* (New York: Abingdon, 1967).

[18] Everett L. Shostrom, *Caring Relationship Inventory* (San Diego: Educational and Industrial Testing Service, 1966). The inventory is discussed more fully in Robert K. Kelley, *Guidebook to Accompany Courtship, Marriage, and the Family,* 3rd ed. (New York: Harcourt Brace Jovanovich, 1979).

Figure 7–1 Selected Caring Relationship Inventory Questions

Question	**T**	**F**
a. I feel deeply her most painful feelings.		
b. My relationship with him is comfortable and undemanding.		
c. My feeling for her is often purely physical and animally sexual.		
d. I have tastes in common with him which others do not share.		
e. I spend a lot of time thinking about her.		
f. I know the weaknesses I see in him are also my weaknesses.		
g. I like to express my caring by kissing her on the cheek.		
h. I feel free to show my weakness in front of him.		
i. My feeling for her has a rough, strong, even fierce quality.		
j. I know him well enough that I don't have to ask for the details of his activities.		

SOURCE: Selected from Everett L. Shostrom, *Caring Relationship Inventory* (San Diego: Educational and Industrial Testing Service, 1966). Used by permission of the author.

lected questions.) And the troubled couples scored higher than the couples who were divorced.[19] In addition, the test results of this sample of approximately 350 couples produced a similar significant difference in scores on actualizing versus manipulative love.[20]

The author has administered the "Caring Relationship Inventory" to over fifteen hundred college students and also to many of their partners. Interviews with the majority of those students have confirmed the usefulness of the inventory in measuring love relationships, particularly on the negative end of the scale. The inventory has also proven to be of value to couples who have moved past the first stages of their love for each other and wish to evaluate their relationship at a more advanced stage. It will soon be issued in a new revision.

Shostrom's careful work may well lay the foundation for a more accurate measurement and understanding of the elusive quality of love. Although it suffers from the deficiencies of any self-reporting inventory (it is possible for the person being tested to give false answers concerning his own feelings), it can still be a highly useful instrument for analysis and counseling. Its greatest strength lies in the attempt to correlate love with particular behavior and thought patterns.

[19]Everett L. Shostrom, *Manual for the Caring Relationship Inventory* (San Diego: Educational and Industrial Testing Service, 1966), p. 8.

[20]For a further description of actualizing and manipulative love, see Abraham H. Maslow, *Toward a Psychology of Being* (New York: Van Nostrand, 1962).

Maturity in Love

The search for enduring love might be characterized as the search for maturity in love. Mature love is the kind of love that does not change with the seasons or with changing circumstances, but accepts life both at its best and at its worst. It is a love that may develop slowly and without fanfare or excitement, but that builds surely and solidly into a deep and meaningful relationship. There are many essential characteristics of mature love. We have noted some of them in discussing the definitions of love and the measurement of love. Let us stress three elements that are basic to mature love.

Personal Worth and Respect

One element is a mutual sense of *personal worth and respect*. If one depreciates his own value and is unsure of his own identity and self-structure, he cannot love truly. Or if the loved one is not worthy of respect and admiration, if he is not seen clearly as a person of value and integrity, then love will not grow and mature. This is a feeling that must be shared by both partners.

Allen and Charlotte were both somewhat shy and lonely people, and when they discovered each other, they fell head-over-heels in love. They had both left college without graduating. Neither had been socially popular on campus. They made some friends at the office where they both worked, but neither became too deeply absorbed in the social lives of either the married or single people they met during working hours.

When Allen and Charlotte began to date, they blossomed out with all the telltale signs of love's transforming influence. They were happier and more enthusiastic about life, although they may have seemed a little dizzy to their fellow employees. Every lunch hour was a romantic interlude, and each date was a high point in the week's activities. In April, when they announced their engagement, their families and friends hoped that the marriage would work wonders for both of them.

Counseling before marriage revealed serious personality difficulties for both Allen and Charlotte. They recognized those difficulties but felt sure that love would overcome them. "I have never known a girl like Charlotte," Allen insisted. "Allen and I will find perfect happiness," exulted Charlotte. They were blind to each other's faults. They married as planned and moved into a house in the suburbs, where their first child was born a year later.

After a year of marriage, the personal inadequacies of the partners began to take their toll. Charlotte realized that much of her image of Allen was a reflection of her own fond expectations that had little relation to his real personality. Allen was immature, careless, and selfish; a temper tantrum would shake the house for an hour. Nor was Charlotte attractive and pleasing in her new role as housewife and mother; her inadequacy in meeting daily family needs was painfully evident. Charlotte was childish, emotional, and jealous; if Allen was fifteen minutes late for supper, she would be a nervous wreck. Their sense of personal worth and value and their respect for each other were seriously impaired. They quarreled and turned to parent figures for emotional support. "Why in the world does Allen say those things?" Charlotte would complain bitterly. "My wife doesn't try to understand me," Allen would counter. Finally, after several unsuccessful reconciliations, they separated and divorced.

The growth of a mutual sense of personal worth and respect cannot be accomplished overnight. During courtship couples often make an extra effort to put forth the best side of their personalities and to accept the loved one with a minimum of criticism or objective evaluation. But one must look carefully for signs of maturity as evidenced by relationships in the parental family, at school, or on the job. Over the year-by-year experiences of marriage, a mature love that values highly both self and partner is extremely important.

Empathy

A second element of mature love is *empathy.* One must have the ability to feel and understand the feelings and attitudes of one's partner. Only rarely are most human beings able to express in words how they feel and think. Most of us count on other people to understand our feelings and our behavior on the basis of nonverbal communication—through our facial expressions, the way we move, or the different tempo with which we go from one task to another. It is not merely that we need someone to sympathize with us; we need to know someone cares and experiences with us our personal needs and problems.

In childhood we express our feelings freely. We cry when we are hungry or tired, reach out for objects that interest us, and ask for attention from parents and brothers and sisters. But society quickly conditions us not to be too expressive in most situations. We sit quietly behind a desk in schoolroom after schoolroom, are transfixed before TV screens hours on end, and accept a job in which we are only a cog in a great machine. We work in a busy factory or in an office where conversation is kept to a minimum. It therefore becomes of prime importance that we find warm and empathetic relationships in our family, particularly with our spouse.

Empathy is a key factor in companionship, a primary goal in modern marriage. Sexual needs and gratification play an important part in initiating love relationships and in binding a couple together. The birth and raising of children is a dominant task in the first years of the marriage, with most families having one or two children before the wife is thirty or thirty-five years of age. But companionship is a basic need for the couple at each stage in their relationship, and an ability to feel and act empathetically with each other will strengthen the bonds between them year by year.

Commitment

Commitment is a third element of mature love. Love is nurtured by a willingness to accept responsibility and to give oneself genuinely to the success of the relationship. Both members of the couple must determine to build and maintain their love and their marriage and to continue their determination through the years. It is partly an outgrowth of parental training and influence; it can also come from observations of the love relationships of those close to us—our relatives, neighbors, and peers. It is often associated with religious conviction and the desire to honor and identify with certain high religious ideals of fidelity, responsibility, and providence. And it can be an outgrowth of personal experience, as husband and wife build depth and meaning into their love for each other.

Richard Hettlinger points out that commitment often is a means to growth, even though we now hear that marriage prevents us from being and finding our best selves. He writes:

> Many marriages survive and grow *because of* rather than in spite of the public commitment and the relative difficulty of separation. Despite the common assertion that "I wouldn't want to stay together simply because we had to," there are many situations in which love is sustained, and eventually deepened, simply because the marriage cannot be terminated at will. Many people find that they only discover what love is really about when they have experienced the kind of crisis that would have led to the breakup of any private arrangement.[21]

[21]Richard Hettlinger, *Human Sexuality: A Psycho-Social Perspective* (Belmont, Calif.: Wadsworth, 1975), pp. 147–48.

Certainly no modern marriage is immune to pressures that test its stability and integrity. Pressures result from the rapidly changing roles of husband and wife in our society, from the need for social advancement and economic gain, from the high-tension schedules that pull husband, wife, and children in ten directions at the same time. A stable marriage reflects constancy on the part of both partners and their willingness to look beyond particular problems or tensions to the enduring bases of their love for each other.

In summary, mature love is in many ways an expression of what we feel most deeply about life and its meaning. When we develop a growing, sharing, trusting, caring, honest, free, and mature relationship with another person, we feel ourselves to be very close to the secret of what it means to be a human being. Can such love be love at first sight? Clearly, all these characteristics cannot develop instantaneously. The development of a mutual sense of personal worth and respect, of empathy, and of constancy will take time. If the couple are well matched and of a reasonable age for courtship and marriage, and if their courtship reveals mutual interests, needs, loyalties, and ideals, their love at first sight may well develop into a lifelong romance. But all of us know of many instances of love at first sight that lasted only a brief period and eventually brought more sorrow than happiness.

Determining Mature Love

What signs indicate that love is strong and mature rather than shallow and immature? How can we determine whether we are in love or only infatuated? Figure 7–2 compares some of the differences between maturity and immaturity in love. A good way to determine whether your own love is mature is to ask yourself these questions.

1. What is the most attractive feature of your partner's personality? Is it consistent with your own personality, or is it attractive to you simply because it is different and exciting?
2. Can you be yourself naturally with the person you love? Does he or she bring out the best in you or the worst? Are you genuinely proud of him or her? Do you enjoy being with him or her in the company of your family and friends?
3. Are you greatly concerned if your beloved is worried, sick, or tired? Is your concern a healthy one, or a desire on your part to make him or her dependent on you?
4. Does your relationship have its ups and downs? How do you resolve tensions between you? Are you better able to talk over your problems and disagreements than you were two months ago? six months ago?
5. Do you have many interests in common with this person? Are they

the kinds of interests that can be sustained in married life, or are they common only to courtship?

6. Do you have free and easy communication with each other, so that you want to share confidences and sincerely feel that you have a great deal of mutual trust in each other?
7. Is this person as physically attractive to you now as at the beginning of your courtship? Does your desire for affection and intimacy overshadow any other part of your relationship?
8. Have you known him or her long enough to be in love, or have you been infatuated for only a short time?
9. Are your family and friends in agreement with your feelings? If not, is it possible that you enjoy this person because the relationship expresses your independence of your family?

These are questions to help you begin your thinking about the love relationship. Are you stimulated by such inquiries, or are you threatened by them? Do you prefer to enjoy the feeling of love without examining it too closely? If so, do you think it is possible to build a marriage on a relationship that you are unwilling to examine closely?

Figure 7–2 Differences Between Mature Love and Immature Love

Immature Love	*Mature Love*
1. Love is born at first sight and will conquer all.	1. Love is a developing relationship and deepens with realistically shared experiences.
2. Love demands exclusive attention and devotion and is jealous of outsiders.	2. Love is built on self-acceptance and is shared unselfishly with others.
3. Love is characterized by exploitation and direct need gratification.	3. Love seeks to aid and strengthen the loved one without constant striving for recompense.
4. Love is built on physical attraction and sexual gratification. Sex often dominates the relationship.	4. Love includes sexual satisfaction, but not to the exclusion of sharing in other ways.
5. Love is static and egocentric. Change is sought in the partner in order to satisfy one's own needs and desires.	5. Love is a growing and developing reality. Love expands to include the growth and creativity of the loved one.
6. Love is romanticized. The couple do not face reality or are frightened by it.	6. Love enhances reality and makes the partners more complete and adequate persons.
7. Love is irresponsible and fails to consider the future consequences of today's actions.	7. Love is responsible and gladly accepts the consequences of mutual involvement.

Failure in Love

The course of love is not always smooth. We must realize that many romances just do not last. The expectations of the couple, so high at the beginning of their relationship, may not be realized. This does not mean that the partners have lost their one true love, but it is an indication that they need to choose more wisely and carefully next time. It is much better to discover that some of the physical attractions we call love are false and unrewarding during dating or engagement than to discover it after marriage. The great love stories tell us that love always has its bright and dark sides. There is no happiness more perfect than that of true lovers, but there is also no misery more profound, or depth of despair greater, than that into which lovers fall when they are frustrated, disappointed, or forgotten. Is it possible to find pleasure without pain? Is it really "better to have loved and lost than never to have loved at all"? This is certainly one of the mysteries of our life.

What can end what seems to be a perfect relationship? There are many reasons a couple may separate after an apparently genuine love has developed between them. While opposites often attract, it may be that after the first attraction wears off the contrasts become more and more pronounced. The couple argue frequently, make impossible demands on each other, and finally break up and go their separate ways. They cherish the excitement and satisfaction of love but lack the maturity and interest to build a permanent relationship. They may find that they are not yet ready for the demands and responsibilities that are involved.

Hollywood, television, and popular novels remind us constantly of the possibility of triangles breaking up a love relationship. The competitive nature of the American courtship system and the fact that business, school, and community life bring us into contact with many potential marriage partners does allow such situations to develop. However, the effect of such outside influences on a couple in love is probably exaggerated. A breakup is most likely a result of the immaturity, instability, or lack of interest of the original couple. When a relationship is weak, unbalanced, or neurotic, a third person merely reveals the dissolution already taking place.

Sometimes parents put pressure on our unrealistic and romantic dreams by opposing our choice of a partner. This is certainly a factor in broken engagements and in the failure of many other heterosexual partnerships. As Richard Driscoll and his colleagues have shown, however, parental opposition may serve to intensify the couple's romantic feelings.[22]

Social pressures and the influence of friends and business associates also contribute to the breakup of many couples. One's partner may not seem so

[22]Richard Driscoll, Keith E. Davis, and Milton E. Lipetz, "Parental Interference and Romantic Love," *Journal of Personality and Social Psychology*, 25, no. 1 (Oct. 1972), 1–8.

perfect when viewed objectively in comparison with a broader range of possible partners. This is one great difficulty with service marriages. The man or woman who marries hastily as a result of a love affair in unfamiliar surroundings, without the guidelines of family or social approval, is looking for trouble. Families or friends are usually criticized for interfering in such matters, but they may actually be doing the couple a service.

No one wants to encourage failure in love. Such failure is often damaging to the ego and frustrating to the spirit of the persons involved. On the other hand, as in all problems involved in one's growth toward maturity, such disappointments may often lead to a more genuine, understanding, and lasting relationship when the flame of love is kindled anew.

SUMMARY

Love is the universal ingredient for marriage, but it is not easy to define. It functions at different levels: It is first of all a physical attraction; at a higher level it is defined in interpersonal terms. Ultimately, it is an adventure, close to the core of the mystery of life.

Love begins in many ways. The initial attraction may appear to be just a passing fancy, but it is not solely a matter of passion and emotion; there are thought processes involved as well. The first spark of love is kindled by powerful unconscious drives, which Freud called the id and the libido.

These drives, as well as our sexual development, begin at birth. But love is more than emotion; it is also conscious and rational.

Social psychology describes love as an exchange of desirable qualities, as both giving and receiving. This exchange must reach some balance, some state of equilibrium. But love is more often described as an interpersonal relationship. In the circle of love described by Ira Reiss, love moves from rapport to self-revelation and then to mutual dependency and personality need fulfillment. The circle of love is an ideal progression; in actual situations, couples often have difficulty developing or maintaining their love.

Love may also be defined as *eros* and *agape*. Eros represents sensual love and is often thought of in negative terms. But erotic love is a normal and healthy part of the whole person. Agape is basically a religious concept. It stands for selfless love that gives far more than it asks. It is the kind of love that gives marriage stability and depth. Both eros and agape are necessary for a lasting and satisfying love relationship. Love has also been described as both romantic and conjugal. Again, both these kinds of love are needed in marriage.

Love is an art. According to Erich Fromm, this art does not come naturally in a materialistically oriented society, but must be learned. Love is not something that suddenly happens to us; it is the result of careful preparation and cultivation. Its essence is giving. Such unselfish love is evidenced by care and concern for those we love, by the acceptance of responsibility for the loved one, by mutual respect, and by knowledge of the real person whom we love. Such a theory of love needs to be matched by practice and is built on discipline, concentration, and patience.

Love can be measured, although the task is not easy. The more precise our measurement, the more mathematical and the less like genuine love it may be. Bernard I. Murstein has proposed that in order to measure love we must recognize the different stages in its development. Zick Rubin has distinguished between liking, which includes affection and respect, and loving, which is basically attachment and caring. And Everett L. Shostrom has devised a test to measure love in five dimensions: affection, friendship, eros, empathy, and self-love. Each dimension can be further defined as either manipulative or actualizing. The use of Shostrom's "Caring Relationship Inventory" shows that there are significant differences among successfully married, troubled, and divorced couples. With such a test, we can begin to answer the question of what love means and how stable and lasting it is.

The search for enduring love has been characterized as the search for maturity. The three most essential elements of mature love are a mutual sense of personal worth and respect, empathy, and commitment. Mature love may or may not develop from love at first sight. Typically it is due to many factors in the backgrounds and personalities of both partners.

Love does not always lead to marital happiness and satisfaction, however. Many factors may doom a relationship to failure. Wide dissimilarities in background and interests or outside pressures on the couple may dissolve their original attraction for each other. If love is not deep enough and strong enough to withstand such situations, the relationship is best relinquished.

SUGGESTED READINGS

Fromm, Erich. *The Art of Loving.* New York: Harper & Row, 1956. An excellent introduction to love by the noted psychologist, with practical advice on achieving a higher state of the "art."

Hunt, Morton. *The Natural History of Love.* New York: Alfred A. Knopf, 1959. Readable treatment of love from a popular and historical viewpoint.

Martinson, Floyd M. *Marriage and the American Ideal.* New York: Dodd, Mead, 1960. Chaps. 7–10. Good treatment of our views on love and marriage in relation to traditional, romantic, and more scientific viewpoints.

Murstein, Bernard I., ed. *Theories of Attraction and Love.* New York: Springer, 1971. Discussion by several authors of love as related to social psychology.

Rubin, Zick. *Liking and Loving.* New York: Holt, Rinehart & Winston, 1973. Introduction to differences between liking and loving, with experimental and survey evidence.

Shostrom, Everett L. *Man, the Manipulator: The Inner Journey from Manipulation to Actualization.* New York: Abingdon, 1967. Discussion of personal growth and development, with close relation to work of Abraham Maslow.

Skolnick, Arlene. *The Intimate Environment,* 2nd ed. Boston: Little, Brown, 1978. Discussion of love, marriage, and family in context of intimate interpersonal relationships.

8 College: Engagement, Living Together, Marriage

- What is the choice among engagement, living together, and college marriage?
- Is engagement a necessary step in courtship?
- What elements of engagement are the best preparation for marriage?
- Why do some couples prefer a trial marriage arrangement?
- What is your personal attitude toward trial marriage?
- Is college marriage a wise choice?
- What happens to the academic career of married students?
- Do women find college marriage more difficult than men?
- Is this the year for you to choose to become engaged, to live with your partner, or to get married while in college?

The Choices

Your teenage years are a time for choices. You must choose whether or not to attend college. Perhaps a business opportunity, a trade school, a position in the family business, or marriage looks more inviting. If you decide to continue your education, you must consider what kind of school you wish to attend: state college, community college, or university. After this, there are also many choices to be made in your personal life. Should you continue to live at home and commute to school, in order to reduce part of the costs of your education? Or should you live in a college dormitory and reap the benefits of meeting and living with a wide variety of people? Or should you take an apartment off campus, or live in a sorority or fraternity, or some other alternative? Each has its assets and liabilities.

At the same time, we have choices in our love relationships. The couple entering college, who are seriously in love, have three alternatives before them. They may announce their engagement to be married at some future time, perhaps after they finish their education. Or they may decide to begin living together so that they can make what seems to them to be the most practical preparation for marriage (we discussed such arrangements in Chapter 2). Or the couple may decide to be married while they are still in ege and merge their educational and marriage plans. Let us consider each f these alternatives.

nent

Engagement has been the traditional preparation for marriage, and it is an elaborate social system. There is the formal engagement announcement, with a date for marriage specified or suggested, which sets the stage for the couple to take their place in the community as a married couple. Today engagement is receiving less emphasis because couples are seriously going steady in high school or college for several months or years before marriage, and many of the features of the engagement period are inherent in such dating patterns.[1] The steady couple have a social status as exclusive dating partners and are often recognized as probable marriage partners by their families. But engagement retains its importance for a large number of college couples. It is still the pattern chosen by the majority of young people, because it offers many advantages to the man and woman who want to begin their married life with a strong measure of support from their families and from the community.

Engagement has both traditional and contemporary meanings. In some families and in some parts of our culture the engagement period today may be very similar to that experienced by our parents and grandparents. For others, the faster pace of modern life and the more varied patterns of work and leisure have given a far different meaning to this premarital period. Let us examine more closely what the announcement of engagement signifies to the couple, their friends and families, and the community at large.

Defining Engagement

Engagement signifies an intention to marry. The element of commitment is an important aspect of engagement, as Mary Hicks has concluded from her study of ninety-four married couples at Pennsylvania State University. Hicks found that the engagement period gave the couple a sense of security as they focused on the future. They were able to improve their problem-solving behavior and to continue the process of mutual personality exploration.[2]

This intention to marry is not as strongly interpreted as it was a hundred years ago; a breach-of-promise suit because of a broken engagement is now a rarity in our trial courts. We move from state to state, from town to town, or from college to college very easily. In a new environment we may enter

[1]See Chapter 3.

[2]Mary W. Hicks, "An Empirical Evaluation of Textbook Assumptions About Engagement," *The Family Coordinator*, 19, no. 1 (Jan. 1970), 57-63.

into an enjoyable and serious courtship very quickly. But changed circumstances may force us to change our intentions just as quickly.

Most engagements result in marriage. But again, it is no longer a disgrace to break an engagement. Friends and family members usually conclude that it is better to break an engagement now than to break a marriage later. When the couple announce their engagement, they have every intention of getting married. But intentions change, and if they do, the couple can cancel the agreement and reenter the courtship system in search of more suitable partners. This flexibility has both positive and negative aspects. It prevents many unwise marriages; but it may also encourage a certain thoughtless and hasty attitude toward engagement.

There is no fixed period for engagement. Although six months to a year may seem to be most suitable, there are many variations. For example, engagement to a serviceman may extend for a much longer period of time since the couple may discover that they do not have too much ease in communication by letter; additional time for their preparation for marriage is needed. A young college couple, on the other hand, may find three months a very adequate engagement period. In a majority of cases today, the maximum limit on engagement is a year.

Engagement should mean the strengthening and deepening of the couple's feelings for each other. Mark Krain has conducted an exploratory study to discover whether or not dating and engaged couples actually make progress in their relationship in terms of more effective and unifying communication between partners. He discusses earlier evidence that teenagers

gradually reduce their hostile, exploitative, and teasing approach to the opposite sex as they become older. However, the results of the Krain study were inconclusive in regard to a definite, positive growth for engaged couples after some period of months in preparation for marriage. Neutral communication always took up a fair amount of time (we all like to talk about the weather), but negative and hostile communication was still present between couples in late stages of the study.[3] Krain's investigation seems to prove that there is no easy method that will build a strong marriage in an engagement period of fairly short duration. Some progress can and should be made, but it is not guaranteed, and it needs to be a continuing development right on into the marriage.

The engagement period is one of pleasurable anticipation. For seven or eight years, since junior high school days, the couple have been caught up in the whirl of the fun-filled but often demanding ritual of American courtship. For the young man, the search for a suitable partner has meant a certain amount of competition and probably a good deal of expense. Engagement shows that he has met the test, has found the partner who meets his needs and expectations, and can now relax a little. His role in the social events leading up to the wedding is minimal. If he is fortunate enough to be engaged to a young woman who is poised and genuinely concerned for his happiness, engagement will be a time in which he makes a smooth transition to the responsibilities of matrimony.

Engagement is even more important for the young woman. She too has had her moments (and perhaps months) of anxiety and concern during the lengthy courtship period from junior high school through high school and college. In her own mind she may have been torn between conflicting feelings about this young man and that one. But now her mind is made up. She is engaged.

In most college circles and in much of the community around us the engagement period will be a memorable one. There will be an announcement party, small or large. There will be the excitement of choosing gowns for the wedding and making arrangements for the ceremony and reception. The couple will be apartment-hunting, or perhaps even house-hunting. There will be plans for a honeymoon, brief or extended, and of course there will be the special feeling of romance that our culture provides for bride and groom.

For both the man and the woman, then, engagement marks a major achievement. Marriage brings a high status in our society. It may not be the most opportune time for marriage, and the choice may be hasty or unwise, but engagement brings hope that the man and woman will begin a new life.

[3]Mark Krain, "Communication Among Premarital Couples at Three Stages of Dating," *Journal of Marriage and the Family*, 37, no. 3 (Aug. 1975), 609–18.

The high status of the married person is thus transferred to the engaged man and woman. We must not minimize this achievement. A good marriage is a worthwhile attainment. School is important, and a job pays well and provides a great deal of stimulus and enjoyment; but to be a wife or a husband brings additional satisfaction.

Purposes of Engagement

Engagement is the culmination of the courtship process, and as such, it serves a number of vitally important purposes in preparation for marriage. Many engagements are terminated some weeks or months before the intended wedding. In those cases, one or more of the purposes of this important final testing stage have not been fulfilled.

PREPARING FOR MARRIAGE

The first and most important purpose of the time of formal engagement is to prepare the couple for their future marriage. The engaged couple should become even more aware of their interpersonal relationship. They should come to feel more and more certain that their mutual choice has been right, and there should be fewer and fewer barriers that prevent them from entering freely into their new partnership. Those couples who have differences in outlook on important questions during engagement will experience difficulty in their marriage. No two people can make a new beginning in marriage unimpeded by prior training and disposition; we are all strongly influenced by our personal frame of reference.

The engagement period requires a number of adjustments by both partners. Marriage is sometimes described as a fifty-fifty arrangement, but more generally it comes out at about sixty-forty. One partner will give in more at one point; the other partner more at another. Perfect balance is rare. Many decisions are the result of compromise, and that process must begin during engagement.

The ability to live life at a routine level must also be developed during engagement. Engagement can be exciting, and there may be a bustle of activity as the wedding date approaches. On the other hand, the engagement may last for from six months to a year, in which case the couple will learn to settle into a more routine relationship, roughly comparable to the one they will have after marriage. The financial realities of married life must be faced together. Compromise solutions to various differences concerning in-laws, religious affiliation, mutual friends, and other important matters need to be tested out. An engaged couple should find satisfaction in these practical tasks during the final stages of their engagement. Some tension and disagreement are natural, as in any human relationship, but basic love, concern, and compatibility should prevent such conflicts from building major barriers between the couple.

STRENGTHENING FAMILY RELATIONSHIPS

A second major purpose of engagement is to involve the parents, family, and friends of the couple in support of this new relationship. It may seem strange to think of these extended networks in a generation when many young adults are living thousands of miles from home. The free choice emphasized in our courtship system gives the couple a clear option to court and become engaged without obtaining the approval of family or friends. The engagement period is the natural time to gain this approval by fostering thorough acquaintance and understanding with families and other significant persons.

Although the traditional pattern of asking for a daughter's hand in marriage seems to be ignored in today's society, in which individual freedom is emphasized, the father still appreciates having a ceremonial part in the decision. When no communication takes place between parents and children, feelings of suspicion and mistrust may develop, such as when a man's parents learn of the engagement after it has been announced.

Ellen discussed her engagement problems with a counselor in October, some two weeks after engagement. Her parents had been opposed to her steady dating of Jerry and had sought in various ways to discourage it. They had limited her dates to weekends, lowered the curfew hour, put him off limits for several lengthy periods, and otherwise tried to break up the relationship. When she mentioned engagement to them, they refused to discuss it. When she became engaged in spite of their objections, she wore her ring proudly outside the home, but never within it.

Her parents' objections seemed to have some validity. Jerry was almost a stranger to them, and so they rejected him without really knowing him. Ellen and Jerry were of different religions, and neither had yet given signs of moving toward the other's faith. He was new in his job, having completed his hitch in the service, and she was beginning a two-year nursing program. Instead of looking for opportunities to discuss her feelings with her parents, Ellen let communication break down. She became engaged to Jerry.

At this point the fears of father and mother were clear. Ellen and Jerry would elope, and the last hope of parental influence and restraint would be lost. They reacted as might have been expected—by tightening the reins as much as possible, hoping to force their daughter to change her plans.

A middle course was proposed by Ellen's counselor to ease the tension. No wedding date had been set, and that had intensified the parents' anxiety. Why not set a June date, some twenty months away, so that both families and the young couple could look at the situation without the pressure of an early marriage on them? Then the potential dangers of their marriage could be examined clearly and objectively, without threat or duress. Ellen could explain the distant plans as a concession to her parents' feelings and bring her parents more easily into communication with her intended partner. And if the engagement did not work out, the problem of picking up new activities at school and work would not be so great as would be the case in a hasty and unsuccessful marriage.

Luckily, the parents' reaction was positive. With the fear of elopement reduced, they were able to relax and take a more reasonable view of the situation. The financial and educational problems facing the couple would be far less formidable after another twenty months had passed; the couple took several positive steps to resolve their religious differences; Jerry got a promotion and a raise, and there was time for both parental families to become acquainted and establish some personal relationships at their own level.

After four months the young couple found their marriage plans were much less complicated. The parents accepted the serious intentions of their daughter and prospective son-in-law and were more realistic in their appraisal of the couple. And Ellen could discuss the possibility of an earlier marriage date more freely.

There are various ways that engaged couples can win more wholehearted support and approval for their marriage. Basically, success depends on a real willingness on the part of the young couple, once they have made their own decision to marry, to involve others in their developing plans. They need to accept the value and worth of the opinion of others. When they take this first basic step of recognition and acceptance, the couple can usually expect a positive response in return.

A dialogue must develop between the couple and their parents if some of the generational differences are to be overcome. What many parents say to engaged couples who are still in college is this:

> You have decided to become engaged. You want to be married next spring. You want to live near the college and finish your education. It

> will be a rough and uphill climb for you the next two or three years. You haven't asked for our advice about it, and you've ignored what hints we have been dropping for the last four months. You wanted to be on your own and you are. Good luck—you'll need it!

It is often wise for the engaged couple to react positively to parental criticism. The future success of the marriage and good relationships with the in-laws might suggest a response like this:

> We are young (and very much in love). Perhaps we were a bit hasty in deciding to become engaged. But this is what we really want. What do you think we should do? Should we leave the date indefinite for awhile and see how the finances work out? Should one of us sell his car and try to do some ride-sharing, so that we can put that money aside for the furniture? Should one of us drop out of school for a semester and save money for the wedding? Should we plan for a small private wedding at home instead of a big church ceremony?

Most parents, when faced with this kind of response, tend to recognize more clearly the problems the younger generation is facing. If the engagement period is a time of genuine communication between generations, they will probably be much more sympathetic toward alternative solutions and much more apt to assist the young couple in making their decisions. Time and patience will accomplish a great deal during the engagement period.

The classic study of one thousand engaged couples by Burgess and Wallin showed that parental opposition was very frequently associated with broken engagements.[4] In the early dating stages, parents are seemingly willing to let the choice of partner be a very free one. When marriage becomes a definite possibility, they become more vocal, and will state their negative opinions more forcefully.

It would be wrong to assume that a young man's family is not interested in his engagement and marriage even though he is an independent young adult. A bridegroom may be closer to his family today than a young man was at the turn of the century. Then he often left home at fifteen or sixteen to work elsewhere, and usually did not marry until ten years later. (See Table 8–1.) Today, by contrast, he is often in school until age twenty-one or twenty-two, and may live at home all these years. When he is married at twenty-three or twenty-four, there is strong input from his family in regard to his plans.

[4]Ernest W. Burgess and Paul Wallin, *Engagement and Marriage* (Philadelphia: Lippincott, 1953), pp. 288–89.

Table 8–1 Life Patterns for Men, 1900 and 1977

1900

Age:	Birth	16	26	36	46
Life Pattern:	Childhood and Education	Full-time Employment	Marriage and Family Formation	Maturity	Death

1977

Age:	Birth	18	23–24	33	67
Life Pattern:	Childhood and Education	College or Technical Education (Service)	Marriage and Family Formation	Maturity Retirement	Death

SOURCE: U.S. Bureau of the Census, *Statistical Abstract of the United States, 1977* (Washington, D.C.: U.S. Government Printing Office, 1977), p. 59.

PREPARING FOR INDEPENDENCE

A third purpose of engagement is to strengthen the couple's sense of independence and freedom. This is important to many college couples. If both the man and woman are living with their parents, they are subject to varying restrictions and limitations. Money for many things—car insurance, college tuition, dormitory expenses, perhaps even recreation—may be largely or entirely controlled by the parents. And the parents may feel that their financial investment in the education of their son or daughter, in addition to the personal and emotional factors involved, entitles them to a certain veto power over the activities of their child. Unfortunately, some parents do not make any appreciable change in the way they exercise their authority as their children mature from the early teens through the college years. They are as demanding or restrictive toward their children when they are nineteen as when they were thirteen.

To men and women of college age, feeling the continued pressure of parental control as they make the transition from adolescence to full adulthood, engagement may offer an attractive way of gaining freedom from these restrictions. If they are engaged, they reason, their parents need not be so concerned about their hours and their activities. And they will probably have a greater say in the bargaining between the two generations over finances. Sexual freedom is involved too.

A final purpose is served by the formal announcement of the coming wedding. In earlier days this was accomplished by the traditional publishing of the banns. A small New England town or a rural village in Virginia would thus receive an almost complete communication about the engagement through the church announcement. There is no comparable announcement today. Still, there is a distinct advantage to the couple, and to society, if their engagement and marriage are recognized and important events in the life of the community.

Necessity of Engagement

Is the engagement period really worthwhile? Or is it another social ritual that should be eliminated? We have to admit that the engagement period presents several potential problems. A partner who seems adequate during early dating may not stand up under the closer scrutiny of engagement. Pressures for and against premarital sex will be a recurrent problem for the engaged couple. Financial problems may become more acute because the expenses of setting up housekeeping must be added to those of the wedding and honeymoon.

Unfortunately, many engagements do not prepare couples adequately for marriage because the couple are not realistic. They do not face the practical problems that must be solved. They do not take time to be with their families, to gain their respect and approval. They fail to tackle problems together in such a way that they can build patterns for mutually shared decision-making.

It must also be noted that many couples do not have an engagement period long enough to serve any useful purpose. The engagement period must be long enough, perhaps two to three months as a minimum, to allow the couple time to approach the wedding day with some measure of assurance and preparation. A brief announcement a week before a private ceremony hardly qualifies as an engagement in middle-class culture.

Sometimes abbreviated engagements are necessitated by pregnancy. In other cases the couple lack the financial resources to become involved in expensive wedding arrangements, or they feel that a formal engagement is too much fuss and bother. Often young couples object to the materialistic show that characterizes many formal engagements and marriages. Since our courtship system is essentially a voluntary one, couples who wish to marry after a very brief engagement are free to follow their own wishes and desires.

Burgess and Wallin, in their study of engaged couples, listed five chief factors in broken engagements: slight attachment, geographical separation of the couple, parental opposition, cultural divergence, and personality problems of one or both engaged persons.[5] However, since this study was completed in 1946, it represents an older generation and needs to be updated. There is much greater tolerance of socioeconomic and cultural divergences today than there was during the Depression and the Second World War. Even if families and friends would not cross social, ethnic, or racial lines themselves, they tend to be more tolerant of the younger generation taking such steps today.

Personality problems include a wide range of difficulties, and they are naturally a continuing factor in broken engagements. In addition, we must consider many factors related to changes in our culture and society. There is the question of anticipated and actual roles in the new relationship, the problems associated with mixing marriage and education, the pros and cons of financial assistance and consequent influence by one or both sets of parents, and the likelihood of immaturity on the part of the couples marrying in their late teens before either partner has had a taste of adult responsibility and achievement. The personal goals and aspirations now held for marriage include hope for a high degree of companionship. The fulfillment of these hopes is not easy. If one feels that the engagement period is not giving clear indication of a smooth course ahead, he or she may decide to break the engagement rather than face the risk of later failure, separation, and divorce.

Living Together

Today, many young couples "in love" live together, in a majority of cases without a formal engagement or firm plans for a marriage date (see Chapter 2). Why are some students turning away from marriage, and replacing it with the living-together arrangement? What is behind this trend now being observed around the country? Obviously, social and peer pressure is a factor. In the same way that various aspects of dating have become almost mandatory over the years, for many couples living together is the natural culmination of courtship. Bower and Christopherson reported in a broad study of students at a number of colleges that there was a great deal of similarity between the college students studied, both cohabiting and noncohabiting ones.[6] The chief differences between the students were found in greater flexi-

[5]Burgess and Wallin, p. 273.

[6]Donald W. Bower and Victor A. Christopherson, "University Student Cohabitation: A Regional Comparison," *Journal of Marriage and the Family,* 39, no. 3 (Aug. 1977), 447–53.

bility on the part of noncohabitors in considering alternative lifestyles, the lower desire of cohabitors for children, and a delay in marriage age for the cohabiting couples.

The idea of trial marriage is not new. It was popularized by Judge Ben B. Lindsay and Bertrand Russell in the 1920s. Lindsay termed it "companionate marriage."[7] But the early innovators were generally ostracized; the real impetus toward our contemporary experience came much later. In 1966 Margaret Mead proposed a two-step plan for marriage: The first step would be a trial period, in which marriage would be "individual," with no children and a simple, easy way of divorce; the second step would be "parental marriage," in which couples would accept the lifetime obligations of parenthood. In essence, states that have liberal divorce laws have made the first step a reality. It is simple for a young couple to step in and out of marriage, especially if they have no children. The concept of lifetime parental obligation, however, is not among our present customs.

Rustum Roy and Della Roy have suggested that what is needed by society today is the institutionalization of premarital sex.

Premarital sexual experience is now rather widely accepted, covertly if

[7]See Miriam E. Berger, "Trial Marriage: Harnessing the Trend Constructively," *The Family Coordinator*, 20, no. 1 (Jan. 1971), 30–43.

> not overtly, throughout our society. . . . The new rise in "keeping-house-together" arrangements in college and beyond is spreading like wildfire. We see an opportunity here for a simple evolution of the monogamous ideal within relatively easy reach. Almost all analysts believe that postponing marriage by two or three years and making it more difficult—with some required period of waiting or even waiting and instruction—would be very beneficial. Traditional marriage in its classical form enjoined a "decent" (six months to two years) engagement period partly for the same reason. One of the main drives toward early marriage is that there is no other way to obtain regular sexual gratification in a publicly acceptable manner. By one simple swish of tradition, we can incorporate all the recent suggestions for trial marriages, "baby" marriages, etc., and cover them all under the decent rug of the "engagement." Engagements with a minor difference: that in today's society they entitle a couple to live together if they desire, and sleep together—*but not to have children.* Thus, engagement would become the first step that entitles one to legal sex—publicly known sex with contraceptive devices. By no means need this become the universal norm. Pluralism of marital patterns should start here, however. Many parents and various social groups may still urge their members to restrict engagements to a noncoital or nonsexual level of intimacy; but even here they would do well to legitimize some advanced level of sexual activity and by so doing they would probably protect their marriage-institution more effectively. . . .
>
> Along with the engagement-including-sex concept could be introduced the idea of training for marriage. Everyone falls for the training gimmick. Driver education, often taken after three years of driving, is still useful, and is induced by the lowered insurance rates. Similarly if society required a "marriage-education" course before granting a license, another important step in improving the quality of marriage would have been achieved.[8]

A study by Henze and Hudson suggests that cohabitors are not different in family background from noncohabitors, but they do tend to be nonchurchgoers, to label themselves as liberals in lifestyle and in their outlook toward drug use. Henze and Hudson do not believe that couples who live together will never get married, but they may marry at a later age.[9]

Miriam E. Berger feels that the living-together trend must be put to con-

[8]Rustum Roy and Della Roy, "Is Monogamy Outdated?" reprinted in *Human Sexuality: Contemporary Perspectives,* ed. Eleanor S. Morrison and Vera Borosage (Palo Alto, Calif.: National Press Books, 1973), pp. 152–53.

[9]Laura F. Henze and John W. Hudson, "Personal and Family Characteristics of Cohabiting and Noncohabiting College Students," *Journal of Marriage and the Family,* 36, no. 4 (Nov. 1974), 722–27.

structive use. If we are to have trial marriage, there must be some professional guidance available so that the people involved can learn from their experience rather than make the same mistakes over and over again. The help of a counselor would be an invaluable asset to such couples. They might ask themselves the following questions:

> What did I learn about myself from this experience? How did I adjust to living with a peer, as distinguished from living with parents and siblings, or alone? What have the problems of adjustment been? Would I have the same problems with another roommate or spouse? How much did I contribute to these problems and how much was the responsibility of the partner? What neurotic games did we play? What hangups did I bring to the relationship that were reinforced by our interaction? What kind of person do I need to live with: dominant, submissive, detached, involved, affectionate, etc? What was our style of communication: constructive, silent treatment, hitting below the belt? How effectively do I communicate my needs and feelings? How did our communication problems affect our sexual adjustment? On the assumption that personal happiness is achieved through satisfying closeness to another human being, what problems did I have in achieving and maintaining that closeness?[10]

Long-Term Results of Living Together

How successful are couples in building stable relationships in the living-together framework? Carl Rogers, who is sympathetic to innovative lifestyles, interviewed one couple who had been living together for several years. They met when she was eighteen and he was nineteen; problems in their courtship included drug usage and conflicts with their parental families. Rogers asked them about their experience living together, and their responses revealed their difficulty in making a commitment to each other during the initial years of their relationship.

> DICK: We never mentioned love in our relationship. And that's for at least three years. We never committed ourselves to loving one another until well into the fourth year, although I don't know *why*. We'd ask each other if we liked each other and placed a great deal of significance on that, but just as significantly we avoided the word "love," and all I remember about the first time we did mention love was that it was kind of a trauma.
> GAIL: I can remember everything. I think we were arguing about us. And Dick was trying to tell me, without telling, that he was leaving me. You know, saying there's this problem and that it's stale and it's . . . and so

[10]Berger, 41–42.

on. And I'm all ready to change and work it out and then he just got frustrated and he said, "But I love you and I really care for you," and then he walked out. That I really couldn't understand. You told me you loved me and walked out and left me! I thought, "Well, that's crazy." I thought that was the nuttiest thing I ever heard. I thought, "Well, does he feel guilty about hurting me and is that why he's saying it?" And if he was all that crazy about me, he wouldn't have been walking out to somebody else! And he didn't tell me, you know, he never told me he had another girlfriend, which bugged me a lot because I thought he could at least do that. And I had to go through this whole painful thing of finding out, when somebody said they saw Dick with this little blonde. And I thought, "Well, if that's true, he's probably at her house," and so I went over there and there they were and Dick was mortified. I was bitchy and I wouldn't go away.[11]

Who Lives Together?

In a recent article Ridley, Peterman, and Avery point out that there are different types of living-together relationships. Probably a majority of couples who live together are not committed to a future marriage.[12] If the partners are basically seeking convenience or ego satisfaction for themselves, the relationship will not be a very valuable one. However, if they are testing out a future marital relationship, they are in a sense going through many of the same feelings and reactions that newly married couples do. This kind of responsible commitment may be the crucial factor when the decision to marry or live together is finally made. Richard Hettlinger has emphasized this point in his book on sex and the college student.

> First, I would ask whether the act of intercourse, with all its unique quality and intimacy, can be rightly or meaningfully experienced apart from the permanent commitment of marriage. Does not love, in any profound sense, remain unfulfilled until the couple are actually responsible for each other? And if so, can the act which expresses and seals the unity of love be justified in advance of that moment? Should the man who has not yet taken the decisive step of committing his future to a girl ask of her this risk to her future? If he does not yet share his economic and domestic life with her, is he ready to share this unity of body with her? There is, after all, a real difference between the relationship of a couple before and after marriage. Before, even in the most sincere and honest engagement, neither is fully and objectively responsible for the other.

[11]Carl Rogers, *Becoming Partners* (New York: Delacorte Press, 1972), pp. 33–34.

[12]Carl A. Ridley, Dan J. Peterman, and Arthur W. Avery, "Cohabitation: Does It Make for a Better Marriage?" *The Family Coordinator,* 27, no. 2 (April 1978), 129–36.

> After the wedding they are legally, socially, and personally committed beyond recall, no longer independent centers of action but "one flesh." Even trial marriage is an entirely different relationship, because in this experiment people are trying each other out, rather than committed to each other. Indeed, a trial marriage is a contradiction of terms, because the essence of marriage is that (at least in intention) it is not a trial at all but a permanent bond. And if the full meaning of sex is discovered in personal relationships, the ultimate intimacy of intercourse should be preserved until the ultimate commitment to another person, which is represented by marriage.[13]

One interesting recent study suggests that couples living together may actually have a lower level of agreement than couples seriously going together but not living together.[14] Couples going together had more compatible and traditional values and high expectations of marriage. Couples living together, however, had some major differences of opinion. The chief difficulty was that the women wanted to get married and felt a real need for their partners, but the men would not make a commitment to marry. The sociologists who conducted the study noted: "to a very striking degree, living-together couples did not reciprocate the kinds of feelings (of need, respect, happiness, involvement, or commitment to marriage) that one would expect to be the basis of a good heterosexual relationship."[15]

One cannot draw final conclusions from such a small sampling of couples. However, we should not assume that all couples who live together will find the experience a positive one in building a sound relationship or in moving from a trial marriage to a permanent one, nor that they will find it a negative experience either.

Legal Aspects of Living Together

There is a legal aspect to these considerations as well. Through the centuries an elaborate legal system has been built up around the institution of marriage and the family. The common-law marriage was the former device used to grant couples living together some of the rights of couples who had a legal marriage. Some recent court decisions seem to suggest that a new body of laws will gradually develop for contemporary living-together couples.[16] Since

[13]Richard E. Hettlinger, *Living with Sex: The Student's Dilemma* (New York: Seabury, 1966), p. 135.
[14]See Judith L. Lyness, Milton E. Lipetz, and Keith E. Davis, "Living Together: An Alternative to Marriage," *Journal of Marriage and the Family*, 34, no. 2. (May 1972), 305–11.
[15]Lyness, Lipetz, and Davis, p. 310.
[16]Barton E. Bernstein, "Legal Problems of Cohabitation," *The Family Coordinator*, 26, no. 4 (Oct. 1977), 361–66.

many living-together couples terminate the relationship at the end of six months or less, legal protections may be scaled down to recognize the more temporary and less binding nature of the relationship.

College Marriage

Another alternative clearly open to the college couple seriously in love is college marriage. At most of our large universities, permanent housing has been made available for married couples and their children, so that husbands and wives can continue their college careers in as comfortable an environment as possible. At small colleges and community colleges, which usually offer no housing for married couples, there are apartments or other living facilities available in the nearby community. Prior to 1941 our colleges and universities catered to the single student. The widespread acceptance of married students today is a result of the influx of married veterans after the Second World War.

But the fact that there are many married students on campus does not answer the question, "Should we get married while we are still in school?" The couple who are thinking of marrying while they are in college should ask themselves, "If we do marry while we are in college, what will be our chances of finishing school, and what effect will college marriage have on our future happiness?" Each couple's relationship is unique, and there is no single yardstick that can be applied to every case. What will contribute to the future success or failure of the relationship? A couple ought to weigh the pros and cons of college marriage and consider what it means to them in contrast to a lengthier engagement or a trial marriage. Some of the differences among the three alternatives are illustrated in Table 8–2.

Benefits of College Marriage

The increasing percentage of married students on campus is looked on favorably by most members of the college community. This is due in part to the fact that some married students are older than their fellow unmarried students. A married student thirty or thirty-five years of age is more mature and settled than an eighteen-year-old freshman. Students have always been noted for letting off steam during their college years, and we are not surprised to find them striking against the food in the college dining hall, taking over a resort town during spring vacation, or staging an impromptu rally after a big football victory. Some people criticize such antics as a sign of immaturity. And immaturity may also be evidenced in more serious ways—

Table 8-2 Engagement, Living Together, and College Marriage

	Engagement
Place of residence	Separate. Couple continue to live at home or college.
Finances	Separate. Joint planning for future expenses.
Sexual relationship	Premarital relationship is determined by couple. Sex may be postponed until marriage, or couple may have premarital sexual understanding. Guilt feelings possible.
Interpersonal relationship	Couple are given increased privacy in which to develop relationship. Problem-solving behavior encouraged.
Relationship with parental families	Continuing relationship encouraged. Social customs involve family members.
Relationship with religious community	High acceptance of couple. Majority of couples choose religious wedding ceremony.
Relationship with society	High acceptance of couple. Couple meet social norms and receive support through traditional customs.
Culmination in marriage	Approximately 50 percent of couples marry. Exact number of successes and failures in marriage unknown.
Success in marriage	Approximately 70 percent of couples who marry remain married. Divorce increasing. Alternative lifestyles being experimented with by some couples.

Living Together	College Marriage
Shared. Some may have both dormitory and private residence.	Shared.
Living expenses shared.	Expenses shared.
Regular sexual experiences. Possible guilt feelings because of lack of social and religious sanctions.	Regular sexual experience.
Relationship developed on daily basis. Some problems combining partnership with education. Many couples unable to stabilize relationship. Counseling available.	Relationship developed on daily basis. Some problems combining marriage with education. Some help available from counselors and parental families.
May be tense. Some families unaware of relationship; some strongly disapprove.	Some in-law problems, often due to parental subsidizing of marriage. Social customs encourage development of couple's independence.
Less acceptance of couple. Some counseling available. Some couples eventually choose religious wedding ceremony.	Good acceptance of couple. Some support and counseling available. Higher degree of acceptance.
May be antagonistic; couple may be antiestablishment. Or may be strong; couple may identify with subculture (other couples living together, student couples).	Good acceptance of couple. Some criticism for not postponing marriage until completion of all or most of education.
Majority of persons do not marry their first living-together partner. No exact percentages are available for those marrying their second, third, or fourth living-together partner. Depth of original commitment a determining factor in whether or not a couple marry.	(All couples married.)
Effect of trial marriage on later marital adjustment unknown. Many studies now underway.	Couple may benefit from shared experience in academic environment. Total effect on later marital adjustment thought to be favorable.

when a student drops out of school without completing courses or gets into serious trouble with the police over a prank that backfires into a public nuisance or a crime.

Married students are apparently above much of this wild-oat sowing. They have a partner, and perhaps children, to go home to. They probably have part-time or full-time jobs to help support themselves and their children. To some people, the married college couple may seem imprisoned by their situation, but they are apparently willing to sacrifice personal comfort and convenience in order to make their family's future secure.

Busselen and Busselen have documented the maturity of married students in their survey of the studies done in this field during the past thirty years. They also note that colleges and universities are much better equipped to assist married students today than they were when such students first appeared on campuses in great numbers after the Second World War.[17]

This social and emotional maturity can be expressed in terms of the satisfaction of ego needs. According to one psychological viewpoint, marriage is partially a result of certain "self needs" of the two persons involved, and a successful marriage results in the satisfaction of those needs: needs for love and affection, for security, for new experiences, and for self-expression that are not always met in single life. (This is, of course, a benefit that accrues to all kinds of marriage; Robert Winch has discussed it in connection with his theory of complementary needs.[18]) If the man is a veteran pursuing his education away from home or the woman is isolated from her family, the encouragement offered by the love and support of wife or husband, together with the steadying influence of regular home patterns, social companionship, and mutual interests, may make the difference between the continuance of college studies and their termination.

All in all, we have to give a favorable vote to college marriage in terms of meeting many of the social, sexual, and emotional needs of the couple. These people are not isolated and alone—they have a loving and committed companion to share the college experience with them. The question of the effect of marriage on one's academic life is more difficult to measure. When the first wave of married students came on campus after the Second World War, they did well in their studies. They were older, more serious, and more dedicated. This trend was seen in some of the studies done ten or fifteen years later. However, a more critical view has been supported in recent studies. Alan E. Bayer, utilizing data from a large subsample taken from 200,000 entering students in more than 250 junior colleges, four-year col-

[17]Harry J. Busselen, Jr., and Carroll K. Busselen, "Adjustment Differences Between Married and Single Undergraduate University Students: An Historical Perspective," *The Family Coordinator*, 24, no. 3 (July 1975), 281–87.

[18]Robert F. Winch, *The Modern Family*, 3rd ed. (New York: Holt, Rinehart & Winston, 1971).

leges, and universities in 1966, indicates that better students do not marry while in college.

> Generally, the more academically able the student, the less likely he or she was to marry early. Men who had both outstanding high school grades and high self-ratings on writing ability were likely to remain single. Women who rated themselves high on academic ability were less likely to marry during college.[19]

The question whether marriage brings academic gains is still open, then. Further evidence seems to be needed before a definite judgment can be made. An older veteran or a married man returning to college to complete his education at some time after marriage will probably have more motivation and drive for academic achievement than many single students. But there is no guarantee that marriage will benefit every undergraduate. A number of social, family, personal, and psychological factors need to be considered before a specific prediction can be made for a particular student.

Margaret Mead has also questioned the value of marriage for undergraduates who may be thus prevented from reaping the benefits of the highest intellectual stimulus and exploration in one's undergraduate years. She writes:

> The university is a unique development of our kind of civilization, and a special pattern is set for those who have the ability and the will to devote four years of exploring the civilization of which they are a part. . . . It includes . . . those who are willing to accept four more years of an intellectual and psychological moratorium, in which they explore, test, meditate, discuss, passionately espouse, and passionately repudiate ideas about the past and the future. The true undergraduate university is still an "as-if" world in which the student need not commit himself yet. . . .
>
> One of the requirements of such a life has been freedom from responsibilities. . . .
>
> This freedom once, as a matter of course, included freedom from domestic responsibilities—from the obligation to wife and children or to husband and children.[20]

[19] Alan E. Bayer, "College Impact on Marriage," *Journal of Marriage and the Family*, 34, no. 4 (Nov. 1972), 602.

[20] Margaret Mead, "Is College Compatible with Marriage?" in *Toward a Sociology of Women*, ed. Constantina Safilios-Rothschild (Lexington, Mass.: Xerox College Publishing, 1972), pp. 116–20.

A word of caution should be said concerning the research that has been done on college marriage. The investigators have detoured around a major problem because they have neglected to consider the student who marries during a vacation period or prior to anticipated reentrance to college and than fails to return to school. Usually no information on the number of married students who drop out of college is provided by researchers. A more comprehensive study needs to be conducted, in which students who marry and fail to continue or complete their education are included. We know that the attrition rate for single students is fairly high; we should seek to determine whether marriage is associated with a higher dropout rate or whether it encourages the student to continue his or her education.

Our present knowledge of the effects of college marriage is, in other words, limited. A couple considering marriage before graduation must rely primarily on their own appraisal of their situation. There are no reliable guideposts to help them make accurate predictions of how their own student marriage will develop.

How do college couples decide when to marry, then? There are many pressures in our society directing students, especially women, toward marriage. And there are equally strong pressures encouraging both men and women toward the highest possible educational achievement. Are those goals mutually exclusive? Most young couples strike some kind of compromise.

Problems in College Marriage

A number of problems are frequently encountered in college marriage. Many of them have been suggested by several of the research studies we have already discussed. They relate to maturity, finances, parenthood, initial marital adjustment, and whether one or both partners are students.

A couple may wish to marry while in college because it seems the thing to do, because many of their friends are married, because it seems an easy and natural outcome of their courtship, or because they covet the status and freedom of married life. But many couples are not really mature enough to accept the full responsibilities involved. They may not realize that there are conflicts between the obligations they will have to each other as husband and wife and their free relationship as single students. They may not recognize the burdens of financial responsibility that will be theirs when they cut loose from parental ties and attempt to balance the budget by themselves. They may not bargain for unplanned pregnancies that put an added strain on their new partnership. They may concentrate on the atmosphere and stimulus of the college community instead of looking deeply enough at their own relationship. Immaturity, which is a danger in any marital relationship, is no stranger to college couples.

The decision to marry in college is a significant one. Most college programs today demand a long workweek. The higher the academic goals held by the students, the harder they will have to work in order to achieve them. It is a well-documented fact that many students cannot meet the competition and fail to finish their college careers. The dropout rate is high. The addition of the full-time job of marriage to the job of being a student is a burdensome one. Although both husband and wife are normally not employed full time, one partner holding a full-time job and the second a part-time job is a common pattern. In most cases both partners need some employment to meet financial needs. Yet the couple must have some time for each other. They cannot be constantly rushing from work to campus and back to work again; they need some social life, some time for relaxation, and some time for their children (if they have any). Unfortunately, some college couples simply cannot make a successful adjustment to the pressure of having two major responsibilities at once.

Another potential source of trouble for college marriages—as for all marriages—is money. The rising cost of a college education has been a matter of increasing concern in the United States. Although the percentage of students enrolled in public colleges and universities, where tuition costs and fees are partially tax supported, has risen steadily in the past twenty years

in comparison with private institutions, it is still very expensive to attend college—probably a minimum of five thousand dollars a year for the student living away from home. The cost is normally regained by subsequent higher earnings, but that does not make the original financial load any lighter. Financing a college marriage, then, is no easy task.

There is usually less parental support for students after marriage. Two together can possibly live as cheaply as two separately, and they may be able to reduce costs, including those of dating. But because they are married, they are expected to be more on their own and to earn, borrow, or receive from scholarships and other sources a much larger share of their budget. If the couple are resourceful and keep expenditures within the limits of the resources available, they can make a successful start toward financial stability. But if they are unused to discipline and sacrifice and are counting on more family support than is likely to be forthcoming, they may be in trouble. More than half the studies of college marriages list finances as a significant or potential source of tension. Financial pressures may discourage the couple and keep them from enjoying and utilizing their college years to the proper extent. And parents may resent the burden of supporting a daughter-in-law or son-in-law in addition to their own son or daughter. It takes a strong and mature couple to handle a heavy financial burden.

Pierre, now twenty-five, and Carole, now twenty-two, met on a four-year college campus, where he was an exchange student from Europe. His scholarship provided full costs for his tuition and living expenses while he was a full-time student in engineering. It also required him to return to his country for a certain term as a civil servant on completion of his studies.

When Carole and Pierre began dating regularly, she was a senior at a nearby women's college. They decided to marry during her last semester, so that she could remain with him during the last two years of his study. After eleven months of marriage, their first child was born two weeks before Christmas Day. This wreaked havoc on their limited budget, since neither had any money saved beyond minimal hospital expenses. They decided that she should seek employment, since he was prohibited under the terms of his scholarship from earning money during the regular semester.

Through home-town friends, Carole was able to find an elementary teaching position at mid-year some thirty-five miles from the college. She arranged to have a college classmate care for her daughter while she commuted to and from work. During the next summer, Pierre sought the most remunerative employment possible, which turned out to be work in a lumber camp out of state. After a summer separated from his family, he returned to college, and they resumed their old routine for the balance of the school year.

Pierre and Carole had an unusually happy marriage. They had many common interests and many mutual friends in the campus community. They planned to return to Europe on his graduation. But few couples would want to marry under such conditions or would be able to adapt to such changing conditions as easily as Pierre and Carole did.

If circumstances become too difficult, both husband and wife may drop out of school. But necessity and tradition seem to dictate that the husband, as the future major breadwinner, take priority in completing his education. However, the college woman may well ask herself, "Will I achieve my expectations by marrying in college? Or will I be a more mature and responsible wife and mother and a more useful and intelligent and concerned member of society if I complete my education before marriage?" Granted, a married woman may make sacrifices gladly, and she may return to school after the financial pressure is relieved or after the children are in school or adequate child care is available. But the woman considering a college marriage should be honest in recognizing that college marriage may not be an aid to her in completing her educational goals.

Sharon Price-Bonham has pointed out that the situation of student couples is different from that of couples in which only the husband is a student. In the past sociologists have put major emphasis on the second group. Price-Bonham analyzed 71 couples in which both husband and wife were students and 125 couples in which only the husband was in school.[21] Her findings substantiated much of the earlier research on characteristics of married students. However, she also discovered that married students showed more individuality when the wife as well as the husband was in college. This showed up in lower marital adjustment scores for those couples on the Marital Adjustment Test developed by Burgess, Locke, and Thomas in 1963.

There are two possible conclusions to be drawn from these findings. One is that individualistic married women students, pursuing their own educational and career goals concurrently with their husbands, will be less satisfied in future years and will in some cases gradually move away from their husbands through psychological or actual physical separation and divorce. The other possible conclusion is that such women will be more stimulating,

[21]Sharon Price-Bonham, "Student Husbands Versus Student Couples," *Journal of Marriage and the Family*, 35, no. 1 (Feb. 1973), 33–37.

exciting, and fulfilled wives, mothers, and partners and that the equality and diversity found in their marriages in their college years will prevent their relationships from becoming stale, utilitarian, and unfulfilling. A great deal more research is needed to determine which conclusion—if either—is valid.

Meanwhile, the feminist movement is questioning the wisdom of a woman giving up her college education while her husband continues his. The "PHT degree"—"Putting Hubby Through"—has little real value to the woman wanting to begin her own career, or forced of necessity to support small children. The increasing emphasis on equality within the marriage relationship and on companionship in marriage makes this problem in college marriage more and more important. If the wife drops out of school and works at a job that is below her potential, she may not be stimulated to think about the same intellectual problems that her husband will face while continuing college. Students considering college marriage need to think carefully about the effect of the woman's dropping out of school.

Another problem of college marriage is handling the responsibilities of parenthood. Most college couples do not intend to have children before graduation, except in the case of forced marriage. Yet a study of any sizable group of married students shows that they often do have children. These frequently unplanned yet important additions to the family are a special concern for the college couple. Can both of them continue their education with an extra mouth to feed? Can they succeed as both students and parents? Although there are many couples who do, it is certainly difficult. Realistically, a couple contemplating college marriage ought to face the possibility that they may have children before one or both of them finish college. If they agree to practice birth control while finishing their education, the problem may not be serious. But the couple ought to talk about what they will do if the woman becomes pregnant and how they will meet the responsibility if they decide to accept it.

Another question is whether or not a college marriage will allow the couple's relationship a natural and successful beginning. The first months of marital adjustment are very important ones; many patterns are set during that period that will have a lasting impact on the marriage. If the couple feel trapped by their situation and by the severe limits on their finances, their free time, and their enjoyment of their new relationship, they may seriously question the wisdom of their marriage.

Making the Choice

Each college couple must make their own choice about engagement, living together, or college marriage. Couples may just continue dating; often they will find their relationship unrewarding and will split up. Others, of course,

may try a combination of two or three of these alternatives, with the decision to marry coming as the final stage in their courtship.[22]

The long-range view may be the most helpful one. If the couple find that they are growing together in their relationship and are able to share mutual hopes and goals, they can take a positive view toward the future. If not, their relationship may need to be carefully and perhaps painfully reevaluated. The choice the couple make will have a major impact on their relationship and on their future marriage and family responsibilities. Their basic values, their moral standards, their relationships to their families, and their place in the larger society are all involved.

Many crucial decisions must be made in life. The decision to become engaged, to begin living together, or to enter a college marriage can certainly be one of the most significant in a person's college career.

SUMMARY

College is the time for decision-making. When you fall in love in college, you must decide how to continue and strengthen the relationship with your partner in the most meaningful way. Will you choose engagement, living together, or a college marriage?

Engagement is the traditional preparation for marriage. It signifies an intention to marry and is a major achievement for both the man and the

[22]See Gerhard Newbeck, "The Decision to Marry While in College," reprinted in *Encounter: Love, Marriage, and Family,* ed. Ruth E. Albrecht and E. Wilbur Bock (Boston: Holbrook, 1972), pp. 138–52.

woman. There are many motivations for engagement; unfortunately, not all of them are good ones.

Ideally, engagement serves to prepare the couple adequately for their marriage and announces their intentions to everyone. The couple should seek to gain the support of family and friends. Bridging the generation gap is important; parental opposition may actually lead to a broken relationship. During this period, the couple should also establish a pattern of joint decision-making.

There are several problem areas in engagement. An abbreviated engagement may not allow the couple adequate time to prepare for marriage. And some couples may become overinvolved with plans for the ceremony and neglect to develop cooperation with each other.

Some contemporary couples choose to live together in a trial marriage rather than to become engaged. Many sociologists have suggested that such arrangements should be given social sanction in order to avoid hasty and unwise marriages. Others suggest that trial marriage should be mandatory. As living together becomes more socially acceptable, it can be examined more objectively. Do the partners really benefit? Many aspects of the trial marriage concept need to be examined more closely. Living together seems to bring problems as well as advantages, however. Emotional attraction may be high, but the couple may not be able to handle their problems and conflicts. Some people question whether any marriage can be successful without one of the most essential elements of love, commitment—an element lacking in trial marriage. And there is some indication that women expect more from trial marriage than men.

College marriage has become an accepted part of campus life since it began after the Second World War. Married students often are older and more mature than single students. However, their academic gains seem more doubtful today than in studies ten or fifteen years ago. The best students do not seem to marry early. Margaret Mead believes that some students may be denied their chance to really explore and experiment in their undergraduate years if they are rushed by social pressure into a college marriage.

Greater emotional maturity is one benefit of college marriage; married students seem better able to cope with their problems. The responsibilities of a family spur the couple on. College marriage also satisfies students' ego needs.

Several problems are typical of college marriage. The couple may not be equal to the responsibilities involved in marriage. Financial demands may force one or both of them to interrupt their education. Children pose another problem. There are serious deficiencies in the research on undergraduate student marriages. As a result, we do not know how many students leave school because of marriage, and we do not know what the effect of marriage in college is on the long-term adjustment of the couple.

SUGGESTED READINGS

Burgess, Ernest W., and Paul Wallin. *Engagement and Marriage.* Philadelphia: Lippincott, 1953. Pioneering study of one thousand engaged couples.

Busselen, Harry J., Jr., and Carroll K. Busselen. "Adjustment Differences Between Married and Single Undergraduate University Students: An Historical Perspective." *The Family Coordinator,* 24, no. 3 (July 1975), 281–87. Review of literature on married students since Second World War. Reflects increasing acceptance of marriage on the college campus.

Hettlinger, Richard E. *Living with Sex: The Student's Dilemma.* New York: Seabury, 1966. Well-written discussion of the sexual attitudes and behavior of college students from the perspective of an Episcopalian chaplain.

Hicks, Mary W. "An Empirical Evaluation of Textbook Assumptions About Engagement," *The Family Coordinator,* 19, no. 1 (Jan. 1970), 57–63. Study of engaged couples at a large Eastern university. Takes a favorable view of the engagement experience.

Newbeck, Gerhard. "The Decision to Marry While in College." Reprinted in *Encounter: Love, Marriage, and Family,* ed. Ruth E. Albrecht and E. Wilbur Bock. Boston: Holbrook, 1972, pp. 138–52. Surveys the positive and negative aspects of college marriage.

Ridley, Carl A., Dan J. Peterman, and Arthur W. Avery. "Cohabitation: Does It Make for a Better Marriage?" *The Family Coordinator,* 27, no. 2 (April 1978), 129–36. Analysis of different types of living-together relationships and their outcomes.

Roy, Rustum, and Della Roy. "Is Monogamy Outdated?" Reprinted in *Human Sexuality: Contemporary Perspectives,* ed. Eleanor S. Morrison and Vera Borosage. Palo Alto, Calif.: National Press Books, 1973, pp. 143–59. Authors advocate more liberal premarital sexual attitudes and suggest revised courtship code to include living together with engagement.

Schulman, Marion L. "Idealization in Engaged Couples," *Journal of Marriage and the Family,* 36, no. 1 (Feb. 1974), 139–47. Survey of engaged and seriously dating couples, with analysis of their romantic, idealistic, and realistic attitudes toward each other and marriage.

Spanier, Graham B. "Romanticism and Marital Adjustment," *Journal of Marriage and the Family,* 34, no. 3 (Aug. 1972), 481–87. Relates romantic attitudes prior to marriage to the actual adjustment patterns of married couples.

9 Variations in Marriage Partnerships

- What effects do the variations in marriage patterns have on the individual and the couple?
- What are the motivations for interfaith marriage? What problems may arise in such marriages?
- What factors have caused an increase in interracial marriages? What effect will this increase have on society?
- Why is there a special interest in black-white marriages?
- How does divorce affect subsequent marriages?
- What other variations in marriage are important? What effect do they have on marital adjustment and happiness?

Some Premarital Decisions

There are many decisions to be made before the final commitment to marry. Decisions that may seem simple when dating or "going steady" become much more complicated when the responsibilities of marriage are seriously considered. Should a person marry someone with a different religious background or with no religious faith at all? Should a man and woman of different races marry? Should a college student marry a divorced person? And what about variations—marriage to a person of a different social class, to a person much older or younger, or to a serviceman? Many people may consider at least one of these possibilities before taking the final step to marriage.

Interfaith Marriage

One common variation in American marriage patterns involves marriage to a person of a different faith. Since America has major Protestant, Roman Catholic, and Jewish groups, as well as many other smaller religious bodies, there is frequent contact between people of different faiths and some crossing of religious lines in both courtship and marriage. We will examine the frequency of interfaith marriages; problems that are common to many mixed marriages; views of religious bodies toward interfaith marriages; and factors that influence a person's decision to marry or not to marry a person of another faith.

Most studies of interfaith marriage stress the following definition of *religious:* "To be religious is to be a member of a religious community." All great living religions have had some institutional form. It is doubtful that Judaism would have survived without rabbis and synagogues, Buddhism without priests and temples, Catholicism without priests, nuns, and churches, or Protestantism without ministers, lay leaders, and churches. However, only 60 or 61 percent of the American population is formally affiliated with a definite church or synagogue in any one year. Still, we customarily list an unaffiliated person as Catholic, Protestant, or Jewish when he states that as his religious preference.

There are many ways of looking at religion—for instance in terms of one's view of God or one's philosophical orientation. But those concepts are difficult to isolate as factors in marital happiness; two people who seem to share the same theology may belong to different classes, cultures, or races. Similarity in religious viewpoint may be a positive factor in marriage, but it is difficult to disentangle from other variables. The most direct sociological measure of religious interest is usually the regularity of church or synagogue attendance. Most studies show that Roman Catholics attend church most frequently, followed by Protestants, with Jews spending the least amount of time within their houses of worship.[1] But the mixed marriage rate is not necessarily directly related to religious interest, undoubtedly because other factors in addition to religious loyalty are involved in the final choice of a marriage partner. Religion might also be thought of in both sociological and psychological terms. Sociology stresses the institutional nature of religion, while psychology is concerned more with commitment or faith.[2] In studying interfaith marriage, it is helpful to make use of both the sociological and the psychological points of view.

Frequency of Interfaith Marriage

There have been a number of sociological studies to determine the frequency of interfaith marriage. In early American life, religion often played a dominant role in courtship and marriage, because many of the colonies, especially in New England, tended to be homogeneous in religious composition.

[1]Gerhard Lenski, *The Religious Factor* (Garden City, N.Y.: Doubleday, 1961), pp. 32–38.
[2]See Charles W. Estes and Michael A. Overington, "The Meaning and End of Religiosity," *American Journal of Sociology*, 75, no. 5 (March 1970), 760–78.

After the establishment of the United States, with continued immigration and expansion to the West, religious homogeneity started to weaken in many communities. The lack of close contact with traditional churches or denominations and the relaxation of social controls caused more mixed marriages to be contracted. However, the more stable and settled communities in the East, South, and Midwest still tended to restrict such mixed marriages.

Study of the interfaith marriage rate is complicated by at least one methodological problem. If, for example, we are studying 10 marriages involving Catholic men and women, we can compute the interfaith rate in two ways. Let us take a sample in which 6 Catholic men marry 6 Catholic women and 4 Catholic men marry 4 non-Catholic women. The rate for interfaith marriages is 40 percent (4 in 10); but the rate for individuals is only 25 percent, since only 4 of the 16 Catholic individuals in the sample married out of their faith. Current research, unfortunately, does not make this distinction clear. There are no comprehensive state or national records of interfaith marriage, since marriage licenses in almost all states do not list this information. Also, it is difficult to discover if there has been a change in the stated religion of one or both partners. A study by Larry Bumpass suggests that the frequency of such intermarriage doubled in the post-Second World War period.[3] The continued mobility of our population, and the increasing secularization of American culture, are undoubtedly major factors in such a rise.

The carefully documented study by Lenski of Protestants, Catholics, and Jews in Detroit showed that 85 percent of the white Protestants and Catholics in the sample reported that their spouses were of the same major faith, which would indicate a 15 percent interfaith marriage rate. But when the couples'

[3]Larry L. Bumpass, "The Trend of Interfaith Marriage in the United States," *Social Biology*, 17, no. 3 (June 1970), 253–59.

religious backgrounds were checked, it was found that only 68 percent of them had been reared in the same faith.[4] Thus 32 percent of the couples were involved in interfaith marriage if family training and influence are considered. A study of interfaith marriage in a medium-sized Midwestern city by Nicholas Babchuk, Harry I. Crockett, Jr., and John A. Ballweg suggested that an even larger number of switches in religious affiliation takes place before and during the early years of marriage, if changes within Protestant denominations are considered. The respondents all had stable marriages of at least ten years' duration and included Catholics, Jews, and some twenty-three Protestant denominations. All were parents of sixth-grade children. The authors found that a change in religious affiliation had occurred in 73 percent (105 of 144) of the marriages in their sample.[5] At that stage 84 percent (88 of 105) of the couples had achieved a common religious affiliation, although many of them were of different backgrounds.

A further study by the same authors in another Midwestern city yielded results similar to their earlier research. There were more Catholics in the second study, so the Catholic intermarriage rate was lower. The church attendance of Catholic wives proved to be uniformly regular, whether or not their marriages were mixed.[6]

Reasons for Interfaith Marriage

What is the motivation that leads men and women to marry a person outside of their own faith? Wade C. Roof has proposed that traditional religion's place in contemporary society depends to a large extent on the network of attachment and interaction within local communities. In accordance with Roof's theory, to be a part of a traditional church would mean that a person feels at home with his church or synagogue group because it satisfies a number of his social as well as religious needs. Roof's measure of religiosity includes the following:

> *Church Attendance.* The frequency of attendance at Sunday [or Sabbath] worship services.
>
> *Religious Organizations.* The number of church groups (e.g., choirs, men's clubs, study groups) in which the respondent regularly participates.
>
> *Congregational Friendships.* Out of the four closest friends, the number who belong to the same congregation.

[4]Lenski, p. 49.

[5]Nicholas Babchuk, Harry I. Crockett, Jr., and John A. Ballweg, "Changes in Religious Affiliation and Family Stability," *Social Forces,* 45, no. 4 (June 1967), 551–55.

[6]Harry I. Crockett, Jr., Nicholas Babchuk, and John A. Ballweg, "Changes in Religious Affiliation and Family Stability: A Second Study," *Journal of Marriage and the Family,* 31, no. 3 (Aug. 1969), 464–68.

Doctrinal Orthodoxy. Scale consisting of orthodox responses about God, Jesus, Heaven and Hell, and the Bible. [Such scales are sometimes hard to measure. This scale was tested and seems to be reasonably consistent and reliable.]

Devotionalism. Scale combining responses regarding frequency of personal prayer and Bible reading. [There is a fairly strong correlation between these two responses.][7]

The implication of Roof's research is clear. If you fall in love with a person who is able to share a number of these associations with you within your own faith (intrafaith), you will not have a strong motivation for intermarriage. But if you can cross over to share with a partner outside your church in some, if not all, of these five areas, an interfaith marriage becomes a distinct possibility.

There are other factors that can be cited, such as mobility. Today's college students travel extensively to areas far away from their homes. The chances of meeting and marrying a person of another faith during travel are much higher than in one's parental home. City living also tends to break down cultural and religious exclusivity. In a small town, social classes and religious groups may live in mutually exclusive areas and mingle very little socially. But in cities like New York, Los Angeles, and Houston, family and religious background do not carry the same weight, especially early in courtship, that they would in a small town or a rural area. In addition, dating and courtship are usually carried on in public rather than at home. Many couples still spend some dating time at home, but the idea of a young man putting in an hour or two at home talking to parents in order to convince them that he is suitable company for their daughter is out of date. The whole trend of courtship in our society is toward a free and unrestricted choice of partner, with few limitations set by parents, society, or established custom. We are not surprised when a local student dates an international student, when a veteran is married to a woman he met overseas, or when two students of different religious or ethnic backgrounds start going steady.

In addition, the greater tolerance of different religions that has come about in the past decade or so is giving a certain de facto approval to mixed marriage. Our democratic system has always given such approval in theory, but in practice there has been considerable prejudice against interfaith marriage, with many social controls operating to prevent it. Now that there is more dialogue between the major religious groups, there is less strong emotional feeling against mixed marriage. However, this tolerance is not universal; some religious leaders still strongly oppose interfaith marriage.

[7]Wade Clark Roof, "Traditional Religion in Contemporary Society: A Theory of Local-Cosmopolitan Plausibility," *American Sociological Review*, 41, no. 2 (April 1976), 206.

The increasing rate of divorce is apparently also contributing to the rise in the interfaith marriage rate. Erich Rosenthal has shown that the proportion of Jewish intermarriages in Iowa and Indiana is higher among couples married more than once than it is among the general population. For example, in Iowa, 34.3 percent of marriages of Jewish men to never-married women were interfaith marriages; 63.6 percent of marriages of Jewish men to twice-divorced women were interfaith.[8]

The frequency of interfaith marriage among Roman Catholics has been a subject of much interest and research. Until the changes authorized by the late Pope Paul VI, the requirement that the Ante-Nuptial Agreement be signed by the non-Catholic partner distinctly put the pressure on the couple to make Catholicism the dominant faith in the family, regardless of the wishes of the non-Catholic. What then motivates Roman Catholics to marry outside their faith? According to John Thomas:

> *Percentage of Catholics.* First, the proportion of Catholics in the total population greatly influences the intermarriage rates of Catholics in different sections of the country. The relative scarcity of prospective marriage mates within one's own religious group leads to a high rate of intermarriage wherever ethnic and/or social status differences do not prevent occupational and social contacts. . . .
>
> *Cohesive Ethnic Groups.* The second factor is the presence of close-knit ethnic subgroups in the community. . . . We have shown how well the prohibition on outgroup marriage operates in those parishes where ethnic solidarity is strong. However, there are many factors combining to produce this effect. . . .
>
> *Socioeconomic Status.* A third factor appears to be the socioeconomic class of the Catholic population in the community. Intermarriage rates seem to be closely related to socioeconomic status. This hypothesis is advanced tentatively since adequate statistical support is still lacking. However, we have made studies of several communities which furnish rather substantial evidence that the hypothesis is well founded. . . . This study gives every indication of a rather close association between socioeconomic status and intermarriage since the percentage increases from 8.5 in the lower rental areas to 19.3 in the suburban parish.[9]

The conclusions Thomas reaches are shared by other sociologists, with a single exception. It has been suggested that the third tentative hypothesis,

[8]Erich Rosenthal, "Divorce and Religious Intermarriage," *Journal of Marriage and the Family*, 32, no. 3 (Aug. 1970), 439.

[9]John L. Thomas, *The American Catholic Family* (Englewood Cliffs, N.J.: Prentice-Hall, 1956), pp. 155–58.

that the higher social classes intermarry more frequently, may not be accurate. Perhaps many women marry into higher social classes and in so doing change their religious affiliations; since they are not married in their original churches, they will not be listed in parish marriage records.[10]

Problems in Interfaith Marriage

Although there are many successful interfaith marriages, there are a number of potential problems that should be discussed and resolved by couples before marriage. Resolution of these problems may be possible after marriage, but the problems may put a severe strain on the relationship.

Interfaith marriage links partners of different religious and cultural backgrounds. There may also be differences in ethnic origin and other social variables. The more widely separated the religious communities of the interfaith couple are, the more serious may be the problems.

Do interfaith marriages have a higher divorce rate than those with no religious difference? In most surveys, the answer is yes. The homogeneous Jewish couples seem to have the lowest divorce rate, with Catholic couples next, and Protestant couples the highest of the three major groups. Ethnic, cultural, and social differences must also be considered here. Are Catholic communities more homogeneous than Protestant ones? More data are needed here. One national study shows a higher divorce rate for interfaith couples, but a smaller difference than in surveys of a generation ago.[11] The results of this study are shown in Table 9–1.

We do not know how many interfaith marriages do not end in divorce, yet within the intact marriage relationship there may be a low level of satisfaction. The stigma of divorce is still strong in many families and groups, so that the partners may feel an obligation not to divorce, and will remain in an unhappy marriage.

One problem in interfaith marriage is in role or value conflict. Closely associated with a religious difference may be differences in family training, ethnic traditions, or attitudes toward employment, politics, or use of leisure time. Each partner may want to play a role quite different from the desires and expectations of the spouse. Value conflicts may occur over attitudes toward sex, birth control, or personal behavior. Most families are able to solve these value problems, although in many cases the solution is simply to drop both religions or to let one partner take all the responsibility for religious life and teaching while the other becomes a silent partner. Some mixed cou-

[10]See also Paul H. Besanceney, S.J., *Interfaith Marriages: Who and Why* (New Haven, Conn.: College and University Press, 1970).

[11]Larry L. Bumpass and James A. Sweet, "Differentials in Marital Instability: 1970," *American Sociological Review*, 37, no. 4 (Dec. 1972), 754–66.

Table 9–1 Stability of Interfaith and Intrafaith Marriages: Percent of First Marriages Among White Women Under Age 45 in 1970 Ending in Divorce or Separation

Religion of Husband	*Religion of Wife*	*Percent of Unstable Marriages*
Jewish	Jewish	4.4
Catholic	Catholic	9.3
Protestant	Protestant	15.1
Other*	Other	15.1
Other	Catholic	13.8
Catholic	Other	18.2
Catholic	Protestant	19.9
Protestant	Catholic	20.6
Protestant	Other	22.6
Other	Protestant	28.1

*Not member of three major groups.

SOURCE: Adapted from Larry L. Bumpass and James A. Sweet, "Differentials in Marital Instability: 1970," *American Sociological Review,* 37, no. 4 (Dec. 1972), 754–66.

ples try to divide the children between the two faiths; but this solution may place great pressure on the children. Other couples compromise on a religion midway between the religions of mother and father. As indicated in the Babchuk, Crockett, and Ballweg study (see page 248), many couples switch to a common religious community either just before or just after their marriage in order to avoid conflicts.[12]

A recent study of the religious affiliation of sons of religious intermarriages, using a sample of army inductees at Fort Dix, New Jersey, showed some interesting results.[13] If the father was Protestant and the mother Catholic the sons were more likely to be Catholic. But the sons of Catholic fathers and Protestant mothers were almost equally divided between the two faiths. The most noticeable difference in the frequency of church attendance was shown by the Protestant sons of Catholic father-Protestant mother marriages. Over 50 percent of them were either nonattenders or irregular attenders.

[12]Babchuk, Crockett, and Ballweg, "Changes in Religious Affiliation and Family Stability."
[13]Sydney H. Croog and James E. Teele, "Religious Identity and Church Attendance of Sons of Religious Intermarriages," *American Sociological Review,* 32, no. 1 (Feb. 1967), 93–103.

Entering an Interfaith Marriage

The decision to enter an interfaith marriage is not an easy one. In addition to the religious beliefs and values of each partner, a number of personal, family, social, and ethical values enter into the decision. Almost everyone has a bias in these cases: a bias in favor of the religious faith of one partner or the other; a bias strongly against one religion or the other; or a bias against facing the issue squarely. However, since so many people contemplate a mixed marriage at one time or another during courtship, a very serious attempt to tackle the problem should be made.

The choice of a partner of a different faith is closely related to the strength and vitality of one's own religious convictions. If a man or woman has a strong and meaningful religious faith, and has been able to develop it both in public worship and relationships and in his or her private life, it is natural to expect that faith will be an important factor in the choice of a marriage partner. If a man or woman has no religious faith or experience, or if religion is only of peripheral value, then religious affiliation will be a minor or unimportant part of the decision to marry.

Fifty years ago many religious groups condemned interfaith marriages unequivocally. We live in a more tolerant age, and some religious leaders are now sounding a more optimistic note.

Paul and Jeanne Simon are optimistic about mixed marriages between Protestants and Catholics. They feel that a family should follow the religion of the more active partner (who is often the wife) but that both faiths can make contributions to the marriage and to family life. The Simons' major guidelines may be summarized as follows.

1. The decision on what religious affiliation a couple will have should ideally be made before engagement, but in any event as quickly as possible.
2. If a couple are religiously indifferent, their children probably will be also.
3. If the answer to what a couple's religious affiliation should be is not obvious, two factors should be considered: which spouse is more religiously active and what the affiliation of the mother is.
4. Nothing derogatory should ever be said around the children about either partner's church.
5. Most home religious activities are things that can be done in common—prayers, devotions, Advent-wreath ceremonies, applying faith to life. A family should do those things together.
6. There is good religious literature that is acceptable to both Protestants and Catholics.
7. A good Protestant-Catholic home presents an unusually fine oppor-

tunity to think through the fundamentals of Christian faith and teach understanding for the beliefs of others.[14]

There may be problems connected with unwanted children in an interfaith marriage. Bean and Aiken have shown that there were "significant differences in the prevalence of unwanted fertility between interfaith couples in the United States," based on a detailed analysis of the 1965 National Fertility Study by Ryder and Westoff.[15] Age and educational heterogamy did not make such a difference, but the differences in values, life goals, and priorities that are associated with religion did make a difference. Here again, the choices that each partner makes, in view of his or her own value structure, are crucial.

SOME GUIDELINES

What guidelines are available to couples considering a mixed religious marriage? During the college years many students have religious doubts and questions. As a result many young adults have no active religious affiliation. They choose to ignore religious considerations in marriage as the simplest, and perhaps the most honest, course. But the responsibilities of marriage, and possible parenthood, cast a different light on the matter. Religious commitment is often a mark of maturity and self-development, and can strengthen the total family relationship. If one enters an interfaith marriage, or marries a person with no religious faith at all, conflicts may develop. The growth of spiritual maturity and understanding may be hindered if the marriage partners are pulling in two different directions. Perhaps there may be a disparity between the spiritual interest and sensitivity of one partner and the disinterest of the other. On the other hand, to marry a person who has a strong religious conviction very different from your own poses another difficulty. If there is any sense of purpose and fulfillment in your religious faith, it will be self-defeating to marry a person who denies or disagrees with that faith.

Interracial Marriage

Interracial marriage is a significant variation in marriage patterns, and it is a subject of great interest to the contemporary college generation. Today, students in colleges and universities meet fellow students of all ethnic and racial backgrounds, and it is natural to have social contact between the dif-

[14]Paul and Jeanne Simon, *Protestant-Catholic Marriages Can Succeed* (New York: Association Press, 1967), pp. 87–88.

[15]Frank D. Bean and Linda H. Aiken, "Intermarriage and Unwanted Fertility in the United States," *Journal of Marriage and the Family*, 38, no. 1 (Feb. 1976), 61–72.

ferent groups. The invalidation of miscegenation laws by the Supreme Court in 1967 removed the legal barriers to interracial marriage that existed for over two hundred years. It seems proper that civil rights should extend to the choice of one's marriage partner, but legal changes will not necessarily bring about rapid changes in the social customs of many American communities. Total acceptance of interracial marriage (and, indeed, other types of mixed marriage) will probably come about only over a long period of time, extending at least one or two generations into the future.

The large metropolitan areas, such as New York, Chicago, Los Angeles, and Philadelphia, will undoubtedly show a greater frequency of interracial marriage than small communities. Nevertheless, even in the impersonal, and therefore relatively tolerant, urban setting, interracial marriages are subject to special tensions and problems. And the great mobility of our society makes the chances fairly high that an interracial couple will be moving to a new home at least four or five times during their married lives and will need to make new adjustments to their neighbors and communities in each of those situations.

Thomas Monahan has made a careful study of interracial marriage in Indiana before and after the repeal of Indiana's law against racial intermarriage in 1965. Table 9–2 indicates the interracial marriage rate from 1962 to 1967 and reflects this change in the law.

Monahan's study shows clearly that there was a significant rise in the interracial-marriage rate when the miscegenation law was repealed. How many of these marriages represented a legalization of common law marriages is not known. The low mixed-marriage rate (only 4.63 percent for blacks with whites in 1967) is much less than would have occurred by chance, and much less than the religious intermarriage rate we have just discussed. Future pro-

Table 9–2 Trend in Interracial Marriage, Indiana: 1962–1967

Year	Percent of Marriages Mixed by Race* Total	White	Negro Total	Negro with White	Other
All Years	.35	.36	2.84	2.65	58.34
1962–1964	.25	.27	1.76	1.66	54.21
1965–1967	.43	.44	3.73	3.46	61.48
1962	.26	.27	1.93	1.90	61.86
1963	.26	.26	1.83	1.65	50.35
1964	.25	.26	1.53	1.47	52.86
1965	.36	.37	2.60	2.41	57.23
1966	.41	.43	3.87	3.62	60.14
1967	.52	.53	4.26	4.63	66.32

*Based on the universe of cases (290,193). Each race was calculated separately.
Results developed from punch cards made available to the writer by Barber and Christensen show the following comparable figures for 1960: .18, .19, 1.10, 1.02, 55.95; and for 1961: .21, .22, 1.35, 1.24, 57.84 percent.

SOURCE: Thomas P. Monahan, "Marriage Across Racial Lines in Indiana," *Journal of Marriage and the Family*, 35, no. 4 (Nov. 1973), 634. Copyrighted 1973 by the National Council on Family Relations. Reprinted by permission.

jections are difficult to make, since a linear rise in the rate cannot be predicted on the small amount of evidence available.

Other trends noted in the Indiana study: More of the interracial marriages were civil ceremonies as compared to the marriages of homogamous white couples; a larger number of interracial couples were involved in remarriages. Men in interracial couples also tended to be older than those marrying within their own race. Monahan, who specialized for many years in data on interracial marriage, further confirmed the rising rate of intermarriage in a study published in 1976. He notes that the civil rights movement, and steps taken to preserve individual privacy, have made it more difficult for the social analyst to examine full and accurate records on the subject of interracial marriage. Some of his conclusions indicate possible trends in this area in the future:

> The differential proclivity of the sexes in regard to entrance into interracial marriage is seen to vary with the particular races concerned. . . In

> the data presented here, in seven out of ten cases of the marriages of Negroes with Whites, the male is Negro; in the marriages of Other Races with Whites, the male partner is more often White. Although the Negro male is in the majority in racial crossings of Negroes and Other Races, an unusual condition appears in the South where, in 60 to 70 percent of the interracially married couples (Negroes with Other Races), the wife is Negro.
>
> . . .The overall incidence of interracial marriage is small but it is rising, particularly the marriages of Negroes with Whites. From the point of view of the minority, biological amalgamation is considerable. As the phenomenon grows, more attention will be given to it, by the minorities if not by the majority.[16]

Black-White Marriages

The most controversial unions in our society have been between blacks and whites. This is probably the case because of both the heritage of slavery and the marked physical differences between blacks and whites. David Heer has made a comparison of census data of marriages between blacks and whites in 1960 and 1970.[17] His study also shows an increase in interracial marriage in most cases during the ten-year period. The totals are represented by type and region in Table 9–3. They show a 26 percent increase for the United States as a whole, but with certain exceptions. The husband-white, wife-black category declined in all tabulations, and all types of interracial marriage showed a decline in the South.

The accuracy of these figures is difficult to verify. Monahan was particularly critical of the interpretation given by Heer.[18] It seems clear that the study of interracial marriage must be continued on two levels: (1) the collection of the most accurate data possible; and (2) an adequate interpretation of these data based on all information available to us.

Interracial marriage is complicated by the different cultural, social, and economic factors involved. Melton and Thomas have attempted to analyze some of these factors in their study of "Instrumental and Expressive Values in Mate Selection of Black and White College Students."[19] They found, for

[16]Thomas P. Monahan, "An Overview of Statistics on Interracial Marriage in the United States, with Data on Its Extent from 1963–1970," *Journal of Marriage and the Family,* 38, no. 2 (May 1976), 223–31.

[17]David M. Heer, "The Prevalence of Black-White Marriage in the United States, 1960 and 1970," *Journal of Marriage and the Family,* 36, no. 2 (May 1974), 246–58.

[18]Thomas P. Monahan, "Letters to the Editor, Critique of Heer's Article," *Journal of Marriage and the Family,* 36, no. 4 (Nov. 1974), 669–71. See also David M. Heer, "Reply to Monahan," 671–72.

[19]Willie Melton and Darwin L. Thomas, *Journal of Marriage and the Family,* 38, no. 3 (Aug. 1976), 509–17.

Table 9–3 Number of Black-White Marriages by Type and Region, United States: 1960 and 1970

	1960	*1970*	*Percentage Change Since 1960*
United States: Total	51,409	64,789	+ 26.0
Husband black, wife white	25,496	41,223	+ 61.7
Husband white, wife black	25,913	23,566	− 9.1
North and West: Total	30,977	51,420	+ 66.0
Husband black, wife white	16,872	34,937	+107.1
Husband white, wife black	14,105	16,483	+ 16.9
South: Total	20,432	13,369	− 34.6
Husband black, wife white	8,624	6,286	− 27.1
Husband white, wife black	11,808	7,083	− 40.0

SOURCE: David M. Heer, "The Prevalence of Black-White Marriage in the United States, 1960 and 1970," *Journal of Marriage and the Family,* 36, no. 2 (May 1974), 247. Copyrighted 1974 by the National Council on Family Relations. Reprinted by permission.

example, that black respondents placed more value on instrumental (functional) dimensions in mate selection, but were much the same as white respondents in regard to the expressive (emotional) dimension.

For generations the case for and against black-white marriages was debated by white leaders and scholars, who often only summarized their own prejudices. Now we can see the picture from the black perspective. Clotye M. Larsson expresses the issue in this way:

> The Negro's response is likewise defensive. Condemned to burn on the pyre of history for three hundred years because of the white man's visions of sorcery, the Negro masses are understandably unprepared to thrust more of their dreams into the flames. . . .
>
> A man under attack learns to be careful. Suffering—unimaginable, unendurable, unremitting suffering—has taught the Negro to walk softly and beware of the big stick. A man under attack learns to measure his goals, to define them with precision, and to outline his means of getting from where he is to where he wants to be by the least perilous route. First things *do* come first. Survival comes first. Food. Clothing. Job. Shelter. Recreation. Creature comforts.

> Free access to hamburger stands and restrooms is for every man. But interracial marriage? That is for the few. The very few. . . .[20]

The whole pattern of racial relationships in our society is a tragic one. Jim Crow laws and social customs served in the past to implement a social, moral, and religious code that condemned mixed marriages. However, the related double standard did not necessarily condemn sexual union between the races, and the large number of mulattoes in both South and North attests to the fact that such unions were fairly frequent.

The social controls that operate to limit racial intermarriage are well known. Although those controls are being lessened through the breakdown of school segregation, the integration of public facilities, and other measures imposed on society by political and legal means, they still have tremendous influence.

Issues in Interracial Marriage

There are a number of important issues involved in interracial marriage. The question of motivation is crucial. Why does one want to marry a person of a different racial and cultural background from his or her own? Why risk the criticism of family and friends by marrying outside one's own racial or national group? A primary motivation in American society, of course, is romantic love. But other factors are certainly influential in the final decision. Is one or both partners highly idealistic and willing to risk personal discomfort or ostracism in order to exemplify the freedom and individuality in which they sincerely believe? Or is rebellion against parents, friends, or rigid social controls a major influence? Does one of the partners favor the marriage because it means a step up in social status? These and other possible motivations should be carefully examined by the couple contemplating interracial marriage.

Greater freedom of dating between different races and nationalities has undoubtedly served as a stimulus toward interracial marriage on college campuses. Very often college communities contain a number of interracially married couples who married during their college years, and decided to remain near an academic environment. But interracial couples often find an urban environment equally favorable, and antidiscrimination laws in housing and employment have made it possible for them to find a welcome in an increasing number of American communities.

Another significant issue in interracial marriage is the reaction of family and friends to the mixed racial marriage. The family of the black spouse may

[20]Clotye M. Larsson, ed., *Marriage Across the Color Line* (Chicago: Johnson, 1965), pp. vii–viii.

be more open to the marriage than that of the white spouse. (The recent upsurge of black consciousness has made racial intermarriage unattractive to many blacks, however.) In most cases the easiest place to find housing is the black residential section, and that may lead to closer contact with the black parental family. However, the problems of interracial marriages seem to be concentrated within adult relationships; the children of the marriages apparently do not have all the traumatic experiences hypothesized for them. And the increasing openness of our society certainly indicates that children of the coming generations will be far less prejudiced than their parents. It is fast becoming unnecessary to talk in terms of incidents of discrimination and prejudice in 1958 or 1968. Today's interracial children, fortunately, are growing up in a far different America.

Still another important issue in interracial marriage has to do with social, ethical, educational, and religious values. It is possible that couples from two different races, with different social, cultural, and educational backgrounds, will also have wide variation in values. The things that are important to one partner may not have the same importance to the other. Similar educational background does not necessarily mean that the couples have identical value structures. Values should be carefully and thoughtfully discussed before

Table 9–4 Proportion of Marriages in Which Both Husband and Wife Married Only Once, by Race: 1970

Husband Black, Wife White	*Husband White, Wife Black*	*Husband Black, Wife Black*	*Husband White, Wife White*
61.1%	67.4%	72.7%	80.7%

SOURCE: David M. Heer, "The Prevalence of Black-White Marriage in the United States, 1960 and 1970," *Journal of Marriage and the Family,* 36, no. 2 (May 1974), 250. Copyrighted 1974 by the National Council on Family Relations. Reprinted by permission.

marriage. The rising educational level of blacks in our society, reflected in the educational level of those in interracial marriages, often contributes to the strength and stability of these marriages.

Another question to be considered is this: How stable will an interracial marriage be? Is there more or less chance of divorce when partners of two different races marry? Heer's study in 1974 indicated that a lower percentage of spouses who entered interracial marriage were in a first marriage than if the partners were of the same race. The tabulation is shown in Table 9–4. This may indicate that divorced persons were more willing to break with tradition and try an interracial marriage for a second marriage.

One piece of evidence suggesting greater stability in marriage for a black-white couple was documented by Monahan in an Iowa study. He stated:

> In the divorce rate analysis it was found that Negro-Negro marriages were twice as unstable as white-white marriages. Most remarkable, however, it was also found that in Iowa mixed Negro marriages were more stable than Negro-Negro marriages, and the Negro husband with a white wife showed the lowest divorce ratio in the four-way comparison [even lower than white-white marriages].
>
> . . . It may well be that at present the racial intermarriage process for Negroes may produce more deliberateness in the marriage decision, and this with other selective factors may create a more lasting bond than generally prevails.[21]

Joseph R. Washington states the case for racial intermarriage in these words:

> The case for black-white unions is fundamentally the case for America, an America rid of its evil past of racism, which strides forward with black

[21]Thomas P. Monahan, "Are Interracial Marriages Really Less Stable?" *Social Forces,* 48, no. 4 (June 1970), 470.

and white fully accepting one another. Full acceptance is what marriage means—union in mutual fidelity and trust, in adversity and good times, until death parts us.

Our need is nothing less than rebirth as a nation. Rebirth of this nation requires dominant whites to perceive our common history through the black experience—to think black, to feel black, to become black. The real question is, can whites become black, not can blacks become white. The latter is the old question which leaves speculation about genetic manipulation or even black self-hatred on dead center. To be black is really a conditioned experience; it is less a matter of genetics. Given the historic argument that one drop of black blood makes one black, it can be safely argued that it is impossible to know who is black, that what matters is for us all to accept our common blackness as the precious value it is.[22]

Marriage to a Divorced Person

The high frequency of divorce in the United States means that there is a large number of divorced persons in almost every American community. The rate has been estimated as high as four out of every ten marriages for young women now in their late twenties. Most divorced men and women remarry, and it is natural that some of them, particularly men in their twenties and thirties, should meet potential partners who are in college. In a later chapter we will discuss more thoroughly the entire subject of divorce. Here we will concentrate primarily on the decision to marry a divorced person and how that decision can be made intelligently.

Major Considerations

The first question asked by a person considering marrying a divorced partner is this: "Will our marriage work out, or will it also fail?" If a man or woman has seen one marriage end in divorce, will it be that much easier for a subsequent marriage to end the same way? There is no certain answer to these questions. The majority of remarried persons are able to achieve stability in their second marriage. But many do not.

The factors that enable some people to succeed where others fail are undoubtedly complex. It would be logical to look for a higher degree of personal compatibility and satisfaction with a divorced person than would be ex-

[22]Joseph R. Washington, Jr., *Marriage in Black and White* (Boston: Beacon, 1970), p. 335.

pected with a person never before married. In our culture, it is assumed that people who marry are in love. But the meaning of love, as we saw in Chapter 7, may be different for different couples. The love one has for a divorced person needs to have particular depth and strength, because it will be tested by situations that do not always occur when marriage is a new experience for both partners.

Another problem is whether the parental family will accept marriage to a divorced person. One reason that society is more tolerant of divorce today is that there is a more general awareness of the stresses and strains on married life. People are less apt to be critical of divorced couples. One's family, on the other hand, may be less hesitant to criticize. They may have strong religious convictions; they may resist involvement in the more complex relationships with a divorced person, and possibly stepchildren. They may have preferred another possible partner.

Some divorced persons try to escape such criticism by moving away from family and in-laws. That helps by minimizing the friction of daily and weekly contacts with family members who do not approve of divorce. But it may be an unrealistic or defensive way of dealing with the problem. Our emotional and psychological ties with our families are so great that it is generally a poor sign if a person is trying to develop maturely and is, at the same time, rudely severing family bonds.

Children of a prior marriage may bring difficulties for the new couple too. When a prospective marriage partner is the father of children in the custody of their mother, a whole set of complications is added to the relationship. If, on the other hand, one is to become a stepmother or stepfather to the children, a new set of responsibilities is involved. There are conflicting loyalties to spouse and children and the problems of affection, discipline, and guidance for children other than one's own. All these complications need to be evaluated carefully. This is one of the most critical problems facing the person contemplating marriage to a divorced person.

And one might raise the question whether the divorced person has the same feeling about marriage and the permanency of the marriage relationship as the person who has never been married before. It is logical to expect those intangible attitudes to affect the success of a marriage.

Chances of Success

Is it possible to have a successful marriage with a divorced person? If you are trying to decide whether or not you should marry a divorced person, you may want to ask yourself the following four questions. The way in which you answer them should help you to determine what decision to make.

First you should ask seriously: "How marriageable are we? Are we really meant for each other?" You ought to score and rescore your strengths and weaknesses in a possible marriage partnership. You need to have a number of plus factors favoring your marriage to overcome the possible difficulties springing from the problems of a prior divorce.

You should also seek an honest answer to the question: "How has this divorced person grown or changed since the divorce?" Was the divorce brought on by immaturity and impulsiveness? What change have two or three years brought in his or her personality? Did he foolishly become involved with a teenage girl while in military service and marry her hastily and unwisely? What indications do you have that he recognizes his failures in that experience and can profit from them in a second marriage? Or take the case of a young woman, married at seventeen because she was in constant conflict with her parents and anxious to be free of their restraint. What indications are there that she now has a more mature and responsible attitude toward her future, and toward that of her two-year-old daughter?

The answers, of course, might be evaluated in light of a third question: "Who was at fault in the broken marriage?" This is legal terminology and also has definite religious connotations. Before the advent of no-fault divorce laws, it was expected that the "guilt" of one party (in terms of desertion, cruelty, adultery, or some other action) would be established before the divorce could be granted. However, although the question of guilt or innocence is important legally and religiously, the real causes for divorce in most cases are not so simple, and we cannot usually make a helpful determination here. Moreover, it is difficult for the person who is falling in love to evaluate objectively the loved one's role in the first marriage relationship. When discussing this experience with the person you are considering as a future partner, you undoubtedly will be prejudiced in his or her favor and eager to accept his or her interpretation of the situation. Nor do legal records always tell the full story about marital discords. It is not easy for laymen to examine court records freely, and the marriage counselor, minister, or psychotherapist who may have the greatest insight into the true cause of the divorce is pledged to keep this information confidential. All in all, this is a difficult question for which to receive an adequate answer.

Finally, in summary, one might simply ask: "Is this to be a marriage governed by reality or by feelings?" Every marriage needs the best that we can give to it. This is also true if one or both parties are entering a second marriage. Such a union will require an extra measure of patience, love, and determination to make it succeed. There are bound to be some rough spots and some disappointments. If the love is all feeling—primarily romantic—the marriage may crumble under the impact of the special pressures inherent in it. Realism should be a major factor in making the final decision about marriage to a divorced person.

Other Factors in Marriage Patterns

There are other variations in marriage that are considered important factors in mate selection. These factors include age, education, social class, and marriage to a serviceman or a servicewoman.

American marriage statistics show that women have consistently married men older than themselves (see Chapter 10). At times the age difference may be ten or twenty years or more. However, the difference in age does not seem to be as important as the exact ages involved. It has been discovered that couples marrying at a very early age (in their teens) have great difficulty in establishing a stable marriage, where older individuals (even with an age difference) have been much more successful. Bumpass and Sweet, for example, find that both age and education are favorable factors to be considered in connection with interfaith marriages; older and better-educated couples form more stable marriages.[23]

The relationship of education to marriage choice is clearly shown in the study of 1970 census figures by Richard Rockwell. Educationally homogamous marriages are now occurring at above chance levels, and they are also following the pattern suggested by the "mating gradient," which means that women will marry above themselves in education and social status. The increasing number of men with a college education makes this possible. A woman will find a number of partners with equivalent education to her own, and others with higher education. Rockwell finds a strong tendency for both husbands and wives not to marry more than one level up or down in education.[24]

It is more difficult to assess the place of social class factors in marriage, since class status is not listed on marriage licenses, and data must be inferred from independent studies of residence, income, and education. Adams states that the general tendency is for homogeneity between mates to persist, in social class as well as in other categories.[25]

Marriage to a Serviceman

Another variation from traditional marriage patterns is that of a woman student to a serviceman. (The converse relationship, marriage of a male student to a servicewoman, is very infrequent.) Although we recognize that many

[23]Bumpass and Sweet, pp. 754–66.

[24]Richard C. Rockwell, "Historical Trends and Variations in Educational Homogamy," *Journal of Marriage and the Family*, 38, no. 1 (Feb. 1976), 83–95.

[25]Bert N. Adams, *The Family: A Sociological Interpretation*, 2nd ed. (Chicago: Rand McNally, 1975), pp. 218–20.

"I *do* love you, Larry. It's just that we look silly together."

Drawing by Tobey
© 1974 The New Yorker Magazine, Inc.

young women who have begun their working careers marry servicemen, our special interest is in the student-serviceman marriage. In a typical case, we would be considering the union of a twenty-year-old woman with a man twenty to twenty-six years of age.

Many students marry servicemen as a normal completion of our democratic courtship system. All teenagers have approximately the same opportunity as others in their peer group to enter the dating system in secondary school and to progress naturally through various stages toward marriage. A young man in the service will tend to move forward to engagement and marriage in the same way as the nonservice members of his peer group as a logical completion of his dating experience. His intended partner would not want it otherwise.

But everything is not smooth sailing for the young couple contemplating a service marriage. The couple should be aware of the special problems involved. What is the present outlook for service marriage?

The creation of a volunteer army, and the consequent end to the military draft, have moved the military situation at a distance from the college campus. However, there are still military installations near certain college campuses, resulting in potential partners for a number of students. As in all marriages, the basic elements in a service marriage are the personalities of the two partners. If they share a mature love for each other, if they have had sufficient time to become well acquainted, if they have similar interests and temperaments, and if they have an engagement period that provides them enough time to prepare adequately for their marriage, they should have every opportunity to make a success of their marriage. But if they do not have these average qualifications of civilian marriage, the added stresses and separations of military life will only intensify their problems.

The circumstances of marriage to a serviceman are important. Does he know what assignment he will have in the next six months or year? Is his branch of the service likely to mean mostly stateside duty or frequent duty overseas? Uncertainty enters into many courtships for today's college couples. The draft is, at least for the present, no longer a threat to young men. But a man may choose to volunteer for some branch of the service, and the couple often will not know for certain where he will be stationed when he enters the service. A man may enlist in the Air Force expecting to be stationed at a large base in a nearby state and discover that he has been assigned to a training field thousands of miles away. With U.S. forces on call in many parts of the world, the couple cannot project future plans for the first months and years of married life with any degree of assurance. One service wife may take these uncertainties in her stride, while another will find it makes her marriage adjustment especially difficult.

Engagement may be a difficult period for the couple who are considering a service marriage. How will the couple get to know each other and their habits of living, thinking, and feeling when their main contact may be through letters and telephone calls? Can a couple carry out a satisfactory courtship and be adequately prepared for marriage if they see each other only for occasional brief weekend visits? Or is it wise to concentrate courtship into a fifteen- or thirty-day leave, during which time normal patterns are broken and each partner may overlook problems and practical considerations in a desire to please the other and hasten the decision for marriage? And living together is not often possible.

The most serious problems with service marriages naturally are associated with a wartime situation. The readjustment for Vietnam veterans, for example, in the economic, social, and personal aspects of their lives will continue to be a national problem. The focus here, however, will not be on the college-age population.

Life does not follow a single course for all couples in love. Careful and intelligent consideration of the variations in one's possible marriage partnership is a sound way to prepare for a creative and rewarding married life.

SUMMARY

There are many choices to be made before marriage. Some of these choices involve variations in marriage partnership. There are many interfaith marriages in the United States. Such marriages often involve the linking of different cultural backgrounds as well as different religious backgrounds. If one counts marriages among different Protestant denominations as interfaith, then a majority of all American marriages may be said to be mixed religiously.

Several factors lead to interfaith marriage. There is great mobility in our society today. Urbanization tends to break down religious exclusiveness. Recreational activities, in which courtship often begins, are not usually religiously oriented. There is also an emphasis on freedom of individual choice in today's society. The mixed-marriage rate of a particular religious group seems to be determined mainly by the proportion of the group to the total population, the closeness of the ethnic groups its members belong to, and the socioeconomic level of its members.

Interfaith marriages do seem to lead more frequently to divorce, and they may bring conflicts in marital roles and family values. Frequently there are conflicts over the religious education of the children. Partners in interfaith marriage may also report marital dissatisfaction that is not serious enough to lead to divorce.

The decision for or against an interfaith marriage is not an easy one. Some honest thinking is required. Paul and Jeanne Simon have drawn up some guidelines for Protestants and Catholics in interfaith marriage and are optimistic about such unions.

Interracial marriage is another significant marriage variation. The fact that the number of interracial marriages in our society is slowly increasing indicates shifts in our social, economic, and cultural life. Most controversial are black-white marriages. Much of our prejudice against interracial marriage is rooted in our national history. But since legal restrictions against interracial marriage have been invalidated, some Americans, both black and white, are urging a more open acceptance of interracial unions. Marriages of black grooms and white brides are more common than the reverse combination.

On the personal level a number of important issues are involved in interracial marriage. What is the motivation for the marriage? What will be the reaction of family and friends? Value conflicts, which make achieving harmony in any marriage difficult, may be a serious problem in interracial marriage. Couples must also give consideration to the environment in which their children will be raised.

In considering marriage to a divorced person, several questions might be raised. Will such a marriage be as successful as one in which both partners are entering their first marriage? How will family members react? What about the children of the first marriage? What intangible attitudes are introduced into the marriage by the prior marital experience of one or both partners?

Other special marital situations include variations in age, social class, and education, and marriage to a person in the service. Each of these has special factors that will affect a couple's adjustment.

SUGGESTED READINGS

Adams, Bert N. *The Family: A Sociological Interpretation,* 2nd ed. Chicago: Rand McNally, 1975. A solid, general introduction to the family, with special emphasis on the role of the family group in the total life of society.

Barron, Milton L., ed. *The Blending American: Patterns of Intermarriage.* Chicago: Quadrangle Books, 1972. A number of chapters deal with religious, racial, and ethnic intermarriage and the impact on the couple and their children.

Besanceney, Paul H., S.J. *Interfaith Marriages: Who and Why.* New Haven, Conn.: College and University Press, 1970. Good summary of the Roman Catholic Church's views on interfaith marriage.

Bumpass, Larry L., and James A. Sweet. "Differentials in Marital Instability: 1970," *American Sociological Review,* 37, no. 4 (Dec. 1972), 754–66. Careful analysis of 1970 U.S. census data for interfaith marriage.

Heer, David M. "The Prevalence of Black-White Marriage in the United States, 1960 and 1970," *Journal of Marriage and the Family,* 36, no. 2 (May 1974), 246–58. Analysis of census data on marriages between blacks and whites.

Larsson, Clotye M., ed. *Marriage Across the Color Line.* Chicago: Johnson, 1965. Discussion of interracial marriage and its history in the U.S. Includes case histories of couples in interracial marriages; valuable for black perspective.

Monahan, Thomas P. "An Overview of Statistics on Interracial Marriage in the United States, with Data on Its Extent from 1963–1970," *Journal of Marriage and the Family,* 38, no. 2 (May 1976), 223–31. Valuable analysis of rising rate of interracial marriage. Monahan notes the differences in intermarriage among several racial groups.

Rockwell, Richard C. "Historical Trends and Variations in Educational Homogamy," *Journal of Marriage and the Family,* 38, no. 1 (Feb. 1976), 83–95. Study that illustrates the impact of education on marriage choice.

Simon, Paul, and Jeanne Simon. *Protestant-Catholic Marriages Can Succeed.* New York: Association Press, 1967. Favorable view of mixed marriage by a Catholic wife and a Protestant husband.

Stuart, Irving R., and Lawrence E. Abt, eds. *Interracial Marriage: Expectations and Realities.* New York: Grossman, 1973. Current perspectives on interracial marriage, with contributions from both lay and professional writers.

Washington, Joseph R., Jr. *Marriage in Black and White.* Boston: Beacon, 1970. Author advocates free choice for both partners in black and white marriages. Discusses the situation of children in these marriages.

10 Weddings and Honeymoons

- How do you know if you are ready for marriage?
- How important is the example of your parental family to your own marriage success?
- What personality factors are important in marriage adjustment? Can emotional maturity be measured?
- What effect do education and career achievement have on a couple's marriage?
- Does an early or a late marriage have an effect on marital stability?
- What purpose does the wedding ceremony serve?
- What are the marriage laws of your state?
- What purpose is served by the honeymoon experience? Has the purpose of honeymoons changed in the last twenty years?

Are You Ready for Marriage?

Marriage is one of the turning points in a person's life. It begins on the wedding day. The entire selection process, which has been operative from the earliest dating experiences through the final days of the engagement period, is finalized by the wedding ceremony. Although the choices that determine the time and place and the type of wedding are all individual ones, reflecting the fact that marriage is influenced by an intricate combination of personal and social factors, all weddings fit into certain observable social patterns.

Despite our high degree of interest in alternative lifestyles, it remains true that 95 percent of American women are married by age fifty-four and 94 percent of the men by age sixty-four. This means an overwhelming number of weddings include the vast majority of our population. Yet the high rate of divorce in our society seems to indicate that many people are not ready to sustain a stable marriage relationship. Were they unaware of the responsibilities of marriage? Did they fail to recognize the many personal and social factors involved? A fulfilling marriage is built on the interaction of two different people, a man and a woman, who each bring their own strengths and weaknesses to the partnership. If the two individuals have experienced sound basic personality growth on their own, they will be equipped to bring strength and maturity to their marriage. Stinnett and Walters suggest that marriage success is built on the Transactional "I'm OK" position, where both partners find a high level of personal satisfaction. The happiness of a partner's former marriage and personal happiness in childhood are also factors related to a happy marriage.[1]

Personality Development

Psychological studies have underscored the importance of personality development in the total life cycle, with particular emphasis on the early years. Patterns set in the preschool years continue to influence us throughout life. Mary Ellen Goodman writes:

> By age six, or thereabout, the child's personality will have assumed enduring contours. Later experiences will develop detail within these contours, perhaps alter them to some or a considerable degree. However, these later developments must occur either within or against the early configuration. There is in much of human development a sequential nature. Each characteristic is built on a base of that same characteristic at an earlier time or on the base of other characteristics which precede it. . . .
>
> . . . The early formation of personality is possible, indeed inevitable, because of human intelligence as well as human sensitivity. Both are strikingly manifest in the young child's perceptivity with respect to the world around him. By age six, often earlier, children are likely to be well aware of the prevalent social categories, quite able and ready to classify individuals in terms of these categories, and well on the way toward full development of the relevant value-attitude systems prevalent among the adults of their society.[2]

Emotional maturity is a basic ingredient for a happy marriage. Courtship and engagement, by their very nature, may be expected to have a fair number of ups and downs. Such anxieties are normal and should be overcome in a happy marriage. But some personality problems may be very difficult to solve. If one or both partners are highly sensitive, their marriage may be a difficult one. It is fortunate if an engaged couple have encountered enough of the stresses and tensions of adult life to be able to judge each other's emotional maturity.

Couples who marry at a young age often face a number of interrelated problems. They have a minimal amount of education, and thus may also

[1]Nick Stinnett and James Walters, *Relationships in Marriage and Family* (New York: Macmillan, 1977), pp. 66-67.

[2]Mary Ellen Goodman, "Influences of Childhood and Adolescence," in Edward Norbeck et al., eds., *The Study of Personality* (New York: Holt, Rinehart & Winston, 1968), pp. 178–79.

have a low income. Marriage does not solve these problems—it may make them more difficult. Reiner and Edwards have pointed out that these couples need a great deal of help from their communities. This may include practical help in getting a job, housing, social assistance, or medical help. It may also mean helping them to get counseling, such as that offered by a recognized marriage and family counselor.[3]

It is important to emphasize the need for balanced personality interaction between the partners, which may also be described as a democratic sharing of important decisions and experiences. If a husband and wife can agree on important decisions and if their personalities balance and blend easily, their marriage is likely to be harmonious.

Love

Love remains the universal element that brings a man and a woman together and supports a fulfilling marriage relationship. We have discussed some of the myriad aspects of love in Chapter 7. A marriage that begins without love is almost certainly doomed to failure. Love provides that extra plus that carries us over many of life's most difficult crises. It is love that draws us to the strength of our partner, rather than to his or her weakness. It is love that helps us to be unselfish, loving, patient, and forgiving. But love alone will be isolated, fragile, and vulnerable, and we need to add to it these other elements that help it to achieve its goal.

Communication

A third indication of readiness for marriage is effective communication between the couple. Communication is carried on at both the verbal and the nonverbal levels, and both are equally important. The major changes in the courtship system in the last thirty years, greater stress on equality in the partnership, progress toward the single standard in sexual behavior, and increasing opportunities for shared educational and career experiences have all given impetus to improvement in the communication process.

What is the secret of effective communication, both before and after marriage? Successful verbal communication requires that one speak clearly and directly. How often have we heard our partner say to us: "You never said that!" "You never said we were going out to dinner tonight!" "I thought you asked me if I liked fish." It takes practice to say what we mean so that others understand us.

Listening is also a key element in communication. There is no value in a short simple statement or in a lengthy explanation of a important subject

[3]Beatrice S. Reiner and Raymond L. Edwards, "Adolescent Marriage—Social or Therapeutic Problem," *The Family Coordinator*, 23, no. 4 (Oct. 1974), 383–87.

if no one is listening. Both partners need to speak, and both need to listen. Feedback is one good device here. Give your partner an immediate response. Let him or her know exactly how you think and feel about a particular matter. This encourages partners to reflect on what they have heard and make sure that communication is really a two-way street. Both partners have a share in making the process a success. This is one mark of the contemporary college generation—couples like to talk to each other.

> Dorothy and I met while I was in the service. She was attending the university and I worked part-time at the Wolf Den across from the university as a short order cook. One night when I was in the Den on my off-duty hours Dorothy was there. I took my coffee and went over to her booth and sat down. We sat and talked, mostly about her family, and then we rode around the countryside for several hours. We found that we had many things in common, among them music, literature, entertainers, similar religious beliefs. Our goals and ideals were quite parallel. This all happened on Wednesday.
>
> On Friday we had our first real date. We went to a movie, and then danced at a small night club outside town. Again, most of the time was taken up discussing ourselves and our families. It was unique to be sitting with someone you had known for just a few days, and feeling as though you had known them for a lifetime. We were both very much relaxed in each other's company, and consequently were able to discuss all sorts of things together.[4]

Not all relationships are so successful, and barriers in the communication process must be overcome. George Bach and Herb Goldberg have incorporated techniques for resolving some of these barriers in their program of fair fighting.[5] It is almost impossible to avoid some conflict in a normal interpersonal relationship. The real question is whether or not to deal with the conflict, and effective communication is the key to doing so.

When there is a low level of verbal communication, nonverbal expressions are even more vital. It is easier to drop off to sleep than to start a lengthy discussion with your partner after a tense evening. Couples must develop techniques to make nonverbal communication more effective.[6] A husband may not feel like entering into a lengthy discussion at home after a hard day at the office, but he can communicate his love and understanding by a touch, a kiss, a loving look. And a wife may have run out of words after closing an important real estate sale, or finishing up an extra hour's work

[4]Student report.

[5]George R. Bach and Herb Goldberg, *Creative Aggression* (Garden City, N.Y.: Doubleday, 1974).

[6]See Ernest J. Green, *Personal Relationships—An Approach to Marriage and Family* (New York: McGraw-Hill, 1978), pp. 215–19.

at the office, or trying to take care of two sick children in the afternoon. Again, her nonverbal communication can tell her husband a lot about how she feels and what she wants to share with him.

Educational and Career Achievements

Another clear indication of marriage readiness is given by one's educational and career achievements. It is sometimes hard to measure achievement, since a number of elements need to be considered. But we can certainly predict a brighter future for a senior honors student than for a freshman who may have to leave college before the end of the first semester. Several studies have shown the correlation between social status and income on the one hand and marital stability on the other. It is no small problem to be poor and uneducated in an affluent society, and the burdens borne by the disadvantaged are reflected in problems in managing a family situation.

Taylor and Glenn have studied the impact of education (and of personal attractiveness) on the achievement of higher social status through marriage. If we look at marriage in accordance with the exchange theory, we might simply assume that an attractive female marries a high-status male and moves up the social ladder in this way. But a woman with more education seems to meet, date, and marry a man who is entering a career in which he will move up the scale. Taylor and Glenn's study of some 300 women did not find any significant relationship of beauty to an increase in social status. There was, however, some support for education. They found that:

> Measures of the association of amount of education with husbands' occupational prestige are moderate and statistically significant for wives of all age levels and in all categories of origin, although . . . they are lower for wives of low-manual origins than for other wives. Nevertheless, the highest estimated effect of education . . . is for the approximately one-third of the wives of low-manual origins who were rated at least above average in attractiveness . . .[7]

The possibility of different gains in status for women has stimulated several recent studies. Felson and Knoke, for example, studied a national cross-sectional sample of 624 men and 536 women.[8] They found that most status still is based on the husband's career and education, and less independently on the woman. Even though she has her own career, she is frequently happy

[7]Patricia Ann Taylor and Norval D. Glenn, "The Utility of Education and Attractiveness for Females' Status Attainment Through Marriage," *American Sociological Review,* 41, no. 3 (June 1976), 494.

[8]Marcus Felson and David Knoke, "Social Status and the Married Woman," *Journal of Marriage and the Family,* 36, no. 3 (Aug. 1974), 516–21.

to identify herself as "Mrs. John Davidson," or "Dr. Romero's wife," rather than stressing her own unique achievements. And apparently it is rare for the husband to attach himself to his wife's work and achievements to bolster his own. The independent married woman, standing squarely on her own two feet, still seems to be in the minority in the reports and interviews studied.

Partners who achieve well in school, who make and keep friends, who have definite ideas about the kind of career that they want, and who can hold a job with some promise for the future are much better marriage risks than those who always come out with the lowest paying and least promising job that is available.

The Marriageable Age

What is the best age to be married? The average age for marriage in this country, after being quite low in the 1950s, is now on the rise. Table 10–1 shows that by 1980 people will be marrying at almost the same median age as they did in 1920.

Marriage ages are especially influenced by demographic trends. For example, if the number of girls born in 1960 is much larger than the number of boys who were born in 1957 and 1958, who might be their logical partners, fewer of these girls may be married some twenty or twenty-one years later, and the marriage age will rise accordingly. Some of these trends in marriage are reflected in Table 10–2.

The percentage of married adults in the population increased steadily until about 1971. The increase in the marriage age is reflected by the fact that the percentage of married adults is dropping again. Table 10–2 clearly indicates the effect of the steady rise in the percentage of married persons into the 1940s and 1950s. For example, using the full 1971 figures, a college woman planning to become engaged to an eighteen- or nineteen-year-old man will find that 92.5 percent of the eligible men are single. If she waits until graduation, and wants to marry a man 20–24 years old, she will find only 57.1 percent eligible single men. Later the 25–34-year-old group shrinks to 20.4 percent, and the 35–44-year-old group decreases to 11.5 percent. The same factors affect a man, although he has greater freedom to marry younger women. Thus there are two contradictory trends evident in these figures. If the marriage age increases, more mature and stable marriages may result. If one, particularly the female partner, waits too long to marry, a suitable partner may be difficult to find.

This proves to be a fascinating subject for the family professionals. In her article "Is There a Best Age to Marry?" Marcia Lasswell is optimistic about

Table 10–1 Median Age at First Marriage, by Sex: 1920–1976

Year	Male	Female
1920	24.6 years	21.2 years
1930	24.3	21.3
1940	24.3	21.5
1950	22.8	20.3
1955	22.6	20.2
1960	22.8	20.3
1962	22.7	20.3
1964	23.1	20.5
1966	22.8	20.5
1969	23.2	20.8
1971	23.1	20.9
1972	23.2	20.9
1973	22.5	20.6
1974	22.5	20.6
1975	22.7	20.8
1976	23.8	21.3

NOTE: Beginning in 1950, figures are based on sample. Prior to 1960, figures exclude Alaska and Hawaii.

SOURCE: Adapted from U.S. Bureau of the Census, *Statistical Abstract of the United States, 1968* (Washington, D.C.: D.C.: U.S. Government Printing Office, 1968), p. 61; *Statistical Abstract of the United States, 1972*, p. 63; and *Statistical Abstract of the United States, 1977*, p. 74.

people marrying at a later age.[9] Her conclusion and advice is: Let women wait until they are 25 to marry, and then have their two children at age 28 and 30. This would have the positive benefits of emotional maturity and financial preparation. Let men marry at age 28 and father their two children at age 30 (sic) and 32. The only problem with this concept is the narrowing choice of partners as one moves from the twenties into the older age brackets.

Two recent studies suggest that the age at which one marries may not be

[9]Marcia E. Lasswell, "Is There a Best Age to Marry? An Interpretation," *The Family Coordinator*, 23, no. 3 (July 1974), 237–42.

Table 10–2 Percentage Married at Ages Fifteen Years and Over (1890–1971) and Ages Eighteen and Over (1972–1976), by Sex and Age, United States

Sex and Age male	*1890*	*1900*	*1910*	*1920*	*1930*	*1940*	*1950*	*1965*	*Sex and Age male*	*1971*	*1972*	*1976*
15 and over	54.1	54.7	56.1	59.4	60.1	61.6	69.0	67.9	15 and over	74.8	73.7	72.2
15–19	.5	1.0	1.2	2.1	1.7	1.8	3.1	2.5	18–19	7.5		
20–24	18.9	21.6	24.2	28.4	28.2	28.0	39.5	46.3	20–24	42.9		
25–34	61.6	60.7	63.0	65.9	68.5	70.3	79.0	83.6	25–34	79.6		
35–44	81.0	78.9	79.3	80.1	81.6	82.8	87.0	87.2	35–44	88.5		
45–54	84.4	82.3	81.6	81.2	81.7	83.1	85.8	88.7	45–54	87.2		
55–64	82.4	79.8	79.0	78.0	78.1	78.9	81.6	83.8	55–64	87.4		
65 and over	70.6	67.3	65.7	64.9	63.7	64.2	66.0	71.0	65–74	79.0		
									75 and over	62.5		
Female									*female*			
15 and over	56.8	57.1	59.0	60.9	61.1	61.4	67.3	63.9	15 and over	68.5	67.6	66.2
15–19	9.5	10.9	11.4	12.6	12.6	11.9	16.8	10.3	18–19	22.2		
20–24	46.8	46.6	49.4	52.5	51.6	52.1	65.8	65.6	20–24	60.5		
25–34	75.3	73.2	75.2	76.8	77.7	77.6	84.8	88.8	25–34	84.9		
35–44	80.7	79.6	80.2	80.5	81.5	81.4	84.5	87.9	35–44	86.7		
45–54	74.0	73.9	74.8	74.3	75.2	76.3	77.8	81.8	45–54	87.0		
55–64	60.4	60.5	62.1	61.4	62.0	63.4	65.3	66.8	55–64	68.2		
65 and over	35.4	34.2	35.0	34.2	34.6	34.6	35.8	27.2	65–74	46.3		
									75 and over	21.8		

NOTE: Includes armed forces overseas during 1940 and 1950; 1965 figures include individuals fourteen and over. No 1971 figures are available for individuals 15 and over.

SOURCES: 1890–1950, reprinted by permission of the author from Paul H. Jacobson, *American Marriage and Divorce,* Copyright © 1959 (Rinehart & Co., Inc.), Xerox Corp. Book Publications, OP 31, 415, Ann Arbor, p. 34, Table 7; 1965 and 1971 figures from U.S. Bureau of the Census, *Statistical Abstract of the United States, 1972* (Washington, D.C.: U.S. Government Printing Office, 1972), p. 37; and 1972 and 1976 figures from *Statistical Abstract of the United States, 1977,* p. 74.

as important as some family sociologists would have it. Vaughn Call and Luther Ott studied a group of 313 men in Lenawee County, Michigan, over a fifteen-year period from 1957 to 1972, beginning at age seventeen. They checked the young men's fathers' occupations and education, mothers' education, and their own academic performance and occupational aspirations. They found that for these men their age at marriage did not have any significant effect on their educational or occupational achievements. In fact, the ones who married earliest had the higher income at the end of the fifteen-year study.[10]

The second study by Gary Lee at Washington State University also calls into question the impact of marriage age on later stability. Lee found that there was a positive correlation between later age and marital satisfaction, but the correlation was small. He concluded that it is not really a strong enough relationship to produce the great differential in the divorce rate between early marriages (as with teenagers) and those marrying later, in their twenties. Is it possible, he asks, that the young divorce quickly because they know there is another partner just around the corner?[11]

Moral and Spiritual Values

Another positive factor in marital readiness is in shared moral and spiritual values. A husband and wife who have moral sensitivity are better able to form a union that has meaning and value beyond the limited circle of their own immediate family. They will have a genuine concern for their friends and neighbors, interest in the political world, and a relationship with the world at large that transcends local and national boundaries. A highly developed sense of the rightness and wrongness of things, seen in the broadest possible perspective, will stand them in good stead when they need to adapt to new situations in their marriage.

James W. Maddock has suggested that morality is an integral part of personal development and self-fulfillment. Values are a way of seeing reality, and morality is the actualization of those values.[12] We must recognize the importance of moral development. Instruction in moral values is vital in the home, the church, and the school.

Stinnett and Walters state that religious belief is positively associated with marriage success. The teachings of the major religions emphasize

[10]Vaughn R. A. Call and Luther B. Ott, "Age at Marriage as a Mobility Contingency: Estimates for the Nye-Berardo Model," *Journal of Marriage and the Family*, 39, no. 1 (Feb. 1977), 67–79.

[11]Gary R. Lee, "Age at Marriage and Marital Satisfaction: A Multivariate Analysis with Implications for Marital Stability," *Journal of Marriage and the Family*, 39, no. 3 (Aug. 1977), 493–504.

[12]James W. Maddock, "Morality and Individual Development: A Basis for Value Education," *The Family Coordinator*, 21, no. 3 (July 1972), 291–302.

values that contribute to this success. Those with an active religious participation are encouraged to share love, respect, support, responsibility, and forgiveness. One's individual growth in these areas is strengthened by the example of others. Religion becomes a family activity for all ages. Friends share the religious life of the church or synagogue. There is a sense of the divine in human life.[13]

The Wedding Celebration

Planning a wedding celebration that will be a joyful and memorable experience for both the couple and their families and friends is a real challenge. It is a way of establishing the tone and direction of the couples' shared life together. When the time comes to set the date for the wedding, the couple may be overwhelmed by the possibilities before them. Should they plan a large church wedding, with a costly reception and all the trimmings? Should it be a quiet home ceremony, with just close friends and members of the family present? There is no binding rule to follow; in our society each couple is given wide freedom of choice in planning the wedding ceremony.

The majority of weddings in the United States are still religious ceremonies. Younger couples are more apt to have a church wedding, while older couples and divorced persons remarrying are more likely to have a civil ceremony. Ties to the church and the community are stronger if the young couple are still living with or near their parents, and are entering into their first marriage.

The wedding ceremony does not in itself determine the outcome of the marriage. One couple may have a very costly and elaborate church wedding and find their marriage a failure after a few short months. Another couple may have a very simple ceremony before a justice of the peace and find happiness in a long and fruitful marriage. Some families put a great deal of emphasis on their own social status. We cannot always make an accurate judgment based on outward appearances. Some general trends can be noted, however. People entering marriage with a religious ceremony will probably be more socially oriented than those who do not; they will often be more deliberate and thoughtful; and they are usually more closely involved with their families and their home communities.

We often wonder just what a couple think when they are about to be married. Do they have feelings of anticipation and optimism, or are they pessimistic and fearful? In states that have a waiting period between the issuance of the marriage license and the performance of the wedding ceremony, some couples apparently change their minds and do not use their

[13]Stinnett and Walters, pp. 76–77.

marriage licenses. One interesting attempt to understand what goes on in the minds of couples about to be married was made by Paul Hilsdale, who interviewed some 80 respondents waiting for their marriage licenses in a large Midwestern city.[14] He found that Catholics would not discuss the possibility of divorce. Eighty-four percent of the final sample (all non-Catholics) recognized that divorce was sometimes necessary. Even they, however, "were firmly agreed that marriage must *begin* with an absolute commitment." Although Hilsdale did not believe the couples were starry-eyed romantics, he felt that they were probably overconfident about their chances for marital success in our contemporary society.

Undoubtedly, more attention and research should be focused on premarital attitudes and decisions. The choices made by two people before the day of their marriage should not be haphazard ones; some careful thought and guidance should be invested at this significant point.

Purposes of the Wedding Ceremony

The wedding celebration has legal and religious meaning and has a significant place in the transition of the couple from single to married status. Some sociologists term the ceremony, together with the customs that surround it, the "rites of passage." The rites vary so much, however, that it is better to discuss the particular purposes served by the wedding and to note how those needs are met by particular kinds of wedding ceremonies.

There are three major purposes of the wedding ceremony. The first purpose is the focusing of attention on the change from single to married status. You can write to the college of your choice and fill out endless admission blanks and even register for courses in advance; but you do not become a student until you enter the college. In marriage too there must come a particular time and place when you change status and actually become the new and different person you want to be. You may have talked about it for a number of months or even years. But no amount of preparation can take the place of the wedding itself; at that moment in time you take the final step and are married. The very fact that every engaged couple does not enter matrimony and the half-humorous, half-serious references to the bride left waiting at the church remind us of the basic importance of this first purpose of the wedding.

The wedding day should mark a definite change in family relationships. The same questions remain, but they are tempered by the realization that the important step has been taken, that the couple are now facing their problems together, and that they deserve some measure of encouragement and

[14]Paul Hilsdale, S.J., "Marriage as a Personal Existential Commitment," *Marriage and Family Living,* 24, no. 2 (May 1962), 137–43.

support. The community also is significantly involved in the new relationship that begins with the wedding ceremony. In a formal and legal way through the marriage license and registration, and in a more personal way through the actual ceremony, the community has given its approval to the new union. The community hopes that the couple will have a long and happy marriage. It accepts the new relationship and focuses on the positive strengths of the young couple.

A second purpose served by the wedding service is the establishment of a basic legal framework for the new family. Centuries of tradition and experience are intermingled in the laws of the several states. Within the legal framework established by the wedding, the family will have the security and protection it needs to guard its interests in the event of death or dissolution of the marital bond.

A third purpose served by the wedding ceremony is the involvement of the bride and groom in a meaningful interpersonal commitment to each other. They have often shown their love for each other in words and in acts of affection, kindness, concern, and appreciation. Now they express those feelings of love in a public commitment: "I will," "I promise," "I do."

In a religious service, the couple seek divine sanction and blessing for their marriage. According to the Roman Catholic tradition, that service is a sacrament of the church. In Protestant churches, the wedding does not have sacramental meaning, but it is symbolic of the church's approval of the union and of God's love and concern for the couple. Within the Jewish tradition, it is a sacred rite, hallowed by thousands of years of tradition and faith. The couple who share in a religious service are seeking to find spiritual meaning and direction for their life together.

In each religious tradition, custom and doctrine have been brought together in particular orders for the wedding service. In some religious communities, only full members of the church or synagogue may share in the full religious ceremony. In others, the particular church or clergyman may decide whether or not the couple may be married with the blessing of a religious service.

Evaluating the Wedding

A great deal of help and advice is available to a young couple in planning the wedding service and reception. Entire books treat the subject exclusively, and wedding manuals and books of etiquette are quick to point out the necessary social functions, announcements, guest lists, and the thousand and one other things they seem to feel are required for the perfect wedding. Fortunately, a number of teachers, marriage counselors, and clergymen are emphasizing adequate preparation through counseling and testing prior to the wedding. Rather than give detailed descriptions of social customs and expectations as they apply to different class, ethnic, and religious groups, let us consider three basic ways in which we can evaluate the wedding plans of an engaged couple. To aid our evaluation, there are several questions we can ask.

DOES THE WEDDING REINFORCE THE ENGAGEMENT?

It has been suggested that during the engagement period the couple make adequate preparation for the future marriage, gain the support of family and friends for the marriage, make formal announcement of the impending wedding in the community, and establish patterns for joint decision-making. Development of the wedding plans should help the couple achieve those purposes.

In many cases the plans for a wedding are so complex and the time available to carry forward those plans so limited that the couple find themselves in conflict during much of the time they are together. "Let's go out to River Park and just sit and talk awhile." "No, Bill, we can't. We have to see the florist again about the plants for the reception, and your mother is coming over to look at the invitation list." Every date and every free afternoon seem swallowed up with some errand or project having to do with the wedding.

The bride is more likely to be faced with the temptation to become overly absorbed in the details of the ceremony. The wedding day is a special one for her, and she wants it to be just so. Her family and friends may encourage her to plan this, add that, and change this a little. It becomes a grand, festive occasion, and every other aspect of preparation for married life is shunted aside. A little less hectic schedule and a little more emphasis on time spent alone with her fiancé may well prove to be an extremely wise investment for her in the long run.

HOW MUCH SHOULD THE WEDDING COST?

Do plans for the wedding celebration fit the families involved? Weddings are big business, and the bridal shops, stores, photographers, entertainers, florists, caterers, and even the churches may all seem to be working together to make the wedding an overly elaborate affair. This commercialization of the rites of passage—baptisms, confirmations, bar mitzvahs, weddings, and funerals—seems to be characteristic of American society. Some guidelines and directions must be set, especially by the bride and her family, if the cost of the wedding and reception is not to be an unrealistically heavy financial burden to everyone. The couple should be certain that the expenses of the wedding are in harmony with their families and their own position in the community.

Costs for the wedding can be computed more accurately if the couple consider together who will be responsible for which items. The traditional

responsibilities of the bride's family include: the wedding and reception; the bride's trousseau and all her clothes, including her going-away clothes; engagement announcements and wedding invitations and announcements; rent for the church or chapel; the bridesmaids' bouquets and the flowers in the church; fees for the sexton, organist, and soloists; transportation for the bridal party from the house to the church and from the church to the reception; all expenses of the reception, including food, flowers, music, rental fees, and so on; the wedding ring for the groom in a double-ring ceremony.

The fact that the bride's family bears most of the expense is related to ancient customs, including the dowry, and is based on the fact that in earlier generations an unmarried woman was a liability to the average family. But today, when a daughter has a well-paying job, her father is likely to regret seeing her leave home to get married. And when a man marries a woman who will continue working after marriage and help to carry any financial burdens, this division of expenses seems grossly unfair.

The traditional expenses for the bridegroom are much fewer than those for the bride and her family. In a small home wedding, they may be practically negligible. In a more formal wedding, they include: the engagement ring; the wedding ring; the marriage license; the bride's bouquet and gift; boutonnieres for the best man and the ushers; the ushers' presents and, in a formal wedding, ties and gloves for the ushers and the best man; corsages for his mother and his new mother-in-law; the fee for the minister; transportation to the wedding for the best man and himself; all expenses of the honeymoon.

It is traditional for the bride's attendants and the best man and the ushers to be responsible for their own wedding costumes, for their wedding presents to the bride and groom, and for any parties they may wish to give for either bride or groom.

In modern weddings, especially when one or both members of the couple are still in college or the groom is in the service, the traditional guidelines for the payment of the expenses are often not strictly followed. More joint planning takes place, and the cost of the wedding and reception may be borne by the parental families or the bride and groom themselves.

WHAT KIND OF WEDDING?

The main consideration in planning a wedding should be the true interests of the couple who are being married. Is this the kind of wedding that they really want and will be happy to remember? Or is this a wedding that is primarily a display put on for the benefit of family members or friends? In some cases, there is so much planning done by the bride's mother or father, the wedding hostess, and other interested people that the bride and groom

seem to be outsiders in their own wedding. In years to come, the couple will look back on their wedding with real satisfaction if it was *their* wedding, not if it was directed and planned by others without their whole-hearted involvement and participation.

In the last decade many young couples have planned ceremonies to fit their innovative lifestyles. Most churches now allow more free and creative wedding services than they did in the past: many couples choose to have guitars and folk music, write their own vows, and break with traditional customs for invitations and receptions. Couples should find it possible to express their personalities and their way of life within the context of a religious ceremony.

The Marriage Contract

The laws governing marriage are varied and complex. Society has established many of the laws in order to have some measure of control over marriage. Culturally, the double standard has favored the man in the marriage contract, so our judicial system has had to intervene to establish a more equitable interpretation of the rights and responsibilities of both partners. The most universal laws governing marriage have to do with the age at which marriage may be contracted, both with and without parental consent; specifications for physical examinations and blood tests for the prospective partners; and in some states, waiting periods before or after the issuance of the marriage license. In addition, some states still recognize common-law marriages. Prohibitions of certain marriages—for instance, when the partners are close relatives or when there is evidence of illness or unsound mind—are also made in many states.

The marriage contract is rooted in the English common law of many centuries ago. The two partners became one, but under the legal identity of the husband. Lenore Weitzman points out that there were four essential provisions in the traditional marriage contract:

1. The husband is recognized as head of the household;
2. The husband is responsible for support of his wife and children;
3. The wife is responsible for domestic services;
4. The wife is responsible for child care.[15]

A wide range of laws is derived from these basic premises. Most of the power and freedom belongs to the man, while the brunt of the burdens of family life (and especially those dealing with childrearing) falls on the wife. The strong support for the Equal Rights Amendment is one indication that people are aware of the problems created by these traditional laws and want to have them changed. In addition, the feminist movement has shown that these laws are unfair to wives in today's society since a majority of young married women are working. This is bound to have an effect on the legal system and bring about changes in the legal marriage contract. There is also a growing number of people living in alternative family structures, and there is an increasing demand for legal protection for such persons.[16]

It may be that new changes in our marriage laws will come about from our changing social customs. It is already clear that many laws, particularly those on sexual behavior, are not strictly enforced. One desirable legal revision would be a standardization of state laws so that couples would not find it advantageous to marry or divorce in states where they are not resident. In that way, the governing agency most closely related to them, with the easiest access to such vital information as marital status, health, and financial responsibility, would also register and supervise their marriage. Moreover, if legal reform were accompanied by a standardization of the vital statistics required for marriage and divorce, the factors involved in the stability and instability of marriage could be more readily studied by sociologists. Our society is now in the incongruous position of recognizing many of the major problems in marriage and divorce while failing to provide the basic information necessary to find the solutions to those problems.

[15]Lenore J. Weitzman, "To Love, Honor, and Obey? Traditional Legal Marriage and Alternative Family Forms," *The Family Coordinator,* 24, no. 4 (Oct. 1975), 531–48.

[16]See Weitzman, pp. 540 ff. Also, see D. Kelly Weisberg, "Alternative Family Structures and the Law," *The Family Coordinator,* 24, no. 4 (Oct. 1975), 549–59.

The Honeymoon

The wedding celebration culminates in the honeymoon, the traditional rite of status passage into the married state. It marks a transition from single life to marriage. During this time, the couple break away from family and friends and have the privacy to give their undivided attention to each other.

Fifty years ago a special honeymoon was highly significant for a middle-class couple. They had probably never traveled and had perhaps been closely chaperoned, and the honeymoon was their first chance to be alone together, the time to initiate their sexual relationship. Today the honeymoon does not mark so strong a break with past experience. Chaperones are practically non-existent, and most college students travel long before they are married. And there is greater flexibility in their relationship before marriage. "Why should we spend $750 on a honeymoon," they may ask, "when that same money would carry us through another semester at school or pay for half the furniture in our apartment?" Still, the honeymoon is important because it marks the beginning of married life. You cannot always remember the first time you met your future wife or husband or how you decided on the third and fourth ushers in your wedding party. But you will remember your honeymoon, be it long or short, and you should strive to make it a pleasant and enjoyable one.

There is no simple way to compress a lifetime of adjustment and growth toward maturity into the few days of the honeymoon. A couple should not expect miracles. Their sexual adjustment will probably not be perfect, and they should not overromanticize it and feel that it should be. Nor will they immediately merge habits in every other phase of life just because they are officially a married couple. However, the honeymoon is a good time to begin compromising on the little things that determine whether married life goes smoothly. And fortunately, most couples do find their honeymoons satisfying and memorable in a majority of ways.

Planning the Wedding Trip

Couples planning their weddings will find that honeymoons are also big business. Carl Gersuny has written with insight on the honeymoon business in the Pocono Mountains area. He describes the multimillion-dollar honeymoon service industry there and the way in which it sells wedding trips to a "Pocono love nest" to thousands of newlyweds annually. In true American fashion, the hucksters of honeymoonism seem to have discovered a need on the part of many newly married couples. Honeymooners want to be sure that their honeymoon will be a success; what more natural way to ensure that than by paying the price to people who will guarantee results?

The honeymoon might be compared with other important rites involving

services to the family. The clergyman or wedding director assists in the plans for the wedding; the doctor and hospital provide assistance for the birth of a child (and discourage childbearing at home). The funeral director provides complete services for the time of death. And the honeymoon hotel provides atmosphere, entertainment, privacy, and even informal counseling to make sure the newlyweds face their initial adjustment to each other with a minimum of risk.

> Society in the United States is characterized by other-directedness, declining average age at first marriage, and relatively high levels of discretionary income. Combined with an increase in the proportion of the labor force in the service sectors, these characteristics are conducive to increasing demand for the specialized services of the honeymoon industry, which will undoubtedly continue to grow.
>
> This is a service industry without constituencies on the order of school attendance districts. Rather, it is a highly competitive, specialized service marked by intense rivalry for clients. As indicated, the entrepreneurs in this industry have elaborated an exceedingly colorful rhetoric to win the hearts and minds of engaged couples.[17]

The honeymoon should be a brief period of rest and relaxation. It does not need to be a month's cruise to Bermuda or six weeks in the Canadian Rockies, but it ought to be at least a short interlude during which the couple

[17]Carl Gersuny, "The Honeymoon Industry: Rhetoric and Bureaucratization of Status Passage," *The Family Coordinator,* 19, no. 3 (July 1970), 260–66.

can relax after the hectic days of preparation for the wedding, take time to enjoy themselves, and just appreciate each other. The honeymoon should be personal and private. A couple need not feel that they must have a honeymoon just like every other couple's. If the couple plan a pleasant trip that meets their needs and falls within their budget, they can expect to find it both enjoyable and fulfilling. They should have privacy and a chance to be themselves on the kind of schedule and in the kind of environment that is most pleasing to them.

SUMMARY

Readiness for marriage is important for a couple's future success. The partnership should be built on the sound personality development of both partners, since emotional maturity and ego strength are vital in a relationship. Love remains the basic element, the extra plus for the union, while communication is another key factor, involving clear and direct speech and careful listening. Communication may be nonverbal as well as verbal.

Achievement in education and career is another indicator of marriage readiness. Success in these two areas carries over into marriage. A balance must be struck between available partners (largest at the younger ages) and increased maturity (into the older twenties and thirties). Moral and spiritual values are crucial factors in strengthening a marriage.

The wedding celebration is a special rite of passage. The majority of couples prefer a religious to a civil ceremony. Careful preparation for marriage is the appropriate goal of all weddings. The wedding serves at least three purposes: it focuses attention on the couple's change from single to married status; it establishes a basic legal framework for the new family; and if it is a religious wedding, it gives the marriage spiritual meaning and direction.

There are a number of ways to evaluate wedding plans. Does the wedding reinforce the engagement, so that the couple have time to be together and prepare themselves emotionally for their marriage? Do the wedding plans fit the families, particularly the bride's? Who plans the wedding? Do the couple really see the ceremony as an extension of their true love and concern for each other? Is the emphasis on things, or on the two persons who are being joined together?

During all the planning for the wedding, the couple may lose sight of the fact that marriage is a legal contract based on English common law. Previously, the husband was favored, but today there is progress toward equality of husband and wife in the marriage.

Finally, careful planning of the honeymoon is needed. The honeymoon is the important beginning of married life. For some couples it means a resort vacation planned by the honeymoon industry. It should, however, be a personal and private experience for the newlywed couple.

SUGGESTED READINGS

Bach, George R., and Peter Wyden. *The Intimate Enemy: How to Fight Fair in Love and Marriage.* New York: Morrow, 1968. Suggestions for constructively channeling aggression; developed in a program with several hundred couples.

Call, Vaughn R. A., and Luther B. Ott. "Age at Marriage as a Mobility Contingency: Estimates for the Nye-Berardo Model," *Journal of Marriage and the Family,* 39, no. 1 (Feb. 1977), 67–79. Interesting study of group of young men from age 17 to 32. Refutes idea of absolute necessity of a college education for success in marriage and career.

Crosby, John F. *Illusion and Disillusion: The Self in Love and Marriage,* 2nd ed. Belmont, Calif.: Wadsworth, 1976, Chapter 9. Special focus on new patterns in the premarital and early marital periods; includes the "two-step" marriage.

Felson, Marcus, and David Knoke. "Social Status and the Married Woman," *Journal of Marriage and the Family,* 36, no. 3 (Aug. 1974), 516–21. Study of over 1,100 men and women comparing family status as it relates to careers of husbands and wives. Majority of couples studied maintain many traditional role patterns.

Lee, Gary R. "Age at Marriage and Marital Satisfaction: A Multivariate Analysis with Implications for Marital Stability," *Journal of Marriage and the Family,* 39, no. 3 (Aug. 1977), 493–504.

Melville, Keith. *Marriage and Family Today.* New York: Random House, 1977. Good introduction to some of the problems of the beginning period of marital adjustment.

Reiss, Ira. *Family Systems in America,* 2nd ed. Hinsdale, Ill.: Dryden, 1976. Discussion of marriage as it affects different social and ethnic groups.

Weitzman, Lenore J. "To Love, Honor, and Obey? Traditional Legal Marriage and Alternative Family Forms," *The Family Coordinator,* 24, no. 4 (Oct. 1975), 531–48. Examines the legal consequences of some alternative family forms. This issue of *The Family Coordinator* includes a number of discussions of variant family forms and lifestyles.

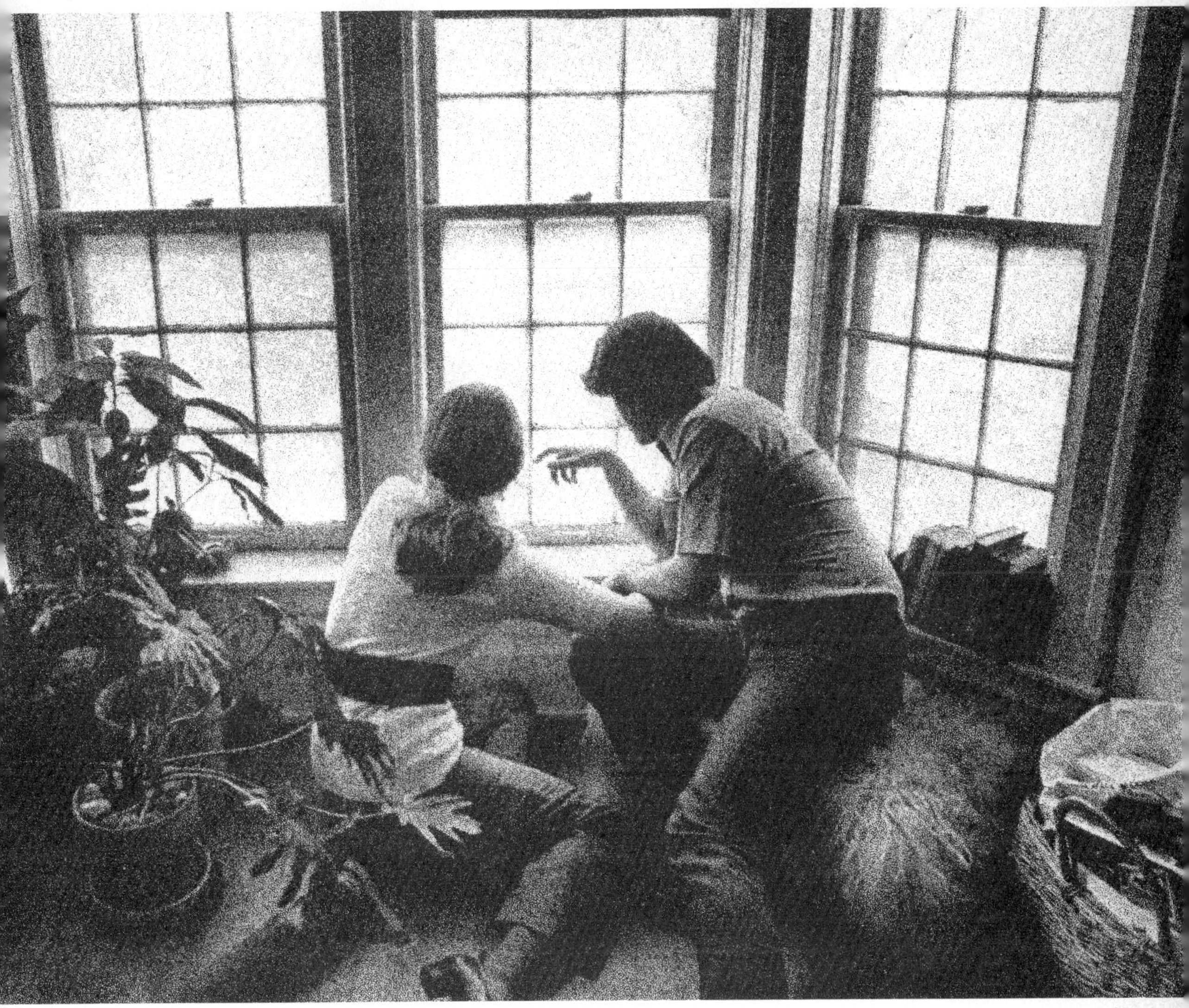

Part IV
Early Marital Adjustment

11 Beginning Marriage

- How would you define successful marital adjustment?
- Are there different levels of marital adjustment throughout the family life cycle?
- What factors are most important in making a good beginning in marriage?
- How do a couple learn to communicate their deepest feelings?
- What are the most important things that husband and wife share in marriage?
- Why are so many marriages filled with tension and conflicts? How can a couple resolve these tensions and conflicts?
- What are the most common patterns of decision-making in a marriage? How do a couple reach a "balance of power" in their marriage partnership?

Strengthening the New Partnership

A good beginning is a helpful thing in many areas of life. When you start a new job or a new college program, it is beneficial to have an open, optimistic, and friendly attitude. It is good to begin a trip to a new city, a new state, or a country overseas with expectations of a safe journey, pleasant experiences, and a rewarding visit. In the same way, you should enter marriage with love, good faith, and high expectations.

The beginning of married life is a unique experience for each couple. Never before have two individuals with these particular experiences, personalities, and expectations been united in marriage and committed to sharing their lives. To begin a life together after an exciting courtship, engagement, wedding, and honeymoon is not always easy, for marriage encompasses the complexity and tension of every aspect of human living. The initial adjustments made by husband and wife will determine whether their marriage lives up to their expectations or whether they meet obstacles in reaching their goals.

The first adjustments will often be casual and taken for granted. The husband unconsciously takes the lead in certain things and the wife in others.

The routine ways of organizing the day's and week's activities may roll along without any major effort on the part of either partner. In other cases couples may require much more effort and a longer period of experimentation before they can learn to compromise. Her family or his may seem to visit too often, which can become a real source of contention between them. His idea of how often they should share the physical expression of their love may be different from hers, especially when the honeymoon is over and she is busy with a full day's work. Her custom of church attendance every Sunday may be far from his preference for a leisurely late breakfast followed by eighteen holes at the county golf course. And he may not have expected to share the housework with her or to have to prepare his own dinner when she is working late at the office.

It is important to realize that adjustment in marriage, during the first year as well as throughout the entire life cycle, is not focused on any single activity. Rather, it comprises big and little decisions on many things. A couple need to establish routines for everyday living, to learn to make purposeful decisions together, and to build new friendships as a couple to replace old friendships severed by time, distance, and their new activities and interests. They must build wholesome and satisfying relationships with both parental families without running the risk of domination or disruptive antagonism. They will have to establish a working family budget, or at least an informal financial plan that will keep the new partnership solvent. They will need to find a mutually satisfying pattern of sexual activity. They will want to share some meaningful expression of their religious conviction and practice. And, if they want children, they should plan ahead for them without either unrealistic optimism or needless anxiety. In all those ways and in many others, husband and wife must learn to give and take, to be both aggressive and submissive and to search for the mutual responsibility and enjoyment that will lay the strongest possible foundation for their future happiness.

Defining Marital Adjustment

It is not easy to define what we mean by marital adjustment. Many diverse definitions have been used in the family field in the last fifty years. Spanier and Cole, in a recent summary of the literature, suggest that adjustment is a process, with several component parts:

> Marital adjustment is a process, the outcome of which is determined by the degree of:
> 1. Troublesome marital differences.
> 2. Interspousal tensions and personal anxiety.
> 3. Marital satisfaction.

4. Dyadic cohesion.*
5. Consensus on matters of importance to marital functioning.[1]

Their work suggests that we have tried to oversimplify our understanding of an adjustment process that is really quite complicated. In order to make valid judgments, Spanier and Cole suggest, we need to use as accurate a measure as possible, taking into account all the information that is available. Our present marital adjustment scales are inaccurate. Better methods and more relevant research are needed in order to help us deal more effectively with individual and marital adjustment processes. We must recognize that some of the factors we are trying to evaluate may need to be re-examined as new and more precise research becomes available. With these reservations in mind, let us consider the first months and years of family life in more detail.

The Family Life Cycle

In earlier chapters, we focused our attention on the couple beginning married life together for the first time. They are probably in their early twenties, the median age for marriage in the United States. But many other newly married couples do not fit this norm. One or both partners may be in a second marriage, so that each partner has a different marital experience and expectation. One partner may be some years older than the other. There may be children from the previous marriage who live with the couple, or with a prior spouse. These and other factors make it useful to consider marital adjustment in terms of the family life cycle, and to evaluate the couple partly in light of their particular stage in the cycle.

There have been several analyses of the family life cycle. An early summary by Sorokin et al. saw four stages in the cycle, with newlyweds at the beginning followed by couples with children, couples with one or more grown, self-supporting children, and, finally, older couples, with grown children out of the home.[2] If each child and its development are included, many more stages are possible.

Evelyn Duvall has proposed eight stages in the family life cycle, and they have proven to be a very practical and logical progression.[3] Her summary

*The increasing closeness of two partners in matters important to their marriage.

[1]Graham B. Spanier and Charles L. Cole, "Toward Clarification Investigation of Marital Adjustment," *International Journal of Sociology of the Family*, 6, no. 1 (Spring 1976), 127–28.

[2]Pitirim Sorokin et al., *A Systematic Source Book in Rural Sociology*, Vol. 2 (Minneapolis: University of Minnesota Press, 1931), p. 31.

[3]Evelyn Millis Duvall, *Marriage and Family Development*, 5th ed. (Philadelphia: Lippincott, 1977), pp. 144–45.

Table 11–1 Duvall's Eight-Stage Family Life Cycle

Stage	*Designation and Descriptive Interval Qualities*
I	Married couples (without children)
II	Childbearing families (oldest child, birth–30 months)
III	Families with preschool children (oldest child, 2½–6 years)
IV	Families with school children (oldest child, 6–13 years)
V	Families with teenagers (oldest child, 13–20 years)
VI	Families launching young adults (first child gone to last child's leaving home)
VII	Middle-aged parents (empty nest to retirement)
VIII	Aging family members (retirement to death of both spouses)

SOURCE: "Duvall's Eight Stage Family Life Cycle" from *Marriage and Family Development,* 5th Edition by Evelyn Millis Duvall. Copyright © 1957, 1962, 1967, 1971, 1977 by J. B. Lippincott Company. By permission of the publisher.

of the eight stages is presented in Table 11–1. The cycle presupposes the birth of children to the couple, and is thus most useful in analyzing the intact nuclear family. Alternative family patterns will have to be evaluated in a somewhat different manner, depending on the circumstances involved.

We have already discussed some of the changes that have occurred in the family life cycle in this country because of changes in the marriage age, the smaller number of children, the independence of young adults, and the much longer period of time allocated to stages VII and VIII in the cycle (see Table 11–1). Naturally these changes have a marked impact on marital adjustment and, as much as possible, should be considered by each family unit as they assess their own lifestyle and expectations.[4]

Marriage and the Family Life Cycle

The romantic image of marriage suggests that the couple who are deeply in love and begin their marriage under favorable conditions will gradually achieve a more and more harmonious relationship. Sociologists have reinforced this hypothesis with studies designed to show the number of ways in which successful couples reach adjustment early in marriage. On the other hand, couples unable to reach such adjustment gradually move apart, some

[4]Duvall has given a detailed study of these factors in her chapter "The Family Life Cycle" *(Marriage and Family Development,* pp. 137–57). A similar approach to change across three generations is shown in the study by Reuben Hill, *Family Development in Three Generations* (Cambridge, Mass.: Schenkman, 1970).

of them into separation and divorce. As J. Richard Udry has shown in his critical summary of marital interaction processes, we simply do not have consistent data that support a single direct and clear-cut interpretation of marital adjustment.[5] There is some evidence that adjustment, understanding, communication, and need satisfaction increase over a period of time; but there is also contrary evidence to suggest that marriage more typically becomes less satisfactory as time goes on. Since there seems to be no immediate solution to this dilemma, we can only highlight the various ways in which marital adjustment must be made and discuss each in view of the relevant findings.

Another crucial question that has not yet been answered satisfactorily, as Udry has pointed out, is the problem of how to define adjustment or happiness or success.[6] What do those terms mean? Can we measure them by the fact that the couple are not separated or divorced and rate themselves as "happy"? Or do we want them to show evidence of their adjustment or happiness by playing golf together, sharing the same friends, going to the same church, or doing the grocery shopping together? Because of the wide range of value standards in our society, we are bound to have divergent views on what adjustment and happiness mean. Undoubtedly this is a reflection of our rapidly changing society and our highly mobile families. The goals and satisfactions a married couple have shared together as newlyweds in an apartment in a small Midwestern town may not seem adequate when the husband has become a successful businessman in suburban Philadelphia and the wife is involved in a wide range of community and social activities.

[5]J. Richard Udry, *The Social Context of Marriage*, 3rd ed. (Philadelphia: Lippincott, 1974), Chapter 11.
[6]Udry, pp. 207–08.

Decades ago, when family life was more stable and many couples lived in the same community all their lives, it was easier to connect the goals and aspirations of childhood with those of later stages in life. The couple's surroundings were more constant, and relatives and friends were more apt to be stable elements in the couple's experience. But today, when families often move every two or three years, it is harder to define adjustment and marital success.

Another way of looking at the problem is to ask whether or not the total impact of marriage is more favorable for the husband or for the wife. Does one get a better break than the other? Jessie Bernard, in her thought-provoking book *The Future of Marriage,* has suggested that it is clearly the male partner who has the best of it.[7] Marriage for the wife involves so much surrender and reconciliation that there is a definite destructive nature to it. Norval Glenn, on the other hand, takes a more optimistic view of happiness as reflected in several national surveys. He reports that:

> The pooled data from three recent U.S. national surveys show that, among whites of both sexes, married persons report greater personal happiness than widowed, divorced or separated, or never-married persons, the difference being somewhat greater for females than for males. Although the association between marital status and reported happiness may be partially spurious, I report evidence which indicates that it is very unlikely to be totally spurious. . . . Pooled data from two national surveys show that white females, as a whole, report about the same level of marital happiness as white males.[8]

Predicting the Family Life Cycle

Can we predict what the family life cycle will be like in the 1980s? We need accurate knowledge of what life will be like as a basis for our expectations of how we will adjust to our marriage partner. Paul C. Glick of the Population Division of the Bureau of the Census has attempted to give us such a basis. In Table 11–2, Glick shows how the final stages of the family cycle are changing and how the greatest impact of this change is on women, particularly in the lengthened period of time between the marriage of the last child and the death of the spouse. This period is now eight times as long as it was in the 1900s. Women are thinking about their marriage in terms of their roles as mothers, but are also looking forward to an increasing number of years without parental responsibility.

[7]Jessie Bernard, *The Future of Marriage* (New York: Bantam), 1972.
[8]Norval D. Glenn, "The Contribution of Marriage to the Psychological Well-Being of Males and Females," *Journal of Marriage and the Family,* 37, no. 3 (Aug. 1975), 599.

Table 11–2 Median Age of Mothers at Selected Stages of the Family Life Cycle

Stage of the Family Life Cycle	80-Year Average	1880s / 1900s	1890s / 1910s	1900s / 1920s	1910s / 1930s	1920s / 1940s	1930 / 1950s	1940s / 1960s	1950s / 1970s
		Period of Birth of Mother / *Approximate Period of First Marriage*							
Median age at:									
First marriage	20.9	21.4	21.2	21.0	21.4	20.7	20.0	20.5	21.2
Birth of first child	22.6	23.0	22.9	22.8	23.5	22.7	21.4	21.8	22.7
Birth of last child	31.3	32.9	32.0	31.0	32.0	31.5	31.2	30.1	29.6
Marriage of last child	53.5	55.4	54.8	53.0	53.2	53.2	53.6	52.7	52.3
Death of one spouse	62.8	57.0	59.6	62.3	63.7	64.4	65.1	65.1	65.2
Difference between age at first marriage and:									
Birth of first child	1.7	1.6	1.7	1.8	2.1	2.0	1.4	1.3	1.5
Birth of last child	10.4	11.5	10.8	10.0	10.6	10.8	11.2	9.6	8.4
Marriage of last child	32.6	34.0	33.6	32.0	31.8	32.5	33.6	32.2	31.1
Death of one spouse	41.9	35.6	38.4	41.3	42.3	43.7	45.1	44.6	44.0
Difference between:									
Age at birth of first and last children	8.7	9.9	9.1	8.2	8.5	8.8	9.8	8.3	6.9
Age at birth of and marriage of last child	22.2	22.5	22.8	22.0	21.2	21.7	22.4	22.6	22.7
Age at marriage of last child and death of one spouse (empty nest)	9.3	1.6	4.8	9.3	10.5	11.2	11.5	12.4	12.9

SOURCE: Paul C. Glick, "Updating the Life Cycle of the Family," *Journal of Marriage and the Family*, 39, no. 1 (Jan. 1977), 6. Copyrighted by the National Council on Family Relations. Reprinted by permission.

Positive Factors in the Beginning Marriage

In the previous chapter we discussed some of the positive factors that are associated with stable and successful marriages. These are elements of living that are important to both single and married people and that contribute to the development of a loving and satisfying marital relationship. They include sound personality development for each partner; the importance of love, the universal element (see Chapter 7); the growth of effective communication; the factors of educational and career achievement; the importance of age in

mature preparation for marriage; and the place of moral and spiritual values. These elements continue to have a central place once bride and groom settle down to married life together. Let us now focus on six other factors that act as positive reinforcements for the beginning marital relationship.

Appreciation

Appreciation is a basic positive factor for the young married couple, and it should have a central place in their marriage. In the courtship process, the young couple often compliment each other. Such compliments have meaning and contribute significantly to the relationship. Psychology has shown us the importance of appreciation, or, in behavioral terms, positive reinforcement. We learn to do those things for which we receive a positive reward, and cease doing those things that are negatively reinforced. It is no surprise, then, to find that appreciation is a key factor in the smooth functioning of the marriage partnership.

Yet this is an ingredient that is often missing in marriage. The couple take each other for granted, and fail to appreciate each other. Their marriage relationship becomes boring, and the romantic element recedes into the background. What is needed is a constant pattern of appreciation flowing between partners. Nick Stinnett, in reporting his study of a group of well-adjusted couples in Oklahoma, listed appreciation as one of four outstanding characteristics of these midwestern couples.[9] These couples found it worthwhile to share with each other their positive feelings, and to make appreciation open and rewarding to all family members. It is a simple key to behavior that will enlarge and strengthen many aspects of day-to-day behavior.[10]

[9]Groves Conference Workshop, Kansas City, Missouri, April 1976.
[10]See also Nick Stinnett and James Walters, *Relationships in Marriage and Family* (New York: Macmillan, 1977), pp. 84–85.

Equality

Perhaps today's generation of college students will mark the end of the double standard in America, and the beginning of a single standard of sexual, social, economic, political, and personal behavior for men and women. The fact that many of today's couples begin their marriage relationship as equals is a trememdous step forward. Equality means that they can strengthen their relationship with input from both partners, with each one contributing the maximum share that is possible to the growth of the partnership.

This equality will be reflected in many ways inside and outside of the couple's home life. It will affect career choice, place of residence, leisure activities, religious activities, and extended family relationships. Gertrude Zemon Gass wants to see equality extend into marriage counseling. She believes what is needed is "equitable marriage." She writes:

> There is, however, an increasing number of marriages in which the partners are attempting to move toward a goal of self-realization, toward a relationship which favors creativity, and toward an interaction in which one person does not achieve at the expense of his or her mate. This attempted shift by many toward a balanced relationship is responsible to a great degree for changing role relationships among married couples who are young, in their middle years, and older couples as well.[11]

If striving for new freedom for women has increased separation and divorce, so the achievement of real equality in marriage can be expected to strengthen the marriage bond. Both husband and wife can become free to be their best selves.

Love and Joy

A major task of the couple throughout their marriage is to continue the development of love and joy in their daily life together. During courtship, engagement, the honeymoon, and the early weeks of marriage there is usually a very strong romantic element in the couple's relationship. This romantic orientation is almost impossible to maintain throughout the course of a lifetime. If a couple's love for each other is to develop and mature over the years rather than become dull and irrelevant, certain definite steps must be taken. The couple must expect and accept the change from romance to routine. A night out at the movies, with a snack at the coffee shop before coming home at 2 A.M., may no longer be feasible when the couple must leave for work

[11]Gertrude Zemon Gass, "Equitable Marriage," *The Family Coordinator*, 23, no. 4 (Oct. 1974), 369–72.

at 7 in the morning. If the budget is being stretched to include a new house, a new car, or a new baby, the couple may have to limit their former taste for steak, lobster, or some other expensive dish. This should not be a letdown; it should be expected.

A couple should maintain the romantic element in their marriage in a number of little ways. He can open the car door for her. He can remember their anniversary and her birthday or comment on her new dress. She in turn can cook a special dish, compliment him on a new tie, or remember his birthday. A wholesome emphasis on a lot of the little things in the marriage will go a long way.

Finally, a couple should strive to preserve the intimacy of their relationship. They seek privacy during courtship and engagement: there is so much to talk about, and so many things each person wants to know about the other. In marriage this note of intimacy can easily be lost. The couple slip into the routine of everyday living and no longer attempt to create special occasions for each other.

The only way to preserve intimacy in our modern marital system is to make conscious provision for it. Arrangements may be made for a reliable babysitter so that there can be a real night out. Or an occasional meal when the children have been fed and put to bed can help to preserve and enhance the intimacy the couple cherished so dearly in courtship. In some definite and planned-for ways, husband and wife must continue to show each other that their own relationship is the primary one and that all other aspects of family life enrich and develop their personal feeling rather than destroy it.

A. Lynn Scoresby stresses the importance of love and joy in building marriage as a place of happiness.[12] She believes that while love can be described as giving, it can also be described as a reciprocal relationship of giving and receiving. This balanced exchange gives each person the freedom to grow and be himself or herself. In such a situation, love and joy reinforce each other.

Shared Goals and Experiences

Another important element in developing the marriage relationship is the creation of common goals and experiences. This is reflected in the strong emphasis on companionship in modern American marriage. Here is an interesting cultural phenomenon. Before marriage we are expected to assert our individual independence and uniqueness. Our maturity is partially measured by our freedom from parental domination, and we strive to build successful life patterns as individuals: to plan our education carefully, to choose a promising career, to make new friends at college and in business. But after marriage we are expected to share all our goals and experiences.

If the married couple build common goals, the bond between them becomes stronger with the passage of time. They often live at a distance from their families and the close friends of their teenage and college years. And they may continue to change jobs or homes frequently enough to break close contacts made through business or the community. If husband and wife genuinely share their leisure time, their love will be strengthened and deepened by their shared experiences.

How does one develop a set of shared goals and experiences? We have so many routine tasks that we fail to point our marriage and family life in the direction we really want them to go. Piercy and Schultz have suggested that couples can build on the current interest in "value clarification" and strengthen their relationship.[13] A number of strategies developed in other disciplines have been found helpful in marriage enrichment programs. Couples can "vote" for their most important values, see their values on a continuum, and recognize the meaning of differences in their values. Open discussion and clarification of the couples' value structures are a significant way of building this aspect of the marital relationship.

One area of early marital adjustment that is often neglected is the need to build new friendships as the marriage begins. Many couples live and work at some distance from their homes or from their college communities just after they are married. There may be no friends or in-laws near enough to visit and enjoy social occasions with the couple. Very typically the husband's

[12]A. Lynn Scoresby, *The Marriage Dialogue* (Reading, Mass.: Addison-Wesley, 1977), pp. 177–78.

[13]Fred Piercy and Kay Schultz, "Values Clarification Strategies for Couples' Enrichment," *The Family Coordinator*, 27, no. 2 (April 1978), 175–78.

work will cause him to be transferred to new communities every three or four years, and the whole process of building friendships and a normal social life must be started all over again. If the couple are skillful at meeting and developing friendships, the breadth and elasticity of their marriage will be expanded. As a couple, if they can build natural friendly links with other couples, they will have a chance to observe their own partnership in better perspective. The couple may think of their own experiences as unique, but through social contact they will discover that their fears, anxieties, and problems are shared by many others.

In large degree, the emphasis in American courtship is on the dating couple rather than on their relationships to others in social settings. There is frequent double dating and a great deal of mass recreational activity, but the focus is on the individual couple in the entire process from the first date to engagement and marriage. Such a pattern is difficult and often frustrating to maintain throughout the course of a marriage. More normal give-and-take with other couples and with both mutual and separate circles of friends is a more mature and stimulating way to live and will give the couple greater resiliency and stability in their own relationship.

Creative Use of Conflict

A mythology that has grown up around marriage is that it will be a continual "honeymoon." The satisfactions of married life, and the realization that the couple now have the opportunity to share all of their life together, has been sometimes enlarged to suggest that the couple will sail smoothly along with no differences at all and, certainly, with no major conflicts. This is an illusion. A couple are bound to have some disagreements. Two people who have strong personalities will undoubtedly find that they do not agree on every aspect of their new partnership.

How can the couple deal with this problem? They should learn the creative use of conflict. Conflict must be recognized, dealt with in a reasonable manner, and settled in a way that is equitable to both of the marriage partners. Such conflict resolution is a key part of the Marriage Enrichment Program developed through the Association of Couples for Marriage Enrichment (ACME) by David and Vera Mace.[14] Conflict has been central in the work of Dr. George Bach in his study of "How to Fight Fair in Love and Marriage."[15] It has been a prominent part of much of the encounter-group and sensitivity training that has been so popular in psychology during the last decade. This is not to say that indiscriminately making marriage a bat-

[14]See David and Vera Mace, *We Can Have Better Marriages, If We Really Want Them* (Nashville: Abingdon, 1974).

[15]See George R. Bach and Peter Wyden, *The Intimate Enemy: How to Fight Fair in Love and Marriage* (New York: Morrow, 1968).

tlefield will bring instant and beneficial results. But a wise and creative use of the conflict situation to bring differences in the partnership into the open, and to resolve them as soon as possible, is of great value.

Making a Commitment

The achievement of a successful marital partnership is a major accomplishment. It requires a working commitment on the part of both husband and wife that takes patience, understanding, energy, a willingness to compromise, flexibility, and lots of good, old-fashioned perseverance. In the marriage relationship, two unique individuals strive to become one and in that oneness to find genuine satisfaction, happiness, and a pattern of human living worth sharing with their children and with tomorrow's world.[16]

The couple must make a genuine and realistic dedication of themselves to the goal of a successful and stable marriage. The motivation for this kind of dedication comes from the love husband and wife have for each other, coupled with a family background that nurtures and encourages this kind of a marriage relationship. Excellent marriages do not just happen. There is abundant evidence that many marriages drag along from year to year, offering no special meaning to the partners and no contribution to their zest for life. If a couple simply drift into marriage because it is the simplest and easiest way to meet their personal and cultural expectations, and allow themselves thereafter to be pulled apart by conflicting social, psychological, and personal forces, the results are easily predictable. They will retain only the shell of a genuine marriage, and if there is any appealing or obvious way to break the marriage bond, they will do so.

Genuine and realistic dedication to the achievement of a rewarding marriage—one that is not just ordinary and will give both partners satisfaction and responsibility—will carry the couple through the inevitable crises of their experience together.

A working commitment is important to the success of innovative lifestyles as well. Rosabeth Moss Kanter, in studying Utopian communities, has suggested that commitment involves continuing the group, building cohesion among its members, anc achieving a degree of control over the group.[17] She points out that a Utopian group must demand a firm positive allegiance on the part of its members; if a strong commitment does not exist, the group cannot achieve its purpose. It is no surprise, really, that the small dyadic group we define as monogamous marriage demands a working commitment too.

[16]See Ernest J. Green, *Personal Relationships: An Approach to Marriage and Family* (New York: McGraw-Hill, 1978), pp. 141–42.

[17]Rosabeth Moss Kanter, *Commitment and Community: Communes and Utopias in Sociological Perspective* (Cambridge, Mass.: Harvard University Press, 1972).

The Family as a System

An important way of looking at the family is as a system. This system has two major characteristics: Its parts are directly related together; and there is a reasonably stable relation between the parts during any particular period of time. Kantor and Lehr have defined *family systems* "like all social systems, [as] organizationally complex, open, adaptive, and information-processing systems."[18] There are many implications in this definition for the beginning months and years of the marriage. Family life is complex, and the closer a couple are to their parental families, and the more intimate and interactive are their relations to their friends, and the sooner children are introduced into the system, the more complex the relationship will become. Openness has already been discussed as a major factor in marriage. The emphasis in systems theory is on openness both inside and outside the family structure. In addition, the family system adapts itself readily to new situations. We are all aware of the constantly changing nature of the larger social environment in which we live. Conflict and stress within the family, and in the relationships we have at work, in our communities, and with our neighbors, means that an ability to make flexible adaptations is a basic need.

Balance of Power in the Family

What is the family power structure? Will power and decision-making be shared, or will one person dominate the other, so that the family is really a dictatorship? Decision-making must be shared by husband and wife. The two must work together, talking about important decisions that need to be made and sharing equally in them. In families in which the "balance of power" cannot be agreed on—in which there is disagreement over dominance—there are likely to be problems.

Why should one partner want to boss the other? Why should a man be adamant about his rights and authority in the home, or a woman insist on managing the money and dominating the family circle? The answers to these questions lie first of all in the personal backgrounds of the individuals, for they have brought certain concepts and habit patterns into marriage. If John's family has been ruled strongly by his father, and mother and children have been asked to give unquestioned obedience to his every wish and command, then John will probably want to have a position of similar control in his own family life. If Betty, on the other hand, has watched her mother raise four children single-handed, she will probably picture herself as having a far more important part to play in family decisions than John expects. There

[18]David Kantor and William Lehr, *Inside the Family* (New York: Harper Colophon Books, 1976), p. 10.

is such a wide variance in the decision-making process in any average sample of American families that husband and wife may well come into marriage with unequal levels of experience and anticipation.

Another reason that one partner may want to boss the other is that marriage involves a large number of working tasks and decisions. Most married couples begin their life together with somewhat limited resources; the number of things they want to possess and the number of places where they would like to go are largely limited by their available time and assets. In other words, there is much to be done, and everything cannot be done at once. The husband wants to improve his job; the wife wants to complete her education; they both would like to have a house replace the apartment for family shelter; and children are desired to make the family circle complete. If one partner or the other takes the lead, perhaps some of these things can be accomplished more quickly. It always takes longer for two people to decide something than for one. Hence, it becomes very easy for one spouse to attempt to dominate the other.

The naturally desired outcome of the family tug of war is for the couple to reach a mutually satisfying adjustment to each other—one that can provide a maximum of achievement and happiness with a minimum of tension and friction. The sizable percentage of marriages that have ended in divorce in the years since the Second World War indicates that many couples cannot develop an acceptable balance of power.

Cromwell and Olson have summarized three domains of family power. Their report from the Missouri Symposium discusses the resources that are available for power in the family, the processes (or interactions) that go on within the family, and the outcomes of power struggles, i.e., who actually wins.[19] Their study reminds us that there is no simple way of describing who is in command of any one particular family situation. Power is always present, but its use must be described and measured in precise terms.

Exercise of Power in the Family

The exercise of power is bound to have a decisive influence on the family, and particularly on the newly married couple. The traditional pattern of dominance gives the bulk of authority and decision-making to the husband. We have discussed some of the characteristics of this pattern in Chapter 5. The husband provided for his family, ran the government, and fought if need be to protect his home and country. The religious tradition was also one of masculine dominance, and in the marital sexual relationship the man was the dominant and aggressive partner.

The wife's activity, on the other hand, is often carried out in the more limited sphere of the home. If she does not work, she will not meet so many new people in any one day or week; nor must she compete with others day by day to prove her success and accomplishment. She may be seen as a consumer of the goods and services that are produced by her husband and others in the outside community. Her training and guidance of the children do not produce as many immediate results, for they are aimed at children's future accomplishments.

Russell was a competent insurance agent, having started work for a large firm after college graduation. He had been promoted to a lucrative suburban territory and was respected as one of the most successful salesmen. He came from a family in which the father had made almost all the decisions and the mother had been quiet and submissive.

When Russell married Susette, a fashion designer for a metropolitan department store chain, he immediately established his place as head of the house. He managed the family income, including Susette's salary, and made all major decisions concerning the choice of home or apartment, automobile, insurance, and so on. He designated a certain amount of money to his wife for a very modest food and household budget. After their three children were born, he continued to make family decisions unilaterally, although he did not take too active a part in the discipline and education of the children.

[19]Ronald E. Cromwell and David H. Olson, eds., *Power in Families* (New York: Halsted Press, 1975), pp. 5–7.

Susette began to realize that she was a second-class citizen in her marriage. She became more aware of her own potential and capabilities. Gradually she came to resent being excluded from family decisions, since she worked long hours at her job and in her homemaking duties.

One weekend Russell announced that he was leaving the insurance firm in order to set up a mortgage and real estate business. He planned to complete special studies for the needed licenses and utilize his wife as secretary and office assistant until the business became self-supporting. "You'll enjoy having your own office and some afternoons off," he said, "and you won't have to drive into town to work in the crowded business district."

Susette was dismayed. She had always avoided office work, since her interests were more creative and artistic. Giving up her fashion design position would cut off a portion of the family income and put both husband and wife into the same speculative business. "How can I give up something I love to do and am paid well for doing," she asked friends in bewilderment, "to take a chance on a job that may not even pay a salary if my husband is unable to begin it successfully? It's impossible, and I won't do it!"

The arguments that resulted from these two different concepts of marital decision-making and dominance finally led to the separation of the couple. The subsequent failure of the mortgage business only intensified the wife's resentment. Although the wife had agreed to be submissive to her husband during most of the early years of marriage, the husband's inability to sense her feelings and his unwillingness to modify any of his thinking about sharing important decisions with her led to an open split between them.

The changes in role behavior we discussed in Chapter 5 are having a strong impact on the balance of power in the family. There have always been dominant women, in every society, but usually they had to maintain their position of power against severe criticism. Because modern women are gaining more freedom and equality, there are bound to be more families today in which the wife's assertion of her abilities and rights leads to her dominance. This is not the most common pattern, but there are a number of ways in which it comes about. The husband may be in the service or be required to travel because of his work, and in his absence the wife fills the power vacuum and becomes accustomed to making most of the decisions. In other families the wife has a higher level of education than the husband, and when the children begin to attend school and the focus of family life centers more on education, the mother may tend to be more influential and respected than the father. It is still too early to say what effects the many changes in the family power structure will have on family life. More research is needed in this area.

Types of Family Power Structures

Trudy Kolb and Murray Straus have attempted to measure family power by observing families in a laboratory situation. They recognized the primacy that has been given to the husband in the family power structure, and sought to ascertain if there is actually a difference in marital happiness for couples who utilize power in different ways in laboratory problem-solving situations. (They utilized reports of college students as one measure of the couples' marital happiness.) Behavior of the families in problem-solving situations was observed and recorded. The study showed an association of marital happiness (as observed in this experiment) for husband-led families.

> The findings show that high *husband* power is associated with high marital satisfaction, whereas high *wife* power is not associated with marital happiness. Similarly, high *parental* power is associated with high marital happiness, but high *child* power is associated with low marital happiness.[20]

Another type of role behavior focuses on an egalitarian pattern of decision-making. Even though couples do not share in all decisions, they certainly find that the area of mutual interest and agreement is growing. In the *syncretic*, or democratically functioning, marriage, greater recognition is given to both spouses, and therefore both tend to be more involved in all decisions that affect family life. In the early years of marriage, the couple may try to do everything together and to make decisions jointly whenever possible. As time progresses, children arrive, and decisions may be shared according to the varying parental responsibilities of wife and husband. It is simpler for children to find means of self-expression in such a family because of the openness of two different personalities and viewpoints. And if one parent should die before the children are grown, the democratic family may be more flexible in reshaping family patterns to meet the crisis.

The increasing influence of the democratic decision-making pattern is clearly reflected in a study of farm families by Herbert L. Smith.[21] In sam-

[20]Trudy M. Kolb and Murray A. Straus, "Marital Power and Marital Happiness in Relation to Problem-Solving Ability," *Journal of Marriage and the Family*, 36, no. 4 (Nov. 1974), 764.

[21]Herbert L. Smith, "Intrafamilial Decision Making and Marital Satisfaction," a paper delivered at the Annual Meeting of the National Council on Family Relations (San Francisco: August 1967).

pling a group of husbands and wives in rural Wisconsin, with an average age of forty-six for the husbands and forty-two for the wives, Smith found that democratic decision-making patterns were followed in five of the seven most common kinds of family decisions. The exceptions were decisions about food and entertainment, which were wife-dominated, and decisions concerned with running the farm itself, which were dominated by the husband. The evidence was overwhelming that husbands and wives made decisions about the children together. However, there was no consistent positive association between democratic decision-making and marital happiness and satisfaction. The ratings of marital happiness were more positive when decisions on childrearing were considered.

Gerald R. Leslie, in discussing common authority patterns in the family, feels that the family in the United States has been moving toward an egalitarian pattern for many decades.[22] The need for dominance by brute strength is decreasing, and thus a more practical and satisfying relationship develops from the shared egalitarian pattern. This certainly does seem to be the more common American pattern, and one which reflects the greater freedom given to women in our culture than in many others.

Constantina Safilios-Rothschild, in an interesting comparison of women in Detroit, Michigan, and Athens, Greece, sees power and love as both resources that may be divided between the spouses. She agrees that there is more exchange possible in the American situation, whereas she finds that only a very small percentage of Greek women with high educational, finan-

[22]Gerald R. Leslie, *The Family in Social Context,* 3rd ed. (New York: Oxford Univ. Press, 1976), pp. 59–62.

cial, and status resources will be able to successfully claim power in their marital relationships.[23]

It should not be suggested that most couples follow a single approach in every choice or decision, especially when the couples are vastly different in background and temperament. Real understanding and patience are needed for each individual couple to work out those balances of power and decision-making that are most suitable for them.[24] One thing is clear—*both* partners cannot expect the other person to carry the load of sympathy and consideration in one situation after another. If neither will play the empathetic role, as appears to be the case with the troubled couples studied, the marriage is likely to be in serious danger.

Jessie Bernard has suggested that what is needed in contemporary marriage is a "shared-role pattern."[25] Women's liberation should not mean that roles are reversed, but that they are shared. This must be bona fide sharing, not a counterfeit substitute. It must involve careers, children, housework, bill-paying, and countless other aspects of family life. This is the shape of the future for marriage.

We need to recognize that each couple must, in the final analysis, develop a system of authority that meets their own needs, expectations, and values. Over the life cycle of the marriage, however, a pattern of increased sharing and equality seems to promise the best results for dealing with those responsibilities and tensions that will affect the entire family unit.

SUMMARY

The beginning of married life is a unique experience for each couple. The initial adjustments made by husband and wife will determine whether their marriage lives up to their expectations or whether they meet obstacles in reaching their goals. It is useful to consider marital adjustment in terms of the family life cycle. Evelyn Duvall's eight-stage family life cycle centers primarily on families with children. Those couples without children will follow a different progression.

The family life cycle of the future will reflect our changing society. Couples are having fewer children, and are thus involved in the child-rearing task for a shorter period of time. In addition, the span is longer, giving a couple more years without their children.

There are many positive factors that contribute to marital adjustment. Appreciation is one key element because everyone needs positive reinforce-

[23]Constantina Safilios-Rothschild, "A Macro- and Micro-Examination of Family Power and Love: An Exchange Model," *Journal of Marriage and the Family*, 38, no. 2 (May 1976), 355–62.

[24]See also Denise B. Kandel and Gerald S. Lesser, "Marital Decision-Making in American and Danish Urban Families: A Research Note," *Journal of Marriage and the Family*, 34, no. 1 (Feb. 1972), 134–38.

[25]Bernard, p. 248.

ment. Equality is a second factor, and a mark of contemporary marriage. A couple should continue to develop love and joy in their daily life. In this way, their marriage will continue to be an adventure. Shared goals and experiences are another plus for beginning marriage. The couple should clarify their goals and values, and establish a satisfying social life. They must also learn the creative use of conflict, since it exists within the family system. Finally, each partner must make a commitment to the greater good of the family.

The family power structure reflects how decisions are made. The couple may follow a pattern where the husband is dominant, the wife is dominant, or the relationship is egalitarian. Today an egalitarian balance of power is becoming more prevalent and seems to hold much promise for the future of successful marital adjustment.

SUGGESTED READINGS

Bernard, Jessie. *The Future of Marriage.* New York: Bantam, 1972. Good analysis of marriage from the feminist viewpoint. Deals with the different perspectives of "his" marriage and "her" marriage.

Cromwell, Ronald E., and David H. Olson, eds. *Power in Families.* New York: Halsted Press, 1975. Articles analyzing different factors of family power and family decision-making.

Duvall, Evelyn Millis. *Marriage and Family Development,* 5th ed. Philadelphia: Lippincott, 1977. See especially Chapter 7, "The Family Life Cycle." Careful analysis of the tasks and responsibilities that face a couple beginning marriage.

Hill, Reuben. *Family Development in Three Generations.* Cambridge, Mass.: Schenkman, 1970. Focuses on the changes in marriage and family life over the past fifty years.

Kantor, David, and William Lehr. *Inside the Family.* New York: Harper Colophon Books, 1976. Detailed analysis of processes within the family with emphasis on a systems approach.

Leslie, Gerald R. *The Family in Social Context,* 3rd ed. New York: Oxford Univ. Press, 1976. See especially Chapter 2, "The Family in World Perspective." Compares American family structure with the family structure in other societies.

Locke, Harvey. *Predicting Adjustment in Marriage: A Comparison of a Divorced and a Happily Married Group.* New York: Holt, Rinehart & Winston, 1951. Pioneering study of two groups of couples that analyzes the factors involved in marital adjustment.

Mace, David R., and Vera Mace. *We Can Have Better Marriages, If We Really Want Them.* Nashville: Abingdon, 1974. The founders of the Marriage Enrichment Program stress positive aspects of marriage, and offer constructive suggestions to improve marriage.

Shostrom, Everett, and James Kavanaugh. *Between Man and Woman.* Los Angeles: Nash, 1971. Popular treatment of the marriage relationship, with discussion of the dynamics of dependence, independence, and interdependence.

12 Family Crises

- How do families meet crisis situations?
- How do married couples deal with conflict?
- What do we know about violence in the family? Do family crises lead to violence?
- What social pressures affect the family?
- How do economic problems affect young couples in particular?
- How do health problems affect family life?
- How does alcoholism affect the family?
- How common is drug abuse in the contemporary family?
- What impact does death have on family life?
- How should a young couple face separation and divorce?
- What are special problems of the one-parent family?

Kinds of Family Crises

Life is like a mosaic that contains many different shapes, colors, contrasts, and patterns. It is unrealistic to imagine that there will not be conflicts and crises in marriage. It is important that we learn how to deal with family stress.

In this chapter we will discuss different kinds of family crises: interpersonal conflict; family violence, social pressures on marriage and the family; health problems, alcoholism, and drug abuse; death; separation, divorce, and single parenthood.

Interpersonal Conflict

Conflict is a very common occurrence in almost every marriage, and over a period of time it may have an escalating effect. An argument or disagreement that occurs early in the marriage may lead to more serious conflict, possibly even violence, and later separation or divorce, or both.

HOW DO ARGUMENTS BEGIN?

An argument is the result of a breakdown in the working partnership between husband and wife. The rational argument the husband intends to pursue or the flawless logic his wife has prepared for their evening discussion may become heavily tinged with personal valuations and feelings. Thus many arguments in marriage become irrational and destructive.

An argument may begin for any number of reasons. When it continues to the point that it becomes hot and heavy, it may affect many parts of the couple's relationship other than the one they are arguing over. A primary source of friction may be the question of dominance. Another cause of marital disagreement may lie in the personality problems of one or both partners. If one partner has severe neurotic problems and is constantly rationalizing his difficulties or projecting them onto others, that will certainly put stress on the marriage relationship. Once more, the emphasis should be on *realism*. Our romantic nature urges us to forget warning signals in our partner's conduct in courtship or the admonitions of parents and friends. To our sorrow, we discover in marriage that a person is basically much the same throughout life, and severe conflict ensues simply because each partner is being himself or herself.

Louis was eighteen when he met Caroline, a high school senior of seventeen. He had quit his part-time job in order to enlist in the Marines but was rejected because of a physical disability. Louis was the fourth son in a large family, and his father, a taxi driver, had had little time to spend with his children. Although he received some intellectual stimulus through his mother and nearby relatives, Louis had never done well in school and at sixteen had dropped out of high school to try his luck as a deliveryman and part-time helper for the local garageman.

Caroline came from a different kind of family. Her father was the manager of a large chain variety store. He did well in the company, and that meant pay increases and new managerial jobs every three or four years. Her mother was active in local business clubs, church activities, and community work. Caroline had three brothers but as the only girl in the family was somewhat spoiled.

Caroline was in the top quarter of her class and had been recommended for a college scholarship. When she started dating Louis steadily, her grades went down, and at graduation she decided to go to work instead of to college. Her parents and friends criticized Louis sharply. "He's not our type," they insisted. "He could never hope to support you with his education," said others. Six weeks after graduation, following some sharp arguments between parents and daughter, the couple eloped and were married by a justice of the peace.

Two children were born to Caroline and Louis in the first three years of marriage. In the first five years Louis had a steady job for only half the time. Even with work that Caroline managed to get before the birth of each child, they were constantly in debt.

Caroline was sure that Louis would settle down and add maturity and financial stability to his obvious charm and good looks. She told her parents, "He will change for me; be patient—it will take a year or two."

Five and a half years after the wedding, sadly convinced that he was still the same kind of person she had refused to recognize in courtship, Caroline sued for divorce. She knew that she would undoubtedly get custody of the children, but she had little hope of receiving alimony or child support.

Many of the adjustments that are required of a newly married couple may lead to arguments between them. Their new apartment may not be all that was expected: The heater is not working properly, no one comes to check out the new refrigerator that doesn't defrost on time, or the family upstairs is so noisy and troublesome that the wife is constantly in the middle of a series of ticklish arguments between old neighbors and new. These similar situations are apt to develop in any family's life experience. The situation itself cannot be avoided; when it develops, family conflict rises to the surface and is compounded.

Fatigue certainly should be recognized as another common cause of tension and arguments in the family. It is a typical factor in a home where the woman is working and is also expected to play the roles of homemaker, wife, and mother. There are limits to any person's endurance, and when that limit is reached, conflict will often be the result. Nor are husbands immune to fatigue, both physical and mental. If a man works at a job that demands heavy physical labor, if he is under heavy pressure to produce a high volume of work, or if he is moonlighting, he may well come home fatigued and ill-prepared to cope with a host of problems left over from the day's school and home activities.

CAN ARGUMENTS BE WORTHWHILE?

It would be a mistake to imply that all of the conflicts and arguments in which we are involved are entirely negative. Some arguments are worthwhile. Psychotherapists have recognized that a person often needs to touch bottom in his experiences before he can find motivation to tackle his problems honestly and arrive at some meaningful conclusions. In the same way, a marital argument may actually clear the air in such a manner that constructive action can be taken by the couple, not only to end the argument but to tackle some of the underlying problems that have been exposed.

One value of an argument is that it allows one or both partners to vent hostile feelings that have been accumulating. Let us consider, for example, a man whose job is not going well. Colortone TVs or Cleanso soap or Jewel cigarettes are not selling well, but the district manager insists that the local distributor increase sales at least 10 percent in the next six weeks. Such a demand is unreasonable in a period of declining sales and is virtually impossible to meet. But if the man contests the order or tries to have it rescinded, he may lose his job in the process. So he stills his protest, buries his resentment, and takes it all home to his wife and family.

Some trivial happening may set off a series of storm warnings at home. Dinner is late or the roast has been burned. "That's the fourth late meal in two weeks," the husband roars. Or, "Billy left his bike in the driveway again, and it almost scratched the car fender." Or, "Sally didn't finish the dishes last night, and now she wants to run off to a movie tonight without lifting a finger to help!" The particular subject that ignites the argument need not be important. The key fact is that the husband has generated a number of hostile feelings at work and has had no opportunity to express them. So the family is the obvious (and the safest) place to do so. When a family argument develops, a tension-producing situation is often brought into the open, and discussion can shift from a trivial subject to the more crucial one. In the same way, an understanding wife recognizes that her husband may have problems at work that he does not always discuss freely with her. If he is caught up in a tense argumentative situation, those problems may come to the surface.

Andrew Selig describes such a process in a case study of counseling with one family. Crisis intervention is extremely valuable in significant periods in life. (Existential psychology stresses the same insight.) In this particular family group—father, mother, two teenage children—a long period of family counseling (ten weeks) failed to produce significant changes in the family's process and structure. The family members were all distant from one another and happiest when alone. There were frequent arguments between mother and daughter, while father and son remained isolated. The death of an uncle, who was close to the father, was the specific crisis which opened the family up to meaningful discussion and family growth. They began to meet together on an informal basis, a rare event in the time preceding counseling. Changes in the unsatisfactory family situation, which had at first been sought only by the mother because of varied problems, now became a goal of all family members.[1]

An argument may help one or both marriage partners to reevaluate themselves. Most of us want to look on the positive side of life, and it is damaging to our self-image if we fail to maintain and defend ourselves. When we are faced with a crisis because of a strong conflict with a person very close to us, we may be willing to take the unusual and threatening step of reevaluating our self-structure. If wife or husband takes the initiative against us, we may be willing to take a sober look at the real weakness within ourselves that is being exposed. If a climate of love and trust has developed between the partners, then there is the definite possibility that some therapeutic value will be gained by the eruption of conflict.

Clark was a draftsman whose work required close concentration during long tedious hours. He was an efficient, highly accurate workman and was employed by an architect who relied on him for a number of the most important drawings for each new contract. Clark rarely socialized with any of the other employees in the firm and depended on his wife, Fern, to build social contacts for the family.

In some ways Clark reflected in his marriage a pattern of feminine dominance that had existed in his parental home. His mother had been a strong, self-reliant woman who managed the home and family competently without much in the way of suggestion or criticism from her husband.

[1]Andrew L. Selig, "Crisis Theory and Family Growth," *The Family Coordinator*, 25, no. 3 (July 1976), 291–95.

The development of a sharp family argument revealed hidden feelings in Clark concerning his marriage and his relationship to both wife and mother. After a hard day's work, Clark and Fern decided to drive to the Valley for supper, leaving their two small children with a neighbor for the evening. On the way to the restaurant, an argument developed over a small item purchased on a charge account by Fern. Clark's anger flared; he twisted the wheel of the car sharply to the right and exclaimed: "That's enough! One more word and I'll drive straight into that embankment and kill us both!"

Fern was so shaken by his anger and the intensity of what seemed to be a minor quarrel that she sought counseling aid to discover the cause of this and other differences between them. Clark agreed to join her in seeking help. Their recognition of the possible seriousness of their difficulties and their willingness to change some of the patterns of their marriage saved the marriage from deterioration.

The most desirable outcome of a family argument is a solution of the problems raised and a drawing together of the couple. Popular folklore tells us not to worry about family problems if in the end we can kiss and make up. However, such success may be illusory. If the wife knows that she must make a scene in order to win concessions, or if the husband must threaten infidelity in order to gain his wife's attention and concern, they may experiment and discover that those approaches are self-defeating. Such contrived quarrels are an emotional drain on the couple, and they may break down feelings of love and trust, replacing them with suspicion and mistrust.

Unfortunately, it is often the egocentric and domineering person who will initiate an argument, and who will push the hardest to come out victorious. The same person, if the couple has an uneven power distribution, will probably take the lead in most decision-making, while the more timid and submissive person will give in to the aggressive spouse more frequently.

PROBLEM–SOLVING

There are positive and negative patterns of marital disagreement. If quarrels are destructive and the marriage is slowly but surely losing meaning for both partners, then an argument will probably run its course with little if any value to the couple. If an argument is to be constructive and helpful, it must take its place as part of a problem-solving sequence. In other words, the couple must use their rational powers to gain some advantage from their point of difference. A problem-solving sequence would include the following steps.

1. Define the problem that causes the disagreement. Does each partner feel that the other is spending too much money? Is the husband lax in disciplining the children? Does the wife resent her husband's sexual advances?
2. Try to understand the underlying causes of the problem. Is the husband unwilling to share authority with others? Does the wife overemphasize her role as a mother? Are in-laws overcritical of new ideas and new personalities?
3. Consider possible solutions to the problem. Can the couple work this out together? Is outside help needed? Can one person solve the problem? Must both work on it? Have any of the possible solutions been tried before?
4. Agree on the best answer to the problem. Will this require a compromise on the part of one or both partners? Will it provide a truly shared approach to the problem? Must one party give in more than the other?
5. Try out the proposed solution. Does it involve changes in the family's life pattern? Or will it be a change in relationship to the husband's work, the community, the neighbors? Is it a difficult solution to put into practice?
6. Review the decision from time to time. Are things working out as planned? Has the husband carried out his part adequately? Has the wife? Should changes be made in light of the experience gained in executing the solution?

Such a problem-solving approach will enable a couple to gain some benefit from a potentially destructive situation. The crucial question is, will one or both partners be able to control their feelings and apply reasonable procedures to the point at issue? Usually one person has to take the initiative, find some way of minimizing the immediate conflict, and begin the process of redirecting energy into a constructive solution.[2]

Family Violence

A more serious problem for the married couple, and for children later in the marriage, is violence in the family. Although this aspect of family life has been neglected in the past, it is now the subject of a wide range of social science studies. The discussion of this topic, of course, is another entry of society into the private world of family life, and thus meets with a high degree of resistance. However, force and violence hamper the growth and freedom of family members, especially wives and children, and may result in trauma, danger, physical and emotional harm, and even death. Suzanne

[2]See Audrey Haber and Richard P. Runyon, *Fundamentals of Psychology* (Reading, Mass.: Addison-Wesley, 1974), pp. 213–16.

Steinmetz and Murray Straus, in introducing their pioneering study, *Violence in the Family*, describe the situation in these terms:

> At one time almost all the major institutions of our society had the right to use violence. Corporal punishment was the rule of the day in the courts and prisons; masters could use physical punishment on apprentices; the church turned heretics over to the civil authorities for burning at the stake. Today, only the police and parents have a clear legal mandate to use violence as a means of social control. In fact, it would be hard to find a group or institution in American society in which violence is more of an everyday occurrence than it is within the family.
>
> . . . We tend to overlook the violence which takes place there. . . . Yet the facts are clear. Studies of murderers and their victims, for example, show that the most frequent single category of murderer-victim relationship is that of family relationship. Another well-documented form of intra-family violence is the use of physical punishment by parents. In every state of the union, it is legal for parents to strike children—that is, use physical punishment. Indeed, most Americans see a moral obligation for parents to use physical punishment as a means of controlling children if other means fail.[3]

There seem to be very few if any limits on possible occurrences of violence in the family. Richard Gelles has reported in a recent study funded by National Institute of Mental Health (NIMH) grants that there are frequent examples of violence during pregnancy.[4] Situations that disrupt the life of newlyweds, of parents expecting their first or subsequent children, and of families where there are older children, may result in the use of force by one or more parents against the children. Other studies of family violence indicate that there is also some abuse of parents by their own teenage and grown children.

WIFE ABUSE

The practice of wife abuse is, of course, linked to the traditionally submissive role of women. It is always easier to use force on a person smaller or weaker than yourself, or one who is afraid or unable to respond in kind. A great many wives have been abused because they were convenient targets for their partner's anger, and also posed little threat of retaliation. Why don't women escape from such situations? Gelles, in a New Hampshire study of violence

[3]Suzanne K. Steinmetz and Murray A. Straus, eds., *Violence in the Family* (New York: Dodd, Mead, 1974).

[4]Richard J. Gelles, "Violence and Pregnancy: A Note on the Extent of the Problem and Needed Services," *The Family Coordinator*, 24, no. 1 (Jan. 1975), 81–86.

in some 80 families, discovered a number of reasons why wives endure abuse from their husbands.[5] The less severe the violence, and the less frequent, the more the woman would attempt to ride out the situation without seeking outside help. If the woman herself had experienced violence as a child, then she was more willing to accept subsequent victimization by her husband. Finally, if she was undereducated, and not employed outside the home (with contacts that would give her support and a feeling of power), she would remain "entrapped" in a bad situation.

Robert Whitehurst has proposed that the violence of husbands toward their wives is a vestige from an earlier period in human history. Men controlled their wives, and if violence was necessary to ensure that control, they could use it.[6] Even if the "modern" husband says that he wants a fully egalitarian marriage, he finds it difficult to accept loss of control over his wife's behavior. This is especially true if she is unfaithful to him and violates the (double-standard) sexual norms. Violence seems to be the easiest way he can even the score.

REASONS FOR VIOLENCE IN THE FAMILY

Discovering the reasons why violence escalates in the family circle was the subject of a thought-provoking study by Murray Straus.[7] He wanted to test the hypothesis that verbal aggression can be substituted for physical aggression. Straus tested a sample of 385 students who had been living with their families during their senior year of high school. He wanted to see if parents who "argued heatedly," "yelled and/or insulted [each other]," or "sulked and/or refused to talk about it" were able by these incidents of verbal aggression to reduce the amount of physical violence between them. Did they end up "throwing something at the other person," "pushed, grabbed, or shoved the other," "hit (or tried to hit) the other person but *not* with anything," or "hit or tried to hit the other person with something hard." Straus made a distinction between those who were described by their sons and daughters as verbally aggressive (the first group of questions listed) or as physically aggressive (the second group of questions). If the hypothesis proved to be true, those who "let off steam" verbally would not need to go on to physical aggression.

The actual results of the survey turned out to be just the reverse. The higher the level of verbal aggression, the higher the level of physical aggres-

[5]Richard J. Gelles, "Abused Wives: Why Do They Stay?" *Journal of Marriage and the Family*, 38, no. 4 (Nov. 1976), 659–68.

[6]Robert N. Whitehurst, "Violence in Husband-Wife Interaction," in Steinmetz and Straus, pp. 75–82.

[7]Murray A. Straus, "Leveling, Civility, and Violence in the Family," *Journal of Marriage and the Family*, 36, no. 1 (Feb. 1974), 13–29.

Figure 12–1 Mean Physical Aggression Score by Amount of Verbal Aggression

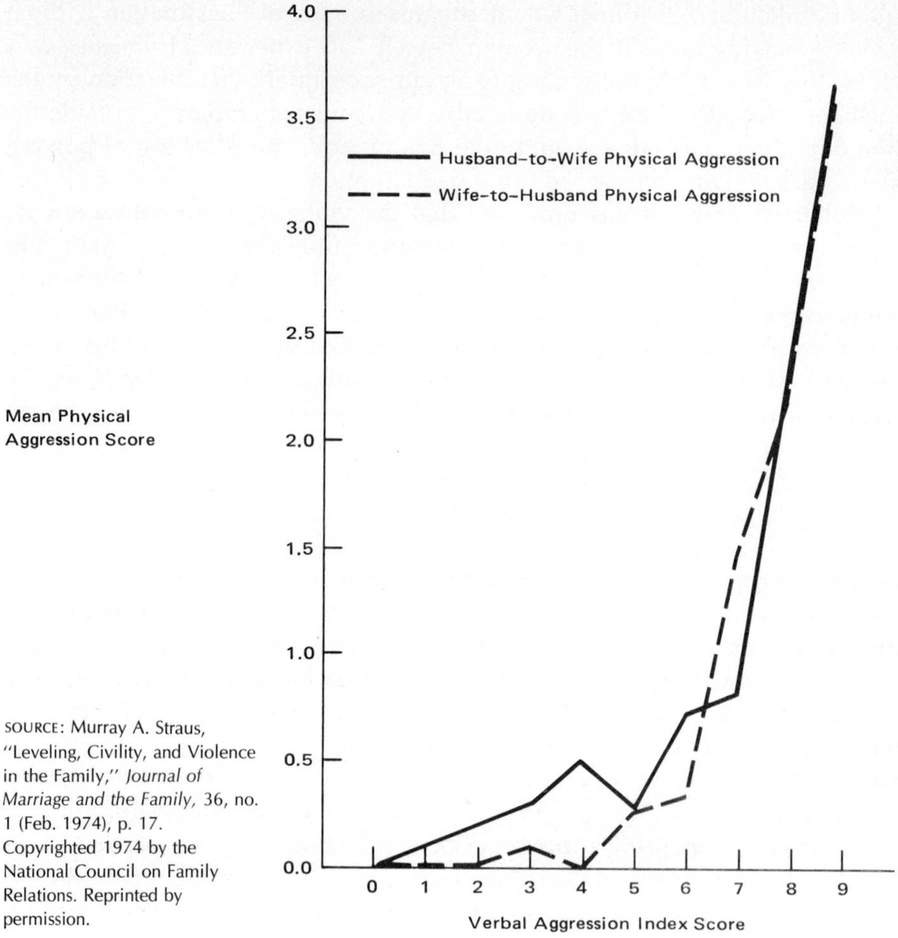

SOURCE: Murray A. Straus, "Leveling, Civility, and Violence in the Family," *Journal of Marriage and the Family,* 36, no. 1 (Feb. 1974), p. 17. Copyrighted 1974 by the National Council on Family Relations. Reprinted by permission.

sion. Figure 12–1 indicates the actual comparison of the two measures of family conflict. The inability to solve problems on the verbal level merely moves the stressful situation up to the next level. And this can be the source of abuse involving many family members.

The list of starting points for family conflicts is probably endless. Issues that are trivial and unimportant in one family may seem to be major ones in another family. We are much more likely to differ on things that have high priority in our lives, in contrast with those which do not. And furthermore, if there are underlying currents of resentment, confusion, hostility, and pain, a seemingly trivial disagreement will touch off a real conflict. This is why it is so vital to discover the key to the creative use of conflict.

Social Pressures

Another major source of tension in the family comes from social pressures. We are speaking particularly of those crises that originate in war, poverty, long-term unemployment, and forced residential mobility. No family is immune from the pressures of society. If the society supports the family's lifestyle, it will be easier for each family member to carry out his or her role as a member of the family group.

ABSENCE OF THE FATHER

Tension in the family can be most clearly seen in a wartime situation where the husband and father, and perhaps some of the older sons, are drafted into the armed forces and forced to leave the family home. Sharon Price-Bonham has explored some of the problems in this country related to the wives of American soldiers missing in action in Vietnam. Her study shows that some wives and families were able to react positively to the ambiguous situation of the missing servicemen, but others were still "marking time" and unable to adjust to the tension of the situation. Even if the husband did return, it is possible that expectations of this second group for harmonious family reconstitution might not be realized.[8] If, in addition, the wife and mother, and older daughters, join the labor force at some distance from home and may no longer share the same residence, family problems will multiply. The impact of wartime conditions can be illustrated by the dramatic rise in the divorce rate immediately following the Second World War, when the full impact of the tensions caused by the war was revealed.

Another situation triggering family tension (especially in developing countries) is the absence of the husband and father because his employment is at a great distance from home. He may even travel to a foreign country to work. In Europe such migration has occurred from Italy and the Southern European countries to Sweden, West Germany, Great Britain, and Switzerland. In the United States we are most familiar with the migration of Mexican farm workers to the United States. These workers leave their families at home in Mexico for six months or longer each year.

POVERTY

Poverty, and its many related problems, is still a major cause of family tension in the United States. There are millions of families who live below the recognized government poverty line, and some of them have been there for

[8]Sharon Price-Bonham, "Missing in Action Men: A Study of Their Wives," *International Journal of Sociology of the Family*, 2, no. 2 (Sept. 1972), 202–11.

generations. Catherine Chilman has identified some basic problems of poor families as a whole. A majority of them are locked in by their particular situation, especially minority families and those family units headed by a woman. She notes a number of problems associated with being at the bottom of the income scale. These families have difficulty in moving to a city or state where they might have a better chance for work. They do not know exactly where to go, and lack money resources to hang on until a new job comes along. Some are older persons who have great difficulty in getting jobs, or are past the retirement age. Poor families lack alternate income from savings, property, stock, or other sources. Physical and mental health are often poor. There is frequent family breakdown as a result of separation, death, and divorce. There is difficulty in effective family planning. These families cannot take advantage of educational opportunities which are offered to them.[9] All in all, the picture is a very discouraging one. Family crises do not occur in these families; instead these families are in a constant crisis state.

UNEMPLOYMENT

Unemployment, resulting in the lack of sufficient income, puts pressure on every part of family life. There is often not enough money, even if the family receives welfare payments, to buy the kind of food that will maintain optimum health; to buy the kind of clothing that the children are proud to wear to school; to buy (or rent) adequate housing in a decent neighborhood.[10] The self-image of husband and wife is threatened, and the whole fabric of family life feels the tension. It is difficult for children to explain why their parents are not employed, and why money is not available whenever needed.

RELOCATION

Forced residential mobility is another kind of social pressure.[11] A family unit that is well-adapted to one neighborhood may not function satisfactorily in a new location, particularly if it is hundreds of miles away in a different state or section of the country. Even if the husband makes a satisfactory adjustment to his new work responsibilities, it may be harder for his wife and children to make the transition. This is suggested by the research of Butler, McAllister, and Kaiser in their study of "Voluntary and Involuntary Resi-

[9]Catherine S. Chilman, "Families in Poverty in the Early 1970's: Rates, Associated Factors, Some Implications," *Journal of Marriage and the Family*, 37, no. 1 (Feb. 1975), 49–60.

[10]See the treatment of "The Family in Poverty," in Gail Putney Fullerton, *Survival in Marriage*, 2nd ed. (Hinsdale,Ill.: Dryden, 1977), Chap. 19, pp. 521–46.

[11]Note the special section, "Moving and the Wife," in *Journal of Marriage and the Family*, 35, no. 2 (May 1973), which includes six special articles on this theme.

dential Mobility."[12] A number of observable factors were not affected by moving, but the mental health of females was. They may have contacts with their immediate neighbors and other people in the new community, but they still feel as though they are "out of it" in comparison with their former neighborhood. Children also may have adjustment problems, particularly in making friends and participating in their new school environment.

Relocation is also a common problem for service families. During wartime, forced separations are common. But even in peacetime, the cost and complications involved in moving a family to a new location can cause family tensions. Jerry McKain studied 200 wife-mothers who had made, on the average, six or more moves as an Army family. He suggests that the focus of the problem often lies in the personality and outlook of the wife-mother.[13] If she is a well-adjusted, happy person, and makes friends easily, she will take the move in stride and help her children to do the same. But if she tends to be alienated from her surroundings and suffers from a sense of rootlessness, then moving will be associated in her mind (and her husband's) as being a time when personal and marital problems began or were intensified. This analysis has been verified in many college and university situations, where the college-student sons and daughters of military personnel show both positive and negative effects and memories of their frequent required family moves.

Health Problems

Adequate health care for American families is a major national problem. Many families are ill-prepared for the expense and time required to meet a major health problem, and this can generate a serious family crisis. In a two-year study of the health practices of a Minneapolis-St. Paul sample of three-generation families, Theodor Litman found that this was one aspect of family life where the younger generation had not stepped ahead of the older generation.[14] They often had less protection for an unexpected major illness in the family than their grandparents had had.

Today, educational opportunities are extended to physically, emotionally, and mentally handicapped persons. Many health and housing facilities are being designed to meet the special needs of the handicapped. It is hoped

[12]Edgar W. Butler, Ronald J. McAllister, and Edward J. Kaiser, "The Effects of Voluntary and Involuntary Residential Mobility on Females and Males," *Journal of Marriage and the Family,* 35, no. 2 (May 1973), 219–27.

[13]Jerry Lavin McKain, "Relocation in the Military: Alienation and Family Problems," *Journal of Marriage and the Family,* 35, no. 2 (May 1973), 205–09.

[14]Theodor J. Litman, "Health Care and the Family: A Three-Generational Analysis," in Marvin B. Sussman, ed., *Sourcebook in Marriage and the Family,* 4th ed. (Boston: Houghton Mifflin, 1974), pp. 268–79.

that as a result of these new programs many of the handicapped will be able to work, have families, and make positive contributions to society. Without these programs, however, the added time, work, and money necessary to make this happen may not be easy for any one family to manage.

How do parents react when it is recognized that they have a handicapped child? The responsibilities connected with the child represent a continuing responsibility through the years. Fortunately, the handicapped are accepted by a majority of families. They go forward with their family life in a positive manner, particularly if there are supporting services in the community that can make the care of the child less of a continual burden on the parents. Dunlap and Hollinsworth, in a study of the effects of a handicapped child on family life in Alabama, found that the effects, rated by the great majority of parents and guardians surveyed, were positive.[15] Table 12–1 shows a summary of their responses. These are encouraging findings, although the fact that the sample was predominantly rural and poor, and had a high percentage of black families, limits its application to a more urban sample.

A more comprehensive study, by Sharon Price-Bonham and Susan Addison, of the impact of mental retardation on the family illustrates some of the additional burdens placed on families with this special problem.[16] Price-Bonham and Addison found that the father has an important role to play in dealing with this family crisis. He plays a large part in the decisions about institutionalization, special home care, and so on. And both parents must share the emotional burden associated with caring for a mentally retarded child. Divorce, desertion, and parental suicide are problems associated with this situation. Clearly, increased education, understanding, and personal and community support are needed.

Alcoholism

Alcoholism is a major problem that affects millions of American families. Americans have ambivalent feelings about the alcoholic. Many still feel he is "morally wrong," or a failure, rather than believing he is suffering from a disease. Research into alcoholism and its impact on the family is still limited. Harry Milt points out that there are psychological and physical views as to the roots of alcoholism. He believes that the physical theories of origin are not scientifically substantiated. He cites a number of studies linking certain basic conditions associated with the disorder. In his view,

[15]William R. Dunlap and J. Selwyn Hollinsworth, "How Does a Handicapped Child Affect the Family? Implications for Practitioners," *The Family Coordinator*, 26, no. 3 (July 1977), 286–93.
[16]Sharon Price-Bonham and Susan Addison, "Families and Mentally Retarded Children: Emphasis on the Father," *The Family Coordinator*, 27, no. 3 (July 1978), 221–30.

Table 12–1 Summary of Answers to Question Relating to the Effects of Having a Developmentally Disabled Member

Question	*Yes*		*No*		*Total*	
	No.	%	No.	%	No.	%
Would you say _____'s handicap has had an effect on whether your family will take a trip, go on vacation, or visit relatives?	127	36	227	64	354	100
Would you say _____'s handicap has had any effect on the family getting out to do such things as going shopping, going to the movies, or going to church?	104	29	255	71	359	100
Would you say _____'s handicap has had any effect on your marriage?	22	7	281	93	303	100
Would you say _____'s handicap has had any effect on the closeness or happiness of your family?	64	19	277	81	341	100
Would you say _____'s handicap has had any effect on deciding where the family will live?	33	9	326	91	359	100
Would you say _____'s handicap has had any effect on the job of the household head?	43	15	239	85	282	100
Would you say _____'s handicap has had any effect on whether the mother will work?	88	28	229	72	317	100

SOURCE: William R. Dunlap and J. Selwyn Hollinsworth, "How Does a Handicapped Child Affect the Family? Implications for Practitioners," *The Family Coordinator*, 26, no. 3 (July 1977), 288. Copyrighted 1977 by the National Council on Family Relations. Reprinted by permission.

People who become alcoholics are psychologically alcoholism-prone, predisposed by two basic conditions. One is an unremitting burden of emotional distress made up of anxiety, depression, repressed anger, aloneness, and low self-esteem. The other is a cluster of personality traits which limit the individual's capacity to deal realistically with emotional problems and the problems of living—low tolerance for frustration and suffering, the need for immediate gratification, poor impulse control, and low coping ability or "ego strength." This person has an urgent need for (1) relief from emotional distress; (2) an easy source of gratification, pleasure, and self-esteem; and (3) a way to deal with the reality he cannot handle. Alcohol provides all of these. It anesthetizes emotional pain, produces euphoria, aggrandizes the ego, and modifies reality so the drinker

does not have to deal with it. Dependency on alcohol for these effects is at first limited, but it expands, crowding out realistic alternatives until, eventually, it dominates the personality completely.[17]

Milt points out that the incidence of alcoholism in women is rising, and that this is often related to problems concerned with female sex functions and family and love relationships. These women doubt their adequacy as women. In upper- and middle-class families, women often drink most heavily at home.

Can alcoholism be cured? Milt takes the optimistic view that we are on the road to solving this critical problem that triggers so many family crises. Some alcoholics recover by spontaneous remission, as they recognize their heavy drinking pattern as nonproductive. We see the same remission in many types of mental illness. Others will be helped in treatment programs. Alcoholics Anonymous continues to have the best track record in this field. The "twelve steps" (see Table 12–2) have value, not only for the alcoholic, but also for family members.

In fact, almost all rehabilitation programs for alcoholics now recognize

[17]Harry Milt, *Alcoholism: Its Causes and Cure. A New Handbook* (New York: Charles Scribner's Sons, 1976), p. 23.

Table 12–2 On admission to AA the new member is introduced to the AA guidelines, known as the twelve steps, and encouraged to follow them at his own pace:

1. We admitted that we were powerless over alcohol—that our lives had become unmanageable.
2. Came to believe that a Power greater than ourselves could restore us to sanity.
3. Made a decision to turn our will and our lives over to the care of God as we understand Him.
4. Made a searching and fearless moral inventory of ourselves.
5. Admitted to God, to ourselves and another human being the exact nature of our wrongs.
6. Were entirely ready to have God remove all these defects of character.
7. Humbly asked Him to remove our shortcomings.
8. Made a list of all persons we had harmed and became willing to make amends to them all.
9. Made direct amends to such people wherever possible except when to do so would injure them or others.
10. Continued to take personal inventory and when we were wrong, promptly admitted it.
11. Sought through prayer and meditation to improve our conscious contact with God as we understood Him, praying only for knowledge of His will for us and the power to carry that out.
12. Having had a spiritual awakening as a result of these steps, we tried to carry this message to alcoholics and practice these principles in all our affairs.

SOURCE: Reprinted by permission of Charles Scribner's Sons from *Alcoholism: Its Causes and Cure. A New Handbook* by Harry Milt. Copyright © 1976, 1972, 1969 Harry Milt. (New York: Charles Scribner's Sons, 1976), pp. 116–17.

the importance of the family relationship in any long-term recovery program. In an official publication, the Al-Anon Family Group points out the impact of alcoholism on the daily interaction of the marriage partners and their sexual relationship.[18] According to Steinglass and Moyer, the wife or husband of an alcoholic must understand the dynamics involved in order to help in the solution of the problems generated, rather than to increase them. They also point out that there is a middle ground between outright alcoholism and

[18] *The Dilemma of the Alcoholic Marriage* (New York: Al-Anon Family Group Headquarters, Inc., 1971).

complete abstinence. What should be considered "normal drinking"?[19] Is there one set of behavior that characterizes the heavy drinker, another for the total abstainer, and a third set for someone midway on the continuum? We simply do not know. Alcohol is obviously associated with a great deal of family behavior, but it has not been studied scientifically and thoroughly enough in order to identify all of the related effects with certainty.[20]

Drug Abuse

Drug abuse is another major problem for American families. In the 1960s national concern and attention were focused on the family's sons and daughters. Today it is focused on husbands and wives as well. Drugs have the ability to alter the individual's psychological state. In addition to changing observable behavior, they produce subjective changes in mood, thinking, and level of awareness. Psychotropic (mind-altering) drugs can be classified in six categories: sedative/hypnotics, stimulants, major tranquilizers, minor tranquilizers, antidepressives, and psychomimetics (hallucinogens). The newly developing science of psychopharmacology has changed much of our thinking about the use of these drugs, particularly in the treatment of mental illness. Our major concern here is drug abuse by an individual that has a negative effect on the individual and on family members. Many factors will enter into the degree and seriousness of such abuse, including the availability of drugs, exposure to drugs, and the social situation of the individual.[21]

How can one deal with a drug abuse problem in his or her own family? There are four important questions to be asked: First, how serious is the problem, and is it recognized by the family member involved? Second, what resources exist within the family to meet the problem? Is there enough trust, love, concern, enough objectivity and understanding in the family unit, to take positive and effective steps? Third, what community resources are available to aid the family? Is there a free clinic, a half-way house, a hospital treatment unit, or some other facility where the family member may gain assistance? Finally, what other professional help is available? Psychiatric counseling or institutional treatment may be the most logical course. The decision must be made whether such treatment will be voluntary or mandatory.

Sidney Cohen points out the complexities of the problem of drug abuse

[19]Peter Steinglass and Janet K. Moyer, "Assessing Alcohol Use in Family Life: A Necessary but Neglected Area for Clinical Research," *The Family Coordinator,* 26, no. 1 (Jan. 1977), 53–60.

[20]See Abion, "Family Structure and Behavior in Alcoholism: A Review of the Literature," in B. Kissen and H. Begleider, eds., *The Social Biology of Alcoholism,* Vol. 4 (New York: Plenum, 1977).

[21]Gordon Claridge, *Drugs and Human Behavior* (New York: Praeger, 1970), pp. 11–20, 224–27.

in our society during the past fifteen years, and gives some of the reasons for the high increase in drug usage. The solution to the problem, he states, must involve the parents, the school, the therapist, the legislator, and the user himself or herself.[22]

Death

Death is the ultimate crisis. The family has to face the difficult task of continuing its life without the contribution of one or more members who played important roles in the primary family group. We have built up an elaborate ritual surrounding death. Often, death has moved from the home to the hospital or another institution. Many psychologists and sociologists have described our primary reaction to the fact of death as one of denial. We do not rival the Egyptian pyramids, but there are many elaborate monuments to the dead, and every funeral director can provide a family with embalming, an elaborate casket protected by a concrete vault, and other symbols to help them to believe that death can be overcome to some degree.

Today a more realistic attitude is beginning to prevail. Perhaps the secularization of our culture is part of the reason for a more open and direct discussion of death and dying. If many Americans do not have a faith that will give them a religious interpretation of the fact of death, then it is cruel to deny them the right to discuss the final crisis of life. If no priest or minister

[22]Sidney Cohen, *The Drug Dilemma,* 2nd ed. (New York, McGraw-Hill, 1976).

is to share the closing days or hours of life with the family, then it is not fair for doctors, nurses, friends, and relatives to pretend that the crisis will never come at all. The work of Dr. Elisabeth Kübler-Ross has given us a much clearer insight into the way in which individuals face the fact and prepare for their impending death. When Dr. Kübler-Ross first began her investigations, she found it hard to find dying patients. There were many people who were very weak, some too sick, and others who didn't want to talk. But none were dying.[23] When she finally was able to overcome the protectiveness of families and staff, she found the patients more than willing to talk. From this and subsequent study, she has described five stages of dying. The stages and patient and family response to each stage are summarized in Table 12–3.

There are many ways that we can prepare families for the experience of death, both as it will affect them personally and as they will carry on life's responsibilities after the death of a loved one. Since most women outlive their husbands by from 8 to 10 years, and widows outnumber widowers by almost five to one, the problems of widows are those most commonly experienced by most families. Harvey and Bahr, in one sampling that included a five-nation group of widows, suggest that the major problems for widows are economic. Their personal, social, and emotional problems may all be secondary to the fact that they are poorer than when married and subject to the stress associated with poverty and less than normal income levels.[24]

James Peterson and Michael Briley discuss some of the most important steps to be taken by the widow in working through the psychological deprivations caused by the loss of her mate. The "subjective grief work" that needs to be done includes dealing with the relationship with the deceased; accepting the pain of bereavement; working through feelings; and expressing feelings. Peterson and Briley stress the need for "a creative approach to being alone" through developing new aspects of one's personality, building a new world of interests and friendships, recognizing the need for growth of the spirit, and dealing realistically with one's financial, romantic, family, and social environment. The same double standard that has made life easier for men in other realms of family life has extended privilege more freely to the widower than to the widow. But the tide is turning, and a greater recognition of both the problems and opportunities facing the newly widowed will help them to find that "life can be fulfilling."[25]

[23]See Elisabeth Kübler-Ross, "What Is It Like to Be Dying?" reprinted in *Understanding Death and Dying,* ed. Sandra Galdieri Wilcox and Marilyn Sutton (Port Washington, N.Y.: Alfred, 1977), pp. 99–111.

[24]Carol D. Harvey and Howard M. Bahr, "Widowhood, Morale, and Affiliation," *Journal of Marriage and the Family*, 36, no. 1 (Feb. 1974), 97–106.

[25]James A. Peterson and Michael P. Briley, *Widows and Widowhood* (New York: Association Press, 1977), p. 206.

Table 12–3 How to Handle the Five Stages of Dying

Patient Behavior	Stage	Family Response
	Denial	
In effect, the patient says, "It cannot be true." Patients often search frantically for a favorable diagnosis.		Understand why the patient is grasping at straws. Patience and willingness to talk are important.
	Anger	
The patient says, "Yes—but why me?" Deep anger follows, and the patient may bitterly envy those who are well and complain incessantly about almost everything.		Consider that the patient is angry over the coming loss of everything: family, friends, home, work, play. Treat patient with understanding and respect, not by returning the anger.
	Bargaining	
The patient says, "Maybe I can bargain with God and get a time extension." Promises of good behavior are made in return for time and some freedom from physical pain.		If the patient's 'bargain' is revealed, it should be listened to, not brushed off. This stage passes in a short time.
	Depression	
The patient grieves, and mourns approaching death.		Attempts to cheer up or reassure the patient mean very little. The patient needs to express sorrow fully and without hindrance.
	Acceptance	
The patient is neither angry nor depressed, only quietly expectant.		News of the outside world means little, and few visitors are required. There will be little talk, and it is time merely for the presence of the close family.

SOURCE: Based on Elisabeth Kübler-Ross, *On Death and Dying* (New York: Macmillan, 1970). Copyright © 1969 by Elisabeth Kübler-Ross. Reprinted by permission of Macmillan Publishing Co., Inc. and Tanistock Publications Ltd. Reprinted from the April 5, 1976, issue of BusinessWeek by special permission, © 1976 by McGraw-Hill, Inc., New York, N.Y. 10020. All rights reserved.

Broken Marriage

Crises that affect another large segment of millions of American families are those involved in separation, divorce, and the resulting single parenthood. In Chapter 21 we will discuss in some detail the impact of separation and divorce on the family. The rising divorce rate indicates that the crises of separation and divorce have become reality for couples at every stage in the family life cycle. Consequently more and more children are affected by the disruption of the marriage and are being raised in single-parent homes. Traditionally, it has been the woman's duty to raise the children following a broken marriage. Today, it is possible, and more socially acceptable, for a man to have the same responsibility.

How many single-parent families are there in America, and how many children live in these families? Table 12–4 shows the totals in March 1976 for both one-parent and two-parent families, including white, black, and Spanish-origin families. The table indicates the high percentage of single-parent families, 18 percent of all families in 1976. The families with a female head outnumber those with a male head by more than ten to one. In keeping with other data regarding economic and family status for black families, the

Table 12–4 Number of Children Living in Families, by Age, Race, and Type of Family: March 1976*

Race of Family and Children's Age	*Total*	*Husband-Wife Families*	*Families with Male Head, No Female Present*	*Families with Female Head, No Male Present*
All Families:				
Total members under 18	64,924	53,366	924	10,635
Total own children under 18	61,697	51,586	710	9,401
Total own children under 6	17,639	15,332	80	2,227
Total own children under 3	8,246	7,374	22	851
White Families:				
Total members under 18	54,266	47,181	719	6,366
Total own children under 18	52,441	45,979	591	5,871
Total own children under 6	15,033	13,650	62	1,320
Total own children under 3	7,068	6,577	18	473
Black Families:				
Total members under 18	9,422	5,109	185	4,129
Total own children under 18	8,123	4,595	102	3,426
Total own children under 6	2,221	1,326	13	881
Total own children under 3	992	619	4	369
Families of Spanish Origin:				
Total members under 18	4,427	3,349	59	1,019
Total own children under 18	4,146	3,182	40	924
Total own children under 6	1,397	1,124	12	261
Total own children under 3	684	569	4	111

*In 1000s.

SOURCE: Kurt J. Snapper and JoAnne S. Ohms, *The Status of Children 1977* (Washington, D.C.: U.S. Dept. of Health, Education, and Welfare, 1978) (DHEW Publication No. [OHDS] 78-30133), p. 5.

report shows 46 percent of all black families headed by a single parent, including 44 percent female-headed families, and 2 percent headed by males.

Benjamin Schlesinger, who has studied the one-parent family extensively in Canada and Great Britain, reports a number of findings related to a broad European research project, the Finer Report, published in England. The parent's social isolation is a major personal problem, together with the frustration of giving up regular sexual relations. In addition, the care of children, especially the young who demand constant attention and older children who have adjustment problems, is a further burden on the parent, particularly the mother.[26] The Finer Report made some 230 recommendations, many of which have been supported by British social service groups working in this area.

Schlesinger is sympathetic toward the plight of single parents. They need greater understanding and sympathy from society and social agencies. He writes:

> Despite their uncertain, not-married-and-not-unmarried status, the one-parent heads of families are conscientious parents striving to bring their children to healthy maturity with as much capability for finding happiness as if they had both father and mother in an intact family. Their job is lonely and endless. It goes on twenty-four hours a day and requires countless decisions, large and small. Seldom is there anyone from whom single parents can expect moral and emotional support, advice, encouragement, praise, or even faultfinding. Isolation from normal community

[26]Benjamin Schlesinger, "One Parent Families in Great Britain," *The Family Coordinator*, 26, no. 2 (April 1977), 139–41.

> life to some degree is the fate of parents without partners—whether they are divorced mothers who have custody of their children, fathers who are struggling to build normal relations with their children when they have visitation privileges only a few hours a month, or widows or widowers with children. They don't seem to fit any of the normal social patterns. They are the self-styled "fifth wheels" of society.[27]

It is obvious that there must be greater concern for single-parent families so that they can meet the heavy responsibilities laid on them. Brandwein, Brown, and Fox have suggested that there are a number of family functions that are endangered in a single-parent family. Because many single-parent families are poor, their economic functions are impaired. Thirty-two percent of female-headed white families and 58 percent of nonwhite families are poor.[28] When a single parent works, there are problems associated with child care. There are problems with authority and respect for the divorced mother. Domestic functions are a problem for divorced fathers. Emotional support is lacking for single parents.

The problem of dealing with divorced or unmarried parents and their children remains a difficult and baffling one. A new strategy for meeting these needs must be developed. Too many assumptions are being made that are unsupported by our present knowledge. Brandwein et al. conclude:

> Over and over the literature assumes that the single-parent state is temporary. Although many women, especially those under 30, do remarry, a greater proportion, especially after the age of 30, remain divorced. Divorced men are more likely to remarry than are their ex-wives. Because of the assumption that divorcees will remarry, society does not feel obligated to provide supports for single parents. Because societal supports are largely unavailable, husbandless mothers come to view remarriage as the only viable alternative to a difficult situation. The situation will remain difficult as long as policies are based on these circular assumptions.[29]

SUMMARY

Family crises are a reality. We all need to understand the nature of these crises, and to know how to deal with them. Interpersonal conflict is one of the most common family crises. Arguments may arise over seemingly trivial

[27]Benjamin Schlesinger, *The One-Parent Family* (Toronto: Univ. of Toronto Press, 1970), p. 10.
[28]Ruth A. Brandwein, Carol A. Brown, and Elizabeth Maury Fox, "Women and Children Last: The Social Situation of Divorced Mothers and Their Families," *Journal of Marriage and the Family*, 36, no. 3 (Aug. 1974), 498–514.
[29]Brandwein, Brown, and Fox, p. 511.

incidents. Or they may be due to fatigue, conflicts over dominance, or personality clashes. Arguments do have some value. Hostile feelings can be released, and crucial problems in the marriage may be brought to light. Helpful self-evaluation may be initiated. Ideally, arguments should lead to a problem-solving process in which the problems are analyzed rationally.

Violence is a serious family crisis. It can include all family members but most often affects children and wives. This is linked to the traditionally submissive role of women and children. Straus's study has shown that verbally aggressive people are often physically violent.

Social pressures such as absence of the father, poverty, unemployment, and relocation can precipitate family crises.

Health problems, alcoholism, and drug abuse are another group of family crises. Health problems may involve unexpected illness, accident, or a physical or mental handicap. Alcoholism affects millions of Americans and, consequently, their families. Effective treatments are being developed, but Alcoholics Anonymous remains the most effective. Drug abuse is a family crisis that is on the increase. There are four important questions for a family to ask when dealing with a drug abuse problem: How serious is the problem; What resources does the family have to meet the problem; What community resources are available; What professional help is available?

Death is a cultural crisis for families in our society. Often, people tried to conceal the reality of death, but today there is a more realistic attitude toward death. Dr. Elisabeth Kübler-Ross's research has been instrumental in helping people to prepare for death.

Broken marriages and the resulting single parenthood are other major family crises. There are millions of single-parent families in America. The parent's social isolation can be a problem, as can the care of the children, both younger and older. Single parents need greater social support and understanding.

SUGGESTED READINGS

Cohen, Sidney. *The Drug Dilemma,* 2nd ed. New York: McGraw-Hill, 1976. A broad view of the drug problem affecting American society, with suggestions for family and community action.

Green, Betty R., and Donald P. Irish. *Death Education: Preparation for Living.* Cambridge, Mass.: Schenkman, 1971. Report of a symposium on death at Hamline University (St. Paul, Minnesota). Practical discussion of a subject vital to the family.

Haber, Audrey, and Richard P. Runyon. *Fundamentals of Psychology.* Reading, Mass.: Addison-Wesley, 1974. See discussions of thought processes and problem-solving.

Kübler-Ross, Elisabeth. *On Death and Dying.* New York: Macmillan, 1969. Pioneering work that is the basis of much of the current interest in death education. Includes the five stages of dying.

Milt, Harry. *Alcoholism: Its Causes and Cure. A New Handbook.* New York: Charles Scribner's Sons, 1976. Practical review of present knowledge of alcoholism and current approaches to rehabilitation of alcoholics.

Robertson, Ian. *Sociology.* New York: Worth, 1977. Basic sociology text with good treatment of social class and poverty.

Steinmetz, Suzanne K., and Murray A. Straus, eds. *Violence in the Family.* New York: Dodd, Mead, 1974. Collection of articles on violence between spouses and kin, violent parents, and the family as a training ground for societal violence.

Straus, Murray A. "Leveling, Civility, and Violence in the Family," *Journal of Marriage and the Family,* 36, no. 1 (Feb. 1974), 13–29. Straus's critique of the theory that verbal aggression is a substitute for physical aggression.

Wilcox, Sandra Galdieri, and Marilyn Sutton. *Understanding Death and Dying: An Interdisciplinary Approach.* Port Washington, N.Y.: Alfred Publishing Co., 1977. Good collection of articles with additional bibliography and study materials.

13 The Two-Career Family

- How may we define the two-career family?
- What are the motivations for women to work?
- Is it possible for mothers of young children to also carry career responsibilities?
- What effects does full-time employment have on a mother's relations to her children?
- Why do so many women choose to work while their children are in school?
- What impact does the wife's employment have on her relationship to her husband?
- What effect does employment have on a woman's self-image?

Trends in Two-Career Families

The number of married women in the labor force has been steadily rising for the past thirty years. Data from government sources show that the number of women in the working force has increased from 28.1 percent of the civilian labor force in 1947 to 41.0 percent in 1977. (Women comprise about 55 percent of the U.S. population.) This is almost a fifty percent increase in the postwar period. This growth is shown in Table 13–1.

We are seeing a change in patterns of employment, and, consequently, we must reconsider the role of married women in our society. The transition of a majority of American families from rural life to urban life in the first half of the century left many traditional roles and life patterns unchanged. However, the transition for so many millions of women from the homemaker role to the career role is bringing many changes in traditional life patterns. In Chapter 6 we took a look at the conditions that existed during the early married years of your parents and grandparents. The number of working women in the 1920s was not nearly as high as it is today; it was rare that women left their traditional jobs as secretaries, housemaids, waitresses,

Table 13–1 Women as Percentage of Civilian Labor Force: 1947–1977

Year	Millions of Workers	Percentage of Total Civilian Labor Force
1947	16.7	28.1
1955	20.5	31.6
1966	27.3	36.0
1977 (Jan.-April)	39.1	41.0

SOURCE: U.S. Bureau of the Census, *Statistical Abstract of the United States, 1977* (Washington, D.C.: U.S. Government Printing Office, 1977), p. 386.

nurses, or schoolteachers in order to take traditionally masculine jobs. Women needed plenty of time for cooking, baking, cleaning, washing, and a multitude of other household tasks. In a way, this new pattern was a continuation of rural patterns, with outside employment taking the place of farming chores. In the 1930s, the Depression economy did not supply enough jobs for men, let alone women.

The 1940s brought rapid changes. That generation grew up during the Depression and left school to face the Second World War. Women went to work to aid the war effort, and their work energy was sorely needed to support the economy. Of course, the increasing number of working wives in the last thirty years cannot be attributed solely to the enlarged defense budget needs of the nation.

Today, the two-career family is becoming the norm for more and more American couples. Women with a college education are much more likely to work than those who have completed less than a high school education, or only the twelfth-grade level. Obviously, these women seek the satisfaction of a more professional and challenging job and a high rate of income. Hopkins and White point out that the highly educated woman is aiming for a reasonable combination of two major interests—a career and a viable family life. This means new and complex family interrelationships, with both the risks and gains involved. A woman must manage her time so that there can be needed leisure time for family activities. In the same way, equity in relations between the husband and wife can be the basis for the development of equitable family systems that will include the children as they grow into maturity.[1]

[1]Jane Hopkins and Priscilla White, "The Dual-Career Couple: Constraints and Supports," *The Family Coordinator*, 27, no. 3 (July 1978), 253–58.

Martin, Berry, and Jacobsen, in an interesting study of husbands and wives who were both Ph.D.s in sociology, discovered that the degree proved to be a definite advantage for the wife. Comparing her with other women sociologists, they found that she had been more successful in obtaining the Ph.D. in the first place, had higher academic rank, gained more promotions, and had a longer professional career.[2] The only disadvantage seemed to be that she might more often have part-time employment. Even this might be seen as a plus for the wife who wanted to give equal time to her family.

Choice of Occupation

This move toward greater equality extends to the choice of occupation for both husband and wife. A man no longer thinks of transferring to a new position simply in terms of his own future; he must consider his wife's as well. Locating a new home near school, church, and shopping center is no longer a woman's sole concern. Now both partners are often in the job market together.

> The executive recruiter was looking for an engineer to fill an opening at an electronics plant in Los Angeles. He found one in Dallas, well qualified for the $20,000-a-year-job—but there was one hitch.

[2]Thomas W. Martin, Kenneth J. Berry, and R. Brooke Jacobsen, "The Impact of Dual-Career Marriages on Female Professional Careers: An Empirical Test of a Parsonian Hypothesis," *Journal of Marriage and the Family*, 37, no. 4 (Nov. 1975), 734–42.

"I'm afraid I have to leave the firm, sir. My wife's company is transferring her out of state."

Drawing by von Riegen

"I'll take it, if you find my wife a job too," the engineer said. The recruiter did.

Meanwhile, at Caltech, a recruiter for a major communications company in the East also was looking for engineers. He found a good prospect, working on his doctorate—but the student said he did not feel like leaving the West Coast because his wife was an assistant professor at another college.

But the recruiter was not put off.

"He asked me about what my wife does, and said maybe the company could be interested in hiring her, too," the student said.

Those are far from isolated examples, personnel men say. The day of women's lib—or at least of working wives—is upon them and the nation's employers are under pressure to adjust to it. Hence, recruiters and personnel officers are finding more often that they have to think of two jobs, not just one, when they want to hire or transfer employees.[3]

Men's feelings are certain to be affected by these new trends. Recently Mirra Komarovsky conducted a study of 53 senior men at Princeton University to see how they reacted to the new feminine competition on campus. (Princeton has recently begun to admit women students; the first women to complete four full years at the university walked off with more than their share of academic honors.) The men had ambivalent feelings about marriage to a woman who was their intellectual equal. Some wanted a woman cast in the traditional feminine mold, but had some reservations about it.

Deprecating remarks about housewifery were not uncommon, even among men with traditional views of women's roles. A conservative senior declared, "A woman who works is more interesting than a housewife." "If I were a woman," remarked another senior, "I would want a career. It must be boring sitting around the house doing the same thing day in, day out."

But the low esteem attached by some of the men to full-time homemaking coexisted with other sentiments and convictions which required just such a pattern for one's wife. . . . [One] young man explained that he enjoyed shyness in a girl and detested aggressive and ambitious women. . . . It is no exaggeration to conclude that this man could not countenance the qualities that he himself felt were necessary for a fulfilling middle-age.[4]

Another study that probed men's and women's attitudes toward the dual

[3] *Los Angeles Times*, April 16, 1972.

[4] Mirra Komarovsky, "Cultural Contradictions and Sex Roles: The Masculine Case," *American Journal of Sociology*, 78, no. 4 (Jan. 1973), 880.

role of the married professional woman clearly showed that men had a negative attitude toward the ability of the woman to cope adequately with her home and work roles.[5] But women are no longer willing to accept an inferior status when they get married. They have set their sights on a different kind of relationship in their marriage, and it seems clear they have made giant strides in the last ten years toward reaching that goal.

Family Size

Another trend related to the increasing number of working wives today is the decrease in family size. The working wife has fewer children for several reasons. The woman with fewer children is able to arrange her work schedule and responsibilities more easily, and the woman who has employment already worked into her lifestyle is less likely to have another child (and perhaps force a change in her work situation). Table 13-2 shows the impact of labor-force participation on family size in a broad spectrum of American families. The "all families" category, which is largely white, shows a lower family size average than that for black families. But in both cases, the mother in the labor force has fewer children than the mother who does not work outside the home.

A comprehensive study by Elizabeth M. Havens shows that there is a constant inverse ratio between fertility and female labor-force participation. However, Havens points out that other factors must also be considered, including variations in trends from one part of the country to another and the effect of "familialism" norms. She defines familialism norms as those that stress cultural goals in terms of the family unit and that define roles in terms of primary sex characteristics. If homemaking is seen as the primary role for women, it will be that much harder for a woman to feel right about leaving her home to take a job. But in every case, Havens concludes, the inverse ratio holds true.[6]

Linda Waite and Ross Stolzenberg, in an analysis of the National Longitudinal Study of the Labor Market Experiences of Young Women, discuss the several variable factors that result in smaller families. They conclude:

> . . . We return to the question posed several years ago by Bumpass and Westoff [in 1970], which sums up the ambiguity in past research on fertility and female labor force participation. "Do women limit their fertility in order to have time to pursue their non-family oriented interests, or do

[5]See Maureen M. Kaley, "Attitudes Toward the Dual Role of the Married Professional Woman," *American Psychologist*, 26, no. 3 (March 1971), 301–06.

[6]Elizabeth M. Havens, "The Relationships Between Female Labor Force Participation and Fertility Rates," paper presented at the American Sociological Association Annual Meeting, Aug. 1972, pp. 1–4.

Table 13–2 Average Number of Children in Family, by Type of Family, Labor Force Status of Mother, and Race: March 1970 and March 1972

Type of Family, Labor Force Status of Mother, and Race	March 1970* Number of Families with Children Under 18 Years Old (Thousands)	March 1970* Average Number of Children per Family	March 1972 Number of Families with Children Under 18 Years Old (Thousands)	March 1972 Average Number of Children per Family
All families				
Husband-wife families	25,547	2.29	25,482	2.22
Mother in labor force	10,210	2.15	10,354	2.10
Mother not in labor force	15,337	2.37	15,128	2.31
Female family head	2,924	2.29	3,598	2.20
Mother in labor force	1,731	2.06	2,062	1.96
Mother not in labor force	1,193	2.63	1,536	2.53
White				
Husband-wife families	23,285	2.25	23,219	2.19
Mother in labor force	8,970	2.10	9,125	2.06
Mother not in labor force	14,315	2.34	14,094	2.27
Female family head	1,994	2.06	2,413	2.06
Mother in labor force	1,237	1.88	1,470	1.86
Mother not in labor force	757	2.34	943	2.36
Black				
Husband-wife families	2,001	2.67	2,002	2.54
Mother in labor force	1,120	2.51	1,106	2.36
Mother not in labor force	881	2.87	896	2.76
Female family head	912	2.77	1,144	2.50
Mother in labor force	485	2.48	571	2.18
Mother not in labor force	427	3.10	573	

*Figures for March 1970 were revised from those previously published.

SOURCE: Adapted from U.S Department of Labor, *Monthly Labor Review*, 96, no. 4 (April 1973), 40.

women work if their fertility permits them to do so?" Our analyses permit a cautious answer to Bumpass and Westoff, and our answer is, yes, women do appear to limit their fertility plans to accommodate their plans to participate in the labor force, and yes, women's fertility expectations do seem to affect their plans for labor force participation. But while the effect of fertility expectations on labor force participation plans would appear to be small, the effect of labor force participation plans on fertility expectations seems to be rather substantial.[7]

A Wife's Career During Various Stages in Marriage

There are differing viewpoints about whether a wife should be working during various stages in her marriage. A high proportion of young women today have working experience before they are married. Even teenage brides usually have had summer or vacation-time employment and may continue to work after marriage. If a young woman has completed high school or college before marriage, she usually has had some working experience. Unless a child comes in the first year of marriage, most women will continue working or look for a new job in their new community.

A number of factors make the wife's employment at the beginning of marriage widely accepted today, especially in working-class and middle-class families. It allows the couple an easier transition to the new patterns of married life; the old routines provide some continuity with the couple's single lives and allow them to put much of their thought and energy into adjusting to other aspects of their life together. Our culture is also putting more and more emphasis on companionship in marriage. Both husband and wife have talents and skills that are of value to society. Each makes a particular contribution through his or her work day by day; each receives a wage or salary in return for his or her services; and each shares with the other in planning family life and deciding how the family income will be used.

In addition, when the wife works at the beginning of marriage, she is able to contribute financially to many important family goals. Those goals may include the completion of or payment for the education of one or both partners, saving for a home or for furniture and major household appliances, or financial preparation for the birth of the first child.

There are two other advantages to the wife's employment early in marriage. It may both prevent her from becoming bored with her new role as a wife and homemaker and enable her to achieve experience and seniority if she wishes to return to the same vocation later in life. If she can teach long enough to gain a credential or win tenure, if she can work long enough to be considered a permanent employee, if she can complete two years of nursing service in one hospital, or if she can gain proficiency with particular office machines, her working experience may prove invaluable to her when she wants to return to work in her thirties or forties. All in all, it seems a

[7]Linda J. Waite and Ross M. Stolzenberg, "Intended Childbearing and Labor Force Participation of Young Women: Insights from Nonrecursive Models," *American Sociological Review*, 41, no. 2 (April 1976), 250.

logical and healthy trend for women to continue their employment after they are married.

Working Mothers of Preschool Children

Should a woman work when she has one or more small children? Traditional and biological reasons are given to support the thesis that every young child needs a mother to give him or her the right kind of start in life. For many years the idea that a child could be adequately cared for by another person seemed incompatible with our understanding of the psychology of child development. Evidence from other cultures and from the experience of upper-class families, who had always provided substitute care for their children, was ignored. However, new evidence is being published that seems to question the old theories. An increasing number of mothers are working full-time and caring for their families. Table 13–3 shows the rise in the number of working mothers since 1950.

Burton L. White and his associates at the Harvard University preschool project have emphasized the role of the mother in the formative first three years of the child's life. They have discovered that certain reinforcing behavior on the part of mothers provides the maximum benefit to the child. White and his colleagues also discovered that these effective mothers were busy people and in some cases held part-time jobs. Still, the emphasis was on part-time rather than on full-time employment. White et al. conclude:

> Effective mothers talk a great deal to their children. . . They make them feel as though whatever they are doing is usually interesting. They provide access to many objects and diverse situations. They lead the child to believe that he can expect help and encouragement most, but not all, [of] the time. They demonstrate and explain things to the child, but mostly on the child's instigation rather than their own. . . . They are secure enough to say "no" to the child from time to time without seeming to fear that the child will not love them. They are imaginative, so that they make interesting associations and suggestions to the child when opportunities present themselves. They very skillfully and naturally strengthen the child's intrinsic motivation to learn. . . . [8]

Jerome Kagan, a Harvard colleague of White's, has taken a more optimistic view of children whose mothers work and are sent to a well-run day-care center. In a recent study of two groups of children, one group raised at home and one group raised five days a week at the center, the researchers did not find major differences between the groups' development. The chil-

[8]Burton, L. White, *The First Three Years of Life* (Englewood Cliffs, N.J.: Prentice-Hall, 1975), p. 242.

Table 13–3 Married Women (Husband Present) in the Labor Force, by Age and Presence of Children: 1950 to 1976

	Labor-Force Participation Rate 1950	1965	1976
Women with husband present	23.8	34.7	45.0
No child under 18	30.3	38.3	43.8
Children 6–17 years only	28.3	42.7	53.7
Children under 6 years	11.9	23.3	37.4
Also with children 6–17	12.6	22.8	36.2

SOURCE: U.S. Bureau of the Census, *Statistical Abstract of the United States, 1977* (Washington, D.C.: U.S. Government Printing Office, 1977), p. 392.

dren entered the center at about four months of age, and stayed until they were about twenty-nine months old. The mothers retained their primary position in their children's attention and affection. The substitution of other nurturing persons during the day did not have the negative effects that had been predicted.[9]

The availability of top-quality child-care centers is of course crucial, but because our society has stressed the desirability of the mother's care of preschool children, alternatives have been explored slowly. Other industrial nations have experimented with a more comprehensive system of care for preschool children than is common in the United States. For example, the Soviet Union is reported to have set up a large number of child-care centers, which are closely integrated with the place of the mother's employment. In Sweden and England, some nursery schools have been set up in proximity to large urban housing developments. In the People's Republic of China, attempts have been made to care for children in community centers, so that the parents will be free to work full-time. It is difficult to evaluate such programs because social conditions in other countries are not comparable to our own. However, a well-administered nursery school is an excellent supplement to the process of education and socialization of the child that is being carried on by the mother and father.

A long-range solution to the problem of child care will involve the establishment of a network of child-care centers. Most of the detailed plans for such centers must be left for future discussion, but there are several

[9]Jerome Kagan, Richard Kearsley, and Philip R. Zelazo, "Day Care Programs," paper, American Association for the Advancement of Science (Boston, Feb. 1976).

important advantages to professionally run child-care centers which should be noted. Most important, better child care could be provided by such centers than any individual mother can provide by hiring a mother's helper, housekeeper or even the practical mother I have just proposed. In a child-care center, there can be greater specialization of skills, better facilities and equipment, and play groups for the children. Second, a child-care center would mean less expense for the individual working mother, and both higher wages and shorter hours for the staff of the center. Third, these centers could operate on a full-time, year-round schedule, something of particular importance for women trained in professional or technical fields, the majority of which can be handled only on a full-time basis. Except in the teaching fields, such women must provide for the afternoon care of their nursery school and kindergarten-age children, after-school hours for older children, and three summer months for all their children. Fourth, a child-care center could develop a roster of home-duty practical mothers or practical nurses to care for the ill or convalescent child at home, in much the way school systems now call upon substitute teachers to cover the classes of absent regular teachers.[10]

The basic question to be answered, then, is whether or not, if both parents are employed, they can successfully raise a family. Must wife or husband give up a job opportunity because there are preschool children at home? Several key conditions need to be met if two working parents are to share responsibility for a family.

[10]Alice Rossi, "Equality Between the Sexes," *The Other Half,* ed. Cynthia Fuchs Epstein and William J. Goode (Englewood Cliffs, N.J.: Prentice-Hall, 1971), pp. 182–83.

First, parenting must be a cooperative task if it is to be accomplished well. If both husband and wife have full-time jobs, they must share responsibilities for parenting. Mutual encouragement and understanding is the key. They will also have to share responsibilities for their home. This may require assistance with the housework from either husband or a maid. It would be incongruous to add a second salary to the family income and then have a house that is never really clean, poorly planned and hastily cooked meals, and little time for leisure activities. With good planning and a smoothly functioning marital partnership, the quality of family living can remain at a high level.

But, if the two partners are always clashing over the wife's career, there are bound to be some serious and continuing problems in the marriage. Catherine C. Arnott has pointed out that the husband's attitude will affect the profit an educated woman gains for her dual role.[11] The total relationship between husband and wife should be a loving, healthy, and growing one. Neither partner should marry his or her career.

ADEQUATE PAY

Second, both partners should receive an adequate financial reward for their employment. If the husband is being paid a fair and adequate wage for his work, the wife should receive the same. Ideally, a woman should not feel that she is just a cog in some large commercial or industrial machine. If her salary is at the bottom end of the scale, she may not earn enough money to help pay the cost of child care, housekeeping, and other services and expenses related to her work outside the home. The feminist movement has had some success in its lobbying for equal pay for equal work.

CHILD CARE

Third, the provision of competent child care is important. If the family accepts the thesis that an adequate substitute can be found for the parents during the working day, then they must share together the task of finding that person or persons. This is not always easy. Grandmother, the woman next door, or the large commercially run day-care center may not be the answer. A couple must periodically review the situation to see if the changing needs of the child are being met.

[11]Catherine C. Arnott, "Married Women and the Pursuit of Profit: An Exchange Theory Perspective," *Journal of Marriage and the Family*, 34, no. 1 (Feb. 1972), 122–31.

TIME ALLOTMENT

Fourth, the two-career family needs to do creative planning for their family activities. Since weekdays are taken up with careers, there must be careful planning to utilize the early mornings and evenings, and especially the weekends. Time for vacations, recreation, family visits, and so forth, needs to be set aside with careful thought and attention.

A working couple, raising young children, need to realistically balance their time and energy. Some people have energy for an eighteen-hour day, and others feel worn out at the end of a nine-hour day. Fatigue can be a major problem when there are heavy work responsibilities on the job as well as at home. There are small children to be fed, washed, and, most important, loved. There are household duties and responsibility for social and community life. The young couple may find that there are simply not enough hours in the day or days in the week to accomplish all these tasks. Even when there is some measure of help with the household work and child care during the working day, the load is a heavy one.

FLEXIBILITY

Finally, the two-income family needs to be flexible. There is no way that every situation and opportunity, both good and bad, can be anticipated. There is unexpected illness, unemployment for one partner, that forces a temporary change in spending plans, or requirements for one partner to travel and be away from home for a longer time than usual. When both husband and wife are sharing the economic and parenting roles, flexibility must be a major factor if they are to keep the family stable. Children learn to recognize and appreciate this need as well. If they see their parents taking minor and major crises in stride, they, too, will learn to adjust. It is a part of drawing up a balance sheet of assets and liabilities for the partnership, and making sure that the bottom line shows a clear recognition of values involved in this major family choice for a dual economic partnership.

In the 1976 Youth Survey conducted by the American Council of Life Insurance, a national sample of 1,025 young women indicated strong support for the lifestyle of a woman as a "successful executive or professional, living with husband and children in good neighborhood."[12] Their choice is reflected in Table 13–4. The survey indicates that the women who see this future lifestyle as most appealing are younger women with some college education who come from high-income families. (Their choice of an "executive" position, of course, is at a much higher level than the positions presently available. Still, it is clear that these young women are moving in that direction.)

The Carnegie Council on Children has proposed some steps that can be taken to help two-career families while their children need extra care. They have studied some of the problems we have been discussing, and reached these conclusions:

> Many mothers do not return to work immediately after the birth of a child but quit their jobs in order to stay home for a few years. That decision has always been a career liability; their seniority rights are lost and their skills can become rusty. The potential risks of child rearing to a career discourage many parents—and we explicitly include fathers—from taking time off when their children could benefit from it. . . .
>
> Existing policies that enable parents to take time out for childbirth without penalty should be expanded to let them take more time off—as much as several years—and then return to work without having lost their former status. . . .
>
> Such policies could have a strong effect on the work patterns of both fathers and mothers, with tremendous benefits to their children. It could encourage women and men to approach their education and early jobs with a firm conviction that they would be free to return to interesting work after an interval away.[13]

[12]American Council of Life Insurance, *Youth 1976 Finance-Related Attitudes* (New York: American Council of Life Insurance, 1976).

[13]Kenneth Keniston and the Carnegie Council on Children, *All Our Children—The American Family Under Pressure* (New York: Harcourt Brace Jovanovich, 1977), pp. 128–29.

Table 13–4 Lifestyle Young Women Find:

	Most Appealing (in percent)				*Least Appealing* (in percent)				*What Young Women Expect to Be in 15 Years* (in percent)			
	1970	*1972*	*1974*	*1976*	*1970*	*1972*	*1974*	*1976*	*1970*	*1972*	*1974*	*1976*
Successful executive or professional, living with husband and children in good neighborhood	26	31	30	34	7	7	7	8	27	28	30	29
Single person with good job, living well in apartment in major city	14	15	17	19	19	16	19	15	6	6	5	8
Life free of obligations, living where and with whom one pleases	10	8	9	10	42	43	42	38	5	5	5	5
Working to solve social problems, little concerned with material comforts	7	11	8	8	19	18	17	17	7	7	8	6
Average housewife, raising children, with time for own interests	42	35	36	25	12	16	15	18	52	53	51	49

SOURCE: American Council of Life Insurance, *Youth 1976 Finance-Related Attitudes* (New York: American Council of Life Insurance, 1976), p. 47.

Working Mothers of School Children

Can a wife carry on her outside employment when her children are in elementary or secondary school? A government report issued in 1976 showed 53.7 percent of the mothers of school-age children at work. This was the group with the highest percentage of working wives in the population. This seems to be the most propitious time for a mother to be employed. The children have school expenses, especially if one or more children are looking forward to college study. The excitement of raising a family of small children early in marriage may not be matched by the experience of sending older children off to school. In this period the mother may find herself crowded out of the lives of her children because of the large number of school, volunteer, and community organizations that demand their time. The mother of school-age children may also feel that she needs to resume a working career in order not to lose her chance to reenter a rewarding and interesting vocation. At age thirty or thirty-five, she will still be able to resume a career since she is only eight or ten years removed from her first experience. However, if she waits another five or ten years, until all her children have finished school, she may find it impossible to begin work again without some additional study or training.

Rosen, Jerdee, and Prestwich have conducted an interesting survey of some 1,500 managers and executives who were asked to give their response to a number of possible incidents regarding job responsibilities and requirements for male and female applicants. When the responses were tabulated, a distinct bias was found against the female applicants in the areas of travel, moving for a new job, promotion, and social support.[14] There is apparently a degree of managerial skepticism about women's abilities to balance the demands of work and family. Managers do not expect a married woman to match up to a married male competitor. And at the same time, they are not too keen on a male applicant who gives his family responsibilities higher priority than his job. Rosen et al. recognize the difficulties in reaching real equity here. And for these reasons the wife with school-age children, who is perhaps just accumulating the experience and maturity to take on a challenging new career responsibility, may find it difficult to seize the opportunity until business and society make a coordinated effort to overcome their prejudice.

Working Wives in the Postparental Period

Women in their forties and fifties are casting a strong vote for the two-career family: More than half the women from forty-five to fifty-four years of age are in the labor force. This is one group of women that is providing strong support for the feminist movement. Those people who have spent a great deal of time in volunteer organizations staffed by early retired homemakers know how difficult it is to utilize all the talents of women who have completed their tasks as mothers. A meaningful career with adequate personal

[14]Benson Rosen, Thomas H. Jerdee, and Thomas L. Prestwich, "Dual-Career Marital Adjustment: Potential Effects of Discriminatory Managerial Attitudes," *Journal of Marriage and the Family*, 37, no. 3 (Aug. 1975), 565–72.

and financial rewards seems to be an excellent role for the majority of these women.

> Too many married women arrive at middle-age without having looked and planned far enough ahead, and experience difficulties in making the transition from motherhood to other socially useful occupations. Ministers, doctors, lawyers—those whose professions give them insights into personal lives—know that there are an appalling number of unhappy over-forty women. They also know that many of these could be helped if they could find sufficient purpose for their lives. These women are simply at a loss to know what to do with themselves when they reach the point where their children are no longer dependent upon them. Usually, these are ones who have been the most devoted mothers. Not a few of them feel a quiet desperation in their desire to be of greater usefulness, but are at a loss to know how. They have not foreseen what their later years would be like and have not planned for them. Too often their only relief is in some form of occasional social diversion which provides them an escape. Integration of the several parts of their lives has not been achieved.
>
> The ever-growing numbers of women past forty in the labor force is evidence that return to work after the early years of childrearing is becoming a well-established pattern. But these statistics do not reveal the conflicts and uncertainties in women's experience in making decisions about reentry into the labor force in their middle years. . . . Women need to modernize their self-image to alleviate the abruptness of such transitions.[15]

We should not forget, of course, that a very large number of women in this age bracket have had careers as homemakers for the first twenty to thirty years of their married lives and have developed outside interests in community activities, volunteer groups, and leisure activities. If they are basically satisfied with this pattern, they will most certainly continue it. However, they ought to be aware of the other options available to them.

RETIREMENT

At only one point is the number of working women declining at present. This is in the over-65 group, where an extended life expectancy, and better retirement plans, both public and private, make a satisfying retirement life-

[15]Gladys E. Harbeson, *Choice and Challenge for the American Woman*, rev. ed. (Cambridge, Mass.: Schenkman, 1971), p. 139. See also Margaret M. Poloma and T. Neal Garland, "The Married Professional Woman: A Study in the Tolerance of Domestication," *Journal of Marriage and the Family*, 33, no. 3 (Aug. 1971), 531–40.

style possible for more and more older women. The declining birth rate, however, has led to predictions that this trend may reverse itself early in the twenty-first century. More older workers will be needed to pay for all of these benefits, since there will be a smaller and smaller proportion of younger working people. (This is certainly a question of interest to young and middle-aged couples today as they try to do some advance planning for their own retirement.)

Motivations for a Married Woman's Career

Why do wives work? A number of major motivations are present. Certainly, financial considerations are important. Money may be needed to pay basic living costs or to raise the couple's standard of living so that they can have more conveniences, a nicer home, a newer automobile, or more social status. A wife may work and utilize a part of her salary to purchase the things she and her family want; or a wife may go to work to pay for things already purchased on credit. Sometimes a wife may work because she is convinced that her husband cannot earn enough money to meet the family's needs. In that case, she and the children may consider the father a failure in his work, which could have disastrous effects on the family climate. Not every husband is pleased with his wife's ability to earn a regular salary. He may see this as a threat to his dominance of the family. However, if the wife is working to save enough money for a down payment on a house or to help the oldest child attend college, and if that goal is a joint one of husband and wife, the common work for the common goal may be a means of drawing the family closer together.

Burke and Weir, in a comparative study of career women and full-time homemakers, and of their husbands, measured six need areas for all four subgroups in their research. They found, in simple terms, that each of the four groups was "strong in carrying out the roles that seemed appropriate to them." The housewife liked to be home, was more submissive, "wanted inclusion," wanted control, and wanted affection. The career woman was lower in these areas, but did score higher on "expressed control" (where her desire to be a dominant figure was indicated). The husbands of housewives, on the other hand, were more anxious to be in authority and dominant, while the husbands of the career women were less assertive and less concerned with power and authority.[16]

The wife's personality is a second key to her motivation for working. Many women have become dissatisfied with the traditional housewife-and-

[16]Ronald J. Burke and Tamara Weir, "Some Personality Differences Between Members of One-Career and Two-Career Families," *Journal of Marriage and the Family*, 38, no. 3 (Aug. 1976), 453–59.

mother role. Mastering the dishwasher, adjusting the cleaning bag on the new vacuum cleaner, and measuring the soap for the washing machine may not fulfill her; compulsive cleanliness or the search for new and fascinating ways to prepare dinner will seem like poor solutions to the problem of boredom. Actually, the working wife who is well-organized and who has some assistance from her husband can often accomplish just as much after hours as she did when she was a full-time homemaker.

Some circumstances facilitate a wife's entering full-time employment. When her children go to school and she is alone much of the day, when her husband is willing to aid in the household work, when babysitters and cleaning women are readily available, when the home is new and modern, and when the community accepts maternal employment as a desirable pattern, it is possible for a woman to work easily and with favorable results.

Most women did not work fifty years ago because society did not encourage them to do so. Their education did not prepare them for a career, and the business world itself had no real place for them. They were happy to be living in the city and to replace much of the heavy farm labor they had known as girls with the pleasant busyness of city life.

Today's mothers, in contrast, have worked a great deal during their mar-

ried lives. They worked because of economic necessity and a desire to see their families move ahead more rapidly. But they did not necessarily work in the jobs that would have been their first choices, the jobs they were educated to pursue.

Today's young wife, then, lives in a society that accepts and may even expect a wife who works. Her mother may have been a working mother. Her neighbors may say: "Why aren't you working? Your children are in second and third grade, aren't they?" The Puritan ethic, with its picture of the ideal farm wife working from dawn until late at night, may have its impact here. Why should a woman have time for two-hour coffee breaks, bridge parties, and television soap operas when her husband is hard at work in the factory or office? Why should she have most of the day off, while he is working? Wouldn't a career be more satisfying to her? Today brides also combine work and marriage in a much more positive way. They have often had specific training for their vocations, and their actual jobs may well be their first choices. When we survey this group of married women in 1985 or 1990, their responses may be quite different from those given by working mothers today.

Effects of a Woman's Career on Her Family

What are the effects of outside employment on the typical American wife and her family?[17] There is no solid evidence that supports the view that would place the blame for most delinquency, school failure, and other personal problems of children on the working mother. When educational level, income level, place of residence, religion, and a number of other variables are controlled, then the results of a wife working have been largely on the positive side. In one such study, for example, King, Abernathy, and Chapman queried a number of black adolescents about their view of a mother's employment. The students reported that they did not view a mother's employment as a threat to the marital relationship, if they had the first-hand experience of seeing their own mother work. If, on the other hand, their mother was a housewife, they did see such employment as a threat to the marriage.[18] The report also showed a trend toward greater acceptance of working wives during the period from 1963 to 1973 by middle-class young people than by those lower on the social scale. Alice Marcella Propper made a similar investigation of the effect of a mother's career on her children. She found that the children did slightly more household tasks, but not too much more than those whose mothers were home all the time. There was also some

[17]See the series of articles, "Women at Work," in the *Wall Street Journal,* Aug. 28–Sept. 23, 1978.

[18]Karl King, Thomas J. Abernathy, Jr., and Ann H. Chapman, "Black Adolescents' Views of Maternal Employment as a Threat to the Marital Relationship: 1963–1973," *Journal of Marriage and the Family,* no. 4 (Nov. 1976), 733–37.

indication that sons of working women are less likely to admire their fathers than sons of nonworking women.[19] More research is needed on the place of the father in two-career families.

Although many questions still must be explored, it seems apparent that present research is not revealing marked differences between children of employed mothers and children of nonworking mothers. The effect of maternal employment may vary with each particular family. Differing reactions on the part of the father and different situations with school and peer groups may be of great significance to some children. For example, one student writes:

> Today I am eighteen years old. I was four when my mother joined the working force as a nurse. To say that her working harmed me would be false. She has certainly helped me to decide on my future.
>
> As I look back, I can still remember certain ages that I feel I needed a full-time mother. Eight, twelve, and seventeen were those years. At eight years of age almost every American girl joins the Brownies or the Blue Birds. My choice was the latter. It seemed as though every mother I knew was a part of that club except mine. . . . At the age of twelve many things begin to happen to a girl. She takes a step closer to womanhood and begins to want to establish a deeper relationship with her mother. A scurrying mother at that time made it very difficult for me to ever fully communicate with her. And at seventeen every student is faced with graduating from high school and making plans for the future. Family counseling is very important because decisions are made that could mean a lot of money for school or a complete break with home life.
>
> In the future I plan to work, but not during those specific times in my children's lives.[20]

Both husband and wife are vitally interested in the effect that part- or full-time employment of the wife will have on their relationship. The records of counseling cases, instances of separation and divorce, and other serious family problems are usually not summarized with the question of the wife's employment in mind. It is necessary to review the samples selected for study, and then try to relate these findings to the contemporary situation.

A recent study by Burke and Weir compared a Canadian sample of working wives with housewives using a sample group of husbands in three professional associations. Their findings showed that the working women,

[19] Alice Marcella Propper, "The Relationship of Maternal Employment to Adolescent Roles, Activities, and Parental Relationships," *Journal of Marriage and the Family*, 34, no. 3 (Aug. 1972), 417–21.

[20] Student report.

"Welcome aboard. This is your captain, Margaret Williamson, speaking."

Drawing by Richter

although under increased stress because of their dual role, came through on the plus side. "Working women appeared to be in better physical and emotional health, held more positive attitudes towards life in general, and towards marriage in particular.[21] On the other hand, the husbands of working wives came out on the minus side on the same characteristics. Thus one must have mixed feelings as to how the dual-career system really works for these couples.

The authors suggested several reasons for these conclusions. When the wife goes to work, her husband loses a part of his support system. At the same time, she feels more important and more fulfilled in the new roles assumed by her. Her partner, however, does not get the same satisfaction from the new roles he picks up at home. What is the socially recognized reward for him in the spotless kitchen, well-vacuumed living room, or neatly set dinner table? Until men are somehow socialized to feel satisfaction in these family role functions that have been thought of as feminine, the identity problems for such husbands in dual-career families will probably continue. When a social revolution of such magnitude occurs, it will take at least a generation or two to create the personal and social attitudes to reinforce and support the new behavioral patterns.

Still another factor that is significant in the marital adjustment of two-career families is the relative satisfaction of husband and wife with their jobs. The woman's job may be stimulating and satisfying and the man's frustrating and boring. Or the woman's job may pay more. To a man with traditional role expectations, such a situation might prove difficult.

[21]Ronald J. Burke and Tamara Weir, "Relationship of Wives' Employment Status to Husband, Wife and Pair Satisfaction and Performance," *Journal of Marriage and the Family*, 38, no. 2 (May 1976), 284–85.

> My father likes his work because of its freedom and its healthy environment. He likes all the time off and the sick leave, and he doesn't have to take his work home to the family. He knows, however, that he will never make a mint in this job, and I think that the fact that he will not progress much farther in his work bothers him just a little. He accepts his job, but I wouldn't say that he is overly enthusiastic about it.
>
> My mother started working about ten years ago. She started out part time at $3.50 an hour, and within a few years she had worked her way up to a $900-a-month job, which was more than my Dad was making with greater seniority. . . . She likes her job quite a bit. She is always eager to go to work and sometimes even goes early. I would say that my mother's work has a greater influence on our family life than any other single thing. Because of her working, my father has had to do some of the household jobs normally done by a mother. We children get stuck with a lot of her jobs, too. . . . We do, however, have a lot of extra money because of my mother's working. Thus we have been able to go on trips across the country and to buy a lot of things we wouldn't otherwise have had.[22]

It has also been suggested that maternal employment is related to arguments in marriage. Nye and Hoffman found that there was significantly more quarreling in homes with a full-time employed mother.[23] But there is some question about what is cause and what is effect here. Do women who have tensions and conflicts with their husbands tend to go to work to escape those conflicts and become more independent? Or do those quarrels begin when the woman leaves the home to take a full-time position? The answer is not clear.

It is clear that when a woman takes full-time employment, some changes will come in family life and power structure. If the family has been living for a number of years in traditional patterns, with the husband as sole wage earner, then the change may be dramatic. Successful marital adjustment in families in which both partners are working requires careful budgeting of time. The chief burden usually falls on the wife. She must anticipate the family's needs for holidays and special occasions, for example, and thus be able to make them pleasant and successful times for the family. And she must be able to budget money wisely. It is still the rare husband who can take over the big job of home management.

[22]Student report.

[23]Ivan F. Nye and Lois W. Hoffman, eds. *The Employed Mother in America* (Skokie, Ill.: Rand McNally, 1963), p. 268.

What Does a Career Mean to a Married Woman?

What does it mean to the wife to have a job and a career of her own? A woman becomes free of a fixed role and starts to stretch her wings and fly.[24] She gets out of a rut, becomes more independent, is rewarded for her talents, has the stimulus of outside (and adult) interests, and is able to function in a much broader and more stimulating environment than at home. A new self-image is created that will continue to expand as time goes on. And in it all, her children will learn from her example, and have the opportunity to become progressive, forward-looking individuals. The husband in a two-career family will also profit from this new and exciting lifestyle.[25]

SUMMARY

The two-career family is becoming increasingly common in the United States. Today, women make up approximately 41 percent of the American work force—a 50 percent increase over the postwar period. This increase in the number of working wives and mothers is a factor in the smaller size of families and greater equality between husband and wife.

Most wives, and especially those with a college education, work at the beginning of marriage. Previously, mothers of preschool children did not work, but now many women are choosing to continue working after their children are born. Such a situation requires cooperation between husband and wife and a willingness to share equally in the parenting role.

About 50 percent of all women with children in school work. A woman's employment can enhance her family's financial position, as well as provide her with the satisfaction of career achievement outside the home.

Many studies have been made of the effect of a mother's employment on her children. No significant differences between children of working and nonworking mothers have been discovered. A mother's career seems to be only one of several important elements in the life of the growing child and adolescent.

The trend of the working mother is a positive one. Greater freedom, a healthy self-image, and an enriched family life are all benefits of the two-career family.

SUGGESTED READINGS

Coser, Rose Lamb, ed. *Life Cycle and Achievement in America.* New York: Harper Torchbooks, 1969. Discusses woman's place in the changing American economic system.

[24]See Letha Scanzoni and John Scanzoni, *Men, Women and Change* (New York: McGraw-Hill, 1975), chap. 6, "The Structure of Marriage," pp. 201–53.

[25]See Constantina Safilios-Rothschild, *Toward a Sociology of Women* (Lexington, Mass.: Xerox, 1972), chap. 4, "The Options of Women."

Harbeson, Gladys E. *Choice and Challenge for the American Woman,* rev. ed. Cambridge, Mass.: Schenkman, 1971. Focuses on the rising expectations of women, and the need for freedom of choice in personal life and the job market.

Hoffman, Lois W., and Ivan F. Nye. *Working Mothers: An Evaluative Review of the Consequences for Wife, Husband, and Child.* San Francisco: Jossey-Bass, 1974. Balanced coverage of research on the employed mother; emphasizes research of the previous decade.

Hopkins, Jane, and Priscilla White. "The Dual-Career Couple: Constraints and Supports," *The Family Coordinator,* 27, no. 3 (July 1978), 253–59. Considers the problems involved in the dual-career lifestyle.

Keniston, Kenneth, and the Carnegie Council on Children. *All Our Children—The American Family Under Pressure.* New York: Harcourt Brace Jovanovich, 1977. Relates parental employment to the needs of children and to current social policy.

Lopata, Helen Z. *Occupation: Housewife.* New York: Oxford Univ. Press, 1971. Focuses on 1,000 urban housewives with young children. Valuable control group for study of employed mothers.

Scanzoni, Letha, and John Scanzoni. *Men, Women and Change: A Sociology of Marriage and the Family.* New York: McGraw-Hill, 1975. Sociological treatment of the family, with emphasis on changing role patterns.

U.S. Bureau of the Census. *Statistical Abstract of the United States, 1978.* Washington, D.C.: U.S. Government Printing Office, 1978. Basic source for data on working women, age of children, family size.

White, Burton L. *The First Three Years of Life.* Englewood Cliffs, N.J.: Prentice-Hall, 1975. Noted child psychologist studies impact of mother's employment and other factors influencing the child's early life.

14 Sexual Adjustment in Marriage

- How do our attitudes toward the opposite sex develop?
- What are the most important elements in marital sexual adjustment?
- Why is there so much ignorance about sex in our culture? How can this ignorance be overcome?
- What are the major elements of male sexual patterns?
- What are the major elements of female sexual patterns?
- What factors play a part in the preparation for sexual adjustment in marriage?
- In what ways has our knowledge of sexual functioning increased in the last fifteen years?
- What are the four phases of human sexual response? Are they the same for men and women?
- What kind of sexual adjustment problems do women have? What kind of sexual adjustment problems do men have?
- What kinds of sexual therapy are available for the treatment of sexual dysfunction?

Factors in Sexual Adjustment

Achieving a satisfying sexual adjustment is one of the primary goals in marriage. Because physical attraction is so frequently emphasized in our courtship system, it is often assumed that early sexual adjustment will be natural and mutually satisfying. However, the research on this subject and the continuing high rate of divorce for the first two or three years of marriage clearly indicate that successful adjustment is not always the case.

Some elements of the development of sexuality in the early years of life have been discussed in Chapter 4. Our basic feelings about our sex and gender identity begin in our preschool years. This initial learning experience is modified by later ones, but it usually remains the predominant one. From the early family environment, then, we should naturally develop a sound acceptance of ourselves and our sex. Such normal development of masculinity or femininity begins in early childhood and is the natural prelude to heterosexual relationships in adolescence, which are a major part of the courtship process leading to marriage.

Sexual response in marriage, is, then, the product of a long process of development that begins early in life. It may be influenced by physical, psychological, cultural, and moral factors. In our contemporary society, none of these elements in marital sexual interaction can be ignored. Each plays a part in building sexual harmony that is satisfying to both partners.

Although we will again focus on the newly married couple, sexual adjustment remains a factor in marriage through every stage of the family life cycle. And though we will primarily discuss sex within marriage, we recognize that many of the problems that married couples have are shared by those who are unmarried and living together. The marital sexual relationship may be understood better, perhaps, if we ask ourselves this question: What do a man and a woman bring into their sexual relationship in marriage?

Self-Image and Sexual Response

Each of us brings into a sexual union our own self-image. What kind of person am I? What opinion do I have of myself? Am I an individual of worth and meaning? We discussed the development of the individual's personality in Chapter 1. It is important to remember that sexual intercourse unites two *persons*. If there is no genuine respect in the relationship—both self-respect and respect for one's partner—the sexual relationship will soon degenerate into an arrangement of physical convenience. No mere accumulation of knowledge or mastery of sexual technique can replace the genuine giving of oneself in the act of sexual union.

One way of explaining the difference in our contemporary view of sexual adjustment from previous generations is to note the increasing complexity involved. We are no longer simply interested in how often one has sex, with whom, when, and where. Instead, we talk about human beings growing and developing in a wide range of behaviors, feelings, attitudes, and experiences. The self-concept each of us has in this total framework is vitally important.

Attitudes Toward the Opposite Sex

An important factor that enters into the marital sexual relationship is a person's attitude toward the opposite sex. Every counselor who has dealt with marital sexual problems knows how varied and complex are the many sexual impressions we gain in childhood. Many of our attitudes toward our parents and siblings of the opposite sex are loving and joyful; but unfortunately, many times they are filled with memories of repression, ignorance, hate, and misunderstanding.[1] We pay a daily price for sexual ignorance; some of us must go back and relearn our attitudes toward sex and toward our partners before we can achieve a satisfactory sexual relationship.

Both husband and wife must be realistic about their attitudes toward the opposite sex. Sometimes a person talking about his or her love for a particular partner emphasizes that it is very different from his or her attitude toward others of the partner's sex. "I love Gordon so much," says Herta, "but I never could get along with my father and my older brother." Perhaps so,

[1]See Helen Colton, *Adults Need Sex Education Too* (Los Angeles: Family Forum, 1972); see also Kenneth L. Jones, Louis W. Shainberg, and Curtis O. Byer, *Sex* (New York: Harper & Row, 1969).

but Herta's relationship will undoubtedly be influenced in many ways by the eighteen years she lived at home with her father and brother.

These built-in attitudes toward the opposite sex are especially important to the sons and daughters of parents who harbored resentment and hatred toward each other whether they divorced or not. If there is antagonism between parents, the children are often caught in the crossfire. Negative attitudes are imprinted then and carry over into all aspects of the person's later marital relationship, including the sexual relationship.

Cultural Conditioning and Sexual Adjustment

As we saw in Chapter 5, cultural conditioning also plays a central role in sexual adjustment. It is not simply the physical act of intercourse that is important; it is also the thoughts and feelings associated with it. A great many young Americans are still raised under fairly restrictive Victorian conditions in regard to sex: They hear very little discussion of sex at home and then only in the most negative terms. They are thus ill prepared to enter into their marital sexual experience naturally and freely.

This difficulty can be described simply in terms of stimulus and response. In a conservative and sexually restrictive atmosphere, the child is taught to repress sexual interest and curiosity and not to be tempted by sexual need and desire. The powerful forces of home, church, and school all combine to warn him against the dangers of sexual activity and interest, which, he is taught, will be damaging to him, will violate his moral standards, can hinder later success in marriage, and might limit his upward social mobility. Under this constant and consistent stimulus (counteracted only slightly by the general society), the individual responds with a restrained and limited mode of behavior in regard to sex, for it is considered wrong to respond otherwise.

After marriage, a different set of stimuli exist. That which was forbidden is now accepted. Sexual intercourse is no longer taboo, but an expected privilege of the marital relationship. The physical attraction of one partner for the other and all the preparatory behavior that comes before intercourse are a natural and wholesome part of the sexual relationship. This change can be verbalized, and husband and wife can accept this new set of conditions in principle; but the strength of earlier response patterns will not be lightly set aside. Thus the couple find many fears and inhibitions hindering a satisfactory sexual adjustment. Sometimes counseling is needed to overcome these problems, which are most seriously exemplified by frigidity in women and impotence in men.

Religious training is an important part of cultural conditioning. Kinsey showed that there are strong religious influences on our sexual patterns. "There is nothing in the English-American social structure that has had more influence upon present-day patterns of sexual behavior than the religious backgrounds of that culture."[2] This influence on sex behavior has been shown in many research studies.[3] More religiously active or devout men and women have less premarital sexual experience and generally a lower frequency of intercourse during marriage. Masters and Johnson found that religious orthodoxy is often a major factor in both masculine and feminine sexual dysfunction.[4]

The mass media also exert a strong cultural influence on our attitudes toward sex. There is much frank discussion of sexual drives and feelings in our society, but it is often very superficial. The exploitation of sex by the advertising industry, radio, television, magazines, tabloids, and books has both overstimulated and deceived us. We might illustrate the way cultural conditioning has changed in our society by examining the popular television show "All in the Family." It gives us an idea of how our views on what is and what is not acceptable in married life can differ in one short generation. Pierson and D'Antonio describe it in these terms:

> Archie and Edith are blue collar people with traditional orientations toward all aspects of marriage. They have clearly defined and separated sex roles, overt sexual and emotional expression is narrowly restricted, Archie has a tavern to which he retreats on occasion, and a TV set to which he retreats when at home. Their personalities seem fixed, and such interaction as there is seems merely to reinforce traditional sex role orientations.
>
> On the other hand, Gloria and Mike are overtly sexual in their behavior, talk about liberation from traditional roles, and their interaction is patterned to suggest that they are concerned about mutual development and gratification. Where Archie emphasizes duty, Mike emphasizes spontaneity; Archie sees Edith as a good housekeeper and cook, and wishes she would keep quiet; Mike sees Gloria as a helpmate and lover and encourages her to share experiences with him. . . .[5]

Thus we are conditioned in many ways by our culture. We are, in fact, influenced as much or more by cultural standards on sex as by biological differences between the sexes.

[2] Alfred C. Kinsey, Wardell B. Pomeroy, and Clyde E. Martin, *Sexual Behavior in the Human Male* (Philadelphia: Saunders, 1948), pp. 465–87.

[3] See J. Anthony Somenfink, "A Study of Some Aspects of Marital Behavior as Related to Religious Control," *Marriage and Family Living*, 20, no. 2 (May 1958), 163–69; and Alfred C. Kinsey, Wardell B. Pomeroy, Clyde E. Martin, and Paul Gebhard, *Sexual Behavior in the Human Female* (Philadelphia: Saunders, 1953), pp. 521–25.

[4] William H. Masters and Virginia E. Johnson, *Human Sexual Inadequacy* (Boston: Little, Brown, 1970), pp. 117–20, 229–33.

[5] Elaine C. Pierson and William V. D'Antonio, *Female and Male: Dimensions of Human Sexuality* (Philadelphia: Lippincott, 1974), p. 298.

We see sexual behavior therefore as *scripted* behavior, not the masked expression of a primordial drive. The individual can learn sexual behavior as he or she learns other behavior—through scripts that in this case give the self, other persons, and situations erotic abilities or content. Desire, privacy, opportunity, and propinquity with an attractive member of the opposite sex are not, in themselves, enough; in ordinary circumstances, nothing sexual will occur unless one or both actors organize these elements into an appropriate script. The very concern with foreplay in sex suggests this. From one point of view, foreplay may be defined as merely progressive physical excitement generated by touching naturally erogenous zones. The authors have referred to this conception elsewhere as the "rubbing of two sticks together to make a fire" model. It would seem to be more valuable to see this activity as symbolically invested behavior through which the body is eroticized and through which mute, inarticulate motions and gestures are translated into a sociosexual drama.

A belief in the sociocultural dominance of sexual behavior finds support in cross-cultural research as well as in data restricted to the United States. Psychosexual development is universal—but it takes many forms and tempos.[6]

Prior Sexual Experience

We must also consider the prior sexual experience of the partners when we examine the pattern of marital sexual adjustment. This usually includes both masturbation and heterosexual experience, either through petting or sexual intercourse. There are marked cultural differences in what we expect from men and women in this regard, and biological differences as well. These factors combine to produce a different record of experience for husband and wife. The move toward sexual equality is erasing some of these differences in our culture, but we are probably two or three generations away from realizing a full single standard in sexual behavior.

MALE SEXUAL PATTERNS

What are the American patterns of male sexual activity? A man's sexual response is easily aroused by a number of stimuli. One of the Kinsey findings, which confirmed earlier studies, was that the American male responded more frequently to audio and visual stimuli than the female and could be ready for intercourse very quickly after stimulation. Both husband and wife should understand this, because it has a very definite effect on their relationship. Since the husband is aroused quickly, and his feeling subsides

[6]John H. Gagnon and William Simon, *The Sexual Scene* (New York: Aldine, 1970), p. 25.

very quickly after intercourse, he may find it difficult to coordinate his response with his wife's.

Because men are more aware of the sexual stimuli in our society, they have in some ways tried to build a subculture that recognizes and satisfies their needs outside the marriage relationship. The institution of prostitution and erotic magazines are examples of social concessions to the sexual aggressiveness and responsiveness of men. In earlier periods of history and in other cultures, such concessions to men have been accepted without question as a normal part of a patriarchal society. In the sexual life of our present-day society, we no longer fully accept the masculine dominance and freedom that created the masculine subculture. Instead we stress the companionship of man and woman in marriage and their mutual interest and satisfaction in sexual intercourse. We prepare them for this type of companionship through long years of courtship, which include steady relationships that link boy and girl together in a variety of situations over many months and years.

This is not to say that our culture has really achieved a complete transition to a single standard in sexual behavior. There are still strong remnants of the old double standard in our culture, and parents usually make clear the distinction between their expectations for their sons and their expectations for their daughters. The contrast in expectation is particularly marked when premarital intercourse results in pregnancy: There is a moral judgment made by most Americans against an unwed mother, while there is little concern with the behavior of an unwed father.

In Chapter 4 we discussed some of the masculine sexual patterns as reported by the two Kinsey studies. Kinsey considered all kinds of sexual response, including orgasmic experience from masturbation, nocturnal emissions, premarital petting, intercourse, homosexual contacts, and animal contacts. He found the frequency of orgasm highest for adolescents, with a median frequency of 3.21 orgasms per week for married men from sixteen to twenty years of age; this dropped steadily throughout life (1.18 was the median frequency for ages forty-six to fifty).[7] In comparison, the median frequency of sexual experiences for the married woman was reported at 2.2 per week for the sixteen-to-twenty age group and dropped to .8 by ages forty-six to fifty.[8] Single men showed correspondingly higher frequencies than single women.

The greater frequency of sexual experience for males, both single and married, can be accounted for by several factors. Men usually begin orgasmic experience earlier, often through masturbation. Men are also more apt to enter into premarital sexual relations either with steady partners or with prostitutes. In addition, men have frequent nocturnal emissions and are

[7]Kinsey et al., *Sexual Behavior in the Human Male,* p. 226.
[8]Kinsey et al., *Sexual Behavior in the Human Female,* p. 549.

more often stimulated by various sexual stimuli, largely because their participation in sexual activities is more culturally acceptable than women's.

One might interpret these facts to mean that men are more highly sexed than women. However, it is more likely that the combination of cultural, psychological, moral, and spiritual influences in our society stimulates men to a higher sexual frequency than women. If we lived in a culture that stressed equal standards, freedom, and responsibility for both men and women, and if the sex education of both boys and girls could be standardized, the difference in the frequency of sex might disappear or even be reversed. Given the complexity of our present civilization and its increasing specialization of thought and function, however, it seems probable that some masculine-feminine differences in sexual response will continue in the foreseeable future.

Another part of our folklore states that men are supposed to have little difficulty with their sex life. In actuality, of course, men have problems. Masters and Johnson have given equal time to a consideration of both masculine and feminine sexual dysfunction. Ira Reiss writes:

> Our culture stresses a "tough" male attitude to sexuality. A male is not encouraged to talk about being scared during this first act of intercourse, about erection difficulties, or about premature ejaculation problems. The male is supposed to be relaxed, cavalier, confident, and hedonistic. Fear, anxiety, and performance difficulties are not discussed. The female role is quite different since her role has been, in the past, defined as a more submissive one. Thus, she is supposed to be less aggressive, and thus she can display fear and anxiety and performance difficulties. . . . Perhaps in the next few years we shall begin to see more complete studies designed to better understand male-female sexual differences and similarities.[9]

FEMALE SEXUAL PATTERNS

There has been an expanding number of studies made in the last fifteen years on female sexual patterns in our culture. One result of the feminist movement has been the liberation of women from stereotypes in sexual behavior. Shifts in attitudes, values, and behavior are reflected in every contemporary survey, popular and scientific. We still have not reached a point of equilibrium in this development. There will be continuing change until the theoretical goal of much greater equity becomes reality.

A generation ago (1953), Kinsey published his report on *Sexual Behavior in the Human Female.* According to his data American women did not seek

[9]Ira L. Reiss, *Family Systems in America,* 2nd ed. (Hinsdale, Ill.: Dryden, 1976), p. 279.

arousal by as large a number of sexual stimuli as men. Their frequency of sexual response was less than the male's at every stage of the life cycle. Whereas the average male, single or married, reached orgasm regularly in his late teens, almost half of all women had no such experience before twenty. After they were married, 75 percent of women were able to reach orgasm during the first year of marriage, but the remaining 25 percent took up to twenty years to do so.[10] In fact, Kinsey found that 10 percent of the women he studied had not experienced orgasm after twenty years of marriage. Although there were some exceptions to these patterns, such sexual behavior seemed to be general enough to indicate why women were said to be less sexually inclined than men.

Many of the features of the feminine pattern of sexual response are remnants of earlier eras, when a double standard of sexual behavior was sanctioned and the desires and interests of men were clearly dominant over those of women. If an adolescent boy developed sexual interest earlier than a girl, it was accepted as natural; and if he sought sexual outlets before marriage, it was just a case of his sowing wild oats. If a girl became involved in that way, she was a "bad" girl and lost her chance to make a decent marriage, unless a particular boy felt obligated to marry her.

For countless generations, then, women, especially in the higher social classes, could conveniently be placed in one of two categories. Either they were "good" and remained virgins until marriage, or they were not. After marriage, they often found very little satisfaction in sexual intercourse with their husbands; it was their duty, and it was not necessarily pleasant. In fact, if a woman took too much pleasure in sex, it was thought that she had been involved in some premarital experience that had awakened her sexually and thus made her a less trustworthy wife.

These patterns remain, most markedly in the lower classes, where new conceptions of marriage companionship and more adequate sex education have not been assimilated. Lee Rainwater has suggested that lower-class women develop patterns either of mutuality with their sexual partners or of rejection of sexuality.

> These two patterns are complex, and they certainly overlap. Some women who fit the mutuality pattern do so only against underlying anxieties about their sexual behavior. Some women who fit the rejection pattern are there despite their wish that they could be more "relaxed" in sexual relations. However, the dominance of one or the other tendency is clear in most of the respondents. . . .
>
> On the whole, not quite half of our sample seems to conform to the mutuality pattern, somewhat less than a third to the rejection pattern,

[10]Kinsey et al., *Sexual Behavior in the Human Female,* pp. 383–84.

and about the same number in the in-between category. In general, mutuality seems more characteristic of the upper-lower class than of the lower-lower as one would expect, given the generally less distant relationship between upper-lower class wives and husbands and the sense of strain and conflict so common among lower-lower class couples. . . . About 40 percent of the lower-lower class women indicate a real rejection of sexuality, compared with only 10 percent of the upper-lower class category.[11]

More recent studies have given us further insight into these data, and have changed some conclusions. Catherine Chilman, in reviewing some psychological aspects of female sexuality, has noted these points:

1. Female sexual response, in terms of its physiological manifestation, is much like that of the male. . . .
2. Females probably have at least as strong a sex drive as males do. . . .
3. The female is more capable of multiple orgasm within a defined time period than the male. . . .

. . .

5. The clitoris is the female analogue to the penis: it, rather than the vagina, is the chief female erogenous zone. Physiologically, there is no difference between so-called clitoral and vaginal orgasm. . . .

. . .

9. Contrary to much psychiatric theory that females who masturbate are likely to have neurotic problems, Fisher found that the small number of married females in his sample who masturbate apparently do so because they are more open to their own sexuality and the pleasure to be derived from it. . . .

. . .

12. It may be that females are more dependent than males in their mate relationships.[12]

Bell and Lobsenz, in summarizing a sample of women who responded to a study circulated through the cooperation of American Sociological Association (ASA) members, found three major conclusions standing out.

[11]Lee Rainwater, *And the Poor Get Children* (Chicago: Quadrangle, 1960), p. 121; see also Lee Rainwater, *Family Design, Marital Sexuality, Family Size, and Contraception* (Chicago: Aldine, 1965).

[12]Catherine S. Chilman, "Some Psychosocial Aspects of Female Sexuality," *The Family Coordinator,* 23, no. 2 (April 1974), 123–31.

Although the sample was overrepresented at the college level, and a larger than average group was employed, these trends are worth noting.

> 1. Most wives enjoy a high level of sexual pleasure in marriage. This is especially true for younger women and perhaps can be linked to the fact that they apparently have a less emotionally complicated and more pleasure-oriented attitude toward sex.
>
> 2. Younger wives are experimenting with a variety of approaches to love-making. Furthermore, those women who do vary their sexual experiences in marriage generally report a greater degree of satisfaction.
>
> 3. Extramarital relationships are increasingly frequent, but they are not as common as the popular press would have us believe. One change, however, does seem significant. For older wives, sex outside marriage is, as it traditionally has been, an expression of unhappiness. But the affairs of a number of younger wives seem to express a philosophy that explicitly rejects sexual exclusivity as part of the marriage commitment.[13]

These factors, and others, Bell and Lobsenz report, are making for the development of a new lifestyle for younger wives. They are moving toward greater freedom, experimentation, and emotional honesty.

There are many complicating factors that enter into the sexual relationship. Why do some women not have sexual experience regularly? One reason frequently cited by women refraining from sexual intercourse is fear of pregnancy. Some women do not wish to assume the responsibility of motherhood at the beginning of marriage, for personal or financial reasons. They hesitate to enter freely into their marital sex relations for fear of becoming pregnant too soon. Or, if they do have children, they may find that the children tend to require all their time and energy. While life for the husband goes on at much the same pace, the wife finds that there are endless tasks connected with motherhood. There are diapers to change, clothes to wash and mend, floors to scrub and wax, and toys to pick up. All these things are not directly involved with marital sexual intercourse, but they are bound to have a profound influence on it. Perhaps this is an important reason that many women find greater satisfaction in their marital sex life in their late twenties and early thirties, when the childbearing phase of the marriage is usually completed.

Are there differences between male and female response? The Kinsey studies suggest that sexual experience is a major conditioning factor, both in its presence and its absence, and is particularly important in explaining the differences between male and female responses.

[13]Robert R. Bell and Norman M. Lobsenz, "Married Sex: How Uninhibited Can a Woman Dare to Be?" Reprinted in John H. Gagnon, ed., *Human Sexuality in Today's World* (Boston: Little, Brown, 1977), pp. 112–18.

> We have, then, thirty-three bodies of data which agree in showing that the male is conditioned by sexual experience more frequently than the female. The male more often shares, vicariously, the sexual experiences of other persons, he more frequently responds sympathetically when he observes other individuals engaged in sexual activities, he may develop stronger preferences for particular types of sexual activity, and he may react to a great variety of objects which have been associated with his sexual activities.
>
> There is tremendous individual variation. . . . We have already observed that the anatomy and physiology of sexual response and orgasm . . . do not show the differences between the sexes that might account for the differences in their sexual responses. Females appear to be as capable as males of being aroused by tactile stimuli; they appear as capable as males of responding to the point of orgasm. . . . We find no reason for believing that the physiologic or psychologic satisfactions derived from orgasm by the average female are different from those of the average male. But in their capacities to respond to psychosexual stimuli, the average female and the average male do differ.[14]

Achieving Sexual Adjustment

Let us now bring our discussion and our research together. What are the most important elements in achieving a satisfying sexual adjustment in marriage? Sexual harmony in marriage is the natural and joyful expectation of every newly married bride and groom. But it does not necessarily just happen; the couple usually move toward sexual harmony gradually. There are several basic steps in developing this sexual harmony.

Love

Sexual harmony is built on love. In our culture, the meaning of sex is lost when love is lost. The expression of self-giving and self-sharing that is sexual intercourse must be nurtured by love in all aspects of the marital relationship.

> If sexual intercourse is defined as lovemaking or the simple act of giving and receiving love, then persons with those abilities are presupposed. The tone of the successful sexual relationship implies a kind of "generosity of body and soul," as described by Simone de Beauvoir. This suggests not simply the sharing of oneself with another, but the ability to

[14]Kinsey et al., *Sexual Behavior in the Human Female,* pp. 687–88.

Table 14–1 Intensity Matrix for the Analysis of an Intimate Relationship*

	Intellectual	*Physical*	*Emotional*
Breadth (range of shared activities)	Telling of the meaningful events in one's day Participating in a political rally Years of interaction resulting in the sharing of meanings (phrases, gestures, etc.) understood only by the partners Decision making regarding management of household	Dancing Caressing Swimming Doing laundry Tennis Shopping Gardening Sexual intercourse Other sensual/sexual activities	Phone calls providing emotional support when separated Experiencing grief in a family tragedy Witnessing with pride a daughter's graduation from college Resolving conflict in occasional arguments
Openness (disclosure of self)	Disclosing one's values and goals Discussing controversial aspects of politics, ethics, etc. Using familiar language Not feeling a need to lie to the partner Sharing of secrets with the partner, and discretion regarding the secrets of the partner	Feeling free to wear old clothes Grooming in presence of the other Bathroom behavior (elimination, etc.) in presence of the other Nudity Few limitations placed upon exploration of one's body by the partner Sharing of physical space (area, possessions, etc.) with few signs of territoriality	Describing one's dreams and daydreams Feeling free to call for "time out" or for togetherness Maintaining openness (disclosure) regarding one's emotional involvement with other intimates Telling of daily joys and frustrations Emotional honesty in resolving conflict Expressing anger, resentment, and other positive and negative emotions
Depth (sharing of core aspects of self)	"Knowing" of the partner Having faith in the partner's reliability and in his/her love Occasional experiencing of the essence of one's self in transcendental union	Physical relaxation, sense of contentment and well-being in the presence of the other	Committing oneself without guarantee, in the hope that one's love will be returned Caring as much about the partner as about oneself

*The matrix represents an analytic cross-section of an intimate relationship at one point in time. Entries in the cells are examples of activities (breadth), freedoms (openness), and qualities (depth) characteristic of one highly intense relationship. The relationship depicted in this figure shows high intensity on each of the three dimensions of breadth, openness, and depth.

Table 14–1 (continued)

	Intellectual	*Physical*	*Emotional*
Depth (sharing of core aspects of self)	Working collectively to change certain core characteristics of the self, and of the partner		Nonjealous supportiveness toward the other intimate relationships of the partner

SOURCE: Carolyn Kieffer, "New Depths in Intimacy," in *Marriage and Alternatives: Exploring Intimate Relationships,* Roger W. Libby and Robert N. Whitehurst, eds., p. 273. Copyright © 1977 by Scott, Foresman & Company. Reprinted by permission.

> accept what is shared by another with oneself. This ability comes in a variety of personality types, from introvert to extrovert and every gradation in between, but it is sometimes absent even in what appears to be the most attractive personality. Somehow, in the process of development, this ability to participate in the sharing experience remains inhibited. Under some circumstances, it is possible for such persons to participate mechanically in sexual intercourse, but they never really "give" or "accept" the experience. For whatever reasons, they can never be "close" to another person, even when their bodies are interlocked. This ability to share with another and to be able to accept sharing from another would seem to be related to the total personal attitude toward sex.[15]

The achievement of successful sexual adjustment in marriage is a complex process. There must be a delicate balance between love and knowledge and between the ideal and the real. Since the sexual relationship is the most intimate and most personal relationship that can be established between two human beings, it requires a continuing growth of interest and concern. Many couples begin marriage with a very satisfactory sexual adjustment but lose it when the husband becomes completely absorbed in his work; when the wife neglects their relationship because of the needs of the children; or when both allow the relationship to become casual or unimportant. A maturing and growing sexual relationship between partners can never be achieved casually; it can develop only when both contribute freely and fully to the marriage, sexually and in many other ways.

Every engaged couple should take adequate time to think together about their marital sexual relationship. The achievement of mutual happiness in sexual intercourse and the ability to build normal patterns of sexual response must begin with a frankness and understanding developed during the

[15]Alfred W. Melton, Jr., "Human Sexual Response," *The Individual, Sex, and Society,* Carlfred B. Broderick and Jessie Bernard, eds. (Baltimore: Johns Hopkins Press, 1969), p. 224.

couple's courtship days. The couple will not be able to find sexual satisfaction if they do not find happiness in other ways; but their companionship will find richer meaning and interpretation through their sexual union.

In much of contemporary literature, there is a heavy emphasis on intimacy, which is seen in terms very similar to many interpretations of love.[16] Carolyn Kieffer has developed a helpful "intensity matrix" to analyze an intimate relationship, including its intellectual, physical, and emotional components (see Table 14–1).

Commitment

Another crucial step toward marital sexual harmony is commitment. The love the couple share with each other must be reinforced by responsible commitment. If either partner is not committed to give himself or herself fully to the other, the union may become superficial. W. Norman Pittenger relates such a commitment to religious ideals.

> The understanding of marriage in lands that have been exposed to Christian influence is that it is lifelong, not subject to rupture whenever one party happens to feel a little bored or tired of the other. Here we have a reflection of love as entailing commitment or dedication. It was Gabriel Marcel, I believe, who once said that one of the unique things about men is that they can and do *make promises*—the world in which they live is of the sort that permits, even demands promise-making, while those who make them are able to intend to fulfill them. But a promise, when it is made in the context of heterosexual love, can only signify genuine commitment when it is "for always." "Till death do us part," says the marriage service. Those words pay a very high tribute to the persons who take them upon their lips. . . . Loving and cherishing: there is the self-giving, the mutuality, the willingness to receive, of which we have spoken; there too is the tenderness ("to cherish") which is the mark of love at its noblest.[17]

Commitment involves sexual responsibility. The adolescent boy who engages regularly in masturbation or who frequently engages in premarital sexual relations probably does so in order to satisfy his own sexual desires. He receives sexual stimuli from his culture and responds to it. No other individual is involved in masturbation; in premarital relations, his partner

[16]Note discussion of intimate relationships in Rosabeth Moss Kanter, Dennis Jaffe, and D. Kelly Weisberg, "Coupling, Parenting, and the Presence of Others: Intimate Relationships in Communal Households," *The Family Coordinator*, 24, no. 4 (Oct. 1975), 433–52.

[17]W. Norman Pittenger, *Making Sexuality Human* (Philadelphia: Pilgrim Press, 1970), pp. 52–53.

may or may not have any permanent significance to him. Therefore, the entire experience may well be an essentially selfish one for him. He has a need, he seeks an outlet, and he is satisfied.

In extramarital relations, the same factors may be involved—with a difference. A married man cannot think only of himself; if he has developed a selfish sexual pattern and persists in it after marriage, it will be difficult for him to maintain a stable marriage. He can do so only if his wife is long-suffering, if she refuses to face the reality of the situation, or if she is having extramarital affairs herself and the couple accept this pattern. Otherwise, tensions will inevitably build up, and open conflict will result.

Support for the concept of commitment comes from Masters and Johnson in their book *The Pleasure Bond—A New Look at Sexuality and Commitment.* They have been strongly critical of the concepts advanced by Nena and George O'Neill, Robert Francoeur, Robert Rimmer, and Rustum and Della Roy, which advocate "open marriage" and freedom in the establishment of extramarital sexual relationships. They feel that the arguments advanced have been shallow and self-serving, ignoring basic physical, emotional, spiritual, and social realities:

> Who sets the "criteria for appropriateness" by which extramarital intercourse is to be judged, the partner who participates or the partner who does not—or do they decide together, and if so, who has the final decision? Whose "human need" is being considered—that of the involved partner, the noninvolved partner or the third party? Moreover who is to define these needs, sexual or otherwise, and then weigh them to determine which deserve to be labeled "paramount"? . . .
>
> To encourage such a belief is to encourage the dangerous and self-serving malady of megalomania. The Roys verge on doing this with their assurance that having extramarital relationships may "serve as the vehicle of faithfulness to God." But since they are aware that men and women caught in sexual triangles are imperfect and vulnerable human beings, they must acknowledge that there are risks. They do so, however, in evasive terms. . . .
>
> It is one thing to repudiate the idea that every instance of extramarital sex is anathema to God; it is something else to advance the idea that in certain cases extramarital sex is a way of being faithful to God. . . .
>
> What is the basis of such counsel? . . . When and where and by whom has this approach to human relationships been observed and how have the effects been measured? Who has ever attempted to follow up the consequences after a lapse of time? . . .
>
> As couples, the question (many) want answered is not what makes extramarital sex right or wrong—but what makes it unnecessary? . . .

Figure 14–1

The Male Sexual Organs

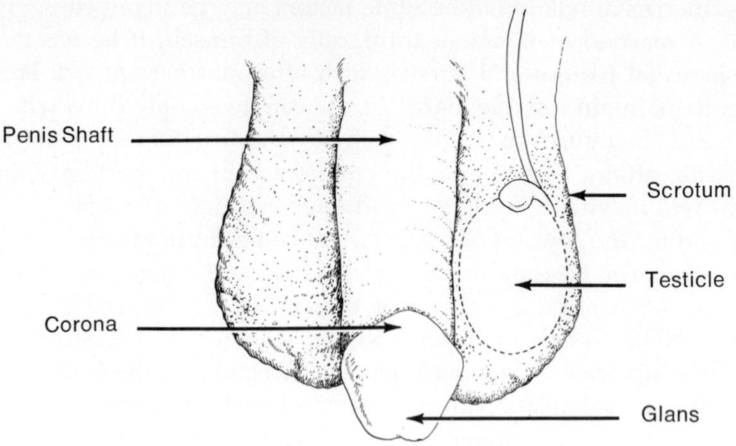

Figure 14–2

The Female Sexual Organs

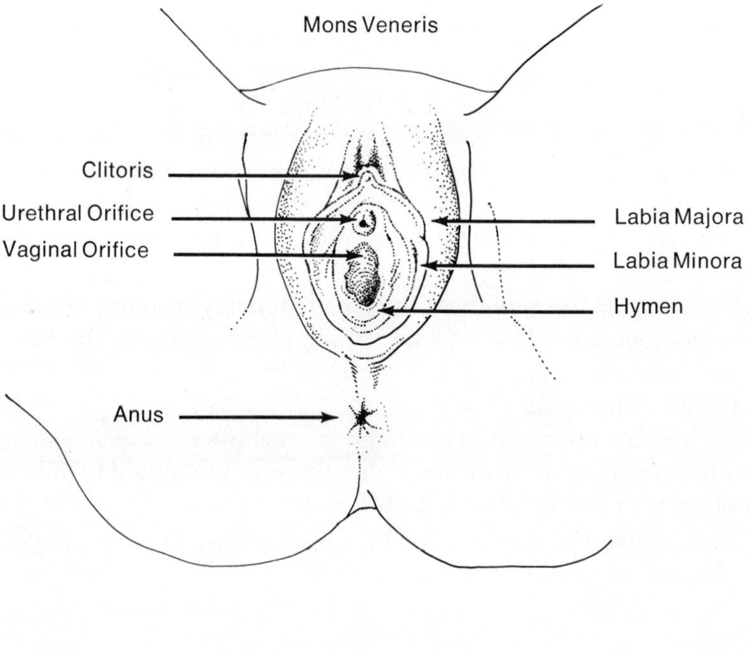

that examines how and why the sense of being mutually committed may contribute to the sexual responsiveness of both partners and to the durability of their exclusive relationship.[18]

Knowledge and Understanding

Sexual harmony grows with increased knowledge and understanding. We now realize the problems generated in the past by sexual ignorance. What we don't know does hurt us. Both husband and wife should have an adequate understanding of the biological and physiological structures involved in sexual intercourse, including the organs of stimulation and arousal that lead both men and women to sexual response. There is considerable evidence that simple ignorance is at the root of much marital sexual maladjustment.[19] Let us consider some of the basic facts a couple will need to know, then.

MALE AND FEMALE SEX ORGANS

The external male sex organs are the *penis* and the *scrotum*. The penis is composed of spongy erectile tissue. During sexual arousal the penile cavities become engorged with blood and the penis enlarges and becomes erect. The skin of the penis is smooth and fairly loose to permit expansion during arousal. The penis has no bone or muscles within it, so an erection cannot be willed.

The main body of the penis is termed the *shaft* (see Figure 14–1). The smooth, rounded head of the penis is the *glans*, the highly sensitive area that is of prime importance in sexual arousal. The ridge at the edge of the glans adjacent to the penile shaft is the *corona*. It has many highly sensitive nerve endings and is a primary source of sexual pleasure and excitement.

[18]William H. Masters and Virginia E. Johnson, *The Pleasure Bond—A New Look at Sexuality and Commitment* (New York: Bantam, 1973), pp. 200–03.

[19]Examples of the problems created by negligent or erroneous sex education are described in the work of John A. Blazer and Leonard J. Friedman. Blazer reported on a study of 1,000 wives who remained virgins after marriage and noted a wide variety of reasons for their failure to begin intercourse with their husbands. Fear of pain, negative feelings about sexuality, and fear of pregnancy were frequently noted. The wives' reports were cross-checked by interviews with their husbands. Blazer concluded that ignorance was the major disruptive factor in the unconsummated marriages, and his study strongly suggested that many married women are ignorant of sexual matters. Friedman reported that sex instruction for such wives early in treatment was successful in 71 percent of the cases he studied. See John A. Blazer, "Married Virgins: A Study of Unconsummated Marriages," *Journal of Marriage and the Family*, 26, no. 2 (May 1964), 213–14; and Leonard J. Friedman, *Virgin Wives: A Study of Unconsummated Marriages* (Springfield, Ill.: Thomas, 1962), p. 139.

The most sensitive area of the penis is the *frenulum,* the thin tissue on the underside of the glans.

The scrotum is a multilayered pouch with two separate compartments, each of which houses a *testicle.* The skin of the scrotum is not especially sensitive to erotic stimulation. The testes may respond to very gentle stimulation; however, manipulation of the testes may easily cause a man pain.

The external genitalia of the female are termed the *vulva* and include the *mons pubis* (or *mons veneris),* the *labia majora,* the *labia minora,* the *vaginal orifice,* and the *clitoris* (see Figure 14–2). The mons pubis is the most visible part of the female genitals, the fatty tissue that is covered with hair. It can be stimulated by contact and pressure. The labia majora are the two elongated folds of skin that appear to close the female genitals. Within the labia majora are the labia minora, which enclose the vaginal orifice (into which the *vagina* opens) and the clitoris. The labia minora, the vaginal orifice, and the clitoris are highly erogenous (sexually sensitive) and tend to open during sexual excitement. The clitoris is a small, cylindrical erectile structure that resembles a miniature penis. The entire clitoris, except for its rounded tip, the *glans,* is covered by the upper folds of the labia minora. The clitoris becomes engorged with blood during sexual excitement and may enlarge to twice its normal size. It is the most sexually excitable area of a woman's body and may be stimulated indirectly during intercourse by the thrust of the man's penis into the vagina (see Figure 14–3) as well as directly by manipulation.

The vaginal orifice is a small opening visible only when the labia minora are parted. Its appearance depends in large measure on the condition of the *hymen,* or maidenhead, which is the fold of connective tissue partially covering the opening. An undamaged hymen was once considered proof of virginity, but in actuality it may be completely absent in a virgin. Petting and the use of tampons will often stretch the hymen. During childbirth, of course, the hymen is almost completely lost.

The vagina contains very few nerve endings that give sexual pleasure; penetration of the penis serves mainly as an indirect stimulus of the clitoris. Masters and Johnson have disproved the old-fashioned misconception that a woman has two distinct orgasms, clitoral and vaginal. Contractions of the vagina during intercourse are caused by stimulation of the clitoris and are only a secondary effect of orgasm, which is experienced by the woman as a climax of feeling in the clitoris.

The pain many women feel during sexual intercourse is generally not the result of physical dysfunction, but is usually psychological in origin. If a woman is not relaxed or willing during intercourse, then the natural processes leading her to sexual pleasure and full orgasmic response are restrained. In much the same way that a man cannot force an erection, a woman cannot force her body to respond to a man.

All normal and healthy human beings respond to sexual stimulation. Our sexual experiences are as broad in compass as all our experiences in life. The manner of stimulation varies widely, and the range and intensity of sexual arousal experienced by each person are extremely varied. There are three major kinds of stimulation: direct stimulation by touch; stimulation by the other four senses; and emotional and psychological stimulation. We have already discussed the primary erogenous zones, the areas of the body that are the most important in direct sexual stimulation. Other erotically sensitive areas of the body include the breasts, the mouth, the ears, the inner and outer surfaces of the thighs, and the buttocks. Still other parts of the body are erotically sensitive, and, in fact, conditioning can produce erogenous sensitivity in zones of the body that are not commonly associated with sexual responsivity.

There is as much variety in positions for sexual intercourse as there is in areas of the body that will respond to stimulation. In addition, oral-genital contact is popular now in our culture. A couple should experiment to find the kinds of sexual expression that are most pleasing to them.

Figure 14–3

The Male and Female Sexual Organs During Intercourse

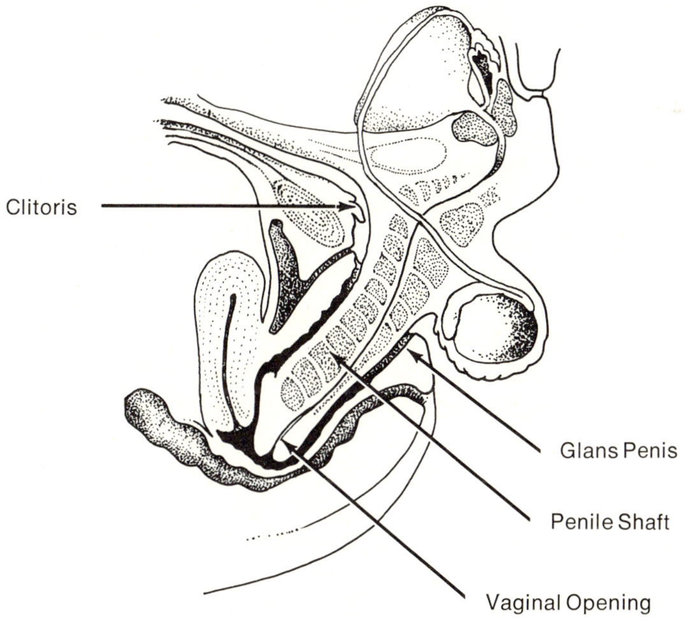

Stimulation through the other senses is a secondary source of sexual satisfaction. Vision, hearing, taste, and smell heighten sexual awareness and response. Visual stimuli are significant, particularly for men, although the effect of cultural patterns must be considered here. (Kinsey found that visual stimuli did not seem to be important to the women he studied; the modern woman's preference for the wearing of long hair by men, however, may be one instance of cultural change in sexual responsiveness to visual stimuli.) In addition, music is an important mood-setter for many couples. And taste and smell are important in oral-genital contact. These secondary means of stimulation are closely connected with emotional and psychological stimulation.

Cultural expectations direct the beginning of sexual excitement. In our culture, the preparation for sexual intercourse varies among married couples from only a few minutes to several hours. Some people, particularly men, approach intercourse and orgasm hurriedly and without apparent consideration for their partners. Others enjoy a great amount of pleasurable foreplay before actually beginning intercourse.

HUMAN SEXUAL RESPONSE

The pioneering work of William H. Masters and Virginia E. Johnson has given us our first accurate understanding of the physiological aspects of the human sexual response.[20] The sexual response of both sexes may be divided into four phases: the excitement phase, the plateau phase, the orgasmic phase, and the resolution phase. The excitement phase is the starting point of the sexual response. It may proceed quite rapidly, or it may develop unevenly. At times it may be discontinued, and the physical excitement then subsides. (Continued failure to complete the sexual union usually creates irritability and restlessness in partners.)

Certain bodily responses are characteristic of the excitement phase: heightened muscular tension *(myotonia)* and engorgement of the blood vessels *(vasoconstriction)*, which causes the surrounding tissues to swell. The most apparent sign of excitement in the male is the erection of the penis. During prolongation of the excitement phase, a man may lose and regain an erection many times. (As a man becomes older, he experiences erection more slowly and less often than he did as a young man. However, healthy men retain their potency throughout life.) The lubrication of the vaginal walls clearly marks the beginning of the woman's excitement phase; other responses occur at about the same time. The labia majora and minora enlarge and become two to three times thicker than their normal size. This swelling

[20]William H. Masters and Virginia E. Johnson, *Human Sexual Response* (Boston: Little, Brown, 1966).

is an indication that the woman's vagina is ready for the insertion of the man's penis. The clitoral shaft also swells during this phase. Additional responses include erection of the nipples, which occurs in almost all women (and about one-third of men), contraction of some involuntary muscles, an increase in pulse rate and blood pressure, and often the appearance of a slight, temporary rash on the abdomen.

In the plateau phase, the increase in sexual tension continues, although the process may be delayed or decreased by limiting stimulation. In women there is a striking color change, called the sex-skin reaction. The enlarged labia minora turn a deep red. Late in the plateau phase, the clitoris withdraws beneath its hood, or *prepuce.* The vaginal walls tighten around the man's penis. Rapid and irregular contractions of the uterus intensify as the plateau phase progresses. Involuntary muscle contractions continue for both men and women, and the heart rate increases still more, sometimes to more than twice its usual rate. Blood pressure climbs. As the plateau phase continues, voluntary control of the progression toward orgasm decreases.

Orgasm is the third phase, the peak of sexual arousal. It consists of a period of a few seconds for the man and up to a minute for the woman when the sexual tension reaches its maximum level and the person experiences an overwhelming sensation of pleasure. There are marked physiological changes, with the breathing rate doubling and the heart rate and blood pressure increasing still more. In women the vagina contracts rhythmically. In men semen—a thick, whitish material—is ejaculated from the penis. There is a loss of voluntary control over the body and a corresponding increase in involuntary muscle tension.

The total function of the orgasm is not fully known. It is the normal way of relieving sexual tension and should bring a feeling of great satisfaction, contentment, and relaxation to the couple. When the desire for orgasm is frustrated, some negative consequences may result.

The resolution phase completes the sexual response. The man returns quickly to his nonstimulated state and is usually unable to achieve a second erection for several hours. Heart rate and breathing return to normal, and the penis gradually returns to its normal size. The woman, however, may be restimulated to further orgasms following the first one; or she may return to her nonstimulated state.

It is generally assumed that men respond more rapidly to sexual stimulation and are capable of reaching orgasm more quickly than women. However, we do not know how much of this apparent difference is physiological and how much largely psychological. We do know that men can learn to control their rate of response in order to achieve simultaneous orgasm with their partners or to allow their partners more than one orgasm.

Simultaneous orgasm is a wonderful experience for a couple, and its achievement has been emphasized by many marriage manuals. But it is now recognized that it is an infrequent occurrence. An undue emphasis on simultaneous orgasm can cause a couple to fail to appreciate their experiences with each other that do not result in simultaneous orgasm. The important thing is for both husband and wife to gain satisfaction in intercourse.

Physical Fitness

Another important aspect of sexual harmony that is sometimes overlooked is physical fitness. Physical attraction is an important part of the courtship process as we have developed it in our culture, and remains an important part of the marital sexual relationship. The physical fitness craze that has swept our society reminds us that each of us, no matter what our age, can retain a great deal of physical vigor, energy, and attractiveness. Physical neglect can have a direct effect on a couple's sexual activity. Sex puts a heavy demand on the cardiovascular system, and an overweight person's heart will have to work that much harder. And sex shouldn't be considered hard work!

Communication

We have discussed in Chapters 10 and 11 the importance of communication in building the marriage relationship. It is just as important where sex is concerned. Frankness and honesty should characterize the marital relationship. This does not mean that a discussion of sex should turn into a confessional session; most counselors feel it is unwise for men and women to attempt to explain and defend their behavior with earlier partners to each other. It is much wiser for a man or woman to seek counseling or religious help in evaluating prior experiences.

Both partners will gain from an open discussion of attitudes. What sexual feelings does she have in response to the beginning of his lovemaking? Is she as much awakened and aroused as her partner? Or does she find it hard to be responsive to him, and is she frightened by his passion and eagerness? What is her basic attitude toward the physical aspects of their sexual relationship? Is she embarrassed and reticent? What are his feelings toward her? Does he expect that she will always simply respond to his advances and never initiate a sexual experience herself? Does he consider her feelings and reactions secondary to his? Is he interested primarily in his masculine conquest, not in her true response of love and affection? What factors in their sex education in family, church, or school might make marital adjustment difficult for them?

Communication is always a major element in successful marital interaction. Masters and Johnson have emphasized the importance of communication in their treatment of sexually dysfunctional couples.[21] One characteristic of some of the lower-class women studied by Rainwater was that they had absolutely no means of communicating with their husbands. They may have rejected sexuality because they had no way of sharing their feelings with their husbands. There are bound to be some problems and misunderstandings that mar the sexual relationship between husband and wife, just as there are tensions in other aspects of their relationship. The couple must find freedom and spontaneity in their sexual relationship and be able to adapt to each other's needs in the same way that they cultivate flexibility and openness on other subjects.

Time and Patience

A married couple need to build their sexual adjustment carefully. Sexual adjustment does not come overnight; it requires time and patience. The couple will need to individualize and personalize the ways in which they express their love for each other sexually.

Our society now places a strong emphasis on mutuality in the sexual relationship; both husband and wife are expected to share in the anticipation of intercourse and in a satisfying orgasmic experience. But such mutuality may not be achieved easily by many couples who have been more strongly influenced by the double standard in sex roles and behavior than by the egalitarian standard. A consideration of the change in women's sexual expectations over the past few decades will help us to recognize the cultural gap that exists today between the egalitarian standard and the double standard many women have been raised with. The expectations of the woman have changed dramatically. Forty years ago, in a pioneering study of marital interaction, Lewis M. Terman reported that married women were not always able to achieve orgasm; in fact, one-third said that they were usually unable to do so.[22] The responses of 760 of the 792 wives included in the research were as follows:

	Frequency of Orgasm	
Never	63	8.3%
Sometimes	191	25.1%
Usually	338	44.5%
Always	168	22.1%[23]

[21]Masters and Johnson, *Human Sexual Inadequacy*, p. 85.
[22]Lewis M. Terman et al., *Psychological Factors in Marital Happiness* (New York: McGraw-Hill, 1938).
[23]Terman, p. 301.

Terman labeled the first and second groups inadequate sexually and the last two groups adequate. He found that there was a positive correlation between the group described as adequate and marital happiness; however, in the group of 792 wives as a whole, only 5.6 percent rated their marriages as below average in happiness.[24] In 1938, in other words, almost one-third of the women studied felt they could attain average or above average happiness in marriage without any frequent orgasmic experience. A husband at that time did not need to be overly concerned with achieving sexual mutuality with his wife; his wife did not seem to miss it.

A man's sexual response in today's society involves much more than it did in earlier generations. It is not enough for him to prove his sexual prowess (although such an accomplishment may mean something in the lower classes). He must also recognize the feelings and responses of his partner and, ideally, be as much concerned for her satisfaction and fulfillment in the sexual act as he is for his own.

> It has been repeatedly observed that in this culture until recently the female half of the human species had much less experience with orgasm than the male. Not more than a hundred years ago, the opinion was held in Western cultures that only evil women ever admitted, even to themselves, that they enjoyed the sexual act. Sexual anesthesia was the price most women paid for the protection and support of their home and children. Society supported the male as ruler of the roost, and the double standard extended to the double bed. The male's sexual needs were gratified according to his, not his wife's, wishes. He chose the time. He felt no need to give. Once satiated, he rarely gave his docile mate a second sexual thought. . . .
>
> The long overdue liberation of women changed all that. Enfranchised, and finding new employment and enjoyment opportunities open to them, women also, at last, expected equality in the marital bed. Many of their husbands then imposed upon themselves an unaccustomed husbandly duty—the sexual satisfaction of their wives. Many, but not all. College-matriculated men are apparently more concerned with wifely sexual gratification than are those with less education. In one study only 7 out of 51 men without college matriculation "expressed the slightest concern with responsibility for coital-partner satisfaction. . . . Out of a total of 261 . . . subjects with college matriculation, 214 men expressed concern with coital-partner satisfaction."
>
> This concern of some men with the sexual satisfaction of their wives is to their credit; perhaps college is a civilizing influence, after all.[25]

[24]Terman, p. 300.

[25]Benjamin A. Kogan, *Health: Man in a Changing Environment*, 2nd ed. (New York: Harcourt Brace Jovanovich, 1974), p. 503. Quoted by Kogan are William H. Masters and Virginia E. Johnson, *Human Sexual Response*, p. 202.

When we consider the cultural patterns that stress equality, openness, and freer sexual expression in America today, we can understand how great has been the change in the sexual expectations of women. Many women still have happy marriages without usually experiencing orgasm; but most women now become worried if they feel that they are experiencing less satisfaction in intercourse than they should. They have read descriptions of what the sexual experience should be and have discussed it with their husbands and with other women, and they want to be normally responsive.

Though modern women desire sexual mutuality in marriage, a great many of them are not able to find full satisfaction in their marital sexual experience for months or years after they marry. The cultural gap between the egalitarian and the double standard that we have spoken of is one reason for this. Psychological and physiological factors may also hinder initial adjustment. In that case, a loving and sympathetic husband can help to awaken his wife to the pleasures of sex by patiently encouraging her. He will need to take great care in preparing his wife for lovemaking and to learn to slow his own reactions in order to keep pace with hers. In time he will be pleased to find that she is becoming more and more responsive.

In order for a husband to be sympathetic to his wife's needs, he must understand how her sexual response differs from his. Behavior that is interpreted as cool or unenthusiastic by inexperienced men often is simply normal learned feminine sexual behavior. The sexual response of a woman is more generalized and less easily aroused than that of her partner. One reason for this may be her biological makeup, but more often her response is psychologically and culturally determined.

> For the human female, orgasm is a psychophysiologic experience occurring within, and made meaningful by, a context of psychosocial influence. Physiologically, it is a brief episode of physical release from the vasocongestive and myotonic increment developed in response to sexual stimuli. Psychologically, it is subjective perception of a peak of physical reaction to sexual stimuli. The cycle of sexual response, with orgasm as the ultimate point in progression, generally is believed to develop from a drive of biologic-behavioral origin deeply integrated into the condition of human existence.
>
> . . . The quantitative and qualitative relationship of these factors appears totally variable between one woman's orgasmic experiences, and orgasm as it occurs in other women. Only baseline physiologic reactions and occasional individually characteristic modes of expression remain consistent from orgasm to orgasm, reflecting the human female's apparent tendency toward orientation of sexual expression to psychosocial demand.[26]

[26]Masters and Johnson, *Human Sexual Response,* p. 127.

A woman's moods and feelings are also crucial to her in her responsiveness to her husband's sexual advances. She will be more apt to withdraw from him if she is tense or depressed or extremely tired or distracted. When tension between the couple erupts into harsh words and arguments, it will be much more difficult for her to restore feelings of love and affection than it will be for him. While he may be ready to kiss and make up in a few seconds, she may take hours or even days to feel that the broken lines of communication and understanding have been restored and be ready to give herself fully and willingly in the sexual union.

It is difficult to compare a woman's sexual response to a man's. While a man's response culminates in the climax of orgasm and in ejaculation, which occur almost at the same time and which are a measure of his sexual interest and activity, a woman's sexual response has many different levels that do not always include orgasm. Feminine sexual response is a unique and personal thing. The responses and feelings of one woman may differ markedly in frequency and intensity from those of a relative or friend, yet both may be well within normal ranges of response. Consider, for example, the experience of walking in the woods on the first warm day of spring. Nothing is more invigorating to a band of city dwellers than to spend an afternoon in such a setting. If a group of ten or twelve people had shared this experience, and you asked each one to describe it to you, you would receive just as many individual reactions. Each person would have walked on the same paths and been stimulated by the same sights and sounds and feelings, but the experience would be different for each one. Similarly, the female sexual response is partially culturally conditioned. Cultural conditioning today differs widely from one person to another and therefore results in a wide range of possible sexual adjustments between husband and wife. The important thing is that a woman be satisfied by her response to her husband, whatever its frequency or intensity.

The achievement of sexual mutuality requires a good deal of effort on the woman's part as well as the man's. A woman must bring to her sexual relationship in marriage a willingness to sympathize with her husband's sexual needs, which may be quite different from hers. As we have observed, the sexual role women are expected to play in marriage is not always a simple one. There is tension between the goals of egalitarianism and the ideals of feminine passivity. Few women would want to build their sexual patterns on nineteenth-century standards, but the new roles demanded by the twentieth century are not always easy to achieve for a woman brought up in a traditional family. Many women need to make a distinct effort to become more in touch with their bodies, to appreciate the sexual experience.

Part of the reason so many people have problems about sex is that sexual feelings are thought to be separate or different from other kinds of feel-

> ings we have. Sex has to do with the body—that alien part of us residing below the neck that has needs and responses we don't understand. But our feelings reside in our bodies. Fears make their presence felt by our pounding heart, our chest caved in, our stomach turning. Joy is tingly—our head feels a little light, our fingers and toes sort of shimmer, and the rest of us feels warm and all in one piece. For some of us anger feels like a pounding in the head, hands tighten and clench, and so on. When you feel these feelings, or any others, try to stop and feel them in your body—below the neck as well as above it. Don't judge, just sense what's happening. It's one way of getting more in touch with you.[27]

A wife needs to gain an empathetic and loving awareness of her husband's moods and feelings. She can do this if she takes a positive approach toward her whole relationship with her husband and allows the depth and fullness of her love to surround their daily life together.

> A woman should be willing to learn. She should not cooperate in anything that proves to be actually distasteful or unpleasant for her after she has attempted it for a time, for it would tarnish their love. But she should have an open mind and adventurous spirit and be willing to try anything that might make the relationship more flexible and gratifying to them both.
>
> . . .
>
> A woman has a profound responsibility in maintaining an active marital relationship. . . . A wife sometimes finds that her husband's spontaneous desire for intercourse occurs more often than she is able actively to respond, no matter how much she would like to. . . . If she enjoys it most of the time, she should certainly participate whenever he needs her.[28]

Of course this advice is not only applicable to women; it is equally pertinent to men. The success of a marriage depends on *both* partners learning each other's needs and responding to them.

Melvin Wilkinson has suggested that we have neglected the concept of linking romantic love with sexual expression. The fact that there is "sexual blockage" because of the cultural restriction on sex during adolescence and outside of marriage does not necessarily make marriage incompatible with sex. Wilkinson sees the maximum amount of romantic love in marriage when: there is a lengthy courtship period; society restricts sex and romantic in-

[27]The Boston Women's Health Book Collective, *Our Bodies, Ourselves: A Book By and For Women* (New York: Simon and Schuster, 1973), p. 24.
[28]Maxine Davis, *The Sexual Responsibility of Women,* quoted in Kogan, pp. 507–08.

volvement outside marriage; and individuals are socialized to believe that romantic love, marriage, and sex belong together.[29]

Problems in Sexual Adjustment

Not all people achieve sexual adjustment without some kind of counseling or medical help. (Some estimates of the number of sexually dysfunctional couples in our society run as high as 50 to 70 percent of the population.) There are several common problems in sexual adjustment. The work of Masters and Johnson has enabled us to identify those problems more clearly and to move toward an adequate medical and psychological treatment of them.

Female Sexual Dysfunctions

Major female sexual dysfunctions include orgasmic dysfunction, vaginismus, and dyspareunia.[30] *Orgasmic dysfunction* is defined by Masters and Johnson as inability to experience orgasm during an entire lifetime. There is no male sexual dysfunction as severe as this one.[31] Many social and psychological factors seem to be responsible for the problem. Parental and religious teaching that sex is bad and that "good girls" do not take an interest in sex is often involved. Research also indicates that very frequently such women are married to men who suffer from premature ejaculation; thus the marital relationship serves to intensify the problem.

Vaginismus is a psychophysiological syndrome resulting in a tightening of the muscles of the vaginal orifice, which makes the entrance of the penis difficult if not impossible.[32] This condition can be observed in routine pelvic examinations as well as during intercourse. Masters and Johnson studied twenty-nine cases of vaginismus and found religious orthodoxy to be a major contributing factor. The condition also is often associated with male sexual dysfunction. Vaginismus can be treated successfully with the cooperation of both husband and wife.

Dyspareunia is pain or difficulty in intercourse; it occurs in both men and women. Dyspareunia may originate from vaginal infections or from criminal abortion techniques or other surgery. It may also be psychosomatic. A variety of methods is used to treat the condition.

Helen Kaplan defines these conditions as general sexual dysfunction (frigidity), orgastic dysfunction, and vaginismus. She discusses in some detail the deeper causes of these problems, including situational factors, and

[29]Melvin L. Wilkinson, "Romantic Love and Sexual Expression," *The Family Coordinator,* 27, no. 2 (April 1978), 141–48.
[30]Masters and Johnson, *Human Sexual Inadequacy,* chaps. 8–11.
[31]Masters and Johnson, p. 227.
[32]Masters and Johnson, p. 250.

dyadic and culturally rooted obstacles.[33] In one case history reported by Kaplan, orgasmic difficulty on the part of the wife was linked to other problems in the marriage. The woman was twenty-nine, had been married for three and one-half years, and had one child. Her husband, a physician, was thirty-eight years old. He had a strong sex drive, and in the beginning of the marriage they had intercourse daily. By the time of seeking counseling, this had decreased to only once every two weeks. Treatment was begun, but then ended in failure and a reexamination of the problem.

Further discussion showed that the wife was in conflict about her commitment to the marriage, because she felt trapped in the situation, where she was her husband's "servant," without goals of her own. She then recognized her need to have some more fulfilling and personal goals for herself. The sexual treatment was resumed successfully, and the woman decided to enroll in graduate school and prepare for a career.[34] Kaplan suggests that the female orgasm needs to be considered over a continuum, with normality here falling within a wide range. (See Figure 14–4.)

Male Sexual Dysfunctions

There are four basic male sexual dysfunctions. *Premature ejaculation* is defined by Masters and Johnson as the inability of the man to satisfy his partner "in at least 50 percent of their coital connections."[35] (There are many variations in marital sexual relationships; the authors feel that their definition allows for normal differences in sexual response.) Premature ejaculation seems to be related to brief and unsatisfactory first experiences of intercourse, often with prostitutes. It may also be associated with use of the withdrawal method of birth control. Most cases can be successfully treated.

Ejaculatory incompetence is inability to complete the sexual act. The seventeen men referred to Masters and Johnson for treatment of this condition had a number of severe psychological problems. Thus the cooperation of the wife was crucial to satisfactory treatment. Therapy was successful for most men. In fact, one divorced couple reunited during therapy and subsequently had two children. Only three patients did not respond to treatment.

Primary impotence has been arbitrarily defined by Masters and Johnson as a lifetime inability to achieve or maintain an erection sufficient to accomplish successful intercourse.[36] Thus primary impotence does not apply to any man who has been successful at some time in either heterosexual or homosexual experiences. During eleven years thirty-two men were accepted for treatment of this condition at Masters and Johnson's clinic. Family influ-

[33]Helen Singer Kaplan, *The New Sex Therapy* (New York: Brunner/Mazel, 1974).
[34]Kaplan, pp. 370–73.
[35]Masters and Johnson, *Human Sexual Inadequacy*, p. 92.
[36]Masters and Johnson, p. 137.

Figure 14–4 Hypothetical Distribution of the Female Orgasm

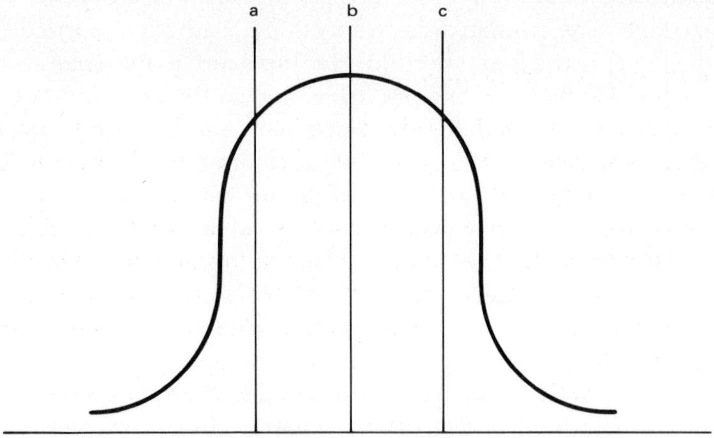

This curve is hypothetical because the actual distribution of the female orgasm threshold is not known. We have no precise data on the question of how many women can achieve orgasm on coitus versus those who are orgastic only on clitoral stimulation. In addition, clinicians differ in their definitions of normalcy. Psychoanalytically oriented clinicians would classify as pathological all orgastic thresholds below point (c), orgasm on coitus. Other therapists, including this author, hypothesize that women who are sexually responsive but require direct clitoral stimulation to reach their orgastic threshold (a) might fall within the normal range from (a) to (c).

SOURCE: Helen Singer Kaplan, *The New Sex Therapy* (New York: Brunner/Mazel, 1974), p. 379. Reprinted by permission.

ences were found to be of some significance in the development of primary impotence, as were homosexual identifications and traumatic psychosexual experiences.

Secondary impotence is failure to accomplish intercourse successfully approximately 25 percent of the time.[37] Men with this condition may have had a long period of successful sexual experience but are no longer able to perform adequately. A total of 213 men were treated for this condition by Masters and Johnson. Contributing factors include severe alcoholic episodes, maternal dominance, paternal dominance, religious orthodoxy, homosexuality, and a number of physiological causes as well. This condition seems to

[37]Masters and Johnson, p. 157.

be one of the most difficult to treat; Masters and Johnson report a 26.2 percent failure rate for the 213 cases.

Treatment of Sexual Dysfunctions

How can problems in sexual adjustment be solved? Masters and Johnson have an intensive treatment program for older couples who have suffered for many years with their problems. It involves spending two weeks at their St. Louis treatment center. For younger couples, a knowledge of this new approach, coupled with careful thought and reading and an early willingness to face and discuss sexual barriers and problems, may forestall such expensive treatment. Let us summarize the key elements of the Masters and Johnson approach.

First, sexual problems are serious ones. The Masters and Johnson program is no quick cure. The Foundation's fee for regular treatment is $2,500 or more, and the two-week stay involves other costs as well. (Some couples are accepted at a reduced rate if their situation requires it.) However, we tend to put monetary values on many things in our society. Today many middle-aged couples have found the money for an affluent way of life, but they may have tended to devalue their marriages and their family relationships. Perhaps it is good that this treatment comes at a high price. "If it costs so much, it must be worth it," many people will reason. And isn't a good marriage worth more than a new car, a new house, or an expensive vacation? Perhaps some priorities will be put in order by such an expenditure.

Second, successful treatment requires that both partners be involved. In the past counselors have usually worked with only one partner. But both partners must work together to achieve sexual adjustment. "If treatment is directed separately toward the obviously dysfunctional partner in a marriage, the theoretically uninvolved partner may actually destroy or negate much therapeutic effort, initially from lack of knowledge and understanding and finally from frustration," warn Masters and Johnson.[38]

Third, the program focuses on the marital relationship; that is the real patient. One partner cannot be sick without the other or become well without the other. Both partners in the relationship are involved; both are helped.

Fourth, a dual-sex therapy team is used: a male doctor (Masters) and a female psychologist (Johnson). Since both sexes are treated, therapists must be able to sympathize equally well with both sexes. This innovative approach has been widely copied.

Fifth, an intensive psychological and medical history of each patient is recorded. Any psychological or medical factors that affect sexual adjustment

[38]Masters and Johnson, *Human Sexual Inadequacy,* p. 201.

need to be carefully considered. Also, a serious study is needed to determine the impact on our culture of this new program, and careful records are therefore a must.

Sixth, the program is intensive: two complete weeks, without a break. The problems treated are of long standing. Surprisingly, brief but intensive treatment has proven highly effective. Although it is hard to measure the results exactly, Masters and Johnson state that positive results are achieved in a majority of cases.

Seventh, there is a careful follow-up of successfully treated patients. The follow-up is now for a two-year period, while originally it was for five years.

> The original research premise emphasized the fact that positive reversal of symptoms of sexual inadequacy during the acute phase of the treatment program was not of great import. If there was to be any clinical claim for positive effect in the Foundation's concentrated approach to symptom reversal, the clinical results would have to be judged in retrospect over a significant period of time, not at the termination of the acute phase of therapy. . . . Failures to reverse symptoms are, of course, considered most significant.
>
> . . . Those marital units whose acute treatment phase was judged inadequate or a failure arbitrarily have not been placed in the five-year follow-up program.
>
> . . . Jules Masserman has so aptly described psychotherapy as "anything that works." This "works" in a healthy percentage of cases.[39]

The Foundation reported a total of 790 male and female patients treated. The success rate in initial treatment was 81.1 percent;[40] the five-year study showed only a small number of subsequent failures, resulting in a revised 80.0 percent rate of positive treatment. This is an unusual achievement.

Eighth, daily round-table discussions are held with therapists. Sexual attitudes and taboos that may never have been mentioned by the couple are discussed freely. This aspect of the program is one that has been widely copied and is being used to prepare engaged couples for marriage by some counselors.[41]

Ninth, a behavior modification approach is used to treat the various sexual dysfunctions. Masters and Johnson stress *sensate focus*, the development of sensory awareness of the natural pleasure of bodily feelings. Touch is the most intense means of psychosexual communication and response; the

[39]Masters and Johnson, *Human Sexual Inadequacy*, pp. 22–23.

[40]Masters and Johnson, p. 361.

[41]See James Maddock, "A Sexual Enrichment Program for Couples," paper presented at the annual meeting of the National Council on Family Relations, Oct. 16–20, 1973, Toronto, Canada.

therapists make specific day-by-day suggestions on how a couple can develop sensory awareness through touch. This is undoubtedly a major factor in Masters and Johnson's high rate of success in treatment of sexual dysfunctions. Both body and mind are helped.

One final point must be made. Masters and Johnson stress that sexual responsivity must develop naturally. Some directions for restraining sexual activity are made during the first three days of treatment, when the stage is being set for the specific methods to be followed. Other than that, no timetable is set for sexual achievements. In some cases, satisfactory results may come weeks or months after the couple leave St. Louis. The development of programs of treatment for sexual dysfunction may well prove one of the major medical and therapeutic achievements of our century. Several treatment centers have been established in major cities, and variations in approach and treatment are being tried. Carefully and deliberately, Masters and Johnson have moved beyond the issues of the two Kinsey reports (What is typical sexual behavior in our society?) and the subject of their own first book (What are the physiological elements of sexual response?) to a question of vital importance for marital sexual adjustment: What can we do to reduce sexual inadequacy and make sexual interaction more satisfactory?

Most of the predictions about sexual relationships are optimistic. Lucile Duberman sees the future in these terms:

> There will be an increase of sexual pleasure in marital coitus by the year 2000. One reason is the heightened awareness of potential satisfaction among women, which will lead to a diminution of inhibitions and a willingness to experiment. At first, this new freedom on the part of women will lead to more self-consciousness, resentment, and even impotence in men, but, ultimately, men will probably accept sexual equality and recognize the benefits it will produce for themselves as well as for women.[42]

Kaplan is more conservative in evaluating the results of the new sex therapy. She feels that further scientific testing and follow-up, under more controlled conditions, will be necessary to validate the claims now being made. The results of all therapy procedures, since they deal with problems usually rooted in some past history of the individual, and since they propose to change his or her behavior in the future, are necessarily studied and evaluated on a longitudinal basis. Kaplan concludes:

> Our current enthusiasm for this approach is unfortunately not based on solid evidence of its effectiveness. Instead this enthusiasm stems, for the

[42]Lucille Duberman, *Marriage and Other Alternatives,* 2nd ed. (New York: Praeger, 1977), p. 63.

most part, from admittedly impressive findings, which, however, derive from uncontrolled studies. It has also been bolstered by publication in both the professional and popular literature of many articles describing excellent results achieved by therapists who are currently employing the new methods.

. . . The new treatment of sexual disorders appears to be of great potential value . . . but . . . we lack substantive proof of its effectiveness.

There can be no doubt . . . that the new methods merit further trial and development. . . . [43]

These new developments, like all sound approaches to the study of marriage and the family, acknowledge the many complex influences on the marital relationship. We must understand what background people bring into their marriage, and we must deal with that background realistically. Moreover, we must help people to clarify the goals they want to achieve and to move in the direction they want to, both as individuals and as couples, in sexual interaction as in the whole of life.

SUMMARY

Sexual adjustment is a basic element in marital happiness. Harmonious sexual relationships do not develop automatically, however, and poor sexual attitudes and training may prevent many couples from achieving a good sexual relationship.

The formation of the sexual response is a complex process. Each person brings his or her own self-image into a sexual partnership. He or she also brings certain basic attitudes toward the opposite sex, formed mainly from family influences and cultural conditioning. Psychological and cultural conditioning are more important than biological differences in determining male and female behavior patterns.

There are certain general masculine and feminine behavior patterns in our society. Kinsey reported earlier and more active sexual development and higher frequency of orgasm throughout life for men. Men also seem to be more easily stimulated than women, although that difference is lessening as our culture becomes more egalitarian. Women may often be more slowly aroused in sexual intercourse than men. They may also require months or years to learn to respond to their husbands' lovemaking. Much of their hesitancy is a remnant of the double standard; women in our society have traditionally been conditioned against sexual pleasure. Women are also more affected sexually by other factors in the marital relationship. Worries over money or the children or quarrels with family members may make it difficult for them to relax sexually.

Achieving sexual adjustment is a high-priority goal for a married couple.

[43]Kaplan, pp. 432–33.

Love, the giving and receiving of true affection and concern, is basic to that goal. Commitment is a measure of such love. Sexual harmony grows too with knowledge and understanding; and basic knowledge of sexual anatomy and the sexual response is indispensable.

There are three major kinds of sexual stimulation: stimulation by touch, stimulation by the other four senses, and emotional and psychological stimulation. The sexual response cycle of both men and women is divided into four phases: the excitement phase, the plateau phase, the orgasmic phase, and the resolution phase. Though the responses of men and women are similar, there are some very basic differences between the sexes. Men seem to be aroused more quickly and easily than women, and once they have achieved orgasm, they are usually unable to respond again for a period of several hours. Women seem to become aroused more slowly but are capable of a series of multiple orgasms.

An important aspect of sexual harmony that is often overlooked is physical fitness. Physical vigor, energy, and attractiveness can have a direct effect on a couple's sexual activity. Communication is another basic ingredient in the sexual relationship. Each partner must be able to talk with the other about sex—especially what does or does not please him or her—in order for a mutually satisfying relationship to develop. And finally, time and patience are needed. Women have moved far beyond the passive sexual response expected of them two generations ago, but women's liberation cannot do away with all acculturated patterns of sexual inhibition overnight. The achievement of sexual mutuality therefore requires a good deal of understanding on the part of both husband and wife.

There are several common problems in sexual adjustment. Major female problems identified by Masters and Johnson include orgasmic dysfunction, vaginismus, and dyspareunia. Premature ejaculation, ejaculatory incompetence, primary impotence, and secondary impotence are major male dysfunctions. Medical and psychological treatment is recommended for these problems.

The Masters and Johnson treatment program offers a highly successful medical and psychological approach to problems in sexual adjustment. Both partners and their marital relationship are treated by a dual-sex therapy team during two weeks of intensive, round-the-clock therapy. Sexual difficulties and psychological hangups are brought out into the open in round-table discussions with therapists. Complete histories are made of both husband and wife, and immediate results are checked through a follow-up survey. Masters and Johnson have found that rapid positive change in sexual adjustment is possible for the vast majority of couples they treat.

Helen Singer Kaplan, in writing about the new sex therapy, is optimistic about its future, but cautions us to seek adequate research evidence for the new programs being developed.

SUGGESTED READINGS

Colton, Helen. *Adults Need Sex Education Too*. Los Angeles: Family Forum, 1972. Popular treatment of difficulties in sexual adjustment on the adult level.

Gagnon, John, ed. *Human Sexuality in Today's World.* Boston: Little, Brown, 1977. Contemporary book of readings including both popular and professional articles.

Kaplan, Helen Singer. *The New Sex Therapy*. New York: Brunner/Mazel, 1974. Prominent psychiatrist describes new treatment of sexual dysfunctions; thoughtful discussion of the origins of these dysfunctions.

Katchadourian, Herant A., and Donald T. Lunde. *Fundamentals of Human Sexuality*, 2nd ed. New York: Holt, Rinehart and Winston, 1975. Comprehensive treatment of the subject. Sets human sexual response in broadest possible perspective.

Kinsey, Alfred C., Wardell B. Pomeroy, Clyde E. Martin, and Paul H. Gebhard. *Sexual Behavior in the Human Female*. Philadelphia: Saunders, 1953. Basic Kinsey volume reporting study of 5,940 females.

Kinsey, Alfred C., Wardell B. Pomeroy, and Clyde E. Martin. *Sexual Behavior in the Human Male*. Philadelphia: Saunders, 1948. Basic Kinsey volume reporting study of 5,300 males.

Masters, William H., and Virginia E. Johnson. *Human Sexual Inadequacy*. Boston: Little, Brown, 1970. Describes program developed for the treatment of sexual dysfunction.

______. *Human Sexual Response*. Boston: Little, Brown, 1966. Original work investigating the physiological and social contexts of the human sexual response.

Morrison, Eleanor S., and Vera Borosage. *Human Sexuality: Contemporary Perspectives*. Palo Alto, Calif.: National Press Books, 1973. Solid collection of articles, including excellent sections on new directions in femininity/masculinity and heterosexual interaction.

Pierson, Elaine C., and William V. D'Antonio. *Female and Male: Dimensions of Human Sexuality*. Philadelphia: Lippincott, 1974. Main emphasis is on intercourse and reproduction. Authors are a physician and a sociologist.

15 Extended Families and Religion in Marriage

- How important is the extended family?
- What are the trends in in-law relationships today?
- What are the most common in-law problems?
- What is predicted for the future of the extended family?
- What place does religion have in family life?
- How does your personal religious viewpoint affect your attitude toward marriage, lifestyle, and contemporary society?
- Does religion contribute to marital happiness?
- What are common problems related to religion in the family? How can such problems be resolved?

The Extended Family

No family lives in a vacuum. We are all part of the social fabric, and we all have roles to play, either by choice or by necessity, in the wider circle of life beyond the four walls of our own homes. The relationships we share with our parents, our brothers and sisters, and other members of our extended family, including aunts, uncles, and grandparents, are mingled with the new relationships we share with our in-laws. There is so much emphasis on the nuclear family in American culture that we may forget we are part of a larger extended family and kin-network system. In marriage, this system links us with relatives of both husband and wife, many of whom may play an important role in our future lives.

Most of us spend a good part of our teenage years trying to get away from our families. There is an elaborate youth subculture in our society that separates young people from their families. Life changes with marriage, however. Suddenly, on the wedding day, both bride and groom inherit a fully developed set of in-laws. There are introductions to Uncle Ben and Aunt Margaret, who flew in from Florida for the wedding. There are two new mothers-in-law and fathers-in-law, and sets of brothers, sisters, cousins, nieces, and nephews. If one has been part of a small and closely knit family, such a panoply of new relatives and kissing cousins may be quite a surprise.

Before the wedding, only one in-law rates much attention: the mother-in-law, a dangerous and threatening figure who is supposed to wreak havoc on the marriage. According to folklore, she is a selfish, talkative, nasty, and troublesome person, and both partners need to be wary of her from the beginning of their married life. The stereotype is not an accurate picture, because she may, in reality, be quiet and friendly, a winsome and lovable woman with a fine sense of humor. Nevertheless, the new son- or daughter-in-law must be on guard. In describing her childhood, one woman recalled the negative influence of a classic mother-in-law.

> Grandmother was in and out of our lives a great deal and was a great one for entering into things, such as quarrels between our parents that might possibly have been resolved but were instead further stirred by her. Many times she would send Daddy's hat sailing after him, and he would pull it down over his head and stomp to the car and drive away. These bitter scenes were followed by remorse and apology. Candy, flowers, or a new hat or dress, often accompanied by a letter or a poem written by Daddy, would soon appear by messenger. I have always wondered how the marriage would have gone if Grandma had not played the role of mother-in-law so well. . . . Ours was not a broken home, but there were so many cracks in the structure I wonder that it held together at all.[1]

This exception to the rule has become an unfortunate stereotype, one that makes an impression on most newlyweds.

A father-in-law may have an important place, particularly for his daughter, and so may a grandfather or grandmother, or some other relative linked closely to husband or wife by residential proximity, common interests, or occupation. Our modern technological society seems to require great mobility from nuclear families, yet many families will not break these kinship ties. The extended family can be very important to the married couple and their children.

But, if this is so, why do problems arise in these relationships? The basic cause is probably our ambivalent feelings toward our in-laws. On the one hand, we would like to be free and independent, completely on our own. On the other hand, we have many ties of affection with our parental families, and it is only natural to want to retain those ties after marriage. The basic problem with in-laws is finding some reasonable and satisfying middle

[1]Student report.

ground between those two feelings. And in the same way, problems with other relatives in our kin-family network arise from the same ambivalence, between duty and freedom, obligation and choice.

Studies of the Extended Family

There have been a number of fascinating studies involving the extended family. Some have been the work of British family sociologists, who have discovered that there are many links that unite working-class families in England.[2] This reflects the more settled family and cultural patterns in many European countries, where the results of industrialization and urbanization have been somewhat mitigated by the smaller size of each country as compared to the United States.

In a study of senior citizens living in the United States, Denmark, Britain, Yugoslavia, Poland, and Israel, Ethel Shanas has illustrated that the older people in all of these countries generally live near their grown children. In every country Shanas found that about four out of every five older persons had at least one living child. "Did you do anything when you were younger to take care of yourself in your old age?" each was asked. "Yes, I had children," was the reply. The study also showed that of the persons who had living children, more than half in each country had children within a distance of ten minutes, and almost three-quarters in every country had seen at least one child "within the last week" (see Table 15–1).

[2]See Elizabeth Bott, *Family and Social Network* (London: Tavis, 1957); and Michael Young and Peter Wilmott, *Family and Kinship in East London* (Baltimore: Penguin Books, 1962).

Table 15–1 The Proportion of Elderly Persons in Six Countries Not Living with a Child Who Saw a Child Within the Last 24 Hours and Within the Last Week

Country	*Percent Who Saw Child Within Last 24 Hours*	*Percent Who Saw Child Within Last Week*
Denmark	53	80
Britain	47	77
United States	52	78
Poland	64	77
Yugoslavia	51	71
Israel	48	76

SOURCE: Ethel Shanas, "Family-Kin Networks and Aging in Cross-Cultural Perspective," *Journal of Marriage and the Family*, 35, no. 3 (Aug. 1973), 509. Copyrighted 1973 by the National Council on Family Relations. Reprinted by permission.

Surprisingly, in an earlier study of family help patterns in Denmark, Britain, and the U.S., Shanas found aged parents in the middle class helping their children to build their own family life, rather than being a liability and burden to them.[3]

Bert Adams studied a group of 799 adults in Greensboro, North Carolina. The group was composed of an all-white sample, married only once, and married not more than 20 years. The group was two-thirds white-collar workers, and one-third blue-collar workers. In this stable grouping, there were still a number of close family ties. Contacts with parents in both working-class and middle-class families ran from 26 to 60 percent on a weekly basis, with blue-collar men who were "downwardly mobile" having the most frequent contact. Affectional closeness to the parents, however, was highest for females, and they also had a closer value consensus with their parents.[4] We cannot apply these findings to all parts of the country, but at least in this southern city, in-laws were still involved at some level in the marriages of their children.

A number of other American studies have emphasized the importance of relationships with the extended family, as well as the close in-laws. Robert Blood and Donald Wolfe studied a number of these interactions in their

[3]Ethel Shanas, "Family-Kin Networks and Aging in Cross-Cultural Perspective," *Journal of Marriage and the Family*, 35, no. 3 (Aug. 1973), 505–11.
[4]Bert N. Adams, *Kinship in an Urban Setting* (Chicago: Markham, 1968), pp. 44, 70.

classic study of Detroit families.[5] In a more recent report, Reuben Hill and his associates studied changes in family patterns over three generations of Minnesota families. Because these families remained in the same metropolitan area for lengthy periods of time, they kept close family ties. Almost three-fourths of the help that they gave and received was to or from relatives. The parents in the middle age bracket, as we might imagine, did the most giving since it went from them in both directions.[6] We can't underestimate, therefore, how strong kinship ties still are in spite of the fact that we live in a highly mobile society.

It has been suggested that close family and kinship ties will be a means of strengthening and stabilizing family life. However, this is not automatically true. Sonya Salamon has made an intensive study of family and friendship relationships in Japan and West Germany. Her report shows that a "nuclear family" may stand in different relationships to the society around it. Both Japanese and Germans have variations of the nuclear family, but the West German nuclear family tends to be much more closely bound to the kin network. When a woman marries, she breaks contact with her own friends and social circle and participates much more closely with her husband's family. In Japan, a wife has more opportunity to share her life with friends outside the family. Thus, she has an outlet for her thoughts and feelings, something not always possible for a married woman in West Germany.

What difference does such a variance in family relationships make in two countries that shared a common disaster at the end of the Second World War, and now share a common prosperity? Salamon writes:

> When comparing the families observed in the two societies we might ask which of the systems described is more likely to draw heavily on the family groups for sources of intimacy, companionship and support? If we examine measures of marital stability, such as divorce rates, we find a striking difference between the two countries. In the early 1950's, Japan and West Germany had nearly identical divorce rates. Starting in the mid-1960's, a period which coincides with the economic boom in both countries, the German rate began to increase more strongly and is now almost 50 percent higher. A factor which might be expected to influence the relatively constant divorce rate in Japan compared with the rising one in West Germany is their respective patterns of family organization and associated interpersonal relationships.[7]

[5]Robert O. Blood, Jr., and Donald M. Wolfe, *Husbands and Wives: The Dynamics of Married Living* (Glencoe, Ill.: Free Press, 1960).

[6]Reuben Hill, Nelson Foote, Joan Aldous, Robert Carlson, and Robert Macdonald, *Family Development in Three Generations: A Longitudinal Study of Changing Family Patterns of Planning and Achievement* (Cambridge, Mass.: Schenkman, 1970).

[7]Sonya Salamon, "Family Bonds and Friendship Bonds: Japan and West Germany," *Journal of Marriage and the Family*, 39, no. 4 (Nov. 1977), 807–20.

Trends in In-Law Relationships

What trends can we observe in the relationship of modern young married couples to their in-laws? Many young couples spend time with their families, and it seems to be an enjoyable time for them. This may be particularly true for those in middle- and upper-class families, where time is spent with the family by choice. In working-class and lower-lower class families, more time may be spent with the in-laws, but usually because no other alternatives are open. Table 15–2 illustrates this preference for time with relatives. It is based on a survey by Helena Lopata of 571 Chicago-area women. The more special the occasion, the more likely that it would be spent with relatives. Murray A. Straus has linked the strength of kin (in-law) relationships with the effects of societal modernization. In his study, four axioms and two theorems drawn from those axioms were tested and proved useful.

Axioms:

1. The greater the geographic mobility, the less the intensity of kinship interaction.
2. Urbanness and middle-class status are associated with higher geographic mobility than ruralness and working-class status.
3. The greater the intensity of interaction with kin, the greater the influence of the kin group on a member.
4. With certain exceptions, the kin group is a transmitter and enforcer of traditional, rather than modern, social-psychological traits.

Theorems:

1. Ruralness and working-class status are associated with higher kinship interaction than urbanness and middle-class status (1 and 2).
2. Regardless of residence or social class, the greater the intensity of interaction with kin, the less the psychosocial modernity (3 and 4).[8]

Straus's study confirms the decreasing importance of kin relationships in the mobile upper-middle-class American family.

Another significant trend is the increasing number of single adults in our society. Frances Kobrin has analyzed census data in this regard, particularly in the growth of "primary individuals." She sees the three stages in the adult lifespan as: premarital independence; marriage/family; and post-family independence. The number of primary individuals is expanding, as shown in Table 15–3. The percentage of single women over sixty-five has more than doubled from 1940 to 1970.[9]

[8]Murray A. Straus, "Social Class and Farm-City Differences in Interaction with Kin in Relation to Societal Modernization," *Rural Sociology*, 34 (Dec. 1969), 481–82.

[9]Frances E. Kobrin, "The Primary Individual and the Family: Changes in Living Arrangements in the United States Since 1940," *Journal of Marriage and the Family*, 38, no. 2 (May 1976), 233–39.

Table 15–2 Contacts with Relatives Versus Friends on Special Occasions

	Occasion			
Spent with	*Vacation Visit*	*Holidays*	*Sundays*	*Sporadic Weekend Contacts*
Relatives	82%	74%	71%	43%
Friends	18	26	29	57
Total	100%	100%	100%	100%

SOURCE: Helena Z. Lopata, *Occupation: Housewife* (New York: Oxford Univ. Press, 1971), p. 329. (Totals limited to those couples who saw either relatives or friends on the specified occasions.)

The Importance of In-Law Relationships

The main reason we need to gain greater understanding of in-law relationships is the continuing psychological importance of the family as the prime influence on the personality and character of husband and wife. We discussed this influence in Chapter 6. A child receives much of its basic personality structure in the first five or six years of life. A boy becomes accustomed to his mother's support and encouragement in a multitude of projects. She is his den mother in the Cub Scouts, his most ardent fan in the Little League, his ever available taxi driver, and so on. Models of Dad as a handyman, sports enthusiast, or successful salesperson are also strong influences. These models are bound to be felt all during the rest of his life. A girl may have the same strong ties with her father or her mother. Psychoanalytic theory would link her more closely with her father, especially when father and daughter share a great many activities together and he has played a strong role in her childhood development. Fathers are sometimes notoriously fussy about the men their daughters wish to marry, and this can be a cause of conflict in marriage. Mother is also an important figure in her daughter's life—even more so when there has been a divorce in the family and the mother has had to play a dual role.

In our homes we learn how and what to eat, when and where to sleep, how and what and when to read, what clothes to wear for many different occasions, how to ask and answer questions, what to think about the world outside the home, how to interpret the universe and its mysteries, how to approach religion and spiritual reality, how to think of sex and how the family expresses sexual feelings, and countless other behavior patterns that will remain with us all through life. When we court and marry a particular person, we are concentrating on the finished product of all this environmental influence. Through talking with and observing our in-laws, both

Table 15–3 Distribution of the Population by Family, Household Status, Age, and Sex: 1940–1970

	Males		*Females*	
	1940	*1970*	*1940*	*1970*
Total, 18 and over	100.0	100.0	100.0	100.0
Family heads	61.7	72.0	64.9	70.3
Family members	24.9	13.6	24.2	13.6
Primary individuals	3.5	7.3	4.3	11.1
Secondary individuals	9.8	7.1	6.6	5.0
Family heads 65 and over	65.5	71.3	49.5	42.5
Primary individuals	10.2	15.6	13.3	33.4

SOURCE: Frances E. Kobrin, "The Primary Individual and the Family: Changes in Living Arrangements in the United States Since 1940," *Journal of Marriage and the Family,* 38, no. 2 (May 1976), 237. Copyrighted 1976 by the National Council on Family Relations. Reprinted by permission.

before and after marriage, we can often identify some of the factors that helped to make our spouse what he or she is in marriage.

TYPICAL IN-LAW PROBLEMS

The very factors that make in-law relationships so important to a young married couple are potential causes of difficulty in marriage. There has not been as much sociological research on in-law problems as we might desire; but we can relate some in-law problems to the changes in family life we have already observed in earlier chapters.

One frequent in-law problem for young married couples is due to the financial dependence of the young couple on their parents. As we have already seen, Americans today still marry early, often before they have become financially independent of their parents. Though there does seem to be a new trend toward dependence among the generations in the middle class, acceptance of such dependence is by no means universal. Our American cultural tradition calls for a clear break between two generations when a new family is begun. Perhaps this tradition dates back to our colonial forebears, when a younger son would leave Europe for America because the older children in the family would inherit all of the valuable property and possessions of the family before he was of age. It could also be related to life on the frontier, when a young couple might stake a claim for virgin land in the West and strike out boldly on their own. This independence between generations is stressed in many ways. Our courtship system is one example; the teenage and college subcultures are another illustration. It is also unusual for a couple to return home to live with their parents after marriage; the break between generations must be maintained. Yet many young couples today are supported by their parents. Thus conflict with traditional values is built into many in-law relationships, at least at the beginning of a marriage.

The middle-class trend toward greater mutual support among in-laws may be a result of the new way of life opening up for us in the last quarter of the twentieth century. In this new life, in-laws may be a source of increasing enjoyment to us. During past generations, we may have rejected our in-laws because of the pressures of day-to-day living. It was difficult enough to care for one's family during the Depression or to keep the family together during a war period without worrying about in-laws. In the 1970s, however, several trends may be combining to make our relationships with our families more pleasant. The many social provisions for the ill and the aged mean that fewer parents will be needy or destitute in their retirement years. (But the specters of inflation and rising housing and medical costs are threatening these advances.) Union and company pension plans will also enable many men and women to retire on comfortable incomes and to have a measure of financial ease and freedom. At the same time, medical advances have made it possible for us to live five or ten years longer than our grand-

parents did. A woman now has a life expectancy of seventy-five years and a man of sixty-nine. Many of our parents will live years beyond that and be healthier and more active than was possible in earlier generations.

Note, then, the shift in external situations as it affects the two generations. Young couples are getting married earlier, with more and more chance of both being in college and without much in the way of savings and job stability. Ahead of them lie ten or fifteen fairly strenuous years in which they must begin their careers, start their family, and establish a home. They will welcome a little help and encouragement. On the other side, their parents and in-laws are perhaps in the very prime of their lives and careers, stable financially, with good health and some excess of time and money. If young couples can establish harmonious relationships with their in-laws, will that not be a beneficial and productive path for them to follow?

The great mobility of our culture has made another contribution to in-law difficulties. If a family moves frequently and thus cannot see their relatives with any regularity, the in-laws may feel neglected. Such neglect of in-laws as a result of mobility naturally is a cause of tension.

Another thing that generates in-law problems is the closeness of mother and child in our culture, which makes it difficult for the mother-child relationship to be broken neatly and cleanly by the marriage of the child. Philip Wylie termed this closeness "Momism," and Edward A. Strecker attempted to chronicle its dangers in his book about American men during the Second World War.[10] A mother can find many reasons to be overly close to her child. It may be because the father is away in the service, traveling for business reasons, or in some other way not able or willing to provide the security and affection she needs. Lacking a close relationship with her husband, the mother tries to substitute for it a close relationship with her child. Or, in other cases, she may try to relive her own adolescent years through the life of her son or daughter.

Janette was the only child of Mrs. Harrison, a divorced woman in her late thirties who had undertaken counseling to help herself adjust to a new job and also to seek advice regarding her daughter. Janette was seventeen, and at that rebellious age in which parental control is often a sore point in family conflicts. For two and a half months she had been dating Peter, about twenty-four years of age, who proved to be a very attentive and thoughtful companion. Mrs. Harrison, however, felt that he was too old for her daughter and made every effort to break up the romance.

[10]Edward A. Strecker, *Their Mothers' Sons* (Philadelphia: Lippincott, 1946).

"I'll protest at the high school," the mother said, "even though I don't feel good about interfering. They shouldn't allow single men to roam the campus during recess and lunch. After school, I'll see to it that she's home on time and doesn't get into any trouble."

One Saturday night the mother's protective instincts were especially strong. After permitting her daughter to go to a party with Peter, she drove three miles across town to check the cars parked outside the home in order to be certain they had arrived.

In less than a year, Janette would reach the legal age for marriage in her home state. She could leave home in the morning and telephone her mother that her marriage was an accomplished fact. Would her protective mother be ready to assume a relaxed, friendly, and helpful role as mother-in-law?

When her son or daughter is grown and married, the overly possessive mother cannot let the mother-child relationship move into a new phase. Here is a large part of the perennial in-law problem.

Still another source of difficulty may be the pattern of give-and-take in family life. Our parents take full responsibility for us when our lives first begin. They feed us, clothe us, shelter us, protect us, and often pamper us. In almost every American middle- or upper-class family, children grow up in fond expectation of many generous gifts from their parents. American parents are used to giving tangible expressions of their love and affection to their children. In many cases they give too much. Children do not learn to stand on their own feet and are afraid of breaking their dependent patterns lest parental subsidies be cut off. In contrast, the things children give their parents are intangible. They are expected to do well in school and athletics and to be popular. Parents enjoy seeing their children succeed.

But when do parents cease to be completely givers and begin to receive appreciation and perhaps tangible aid from their grown children? When does the tide begin to flow in the reverse direction? Will a change come at the time of their child's marriage? When grandchildren are born? When the grandchildren are in school or in college? It is too easy for grown children to ignore the needs of their parents. Parents are expected to yield status and authority gladly to the younger generations. When the children are in their late forties or early fifties, and their own personal and financial situation seems secure, they can think of doing something really nice for their parents. But after forty-five years of being on the receiving end, will they really do such things? There is often a wide gap between the actual and the ideal for retired people in our society.

The best-known study of in-laws was done by Evelyn Duvall. She found that mothers-in-law did not criticize their children excessively, but when they did so, indifference and thoughtlessness were the two most common complaints.[11] Young couples are too busy living their own lives to find time for the older generation's needs and interests.

A final difficulty that triggers in-law problems is that we often overstress the importance of the child in the family. We choose a home in order to be near a certain school. We won't go on vacation in July because the children have swimming lessons and Little League games. In many ways the contemporary American family often defers to the children. When new babies arrive, grandparents are dropped, and the focus of attention is on the new generation. If Grandmother is available as a babysitter, things may work out well; but in many cases the addition of a young child merely adds to the forces driving the older generation out of the picture.

It has been said that most in-law problems develop with the female members of the family—mother-in-law, daughter-in-law, and sister-in-law. This was perhaps a reflection of our traditional patterns of living since women dominated the home scene. But today more women are in the business world, with little possibility of conflict over domestic affairs.

But Mirra Komarovsky has taken exception to the theory of feminine monopoly of in-law problems. Her intensive study of 58 working-class marriages revealed that in-law problems were as frequent among lesser-educated husbands as among their wives. Strain in in-law relations was felt by one-third of the men, as well as by an equal number of wives. Mother-in-law (the wife's mother) was again the key conflict figure.

Several conditions were found to be associated with poor relationships between husband and mother-in-law: marriage to a better-educated wife, conflict between the wife and her mother, emotional dependence of the wife on her mother, and economic and social interdependence of the couple and their relatives, including joint residence. Unfortunately, these low-status husbands found it difficult to deal with in-law problems as they arose. They simply did not have the interpersonal competence to escape conflict-producing situations.[12]

Building Positive Relationships

There are many ways to develop harmonious and satisfying relationships with in-laws. If a young couple think clearly and objectively about their situation and try to create the proper circumstances, they have every right to expect their families to share in the happiness they find in their marriage and to strengthen rather than hinder the growth of their family life.

[11]Evelyn Duvall, *In-Laws: Pro and Con* (New York: Association Press, 1954).
[12]Mirra Komarovsky, *Blue-Collar Marriage* (New York: Vintage, 1967), p. 261.

> We often visited father's parents, brothers, and sister. They in turn often remembered us on birthdays and Christmas. My grandparents came to live with us soon after they retired. They lived with us or near us until their deaths. My grandparents were very much loved by all of us. "Papa" especially loved all children, strangers and friends alike. Upon meeting anyone, he would greet them with a huge bear hug and kiss, quite frightening to some people. . . . Some of my fondest memories center around them. Papa took great delight in making a tub of popcorn for his grandchildren. We would all gather around him, eat popcorn and listen to the radio. After church my brothers, sister and I would race each other home to have one of Papa's French pancakes. Grandmother, in turn, took us to the movies, to bingo parties at church, and visiting.[13]

Another important positive step is recognizing the importance of your partner's family early in courtship. The sooner you establish friendly relations with them and try to enjoy your visits with them, the easier will be your family life in the future. If you ignore them, try to date without considering family interests or plans, and move ahead into engagement and marriage without letting them in on your plans and seeking their advice, you are sowing seeds of friction. Moreover, if there are differences in background between you and your future spouse, it is all the more important that you try to be compatible with both families in order that those differences can be faced honestly and smoothed over.

It is wise to stress the common elements in the two parental families that your marriage and family will be built on in the future. Are both families interested in music, especially symphony concerts? Are both fathers avid football fans? The more the common interests in the two families, and the more they are cultivated, the less likelihood there is that in-law friction will develop.

Another way of making life with the in-laws easier is to minimize potential danger spots in the relationship. Young couples should use judgment and common sense in avoiding conflicts over trivial matters or things that cannot be changed quickly or simply. In-laws in their forties and fifties are not going to suddenly switch politics, religion, or habits of recreation or work simply because the suggestion comes strongly from a daughter- or son-in-law. It is human nature to change slowly, and perhaps increasingly slowly as we grow older. Perhaps the best thing that both older and younger generations can do in the case of substantial differences between them is to attempt to build bridges in some ways, no matter how difficult it is to begin the process. An overemphasis on difficulties and constant focus on problems is self-defeating.

[13]Student report.

There is still a great deal of help and encouragement that comes from various members of the extended family. They are the natural ones to whom to turn. A revealing study of families in crisis was done by Thomas E. Drabek and Keith S. Boggs, who sampled some 3,700 families evacuated from their homes before a massive flood in the Denver metropolitan area in 1965. Drabek and Boggs found that many of the public shelters were not needed, for the families preferred to take refuge in the homes of relatives and friends. The strength of working-class families was evident here. They were more likely to go to the homes of relatives than those on higher social levels. Spanish-American families went to their relatives more readily than Anglo-Saxons. The older the family members, the greater was the tendency to go to the homes of relatives. And of course those people who were in more frequent interaction with their relatives would also be more likely to call on them in time of crisis.[14]

A final help in building sound in-law relationships is to "join the family." Theoretically, one becomes a member of the spouse's family at marriage. In reality, however, that is not always true. There may be some question whether a person of this religion or that ethnic background or political persuasion will be able to fit into the already established family circle. In some cases, such different personalities remain on the periphery of family life. In order to join the family, you must find ways of building the family's confidence in you as a worthwhile addition to it. Ideally, this process should begin in courtship; but if it has not occurred before marriage, it should begin as quickly as possible afterward.

Religion

Building a religious partnership in marriage can be a satisfying joint venture for the newly married couple. It can give them a sense of purpose and direction that will enable them to find their path together in a meaningful and thoughtful manner, and it can help them to guide their children into a pattern of family love, service, and sharing. On the other hand, religion is a potential source of tension and conflict.[15] Let us consider what assets may come to the family through religious faith and conviction; how such a religious partnership can be established; how religion will affect the family's life; and what problems may arise if a couple fail to achieve religious integration.

[14]Thomas E. Drabek and Keith S. Boggs, "Families in Disaster: Reactions and Relatives," *Journal of Marriage and the Family*, 30, no. 3 (Aug. 1968), 443–51. See also Thomas E. Drabek, William H. Key, Patricia E. Erickson, and Juanita L. Crowe, "The Impact of Disaster on Kin Relationships," *Journal of Marriage and the Family*, 37, no. 3 (Aug. 1975), 481–94.

[15]See chap. 9

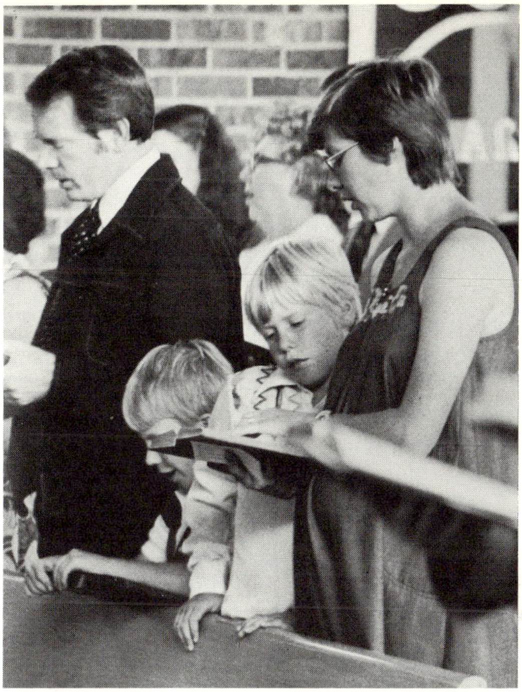

In the United States, religion is closely related to the national culture and supports its dominant values. In contrast with European churches, which are often reactionary and are thus ignored by the majority of people (particularly the urban working class), American churches have retained their vitality and influence.[16] There are many ways of categorizing the different American churches. In his discussion of the contemporary religious scene, James A. Peterson has suggested a six-way classification: the "sect groups," which include many recently organized groups, especially those that serve the lower classes without benefit of established traditions or social status; the conservative-orthodox group, which includes established Protestant churches like the Episcopalian, Presbyterian, and Congregationalist churches; the institutional-authoritarian group, which is Roman Catholic and Eastern Orthodox; the liberal churches, once identified as Unitarian and Universalist but now including other liberal groups; the Jewish denominations, including Orthodox, Conservative, and Reform; and the agnostic, or nonchurch, groups, which have the largest number of adherents.[17] Another classification of religious groups would be more appropriate for college students. One campus survey identified eight major groups that hold the al-

[16]Benton Johnson, "On Church and Sect," *American Sociological Review*, 28, no. 4 (Aug. 1963), 544–45.

[17]James A. Peterson, *Education for Marriage* (New York: Charles Scribner's Sons, 1964), chap. 18.

Table 15–4 Characteristics of the Major Religious Groups

Religious Group	*Lifestyle*	*Attitude Toward Premarital Sex*	*Concept of Marriage*	*Marital Roles*
Traditional Protestant and Catholic	Tends to be conservative.	Discouraged. Some changes evident.	Lifelong commitment.	Traditional. Becoming more flexible.
Liberal Protestant and Catholic	More permissive than traditional Protestant and Catholic; open to new trends.	Open to new viewpoints. May accept trial marriage.	Divorce becoming more acceptable.	More equality and flexibility in sex roles than traditional Protestant and Catholic.
Agnostic and atheistic	Casual and inner-directed.	Accepted. Some traditional parental influence.	Divorce acceptable. Parental influence may have weight.	Wide range of roles accepted.
Jewish	Liberal, but some strong traditional patterns.	Some acceptance. More restrictions on women than men.	Emphasis on lifelong marriage. Strong pressure to marry within faith.	Traditional in many ways. Many wives career-oriented.
Nontraditional ("free") cults	Casual. Experimental approach to group and family living.	Accepted, except in strict communes.	Casual and faddish. May espouse trial marriage or communal living.	Wide range of roles. Often strictly traditional.
Charismatic groups	Conservative, but youth subculture styles accepted. Anti-drugs and anti-liquor.	Strictly discouraged.	Lifelong commitment (most couples young).	Often highly traditional.
Other, including Eastern religions	Varied patterns; wide range of beliefs and behaviors in different groups. Eastern			
Nonaffiliated	Varies widely. Strongly influenced by culture.	Accepted.	Determined by parental influence.	Tends to be egalitarian. Influenced by parental family.

Attitude Toward Abortion	*Childrearing Practices*	*Political Views*	*Social Class**	*Social Views*
Catholics strongly negative. Protestants undecided.	May be conservative. Obedience stressed. Social-class influence may have weight.	Catholics divided. Protestants tend to be Republican.	Wide range for Catholics. Protestants middle and upper-middle class, some working class.	Favor establishment. Often highly conservative.
Tend to approve.	Permissive. Freedom of development stressed.	Tend to be liberal or Democratic.	Frequently upper-middle class. Some wealthy social reformers.	Tend to advocate social change.
Seem to approve.	Generally permissive. Family background may be conservative.	Wide range of opinion. Some radical influence.	Scattered; most middle or upper-middle class.	Tend to be nonestablishment. Some technocrats.
Will consider, but do not generally approve.	Permissive, but children must meet high goals. Strong emphasis on education.	Liberal or Democratic.	Tend to be middle and upper-middle class. Many professionals.	Strongly support democracy.
Often strongly positive.	Usually permissive, especially in communes.	Often radical, strongly antiestablishment.	Class system often rejected. May have good education and income.	Wide range of opinion. Sometimes strongly antisocial.
Generally negative.	Difficult to judge. Seem traditional.	Not vitally interested in politics. Seem to vote conservative.	Usually middle class. Some live simple life in communes.	Tend to withdraw from society, but accept many middle-class values.
religions often highly traditional. Often not involved in mainstream of American culture.				
Generally approve.	Tend to be permissive.	Wide range of opinion.	Scattered.	Tend to be other-directed.

*Upper-class families are often traditional or liberal Protestant or Catholic; Jewish; or Nonaffiliated.

legiance of contemporary students: traditional churches (Protestant, Eastern Orthodox, and Roman Catholic); liberal churches (Protestant and Catholic); agnostics and atheists; Jewish groups; nontraditional ("free") cults; the charismatic Christian movement; other groups, including Eastern religions; and nonaffiliated persons.[18]

In addition to the varying ways in which religions may be categorized, there is a wide internal variance in religions between communities in America. To be Protestant or Catholic or Jewish may have very different meanings in different areas of the country. Religion is a word that needs careful definition, for it is a concept that varies according to our prior experience of it (see Chapter 9).

Each of the religious groups in America has views that will affect a young married couple's outlook on life—including their marriage goals and their views on society, sex, birth control, abortion, and parenthood—and relate to their socioeconomic place in the community (see Table 15–4). One of the most thorough studies of the influence of religion on American life, conducted in the Detroit area by Gerhard Lenski, has illustrated the social impact of religion on people. Lenski's study covered four major groups: white and black Protestants, white Catholics, and Jews. He found that religion had a constant and significant influence on the daily lives of the individuals and families he studied. Religious organizations constituted a vigorous and influential social force that had an impact on all the other institutions in the community.

> Depending on the socio-religious group to which a person belongs, the probabilities are increased or decreased that he will enjoy his occupation, indulge in installment buying, save to achieve objectives far in the future, believe in the American Dream, vote Republican, favor the welfare state, take a liberal view on the issue of freedom of speech, oppose racial integration in the schools, migrate to another community, maintain close ties with his family, develop a commitment to the principle of intellectual autonomy, have a large family, complete a given unit of education, or rise in the class system.[19]

You may want to make an informal survey on your campus to ascertain the size of each religious community in your area. Undoubtedly the strength of the various groups will correlate with the views of people in your area on many of the vital family-oriented issues represented in Table 15–4, as well as with their socioeconomic status.[20]

[18]Survey taken by the author at Fullerton College, Spring 1973.

[19]Gerhard Lenski, *The Religious Factor* (Garden City, N.Y.: Doubleday, 1961), p. 289.

[20]Note a more sophisticated rating of belief designed by Charles Glock and Rodney Stark, termed "Orthodoxy Index," in Rodney Stark and Bruce K. Foster, "In Defense of Orthodoxy: Notes on the Validity of an Index," *Social Forces*, 48, no. 3 (March 1970), 383–93.

What is the future of religion in our family and community life? It is difficult to predict what course it will take. Historically, religious movements seem to move in cycles. As they rise and fall they have differing impacts on marriage and family life from generation to generation. The daring and faith and enthusiasm of one generation are counted as foolishness by another. War, famine, revolution, depression, or some other major historical crisis leaves its impact on the religious community and, consequently, the family.

Robert Wuthnow points out that there were indications of a religious revival in the postwar period of the 1950s, but this was followed by a declining interest in religion in the 1960s and the early 1970s.[21] (However, there are some indications that the charismatic churches and the more conservative religions are growing in strength today.) Using "Indicators of Religious Commitment"—Table 15–5— Wuthnow summarizes the recent trends in types of religious commitment. Wuthnow explains this as part of the response to the counterculture movement in the 1960s. The point is made that religious influence in our culture and in our family life does not follow any consistent pattern. The religious interest of one generation may be ignored by the next, and yet reborn in a different way in the third generation.

Contributions to Family Life

Religion may be approached in a number of ways. It may be considered the one thing of greatest importance and value in the life of an individual; it may be thought of as the individual's view of God and his commitment to a particular faith or creed; it may be defined as membership in a religious community. Although most sociological studies emphasize the last interpretation, the first two are also of importance when we consider the ways religious faith actually makes its contribution to family life.

One major contribution of religion to family life is the spiritual ideals it gives the couple and their children. In the Judeo-Christian tradition, man is created in the image of God. In human form and personality, in a mysterious way, man bears the stamp and image of the Divine. In the religious concept of marriage, the same lofty view of human nature is expanded to include the sexual relationship and the life of the family. This idealization of the family can be seen in the writing of John L. Thomas, a noted Catholic sociologist.

> The contents and the nature of the marriage contract have been established and ordained by the Creator. Individuals are free to enter the contract or not, but they cannot alter its contents. . . . In marriage, male and

[21]Robert Wuthnow, "Recent Patterns of Secularization: A Problem of Generations," *American Sociological Review*, 41, no. 5 (Oct. 1976), 850–67.

Table 15–5 Indicators of Religious Commitment, 1950–1972

	Average for Years:				
	1950–1954	*1955–1959*	*1960–1964*	*1965–1969*	*1970–1972*
1. Value of construction of new religious buildings (constant dollars)	$ 652 mil	$ 994 mil (52.5%)*	$1,112 mil (11.8%)	$1,101 mil (−1.0%)	$ 735 mil (−33.2%)
2. Contributions (constant dollars)	$1,579 mil	$2,580 mil (63.3%)	$3,057 mil (18.5%)	$3,318 mil (8.5%)	$3,531 mil (6.4%)
3. Religious degrees awarded	6,950	8,359 (20.3%)	8,843 (5.8%)	8,707 (−1.5%)	9,878 (13.4%)
4. –as percent of all degrees	2.1%	2.5% (19.0%)	2.1% (−16.0%)	1.4% (−33.3%)	1.2% (−14.3%)
5. Religious books published	788	987 (25.3%)	1,508 (52.8%)	1,847 (22.5%)	1,878 (1.7%)
6. –as percent of all books	6.8%	7.4% (8.8%)	7.0% (−5.4%)	6.8% (−2.9%)	5.2% (−23.5%)
7. Church membership as percent of population	58.4%	61.6% (5.5%)	63.6% (3.2%)	63.6% (0.0%)	63.5% (−0.2%)
8. Weekly church attendance	43%	48% (11.6%)	46% (−4.2%)	(−4.3%)	40% (−9.1%)

*Net change as percentage of previous time period in parentheses.
SOURCE: *Yearbook of American Churches, 1960–1973; U.S. Statistical Abstract, 1952–1974; United Nations Statistical Yearbook, 1953–1972;* Gallup (1972).

female are united as one principle for the purpose of procreation. This is the primary object of the contract. The conjugal union, to be sure, should be based on mutual love and affection; it supplies a suitable foundation for the control and expression of the sexual drive; it results in mutual actions providing pleasure of the highest kind; but all these things presuppose and take for granted the primary object of marriage . . . the generation of children.

Catholics believe that when marriage is contracted by baptized Christians capable of making the contract, this marriage contract is sacramental since Christ has raised matrimony to the dignity of a sacrament. . . . This doctrine has far-reaching significance in the Catholic concept of

> marriage. First, the grace which is supplied is that which is needed for a union worthy of Christians. . . .
>
> Although the demands of the Catholic marriage ideal are very high, God's help is made available to the wedded couple through the sacrament.[22]

While the Jewish and Protestant faiths do not have a sacramental view of marriage, both also hold a highly idealistic concept of the marital union.

In support of the high religious ideals of marriage, love, kindness, and forgiveness are stressed. Marriage is built on the true love and fidelity of both partners. If the vows of love and faithfulness are broken, the couple are governed not by harsh law and unbending justice, but by tenderness and forgiveness. Religious faith, then, is of great help in resolving marital differences and tensions.

When life is governed by such spiritual ideals and goals, the roles of husband, wife, and parent are more clearly defined, and they are considered in a larger perspective. In one sense, a father has less ultimate responsibility for the support and protection of his family, since he is not expected to carry out his duties alone. However, since his role is related to the Divine purpose, it gains stature and meaning.

Another contribution of religion in the life of the family is seen in the emphasis on commitment. This is a controversial area. Should a couple take

[22]John L. Thomas, *The American Catholic Family* (Englewood Cliffs, N.J.: Prentice-Hall, 1956), pp. 70, 77–78.

their marriage vows seriously? Or does a new era call for a new approach, in which the impact of smaller families, greater affluence, higher education, effective contraception, and other factors make commitment out-of-date? The traditional view of marriage reinforces the marital vows by giving them divine sanction and by stressing the permanence of the marriage bond. Since the traditional religious view of marriage is the oldest in Western society, it is closely related to many stable elements in our culture. Marriage is customarily sanctioned in a religious ceremony, in which approval of the wedding by the religious community reflects the approval of society. The actively religious couple reinforce their religious vows through attendance at worship and through their participation in the life of their church or synagogue. When children come, they too are included in the concern of the religious fellowship, and their religious education becomes a joint endeavor of church or synagogue and family.

Mueller and Johnson have shown that religious participation was high for Protestant and Catholic married couples with children who had more education than the parents. They see this as an indication of the importance of religious training as a social norm.[23] Fairchild, in describing some of the characteristics of Protestant family life, notes the emphasis on achievement in these families. He writes:

> These data help to explain a finding from the United Presbyterian family study which seemed incidental until now. Parents had consistently placed first, in a list of twenty-five problems by 845 families, the item: TV and radio listening habits. This appears a relatively superficial concern until one links it with the compelling Protestant image of achievement and career orientation. Passive viewing and listening is not seen as constructive or productive; it seems to these parents not to contribute to future achievement. Indeed, it may be a deterrent to those activities which seem to give training for the future.[24]

Choosing a Religious Community

A discussion of religion in marriage cannot ignore the fact that Americans often marry outside their faiths. Fortunately, many of them realize the importance of religion in marriage and take steps to achieve a common religious allegiance. But other young interfaith couples have difficulty choosing a

[23]Charles W. Mueller and Weldon T. Johnson, "Socioeconomic Status and Religious Participation," *American Sociological Review*, 40, no. 6, 785–800.

[24]Roy W. Fairchild, "Parental Stress in Protestant Homes: Clues from Research," in John Charles Wynn, ed., *Sex, Family, and Society in Theological Focus* (New York: Association Press, 1966), pp. 107–08.

common religious community. They are confused by the options open to them and torn between the practices and allegiances familiar to them and the desirability of a common faith. The decision is not easy. Family and friends, as well as religious leaders, encourage them to choose quickly. But certainly adequate time is needed for such an important decision, particularly if the couple are looking forward to parenthood and want to raise their children in a church or synagogue that is a spiritual home for the entire family.

The high percentage of couples who change their religious affiliation after marriage is indicated by a sample of Midwestern parents taken in 1965 and 1966. The study showed that the majority of couples changed churches in order to achieve a common religious affiliation. "About 84 percent (88 of 105) of such couples [those who converted] achieved a common religious affiliation. Change in religious affiliation occurred in 73 percent (105 of 144) of the marriages in our sample, suggesting that such change is very common among American couples."[25] Undoubtedly the needs of children in the family stimulated some of the change toward a common allegiance, because many couples changed religions before their first child reached ten years of age.

There are many considerations that enter into the choice of a religious faith. Worship is a basic element in every faith. Through worship the individual has a means of expression of thanksgiving, penitence, praise, and dedication. He has a way of affirming those religious truths he believes in. In worship he is inspired by the great music, art, and literature that express the doctrine and history of his religious community. Certainly a person's choice of faith will be influenced greatly by his personal beliefs and his manner of expressing them.

A second consideration is the way in which the religious community interprets and exemplifies a particular religious faith. In one sense, God can be worshiped as above and beyond all human thought and anthropomorphic interpretation. In a practical sense, however, we are all strongly influenced by those who are more mature and experienced than we are. Some communities, like the Quakers, may stand the test of time and win an honored and respected position in the ranks of the established churches even though they are few in number. Others may seem to have a great deal of power and influence but little strength in terms of ultimate sacrificial allegiance on the part of their adherents.

Religious education is also crucial in choosing a faith for the entire family. In our culture, the family seems to take little responsibility for formal reli-

[25]Nicholas Babchuk, Harry J. Crockett, Jr., and John A. Ballweg, "Changes in Religious Affiliations and Family Stability," *Social Forces*, 45, no. 4 (June 1967), 553.

gious education; the parochial school, the yeshiva, the church Sunday school, and church-sponsored youth programs perform that task. Although the parents guide the children in worship and prayer by precept and example, most families look to their church or synagogue for a more complete religious education.

It is difficult for children, and disrupting to the life of the family, when they are shunted back and forth between two different religious communities and are never able to build a consistent set of religious values. In fact, this is probably an important reason for the higher divorce rate in families with basic religious differences. The conflict of parents in this area cannot help but affect their children.

Another significant consideration in choosing a religion is the ethical and social outlook of the religious community. The things an Amos, a Jeremiah, or a John the Baptist suffered for have come to be a part of the core of traditional religious teaching. Religion would be infinitely poorer without the contributions of its great prophets. Every modern church or synagogue, in its broadest conception, must have both its priests and its prophets; in a day of social crisis and change, it is highly important that the prophetic note in religious life be retained.

The religious community may be related to the moral and social life of our day even when it emphasizes an otherworldly approach to life. Benton Johnson, in an interesting inquiry into the influence of Holiness sects (which are often numerous and active in low-income neighborhoods and ghettos),

concluded that in addition to its emotional and otherworldly appeal, holiness religion "may also function as an agency of the socialization of the lower class in the dominant values of American society."[26] In other words, even in groups that may seem to stress an escape from life's problems, we cannot disregard the ethical and social implications of religious belief.

A final element to consider is the impact of a religious faith on day-to-day family living. Roy W. Fairchild and John C. Wynn, in a recent study of Protestant families of various American denominations, discovered that the most common form of family religious observance was grace at meals.[27] The traditional Protestant pattern also included family worship, which was led by the father. In Catholic and Jewish families, particular holy days and festival observances have great meaning. These observances are an important means of drawing the family closer together and are part of the strong emotional contribution that religion makes to marriage.

Difficulties in Religious Adjustment

A shift in religious affiliation is not easy, particularly when a person has been an active and involved member of a strong religious body before marriage. Religion is often linked with traditional and conservative outlooks; religious people are thus likely to view change with suspicion. Although the contributions of religion are for the most part positive and constructive, it would be unrealistic not to recognize the points of tension that do exist.

One problem in religious adjustment is generated by the wide range of religious groups in America. There are many different religious bodies, including over two hundred Protestant denominations, large and small; countless local and individualistic sects; the Roman Catholic and Eastern Orthodox Catholic churches; the Reform, Conservative, and Orthodox Jewish groups; Buddhists; Mohammedans; and so on. What one person might honor as an important and valuable religious belief might well be termed heresy by another.

Religious adjustment may be further complicated by the fact that religion generates both tolerance and intolerance. One of the values of a meaningful religious experience is that it helps to build an understanding of the value of the human personality. Most religions stress the common heritage of humanity and the possibilities of brotherhood and peaceful relationships between people of different races and nations. This can be seen in our society in the increasing dialogue being carried on among Catholics, Protestants, and Jews and in the consequent growth of ecumenical feeling.

[26]Benton Johnson, "Do Holiness Sects Socialize in Dominant Values?" *Social Forces,* 39, no. 4 (May 1961), 309–16.

[27]Roy W. Fairchild and John C. Wynn, *Families in the Church: A Protestant Survey* (New York: Association Press, 1961).

But it must also be recognized that religion sometimes builds an intolerant spirit; by its very nature it claims exclusive allegiance. When one is a sincere and convinced Roman Catholic, all other religions appear to fall short of truth and authority. If one is a dedicated and zealous Baptist, no other faith can match its message and appeal. And if one is born and raised within a Jewish community, affiliation with the Jewish synagogue is natural and inherently right; any other religion will seem foreign. But strongly religious people often make the mistake of thinking that the faith that is right for them will prove right for everyone else. A church that is active and growing may assume its validity is proven by its success. In some cases, a person who is convinced that his faith is *the* right one and that the only satisfactory arrangement for the entire family is for them to adopt it as their own is bound to cause tension by expecting everyone else to do the compromising and refusing to give an inch himself.

One of the problems that came up in the early years after my parents' marriage centered around religion. Mother's parents were very religious Baptists and had certain aggressive tendencies. They believed it was not good enough for a person to be content with just his own personal salvation; if one believed, his belief would manifest its quality in an overt desire to spread the Gospel. In Mother's case, this meant that she had a religious obligation to curb Father's religious indifference. For him, the ultimate question whether or not there was a God held little importance in the overall scheme of life. It was, he felt, much more important for man to invest his intellectual energies in making here-and-now improvements in daily living on earth. Then if the God above was as merciful as the Christian religion claims, anyone who felt the real existence of a Heaven would go there. He criticized the majority of religious bodies as wallowing in quagmires of sentiment and refused to associate with them. Mother's views were such that there was no outward concern or conflict. But Grandmother was concerned! She recognized only two kinds of men—the ones who were saved and the ones who were not. Father was not saved, and she believed that unless Mother put the pressure on him and got some changes made, she was backsliding.

If this conflict of views ever boiled into open antagonism, it was well concealed from other relatives and the children. That it existed is certain, for Grandmother was more than anxious to expose her way of life to her grandchildren. Her home was, and is today, a Christian home, with prayers at meals, end of day, and between times. She also has religious artifacts, music, and social circles. The situation has been gradually resolved. In the years since their marriage, Mother and Father have never clashed openly on religious views. Grandmother has always done her best to be an influence by example on the grandchildren. She often expressed concern about their souls' future, but never (at least before the grandchildren) her doubts or concern for her daughter and son-in-law.[28]

Such tensions within a mixed marriage are very common. When questioned by family and friends, for example, a wife in a divided family might say:

> I know that my husband was not a [Methodist, Catholic, Episcopalian, or Baptist] when we were married. But we love each other very much, and I am sure that he will soon come to know and understand my faith and want to adopt it as his own. There may have been negative factors in his parental home, or in his childhood or adolescent experiences, that have prevented him from joining our church. I am trying my very best to convince him that he should join me in my church, and I expect that he will want to do so very soon. If I fail, it will be a reflection also on me.

The husband, however, may not share such sentiments, and his reply to his wife might be direct and difficult to answer:

> When we first met and fell in love, you had the same religious convictions that you have now. But I did not, and this seemed no barrier to our courtship, engagement, and marriage. You said that it was fine and that you were perfectly willing to let me take my time and make up my own mind.
>
> Why is it now so important that I become a member of your church? Has your faith changed in the five years since we were married? Are you trying to say that you loved and accepted me as a husband on our wedding day, even though I was not of your persuasion, but that you cannot accept me today? If so, you are not very consistent.

It is small wonder that many wives and husbands who profess to be strong adherents of a particular religious faith are beset by feelings of guilt and misgivings when they are forced into such discussions in a mixed marriage.

Religion encourages individuality because it recognizes that men and women have different gifts and abilities which may be expressed in different ways. One of the strengths of the Roman Catholic tradition over the centuries, for example, has been its ability to allow expression within its ranks of a number of different religious orders and traditions, all owing allegiance to one Church. Some Protestant groups, particularly the free churches like the Baptists and Congregationalists, have also been noted for their encouragement of widely differing theologies and customs within a single denomi-

[28]Student report.

national grouping. The modern liberal movement has emphasized strongly the freedom of clergymen, churches, synagogues, and lay people to choose their own religious patterns.

At the same time, religion, and particularly strong and purposeful religion, emphasizes conformity to group norms and standards. In our American tradition, the earliest and most prominent example of such conformism was the Puritan settlers of New England, religious men and women with high ideals, a willingness to endure hardship and suffering in order to achieve their goals, and a closely knit fellowship that rigidly structured much of their day-by-day living. The same kind of religious control over behavior was evident in Quaker, Presbyterian, and Brethren settlements and can still be observed in many religious communities today.

A clash will occur when one partner in marriage comes from a religious background that emphasizes diversity and the other spouse comes from a religion stressing conformity. It may be a Protestant-Catholic marriage, a Protestant-Protestant marriage, a Jewish-Catholic marriage, or any one of a dozen other possible combinations. If this significant difference in religious spirit exists, it is bound to bring conflict into the marriage. Fortunate is the couple whose diverse backgrounds are in harmony.

Alex was reared in a Protestant family in an Eastern community that was over 90 percent Roman Catholic. His family attended a small Protestant church of less than two hundred members. In order to meet the problems imposed by this situation, the family, in common with most members of their small church, adopted a consistent approach. Children in the family were taught: "We belong to a small church, while most of our neighbors belong to a different church. We are not as wealthy as they are, and we do not have as imposing and beautiful a church as they do. However, we believe that one can worship God sincerely in any kind of surroundings. Therefore, we will be true to our faith, in spite of the obstacles. This is a free country, and every man and woman has a right to choose his or her own religion."

Gloria, Alex's fiancée, was born and raised in Texas and was of the same ethnic group. Her family, however, was Roman Catholic in a small town that was almost completely Baptist and Methodist. The Catholic families had to travel some miles to a small chapel where people from several communities met to celebrate Mass. To meet this situation, Gloria and her brothers and sisters were taught: "We are Roman Catholics, and most of our neighbors are Protestants. But we are true to our own religion and do not wish to be pressured into another faith. God will honor all those who worship Him in reverence and truth. It does not matter how many people are gathered together or how large and beautiful the church is. This is a free country, and every person should have a right to follow his or her own religious convictions."

With similar backgrounds in minority church groups in their home communities, Alex and Gloria found little difficulty in merging their religious interests after marriage. If he had been Protestant in Texas and she Roman Catholic in the Eastern community, the results would have been far different.

Husband and wife may also have differing expectations of how much emphasis should be placed on religious teaching and how much the contrast between the ideal and the real can be minimized. Much religious practice is not actually inherent in the ethical standards set up by religion, but represents the sanctification of customs by the religious community. Many of our Christmas observances, for example, are in that category. They may fall short of the ethical ideal (giving gifts to one's own family and loved ones, for instance, instead of to those who are in real need), and at times they may conflict with that ideal.

The clash between the ideal and the actual is evident in many other ways. Religious teaching may hold up a standard of behavior concerning sexual relations, birth control, entertainment, or childrearing that is far different from the actual experience of life. To one person, religious faith may be a motivating force helping him to strive for high and lofty ideals. To another, religion may mean being more acceptant and forgiving of human shortcomings. A mixed marriage often generates serious problems when these different ways of looking at life meet head-on.

John Larsen has suggested that marriage and family counselors need to take some of these possible difficulties into account when working with religious families. The religious framework and dimension cannot be ignored. In the evangelical family, he notes, there are certain characteristic views of religious belief, religious practice, lifestyle, and the authority of the Bible. Parents will often cope with conflicts with their children in a way consistent with this religious background. Larsen writes:

> The therapeutic strategy herein recommended for dysfunctional evangelical families is not to change religiously based values that may be incompatible with therapeutic objectives but to reorder the value structure in a way that facilitates the goals of therapy without compromising the family faith. . . .
>
> . . . a willingness to work within the religious framework allows the

family to tap powerful religious resources that can be mobilized to advance the goals of therapy.[29]

We can expect to find some problems of adjustment in the area of family religious life. Fortunately, the resources needed to meet these problems are available in our society, and means of counseling and supportive therapy are a part of the group life of almost every religious community.

SUMMARY Almost every newly married couple will have an extended family. A large number of individuals and relationships may be involved. Surprisingly, many extended families retain their closeness in spite of our mobile industrialized society. Ties with older parents and grandparents are maintained. If we can maintain such connections, without unhealthy control by any generation, life is enriched and benefited. Such relations with the extended family are also important for the growing number of single adults.

In-law relationships are important because they are a part of a spouse's life. We can share more honestly with our partner if we are big enough to share with his or her family. Typical in-law problems include conflict between the independence expected of newlyweds and continued dependence on parents. A clean break between generations is traditional in America, but parental families have a continuing psychological importance in the life of married children. And the close ties between mother and child in our culture contribute to the tendency toward overdependence on in-laws. Still another problem is related to the pattern of give-and-take in American family life: we often accord children a place of excessive importance in the family and neglect grandparents.

The majority of in-law problems seem to occur among women. The greater importance of the home and family to women results in a greater likelihood of conflict. Working-class men, however, also seem to have a high degree of conflict with their in-laws.

Better health and longer life expectancy now mean that in-laws can be a source of enjoyment rather than a burden to us. And in-laws may prove to be very helpful in times of crisis. Successful in-law relationships can be built through certain positive steps. Couples should try to develop an optimistic and positive attitude toward their in-laws. They should "join the family" in an emotional and personal sense. Elements common to both parental families should be stressed; potential points of conflict should be minimized.

Religion also makes a number of positive contributions to family life. Religion motivates the family to seek spiritual ideals. It strengthens a couple's commitment to each other. And religion is often linked with established social pat-

[29]John A. Larsen, "Dysfunction in the Evangelical Family: Treatment Considerations," *The Family Coordinator*, 27, no. 3 (July 1978), 266.

terns and dominant values. It gives practical encouragement to the family in daily living, particularly in the education and guidance of children.

In America there are a number of distinctive religious communities with varying views on marriage and family life: there are traditional Protestant and Catholic groups, liberal Protestant and Catholic groups, Jewish groups, nontraditional ("free") cults, the charismatic groups, the Eastern religions, and agnostics and atheists. The choice of a church or synagogue is an important one for a newly married couple. Many people change their religious affiliations after marriage. Some conform to their partners' faiths, and others choose a completely new affiliation. Many considerations enter into the choice: mode of worship; the influence of a faith on the lives of its members and the daily life of the family; the program of religious education offered; and ethical and social outlooks.

Religious adjustment may be difficult for some couples; a shift in religious affiliation is not easy. Religion often generates intolerance toward other faiths. And different religious traditions may give rise to differing expectations of the importance of religious faith in family life and the necessity of adherence to religious teaching and ideals. Such problems are often intensified in the interfaith marriages of partners with wide differences in religious background.

SUGGESTED READINGS

Adams, Bert N. *Kinship in an Urban Setting.* Chicago: Markham, 1968. Study of family relationships in a sample taken in North Carolina. Illustrates continuing family ties.

Drabek, Thomas E., William H. Key, Patricia E. Erickson, and Juanita L. Crowe. "The Impact of Disaster on Kin Relationships," *Journal of Marriage and the Family*, 37, no. 3 (Aug. 1975), 481–94. Study of kin relationships following a disaster in Topeka, Kansas.

Hathorn, Raban, William H. Genné, and Mordecai Brill, eds. *Marriage, An Interfaith Guide for All Couples.* New York: Association Press, 1970. A priest, a minister, and a rabbi highlight the positive features of Roman Catholic, Protestant, and Jewish traditions.

Hill, Reuben, Nelson Foote, Joan Aldous, Robert Carlson, and Robert Macdonald. *Family Development in Three Generations: A Longitudinal Study of Changing Family Patterns of Planning and Achievement.* Cambridge, Mass.: Schenkman, 1970. Details the kinship relationships of a stable group of Minnesota families.

Lenski, Gerhard. *The Religious Factor.* Garden City, N.Y.: Doubleday, 1961. Classic study of religious influence in a group of Detroit families, white and black Protestants, white Catholics, and Jews.

Shana, Ethel. "Family-Kin Network and Aging in Cross-Cultural Perspective," *Journal of Marriage and the Family*, 35, no. 3 (Aug. 1973), 505–11. One of several studies by the same author investigating closeness of the elderly with their adult children.

Wuthnow, Robert. "Recent Patterns of Secularization: A Problem of Generations," *American Sociological Review*, 41, no. 5 (Oct. 1976), 850–67. Valuable study of religious trends as they affect different age groups in society.

16 Financial Partnership in Marriage

- How does marriage resemble a business partnership?
- Do financial needs vary in different stages of the family life cycle?
- Can we learn about financial management from our parents?
- What major family goals are important to young couples?
- How do the career choices of husband and wife affect their financial partnership?
- What are the most effective means of planning and following a family budget?
- How can a young couple establish a credit rating and utilize credit wisely?
- What are the financial advantages of different types of housing?
- What are the basic family insurance needs?
- How can the family become an effective consuming unit?
- What savings programs and investments are wise for young married couples?
- How should a couple plan for the retirement years?
- How important is a will to the family's financial partnership?

Financial Planning

A partnership is one of the most difficult business arrangements to run successfully. The future of the entire business depends on the ability of the partners to work together smoothly without unnecessary conflicts about whom to employ, what products to sell, or what days and hours to be open for business. If the partners ever start pulling in opposite directions, the firm is in serious trouble.

It is not surprising, then, that the financial partnership of marriage is often a difficult one to operate successfully. There also, the two partners must learn to work together smoothly or the whole enterprise is in trouble. Any young couple about to begin managing a family income must be realistic about their financial situation. If the husband insists on continuing the use of his money in the same way he did before marriage, or if the wife imagines that she can maintain the same standard of living she was accustomed to in her parents' home, where her living expenses were paid for her and her whole income was available for her personal expenses, both are in for a rude shock. They must recognize that it takes intelligence, a certain amount of time, and a good deal of common sense to build a working financial partnership in the family.

Financial planning meets differing needs of the family during different stages of the family cycle. The first ten years of married life will be financially difficult ones for a young couple. These are years when expenses for home, furniture, children, and other fixed items are heavy. If children begin to arrive in the first two or three years, as they often do, the family will have little opportunity to accumulate savings, equity in a home, or other assets. At the same time, the family's income is usually fairly low, because husband and wife are new entrants into the labor force.

During the next decade costs increase gradually as the children enter school, and expenditures that were postponed during the childbearing period must be undertaken. A larger home, new furniture, more adequate insurance coverage, and a better car are all typical items that dent the family budget in this period. Fortunately, in the average family, income will be rising and should keep pace with the increasing costs. The number of working women rises at this stage, so that more income can be expected from this source.

During the third decade of marriage (which would place both husband and wife in their forties in the average American family), costs continue to rise. There may be sharply increased costs if the children are attending college, especially if the parents must pay for room and board as well as tuition. There may be a wedding or two, and some help may be extended to the newly married children. Income may level off during these years, as the careers of husband and wife settle into a more fixed pattern. It is not unusual, in a rapidly changing economy, for a middle-aged man and woman to find that their skills and experience have suddenly become obsolete.

In many cases, however, this third decade can also be a very prosperous period for the family. If the home mortgage has been paid off, or if the family decides that a smaller home or apartment will be adequate, more money will be left over for other expenses. Income from savings, investments, or profit-sharing plans may provide surplus funds for the family's use. And if both husband and wife work full-time, their double income will provide a much more comfortable standard of living than they had in earlier years.

The fourth and subsequent decades of marriage present more new financial needs and opportunities for the family. For the college-educated couple, the last twenty years of work before retirement should be profitable and challenging ones. The final stage in the life cycle, the retirement years, is assuming increased importance as life expectancy lengthens and Social Security, company pension plans, and other income provisions make possible a more active and enjoyable retirement. (We will treat this subject more thoroughly in Chapter 22.) The needs of the retired members of the family, of course, have their impact on the children and grandchildren. If special medical care is needed, or if grandparents come to live with their children, family expenses will go up.

We have been looking at the family's financial life cycle largely in terms of the college-educated couple. For those in the working class, and for millions of families near or below the poverty level, the situation may be far different. There is less freedom of choice as we go down the economic scale—a mechanic or factory technician will have to plan his family's financial future within stricter limits, and will probably be more affected by changes in the nation's economy.

There are several important guidelines for establishing sound financial partnership throughout the family life cycle. They include one's family back-

ground and one's future goals as well as the more widely accepted formulas for income budgeting. Let us concentrate on the most fundamental guidelines, the ones that will affect most family financial partnerships.

Family Financial Background

One of the first confrontations with reality for an engaged couple is a comparison of their prior financial experiences. Does he come from a very conservative family, in which money has been carefully saved and wisely spent and credit buying, long-term home mortgages, and other forms of borrowing are avoided whenever possible? Does she come from a much more liberal family, in which income and expenditures are rarely balanced and the books are juggled from payday to payday? The experience each partner has had with money in his parental family and the financial habits each has formed during full-time employment will be crucial factors when husband and wife sit down to work out the family budget. Many students may have been puzzled by some of the economies (or extravagances) of their parents, and then are surprised to see themselves repeating the same patterns in their own marriage.

Financial adjustment is probably easier when a woman marries up to a higher status than when the reverse is true. Few women should have trouble adjusting to a higher income—unless a husband is accustomed to spending money in an irresponsible way. The world of literature is replete with brides who married, Cinderella-like, into great wealth and fortune. Those stories generally have happy endings. But the stories of men who marry above themselves are few and far between and have less happy consequences. It may be that there is still an element of truth to such literary portrayals.

Primary Values and Financial Goals

Money is a medium of exchange. Unless one inherits a certain income or sum of money, he usually earns his money by his production or services. If he works hard and produces a great deal, or if he is able to render a much needed and highly valued service, he will receive a substantial amount of money. If he works less, or if people do not want or need his services, he receives less. We all have a certain monetary value in the marketplace.

When one first begins to earn a full-time salary, the amount received per week or per month may seem small. A change of jobs or a promotion may seem quite desirable. But when one begins to recognize how much effort it really takes to assume a new job or to accept added responsibilities in the plant or the office, he can then better evaluate how much the actual increase in income is worth. For example, if a woman is earning $150 a week for forty hours of work in a local real-estate office, how much is it worth to her to be offered a job downtown with more responsibility, longer hours and travel time, and higher prestige? Is $190 a week sufficient to be worth the extra effort and energy? Or $250 a week? The decision will depend largely on the values one holds. Some people will give up their wishes very quickly when they see that hard work and sacrifice are necessary to attain them; others will redouble their efforts. Both those reactions are value judgments.

Donaldson and Pfahl, in their discussion of personal finance, place first importance on goals for the family economic unit. Without such goals, no sensible plan can be developed. They write:

> The most fundamental institution in the American economy is the family unit. Each family, in planning its financial affairs, must answer two basic questions. First, what are the goals for the family unit? Second, how can these goals best be achieved? The answer to the second question can only follow the answer to the first.
>
> . . . [There is] no recommended objective or group of objectives determined for any particular individual. One of the great advantages of a free society is that each person and family may work toward different objectives.[1]

A consideration of values enters into every major choice the newly married couple will make. Should they live in the north end of town or downtown near the shopping center? Should she drop her full-time job at the department store and stay home with the children next year, or do they need the two salaries to support the family? The answers to these questions will

[1]Elvin F. Donaldson and John K. Pfahl, *Personal Finance*, 5th ed. (New York: Ronald Press, 1971), pp. 9–11.

be determined by whatever is most important to the couple—that is, their values.

Stuart was a young management trainee working full time in a chain store while completing his college work in business administration. His salary was approximately $9,000 a year, with annual increases as he gained seniority and additional college credits. He and his wife, Rachel, had two small children. She worked about fifteen hours a week and was also taking courses at college. Both parental families lived in the area and provided ideal babysitting service.

Halfway through the spring semester, Stuart received an offer to become assistant manager of one of the company stores some three hundred miles from home. The transfer would be immediate; he could bring his family to the new location in the summer if he preferred. The base salary was $11,000 yearly and represented another step up in the management program. But he would lose credit for three courses and in the small new community he would be able to continue his college work only by correspondence.

Stuart and Rachel studied this offer carefully. The promotion was a vote of confidence in his work, and the raise would help to pay for a needed car and some overdue medical bills. Housing costs in the small community would be lower, so they would soon be able to have a home of their own. But there were several disadvantages to the transfer, and they were so strong that they finally led the husband and wife to decide against his taking the new job. Stuart and Rachel would have to drop out of college, and their education might be completely interrupted for two or three years. Ties with family and friends would have to be cut. Educational and cultural opportunities for the children would be fewer. The cost of moving and the need for help with the children if Rachel were to work might eliminate part if not all of the increase in pay. The couple decided which aspects of their business and personal lives were most important to them and refused the job offer.

Our values enter not only into the major financial decisions we make in marriage, our choice of vocation, the kind of home we live in, and the number of children we have, but into many of the small daily money decisions that help to establish patterns for the family budget. For example, food costs, which may run as high as 30 percent of the budget, are often largely determined by what we want and what we think is important rather than by our actual physical needs. "Shall we buy expensive cuts of meat for dinner next week, or can we get by just as well with meat loaf, hot dogs, and stew?" The actual proteins, vitamins, and calories may not differ greatly, but there is a wide variance in the importance attached to certain foods by different individuals. "I want a tender steak for dinner," one husband asserts, "because I work hard and I need the energy." "No child of mine is going to grow up eating beans and hot dogs all the time," says another. "Let's get some real meat on this table, even if it does cost a little more." If the choice of food is important to the husband and wife, their pattern of spending will reflect it.

We have to recognize that every goal we set for ourselves will not be attained: the new house or car, the trip that we have been talking about for years, the van that is specially equipped for the kind of vacation we have always wanted. Perhaps it is good to wish for some things that we will never get. But the key is again a question of values. Perhaps the home is the most important because the children are going to school and we want to have more room for them and to live in a good neighborhood not too far from school. Or the most important goal may be that terrific vacation, because we have skipped vacations a couple of summers. What is most important to us? That goal will determine much of what we do with our income in the years ahead.

Job Satisfaction and Marital Happiness

Can you have a wonderful family life if you work at the world's toughest and most unpleasant job? Can you be full of spontaneity and enthusiasm at home if everything you do at work makes you unhappy? Probably not. There is a great deal of interaction between our jobs and family life. Men and women who enjoy their work, and feel that they are really accomplishing something every day, have a head start on having an enjoyable family life as well. There has been a limited number of studies of the effects of specific occupations on marital success. One such study was made early in the Depression.[2] Although occupations have changed a great deal since that time, it is interesting to note the high rates of happiness for engineers, professors and teachers, and ministers, and the low rates for traveling salesmen, unskilled laborers, musicians, real-estate salesmen, and others. Carl Ridley attempted to measure the same factors in a study of married female teachers and their husbands in Florida. There were 208 teachers in the study group, including about one-fifth who had student husbands. The Bullock Scale of job satisfaction was used to measure the degree of job satisfaction of the wives, together with measures of their job involvement and their marital

[2]Richard A. Land, "The Rating of Happiness in Marriage," unpublished M.A. thesis, cited in Ernest W. Burgess and Leonard S. Cottrell, *Predicting Success or Failure in Marriage* (Englewood Cliffs, N.J.: Prentice-Hall, 1939), pp. 139–46.

Table 16–1 Relationship Between Teachers' Job Satisfaction and Teachers' Marital Adjustment

Job Satisfaction	*Marital Adjustment* *Low*		*Medium*		*High*		*Total*	
	No.	%	No.	%	No.	%	No.	%
High	8	14.8	22	40.7	24	44.4	54	99.9
Medium	22	31.0	30	42.3	19	26.8	71	100.1
Low	20	24.1	35	42.2	28	33.7	83	100.0
Total	50		87		71		208	

SOURCE: Carl A. Ridley, "Exploring the Impact of Work Satisfaction and Involvement on Marital Interaction When Both Partners Are Employed," *Journal of Marriage and the Family,* 35, no. 2 (May 1973), 233. Copyrighted 1973 by the National Council on Family Relations. Reprinted by permission.

satisfaction. The results are shown in Table 16–1. Those women who had the highest job satisfaction also had the highest marital satisfaction rating. Surprisingly, many teachers who had low job satisfaction scored high on marital adjustment. The reasons are complex. Both men and women have many different ways of looking at their jobs, and apparently, the same job responsibilities may be supportive for one marriage but interfere with the happiness of another.[3]

Teachers may have a special relationship to their families not shared by other women with careers. They may have a schedule that matches their children's, and they have longer vacation periods. The mother of teenagers may have a lot of fun with them after being with first graders all day, and the mother of preschoolers may find her English class of high school seniors a pleasant contrast. And, as Ridley discovered, there may be a point of high involvement, for both husbands and wives, that may interfere with marital adjustment, no matter how satisfying the job may be to husband and wife.

In general we can expect that jobs that provide a high level of intellectual or creative satisfaction, good income, regular hours, and security will create conditions most favorable to marital happiness. The little research available seems to indicate that such conditions as low income and low status (as for unskilled laborers), job or income insecurity (as for musicians or real-estate salesmen), and considerable time spent away from home (as for traveling salesmen) produce tensions that are likely to carry over into the home life.

[3]Carl A. Ridley, "Exploring the Impact of Work Satisfaction and Involvement on Marital Interaction When Both Partners Are Employed," *Journal of Marriage and the Family,* 35, no. 2 (May 1973), 229–37.

However, we should recognize that since occupations change rapidly with changes in the economy, an occupation that appears stable and rewarding today may be much less appealing five or ten years from now. Conversely, with pay for many blue-collar jobs increasing rapidly, and with contracts now guaranteeing medical help, retirement income, and other fringe benefits, the social position of many skilled workers is becoming more secure.

The long-term benefits or disadvantages of a particular career, then, cannot be predicted with absolute certainty in our rapidly changing society. Nevertheless, couples should think seriously about their work and careers, and try to make sure that there is a real satisfaction for both partners, mentally and monetarily. Money is important in marriage; a couple who cannot achieve their desired financial goals will be frustrated. But will a larger salary compensate for an unhappy relationship? In our materialistic society, there are too many couples who, in Oscar Wilde's words, know the price of everything and the value of nothing.

The total family income, of course, will be a major factor in the reaction of both husband and wife to their career responsibilities. A husband may be willing to stay with a job that is not his first choice because his wife's salary is basic to the family budget, and she really likes her work. Or, on the other hand, a wife may turn down a transfer or a promotion in her work because this would endanger her husband's position and cause a loss of income. Such decisions are difficult for many couples to make because there are so few precedents to guide them.

Family Budgeting

If the couple are to gain some measure of control over their financial life and future, they will need to learn to budget their incomes effectively. This is not a simple task. In order to achieve such an objective, the couple need to plan and organize a workable system of disbursing funds, and restrict unnecessary or unwise purchases. Regardless of their experience before marriage, or during the beginning months and years of marriage, any couple can turn their financial situation around if they are strongly motivated to do so. Donaldson and Pfahl note:

> Everyone has a financial management program. Most personal programs, however, are poorly planned and accomplish little for the individuals involved. While most people realize the importance of financial planning on the part of governmental agencies and business units, the majority of individuals fail to recognize the equal importance of personal financial planning.
>
> Some people put their financial plans on paper, budget carefully, and

keep an up-to-date record of expenditures. Others use a less formal program but are still familiar with the basic objectives of their personal financial plans and the ways in which they intend to accomplish them. Regardless of the formality of the financial program, the family with a wise financial plan for spending and saving has fewer financial problems and thereby enjoys greater peace of mind.[4]

There are many different ways for a newly married couple to create a sound financial plan. The best way to begin is to become acquainted with the spending patterns that are already in operation. Many banks and credit unions provide record and account books for their members, and the couple can use these to accumulate the information needed to build a good, working financial system. No one system is suitable for every family, but one plan, or a combination of several, will help to make the family financial partnership run smoothly.

A simple method of money management is for either husband or wife to handle all of the family's income. That one person is thus responsible for allocating weekly or monthly income for all major budget items. He or she usually then releases to the other partner whatever cash is necessary for daily living expenses. If the husband serves as the family treasurer, for example, he will probably give his wife a weekly or monthly food allowance and perhaps another sum of money for incidentals, gifts, personal clothing, and so on. He will pay the monthly bills, take care of the family savings, and keep just enough cash to meet his daily expenses. Or if the wife handles the family money, she will receive her husband's salary and he will operate on a certain weekly or monthly allowance for cash spending. If a man has few cash expenses in his work and uses credit cards for gasoline purchases, business meals, and the like, this system may work very smoothly for the couple.

My mother acts as secretary to the corporation and writes all checks and balances the bank account. As soon as we all were old enough to subtract, we took turns bringing her checkbook up to date as she wrote the monthly checks. She believes that is the best way for children to see how the family's money is spent. Throughout the years we all had allowances and were expected to manage them wisely. There are no financial secrets from us. We all know how much money we have in savings accounts and what the checking-account balance is at all times.

When it comes to spending money, much thought is given to each purchase. Although we children wanted a color TV for Christmas last December, we didn't get it until October of this year. My father and mother do not believe in buying anything on time. So all purchases are

[4]Donaldson and Pfahl, p. 38.

carefully considered, checked, and rechecked before we venture forth with checkbook in hand.[5]

Another system that is common in two-income families is for the couple to have a joint checking account or two separate checking accounts and to pool their income for some major expenses while paying for smaller personal items from their separate accounts. For example, the couple might use one-half of the husband's salary and one-half of the wife's to pay for food, housing, insurance, and utilities. With the balance of his income the husband might be responsible for a systematic savings program, automobile maintenance, vacations, and his own miscellaneous expenses. The wife, utilizing the balance of her salary, might be responsible for entertainment, gifts, and her own personal expenses.

No single method of management will fit every family, but to avoid any plan at all is to invite chaos. Many young couples begin their married life without any fixed budget or system of money management. This may not bring financial disaster, especially if both are working. But it is a postponement of some important decisions that will affect every stage of their marriage and may be symptomatic of a desire on the part of one or both of them to avoid difficult or unpleasant tasks. Sometime early in the marriage the couple should be ready to move into a more effective budgeting system so that they can make more definite progress toward their financial goals. With the experience gained from their initial financial record-keeping system, they should move easily to this level. In most families a pattern will emerge and the couple can begin to draw up a permanent budget. At the end of the year, or some more convenient time, they can revise the budget on the basis of longer experience.[6]

A certain resistance to budgeting seems to be growing among young married couples, probably for two reasons. First, the budget may seem to exercise some kind of control over the couple's expenditures, preventing them from buying what they really want to buy. We live in an era that stresses freedom and independence, and we don't want to be dominated, even by such an impersonal thing as a budget. Second, the rising level of prosperity in our country means that most families have had higher and higher incomes to live on and have been able to raise their standard of living during the family life cycle. Their grown children are unused to being denied.

It is difficult to project budget costs for an average family because of the built-in inflation factor, which seems to continue as a constant in the Ameri-

[5]Student report.

[6]For a fuller discussion of budgeting, see Robert K. Kelley, *Guidebook to Accompany Courtship, Marriage, and the Family,* 3rd ed. (New York: Harcourt Brace Jovanovich, 1979).

can economy. However, certain fixed principles remain. The family cannot keep increasing its debt load indefinitely. The only possible end result would be bankruptcy. Nor can a couple improve their standard of living if they spend most of their money for food, entertainment, clothing, and other items that do not add to the family's "capital." There must be a balance of expenditures for such items as purchasing a home, providing good furniture, buying life insurance, buying a durable automobile, beginning a savings program.

Regardless of the method, the couple should decide at once to choose *some* workable plan for money management. If it does not operate as well as anticipated, they can switch to another. Many couples use different systems during different periods in the family life cycle. The important thing is for the couple to make a careful decision together and then to give the method they have chosen a fair trial. If they cannot do that, they are bound to be headed toward arguments about money.

Credit and Charge Accounts

The lifetime income of the typical American husband may run from $500,000 to $600,000, depending on the rate of inflation. His wife may match that total or, in accord with the national average, earn about half that much because of a shorter working life span (after raising two or three children). This means a family lifetime total income that may approach a million dollars.

This is a large sum of money. The way it is handled will play a large part in determining whether the family is financially secure and can adequately meet its basic needs, or whether it will be plagued by financial problems, intermittent quarrels over money, and insecurity in the retirement years.

Most young couples accumulate some debts during the first years of marriage. One survey found that five out of ten families had personal debt, with young couples appearing on the list most frequently. Two out of three spending units headed by persons twenty-five to thirty-four used installment credit. The financial patterns of older groups were different; more than two-thirds of those over fifty-four and almost all of those over sixty-four had no installment credit.[7] In other words, credit, as a way of using family income, has been rising sharply in the last fifty years. Our grandparents did not expect to owe money, particularly for clothes and other everyday items; young couples today accept such debts as a matter of course.

[7]Jerome B. Cohen and Arthur W. Hanson, *Personal Finance: Principles and Case Problems,* 4th ed. (Homewood, Ill.: Irwin, 1972), p. 188.

Establishing Credit

The establishment of credit is based on your ability to repay the money borrowed for a purchase. The seller, bank, or other lender might be able to repossess the furniture or other item financed, but he does not prefer to do that. (He would then have to sell the item.) Your ability to pay is judged by your past performance in earning or saving money and then in paying your bills promptly in accord with your contract agreements. Certainly your credit would be good, for example, if you had saved $500 a year for ten years and could thus list a savings account of $5,000 plus interest as an asset. You wouldn't need to have a long string of charge accounts to prove that you were a good credit risk for an average loan. The savings account would prove that. But you could also build credit by using a gasoline credit card, a small thirty-day charge account at your local drug store, or a rotating charge account at a large department store. The important questions are: What did you purchase from the store or company; when did you agree to pay them for it; and did you repay the money as promised?

Because of the passage of the federal Fair Credit Reporting Act, you now have access to the credit records kept on you, whether they are handled by a giant nationwide bureau like Thompson, Ramo, and Woolridge Credit Data, which has files on some thirty million consumers, or a small local credit office. You can discover what went wrong if your credit application is refused, and in doing so get errors in your record corrected or prevent yourself from making the same mistake twice. (After a period of time, your record will be purged of negative ratings. Even bankruptcies are eliminated after fourteen years.) A visit to your local credit bureau will be well worth your while.

One result of the feminist movement has been the drive to extend equal credit to women. Women can now have credit cards issued directly to them in their own names, thanks to the 1974 Equal Credit Opportunity Act. They are able to make direct loans, purchase homes, and carry on a number of important business functions that were in the past denied them. Martha Garrison suggests that women need to be aggressive in seeking the right to credit in their own names, in order to overcome past and present barriers of discrimination and neglect.[8]

The Use of Credit

What should you buy on credit plans, charge accounts, and time-payment plans? Think of your family partnership as a business concern. What do you need most to make your business a success? Education, of course, is a basic

[8]See Martha L. Garrison, "Credit-Ability for Women," *The Family Coordinator*, 25, no. 3 (July 1976), 241–48.

requirement. If one or both partners need to finish school, a loan is a reasonable way to help give the family business a stable foundation. Do you need transportation to and from a particular job? Perhaps you can't support the family otherwise. In such a situation, it makes good sense to borrow money to buy a car. A few dollars a month invested in an automobile may pay big dividends in terms of a good on-time job record, flexibility in making business appointments, and ability to handle special assignments. In the same way, certain basic furniture items may be so necessary that they merit a credit purchase. Or rent may be substantially less for an unfurnished apartment than for a furnished apartment, in which case you would profit by buying your own furniture.

Once basic necessities for the family are purchased, the use of credit for other items should be scrutinized carefully. The typical department store, furniture store, or clothing store charges interest at the rate of about 1½ percent per month on the unpaid balance due. At first glance that seems low, but a second look reveals that it is an annual rate of 18 percent, which is considerably higher than the interest on a typical bank loan. We all know that most young Americans have not been raised to deny themselves something in order to gain it more cheaply, or to appreciate it more after a year or two of waiting. We want to enjoy things now and pay for them later. But we must weigh our need for a purchase against the higher cost of buying it on time. And finally, it is often far too easy to commit ourselves for more than we will be able to pay. What we are talking about, of course, is consumer economics. Every family needs to spend a certain share of its time and thought in looking over the pattern of its consumption. It is foolish to earn $12,000 or $17,000 a year and be continually in debt—especially when your next-door neighbors are earning less than $9,500 a year and seem to be in much better shape financially than you are.

The Cost of Credit

How much does it cost to use credit? Let us consider a young couple with a yearly take-home income of $12,000. Financial counselors would recommend a maximum limit of 20 percent of that amount for principal and interest on debts and charge accounts, other than mortgages, totaling $2,400. A figure of 10 percent or 15 percent would be much better (particularly if they were looking forward to raising a family). If the husband is twenty-four years old, it is entirely possible that the family might keep on paying off charge accounts and credit items for the next twenty years, while expenses for children, house, and entertainment keep rising. If they were fortunate enough to borrow from a credit union at 12 percent annual interest, about $2,200 of that $2,400 would be credited against the principal and $200 kept by the credit union as interest. (If they were paying at the department-store rate, however, $300 would be charged for interest and only $2,100 credited against the principal.) If they kept this out on a "revolving charge," they would keep buying new items as old items were paid off. Looking over the entire twenty years, then, they would be spending from $4,000 to $6,000 for interest on those accounts. If they had been able to resist the lure of the credit offered the first year, that $2,400 would have given them a nest egg to buy all their purchases for cash the next and subsequent years. They would be able to save the interest payments over the twenty years, and have interest earned on their savings as well.

All this is simply capitalism. A family partnership needs working capital in the same way that a business needs capital. If too much of a couple's money is committed, they will not have the flexibility to adjust to changing circumstances. The logical way to gain capital at minimum cost is to postpone a purchase today so that some money will be available to buy something at a bargain or to meet an unexpected emergency tomorrow. This was the secret of success for the early New Englanders, for the industrial giants of the nineteenth century, and for successful corporations. Of course, every couple will have their own idea of how much cash reserve is enough. But they must understand what they are getting themselves into when they buy on credit. If they do, they will be unlikely to regret their obligations after making them.

Where can you borrow money, if you must? Interest rates vary greatly. The cheapest way to borrow money is to use your own savings account or insurance policy (if it has cash value) as collateral. You may be able to borrow on them for from 6 to 6½ percent interest a year. Or you may belong to an employees' credit union, which will grant loans at 12 percent or less. A full-service bank will charge more—usually 12 to 18 percent. Stores themselves offer credit at the same rates (12 to 18 percent), depending on local and state regulations. The most expensive form of credit is offered by loan companies; their rates go to 36 percent or higher. Needless to say, the banks that offer loans at low interest rates can afford to be choosy; they lend only to customers with good credit ratings. The companies that lend money to bad credit risks charge higher rates in part because some of their customers default on payments. Thus the more conscientious you are about making your payments on time, the better chance you will have of obtaining subsequent loans at reasonable rates.

If you are fortunate enough to have had a good college course in consumer economics, you should have an understanding of the ins and outs of modern charge-account and credit living. But many people learn about money the hard way. There is no real substitute for talking to flesh-and-blood people about your money, their money, and what you want to buy (or shouldn't want to buy) on your income. Credit counseling, available through banks, credit unions, and consumer groups, should be utilized by a family that has difficulty in handling this aspect of the financial partnership.

Developing a Family Insurance Program

Every family should have an adequate insurance program as protection against unexpected crises. Accidents, illness, death, or property loss may come when the family is least able to bear an added financial cost. A well-planned insurance program can prevent financial disaster.

Life Insurance

In *Youth 1976—Finance-Related Attitudes,* insurance companies report that financial protection for dependents is the major reason given for purchasing life insurance.[9] A summary of the responses of those in four age brackets from fourteen to twenty-five years of age is given in Table 16–2. The survey showed a generally positive attitude toward insurance coverage, and an increase in the purchase of individual life insurance policies. In 1976, 24 percent of the young people surveyed had made such a purchase, as compared with 22 percent in 1974 and 21 percent in 1972.

Life insurance programs can be conveniently divided into four categories: protection of life, health, and property and protection against emergencies. The federal and state governments are moving into the insurance field more actively, and many employers, unions, and other associations also offer protection plans. But let us consider insurance primarily from the standpoint of the private citizen as purchaser.

Life insurance is a basic requirement for every family. Rates are lower for younger men and women, so it is wise to begin buying insurance at once. Protection is especially vital once children are born, because the wife would have an extremely difficult time raising the family if the husband died without leaving adequate insurance. The financial consequences of a death are staggering. The family's debts must be paid. There may be medical bills in connection with an accident or illness. There are funeral costs and the possible expense of moving to different living quarters. Above all, there are the problems created by the loss of the husband's income. Unfortunately, many young families today are very poorly covered.

There are many different kinds of policies with varying advantages for

[9]American Council of Life Insurance, *Youth 1976—Finance-Related Attitudes* (New York: American Council of Life Insurance, 1976).

Table 16–2 Major Reason for Buying Life Insurance

New Question	*Total*	*14-16*	*Age 17-18 (in percent)*	*19-21*	*22-25*
Provide financial protection for my dependents	48	38	49	54	51
Give my family a feeling of security	16	20	18	13	13
Provide money in case of emergency	12	18	13	11	8
Give me a feeling of security	11	16	12	10	8
Cover my burial expense	7	4	5	7	10
As a kind of forced saving	4	1	1	4	8
Because I'm expected to	2	2	2	1	1

SOURCE: American Council of Life Insurance, *Youth 1976—Finance-Related Attitudes* (New York: American Council of Life Insurance, 1976), p. 25.

the younger husband and father, the father of a large family, or the man nearing retirement. One can purchase term insurance, straight life insurance, limited-payment insurance, and endowment insurance. The decision should be made with competent insurance counsel. It is generally agreed that insurance for the wife must also be included, particularly if she is working and her income is a regular part of the family budget. (In the past, many women were covered only for the cost of a funeral. But today homemakers' insurance, which provides a husband money to hire a mother substitute for his children in the event of his wife's death, is becoming popular.) Generally speaking, insurance for children is not needed for protection but rather as a means of saving for future education, travel, or other special requirements.

Term insurance provides the maximum protection for the minimum cost. It is written for a definite period, usually five or ten years, and then it expires. For example, at age thirty-five, a man would pay about $65 a year for a five-year term policy for $10,000. At each renewal date, the cost would be higher. This would be *level term insurance,* with the coverage remaining the same during the life of the policy. With *decreasing term insurance,* which you might obtain for a house mortgage or automobile loan, the amount decreases yearly as your loan obligation decreases.[10] The disadvantages of term insurance are several. You do not build up any equity* in the policy and thus cannot use it as collateral for a loan. The rates keep going up with each renewal, and if medical problems arise between policies, you may be ineligible for further insurance. For these reasons term insurance should not be your only life insurance; but it is an excellent supplement to other plans.

Straight life insurance is designed to provide the policyholder with permanent protection. Its cost at age twenty-five would be approximately $13 per thousand per year, a cost that is fixed for life. The policy has loan and cash-surrender value. This is in effect a forced savings plan in which the individual pays more than is needed for protection at first in order to keep the premium low in later years.

Some policies combine features of both term and straight life insurance by offering straight life insurance protection at a lower cost at the beginning (perhaps at age twenty-five or thirty) and then automatically increasing the premiums after five or ten years when a person's income would normally be higher.

The *limited-payment policy* is also a variation of straight life insurance, combining lifetime protection with short-term payment. A ten- or fifteen-year payment policy, for instance, would be wise for a professional athlete, who expects a high income for a short period. It is in effect forced savings for him—building an insurance reserve in the years when he can best afford it.

The *endowment policy* is similar to the limited-payment policy, but it emphasizes the company's payment of the face amount, if desired, at a certain age rather than on the policyholder's death. A $2,000 endowment policy, to mature when a child is twenty, is often recommended to parents who wish to provide money for a child's education. (However, it should be pointed out that the insurance company profits from providing a forced savings service. A couple with willpower can save $2,000 without the aid of an insurance company, at no cost to themselves.) The face amount is also payable if the child dies before the policy matures.

There are many other kinds of life-insurance protection. Insurance companies are offering a number of new options and plans to meet family needs more effectively. In addition, many business and employee groups offer plans that afford economical group rates. Every young couple should make sure that they have adequate insurance. It is true, however, that one can become "insurance-poor." A balance must be struck between the ideal coverage for every eventuality and the amount of money the family can realistically budget for insurance coverage.

[10]See Sylvia Porter, *Sylvia Porter's Money Book* (Garden City, N.Y.: Doubleday, 1975), pp. 702–03.
*The cash value of the policy if you choose to relinquish it before maturity.

Health Insurance

Health insurance is becoming more popular (and more necessary) in our country, and the combination of business, union, private, and government plans has made possible protection for every family above the lowest wage bracket. In fact, it seems that the company health plans and government health plans will gradually make it more and more difficult for the individual to "self-insure" himself in this area. In the insurance survey noted in Table 16–3 more than two-thirds of the youth surveyed expect the employer or the government to be responsible for health insurance.

One problem with most health insurance plans is that they do not cover the entire cost of hospital care or physicians' fees. In most cases, fixed amounts are set for hospital costs, office visits, and surgery. The actual billing to the patient may be higher than the amount allowed by the insurance. Another problem is that certain medical services, such as maternity, dental, optometric, and psychiatric care, are excluded from some policies. And unfortunately, some hospitals are not approved for particular insurance plans. Finally, inflation has sent medical costs skyrocketing.

The increasing popularity of health coverage despite these problems is a response to the rising cost of medical services and to the fact that both employer and employee benefit when the latter and his family are able to afford and obtain needed medical treatment. The crushing economic burden that can occur if health insurance is lacking can cause severe problems.

Property Insurance

Property insurance is important because every family has certain properties it cannot afford to replace. The theft of an automobile or its loss in an accident would involve a heavy replacement cost for the average family; automobile insurance is therefore a must. So also is fire and comprehensive coverage for the family dwelling, furniture, and personal belongings. Expensive tools needed at work or valuable equipment used in business needs to be covered by the proper insurance. Depending on the number of items a family owns and the risk involved in protecting them, the cost of property insurance may be substantial. But to omit such protection would be extremely unwise.

Other Insurance

Finally, every family needs protection against emergencies. This includes liability insurance for the automobile and home as well as accident insurance, travel insurance, income-guarantee plans, and so on. Once more, the family must strike a balance between the dream of complete protection

Table 16–3 Youth Survey of Preferred Health Insurance Source

Who should be responsible for providing most of a person's health insurance needs?	*1974*	*1976*
	(in percent)	
The employer, as part of a person's overall benefits package	44	43
The person himself, through private purchases	30	28
The government, through programs funded by taxes, like Social Security	25	28

SOURCE: American Council of Life Insurance, *Youth 1976—Finance-Related Attitudes* (New York: American Council of Life Insurance, 1976), p. 41.

(which is almost impossible in our complex society) and the nightmare of inadequate protection. A practical compromise is to pay premiums for the basic emergencies—those that occur to a great many people and that may entail legal responsibilities. Automobile liability insurance, for example, is a high-priority coverage that has been recognized by the passage of certain state laws requiring insurance or evidence of financial responsibility on the part of automobile owners. Other coverages will depend on a family's income and circumstances.

Housing

The last fifteen years have seen dramatic shifts in American housing patterns. A large number of apartments have been built, including an increasing number of condominiums, particularly in Florida and California. Mobile homes are becoming more popular, especially among young couples and retired couples. Other trends include the purchase of second homes, or motor homes, for recreation and retirement. Here again, changes in the life-style of the younger generation are having an economic impact on industry.

For most newlyweds today, housing means a suitable furnished or unfurnished apartment conveniently located near their place of employment. Some communities also have houses for rent at moderate prices. And a few couples will feel well enough established to purchase a new home at once; the availability of houses and adequate financing will help to determine whether that is a valid option for them. A rough guide to follow is that twenty to thirty percent of the family's take-home income should be spent on housing. (If both husband and wife are working, they may not want to spend the maximum thirty percent.) In a very few cases, the couple will live with one of the parental families (an arrangement that was more common in previous generations). But few marriage counselors would advise living with a parental family for newlyweds, except in unusual circumstances.

The choice of a first apartment or a rented home is very important. It is often indicative of whether the couple will be able to face financial problems together and plan jointly for their common good. The choice should be a mutual one, and the couple should enjoy searching for and finding the right place. This is good preparation for family financial teamwork. The couple will also gain a great deal of experience in their first home or apartment; they will get some idea of the cost of heat, light, gas, water, and other basic housing expenses. They will thus have a background of experience to aid them in their decision to purchase a house.[11]

The question of home ownership has become a very difficult one because of rising costs and inflation. In some desirable locations, houses have doubled or tripled in value in less than six years. In new suburban areas, it is often impossible for a family to purchase a suitable home anywhere near the husband's or wife's employment. When they purchase less expensive hous-

[11]See Donaldson and Pfahl, chap. 10.

ing at a distance, they must commute to work and thus consume precious energy at considerable cost. In spite of this, the proportion of American families who own their own homes has been rising steadily. The purchase of a home with a mortgage loan offers great long-term advantages. Though the interest charges on a mortgage amount to quite a lot of money, they do allow a couple to acquire over a period of time a house that is a financial asset as well as a necessary shelter for the family. Thus the couple who make payments on a mortgage are in effect making payments to themselves rather than to a landlord; after twenty years or so they will have a very valuable possession that will stand them in good stead financially when they retire. (The couple who rent a home or an apartment, however, have nothing to show for their rent payments; their home is still the property of the landlord when they move out, no matter how many years they have been paying rent.) But the problem of obtaining sufficient funds to purchase a home may seem so difficult that newlyweds will accept a high interest rate, overlooking the actual cost of financing the house for the total mortgage period of from twenty to thirty years. The total payment for the house thus may be more than twice the purchase price. And the interest rate is doubly important, because it makes up the major part of the monthly payment for the house in the first five years of the contract. The problem of selling the house quickly if a move becomes necessary should also be taken into consideration. The decision to buy a house must be very carefully made, then. There is no single rule to determine whether a couple should purchase a home or continue renting; the final decision can be made only by the couple themselves.

If a couple decide to purchase housing, a choice must be made between a new house or an old one, a condominium, a semidetached (or duplex), or other alternatives. Buying a single-family home is still the most desired goal for most families.

The purchase of a home in a tract development offers the advantage of many modern conveniences plus savings made possible by mass production in the building process. Social life may be built easily around neighborhood groups. On the other hand, older houses are usually bigger and better built, and their neighborhoods are usually more varied in character.

Related to the age of the house is the cost of maintaining and operating it. Is the house well-insulated, so that heating and cooling costs will be reasonable? Is the heating unit well-designed and economical? Is the electrical system adequate and properly installed? Is the plumbing good? Are the appliances in good condition? Is the house structurally sound and able to withstand normal wear and tear from rain, windstorms, or snow? Or will home maintenance and repair mean a substantial yearly cost to the family?

Finally, the resale value of the house must always be considered. Most young families usually move from their first house after the children arrive and require extra rooms and a play area. A change in the neighborhood or

in general economic conditions may make this a hard house to sell. Professional advice is worthwhile before the purchase.

The Family as Consumers

Another important element in family finances is the purchase of consumer goods. We have discussed the cost of housing and the purchase of goods on credit. Since so much money is expended for the goods we consume from day to day and month to month, it is vital to know where the money is going and how the family can get its money's worth. Let us look briefly at several important guidelines to successful use of this important segment of the family budget.

Weekly expenditures form a major part of the family budget. Most families spend a great deal of money in cash for food, incidentals, recreation, transportation, children's allowances, and entertaining. Since these expenses recur week after week, they may be thought of as fixed. In actuality, there is usually a great deal of room for change in most weekly family spending. Food costs can go down as much as 15 or 20 percent very easily if the family is willing to eat inexpensive meat dishes instead of expensive steaks and chops and if some real thought is given to the purchase of economy sizes (when they *are* economical) and seasonal produce items. Pocket spending money is another variable item. One man may easily spend twelve to fifteen dollars a week for cigarettes, snacks, tips, and so on, while another may spend only five dollars a week. The weekly expenditure for all such items should be considered carefully if family savings are really desired.

Careful control of weekly expenditures is becoming more and more important due to inflation. Government attempts to control inflation through wage and price controls have proved ineffective. This makes it doubly important for each family to get maximum value for their consumer dollar. One cannot usually find a bargain in the price of water or electricity; but many other items that we consume day by day do vary widely in price. And we can make sure that we do not waste such vital natural resources as water, coal, oil, and other energy sources.

Quality is a key factor in consumer economics, particularly in the purchase of such items as clothes, furniture, automobiles, and small appliances. One suit may wear well for only two or three years because of poor materials and inferior workmanship, while another that is perhaps slightly higher in price is better made and will wear twice as long. One electrical appliance barely lasts through the ninety-day guarantee period, while a second will give good service for five or ten years. Although planned obsolescence seems to be an accepted part of our economy today, there are still many durable consumer goods on the market. The purchaser will do well to seek maximum value for the purchase price whenever possible.

Another way to gain the most from regular purchases of consumer goods

is to keep accurate records. When does the guarantee on the vacuum cleaner you purchased last year expire? How much did you spend on food last year compared with the year before the baby was born? How soon should you have the brakes and wheel alignment checked on the four-year-old car you bought last Thanksgiving? You must keep accurate records of how you spend your money and what you can expect to receive for your purchases, especially of appliances, furniture, and durable goods.

Still another way to get the most from your dollar may be described as "playing the consumer game." The perceptive consumer is sensitive to the appeals of manufacturers and sellers and takes advantage of new merchandising methods, advertising offers, and distribution methods, such as discount stores and wholesale outlets. He also does not take everything he reads in an advertisement at face value; he does comparison shopping to make sure the bargain he read about is really a bargain. And there are local and national consumer organizations and consumer journals such as *Consumer Reports*[12] and the *Consumers' Research Bulletin*.[13] The most reliable way to test the real value and quality of a product to be purchased is to check the ratings in these reputable consumers' guides. The difference in ratings for two similar items selling for the same price in the same store may surprise you.

You can also save money by being aware of the seasonal needs of the merchandiser. For example, consider the purchase of a new refrigerator. The one you would like to buy is priced at $350, which is more than you have planned to spend. Two weeks later, however, the new year's models will come out, and the old model will be reduced to $300. The old model will have the same motor as the new model, and most other mechanical features will be the same. If you are willing to sacrifice the slight change in style and perhaps a minor new convenience, you will save the family $50. Such wise shopping can save you hundreds of dollars during the course of a year.

Savings Programs and Retirement Plans

It is not easy for a young couple to start a family savings program. The early years of marriage are years of heavy responsibilities and expenditures. Yet if a couple cannot establish the habit of saving money in the beginning of marriage, they may make little progress until the children are grown. A way must be found to set aside some portion of the family income for the future so that the couple can have a secure retirement.[14]

In the early years of marriage, couples should build up their savings account so that it is adequate to meet unforeseen emergencies, such as a se-

[12]*Consumer Reports,* Consumers Union, Mount Vernon, N.Y.
[13]*Consumers' Research Bulletin,* Washington, N.J.
[14]See Leonard M. Groupe, *Going Broke and How to Avoid It* (New York: Thomas Y. Crowell, 1972).

rious accident, hospitalization, or the loss of a job. A savings account equal to about three months of the husband's income is the amount usually suggested as a minimum; that amount would make it possible for the family to meet the immediate needs of a crisis without going deeply into debt. Life insurance policies will also build up a certain cash value, which can be borrowed against at a low rate in time of emergency. And the equity, or payments against the principal, built up in a home is another asset that might be called on in time of emergency.

When initial family needs have been met and extra funds are available for investment, most families above the median income level will make some investment in stocks or bonds—whether government bonds, mutual funds, or some other conservative investment. The goal is to have some protection against inflation. The cost of living is almost bound to go up; invested funds rise in value at a rate that should equal or better the cost of living. A home is a similar protection against inflation. Some couples, especially those who are knowledgeable about business, may wish to invest in more speculative stocks, such as growth funds. Expert counsel is needed for that kind of investment. And couples who work for stable companies that offer good employee stock option plans may want to take advantage of the opportunity to buy stocks cheaply.

The most difficult investment to make is an investment in which the couple themselves are the sole determiners of the risk involved. Such investments include the purchase of land for later resale, the purchase of apartments or houses for rental, and investment in a particular business, project, or company. Couples are really entering into a business partnership, taking their own savings and launching out into the business world. If the couple work well together and have been successful in their earlier financial planning, they will be prepared for such an endeavor. If they have not functioned smoothly in earlier financial dealings, however, it will probably be difficult for them to make joint decisions about speculative investments.

The family's savings and investment program, together with Social Security and employee retirement plans, need to be integrated into a comprehensive retirement program. In such a program, the couple's monthly income for medical bills, housing, and emergencies will be assured them in their retirement years. Such careful planning makes possible the active retirement that is so widely sought by today's senior citizens.

Finally, couples should not overlook the need to make a will. This is an extremely important duty that many married couples neglect. Just as life insurance is needed to protect spouse and children in case of death and resulting loss of income, a will is needed to protect the family from loss of their life savings. Many states have laws that provide for the disposition of property by the state if the head of a family dies without leaving a will. Such state disposition of family property usually results in the family savings being eaten up by lawyers' fees. Thus a man who neglects to provide a will is putting his family in real jeopardy. All of us will agree that it is unpleasant to contemplate one's own death; but maturity is to a large degree the ability to face the unpleasant tasks in life when necessary. The sooner the need to make a will is faced, the sooner a family's future will be provided for.

The success of the family financial partnership is a key ingredient in a harmonious marriage and family life. Every family unit must devote a reasonable amount of time to studying and evaluating its use of money and financial resources. By paying special attention to what is being done today, and by planning for the future, financial partnership can provide real assets for the entire family.

SUMMARY

The family may be considered as a financial partnership. The early years of marriage are the natural time for husband and wife to build a sound financial basis for family life. Achieving such a goal calls for a realistic recognition of the varying needs of the family during the different stages in the family life cycle. The family's finances are also closely related to their socioeconomic status in the community.

A couple should consider what their financial experiences in their parental families have been, for past experience will have a strong influence on their financial expectations in marriage. A couple should also recognize that one's financial goals and methods are closely related to one's value structure. We earn and spend money for the things we think are important.

Financial planning must also take into account the job satisfaction of both husband and wife. Some of the most important rewards of working are not monetary, but intangible. Therefore a job should never be taken for financial reasons alone. Conversely, a job that is taken for the personal satisfaction it brings should afford sufficient financial reward.

Couples should select a plan for money management early in marriage. One partner may serve as family treasurer and take care of all bills; or the couple may divide their income and responsibilities and maintain a joint checking account. Or they may work together on a shared family budget.

Credit and charge accounts must be used wisely. Most young couples incur some installment debt; the problem is to develop sound habits and a workable plan to govern credit purchases. Otherwise, credit can eat up a disproportionate share of the family income with interest payments and installment costs.

Insurance is a necessity for the modern family. Protection of life, health, and property and protection against emergencies are vital. Without adequate insurance, death, illness, or some other crisis may leave the family financially crippled. Competent professional counsel is the best way to build an insurance program to meet family needs.

Another important financial consideration is housing. Should a couple rent an apartment or buy a home? Since young couples move frequently, the decision on what housing is best is often perplexing. Most young couples will choose to rent when they are first married; but purchase of permanent housing is often a sound long-range investment. If a purchase is to be made, a couple must consider size, age, and kind of house; financing; cost of maintenance; and potential resale value.

The family is a group of consumers. As such they should try to spend their money wisely. Careful examination of weekly expenditures, shopping for quality as well as price, keeping accurate records, and taking advantage of changing marketing conditions are all good means of saving money.

Finally, some means of accumulating savings should be found. Savings accounts, investment programs, and speculative business ventures are all worth considering. The way a couple saves for the future will be a key factor in determining the kind of retirement they will have.

SUGGESTED READINGS

Cohen, Jerome B., and Arthur W. Hanson. *Personal Finance: Principles and Case Problems,* 4th ed. Homewood, Ill.: Irwin, 1972. Basic personal finance text with family budgeting suggestions.

Consumer Reports. Mt. Vernon, N.Y.: Consumers Union. Monthly magazine with consumer evaluations and recommendations.

Donaldson, Elvin F., and John K. Pfahl. *Personal Finance,* 5th ed. New York: Ronald Press, 1971. Sound analysis of personal and family financial programs.

Koprowski, Eugene. "Business Technology and the American Family: An Impressionistic Analysis." *The Family Coordinator,* 22, no. 2 (April 1973), 229–34. Raises significant questions about the relation of American business to the family structure.

Markstein, David L. *Manage Your Money and Live Better.* New York: McGraw-Hill, 1971. Practical advice for family financial management.

Porter, Sylvia. *Sylvia Porter's Money Book.* Garden City, N.Y.: Doubleday, 1975. Popular columnist gives a broad range of suggestions for family spending and budgeting.

Ridley, Carl A. "Exploring the Impact of Work Satisfaction and Involvement on Marital Interaction When Both Partners Are Employed," *Journal of Marriage and the Family,* 35, no. 2 (May 1973), 229–37. Valuable study relating job and income to marital satisfaction.

Troelstrup, Arch W. *The Consumer in American Society: Personal and Family Finance,* 4th ed. New York: McGraw-Hill, 1970. Solid approach to building sound family financial management.

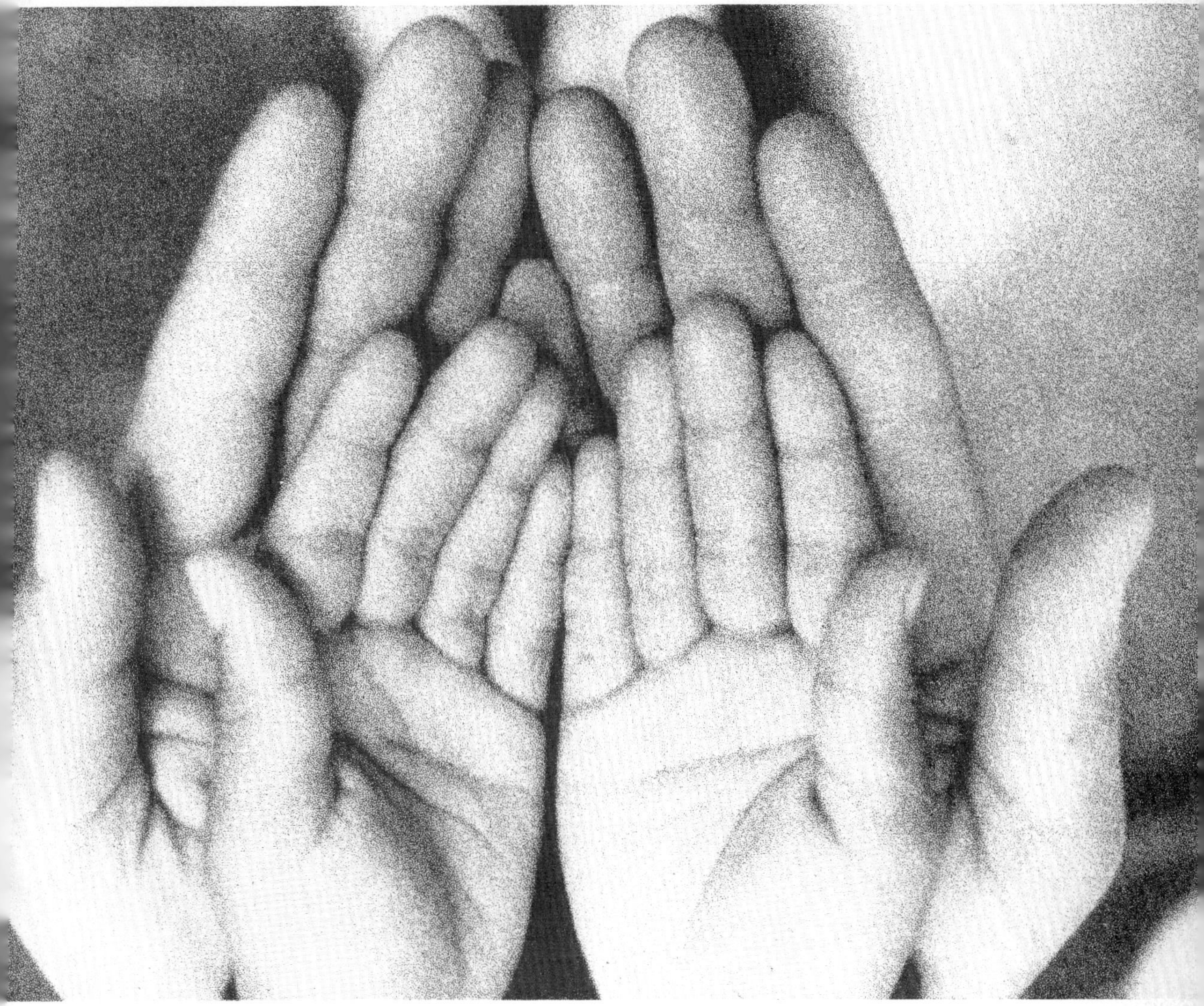

Part V
The Developing Family

17 Parenthood: The First Child

- What is the motivation for parenthood?
- What factors most influence a couple for or against having children?
- What effect will the increasing number of childless couples have on American society?
- Explain the genetic transmission of characteristics from parents to child.
- What are the basic processes in reproduction?
- What are common difficulties that hinder conception, and how can they be overcome?
- What is the normal course of pregnancy?
- What are the three phases of childbirth?
- What is natural childbirth?
- How can a couple build a marriage partnership that will provide a healthy environment for children?

The Decision Not to Have Children

The 1970s have produced a new type of couple in our society—those who are childless by choice and are frankly happy with their choice. Margaret Movius has suggested that voluntary childlessness is the ultimate liberation for women. As long as women are tied to the responsibilities of homemaking and child care, they cannot hope to be completely fulfilled in other ways. Society puts pressure on women to bear children, and in so doing prevents them from achieving outside the home.

> Perhaps the most frequently mentioned reason for remaining childless is the feeling of freedom it affords. . . . This freedom may be in the form of allowing the opportunity for trying new experiences, but is more commonly associated with being able to travel. Although child-free couples experience many of the same limitations as those of parents . . . they have a significantly smaller number of limitations and complications. Without the conventions imposed by having children, child-free couples have more latitude with respect to behavior, language, and hours. Whether the child-free take advantage of their greater freedom is relatively unimportant. More than the reality, childless couples place value on the feeling and potential of freedom.[1]

[1]Margaret Movius, "Voluntary Childlessness—The Ultimate Liberation," *The Family Coordinator*, 26, no. 1 (Jan. 1976), 59.

There are a number of ways to study childless couples. We need to consider the voluntary and involuntary couples in this category. We can also make a distinction between those women who have never been pregnant and those who have begun a pregnancy but terminated it before the birth of the child. S. L. N. Rao of Brown University has made an interesting study of childless women in three age groups, those under 30, those 30 to 49, and those 50 and over. The results of Rao's study are shown in Table 17–1. The data show that the impact of the Depression was felt in the older group of women, where 19 percent remained childless. In the 30 to 49 group, who had their children in the 1950s and 1960s, only 7.6 percent remained childless. The youngest women (under 30) are still bearing children, and the final percent remaining childless is not yet known. The division between those childless by choice and those childless because of physiological reasons is also not certain.

Table 17–1 Percent Childless and Percent Never Pregnant by Age, Ever-Married Females, Rhode Island: 1967–1969

Age Group	*Number of Women*	*Percent Childless*	*Percent Never Pregnant*
15-19	25	28.0	17.4
20-24	152	32.9	23.7
25-29	170	15.3	10.1
Under 30	*347*	*23.7*	*15.3*
30-34	155	7.7	5.8
35-39	156	5.8	4.6
40-44	194	7.7	6.6
45-49	140	9.3	8.3
30-49	*645*	*7.6*	*6.0*
50-54	143	17.5	12.4
55-59	153	18.3	16.4
60 and Over	465	19.6	19.0
50 and Over	*761*	*19.0*	*16.1*
All Ages	1753	15.7	11.9

SOURCE: S. L. N. Rao, "A Comparative Study of Childlessness and Never-Pregnant Status," *Journal of Marriage and the Family*, 36, no. 1 (Feb. 1974), 151. Copyrighted 1974 by the National Council on Family Relations. Reprinted by permission.

What will be the result of this trend toward childlessness? Linda Wolfe suggests that a "baby boom" is a possibility, as the birth rate continues to fall to an as yet undetermined low. When the birth rate is at its lowest, the demand for babies will be so great that the birth rate will rise in response. This is a reflection of economic supply and demand and the "economics of security" that affects those in small birth cohorts. Here is how it is explained by Richard Easterlin:

> It isn't the economics of one's maturity that determines whether or not one will have a large or a small family, but the way in which the economics of one's maturity differs from one's childhood expectations. Depression children expected the worst, but when they grew up they discovered they were better off than they had expected to be and thus they had lots of babies. Their children grew up in affluent times and expected the best—yet when so many of them descended on the work world, they did poorly. As a result, they had few babies. Now their children, expecting hard times, are about to look for work—and are about to discover that, by virtue of their small numbers, things aren't so bad after all.[2]

The trend toward childlessness makes us ask: How important are children? Are they the basic foundation for happiness in the marriage? Or is the choice to remain childless a realistic opiton that means greater opportunities and a satisfying lifestyle for more and more couples in the future?

The Decision to Have Children

Why should a married couple decide to have children? Why should they move from the less restrictive roles they enjoy as husband and wife and assume the responsibilities and limitations of parenthood? What does it mean to choose to have a child, and to begin the creation of a new generation and a new structure for the family unit?

Although family size has been declining, there are still powerful influences that encourage couples to have children. A recent census report predicts only 4 to 6 or 7 percent of the women married in the 1960s and 1970s will remain childless.[3] Bernard Berelson lists six personal reasons that help to explain why couples want children. Here is his list in abbreviated form:

[2]Quoted by Linda Wolfe in "The Coming Baby Boom," *New York Magazine*, Jan. 10, 1977.

[3]Paul C. Glick and Arthur J. Norton, "Marrying, Divorcing, and Living Together in the U.S. Today," *Population Bulletin*, 32, no. 5 (1977), 20.

1. *Personal power.* Having children sometimes gives one parent power over the other. More than that, it gives the parents power over the child(ren) . . .

2. *Personal competence.* Becoming a parent demonstrates competence in an essential human role . . .

3. *Personal status.* Everywhere parenthood confers status. It is an accomplishment open to all, or virtually all, and realized by the overwhelming majority of adult humankind . . .

4. *Personal extension.* Beyond the family line, wanting children is a way to reach for personal immortality—for most people, the only way available . . .

5. *Personal experience.* Among all the activities of life, parenthood is a unique experience. It is a part of life, of personal growth, that simply cannot be experienced in any other way . . .

6. *Personal pleasure.* Last, but one hopes not least, in the list of reasons for wanting children is the altruistic pleasure of having them, caring for them, watching them grow, shaping them, being with them, enjoying them . . . [4]

[4]Bernard Berelson, "The Value of Children, A Taxonomical Essay," in J. Gipson Wells, ed., *Current Issues in Marriage and the Family* (New York: Macmillan, 1975), pp. 172–73.

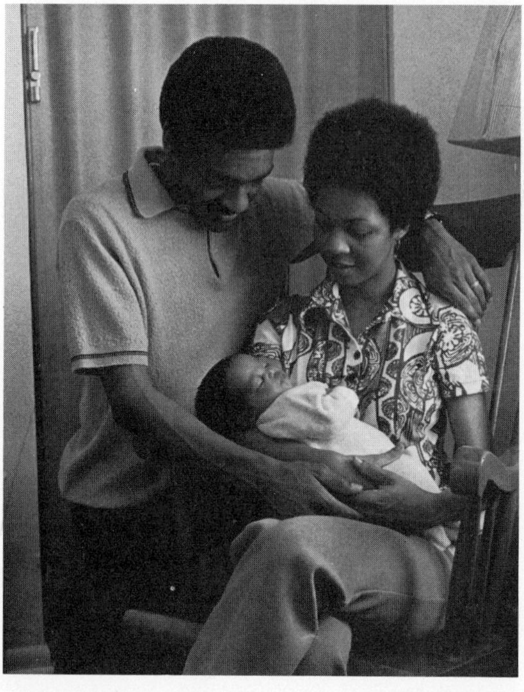

To become a parent is a unique experience. For a young marrie
the birth of the first child is a high point in marriage. It expresses i
new life the strength and vitality of the invisible bond of love betw
band and wife. For the woman, the coming of a child is a confirm
her womanhood, a fulfillment of the unique role she alone can perfo
the man, a child is a confirmation of his manhood. Together, the cou
the nursery, attend classes for expectant parents, buy clothes, and c
name. The birth of a new child symbolizes the high hopes and expec
the family has for the future.

This is not to say that the high expectations of new parents are always realized. E. E. LeMasters, long a perceptive critic of American family life, has noted some negative consequences that recent social changes have had on the parenting role. It is not easy to be a parent in our society. The role is not clearly defined, and everyone is expected to be a success. People get little preparation for their work as parents, and the job is often over-romanticized. Parents are held responsible for their children, but the parental role has lost its place of authority. Doctors, teachers, and family professionals tell the parents what to do, and then blame them if it doesn't work. Other roles have assumed importance, particularly the occupational roles of women. Yet, there is no way out of the parental role. Today's parents don't have to equal the job their parents did; they have to surpass it.[5]

LeMasters seems overly pessimistic. Granted, not every child grows up to meet all the expectations of society. Yet parenthood is chosen by most couples, and today college-educated men and women in particular seem to be planning the birth of their children with great care. Such planning and concern seems to evidence favorable experiences during their childhood and an optimistic view of their future as parents.

Alice S. Rossi has suggested that we need to examine the transition to parenthood more closely. She thinks that some of the adjustment problems faced by new mothers can be eased with increased equality between marriage partners: Women will sustain less of a break in their careers and receive more help from their husbands. Rossi sees four reasons for difficulty in adjustment to parenthood:

1. Lack of preparation for parenthood. Few people are formally prepared for parenthood. Our society stresses cognitive skills and neglects formal training in everyday living. The home is supposed to provide such preparation, but if it fails, the schools offer no help.
2. Limited learning during pregnancy. A few visits to the doctor by the wife and informal discussions with family members or other people

[5]E. E. LeMasters, *Parents in Modern America,* 3rd ed. (Homewood, Ill.: Dorsey Press, 1977), pp. 5–13.

generally are all the guidance expectant couples get. No wonder they often see parenthood as a crisis.

3. Abruptness of transition. When the baby comes home from the hospital, there is no escape. Newborn babies need to be fed in the middle of the night, regardless of the parents' need for rest. Particularly for a young and dependent mother, the suddenness of the total responsibility of motherhood can be very difficult to cope with.

4. Lack of guidelines for successful parenthood. What should one's child become? Is middle-class conformity the answer? Rossi points out that in our society not all successful adults come from loving and supportive "developmental" families. Authority as well as support may be most strongly related to a child's achievement.[6]

The need for careful preparation for parenthood seems obvious. Let us study the development of the family, then, beginning with the process of conception, the course of pregnancy, and the actual birth of the child.

Heredity

Conception takes place when the female ovum is fertilized by the male sperm. The entire potential of the future individual is contained within those two tiny cells; their hereditary components determine the physical and mental characteristics of the developing child.

Each sex cell contains *chromosomes,* which are composed of a number of genetic units called *genes;* the genes determine the hereditary traits that are passed on to the child. The normal human cell has 23 pairs of chromosomes. The sex cells (ova and sperm), however, divide during their development, so that each mature sex cell has only one of each pair of chromosomes, or 23 *single* chromosomes. When a sperm and an ovum unite during fertilization, therefore, the new cell (the *zygote*) receives the full complement of 23 pairs of chromosomes—the normal makeup of a human cell. The new child receives half its chromosomes (and therefore half its genes) from the father and half from the mother.

Genes, which determine the physical characteristics of the new human being, may be either dominant or recessive. For example, let us call the gene that determines Caucasian hair color *A*. We will refer to the dominant gene (for brown hair) as *A* and to the recessive gene (for blond hair) as *a*. If a father carries two dominant genes, *AA*, and a mother two recessive genes, *aa*, then all their children will inherit an *Aa* genetic combination (see Figure 17–1). Because the *A* gene is dominant, their children will all have brown

[6]Alice S. Rossi, "Transition to Parenthood," *Journal of Marriage and the Family,* 30, no. 1 (Feb. 1968), 35–36.

hair, but they may pass on to their children the recessive *a* gene inherited from their mother.

Now suppose the parents each have one dominant gene and one recessive gene for hair color—that is, each has the *Aa* combination. Although each parent would have brown hair, each would be carrying a gene for blond hair. If one of their children inherits a recessive gene from each of his parents—the *aa* combination—he will have blond hair. Statistically, the chance of this happening is one in four. If the child inherits a dominant gene from each of his parents (also one chance in four), he will, of course, have brown hair. And if he inherits a dominant gene from one and a recessive gene from the other, he will, like his parents, have brown hair (and the potentiality for producing blond children). Figure 17–1 illustrates the possible genetic combinations when both parents carry one dominant and one recessive gene.

Figure 17–1 Genetic Transmission Ratios

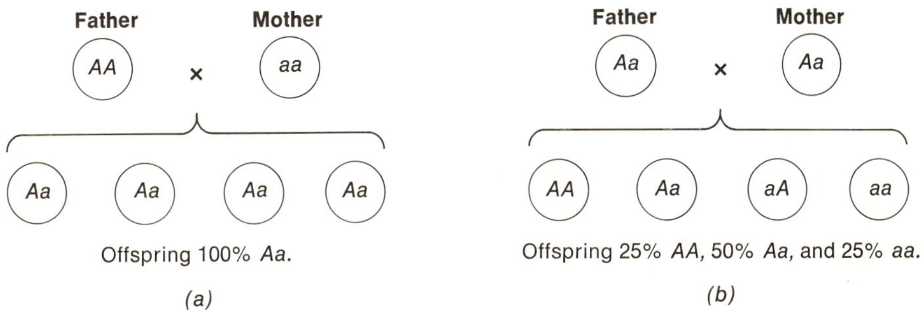

A—dominant gene, brown hair
a—recessive gene, blond hair

This description of the determination of hair color is a simplification of the real process. Actually, more than one gene is involved in the determining of hair color, which is closely related to skin color. But the example does give some idea of how human traits are passed on from generation to generation.

A child's sex is determined by special sex chromosomes. The sex chromosomes differ in male and female, both in size and composition. The female has two *X* (female) chromosomes *(XX)*; when the sex cell divides into two mature ova, one *X* chromosome goes to each ova. The male has one *X* and one *Y* chromosome (one female and one male); 50 percent of the mature sperm will thus carry an *X* chromosome and 50 percent a *Y*. When a sperm carrying a *Y* chromosome unites with an ovum, the child will be a male. Thus the chances of a child's being male or female are statistically equal. (In fact, however, more males are born than females. Chemical conditions in a woman's vagina may favor the *Y* sperm.)

Again, this description of the genetic process has been simplified. Couples should be aware that their baby may not receive a normal *XX* or *XY* chromosome combination, and thus that their child may have sex abnormalities. In such a case, the child's sex may be misclassified at birth. Children who receive abnormal sex chromosome combinations at birth may account for a substantial number of people who desire to change their sex later in life.

Recent research has given us vital information about the DNA molecule, which is the principal component of genes. The day when it will be possible to alter defective genes and thus minimize the risk of birth defects may not be too far off.

The Human Reproductive System

The Male System

The male reproductive cells, or sperm, are formed in the *testicles,* two oval organs contained in the *scrotum* (see Figure 17–2). Sperm are produced throughout most of the lifetime of the male, from puberty into old age; the testes produce billions of them each year. Certain biological features of the testes, including a lower-than-normal body temperature, make possible the formation and storage of the sperm, which cannot live long at the normal human body temperature. During sexual excitement the sperm produced in the testicles pass into the *epididymis* and then into the *vas deferens* and then, during ejaculation, into the *urethra.* In the urethra they are mixed with seminal fluid secreted by the *seminal vesicles, the bulbourethral glands,* and the *prostate gland;* and the semen is then ejaculated from the penis.

The sperm become active at the time of ejaculation, although exactly how they do so is not known. Their life span is short; they probably remain active in the female genital tract for only a day or two (some investigators believe they may remain active as long as six days, however). The large number of sperm discharged into the vagina move in many directions. Some move up into the uterus and the Fallopian tubes, where, if an ovum is present, fertilization may occur. It is theorized that electrical or chemical attraction may move the sperm toward the ovum.

The Female System

The female reproductive system is more complex than the male's. The major reproductive organs are internal (see Figure 17–3) and serve to carry on the process of reproduction after the fertilization of an ovum. The female reproductive cells are produced in the *ovaries,* two small organs an inch or two in length located on either side of the *uterus.* Apparently the ova exist in the female from the time of her birth, the vast majority of them being immature and unusable at that time. During her reproductive years, from puberty to the time of menopause, a woman ovulates almost five hundred times. About once a month an ovary releases an ovum into one of the *Fallopian tubes,* through which it passes into the uterus. During the development of the ovum, the ovary secretes the hormone *estrogen,* which causes certain changes in the lining of the uterus. Then, after ovulation, the ovary releases the hormone *progesterone,* which causes further changes in the uterus in preparation for the reception of the zygote (the fertilized ovum) if conception should take place. The ovum moves slowly down through the Fallopian tube toward the uterus; the passage takes about a week.

There is a good possibility of a sperm uniting with the ovum if the sperm enter or are in the Fallopian tubes when the ovum is being discharged. It is believed that the ovum can be fertilized only during the period of a day after ovulation—it must unite with a live sperm during that period if conception is to take place. Once conception has occurred, other sperm seeking to enter the ovum (now a zygote) are rejected.

If the ovum fails to unite with a sperm, it dies and is eliminated from the body during menstruation. Menstruation takes place when the woman does not conceive and the reproductive cycle is therefore not completed. The uterus has been prepared for the implantation of the fertilized egg, but when fertilization is not accomplished, the material that has been accumulated in the lining of the uterus to support the zygote must be discharged. This discharge, which lasts about five days, occurs fairly regularly, once every twenty-eight days on the average, although menstrual periods may vary from twenty to as many as forty or fifty days.

When a sperm does meet an ovum, its head penetrates the covering of the ovum and its nucleus fuses with the nucleus of the ovum. The full complement of 23 pairs of chromosomes for the new child is thus established. Once the sperm head enters the ovum, the tail drops off, and additional sperm are prevented from entering. The fertilized egg continues its journey to the wall of the uterus, which is ready to receive it. It completes the process of implantation several days later.

Pregnancy may be confirmed as early as 3 to 10 days after the first missed period, depending on the method used by a physician. Symptoms may include breast fullness or tenderness, feelings of nausea, and an increased frequency of urination.[7] The full term of pregnancy, from the time of fertilization until birth, is called the *gestation period* and normally takes from 266 to 280 days. In some cases, of course, pregnancy is terminated prematurely by miscarriage, abortion, or premature birth.

[7]See Elaine C. Pierson and William V. D'Antonio, *Female and Male: Dimensions of Human Sexuality* (Philadelphia: Lippincott, 1974), pp. 144–45.

Figure 17–2 The Male Reproductive System

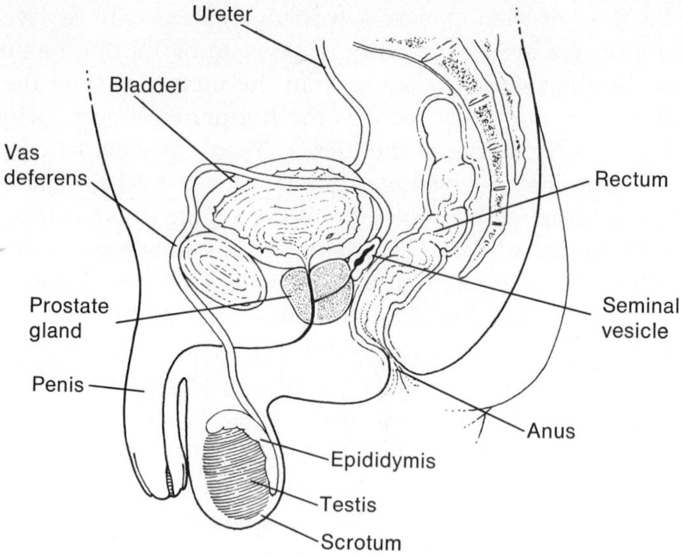

A pregnant woman's role is in many ways an ambiguous one in our society. She is encouraged to be healthy and carry on all normal activities during her pregnancy, but many people want to treat her as sick, and give her special protection and exempt her from responsibilities. A woman's behavior during pregnancy is often shaped by the expectations of her husband, her family, and her associates. Laws and Schwartz point out that many obstetricians foster a protective role by charting and monitoring the woman's life for twelve months.[8] In recent years, an increasing number of women have begun to take more assertive roles during their pregnancies.

Difficulties in Conceiving

Most couples who wish to have children have no trouble conceiving. In fact, 90 percent of all couples desiring a child will conceive in one year or less. Of the remaining 10 percent, about half will never conceive without medical help. A couple who do not conceive within a year's time, then, should see a doctor.

A doctor's help is advised because there are so many variables to be taken into account that a couple cannot be certain that all the necessary conditions

[8]Judith Long Laws and Pepper Schwartz, *Sexual Scripts—The Social Construction of Female Sexuality* (Hinsdale, Ill.: Dryden, 1977), pp. 87–91.

Figure 17–3 The Female Reproductive System

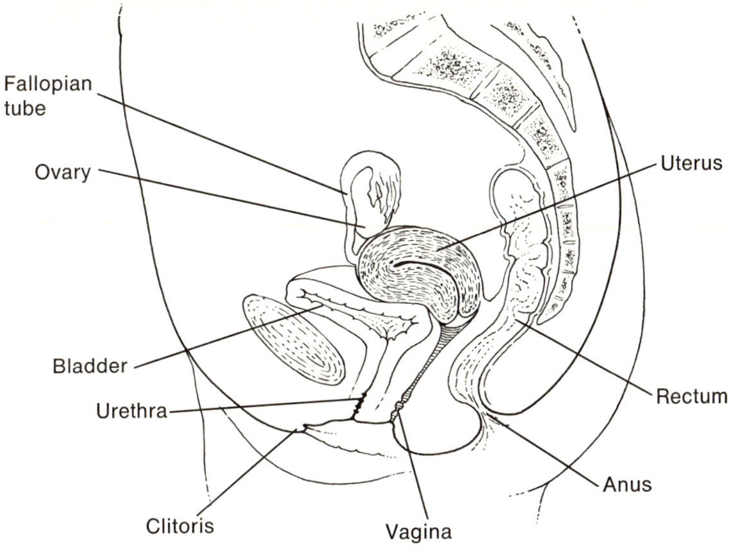

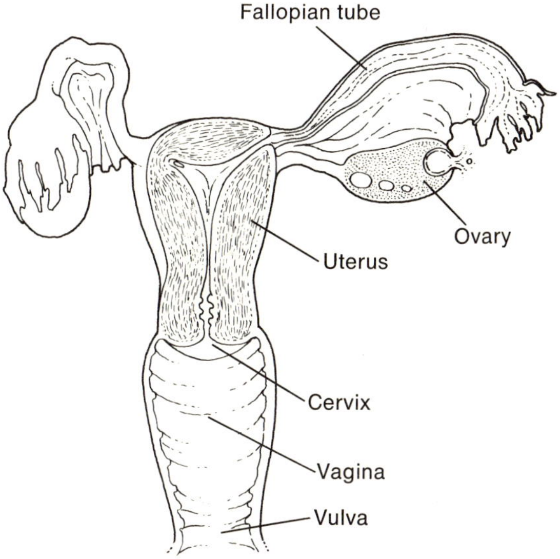

for fertilization exist. For one thing, the fertile period in each cycle is very brief, comprising only one day somewhere in the middle of the cycle. Failure to conceive may also be due to the infertility of the husband. Medical tests will show whether or not that is the problem; if it is, it probably can be corrected. In all, Dr. Alan F. Guttmacher lists seven prerequisites for conception and two more for successful childbearing. If one or more of these requirements are not met, parenthood cannot be achieved.

> There are at least *nine* biological prerequisites for achieving parenthood in the usual manner. Four pertain to the male: (1) Production of healthy live sperm in sufficient numbers, by at least one testicle. (2) Secretion of seminal fluid—the whitish, sticky material ejaculated at orgasm—in the proper amounts and composition to transport the sperm. (3) An unobstructed seminal "throughway" from the testicle to the end of the penis. (4) Ability to achieve and sustain an erection and to ejaculate within the vagina.
>
> The other five biological requirements for reproduction pertain to the female: (1) At least one ovary that functions normally enough to produce a mature egg. (2) A normal womb, properly prepared by chemicals fed into the bloodstream to become the "home" of the developing fetus. (3) An unobstructed genital tract—from the vagina up through the Fallopian tubes to the ovary—enabling the egg to pass down and the sperm cells to pass up. (4) A uterine environment which adequately nourishes and protects the unborn child until it is able to live in the outside world. (5) Safe delivery of the infant.[9]

Other physical reasons for difficulty in conceiving are vaginal secretions that are either too acidic or too alkaline for the survival of the sperm; the use of certain medications by the couple; and too frequent intercourse, which may lower the sperm count.

The widespread use of legal drugs by pregnant women poses a major threat to the health of the fetus in the prenatal period. Vander Zanden estimates that 10 to 15 percent of all conceptions result in spontaneous abortions or stillbirths, and another 6 to 7 percent are born with birth defects, some of which are due to environmental factors. Oral contraceptives used early in the pregnancy have been linked to birth defects. Vander Zanden writes:

> The incidence of drug usage among pregnant women is staggering. One study reveals that expectant mothers take an average of three different drugs during the first three months of pregnancy—the period when the embryo is most vulnerable. During the course of their pregnancy, 65 percent of the women took analgesics (including aspirins and related compounds), 42 percent antibiotics, 27 percent appetite suppressants, and 21 percent tranquilizers. According to current medical opinion, pregnant

[9]Alan F. Guttmacher, M.D., *Planning Your Family* (New York: Macmillan, 1964), pp. 219–20.

> women should not take drugs except when they have conditions that seriously threaten their health, and then *only* under the supervision of a physician. Some authorities even advise against extra vitamins unless they are prescribed by a physician.[10]

Additional hazards are illegal drugs, marijuana, tobacco, and alcohol, as well as occupational hazards and pollutants. Our advances in medicine sometimes seem to be canceled out by negative factors produced by our advances in technology.

Overcoming Fertility Problems

There is now a great deal of hope for couples who have difficulty in conceiving children. Most major medical centers have fertility clinics, and the range of services available to childless couples is steadily expanding. The birth of the first "test-tube" baby in 1978 indicated that it may soon be possible to give assistance in childbearing to many couples who would have been unable to have children in the past.

It is not always clear what causes infertility. Frequently doctors find no physical cause for infertility in husband or wife. In such cases all the couple can do is try to determine when the woman ovulates and time their sexual intercourse accordingly. The time for release of the ovum from the ovary is near the middle of the menstrual cycle; thus a woman may be able to determine the approximate time of ovulation by keeping a record of her menstrual periods. For instance, let us assume that a woman's menstrual cycle comes regularly every twenty-eight days. The average woman will ovulate twelve to sixteen days before her next menstrual period begins—that is, between the thirteenth and seventeenth days after the beginning of menstruation. If the couple have intercourse during those five days, the woman is most likely to become pregnant. But cycles are generally not that regular, so some days should be added at both ends of the five-day period to increase the possibility of conception. This would result in a schedule something like the one shown in Figure 17–4. However, if a woman's cycle is not regular, calculation of the fertile period by this method is impossible.

Another method of calculating the time of ovulation involves noting the woman's basal temperature. There are indications that a woman's temperature rises at about the time of ovulation. If for several cycles a woman keeps an accurate record of her temperature before rising in the morning, she may be able to predict the approximate time of ovulation. Sometimes the temperature drops the day before it rises; that day and the day of the rise in temperature are thought to offer the best possible opportunity for concep-

[10]James Vander Zanden, *Human Development* (New York: Alfred A. Knopf, 1978), pp. 165–66.

Figure 17–4 Typical Menstrual Cycle

Days										Period
1	2	3	4	5	6	7	8	9	10	Infertile Period
11	12	13	14	15	16	17	18			Fertile Period
19	20	21	22	23	24	25	26	27	28	Infertile Period

tion. Still another method of testing for fertility has been developed by the Thorenberg Laboratory, which manufactures a fertility-tester kit available in many pharmacies.

There is a drawback to this method of increasing the probability of conception. Many couples seem to try too hard emotionally. There is no conclusive evidence of psychosomatic infertility due to anxiety, but many doctors strongly suspect that it exists. More than a few couples have spent years trying to have children, given it up in despair, and then, to their surprise, conceived a child!

Although it is commonly thought that sterility is a female problem, about 40 percent of infertile marriages are caused by male sterility. The most common problem lies in a low sperm count. A sperm count of less than 100–150 million sperm per ejaculation is generally too low to result in fertilization of the egg.[11] Once a correctable problem has been found, then treatment can begin.

Psychological attitudes can also hinder conception by lowering a couple's frequency of intercourse. Some women suffer physical and emotional strain during certain phases of their menstrual cycles. They become tired and irritable; they cry easily and are worried and oversensitive. These symptoms may be caused partially by the physical changes the body goes through during the menstrual cycle, but more frequently they are related to social and psychological conditioning: Repression of sexuality, sexual ignorance, and fear of pregnancy do take their toll. But women with strong and active physical makeups and a healthy attitude toward their femininity seem to have few difficulties with their menstrual cycles. Fortunately, physicians can prescribe treatment for women who suffer from psychosomatic impairment of the reproductive process.

Sometimes couples do conceive, but the woman miscarries so early in

[11]Herant A. Katchadourian and Donald T. Lunde, *Fundamentals of Human Sexuality, 2nd ed.* (New York: Holt, Rinehart & Winston, 1975), pp. 120–22.

pregnancy that she does not realize she has been pregnant. The zygote may not become attached successfully to the wall of the uterus. Or the uterus may abort the embryo during the first month after conception. Such early miscarriages are probably quite common.

As we said at the beginning of this discussion, a couple who have difficulty in conceiving should see a doctor. If they do not have a family physician who is able to take the time for medical tests and a thorough follow-up counseling program, they might enter a treatment program such as the one offered by the infertility clinics affiliated with the Planned Parenthood Federation in New York City. Both members of the couple will need to share fully in the therapy program. Perhaps nine out of ten cases of infertility will be found to be psychological in origin (due to childhood conditioning or inadequate sex education) rather than physical. In addition, genetics clinics provide research and consultative services for couples who have questions about hereditary defects that may be transmitted to their children.[12]

The conception of a child should be an experience fully shared by husband and wife. Many men, especially those who have been brought up with traditional role expectations, refuse to see a doctor to discover whether there is some physical difficulty on their part that is preventing conception. They see a physical examination as a questioning of their manhood. Such an attitude is childish, to say the least; but when it results in a lifelong denial of a woman's desire for motherhood, it is cruel. A thoughtful husband will accept a visit to the doctor for what it is: a routine adult responsibility.

Couples who remain childless, after receiving competent medical counsel and assistance, have several options open to them. We have already discussed the role of the childless couple in contemporary society. They may wish to seek to adopt a child, or care for foster children in their home, if this would be a fulfilling "parental" role for them (see Chapter 19). And many men and women find similar satisfactions in occupations that relate to children. There are many ways of expressing our love and concern for children without raising sons and daughters of our own. Most large cities and towns have foster-home programs for the placement of orphaned and neglected children and are actively seeking additional homes. A woman may express her love for children through teaching, library work, playground supervision, scouting programs, and church youth programs. And organizations working with boys are always on the lookout for men who can give both volunteer and professional leadership to their programs. It is interesting to note that many of these youth organizations report that their best leadership is sometimes provided by men and women who do not have children of their own.

[12]See the list of laboratories studying human genetics in Corcado, Mexico, and the United States in Robert C. King, *Genetics*, 2nd ed. (New York: Oxford Univ. Press, 1965), pp. 425–26.

The Course of Pregnancy

The unborn child requires approximately nine months to develop in the uterus before birth (see Figure 17–5). During that period, the mother should be under the care of a physician so that prenatal complications can be avoided and the mother can be adequately prepared for the birth of her child. Blood tests must be taken to detect venereal disease and to determine the woman's Rh factor. If treatment is required, it can be initiated early in pregnancy.

After the zygote attaches itself to the uterine wall, the *placenta,* through which the infant will receive nourishment from the mother, begins to form. The zygote divides rapidly; certain body structures begin to appear, and soon the heartbeat can be distinguished. By the end of the first month, the *embryo* (the multiplying cells that originated with the zygote) is about one-quarter of an inch long. In two months, it has lengthened to about one and a quarter inches and is beginning to resemble human form. At the end of the third month, the embryo has survived the most dangerous period of development and is quite recognizably human; from this time until birth it is called a *fetus.*

During this period, the woman should continue her regular daily activity. It is true that some women must restrict their physical activity during pregnancy, and some are even confined to bed in order to protect the unborn child. But those cases are unusual; most physicians place as few limits as possible on the activity of the future mother. The woman may be troubled

Figure 17–5 The Pregnant Mother

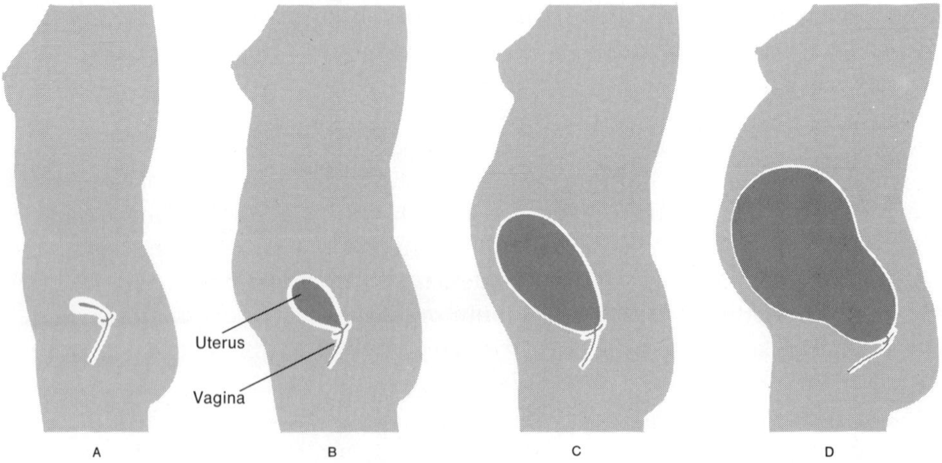

by nausea, or "morning sickness," as it is popularly known, but that condition can now be treated medically.

Nature's provision for the child's growth in the uterus is remarkable (see Figure 17–6). The uterus expands to accommodate the fetus, which is thoroughly protected and insulated by the *amniotic fluid* that surrounds it. The fetus is firmly attached to the wall of the uterus by the placenta, whose fibers penetrate the uterine wall. Nourishment comes to the fetus through the placenta, and waste materials are expelled through the placenta into the mother's blood. The mother's blood does not circulate in the fetus itself, which has an independent circulatory system. Thus the child is protected from numerous diseases and other harmful substances that may be carried in the mother's blood. (However, certain diseases—such as syphilis, mumps, and measles—and drugs and alcohol can pass to the fetus and threaten its health and normal development.)

A problem may arise in cases in which a mother with a negative Rh factor in her blood conceives by an Rh positive father and has an Rh positive child. There is a slight chance that the blood of mother and baby may mingle during pregnancy, with grave consequences for the child. Fortunately this condition can be detected by periodic tests, and the baby can be saved by blood transfusions at birth. Perhaps only one in three hundred of such pregnancies develop this condition.

Figure 17–6 Nature Provides for the Unborn Child

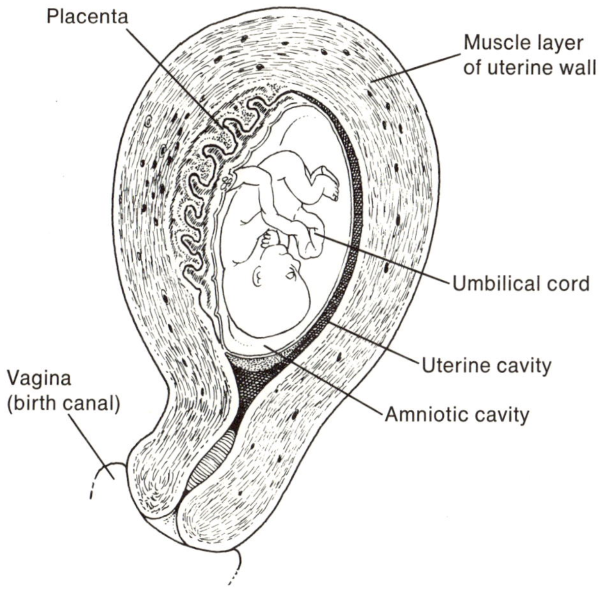

The age of the mother may be another factor in determining the health and vitality of the child. A young adult mother in excellent health normally produces a healthy baby. But a woman in her late thirties or early forties, although she transmits the same genes to her baby, might suffer from the effects of past diseases or have internal disorders. Some inherited defects appear more frequently when the mother is past forty; this is true of Down's syndrome (often called mongolism). And a mother who is too young may face special risks in pregnancy. Teenage girls are capable of conceiving children, but their reproductive systems do not seem to be ready for childbearing. Ideally a mother should be over twenty. But even the risk run by women below and above the normal childbearing age is not too great: about 6 percent of these births are defective, as opposed to about 2 percent of births among women of normal age.

Natural, or spontaneous, abortions are common during the early months of pregnancy. The body may abort some embryos that are defective and would not be fully capable of survival. Some women have a number of unsuccessful pregnancies before they carry a child for the full term.

According to a report by Gabriel Stickle, Vice-President of the National Foundation—March of Dimes, many of the risks that should be identified during pregnancy are not discovered because the women who have the most potential problems often come under medical care last. The uneven distribution of medical services, together with problems in providing adequate food, clothing, and shelter for those families at the lower end of the socioeconomic scale, are critical issues.[13]

Myths About Pregnancy

Every mother receives a great deal of advice about what to do during pregnancy. Often it includes helpful tips to enable her to meet the physical and emotional demands on her. But the common superstitions about her thoughts, dreams, and actions having a direct effect on the child, in the form of birth marks, personality traits, or physical characteristics, are unfounded. The child's central nervous system is completely isolated from the mother's. Naturally, the health of the child is largely dependent on the mother's strength and health. She may face severe emotional problems that drain her strength and may endanger both her and her unborn child. But there is a large margin of safety, and many women are overly concerned about normal occurrences that cannot possibly have any effect on the child. The care of an experienced and understanding obstetrician or family physician will help a

[13]Gabriel Stickle, "The Health of Mothers and Babies: How Do We Stack Up?" *The Family Coordinator*, 26, no. 3 (July 1977), 205–10.

woman to discriminate between what she should and should not be concerned about.

The Birth of the Child

During the birth of the child (see Figure 17–7), the fetus usually shifts into a lower position in the pelvis, with its head downward. (If the baby is in the breech position, buttocks first, the obstetrician may be able to turn the child while it is still in the uterus to avoid a difficult delivery.) When labor begins, the muscles in the uterus begin to contract, and their pressure on the baby gradually forces it out through the *birth canal* (vagina). The structures in the uterine area relax in order to permit the passage of the infant. The total time of labor is seven to ten hours on the average for the first child. In some cases it may be shorter, or it may last as long as twenty-four hours. The more unusual the physical conditions are, or the more fearful and nervous the mother is, the longer the labor period may be. In subsequent deliveries the time of labor is normally shorter by several hours.

There are three major stages in labor. In the first, the labor pains come at intervals of twenty minutes or more; pain is slight; and the contractions are similar to those a woman experiences during menstruation. In this first stage the *cervix* widens in order to allow the expulsion of the child. The stage is completed when the cervix is fully dilated.

In the second stage, the child moves downward through the birth canal; the contractions of the uterus continue at shorter intervals. This is the most difficult part of labor. The second stage ends when the head is expelled from the vagina and the child is born.

In the third stage, *afterbirth*, the placenta is expelled from the uterus and the umbilical cord is cut and bound. After the delivery, the mother's uterus begins to contract. In about six weeks the uterus and the surrounding muscles return to their normal size and shape.

An obstetrician will generally measure the mother's pelvis before delivery to make sure it is large enough; an X-ray may be taken in order to get exact measurements. In cases in which the passage of the infant through the birth canal seems dangerous or impossible, the doctor will recommend a Caesarean section, in which the child is removed surgically through the abdomen. This is a major operation and should be performed only when absolutely necessary. Usually the operation is scheduled several days before the expected delivery; in some cases the physician may wait until labor begins.

There have been many changes in the hospital care of expectant mothers in the last fifty years. Diagnostic services have been greatly expanded. The period of confinement following pregnancy has been shortened. And in

Figure 17–7 Birth

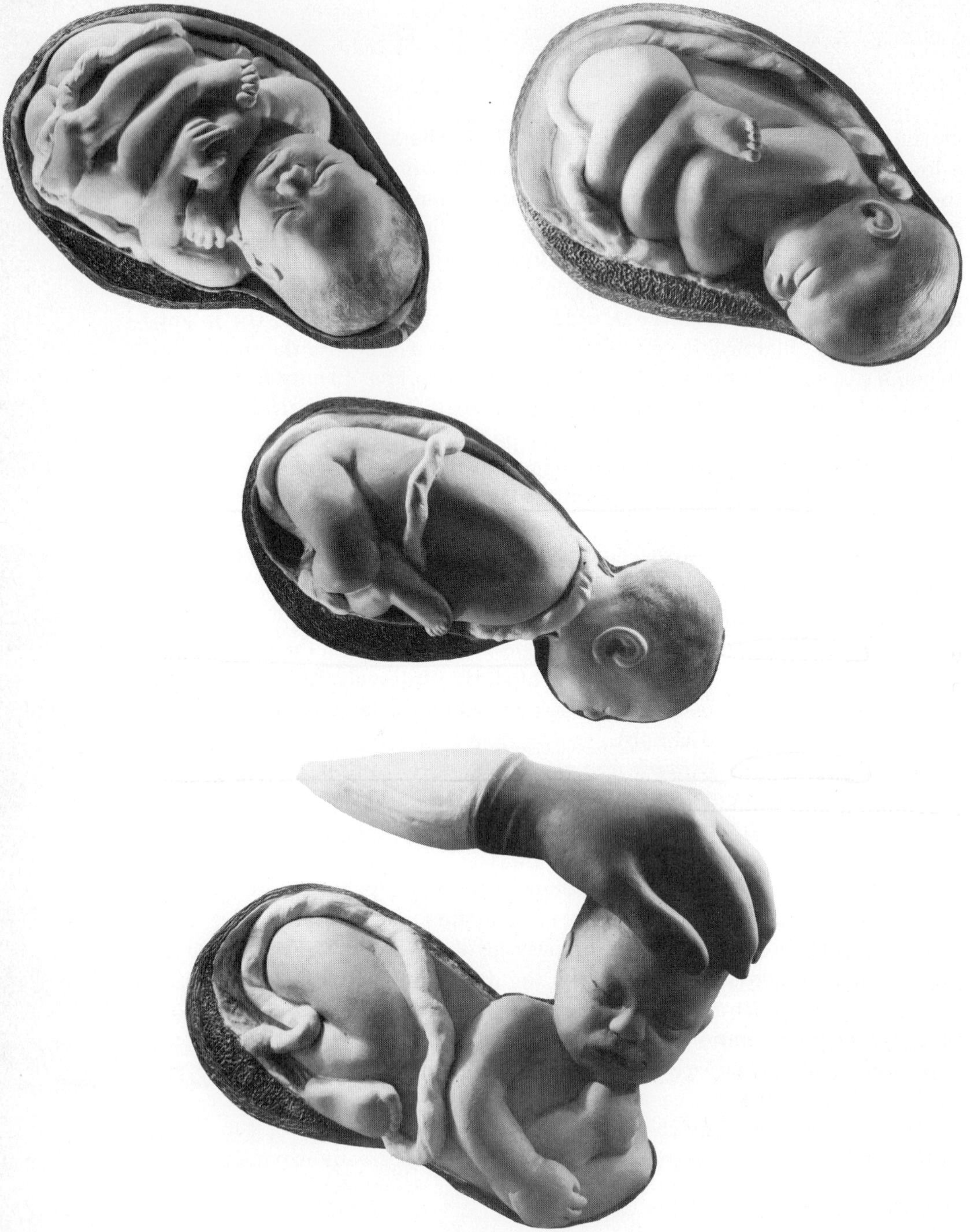

some hospitals the husband is permitted to be in the delivery room with his wife in order to lend her his moral support.

Most young women are interested in the methods of natural childbirth, which have been publicized by Dr. Grantley D. Read[14] and others. This kind of delivery stresses the physiological and psychological preparation of the mother and father so that the child can be delivered without anesthesia (which can be harmful to the child). Plans for such a delivery should be made in cooperation with a physician. Natural childbirth requires a great deal of preparation and a unique partnership between wife and husband. Unfortunately, many doctors are not willing to take the extra time to deliver a baby by this method.

The movement toward natural childbirth received added impetus from the introduction of the psychoprophylactic, or Lamaze, method in the United States. First used in France in 1951 by Dr. Fernand Lamaze, the method is now utilized to prepare almost half the expectant mothers in that country, where costs for training are paid for by the public health service. This technique emphasizes muscle control and respiratory responses that lessen the pain of labor.[15] Interest in this method is high among young mothers and young physicians.

Another trend in natural childbirth methods is the development of Al-

[14]Grantley D. Read, M.D., *Childbirth Without Fear* (New York: Harper & Row, 1953).
[15]Fernand Lamaze, M.D., *Painless Childbirth* (London: Burke, 1967).

ternative Birth Centers. Dr. Boyd Cooper, of Hollywood Presbyterian Hospital in California, which opened such a center in 1978, explains that the center was an outgrowth of patient demand. Patients wanted the option of having a child without anesthesia, and the hospital, faced with a declining maternity population, decided to try the new approach. Cooper is enthusiastic about the results:

> It was only four or five years ago . . . that women in numbers started asking for alternatives to the clinical, impersonal delivery room birth, where the mother is strapped down, monitored, screams for medication and gets bombed out of her skull. Periodically someone tells the husband what's going on. The unknown is frightening. Two or three days later she's awakened and told she has a baby boy.
>
> Meanwhile, . . . the doctor would come out and tell the husband he has a boy. That was the beginning and the end for him.
>
> The women's major complaint: Lack of knowledge of what was going on. They wanted the veil lifted from the mystery.
>
> And they wanted the father to share in the awesome experience of birth.
>
> The husband holds his wife in his arms, loves her, fondles her—it's just got to make it easier. . . . There's someone there to hold her and care for her and love her.[16]

Many teachers of childbirth education not only urge the participation of the husbands in preparation for childbirth and in the delivery room, but also to room with his wife and baby in the hospital for the first day or two. The idea of a husband having maternity leave may seem a bit unusual, but the answer to any objections is twofold. First, couples (especially husbands) who have roomed together in the hospital approve overwhelmingly. The experience draws the family much closer together during the critical transition period when husband and wife become father and mother. "I was there," the father realizes. Second, financial costs are relative. If becoming a father is important to a man, he has every reason to spend extra money to be a part of the experience.

Prospective parents should face the possibility that they may give birth to a defective child. This is not a judgment on them; it is rather a real and crucial test of their human sympathy, love, patience, and understanding. The resources of modern medicine (including special clinics and hospitals), special training schools and classes for the exceptional child, and better employment opportunities in business and in "sheltered workshops" are

[16]Beverly Boyette, "Warm Welcome from a Waiting World—Alternative Birth Center: How It All Began," *Los Angeles Times,* Aug. 20, 1978.

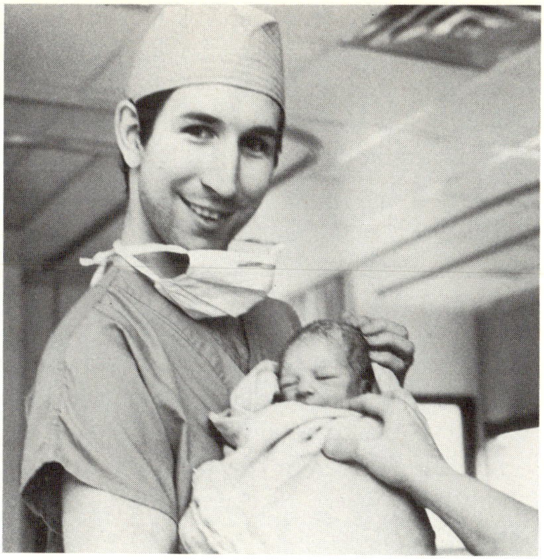

opening up new vistas for the handicapped. No couple should be unable or unwilling to meet the challenge of a handicapped child.

The Challenge of Parenthood

All in all, we have every reason to be proud of the tremendous advances that have been made in the field of obstetrics in the last fifty years. In earlier generations, the bearing of a child was one of the major risks to life for a woman. A mother might die while giving birth to one of her children, or she might find her life shortened by fatigue and illness from too many pregnancies. A stillborn child might be seen as evidence of God's wrath, a physical or mental deficiency as a sign of the sin or weakness of father or mother. Today, the bearing of a child is no longer so dangerous. There has been a steady decrease in both maternal and infant mortality rates in this century.[17] And the mystery and superstition surrounding the birth of the infant have been greatly reduced. We recognize the true hereditary and biological causes of many unusual physical or mental characteristics. If a birth is not normal in every respect, we do not blame the parents.

The safe delivery of the child is thus not the point of greatest anxiety. We recognize that the primary and most difficult task of mother and father must *begin* at the child's birth. The child needs to receive adequate love and af-

[17]Walter M. Ballard and Edwin M. Gold, "Medical and Health Aspects of Reproduction in the Adolescent," *Clinical Obstetrics and Gynecology,* 14, no. 2 (June 1971), 340–42.

fection, firm discipline and wise guidance, and a stable and happy family environment in which to develop its potential to the fullest. Both father and mother must share in family planning, preparation for the child's birth, and the care, training, and guidance of the child. This is the greatest challenge a couple face as they look forward to bringing children into the world.

Parent Education

One of the most promising developments in the family field in the last ten years has been the growth of parent-education classes. Classes in marriage and family-life education have been part of the college curriculum for more than forty years, but the number of courses in parent education is more limited. Perhaps this comes from the fact that we retain an image of the college student as single and not child-oriented, whereas in fact there are married couples with children on almost every campus.

Kerckhoff et al. report on "Parent Education as Provided by Secondary Schools" in a survey of courses in forty states and five Canadian provinces. A wide range of subjects is being taught at the secondary level, including units on child development, discipline and guidance, communication, stages in marriage, child care, feelings, the self-concept, and family planning. These courses are recommended for basic requirements in the secondary school.[18]

Kerckhoff, Ulmschneider, and Adams provide a similar survey of courses at the college and university level.[19] They do not report a wide variety of courses being offered, although basic "parenting" courses were well received, especially in Home Economics departments. Enrollment remains largely female, the average enrollment being only 13 percent male. Most teachers reporting on these courses indicated that a lack of suitable materials was a problem. The same problems were reported in a further article by Croake and Glover. They see two focal points in the emerging programs: one an emphasis on behavior modification techniques for discipline and influence, and the second the interest in democratic discussion groups as a means of improving family sharing and communication.[20]

Parent education is being stressed in a community college program being developed at Cuesta College in San Luis Obispo, California, by Arlene Chandler. The course seeks to aid students to "promote parenting skills and improve parent-child relationships, thus facilitating the raising of happy,

[18]Richard K. Kerckhoff, Myrna Habig, and the Family Life Educational Panel, "Parent Education as Provided by Secondary Schools," *The Family Coordinator*, 25, no. 2 (April 1976), 127–30.

[19]Florence G. Kerckhoff, Ann Ulmschneider, and Connie Adams, "College and University Programs in Parent Education," *The Family Coordinator*, 25, no. 2 (April, 1976), pp. 131–33.

[20]James W. Croake and Kenneth E. Glover, "A History and Evaluation of Parent Education," *The Family Coordinator*, 26, no. 2 (April 1977), 151–58.

responsible, cooperative children and the development of gratifying family life."[21] The course offered in the Family Studies department also has a goal of helping students to "develop a philosophy of parenthood . . . and to help students develop parenting behavior which will enable them to competently relate to children. . . ." As with similar courses, the enrollment includes single parents and married women returning to school, and a good representation of younger single men and women in the college. One unique feature of this program is a required course project that includes a semester's interaction with and a report on a particular child. Students are thus involved in a wide range of "trial parenting" experiences during the semester.

Many family-life educators have been advocating a broader interest among both students and faculty in the Marriage and Family Life course. Perhaps the Parent Education course is a natural way to spark these related "family" interests, and to provide parents with help in doing the task they share: the education, growth, and development of their children.

SUMMARY

Every couple should consider whether or not to become parents. There are strong motivations to have children, but an increasing number of couples deliberately choose to remain childless. Both sides must be considered: Society must recognize the free choice of people to remain childless while at the same time it must prepare those who wish to have children to be parents.

The coming of the first child is a significant event in the lives of both husband and wife. It expresses their union in a new and dramatic way: It marks the beginning of a new generation.

Heredity determines the basic physical characteristics of a child. The male sperm and the female ovum each contain 23 chromosomes, which carry the genes that determine the child's traits. The sex of the child is determined by the sex chromosome inherited from the father of the child.

Conception occurs when a sperm ejaculated into the vagina enters one of the Fallopian tubes and fertilizes the ovum. Since sperm can live in the female body for several days, conception may take place even if a woman ovulates after intercourse. If the ovum is not fertilized, it dies and is discharged during menstruation.

Most couples have no trouble conceiving children, but about 10 percent do have some difficulty. There are many reasons why couples desiring children may be unable to conceive. The husband may be infertile; the wife may not ovulate at regular intervals; or various other emotional and physical factors may affect a couple's fertility. Fortunately, competent medical advice can often help a couple to overcome these difficulties.

[21]Arlene Chandler, Report to the California Council on Family Relations, annual meeting, August, 1978, Santa Clara, California.

After implantation in the wall of the uterus, the zygote develops into an embryo and then a fetus. Sound health and a normally active schedule are usually the best prescriptions for a mother during pregnancy. Some possible threats to the health of the fetus in the prenatal period include legal drugs, illegal drugs, marijuana, tobacco, and alcohol. The regular prenatal care of an obstetrician or family physician will help a mother to avoid prenatal complications and to measure her progress accurately.

There are three stages in the birth of a child. The first includes the labor contractions that begin the expulsion of the child from the mother's body. In the second the baby moves through the birth canal (vagina) and is born. In the final stage the placenta is expelled and the physical link between mother and child is severed. Medical advances have sharply reduced the maternal mortality rate in the United States and made childbirth a remarkably safe process. However, the challenge to provide excellent care for all expectant mothers, including those at the lowest socioeconomic levels, remains.

Modern childbirth education offers father and mother the opportunity to prepare together for the birth of their children. The Lamaze method is followed by many young couples in preparing for natural childbirth. And educators are now suggesting that it is wise to involve husbands in the total birth process and are encouraging their presence during delivery.

In spite of every effort to ensure normal conception and prenatal development, some children are born with mental and physical disabilities. But in most cases today's parents can raise handicapped children successfully by availing themselves of professional help and government and community aid designed to assist in the full personal development of the handicapped. Raising a handicapped child is really a special form of the challenge to encourage the growth and development of a new life that every parent must face.

Parent-education courses are becoming more popular in schools and universities. Many of these courses help married and single students to promote their parenting skills and thus ensure the successful development of children and family.

SUGGESTED READINGS

Croake, James W., and Kenneth E. Glover. "A History and Evaluation of Parent Education." *The Family Coordinator,* 26, no. 2 (April 1977), 151–58. Summary of present programs for parent education. Focuses on behavior modification and discussion-group format.

Glick, Paul C., and Arthur J. Norton. "Marrying, Divorcing, and Living Together in the U.S. Today." *Population Bulletin,* 32, no. 5 (1977). Summary of trends in family size, marriage choice, and parenthood.

Guttmacher, Alan. *Pregnancy, Birth and Family Planning.* New York: Viking Press,

1973. Summary of basic information on pregnancy and childbirth by a leader in family planning.

Kerckhoff, Florence G., Ann Ulmschneider, and Connie Adams. "College and University Programs in Parent Education." *The Family Coordinator,* 25, no. 2 (April 1976), 131–33. Review of materials and programs in parent education.

King, Robert C. *Genetics,* 2nd ed. New York: Oxford Univ. Press, 1965. Reviews genetics and its effects on the family.

Lamaze, Fernand. *Painless Childbirth.* Trans. L. R. Celestin. Chicago: Henry Regnery, 1970. French physician explains the psychoprophylactic method of childbirth.

Laws, Judith Long, and Pepper Schwartz. *Sexual Scripts—The Social Construction of Female Sexuality.* Hinsdale, Ill.: Dryden, 1977. Helpful discussion of the social view of woman's role in pregnancy.

LeMasters, E. E. *Parents in Modern America,* 3rd ed. Homewood, Ill.: Dorsey Press, 1977. Critic of our social framework turns his attention to the problem of parents who attempt to meet the high expectations our society sets for them.

Wells, J. Gipson, ed. *Current Issues in Marriage and the Family.* New York: Macmillan, 1975. Good section of readings on having or not having children.

18 Family Planning and Birth Control

- Is birth control still a controversial topic in our society?
- What methods of birth control are the most effective and the least harmful? Which methods have negative health factors associated with them?
- What is the "natural" method of birth control?
- How did oral contraceptives revolutionize birth control?
- What health problems are associated with oral contraceptives?
- Why do some couples choose sterilization as a method of birth control?
- Explain the different types of abortion. What are the long-term and short-term risks?
- What are the arguments for and against abortion?
- What can Americans do about the world population crisis?
- What are the significant trends in family planning for the future?

Importance of Family Planning

No couple can ignore the importance of family planning today. If our attention is focused on the energy shortage, the food shortage, the water shortage, or on the lack of education, medical services, and an adequate standard of living for billions of people in the world today, we have to come back to family planning as central to all these problems. Certainly this issue is very much in the center of American thought and discussion today. Although America is not one of the overpopulated countries of the world, we are already feeling the pressure of too many people in our great metropolitan areas and in the mushrooming suburban communities of the Eastern seaboard, Florida, Texas, and California. Families are jammed together in high-rise apartments, in tiny tract houses, and in slum areas; the pressure for adequate room for development is constant. At the same time, the discovery of better birth control device has made it possible to control the population explosion. Most newly married couples ask themselves the question, "How many children should we have, and how soon?" Or, "Should we have children at all?"

Birth Control

There are many methods of birth control. They vary widely in their effectiveness and in their acceptability, from both a personal and a religious point of view. Ideally, a birth control method should be as reliable as possible; it should be as harmless as possible to the user, under proper medical supervision; it should be available to people on all socioeconomic levels, which means it should be cheap and easy to use; it should not prevent the couple from conceiving at a later time; and it should not interfere with or change the character of the sexual act itself. In actuality, no known method of birth control offers all these advantages unqualifiedly. Let us discuss the most frequently used methods and their advantages and disadvantages.

The Natural Method

One of the most widely used birth control methods is the natural, or rhythm, method. It has been estimated that in a year's time, about one out of every four women using this method will conceive.[1] The development of the rhythm method came about in the 1930s when it was discovered that conception is possible only during a short period of each menstrual cycle, just after the ovum has been released from the ovary (see Chapter 17). If intercourse does not occur around that time, conception will not occur. The natural rhythm of the reproductive cycle can be defeated.

What this method requires is the exact determination of when the woman will ovulate and abstinence from intercourse both before and after that time. Abstinence for a time prior to ovulation is required because sperm can live within the female for at least two (and possibly four to six) days. The date of ovulation itself can be predicted by keeping a record of menstrual periods for a year. Subtracting 19 from the length of the shortest cycle gives the number of days in the safe period in the beginning of the cycle. Subtracting 11 from the length of the longest cycle gives the number of days in the safe period at the end of the cycle.

Another way to establish the exact day of ovulation is for a woman to chart her temperature every morning before rising. A woman's temperature normally rises about half a degree at about the time she ovulates. Thus the safe periods and the fertile period can be double-checked.

It must be emphasized that a large number of women, perhaps one in every seven, do not menstruate regularly enough to use the rhythm method reliably. And menstrual cycles are not regular in the months immediately following childbirth. When the rhythm method is used carefully under a doctor's guidance, it can be about as effective as the condom or the diaphragm. However, it requires a high degree of self-discipline—which, considering the failure rate, most couples do not seem to have. And, of course, couples who do not use the correct formulas for calculating the fertile period will not have much success with this method.

[1]Benjamin A. Kogan, M.D., *Human Sexual Expression* (New York: Harcourt Brace Jovanovich, 1973), p. 111. Adapted from "Contraceptive Methods Requiring Consultations with Physicians," Searle and Co., San Juan, Puerto Rico.

> Rhythm requires self-control of the sexual urge. This objective alone would not be crippling, perhaps, but in addition the rhythm method requires fairly elaborate mental gymnastics. Users must keep track of numbers of days or take temperatures. . . . Most lower-class people have some notion that there are safe days, but have widely differing and sometimes quite incorrect ideas as to just when they come. They may attempt rhythm, but have little confidence in its effectiveness.[2]

The Roman Catholic Church is the strongest advocate of the use of the natural method of birth control, but in the United States, it has become apparent that many Catholic women utilize alternative methods of family planning. Despite this fact, it is not anticipated that there will be a major change in the Church's policy in the near future.

The Condom

Another method of limiting conception is the use of the condom, a rubber sheath that covers the penis and prevents the entry of sperm into the vagina. Condoms are widely available for purchase without prescription. When used properly and consistently, they offer a high degree of protection. Failures are due to tearing of the sheath or its slipping off after ejaculation.

In the 1970 National Fertility Study conducted by the Princeton University Office of Population Research, the condom was utilized by about 14 percent of the total sample of couples under age 45. It is the second most popular method of contraception used by these couples. The totals, including both black and white subsamples, are listed in Table 18–1.

Many men report that the use of the condom lessens their physical pleasure in intercourse. However, the condom offers protection against the transmission of venereal disease. Using a condom with spermicidal jelly or cream increases the rate of contraceptive effectiveness.

The Diaphragm

Another commonly used contraceptive device is the vaginal diaphragm, a small rubber cup or dome fitted specifically to the individual woman. It can be obtained with a doctor's prescription and must be used in conjunction with a spermicidal jelly or cream in order to be effective (the diaphragm itself is not a contraceptive, but merely a vehicle for the spermicide). According to the 1970 National Fertility Study, the diaphragm is used by only 4 percent of the couples practicing birth control today. If it is accurately fitted and used

[2]Edward H. Pohlman, *Psychology of Birth Planning* (Cambridge, Mass.: Schenkman, 1969), p. 386.

Table 18–1 Methods of Contraception Used Currently by Married Couples by Age and Race[a]: 1965 and 1970

Current Method	Under 45						Under 30						30–44					
	Total[b]		*White*		*Black*		*Total*[b]		*White*		*Black*		*Total*[b]		*White*		*Black*	
	1965	*1970*	*1965*	*1970*	*1965*	*1970*	*1965*	*1970*	*1965*	*1970*	*1965*	*1970*	*1965*	*1970*	*1965*	*1970*	*1965*	*1970*
Number of users	3032	3810	2441	3273	554	462	1215	1800	922	1540	276	222	1817	2010	1519	1733	278	240
Percent total	100	100	100	100	100	100	100	100	100	100	100	100	100	100	100	100	100	100
Wife sterilized[c]	7	8	6	7	14	19	3	3	3	3	7	5	9	13	8	12	22	32
Husband sterilized[c]	5	8	5	8	1	1	3	3	3	3	*	*	6	12	7	13	1	2
Pill[d]	24	34	24	34	22	37	41	49	42	49	31	54	13	21	13	20	13	22
IUD[e]	1	7	1	7	3	8	2	9	1	9	5	10	1	6	1	6	1	5
Diaphragm[f]	10	6	10	6	5	5	6	4	7	3	3	4	12	8	13	8	7	7
Condom[g]	22	14	22	15	17	7	19	11	19	12	18	6	24	17	24	17	16	7
Withdrawal	4	2	4	2	2	1	2	2	2	2	2	*	5	2	5	3	2	1
Foam	3	6	3	6	6	6	5	8	4	8	8	7	2	4	2	4	4	5
Rhythm	11	6	12	7	2	2	7	4	8	4	3	1	13	8	14	9	2	2
Douche	5	3	4	3	17	8	5	2	4	2	15	6	5	4	4	4	20	10
Other[h]	7	5	7	4	10	6	6	4	6	4	8	7	8	5	8	5	12	6

*Less than 0.6 percent.
[a]Currently living together.
[b]Includes non-whites other than blacks.
[c]Surgical procedures undertaken at least partly for contraceptive reasons.
[d]Includes combination with any other method.
[e]Includes combination with any other method except pill.
[f]Includes combination with any method except pill or IUD.
[g]Includes combination with any method except pill, IUD or diaphragm.
[h]Includes other multiple as well as single methods and a small percentage of unreported methods.

SOURCE: Charles F. Westoff and Norman B. Ryder, *The Contraceptive Revolution*. Copyright © 1977 by Princeton University Press, II-3, p. 19. Reprinted by permission of Princeton University Press.

and cared for properly, the diaphragm is an effective method of contraception.

Since spermicides are only effective for about an hour, the safest way to use a diaphragm is to insert it just before intercourse. Many women object to diaphragms because they do not like handling messy creams or jellies when they are on the verge of intercourse. The use of a diaphragm is generally much more acceptable if the man inserts it as part of sexual foreplay. It is recommended that the diaphragm be left in place for six or eight hours after intercourse.

Though the diaphragm and the condom are hardly foolproof contraceptives, they are highly effective when used together. Even a condom and vaginal foam (without a diaphragm) are very effective in combination. Couples should realize that they are not restricted to using only one contraceptive method at once. And indeed, if husband and wife each use a contraceptive or share in the use of a diaphragm, resentment of the responsibility involved will probably be considerably lessened; one spouse will not feel that he or she is constantly sacrificing the pleasure of spontaneity while the other partner simply relaxes and enjoys himself or herself. Finally, any contraceptive is only as effective as the user allows it to be—that is, if a method is used correctly and faithfully, it will be much more effective than if it is used haphazardly and halfheartedly. "Let's forget it this time" is the way many couples use—or rather do not use—their contraceptives. In fact, differences in the failure rates of the various contraceptives are due in large part to their degree of dependence on human will power.

Spermicides

Another method used by a small number of couples (6 percent in the 1970 study) are the various foams, creams, jellies, and suppositories that can be used as spermicides. Usually they are sold with a plastic applicator that a woman uses to introduce the substance into her vagina before intercourse. However, the failure rate for these applications, when used without a condom or a diaphragm, is high, perhaps 20 to 30 percent.

Oral Contraceptives

The most widely discussed birth control method now in use is the oral contraceptive—the birth control pill. Birth control pills actually suppress ovulation. According to published reports, tests have shown them to be the most effective known method of preventing pregnancy when taken regularly as directed. (Oral contraceptives were tested in Puerto Rico and a number of cities in the United States before they were approved for general use by the Food and Drug Administration in 1960.) Since women who began using oral

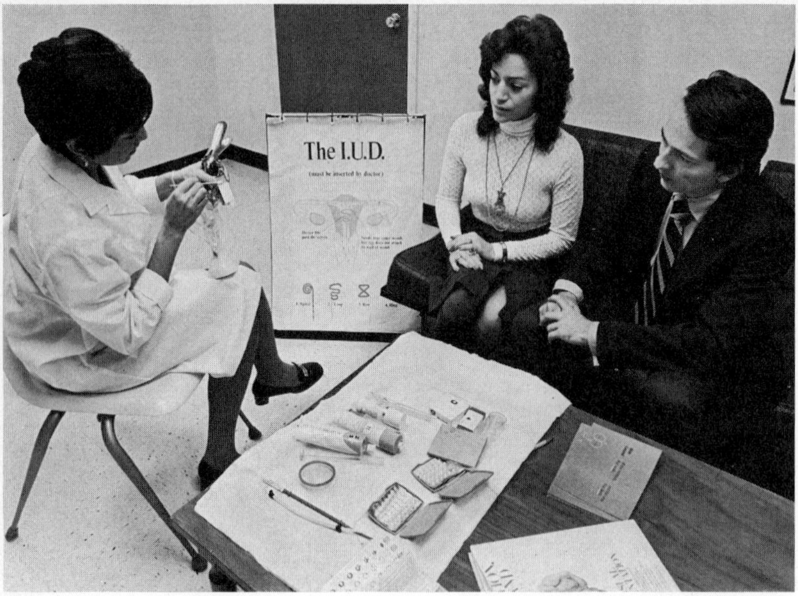

contraceptives in 1960 would now be entering their forties, we cannot be sure what the long-term results of using the pill during potential child-bearing years will be. But doctors have learned a good deal about the pill's short-term effects. They now tend to be more cautious about whom they prescribe the pill for, and more frequently prescribe alternate methods of birth control. In addition, doctors are now better able to discriminate between brands and doses. They recognize that a particular dose or kind of pill will have widely differing effects on women of different physical makeup, and they are beginning to be able to predict what those effects will be.

It should be clear that only a doctor can determine what pill a woman should take and whether she should continue to take it. A woman who has any of the conditions listed below probably will be denied a prescription for oral contraceptives, since these conditions seem to be associated with dangerous side effects.

Heart disease and any abnormality associated with the circulation, including very high blood pressure
Liver disease, such as hepatitis
Kidney disease
Diabetes
Cystic fibrosis

Epilepsy
Migraine headaches
Tumors and cancer of the breasts, ovaries, or uterus
Severe emotional disturbance, particularly after the birth of a baby
Asthma[3]

In addition to seeing her physician regularly—once every six months—a woman taking birth control pills should inform her doctor of any of these symptoms:

Severe depression
Frequent, severe headaches
Very heavy menstrual periods, and heavy or persistent bleeding between periods
More than two missed menstrual periods (if the pills have been taken properly, there is almost no chance of pregnancy; the hormone levels may be too high and are probably suppressing the menstrual period)
A high degree of water retention, as may be manifested by swollen legs, feet, or hands, a large weight gain
Jaundice (yellowing) of the skin or eyes
Any change in vision, especially double vision or loss of vision
Overly tender breasts and the secretion of milk or fluid from the breasts
Weakness in the arms or legs and sudden pain in the chest followed by coughing[4]

Moreover, if nausea, slight bleeding between periods, or short heavy periods (all normal symptoms when a woman first begins to take the pill) persist after three months, a woman should see a doctor.

The 1970 National Fertility Study (see Table 18–1) indicates that 34 percent of all American women sampled used the pill. Almost half (49 percent) were women in the "Under 30" age group, more than double the 21 percent indicated for women in the 30–44 age group. This indicates the wide acceptance of the pill by younger women, and also the fact that many women switch to other forms of contraception after they are in their thirties.

There has been much publicity on deaths and severe side effects linked to the use of oral contraceptives. Such reports generally exaggerate the danger involved. If a woman uses the pill carefully and sees her doctor regularly, she should continue in good health. In fact, it is reassuring for most women to note that the mortality rate for users of oral contraceptives is even lower than the very low mortality rate for pregnant women.

[3]Kogan, p. 115.
[4]Kogan, pp. 115–16.

> [This is] what I think is one of the most logical approaches to the problem. If one selects a model population of 100,000 fertile women who use no contraceptive agents, in one year there will be 50,000 babies born with 15 maternal deaths; the maternal deaths are calculated on the basis of United States Vital Statistics currently available. If the same 100,000 women all use diaphragms there will be 10,000 births with 3 deaths, calculated on the same basis. Now, if these 100,000 women use oral contraceptives there will be 3 deaths, based on the available British statistics. With tongue in cheek one could perhaps say that the oral contraceptives are as safe as the diaphragm.[5]

The reliability of the pill, as with any birth control method, depends on proper and regular use. Pierson and D'Antonio, reporting on Planned Parenthood statistics from southeastern Pennsylvania, state that of 305 girls who reported they were "using" the pill, some 143 were pregnant![6] Obviously, these are far different statistics than are usually given for effectiveness of the oral contraceptives, and need some careful evaluation. The age of those surveyed is certainly a factor. What these girls claimed to be doing in the way of contraception was not a completely accurate report of their behavior.

In addition to the familiar daily pill, new kinds of oral contraceptives are being developed, and some are becoming available to the general public. The "morning after" pill is prescribed by some university health clinics. It is nothing more than a high dosage of estrogen that is taken for several days following intercourse without a contraceptive; large quantities of estrogen tend to irritate the lining of the uterus and prevent implantation of a fertilized ovum. Sudden doses of estrogen do cause side effects that range from the unpleasant to the dangerous, however, so this method of birth control should not be resorted to often. Research is also being done on a once-a-month pill that would be less expensive, easier to use, and more effective in developing countries and areas where regular daily schedules are difficult to maintain. Also proposed has been a "reversible" pill that would suppress ovulation and prevent pregnancy for a long period of time until a second pill (or injection) would make it possible for a woman to become pregnant.

The question at issue is whether or not women are willing to entrust their total health and safety in these matters to the direction of their doctors and medical advisors. In a culture that relies so heavily on drugs for many purposes, and in which the medical profession has such a high status, our answer must be a qualified yes. If a doctor strongly recommends a pill, or some other form of medical treatment, and if this treatment is socially acceptable,

[5]Louis M. Hellman, "Oral Contraceptives: Safety and Complications," *Family Planning Today*, ed. Alan Rubin (Philadelphia: F. A. Davis, 1969), pp. 40–41.

[6]Elaine C. Pierson and William V. D'Antonio, *Female and Male* (Philadelphia: Lippincott, 1974), pp. 193–95.

our prediction would be that women would utilize new and more effective forms of contraception.

The Intrauterine Device

A contraceptive that is used by a small percentage of women is the intrauterine device, a small object made in a variety of shapes that is fitted to the woman's uterus. The IUD works by irritating the cells that line the uterine wall. The uterus then contracts and expels the zygote before it becomes implanted. The IUD does not prevent conception itself.

The IUD was being used by 7 percent of those in the 1970 National Fertility Study, a sharp increase in a five-year period. The reliability rate of the IUD has been placed above 95 percent when it is properly used. Like oral contraceptives, there are certain limitations to its use: women with abnormalities or infection of the uterus cannot be fitted for IUDs. And some women's bodies expel the IUD, especially if it is inserted immediately after childbirth. For women who can use the IUD, however, it is an extremely convenient method. After it is inserted, a woman need only check its position once a week. The IUD can be advantageous in developing countries where it can be fitted by health personnel and provide contraceptive protection for a period of six months or more. The IUD should be checked and replaced periodically.

Sterilization

Sterilization is the most certain method of preventing pregnancy, and it is usually final. There are two major methods for women. Most common is the *tubal ligation,* by which the surgeon disconnects the Fallopian tubes from the uterus and thus prevents fertilization of the ovum. The ovaries continue to release an egg each month, but it is soon reabsorbed into the body.[7] Monthly menstrual periods continue, and a woman's ability to achieve orgasm is unimpaired. Tubal ligation is major surgery and as such is fairly risky and quite expensive. A less serious operation, *tubal cautery by laparoscopy* (popularly called "Band-Aid sterilization"),[8] involves cauterization of the Fallopian tubes. It requires one small abdominal incision.

For a man, sterilization can usually be accomplished by a simple operation known as a *vasectomy,* which involves the cutting of the vas deferens. Both the semen and the seminal fluid continue to be produced, but the sperm are prevented from entering the penis. A vasectomy requires no abdominal incision, is done with a local anesthetic, and takes only about half an hour.

[7]See Evan McLeod Wylie, *A Guide to Voluntary Sterilization: The New Birth Control* (New York: Grosset & Dunlap, 1972), pp. 62–63.
[8]Wylie, p. 63.

It is much less dangerous than female sterilization and has no effect on a man's ability to achieve orgasm.

According to the 1970 National Fertility Study, the number of men and women choosing sterilization as a means of birth control was 16 percent. That number increased during the 1970s. Undoubtedly this is a further reflection of the desire of some couples to have a smaller family, and of some couples to remain childless. One large-scale study of the reasons men give for wanting a vasectomy is summarized in Table 18–2. The survey of some 1,010 men who participated in the Simon Population Trust's vasectomy project in the United Kingdom included the responses a year or more later of 93 percent of the men who underwent the operation. A number of reasons were given by most respondents (a total of 3,489 reasons for 1,010 men).[9] Dislike of contraception was the most widely given reason. But it is also noteworthy that almost as many men gave another reason: "to spare respondent's wife." And half the men gave concern for the wife's health as a reason. On the other hand, very few men (6.3 percent) gave their own health as a reason for seeking the vasectomy.[10]

Since many men are fearful that they may wish to father children at some future time, frozen sperm banks have been established in several major centers in the United States, and reports are now being received on fairly large samples of children conceived with frozen sperm.[11] Results to date seem to be largely favorable. There is some question how long the sperm may be stored and whether the children conceived will be born defective. But there has been no reported increase in birth defects among the several hundred children so conceived in the United States and Japan.

Eduardo Roberto has reported on a study of men who were potential vasectomies in the Chicago area. A number of positive factors appeared to be important to these men when considering the operation: strengthened marital fidelity; admiration of peers; feeling of fulfillment; higher living standard; more sexual response from spouse; better child care for present children; happier family life; relieving wife of contraceptive burden; freedom from worries of unwanted pregnancy; and others.[12] Roberto is also involved with the family-planning communications program of the Midwest Population Center in Chicago. Prior research has helped the center to develop advertising campaigns to promote greater utilization of the vasectomy method of

[9]See the discussion of the Simon Population Trust's project in *Foolproof Birth Control,* ed. Lawrence Lader (Boston: Beacon, 1972), pp. 72–76.

[10]See also Norman Fleishman and Peter L. Dixon, *Vasectomy, Sex, and Parenthood* (Garden City, N.Y.: Doubleday, 1973).

[11]Wylie, pp. 43–57.

[12]Eduardo L. Roberto, "Marital and Family Planning Expectancies of Men Regarding Vasectomy," *Journal of Marriage and the Family,* 36, no. 4 (Nov. 1974), 698–706.

Table 18–2 Reasons for Seeking Vasectomy

Reasons for seeking vasectomy given by 1,010 respondents	*Total number of times each reason was given*	*Percentage of 1,010 respondents giving each reason*
Dislike of contraception	802	79.4
To spare respondent's wife because the operation on the male is less serious	769	76.1
Financial considerations	539	53.4
Health reasons affecting respondent's wife	510	50.5
Failure of contraception (unwanted pregnancy)	508	50.3
Other particular reasons	205	20.3
Health reasons affecting respondent	64	6.3
Blood incompatibility (including rhesus incompatibility)	55	5.4
Fear of transmitting unfavorable hereditary conditions	37	3.7

Total Reasons: 3,489
Total Respondents: 1,010

SOURCE: Simon Population Trust, in *Vasectomy: Follow-up of a Thousand Cases,* p. 10, December 1969, Cambridge, England.

family planning. Is such use of persuasive appeals in keeping with an ethical approach to family planning? Do men need to be sold on having a vasectomy, or should we concentrate on publicizing the facts concerning various aspects of the procedure, and then emphasize a counseling approach to each potential applicant, which would give him every opportunity to make his own choice in the matter?[13]

[13]Roberto, pp. 704–05.

Other Methods

A number of other old-fashioned methods of birth control are still in use, but they are so ineffective that one hesitates to mention them in the same breath with more reliable methods. Any couple who depend on one of these haphazard devices are not seriously interested in birth control. There is the *withdrawal* method, or *coitus interruptus,* which depends on withdrawal of the penis from the vagina before ejaculation. It is unnatural and can cause psychological difficulties. It also can fail quite easily. *Douching,* or cleansing of the vagina, lowers the sperm count but also propels sperm toward the uterus.

One thing generally overlooked by couples practicing birth control is that sexual experience need not include genital-genital contact. Mutual masturbation, either manually or orally, can be practiced without any danger of conception, as can anal intercourse. Couples who are at home with their sexuality and can overcome the traditional taboos associated with this kind of sexual experience may want to use it as a contraceptive.

Religious Teachings on Birth Control

A great deal of the discussion of family planning and birth control centers on the different religious views on the subject. The largest single Christian community, the Roman Catholic Church, has endorsed only a single method of birth control, the natural, or rhythm, method. Protestant churches have generally approved of family planning, although some do not state clearly their views on the subject. Jewish religious leaders have also generally been in favor of family planning and birth control. A typical summary of the traditional Roman Catholic position on family planning and birth control has been presented by Dr. William J. Egan.

> In the positive act of procreation six steps are necessary: (1) preparation for the act; (2) penetration; (3) insemination—the deposition of the seed; (4) fertilization; (5) pregnancy; (6) labor and delivery. The first three steps comprise the voluntary contribution of the married partners. After the third step, nature takes over. If an egg is present, steps four to six follow naturally. If no egg is present, nature, still operating normally, voids steps four to six. But the six steps are *one natural continuity*. The first need not be taken. Once it is taken, any interference with or omission of the subsequent steps is a violation of the natural continuity, vitiates nature, and hence is wrong.
>
> . . .
>
> In sum: God's laws of procreation are deductible from reason and any

revelation. Any act performed in accordance with them is right; all other acts in the sex life are wrong. The sanction imposed by God is graphically noted by St. Augustine: "Intercourse even with one's legitimate wife is unlawful and wicked where the conception of offspring is prevented."[14]

Unfortunately, the rhythm method is generally conceded to be both unreliable and psychologically inhibiting. There has been a great deal of discussion of this problem in Roman Catholic circles under the impetus of the Vatican Councils called by Pope John XXIII and Pope Paul VI. One Catholic woman summarized her viewpoint this way:

> Psychologically, rhythm is the most negative of all methods of family limitation because it hangs constantly over your head. Every day you must take your temperature, test your glucose, and fit the data into the calculations of the ever present chart. The man and woman using rhythm live beneath the overarching tyranny of the "safe period" and the "dangerous period." The nagging question intrudes itself into every act of love. "Did we calculate right?" Every time the menstrual period is late or the daily tests show something that seems to diverge from the previous forecast, there is a period of panic. I consider this among the most inhuman tyrannies over the self and the natural creative instincts that has ever been devised. . . .
>
> I submit both from my experience with rhythm and my experience with the birth-control pills that the latter represent an enormous psychological gain over the former. With rhythm you helplessly assume that you can't keep from having children, and all your energies are expended on keeping from having a dozen. The negative dominates. In the second case you know that you are the master of the situation, that you can choose to have a child as a free act of maternal desire. Psychologically there is an enormous gain when a child is not an accident, but is wanted. . . .[15]

The 1970 National Fertility Study made a separate analysis of Catholic women and the birth control methods they used. Apparently, as reflected in Table 18–3, a large number do not conform to the teaching of their church on birth control methods. This is espcially true of those who tend to be inactive in their church, and receive Communion less than monthly. Of white Catholic women under 30 who are inactive in their religion, 80 percent use the pill and other nonapproved methods.

The American Friends Service Committee takes a more positive rather

[14]William J. Egan, in *Religion and Birth Control,* ed. John Clover Monsma (Garden City, N.Y.: Doubleday, 1963), pp. 37–38, 39.

[15]Rosemary Ruether, *What Modern Catholics Think About Birth Control,* ed. William Birmingham (New York: Signet, 1964), pp. 238–39.

Table 18–3 Percentage of White Catholic Women, by Age and Frequency of Receiving Holy Communion, Who Have Never Used Any Method or Who Most Recently Used Rhythm, the Pill, or Other Methods

Most recent method	*Receive Communion at least monthly*						*Receive Communion less than monthly*					
	Under 45		*Under 30*		*30 to 44*		*Under 45*		*Under 30*		*30 to 44*	
	1965	*1970*	*1965*	*1970*	*1965*	*1970*	*1965*	*1970*	*1965*	*1970*	*1965*	*1970*
None	25	23	24	15	25	29	21	17	22	14	20	21
Rhythm	42	23	38	18	45	27	12	8	12	5	12	11
Pill	11	26	20	37	5	18	14	30	28	39	6	19
Other	22	27	18	30	25	26	53	45	39	41	61	48
Total not conforming	33	53	38	67	30	44	67	75	67	80	67	67
Number of women	558	554	207	221	351	323	525	706	199	378	331	328

SOURCE: Charles F. Westoff and Norman B. Ryder, *The Contraceptive Revolution*. Copyright © 1977 by Princeton University Press, II-8, p. 28. Reprinted by permission of Princeton University Press.

than restrictive approach to birth control and family planning. A working party statement published in 1970 states:

> We believe that the population crisis is so threatening to the quality of human life that for the sake of the individual, the family, and society, we must bring population and resources into balance by learning to control our fertility. Toward this end, we believe that contraception is by far preferable to abortion. But we also believe that abortion, performed under proper conditions, is preferable to the birth of an unwanted child.
>
> We believe that every child should be wanted by and born into a family that is able to feed, clothe, educate, and above all, love him; that the family is the basic unit of our society and that the married life of the parents should encompass sexual activity whether or not for purposes of procreation; that appropriate contraception, which spaces children and eliminates the fear of unwanted pregnancies, strengthens family ties and establishes a sense of responsible parenthood; that in view of the problem of overpopulation, every couple has a responsibility to society, as well as to their own family, not to overburden the world with more lives than it can sustain. . . .[16]

[16]American Friends Service Committee, *Who Shall Live?: Man's Control Over Birth and Death* (New York: Hill and Wang, 1970), pp. 58–59.

Abortion

Perhaps the most revolutionary change in the field of birth control in the last ten years has been the legal use of abortion as a primary means of birth control. Abortion itself is nothing new. Abortions have always been performed, in spite of the severe legal restrictions on them that have existed in the United States for over a century. Unfortunately, the desperation of women for abortions in the past led to many a death at the hands of quack abortionists who were all too willing to risk the legal censure a certified physician would not—for a price. But changes in the laws in New York and other states and a 1973 Supreme Court decision that invalidated forty-eight state laws against abortion have made abortion a safe procedure that can be done by a licensed doctor under good medical conditions. Thus abortion can now be seriously discussed as a viable method of birth control.

The Medical Facts

The method used for an abortion depends on the length of the pregnancy. If the pregnancy is of less than twelve weeks' duration (if the unborn child is still an embryo), abortion is fairly simple. The usual methods include *dilatation and curettage,* a procedure in which the cervix is dilated and an instrument is inserted through the cervix to scrape the pregnancy tissue from the walls of the uterus; and vacuum suction. If the pregnancy is of longer than twelve weeks' duration (if the unborn child has reached the fetus stage), a saline solution is injected into the amniotic sac, or the doctor performs a *hysterotomy* (surgical removal of the fetus through the abdomen). Or abortion may be induced by injection of the hormone *oxytocin,* which causes labor contractions. Abortion after twelve weeks is more dangerous than early abortion. Indeed, the risk rises progressively until, at twenty-four weeks (six months), it becomes so high that most doctors will refuse to perform an abortion, except to save a woman's life.

Figures summarized by Betty Sarvis and Hyman Rodman show low mortality rates for legal abortion in most countries (see Table 18–4). The mortality rate for abortion in the United States is just slightly higher than the very low mortality rate for use of oral contraceptives (about 8 per 100,000 compared to 3 per 100,000). It is a good deal lower than the mortality rate for childbirth (3 per 10,000). Thus the operation would seem to involve little risk.

But the immediate risk of an abortion is not the only risk. Long-term risks are just beginning to be identified due to the legalization of abortion (formerly, of course, most abortions were illegal and were not recorded). Dr. Benjamin A. Kogan has warned of serious medical complications in abortions of first pregnancies and has shown quite clearly that under no circum-

Table 18–4 Mortality Rates for Legal Abortion

Country	*Period*	*Mortality rate per 100,000 abortions*	*Number of abortions*
Denmark	1961–65	41.0	21,700
Sweden	1960–66	39.0	30,600
England, Wales and Scotland	1968–69	21.0	40,466
U.S.—(JPSA*)	1970–71	8.2	72,988
New York City	July 1, 1970–Dec. 31, 1971	4.3	278,122
Japan	1959–65	4.1	6,860,000
Czechoslovakia	1963–67	2.5	406,000
Hungary	1964–67	1.2	739,000

*The Joint Program for the Study of Abortion (JPSA) includes sixty-six institutions (sixty teaching hospitals and six clinics). Almost one-half of the hospitals and five of the clinics are located in New York State.

SOURCE: Betty Sarvis and Hyman Rodman, *The Abortion Controversy* (New York: Columbia Univ. Press, 1974), p. 123. Compiled from Diggory et al. (1970: 288, 290) for England, Wales, and Scotland; Tietze (1970: 198, 208) for Denmark, Sweden, Czechoslovakia, and Hungary; the Health Services Administration of New York City (1972: 2) for New York City; Tietze (personal communication) for Japan; and Tietze and Lewit (1972: 98) for the U.S.—JPSA.

stances should abortion be considered anything other than a last resort when other reliable methods of contraception have failed.

> "Why use a contraceptive this time?" a young wife may ask herself. "Abortions are quick and easy and cheap and no trouble." But abortions can be trouble. An induced abortion temporarily interferes with the body's hormonal system. Although return to normal is the rule, post-abortion medical help may be needed. Moreover, even skillfully induced abortions may be unavoidably connected with future problems. There is reliable opinion that the physical trauma of repeated induced abortions may be associated with both a later inability to conceive or to carry a child to full term. In Hungary, Rumania, and the Soviet Union the most recently available records show a higher number of induced abortions than live births. In Hungary the rate of premature births is also rising, and that country now has the highest rate in Europe. "It is widely felt that this change is the result of the free recourse to abortion possible in Hungary and particularly to the termination of first pregnancies." This

opinion may be particularly applicable to a growing experience in this country. In both California and Delaware, the first pregnancies in single women are the ones most frequently terminated. During the first two years of California's revised abortion law, girls younger than twenty years of age constituted almost 33 percent of all abortion cases. Fifty-three percent of all abortions were performed on childless women. In Colorado, more than 50 percent of all abortions are performed on women who have yet to bear their first child. Physicians are concerned about the one-child-sterility syndrome—couples are unable to have a second child. Although not proven, it has been theorized that this may be due to low-grade infection. Such infections can occur following abortion.

Although most abortions are surely justifiable, they should never be regarded as a substitute for a reliable contraceptive.[17]

The Sociological Data

Studies of abortion patients that are now being made will give us some idea of the kind of person who seeks an abortion. But we cannot be certain that the women seeking abortions five, ten, or twenty years from today will have the same circumstances and attitudes as the ones seeking them today. A changing social environment and better sex education may mean that abortion will be sought by a different population.

A study conducted in June and July of 1970 in Honolulu offered some interesting comparisons between maternity and abortion patients there. The 272 abortion patients studied were twenty-two and a half years of age on the average; the maternity patients were an average of twenty-four years old. Many abortions were first pregnancies; the women who had them were most commonly single and apparently could not or did not want to marry the father of the child. Nearly half the maternity patients reported that they were housewives, and they had a higher average income than the abortion patients. But a significant number of the maternity patients were unmarried, including some 22 percent of those from twenty-one to twenty-five years of age.[18] (Some of those women may have had a living-together commitment with the father, however.) Table 18–5 summarizes the differences between the abortion and maternity groups studied. A question for us to ask is this: "What if such trends continue across the country over the next several decades? What will happen to our families?" If children are wanted, born into families with adequate incomes, with both parents in the home, and with

[17]Kogan, p. 136. Based on Melita C. Gesche and Donald G. Dickinson, "Abortion and the Young," *Health News*, 47, no. 8 (Aug. 1970), 6, 13, 14; and Carl Djerassi, "Fertility Control Through Abortion: An Assessment of the Period 1950–1980," *Science and Public Affairs: Bulletin of the Atomic Scientists*, 28, no. 1 (Jan. 1972), 12.

[18]See Patricia G. Steinhoff, Roy G. Smith, and Milton Diamond, "The Characteristics and Motivations of Women Receiving Abortions," *Sociological Symposium*, no. 8 (Spring 1972), 83–90.

Table 18–5 Comparison of Maternity and Abortion Patients (Honolulu, Hawaii)

Abortion patients	*Data*	*Maternity patients*
22.5 yrs.	Age	24.0 yrs.
65% married	Marital State	87.2% married
55%	First Pregnancy	38.7%
20 yrs.	Age at First Pregancy	22 yrs.
37.4%	Income under $6,000	27.7%
28.7%	Income: $6–9,000	33.9%
33.9%	Income: $10,000 & over	38.3%
41.5%	Employed	19%

SOURCE: Patricia G. Steinhoff, Roy G. Smith, and Milton Diamond, "The Characteristics and Motivations of Women Receiving Abortions," *Sociological Symposium*, no. 8 (Spring 1972), 83–90.

a commitment to childrearing, the results should be positive. Women who do not want to be mothers would remove themselves from this task by abortion. The quality of family life for those remaining should improve.

The Honolulu study may have overstated the number of low-income women applying for abortions, because some women were students. Other studies suggest that women from low-income families and from minority groups are less apt to see pregnancy out of wedlock as negative and are not so anxious to terminate it. Some sociologists think that black women will not avail themselves of the new opportunities for abortion, but Sarvis and Rodman disagree.

> Most convincing are the abortion rates for blacks (per 1,000 live births) in the states with the most liberal abortion laws and practices. These rates have gone up dramatically, and in some instances they have moved very quickly from being much lower than the white rates to being higher than the white rates. This suggests that the attitude differences may have been exaggerated and that in any case a demand for long-denied abortion services exists despite less favorable attitudes. The danger is that policymakers will use attitude differences between blacks and whites or the poor and nonpoor as a justification for denying "unwanted" services.[19]

[19]Betty Sarvis and Hyman Rodman, *The Abortion Controversy* (New York: Columbia Univ. Press, 1973), pp. 182–83.

The danger of discrimination between patients of high and low incomes or of different races that Sarvis and Rodman speak of is a very real one that has been documented. A doctor brings to the abortion controversy his own moral and religious standards, the bias of his medical training, and his experience in his own practice. The lawyer, social worker, clergyman, counselor, and politician also each have their own viewpoints. On such an important public issue, it is very difficult for any professional to have a value-free opinion. Our society has accepted strong legal sanctions against abortion without question for many decades because they seemed to be a logical expression of the moral codes of Western society. Let us examine the moral and theological controversy over abortion from a theoretical point of view—bearing in mind, however, that in our society theory somehow always seems to favor the powerful.

The Moral and Theological Controversy

Abortion is the most controversial method of birth control. Advocates of both stricter or more liberal abortion laws are highly vocal in support of their positions. Much public interest in other forms of contraception, such as oral contraceptives, seems to have refocused on the pros and cons of abortion. A large number of books have been published on the subject. The change in public attitudes and in the legal statutes governing abortion has come so suddenly that it is difficult to assess the situation objectively.

The Roman Catholic Church has remained the most consistent opponent of liberalized abortion. John T. Noonan, Jr., reflects the traditional thinking of Catholicism when he asserts that the embryo is completely human from conception and that abortion is therefore a denial of the human right to life.

> The positive argument for conception as the decisive moment of humanization is that at conception the new being receives the genetic code. It is this genetic information which determines his characteristics, which is the biological carrier of the possibility of human wisdom, which makes him a self-evolving being. A being with a human genetic code is man.
>
> This review of current controversy over the humanity of the fetus emphasizes what a fundamental question the theologians resolved in asserting the inviolability of the fetus. To regard the fetus as possessed of equal rights with other humans was not, however, to decide every case where abortion might be employed. It did decide the case where the argument was that the fetus should be aborted for its own good. To say a being was human was to say it had a destiny to decide for itself which could not be taken from it by another man's decision. But human beings with equal rights often come in conflict with each other . . . the right of the fetus regularly at stake is the right to life itself.[20]

Raymond J. Adamek, in a summary of arguments in favor of abortion, points out that each seems to have some equally strong points on the negative side. "A woman has a right to control her own body" is the pro argument; but one can just as well argue for the independent existence of the fetus, with its own chromosomal makeup and life. "Abortion is necessary to protect the physical, mental, or social health of the mother," and yet there is no proof that abortion cures mental illness, or that pregnancy (especially if a child is given up for adoption) causes it. Adamek concludes:

> We have adopted a permissive abortion policy to solve certain personal and social problems. In my view, it is an extreme policy and is based upon inadequate evidence as to its necessity and efficacy. It is a "solution," moreover, which involves the destruction of human life. Certainly, we can utilize our professional efforts and knowledge, our organizing ability, our charity and tax dollars to develop programs which nourish all human life, and which make the choice of life more feasible, desirable, and honorable for our citizens. . . .
>
> Personal freedom is truly enhanced, it seems to me, only by helping people appreciate the facts of the situations they find themselves in, and

[20]See John T. Noonan, Jr., ed., *The Morality of Abortion* (Cambridge, Mass.: Harvard Univ. Press, 1970), p. 57.

encouraging them to deal with the facts in ways which permit self-acceptance and personal growth toward others.[21]

The position of the United States Supreme Court was stated in a landmark decision on January 22, 1973: The court ruled that the state may take an interest in the welfare of the fetus only after the sixth month of pregnancy, when a premature child is capable of surviving outside the mother's body. State regulation of abortion before that time, except to protect the health of the mother, was ruled an unconstitutional invasion of a woman's privacy.

In the 7 to 2 decision (Justices Byron White and William Rehnquist dissenting), the Court overruled all state laws that prohibit or restrict a woman's right to obtain an abortion during the first three months of pregnancy. The Court held that "the right of privacy . . . is broad enough to encompass a woman's decision whether or not to terminate her pregnancy." After discussing some of the reasons why a woman might decide

[21]Raymond J. Adamek, "Abortion, Personal Freedom, and Public Policy," *The Family Coordinator*, 23, no. 4 (Oct. 1974), 411–19.

to have an abortion, the Court said, "All these factors the woman and her responsible physician necessarily will consider in consultation."

The Court held that after the end of the first trimester of pregnancy, the state may have a compelling interest in the health of the mother, because abortion becomes more dangerous at that point. Justice Harry Blackmun, speaking for the Court, declared that "from and after this point, a State may regulate the abortion procedure to the extent that the regulation reasonably relates to the preservation and protection of maternal health." Reasonable regulation, according to the Court, may be concerned with such things as the qualifications of the person who performs abortions and the facility where the abortions are performed.

In dismissing the contention that the State has a compelling interest in protecting the embryo from conception on, the Court concluded: "In short, the unborn have never been recognized in the law as persons in the whole sense." The State's interest in potential life arises only at viability—which the Court defined as starting from 24 to 28 weeks of gestation. During this final period, the Court held: "If the State is interested in protecting fetal life after viability, it may go so far as to proscribe abortion during that period except when it is necessary to preserve the life or health of the mother."[22]

A negative position has been expressed by Richard Stith. In language somewhat similar to the earlier statement by the Society of Friends, he develops "A Secular Case Against Abortion on Demand."[23] He feels that the question is more than a political one, or a question to be settled strictly on personal or religious grounds. He sees the basic issue as "respect for human life and for their fellow citizens." The potentiality is there when conception takes place. Can we ignore all of the possibilities in the fetus, because there is an arbitrary determination that worthwhile life and personhood has not yet begun?

How can a final decision be made? What is meant by an "unwanted pregnancy"? Except for rape or incest, the question is raised of a potential interest in parenthood, and a feeling of final responsibility, in every act of sexual intercourse, no matter how casual.

Many medical and social workers in the field of family planning have come to feel that there is almost no such thing as a totally unwanted pregnancy. No matter what we feel about our sexual activity, no matter how we respond to the notion of having a child, something in us as women—in our minds, our hearts, our glands, our wombs—seems to welcome

[22]Jimmye Kimmey, "How Abortion Laws Happened," *Ms.*, April 1973, 118.
[23]Richard Stith, "A Secular Case Against Abortion on Demand," in J. Gipson Wells, *Current Issues in Marriage and the Family* (New York: Macmillan, 1975), pp. 193–99.

the fact of being pregnant. As a result, no matter how firmly a woman feels that abortion is the best choice for her, she almost surely will also feel some resistance to the idea, consciously or unconsciously. And if she is not aware that this ambivalence is totally natural, she can let it build in her until she feels she is being torn apart.[24]

The most frequently cited reasons for seeking abortion often involve a feeling on the part of the mothers that they would not be able to provide for the child or that they would be torn between the interests of the child and their education or career. In a very real sense, the reasons they give are a moral argument for abortion; in essence, they are saying: "I do not want this child. The father will not marry me. I would have to go on welfare to support the child or give the child up to an uncertain future with adoptive parents I don't know. I might fail to complete my education or lose my chance to make a good marriage if I did not have an abortion, and I might resent the child for it. I think I would make a poor mother under such circumstances, and I do not want the child to suffer for it." To many people, the voluntary elimination of such mothers from the parent population represents a contribution to society.

When the person involved is a teenage girl, there are other needs because she is subject to all of these pressures and yet may have a minimum of experience and maturity. She may need special help and counseling. Any woman may feel the need of a "real friend," whether that person is a doctor, a counselor, a neighbor, or a relative.[25] Nurses are now becoming involved in such counseling, and the nursing profession is taking this function with increased seriousness.[26]

The World Population Problem

The problem of world population control can be simply stated. The "have" nations are willing and able to institute patterns of population control; the "have-not" countries, which need birth control the most, have so far been unable to do so. World population has already passed four billion, and is increasing year by year. One part of the population problem lies in maintaining some kind of ecological balance with our world environment. Natural

[24]Beth Richardson Gutcheon, *Abortion: A Woman's Guide* (New York: Abelard-Schuman, 1973), p. 25.

[25]Diane B. Brashear, "Abortion Counseling," *The Family Coordinator*, 22, no. 4 (Oct. 1973), 429–35.

[26]Lois Monteiro, "Nursing's Acceptance of the Function of Family Planning Counselor," *The Family Coordinator*, 23, no. 1 (Jan. 1974), 67–72.

resources are not unlimited, and we must monitor consumption so that there is something left for the future. Martha Willing expresses the problem in these terms:

> We can restore the ecological balance we have been so busily destroying only if we care enough. For us to care that much, we must believe that human life will continue, but for how long? This is an interesting conundrum. If changing our ways will buy only fifty or a hundred years, life might as well wag merrily on, callous, unequal, flamboyant and disintegrative. . . .
>
> If we look forward to human use of the earth for five thousand years or more, the rationing problem becomes quite different from planning for five hundred. No matter what technology and energy resources may be developed in the future, a longer cruise is obliged to carry fewer people than a short one. We can get control of the rationing process by cutting our numbers nearly in half over the next hundred years . . . .[27]

Overpopulation has been receiving increasing attention from demographers, sociologists, and psychologists, as well as from the press and popular movements such as Zero Population Growth. Frank Notestein sees zero growth as a desirable goal for Americans and estimates population stabili-

[27]Martha Kent Willing, *Beyond Conception: Our Children's Children* (Boston: Gambit, 1971), p. 215.

zation can be reached at 300 million. And indeed, recent drops in the American birth rate have caused demographers to revise their original estimate of 300 million for the year 2000 to 270 million. But the situation is much more crucial in the less developed regions of the world.

> The situation of that two-thirds of the world's population living in the less developed regions contrasts sharply with that of the United States. In general, in the less developed regions the economy rests heavily on subsistence agriculture and other extractive industries; per capita income and literacy are very low, birth rates are very high, and death rates range from the world's highest to the world's lowest, as does the density of population. Rates of growth vary from a little under two percent to well over three percent. Moreover, where the increase is relatively low, as in parts of Africa, it is clear that it will rise as soon as rudimentary health protection can be introduced.
>
> . . . Indeed, I think that there is grave danger that population growth will so retard economic transformation and the improvement of living conditions that there will be a breakdown of civil order in a number of large countries. This risk gravely threatens the lives of tens, perhaps scores, of millions of people.
>
> It seems difficult to exaggerate the importance of reducing the rate of population growth as soon as possible throughout most of the less developed regions. . . . Zero growth, as a meaningful proposal in the near term, is idle talk. It could only be achieved by a rise in the death rate, which no one will accept as a goal of policy for his own people.[28]

The developing countries are beginning to realize the seriousness of the population program. Cuca and Pierce, in reporting on a number of experiments in family planning in the developing nations, show that with proper planning of the contraceptive program, oral contraceptives were utilized in India in urban, rural, and slum communities. The results are summarized in Table 18–6. Even the women in rural areas, likely to be illiterate, did accept the pill. The People's Republic of China has also instituted a number of programs of population control. Later marriage and smaller families are stressed. China hopes to be able to limit future population growth to 8 million persons annually. An all-out campaign to educate the Chinese public in family planning features the slogan "One child is too few, two children are just right, but three are a major error."[29]

[28]See Frank Notestein, "Zero Population Growth: What Is It?" *The American Population Debate*, ed. Daniel Callahan (Garden City, N.Y.: Doubleday, 1971), pp. 39–40.
[29]*Los Angeles Times*, Oct. 28, 1973.

Table 18–6 Acceptance of Oral Contraceptives and Continuation Rates Among Urban, Rural, and Slum Women in West Bengal, India

Place	*Observations*	*Number of acceptors*	*Percentage accepting*	*Percentage of acceptors continuing 12 cycles*	*18 cycles*
Urban	Majority were acceptors prior to visit	609	42.7	77.6	66.7
Rural	Most accepted after one contact	318	24.4	87.7	85.1
Slum	Most accepted after two contacts	474	31.8	47.4	33.3

SOURCE: Roberto Cuca and Catherine S. Pierce, *Experiments in Family Planning* (Baltimore, Md.: Johns Hopkins Univ. Press, 1977), pp. 122–23. Copyright 1977 by Johns Hopkins University Press. Reprinted by permission.

Hope for the Future

The population problem is a highly significant aspect of our relationship with the rest of the world. Unless some method of educating people about birth control can be found, the billions of dollars expended in military and foreign-aid programs and the Peace Corps, the CARE program, and religious and welfare programs will be largely negated. We know that there is ever widening knowledge about birth control. Organizations devoted solely to that purpose, school educational programs, articles in newspapers and magazines, and radio and television programs all help to make more information available to the general public. However, the gap between the ideal and the actual achievement in the education and awareness of the entire population is still large. Those who seem to need to limit their families most often fail to do so.

Family planning is a topic that has personal significance for every couple sharing a relationship, whether they are married or not. It is also a subject of major significance for the entire world, since the sum total of the choices of hundreds of millions of couples leave its mark on the future history of our planet.

SUMMARY

Family planning is a subject of individual and social importance, one that is significant both to Americans and to the world community. Every couple should decide how many children would be best for their family and choose a birth control method in keeping with their religious convictions.

There are a number of methods of birth control available today. The natural, or rhythm, method is recommended by the Roman Catholic Church. It is extremely difficult to use effectively, however. The condom and the diaphragm, used in combination with spermicides, are more effective and are thus more widely accepted by the general public.

Oral contraceptives are now the most popular means of birth control in the United States. Introduced in 1960, they have since been modified to make possible varying prescriptions for specific patients. When used under the continuing supervision of a physician, the risk involved in taking the pill is small. The intrauterine device is another birth control method that is convenient to use.

Sterilization is a permanent method of birth control that is becoming more accepted in our society. New conceptions of masculinity and the male role are closely related to this trend. Two main methods of sterilization are used for women: tubal ligation and tubal cautery by laparoscopy, both of which involve abdominal surgery. In a man, sterilization is accomplished by vasectomy, a minor operation that can be done in a doctor's office. None of these methods of sterilization impairs the patient's sexuality. Several studies of vasectomy patients show favorable responses to the results of the operation. Some men who undergo vasectomies store sperm in frozen sperm banks in case they should ever wish to father a child.

Religious teaching is still an important factor in the use of contraceptives. The Roman Catholic Church opposes all forms of birth control except the natural, or rhythm, method. However, there have been efforts within the church to liberalize this position. In fact, the 1970 National Fertility Study showed that 80 percent of young Catholic women used the pill and other nonconforming birth control methods, although these women were usually inactive in their religion. Protestant groups, on the other hand, do accept several different birth control methods.

Recently there has been a rapid increase in the use of abortion as a method of birth control. Several methods of abortion are used, depending on the stage of pregnancy of the patient. Dilatation and curettage is one common procedure; hysterotomy and the injection of the hormone oxytocin are also employed. The mortality rate for legal abortions is quite low—lower than the rate for childbirth. However, postoperative risks must also be considered: young women may find it difficult to carry a child to full term after abortion of a first pregnancy. In no case should abortion be considered a primary method of birth control.

Initial sociological data on abortion patients are now being received. Young single women in the lower-income brackets seem to predominate. A number of older women and women who already have families are also receiving abortions, however. Discrimination against some women who seek abortions persists.

Abortion is controversial. Both pro-abortion and anti-abortion groups are strongly committed to their own points of view. The Supreme Court has overruled state laws that prohibit abortion during the first two trimesters of pregnancy. However, Congress and several state legislatures are restricting funding for abortions, which makes this method of birth control unavailable to many poor women.

The world population problem is a critical one. Population growth may soon outstrip the world's natural resources. The crisis is particularly acute in the underdeveloped nations of the world. Family planning is thus a must, not only in the United States but in the rest of the world community.

The decision to assume parenthood is a crucial one. A couple should take time to adjust to each other before beginning their family so that their children will be planned and wanted.

SUGGESTED READINGS

Adamek, Raymond J. "Abortion, Personal Freedom, and Public Policy." *The Family Coordinator*, 23, no. 4 (Oct. 1974), 411–19. Discusses the pro and anti-abortion factors and the implications of new public policy concerning abortion.

American Friends Service Committee. *Who Shall Live?: Man's Control Over Birth and Death*. New York: Hill and Wang, 1970. Thought-provoking report of Quaker study of birth control, with particular emphasis on abortion.

Fleishman, Norman, and Peter L. Dixon. *Vasectomy, Sex, and Parenthood.* Garden City, N.Y.: Doubleday, 1973. Good discussion of male sterilization and its relationship to parental responsibilities.

Gutcheon, Beth Richardson. *Abortion: A Woman's Guide.* New York: Abelard-Schuman, 1973. From Planned Parenthood of New York. A discussion of the various methods of abortion available to women.

Hardin, Garrett. *Mandatory Motherhood: The True Meaning of "Right to Life."* Boston: Beacon, 1974. Critique of the "right-to-life" movement; argues in favor of availability of abortion.

Kogan, Benjamin A. *Human Sexual Expression.* New York: Harcourt Brace Jovanovich, 1973. Basic text on human sexuality. Includes good discussion of the various birth control methods and their effectiveness.

Luker, Kristin. *Taking Chances: Abortion and the Decision Not to Contracept.* Berkeley, Calif.: University of California Press, 1975. A study of 500 women seeking abortions that examines their reasons for not using contraceptive methods.

Ruether, Rosemary. *What Modern Catholics Think About Birth Control.* New York: Signet, 1964. Critique of the Roman Catholic position on birth control from one woman's point of view.

Sarvis, Betty, and Hyman Rodman. *The Abortion Controversy.* New York: Columbia Univ. Press, 1973. Broad coverage of the arguments for and against abortion. Includes social, legal, and medical viewpoints.

Westoff, Charles F., and Norman B. Ryder. *The Contraceptive Revolution.* Princeton, N.J.: Princeton Univ. Press, 1977. Discussion of current birth control practices; emphasis on 1965 and 1970 National Fertility Studies.

Willing, Martha Kent. *Beyond Contraception: Our Children's Children.* Boston: Gambit, 1971. Discussion of contraception and its impact on the future populations.

Wylie, Evan McLeod. *A Guide to Voluntary Sterilization: The New Birth Control.* New York: Grosset & Dunlap, 1972. Discussion of male and female sterilization. Provides detailed information about hospitals and clinics where sterilizations are performed; sperm banks; doctors; and insurance against possible fertilization.

19 Parenthood and Adoption

- How can parents best prepare for the arrival of their first child?
- Is parenthood a crisis? Why do parents have negative reactions to parenthood?
- What are the most important role functions of the father?
- What are the most important role functions of the mother?
- What basic needs of the child must be met by the family?
- What function does adoption serve in our society?
- What factors should a couple consider before seeking to adopt a child?

The Developing Child

The inherited characteristics of the human infant are established at the moment of conception, when sperm and ovum unite. But, of course, life patterns are not developed solely on the basis of inherited characteristics. The influence of environment, especially the home environment during the first years of life, is enormous. In this chapter we will discuss the way in which husband and wife grow into their crucial role as parents and the early development of the child.

The early years are crucial for the child because he learns patterns of behavior and emotional response that will be his for the rest of his life. During these first years, a child undertakes many tasks that will move him along the road from dependent infancy to mature independence. Evelyn Duvall, in discussing the child's development in the family, has outlined nine developmental tasks of infancy and early childhood. They are:

1. Achieving physiological equilibrium following birth . . .
2. Learning to take food satisfactorily . . .
3. Learning the know-how and the where-when of elimination . . .
4. Learning to manage his body effectively . . .
5. Learning to adjust to other people . . .
6. Learning to love and be loved . . .
7. Developing systems of communication . . .
8. Learning to express and control feelings . . .
9. Laying foundations for self-awareness . . .[1]

This is a comprehensive list and, interestingly, contains four items dealing with physical capabilities, four dealing with social interactions, and only one dealing with the mental, emotional, moral, and spiritual life of the infant. Perhaps this is a way of recognizing that we can observe how a baby handles his body, and how he reacts to other people, but we cannot know what goes on inside the baby's mind because of the lack of language and communication skills. Yet the inner development of the child is important, just as the total growth and development of the child is crucial.

When we consider how broad are the basic tasks the child has to achieve in the first year or two of life in comparison with the relatively gradual adjustments the child is required to make in later life, we see why these beginning years are so important. Facing these developmental tasks is a part of the child's individual personality development. There is no inflexible schedule that tells when a boy or girl will be ready to take a particular step toward greater maturity. A child's readiness will be determined both by his own makeup and his family environment. George E. Gardner discusses the growth of the child from two to five years of age this way:

> Our expectations regarding psychological development must always be measured against the background of the individual child. Is his society willing and has it the capacity to give him opportunities to learn? By his society I mean his parents primarily, of course, but also the other persons of his immediate environment. Will his curiosity and his explorations bring him useful and instructive feedback from them? The amount of feedback flowing from adults to children varies not only from family to family but also from social group to social group, too often depending, sad to say, upon their economic and educational status. How much stimulation the child gets from his environment will influence the rate at which he will progress along the several ladders of development: physical, interpersonal, intellectual, and moral. . . .[2]

[1]Evelyn Millis Duvall, *Marriage and Family Development*, 5th ed. (Philadelphia: Lippincott, 1977), pp. 220–21.
[2]George E. Gardner, *The Emerging Personality* (New York: Delacorte Press, 1970), pp. 37–38.

Sandra Titus conducted an interesting study using family photographs to determine what actually occurs in the early years of family life. She selected a small sample of 23 families in a small midwestern community. She was able to interview them and note the differences in their photographic records of their children, including at least one child who was between 4 and 11 months of age. All families had photos of their first child, and almost all had photos of the most recent child, but there were significantly more photos of the first child than the younger children. Perhaps the whole child-caring pattern is more exciting the first time around. The pictures reflected what the parents were interested in (and proud to share). Both mothers and fathers were photographed in the caretaking roles for the first child (holding, feeding, bathing, diapering). Within the limitations of picture taking (expense, equipment, posing, having third party available), the photos gave an indication of how the parents carried out their new responsibilities, and perhaps, Titus speculates, even increased the parents' commitment to their new role.[3]

Preparing for Parenthood

How do parents learn how to be parents? What changes occur in their thinking and behavior? How do they meet the necessity for change in their outlook and their patterns of daily life? The process begins with the adjustments the couple make as they prepare for the birth of the first child.

We have discussed in Chapter 17 some of the elements of choice that should guide a couple into the experience of parenthood. As birth control and family planning become more and more the norm in our society, the role of the parent assumes a place of greater importance, and consequently is more carefully considered and given greater priority in the lives of both husband and wife.

Preparation for the New Child

There are many other ways in which parents prepare for the birth of a child. The most obvious is in the alterations they make in their home or apartment. The den is transformed into a nursery, or a corner of the parents' bedroom rearranged to make room for a crib. Perhaps a new house or apartment is considered. Certain changes are made in the family budget as well: extra money is set aside for doctors' bills and hospital expenses, and the purchase of a new car, a color television set, or some other item not essential to the life of the child is postponed. The wife usually leaves her job, and the couple

[3]Sandra L. Titus, "Family Photographs and Transition to Parenthood," *Journal of Marriage and the Family*, 38, no. 3 (Aug. 1976), 525–30.

spend their leisure hours getting ready a thousand and one things that may (or may not) be needed by a brand new baby.

But the best preparation the couple can make requires no special effort at all. They must be themselves if they are to be the best possible parents for the child. If husband and wife are genuine, honest-to-goodness people with a deep and real love and concern for each other, they have made the best possible preparation for a third member of the family circle; they will be ready to share their own happiness with their child.

A preparation of prime importance is the desire of parents for the coming child. Unfortunately, some first children are unwanted; they are conceived before marriage, or perhaps before the time chosen by their parents. The father is resentful because the child represents a loss of freedom for him. He may find the new financial obligations extremely heavy. And his frustration may be shared by his wife; her natural joy and expectation may be dimmed by the recognition that the child will limit her personal activities in the coming months and years. There is a different feeling in a home where both father and mother are eagerly awaiting the birth of their new child. They share concern for the wife's health and strength during pregnancy and find much time to talk together about their hopes and dreams for the future.

Still another vital preparation for a new child is a real willingness to share one's future with the child. A childless couple in our prosperous and mobile society have many opportunities to seek advancement in business or a profession and to live in the area most acceptable to them. The coming of children, however, means that major decisions can no longer be made on the basis of parental preferences alone. The welfare and development of the children become major considerations. And parents must also accept the fact that a child has a mind of his own and will not always agree with them. Unfortunately, some parents share their lives with their children grudgingly. They expect their children to be what they want them to be and are unwilling to adapt to new points of view in the family. Happy is the child who is born into a family in which he is loved and cherished for what he is as an individual and for what he is to become, small or great, in the years ahead.

Parental Reactions to Childbirth

The beginning of parenthood is an exciting time. Is it also a time of crisis? It is a fearful and wonderful thing to carry your first child across the threshold and realize that your marital life is finally and irrevocably altered. In the hospital, fathers may seem to be a needless accessory, and even some mothers may feel that the baby is better off being taken care of by doctors and nurses. But soon the brief days of the hospital stay are over, and father and mother are at home again with a very demanding new member of the family. The first nights are interrupted by insistent cries for feeding or changing, and the parents realize that they are totally responsible for this helpless new person.

There is a real sense of pride and achievement for most parents when they finally settle down and appreciate the fact that this is *their* baby, a visible sign of the continuity of their life together. Relatives, neighbors, and acquaintances voice words of friendship and concern. Certainly the seed of family pride and solidarity is nurtured and blossoms naturally under such conditions.

At the same time, parenthood is bound to bring its fears and anxieties. "Did the baby sleep at all this afternoon?" the anxious husband inquires. "Did you ask the doctor how her tests came out?" inquires another worried husband. Nor is the wife immune to attacks of uncertainty and confusion. "Is that just a nighttime cough, or is she coming down with pneumonia?" "Why doesn't that rash on his leg go away?" "Is he eating enough during the day to be able to skip that 2 A.M. feeding?" Everything is a new experience, and parents are bound to be perplexed and anxious if there is any indication that the infant is not growing normally.

As we saw in Chapter 17, one sociologist, E. E. LeMasters, has spoken of the arrival of the first child as a parental crisis.[4] LeMasters first hypothesized that the addition of a new member to the family might prove an upsetting experience for the parents. He then selected a small sample of 46 couples under thirty-five years of age, all typical middle-class respondents. The husbands were college graduates and the wives were housewives at the time of the study. The first children were less than five years old. LeMasters interviewed the couples over a three-year period.

LeMasters used a five-point scale ranging from *1* for no crisis to *5* for severe crisis to code his interview data. Although the marriages were generally functioning well and the children had been either planned or desired, 38 of the 46 couples reported an extensive or severe crisis when the first child arrived. The great difficulty, as LeMasters saw it, was that the couples had romanticized parenthood. They found themselves tired or exhausted; they discovered the confining effects of the ever present responsibility of children; they missed their jobs and social contacts outside their home; and they were surprised by the volume of work and the difficulty of returning to normal family and social life.

A different perspective on this period is provided by Candyce Smith Russell. She recognizes that much of the parent "crisis" literature has focused on the negative impact of the new third member of the family, who is seen as disrupting a couple's affection and intimacy. Russell conducted a study of 296 wives and 272 husbands whose infants were about 29 weeks old at the time of the study. She inquired about the parental crisis situation.

[4]E. E. LeMasters, "Parenthood as Crisis," *Marriage and Family Living,* 19, no. 4 (Nov. 1957), 352–55.

Russell also added a "Gratification Checklist" to her study, which attempted to measure the positive side of parenting. It also directed the parents to think of both the good and the bad in parenting. The net result on the "crisis" measure is shown in Table 19–1. The vast majority in Russell's study showed only a "slight" or "moderate" crisis (over 90 percent of both fathers and mothers), and a very small number (less than 4 percent of the total sample) checked "extensive" or "severe" crisis. She did find that the more highly educated parents seemed to be less satisfied with their new role. Perhaps this was because both parents saw their parenting role as competitive with what they were trying to achieve for themselves in their careers and in society.

A similar, more positive, conclusion was reached by Daniel Hobbs in studies conducted in 1965, 1968, and 1975. In a 1976 report, using a random sample drawn from public birth records, and utilizing surveys and interviews, Hobbs and Sue Peck Cole suggested that beginning parenthood is not a crisis, but rather a transition with some accompanying difficulty. There was little statistical significance in the varying problems that were identified with parenthood.[5] More research needs to be done to be able to predict with any certainty who will react to the parenthood transition most easily.

Hobbs and Jane Maynard Wimbish followed the same line of investigation with black couples, and found that they experienced slightly greater difficulty than white parents, and that the mothers had more problems in adjustment than the fathers. Still, "crisis" was too strong a description of their reaction to their new status as parents.[6] Comparative studies of whites and blacks are especially valuable because there is, at present, little reliable data on the significant differences in family patterns among various racial groups.

It is too easy to focus on the problem situations and ignore the many families in which life is marked by real joy and achievement. Stella Chess, Alexander Thomas, and Herbert Birch take a more optimistic view.

> Parents—as a harried mother once pleaded—are people, too. They share the human characteristic of being different. They are at least as different from one another as are their children.
>
> Men and women vary enormously in the way they play their parental roles. This is not surprising. Adults are first of all different individuals before they become parents. . . .
>
> There is no mystery about good parenthood. If parents cultivate with

[5]Daniel F. Hobbs, Jr., and Sue Peck Cole, "Transition to Parenthood: A Decade Replication," *Journal of Marriage and the Family*, 38, no. 4 (Nov. 1976), 723–31.

[6]Daniel F. Hobbs, Jr., and Jane Maynard Wimbish, "Transition to Parenthood by Black Couples," *Journal of Marriage and the Family*, 39, no. 4 (Nov. 1977), 677–89.

Table 19–1 Crisis in Parenthood

Degree	Males	Females
None	3.3%	0.3%
Slight	75.1	57.5
Moderate	16.8	39.1
Extensive	1.1	3.1
Severe	3.7	0

SOURCE: Candyce Smith Russell, "Transition to Parenthood: Problems and Gratifications," *Journal of Marriage and the Family,* 36, no. 2 (May 1974), 296. Copyrighted 1974 by the National Council on Family Relations. Reprinted by permission.

> their children the qualities they use to make their other close and deep relationships work, there will probably be no need to worry about whether the child is sufficiently loved.
>
> Sometimes parents seem so weighed down with instructions and commandments that the joys of parenthood are quite obscured. This is indeed sad. Children are one of the most reliable and richest sources of pleasure in life.[7]

Parenthood must be kept in perspective. Parents ask: "What do we really expect when a new child enters our home? Do we recognize the changes that will come as a result of this new responsibility? Do we realize that the family's interest and attention will refocus on the child and that our closeness may be diminished as a result?" Couples should face parenthood seriously and thoughtfully. But they should also be confident in their ability to deal with it.

> My husband and I have always felt that family love and affection are highly important, and this has helped us to overcome some very trying circumstances. We have learned that no one party has to be "bad," or deliberately cause dissension in a marriage. Differing priorities that may fit one person may be difficult for another to follow.
>
> Love for the children can become an obsession very easily, especially with women. Men may temper their love for children with strict attitudes to help them become more self-sufficient. . . . My husband has accused

[7]Stella Chess, Alexander Thomas, and Herbert G. Birch, *Your Child Is a Person* (New York: Viking Press, 1965), pp. 196, 202.

me of preparing our children for Disneyland instead of the real world that awaits them. However, I feel that dreams are important, whether they are attained or not.[8]

Models for Parenting

What is expected of us when we become parents? What will give us guidance and direction in taking on this new role? How can we go about being the kind of parents we ought to be? LeMasters says there are at least five models that have been followed by American parents. The first is the *martyr* model. This model is characterized by guilt and overprotection, and a combination of revolt or submission and hostility and resentment by the child toward the parent. This model is destructive for both the parent and the child. A second model is the *buddy* or *pal* model. This is developed around equality, democracy, and sharing between the children (primarily teenagers) and the parent. LeMasters suggests that some of these parents married young, and the children and parents have grown up together.

A third type is the *policeman* or *drill-sergeant* model. Its exponents would explain that this is an effective method of controlling children and of keeping them out of trouble. However, it is not too successful with teenagers. The adolescent peer group has a powerful antiauthority influence. In this kind of family structure we can see the genesis of youth rebellion against authority.

A fourth model is the *teacher-counselor* model. In such a role the parent stresses the child's development. This seems to be the dominant middle-class model, and has many historical roots in our culture. But it may be too permissive, produce anxiety and guilt in parents, and fail to recognize clearly the needs of the larger society. In the same way, the *athletic coach* model is culturally attractive, especially for fathers. They can relive or reshape their own childhood experiences by stimulating the kind of behavior in their children that will create what they consider the best results.[9] LeMasters suggests that these models are valuable in parent counseling since they help parents to see what they are doing to their children and where the parent-child relationship is going. It is interesting to note that parents (and especially fathers) will choose a model when the child is very young, and build on it. Fathers strive to be pals to their young sons, dress alike, spend time constantly together, and favor them in every way possible. Mothers may choose the counselor role, and utilize this for a too permissive and adult approach to their young children. It always helps to have a clear model for behavior,

[8]Student report.
[9]LeMasters, pp. 192–203.

and to have enough self-understanding to evaluate and modify one's actions if necessary.

The Husband's New Role as Father

One of the failures of our present dating and courtship system is that it has practically no relation to the duties and responsibilities of parenthood. But parent education is as important as education for any other role in life. Home economics classes represent one serious attempt to prepare people for the parental role. Unfortunately, the vast majority of students so far have been women; preparation for fatherhood has been neglected.

The new responsibilities a husband assumes with parenthood give him an opportunity to play an enlarged role in family life. As a married man he has learned to share life with his spouse, but he has retained a large measure of independence. When he becomes a father, however, he finds that his wife must assume many new responsibilities and for that reason relies more heavily on him for physical help, encouragement, affection, and security. This partnership between husband and wife is basic to their role behavior as parents. When they are working together successfully in a loving and caring relationship, this security will be communicated to their children.

> A healthy parent-child relationship that is nonexploitative and that provides the child with security can develop when the parental relationship is a healthy, loving one. The mother's comfort depends to a considerable extent upon the nature of the relationship she has with her husband. Her feelings of being valued, loved, and respected and her acceptance of herself and her femininity are heavily affected by her husband's acceptance of her and her roles. The mother-father relationship, then, is one that determines and pervades all others.[10]

A father's first task is to accept the responsibility of his fatherhood. In contemporary society, it is not enough to father a son or daughter and then leave the task of raising and educating the child to the mother. In earlier generations, that may have seemed appropriate; a man's working day was so long that he had little time left for his children. He might even have to be gone from home for weeks or months at a time. Today such absence, except because of military service, is rare. Even the traveling salesman can telephone home from anywhere in the country. And most middle-class families do manage to see that the husband's work will not require long absences from home. A man ought therefore to be involved with the raising of his

[10] Ira J. Gordon, *Human Development from Birth Through Adolescence* (New York: Harper & Row, 1969), p. 51.

children. Children soon become aware of how well a father accepts his basic responsibility in the family. One black student, writing of his home and family, described his father in this way:

> Throughout the years, my father has been a hard worker and a good provider for his family. He has worked on tough jobs—from construction work to shipyard employment. My father has a great deal of pride in himself and his family. He has admirably fulfilled his role as head of the household for many years.
>
> Even during the Second World War, when working hours were hard and long, he maintained his zest for life. He has remained youthful and young at heart until this day. He has striven to give us many things that a large family such as ours would not normally have. . . . He has instilled this pride of providing and working for a better standard of living in his children. I give my father a great deal of credit for his fortitude and his ability to withstand the pressures on a man with a large family in our society. . . .[11]

Maureen Green has pointed out that the last twenty-five years have seen a decline in the importance of the father role. The change and initiative have been in the hands of women. The emphasis on individual choice has freed both husbands and wives from lifelong obligations to each other and their children. What is left? A father should be an example to his sons, and should

[11]Student report.

build a strong relationship with them. And he plays an important role with his daughter. Green writes:

> As a teacher of the traditional sexual roles . . . father can be a doubtful blessing to his daughters; but as an individual to love and understand he suffers from no such handicap. Father is, after all, the first man a girl ever loves. He is the man who first makes her feel her mother as a rival and enact the famous triangle of love and jealousy that Freud has pinpointed as crucial in emotional development. And father, above all, is the first man who shows her men. . . . Because they are reared and taught in their early years by women, and realize very early that they will grow up to be just like mother one day, there is very little motive for them to find out at all that another sex exists. They can live quite cheerfully without knowing that there are men. It is father who has to represent for them this extraordinary and different kind of human being.[12]

A second task for a new father is to accept the change in his relationship to his wife. We discussed marital role expectations in earlier chapters. There are many ways in which marriage brings a great deal of ego satisfaction to a man. Especially if he feels that his relationship to society is largely impersonal, he will treasure the sense of importance and value he gains from the love and affection of his wife. In the office or store or factory he may feel that he is valued only as a cog in the wheel; at home he holds the place of central importance. But when a child comes, he must share this place in his wife's affection.

The shift in the relationship of husband and wife is a matter partly of time and partly of personal relations. There are only twenty-four hours in the day, and the care of a young child or of two or three small children is bound to occupy much of a woman's time. A husband should have the maturity to see that love given to a child is not love taken away from him. Father and child are not in competition for a mother's attention and love.

Such changes must not only be accepted graciously by a husband; at the same time, he and his wife must work to create ways to be together without the interference of the children. Time and money can be found for leisure activities outside the home so that they can maintain their identity as a couple.

Another task for the new father is to assume an emotionally supportive role in the family. He needs to express his love for his wife freely so that she can meet her new responsibilities to her children. In a way, each human being is a reservoir of energy, intelligence, and emotional warmth and strength. This reservoir is not inexhaustible; at some point we can be

[12]Maureen Green, *Fathering* (New York: McGraw-Hill, 1977), pp. 101–02.

drained dry and become incapable of meeting new demands. But if a father gives his family his love and support, they will more than return it.

A study by Samuel Cox of a number of sixth-, seventh-, and eighth-grade children in a white middle-class community seems to confirm the importance of a father's emotional support. Students were rated by their peers and divided into two groups of high and low peer status. They were then tested on how they felt about their parents, and their parents gave reports on their own behavior. It is interesting to note that the children with high peer-status ratings were more apt to have parents who would participate in such a study: 45 out of 52 families agreed to participate. Of the low-status children only 30 out of 48 had intact families in which both parents would agree to participate.[13] Cox found that "data in this study strongly support the observation that the father's affectional behavior has more influence than the mother's affectional behavior on the child's behavior, provided the measures of parental affectional behavior are based on the child's perception of those parental behaviors."[14] In addition, Cox cited other studies that indicated the importance of the father's acceptance of a child to the child's adjustment, behavior, and even scores on intelligence tests.

The need for a father's affection is especially important now that many outside influences are pulling husband, wife, and children away from the home (see Figure 19–1). The basic economic unity and interdependence characteristic of the traditional farm family no longer hold family members together. School, church, and community, together with economic factors, peer groups, television and mass media, and recreational activities, pull the family in many different directions. A father who plays a strong supportive role can do much to hold a family together.

The Wife's New Role as Mother

The tasks a wife must assume in her new role as a mother are just as varied and perhaps even more important than those assumed by a father. The new mother has a major task before her in shifting her interest from the broader community to the home itself. If she has had full-time employment, which is customary for most young wives in our culture, it may have been a profession for which she had several years of training. A career can be challenging and rewarding. With the arrival of the first child, many women will become full-time homemakers for the first time in their marriage, and the switch may not be easy. If she is used to the hustle and bustle of a busy office, hospital, or factory, she may find being at home alone depressing. If others have been dependent on her for professional help, she may not be inspired

[13]See Samuel Cox, "Intrafamily Comparison of Loving-Rejecting Child-Rearing Practices," *Child Development*, 41, no. 2 (June 1970), 437–48.
[14]Cox, p. 446.

by the necessity of cleaning the kitchen or preparing formulas. The ease with which a mother is able to switch from one role to the other will vary from woman to woman; in every case, there will be some major adjustments to be made.

A growing number of women will return to their jobs soon after their baby's birth. Some of the pros and cons of this were considered in Chapter 13. Some couples are able to obtain first-class day care for their young children or full-time care in the home, while other couples may have difficulty finding someone to care for their children. One recent study estimates that forty percent of women with children under six are working. The question is raised whether there are enough quality day-care centers to meet the needs of the large number of two-income families, or if day care is really the solution for the need of the child. Many experts still see the need for more "mothering," and for less of a highly structured and impersonal nursery school environment.[15]

The new mother needs also to expect some changes in her physical strength. Few mothers return from the hospital and resume a normal schedule within a week or two; most find that a much longer period goes

[15]See Earl C. Gottschalk, Jr., "Women at Work: Day Care Is Booming, but Experts Are Split over Its Effects on Kids," *The Wall Street Journal,* Sept. 15, 1978, 39–42.

Figure 19–1 Outside Influences on the Contemporary Family

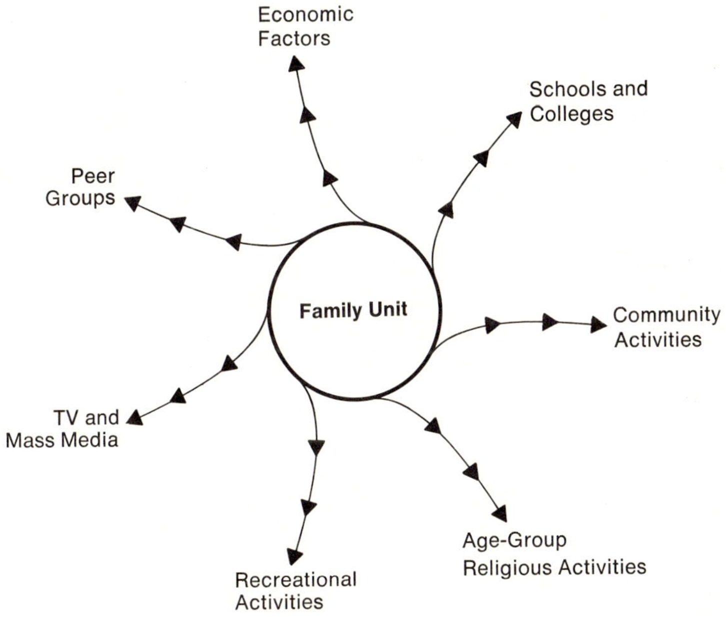

by before they regain their full strength and vitality. The important thing is for both husband and wife to recognize that there may be a physical and emotional letdown *(post-partum depression)* following the birth of a child and to be prepared to take the time necessary for recovery. The more fully the mother (and the father) have shared in the preparation for birth of their child, the more quickly health and vitality will return. And at the same time, such sharing will accelerate the return to their normal pattern of sexual activity.

Finally, a woman must learn to balance her roles as wife and mother. It is natural to expect a shift in the relationship between husband and wife. But the wife needs to be aware of the dangers involved. She must make the transition as smooth as possible. An evening's recreation without the baby, an emphasis on certain enjoyable experiences that husband and wife can share, and some special attention that stresses the importance of the husband to her will help maintain a husband's feeling of security.[16]

A wife and mother will normally be thinking more seriously than her husband about all these changes. As a girl she will have taken more interest in home life and children than her husband. As a babysitter she may have observed and tried to understand different parents' reactions to their responsibilities. As a college student, she may have taken courses in home economics, psychology, or sociology. Throughout the years ahead she will naturally observe the patterns of family life and note signs of possible trouble. If she does not take a happy home life for granted, but consciously nurtures it, she will be contributing more than she knows to the lives of everyone in the family.

The Child's Basic Needs

The new baby has many needs. He turns first of all to his mother to meet these needs; but very early he recognizes that his father is also a source of satisfaction. Soon he begins to interact with grandparents, babysitters, nursery-school teachers, and other substitutes for his parents who can help to supply his requirements. And indeed, his requirements are many.

In the beginning the focus is almost completely on the baby's physical needs. He needs to be fed, kept clean and warm, allowed to sleep comfortably, and so forth. But his psychological needs will soon be felt as well. We have all seen a child become frightened when his mother leaves the room. Or we have observed a baby kick and fuss when his father tries to let a stranger hold him. Maslow has discussed these varying levels of need in his "hierarchy of needs."[17] But as the child grows, other, more significant social,

[16]For further discussion of the young mother's role, see Duvall, pp. 223–26.
[17]See Chapter 1, pp. 13–14.

psychological, moral, and spiritual goals are recognized. Once the process of development begins at birth, it continues in many different ways throughout the life cycle.

The child needs both nurture and control from his parents. He needs support so that he can face with confidence and strength the many tasks thrust on him, and he gains it from his parents as they give him love, affection, interest, and attention. Gradually his sense of self-respect and value grows. He is willing to try new things and face new experiences because he has his parents' reassurance. Children who do not receive enough love will have a difficult time growing up. Catherine Landreth has reported on the development of two groups of children, one reared in an institution in which they received little love and the other reared in foster homes.

> The group who spent the first three years of their lives in institutions had many problems of adjustment when they were later placed in foster homes. Twelve of them, in fact, had to be replaced into other foster homes, some as many as three times, during the three-year period of this study. In contrast, the group who spent the first three years of their lives in foster homes had few problems of adjustment in the ensuing three years, and only one had to be replaced. There were, moreover, twice as many behavior problems in the institutional group, and the problems were of a different kind from those of the group of foster-home children.

> The institutional children were disobedient, hyperactive, restless, distractible, and unable to concentrate. Behavior problems of the foster-home group were of a more passive, moderate type.[18]

A child needs control as much as he needs support. The child will probably want to assert his independence and be as free of parental control as possible. But every child needs and at least unconsciously wants the reassurance and guidance of parental control. The secret is to achieve a good balance between too much control and too little. That golden mean may be hard to find. It will be reached most easily if the parents cooperate with each other in giving the child both love and discipline. One parent should not be responsible for all the love or all the control.

Norman Denzin has documented the wide range of childhood socialization in the development of language, social behavior, and identity. He sees interaction as crucial to the child's normal development, and feels that we often underestimate the child's ability to share in his own responses and have a part and choice in his maturing life patterns. Denzin describes the importance of play and games, and shows how children move from one stage of activity to another. Here is his summary:

> Three forms of play have been distinguished and they range along a continuum . . . . *Playing at play* describes the free-floating interactions of the young child who moves from place to place, playing at whatever concerns him at the moment. *Playing at a game* describes the young card player who draws and deals and forms pairs, yet has no firm knowledge of how a specific game of cards is played. A good deal of the play of young children from the ages of three to seven falls in this category. *Playing a game* describes the skilled game player who works within the rule-constructed boundaries of a specific game wherein matters of skill and chance are rigidly controlled.[19]

Another need that is increasingly important for American children is the development of independence. Sooner or later children must learn to live on their own. They must be able to move into new situations with no immediate parental presence or support. Such situations will be rare when the children are very young, but they will grow more and more common as the years go by. Parents must adjust accordingly. How many parents succeed in caring for their children when the children will accept a dependent status but fail when they see signs of independence!

[18]Catherine Landreth, *The Psychology of Early Childhood* (New York: Alfred A. Knopf, 1959), p. 363.

[19]Norman K. Denzin, *Childhood Socialization* (San Francisco: Jossey-Bass, 1977), p. 159.

There are two important attributes of independence. The first is that the development of independence can be inhibited or prevented, but it cannot be forced. The second is that independence is best permitted to grow at its own rate, but not so fast that it results in serious harm to the child or to his environment. . . .

Allowing a child to make decisions of thought or action before he is capable of understanding the consequences, if the consequences could be dangerous or serious, is not realistic or appropriate. . . .

It is also fair to point out that, in the enthusiasm for promoting the development of independence, it is not realistic or necessary to permit damage to valuable property. Harm to the feelings of the parents may properly be considered "serious damage" of "valuable property" and not tolerated in the quest for independence.[20]

A child's individuality needs also to be recognized. Every child has a unique appearance, a certain energy level, and particular abilities that are different from his siblings' or his peers'.[21] Children's emotions develop partly through natural maturation and partly through learning. As teachers who work with emotionally handicapped children know so well, overnight changes in a child's personal and emotional responses are extremely rare. But a change in the learning environment and patient work to develop productive avenues of emotional behavior can bring worthwhile results.[22] Parents should do all they can to help a child grow, but they must recognize that every child has certain limits and certain weaknesses, and they must be understanding.

Child Spacing and Sibling Relationships

We have a strong contemporary emphasis on the planned family. How large should it be? How many years should intervene between each child? Is it better to have one child, or two or three? The number and spacing of the children are related to the couple's vocation and career plans. Carolyn C. Perrucci has shown that engineers with the most education and highest career aims tend to marry later and have children after a longer interval than less educated men.[23] The expense of an advanced degree and the need to

[20]William E. Homan, M.D., *Child Sense: A Pediatrician's Guide for Today's Families* (New York: Basic Books, 1969), pp. 56–58.

[21]See Ronald C. Johnson and Gene R. Medinnus, *Child Psychology, Behavior and Development*, 2nd ed. (New York: Wiley, 1969).

[22]See Catherine Landreth, *Early Childhood: Behavior and Learning* (New York: Alfred A. Knopf, 1967), pp. 135–43.

[23]Carolyn C. Perrucci, "Social Origins, Mobility Patterns and Fertility," *American Sociological Review*, 32, no. 4 (Aug. 1967), 615–25.

move to a new community to accept job opportunities may be factors in this delay of parenthood.

Delayed parenthood seems to be related to many other factors of importance in marriage. On the one hand, society in general, and often grandparents and other relatives in particular, look favorably on the early growth of the new family. On the other hand, marital stability and other valuable goals may be reached more easily when parenthood is delayed for several years, and the couple are able to achieve greater maturity and readiness for parenthood.

Bahr and Leigh have conducted a comprehensive study of the relationship between family size, intelligence, and expected education. They were able to work from a sample drawn from the National Longitudinal Surveys of Labor Market Experience conducted at Ohio State University, and utilized a sample of 700 black females, 600 black males, 2,700 white females, and 2,700 white males. In contrast to some earlier studies, they found that "family size in and of itself has little effect on intelligence or expected education."[24] The best predictor of how well a student would do was educa-

[24]Stephen J. Bahr and Geoffrey K. Leigh, "Family Size, Intelligence, and Expected Education," *Journal of Marriage and the Family*, 40, no. 2 (May 1978), 331–35.

tional encouragement. Other factors were slightly positive, but the study clearly did not show any strong negative effects from being in a large family. Other factors (family income, time with each child, lack of adequate housing) might be the subject of future study, but were not tested here. Simply stated, a child is better off (in terms of intelligence and expected education) if he comes from a family where his parents encourage him to study hard and do well in school.

Two extremes in child spacing obviously create some difficulties. If there is only a year between births, the mother may have negative reactions because of the constant drain on her energy. And of course the financial burden is heavier when the expenses of bringing two children into the world come within such a short time. Competition between siblings may be injurious to the younger child or to the one less favored in intelligence or appearance. But at the same time, the children may be able to share a great many things and to create a children's world in which they can play without great dependence on their parents.

If the children are six, seven, or more years apart, other problems will arise. The children will have few playmates in common and will find it hard to share the same interests and activities. And it works a hardship on the parents, who must, in effect, raise two or three separate families. Such wide spacing does mean, however, that each child will have the benefit of more individualized concern and attention from the parents.

Child spacing that creates the ideal relationship between the children lies somewhere between the extremes. The children should be close enough together, perhaps two to four years apart, to have many things in common. At the same time, they should be widely enough separated for each child to be able to stand on his own feet and build an independent and distinctive life. Of course, age is not the only factor involved in sibling interaction. Sibling relationships will also be affected by the sex of the children. Two girls only two years apart may find a high degree of common interest and companionship, but a boy and a girl two years apart may not get along so well. The sex of a child may also have a great deal to do with whether or not he is pampered or neglected or whether he feels competition from his siblings very keenly or is untroubled by it. A daughter who has two or three older brothers may receive a great deal of attention and affection from parents and siblings because she is the only girl in the family. But if the youngest child in a similar situation is a boy, his environment will be quite different. He will have hand-me-down clothes to wear and several older brothers to give him orders and perhaps tease him. But certainly in this regard no two families are alike.

Knox and Wilson studied 144 mothers who had only two children, with the second child under five years of age. The mothers were given a forty-nine-item questionnaire to test their responses to the addition of a second child to the family. The answers from this sample in North Carolina, composed largely of white, Protestant, middle-class, and traditional wives and mothers, was uniformly positive. Exactly half reported that they had enjoyed the first child and wanted to repeat the experience. One-fourth reported that they desired a companion for the first. Some 45.5% reported that they had decided to have a second child before they had the first. They seemed to agree that there was more adjustment in caring for the first child than in adding the second to the family. All in all, the Knox and Wilson study seemed to confirm the strong support many couples have in favor of the two-child family.[25]

Adoption

When a couple in our society desire to have children and are unable to do so, a logical step for them to take is to adopt a child. In that way they fulfill all the normal responsibilities of parenthood with the exception of the actual conception and birth of the child. In addition, they will help to solve the social problems created by the birth of children who do not otherwise have the opportunity for a normal home life.

There were approximately 169,000 adoptions in the United States in 1971, double the number recorded in 1952, but slightly less than in 1970. They included 86,000 children adopted by relatives, 17,000 children adopted privately, and 66,000 children placed by agencies.[26] Although the number of children awaiting placement in any given year exceeds this figure, most adoption agencies have a waiting period of from six months to a year or more. Some delay is necessary (applicants' suitability must be checked, for example), but the biggest problem is that the demand for children is not matched by the supply. There are not as many babies, especially white babies, as there are couples wanting to adopt them; and there are often more handicapped children and older children than there are couples willing to accept them.

At the same time that adoptions are becoming more frequent, increasing concern is being shown for the unmarried parents of illegitimate children. In addition to discussing the adoption of children, we must discuss the natural parents of the children who are being placed for adoption. It is estimated that eight million or more Americans have been born out of wedlock, and the number is still increasing.

Kadushin has studied 91 Wisconsin children who were adopted between

[25]David Knox and Kenneth Wilson, "The Differences Between Having One and Two Children," *The Family Coordinator*, 27, no. 1 (Jan. 1978), 23–25.

[26]U.S. Bureau of the Census, *Statistical Abstract of the United States, 1977* (Washington, D.C.: U.S. Government Printing Office, 1977), p. 353.

the ages of 5 and 12 years. He found that the result of this experience, which is not so typical as infant adoption, was generally good. Two-thirds of the adoptive parents were willing to repeat the experience. Some had more problems than they expected, and some were greatly disappointed. The most typical problem was that school achievement was not so high as desired. When the adoptive parents made the effort to initiate and carry out such an adoption, they apparently had high hopes for their new son or daughter. The parents were often in their forties, and did not have children of their own. Still, the study suggests that such adoptions are well worth trying, from a social standpoint, if they provide a healthier environment for the child, and a fair measure of satisfaction for the parents.[27]

Adoption places more emphasis on the parenting skills of father and mother, and the family atmosphere they create, rather than on hereditary factors. Adoption experiences help us to understand the possibilities that exist for people to make a permanent contribution to the development and maturation of a child who is not their biological inheritor, but who nevertheless receives major direction in life from them.

Adoption is a privilege and with that privilege comes responsibility. One Protestant church group has expressed the relationship in these terms:

> Responsible marriage and parenthood extend to the adoption of children who need homes and loving, understanding parents. Adoption is not to be taken lightly. It involves serious, lasting decisions, legal responsibilities, many risks and adjustments, and the lifelong well-being of adoptive parents and children. Nevertheless, couples who have emotional maturity and love for each other have much to give a child, and will themselves be blessed by adopting children. Adoption is a way of expressing gratitude and love. It is also a means of discovering and fulfilling God's purpose for a man and wife.
>
> Adoption brings into existence mutual rights and responsibilities between the adoptive parents and the adopted child identical with the rights and responsibilities which exist when children are born into a family. Accepted adoption policies and practices take into account the circumstances, rights, needs and feelings of the child, the child's own biological parents, and the adoptive parents. Social agencies which place children for adoption are in a position to weigh all of these features, and are committed to the three-fold responsibility of providing help and counsel to the parents, children, and adoptive parents. They do not serve as agents for one person or set of persons to the exclusion of concern for the needs and rights of the other parties involved.[28]

[27]Alfred Kadushin, *Adopting Older Children* (New York: Columbia Univ. Press, 1970).
[28]United Presbyterian Church, "Responsible Marriage and Parenthood" (Philadelphia: 1962).

There are many important questions in adoption. Should the adoption be arranged through a social agency or through private parties? What factors will be of importance to an adoption agency in approving a couple as adoptive parents? What questions should the adopting parents ask themselves before making application for a child? How is the adoption procedure carried out? Finally, what problems may arise several years later in the family with an adopted child?

The Decision to Adopt a Child

Adoption is a natural part of the emphasis on family planning. There are many motivations for the adopting couple. When the child is a relative, and adopted by some other family members, the sense of family responsibility is of course high. But when a childless couple seeks to adopt, they ought to examine their feelings and motives deeply. There are certain basic questions a couple should ask themselves. The primary question, of course, is: "Do we honestly want to adopt a child?" Do they wish to adopt because of their own desires or because of social pressure, a desire to carry on family traditions, an antidote to boredom, or because of the expectations of one spouse of the other?[29]

[29]See Joan McNamara, *The Adoption Adviser* (New York: Hawthorn, 1975), pp. 6–14.

A further question, one that probes a couple's understanding of life, is "Will we accept our adopted child for what he is, not for what we want him to be, a carbon copy of one of us?" We all wish we could know how our children will turn out. In adoption, we know at least whether the child is a boy or girl. But all the other questions will be answered only with time. We must be willing to adopt the child for himself. At the same time, he deserves a normal place in relation to prior or subsequent natural children in the family. It is equally unwise to favor an adopted child or to deprive him of normal love, discipline, and concern.

One question potential adoptive parents should ask themselves—one that is high on an agency's list of considerations—is: "How stable is our marriage? Are we mature enough and flexible enough to welcome an adopted child into our home and to meet the special situations that may arise?" Most couples are ready to give a tentative "yes" to this question before they begin adoption proceedings. Their willingness to seek professional evaluation of their suitability would be in itself a good sign of their maturity and stability.

Finally, the couple will wish to ask themselves: "Will we meet the necessary personal, legal, and agency qualifications for adoption? Realistically, are we the kind of couple to whom the agency will want to grant a child? Or will we meet the specific requirements of a private adoption?" Basic qualifications, including age, financial stability, good health, and emotional maturity, are the practical matters to be considered.

Advantages of Agency Adoption

Social agencies in most areas of the country place a little less than half the children approved for adoption by the courts each year. Since agencies are often slow in accepting and processing applications, many couples feel that a private adoption is much easier to accomplish. An unwed mother may also feel that it is more natural to discuss this problem and its solution with her doctor than to turn to what seems like an impersonal social agency. We have a natural reluctance to discuss our problems with strangers and a tendency to make decisions on such personal questions with those we know and trust. A private adoption may be completed quickly with a minimum of publicity. And adoption is, after all, a big step for a couple to take. Most of us are inclined to draw back from ventures into the unknown, and that may be a good part of the motivation for private adoption through a doctor or a lawyer. The family doctor is our good friend. He knows us and our needs and problems, and he knows something about the baby who is eligible for adoption. He will do the right thing for us.

The process of private adoption is, in a sense, the operation of the free market system. Certain couples wish to become adoptive parents; there are infants who need families to care for them. If they have a fine group of field representatives working for them (doctors, lawyers, court officials) and if they have financial assets that guarantee their ability to provide for the child (and meet the costs of their representatives), then they will obtain a fine baby, perhaps in a very short time.

The major advantage of an agency adoption is that the agency represents the child first. It does not recruit parents and then search widely for a child to join them; it accepts the child first and then examines the homes to which he might go. Adoption is a legal matter; the child is a ward of the agency and remains so until the adoptive parents convince the agency and the court that they are suitable permanent parents for him. He is not permanently adjudged to be a part of a new family until it is shown that it is in his best interests.

Another advantage of agency placement is that the staff of an adoption agency is professionally trained to assist in adoption. Physicians and lawyers have the benefit of their own particular experiences in the field of adoption; but they usually are not specialists in the field, nor do they have the time to be of help to the new parents and the natural parents that an adequately staffed adoption agency has.

Adoption through an agency also is more of a public matter, so it must meet the test of public interest. In our society, we recognize more and more the need for adequate examination and evaluation of the relationships between many groups. And we attempt to test and adequately counsel young people entering new vocations or the armed forces. Is it not logical for society to exercise careful supervision over the process of adoption, since it determines so much of the course of life for the child involved? This is only one of many aspects of adoption that need to be evaluated more thoroughly. When relatives are involved, society hesitates to interfere, but the potential dangers of private adoption may make it advisable for the state to establish certain standards. Both prospective parents and unwed mothers should receive the best possible counsel on adoption.

Typical Concerns in Adoption

There are several concerns in adoption. First, of course, is our interest in the natural parents of the child, particularly the mother. How will she feel when she relinquishes her baby to new parents? The advantage of agency placement of a child is readily apparent here. An unwed mother needs wise and competent counsel if she is to be able to interpret her experience meaningfully and learn from it for the future. Although she may receive such counsel in connection with an independent placement, she is more likely to receive it in a placement through a reputable adoption agency.

A second question that occurs to adopting parents is: "What will we do if our child is completely different from what we expect? What if he cannot match our hopes and dreams for him or if he disappoints us and fails to fit in with our family? Will we be able to handle such situations?" The answer, of course, is the same answer that must be given to natural parents: we have no way of guaranteeing the future. The future is unknown. We cannot be positive that our children will accept our manners, our values, our politics, our religion. H. David Kirk has described adoption perceptively as a "shared fate": the lives of all the members of the family are transformed by the experience.[30] We must have faith that we are going to be the best possible parents for our children. And as for our uncertainty, fears and anxieties are to be expected. In fact, they should be seen as evidence of parental concern.

Couples considering adoption will be happy to know that the evidence seems to indicate that adoption has many positive results. Benson Jaffee and David Fanshel made an intensive study of one hundred adult adoptees, divided into "low problem," "middle range," and "high problem" categories (groups 1, 2, and 3). Table 19–2 indicates how those adults saw their relationships to their adoptive parents. Three-quarters of the adoptees, including even the high-problem group, reported that they were "very close" or "somewhat close" to their parents. This is an encouraging response.

One benefit of the smaller number of children available for adoption is that the child with special needs has a much better chance of being adopted. Today new opportunities for children with physical handicaps and children who are the product of interracial marriages are opening up because more parents seeking to adopt consider such children, as well as those in the older age levels who could not be placed ten or twenty years ago.[31]

Another concern is when a child should be told that he is adopted. Should it be done early in life before anyone has raised the question, or should it be postponed until the child is old enough to understand the meaning of adoption? This question has been a perennial one with adoptive parents. It is of great concern to those who have made private placements of their children. If a child discovers that he is adopted as the result of a playmate's taunt or an adult's criticism, it may be an unsettling experience.

It is generally thought that a child should be told he is adopted while he is young. As a child goes to school, and especially as he enters adolescence, he becomes more sensitive to his self-image and to the relationships he has with his peers. Although he is intellectually better able to wrestle with the facts and implications of his adoption when he is older, it will be more difficult for him to deal with emotionally and psychologically. For this reason, the knowledge of his adoption should be a natural part of his growing up.

[30]See H. David Kirk, *Shared Fate: A Theory of Adoption and Mental Health* (New York: Free Press, 1964).

[31]McNamara, pp. 29–42.

Table 19–2 Current Closeness Between Adoptees and Parents

	Group 1	*Group 2*	*Group 3*	*Total*
Very close	91%	67%	34%	64%
Somewhat close	9	15	12	12
Casual—neither close nor distant	—	6	6	4
Somewhat distant	—	—	9	3
Very distant	—	3	18	7
Disparate response	—	9	15	8
Not covered/Unable to determine	—	—	6	2
(Total cases)	(33)	(34)	(33)	(100)

SOURCE: Benson Jaffee and David Fanshel, *How They Fared in Adoption: A Follow-Up Study* (New York: Columbia Univ. Press, 1970), p. 202. Reprinted by permission of Columbia University Press and the Child Welfare League.

New discussions of the rights of individuals have raised still another question. Should the adopted child be able to examine the court records of his adoption when he becomes of legal age? How would it affect him, his natural parents, and his adoptive parents? Several organizations are being formed to advocate changes in state laws to allow such examination of records. The legal questions involved are still being tested. Here again, there seem to be advantages to the careful and thoughtful procedures associated with agency adoption.

Unmarried Parents

The problems generated by unmarried parents are not new; the social problems and care of illegitimate children have been a major concern throughout history. Only in the last twenty-five years has scholarly attention been given to this important subject.

The number of children born to unmarried parents has risen sharply in the last twenty years. A majority of the births are to mothers from ages fifteen to twenty-four. This problem is a major one for black and other nonwhite groups. The minority groups actually account for a majority of the illegitimate births in the United States. A number of cultural, socioeconomic, religious, political, and political factors are involved here.[32] Although many of the mothers of these children are eventually married and share parenting responsibilities with their husbands, the difficulties of early childhood for these boys and girls are evident.

The Unmarried Mother

The image our society has of unwed mothers is a negative one. They are usually considered either unfortunate innocents who have been wronged by the irresponsible fathers or sexually promiscuous women. In the latter view, their pregnancy is considered evidence of their weakness; their removal from home and friends to bear the child in some other community and their willingness to give the child up for adoption are seen as proof of their guilt.

A thorough study of unmarried mothers, by Clark E. Vincent, has shown that the single woman herself may react to her pregnancy in several ways.[33] She may become disgusted and disillusioned; she may feign casual indifference; or she may describe her experience as one of love and fulfillment. The sexual relationship preceding pregnancy was described as an affectionate one by over half the women Vincent studied (see Table 19–3). Vincent found that only a small fraction of the women (3 percent) reported that their pregnancy was a result of rape, force, or incest. He attributes the incidence of pregnancy out of wedlock mostly to "fun morality," which encourages sexual activity and then condemns the woman who gets "caught" by her pregnancy.

Some hopeful approaches to the problems of unwed mothers include group therapy programs and counseling that brings in the unmarried father. There is no single pattern of adjustment that is followed by people who become unmarried parents. Greater freedom for women and greater possibilities for supporting children of single-parent families mean that unwed mothers are no longer under as much pressure to give up their children for adoption. One study of a group of unwed mothers in New York has shown that a choice of a variety of lifestyles may be made by unwed mothers, particularly in regard to job opportunities, child-care arrangements, and later marriage.[34] If present trends continue, we may hope to see a lessened number of children who are raised by unmarried parents in highly unfavorable circumstances and a greater number who have good opportunities for growth and development. This is not to say that society can replace the

[32]For a helpful analysis of this difference, see Hallowell Pope, "Negro-White Differences in Decisions Regarding Illegitimate Children," *Journal of Marriage and the Family*, 31, no. 4 (Nov. 1969), 756–64.

[33]Clark E. Vincent, *Unmarried Mothers* (New York: Free Press, 1961).

[34]See Mignon Sauber and Eileen M. Corrigan, *The Six-Year Experience of Unwed Mothers as Parents* (New York: Community Council of Greater New York, 1970).

Table 19–3 Sexual Relationships Preceding Pregnancy Out of Wedlock

Relationship	*Number*	*Percentage*
A love relationship of some duration	344	32
A close friendship relationship	248	23
A casual relationship	258	25
No answer	182	17
Rape, force, incest	30	3
Total	1,062	100

SOURCE: Reprinted with permission of the Macmillan Company from *Unmarried Mothers* by Clark E. Vincent. Copyright © 1961 by The Free Press.

two-parent family without major difficulty, but rather to make a plea for more effective help, counseling, and guidance for all single parents, including the divorced and widowed, who have the responsibility of raising children on their own.

The unmarried mother needs all of the help and encouragement she can obtain, yet our society does not always respond. The birth rate has been going down for all age groups except the unwed teenager. One estimate places the number of teenage out-of-wedlock births in 1974 at 221,400.[35] Careful and concerned counseling is needed. Many adoption agencies are spending more time with the pregnant teenage girl, even if she does not intend to give up her child. School districts are also providing more programs for teenage mothers, and offer opportunities for guidance to the fathers as well.

> The problems of teenage parenting are varied. They demand from us not only our traditional skills, but new knowledge more relevant to the particular needs of adolescents. Our goals should be to prevent teenage pregnancies in the first place, to help teenage parents and their child, and to help the teenage mother not to have a repeat pregnancy. . . .[36]

Supportive counseling is the need. It must be readily available, low in cost, and given in a nonjudgmental atmosphere so that the mother (and the father) can feel a sense of trust and acceptance.[37]

[35]See Alice S. Honig, "What We Need to Know to Help the Teenage Parent," *The Family Coordinator*, 27, no. 2 (April 1978), 113–19.
[36]Honig, p. 119.
[37]See Ruth I. Pierce, *Single and Pregnant* (Boston: Beacon, 1970), pp. 138–51.

There has been very little research done on unmarried fathers—the material we have on them is much less than the amount of material on unwed mothers. The reasons for this are obvious. The double standard allows a man sexual freedom but condemns the female. That is, society maintains the standard of premarital chastity by censuring the unwed mother. While unwed mothers draw welfare assistance, the father needs no such support. And unwed mothers are readily available for study in homes, institutions, or hospitals; the fathers are not.[38]

Unwed fathers are typical American men, and in most cases are normal dating partners for the women involved. Relationships between the two partners are usually favorable until pregnancy occurs. Then the men may experience conflicting feelings if they find they are unable to assert their fatherhood. They may try to resolve the conflict they feel by condemning the mother. But since they are not vitally involved in the pregnancy and birth, their guilt feelings are prolonged. There is no clear-cut crisis and release from guilt for the man like the experience of giving up the child that the mother goes through.

To conclude, the problems of unmarried parents are not peculiar to our society. They seem to exist in most contemporary cultures. A study of illegitimacy in Great Britain shows a tripling of the rate in the United Kingdom from 1938 to 1962; the rate exceeds the rate immediately following the Second World War.[39] Further studies must be made so that we may better understand the motivations leading to pregnancy outside marriage and the means that might reverse the present upward trends.[40] Honest and constructive recognition of the basic human concerns involved here is essential.

SUMMARY

The early years of a child's life are crucial to his development. Many major learning tasks must be accomplished during infancy and early childhood. The home atmosphere created by parents will have great significance throughout all their child's future experiences.

Husband and wife must grow into parenthood. They can prepare for the coming of their children in many ways. Certain changes must be made in the physical environment of the home, of course. But the best thing parents can do is relax and give the child a feeling of belonging and acceptance. Anxiety and a certain sense of inadequacy seem to be fairly common among young parents. But these worries need to be kept in perspective. There are

[38]Vincent, pp. 3–5.

[39]Shirley M. Hartley, "The Amazing Rise of Illegitimacy in Great Britain," *Social Forces*, 44, no. 4 (June 1966), 533–45.

[40]See Clark E. Vincent, C. Allen Haney, and Carl M. Cochrane, "Familial and Generational Patterns of Illegitimacy," *Journal of Marriage and the Family*, 31, no. 4 (Nov. 1969), 659–67.

many gratifying elements in the parenting experience. There are several different models for parenting: the martyr; the buddy or pal; the policeman or drill sergeant; the teacher-counselor; and the athletic coach. These models are valuable in parent counseling since they help parents see what they are doing to their children and where the parent-child relationship is going.

A husband acquires new responsibilities as a father. His relationship to his wife is changed and in some ways redirected. Ideally a husband is secure enough emotionally to be able to adjust to the new claim on his wife's attention without resentment and contribute positively to family life.

A woman also finds her role modified when a child arrives. She must balance her roles as wife and mother and career woman, giving due regard to each. In many cases, she is more active than her husband in developing a happy and secure home atmosphere.

A new baby has his own needs, both physical and psychological. He must build relationships with the outside world and learn basic human values. He must also develop independence. His parents should give him both nurture and control and should recognize and encourage his unique capabilities. They must gradually decrease their authority so that he is able to learn to live on his own.

The number and spacing of children in the family are important. Every child has a right to be wanted and cherished for himself. Firstborn children have been studied frequently to determine whether they have an advantage over other siblings, but we have little clear evidence that they do. Small families do seem to offer greater opportunities to children, however.

Adoption serves a highly useful social purpose in bringing couples who desire to be parents together with children who need homes and parental love and concern. The process of adoption does pose certain problems for adoptive parents, natural parents, and children, but couples with determination can deal with them successfully. Agency adoption offers the advantage of full representation of the interests of the child and a trained professional staff whose primary function is to serve all parties involved in the most thorough way. Factors considered by an agency reviewing an adoption request include the stability and happiness of a marriage, the ages of the couple, their financial circumstances, their similarity to the child they desire to adopt, and state racial or religious requirements.

There are several typical concerns in adoption. How will the natural mother feel about relinquishing her child? What if the child does not match the expectations of the adoptive parents? When should a child be told that he is adopted?

The number of children born to unmarried parents has increased sharply in the United States in the last twenty years. Unmarried parents represent a cross-section of American life; they come from all racial and religious groups, all classes, all backgrounds. A more sympathetic approach to the problems of unmarried mothers and fathers and their children now seems to be developing. More effective counseling and assistance both for unmarried parents and single parents is becoming available.

Unfortunately, until now unmarried fathers have been neglected by both sociologists and counselors. The limited data we have indicate that such fathers are fairly typical of the general population. We need to know much more about the conflicting feelings they have about their fatherhood in order to help them.

;GESTED .ADINGS

Denzin, Norman K. *Childhood Socialization.* San Francisco: Jossey-Bass, 1977. Analysis of childhood development in terms of language, social behavior, and identity.

Duvall, Evelyn Millis. *Marriage and Family Development.* 5th ed. Philadelphia: Lippincott, 1977. Describes family development in terms of the needs of father, mother, and child.

Gardner, George E. *The Emerging Personality.* New York: Delacorte Press, 1970. Basic study of child development with sound psychological treatment.

Green, Maureen. *Fathering.* New York: McGraw-Hill, 1977. Journalist examines role of the contemporary father; takes positive view of the changing expectations for him in the family.

Jaffee, Benson, and David Fanshel. *How They Fared in Adoption: A Follow-Up Study.* New York: Columbia Univ. Press, 1970. Intensive study of 100 adult adoptees and their relationships with their adoptive parents.

Kadushin, Alfred. *Adopting Older Children.* New York: Columbia Univ. Press, 1970. Study of 91 Wisconsin children adopted at an older age. Concludes that the results were generally favorable for most families.

Leichter, Hope Jensen, ed. *The Family as Educator.* New York: Teachers' College Press, 1974. Collection of stimulating essays that examine the role of the family in the educational process.

McNamara, Joan. *The Adoption Adviser.* New York: Hawthorn, 1975. Practical manual outlining adoption policies and procedures.

Munsinger, Harry. *Fundamentals of Child Development,* 2nd ed. New York: Holt, Rinehart & Winston, 1975. Emphasizes the process of change and growth in each phase of child development.

Pierce, Ruth I. *Single and Pregnant.* Boston: Beacon, 1970. Focuses on the choices, such as abortion and adoption, facing the unwed mother.

Russell, Candyce Smith. "Transition to Parenthood: Problems and Gratifications." *Journal of Marriage and the Family,* 36, no. 2 (May 1974), 294–301. Favorable view of the transition to parenthood. Does not view it as a crisis experience.

Sauber, Mignon, and Eileen M. Corrigan. *The Six-Year Experience of Unwed Mothers as Parents.* New York: Community Council of Greater New York, 1970. Studies women living in an urban environment who chose to raise their children by themselves.

20 The Family with Older Children

- How is the "balance of power" in the family rearranged as the children reach their teenage years?
- How does a family define its standards and values? Do the children share in this process?
- What role does social class play in setting family goals?
- What are the characteristics of a democratic family? Are there advantages to growing up in such a family?
- What effect does the community have on the family?
- Why is sex education a difficult task for many parents? Can school sex education programs replace parental instruction and guidance?
- What are the special needs of the single-parent family? How can these needs be met?

The Middle Years

Our primary interest during the preceding chapters has been in the exciting process of courtship, marriage, and early marital adjustment. We have focused on the two individuals who marry and how they handle the first challenges marriage brings to them. The following years of marriage are more routine in many ways. The romance and the pride of starting a family have worn off by that time, and couples must adjust to the less fascinating tasks of attending PTA meetings, chauffeuring the children to and from their activities, and intervening in disputes over what television program to watch. Some couples accept this change more graciously than others. It is easy to romanticize our younger years and to be too harsh on the present.

For a couple of years before I married Milton—before those fights and those kids and those baby-sitters—I dwelled in the wicked city of New York. I was there to burn my candle at both ends, live life to the hilt, and do all of those other wild, delicious things that my mother would never allow me to do in New Jersey.

"Ah, those were the golden days," I always tell Milton.

Or, as I asked myself only last week, were they?

It was one of those weeks when all three kids had come down simultaneously with a stomach virus and the chicken pox, and my husband kept pointing out dust on the blinds and the baseboards, and my four-year-old drove his tricycle over my wristwatch, and my husband remarked that my dinners were quite uninventive, and my in-laws phoned me to tell me I never phoned them, and I said to myself, "For this a person gets married?"

. . . Wasn't it better, I asked myself, back when I was single, back when I lived on my own in Greenwich Village, back when I could roam heedlessly through spring rains with a pounding heart and a throbbing pulse and lots of agony and ecstasy? Wasn't it better before?

The answer is no.

Not "I don't think so."

Not "It's hard to say."

Just . . . plain . . . no.

. . . First of all, there were never any noblemen. Instead there was Herbie Prince, whose only claim to nobility was his name. Poor Herbie, I well recall, was a hypochondriac, and we never got to roam heedlessly through spring rains because he was terrified of developing bronchitis. . . .

As for living on my own in Greenwich Village, I'm afraid I never had any of those searingly beautiful—or was it beautifully searing?—experiences I claimed to be looking for when I moved away from the suburbs of New Jersey. . . .

The end of a romance always seemed to leave me with bleeding gums and pimples on my chin, in addition to the standard signs of heartbreak like sleepless nights. . . .

What I wanted was . . . one night . . . he'd stop the car and ask did I want lots of children; and I'd know that he was asking to marry me and that I'd say yes.

And I did.[1]

What really happens when we enter the middle stage in the family life cycle? In this chapter we will consider family life as infants become children and start school and as children become adolescents and begin to reach out for the experiences and opportunities of adult life. We will think about how life is viewed from the standpoint of the child and how the relationships among father and mother and children are modified and enlarged as the children enter inceasingly into family activities, discussions, and decision-making.

[1]From *Yes, Married: A Saga of Love and Complaint* by Judith Viorst. Published by Saturday Review Press/E.P. Dutton & Co., Inc., and used with their permission.

The Changing Balance of Family Power

As the family moves into the middle stages of family life, new centers of interest develop. The concerns and activities of the children, especially as they become teenagers, assume a place of greater importance in the family. The "balance of power" in the family shifts. Such a change in the balance of power in a family, as in any human group, is bound to be accompanied by some tension and conflict. The children seek to find their own independent place in the family structure, while the parents in turn strive to retain their place of control and authority. It takes wise and understanding parents to recognize that the successful progress of this period of change lies largely in their hands and that they must anticipate and share in the way their children move from early dependence into later independence and maturity.

Leonard was a junior in college when he met Trudy, an attractive secretary in one of the college offices. After a courtship of nearly a year, they were married about four months before his graduation. Leonard had completed his military service before entering college. He took a position with a large manufacturing firm, where he worked in the lower echelon of management.

Trudy was energetic and active in neighborhood and community affairs. With the birth of their three sons, their family seemed complete. Both Leonard and Trudy enjoyed doing things with their children, and they were known as a very closely knit family. Family dominance was somewhat patriarchal, and the father prided himself on the fact that his sons were being brought up "as boys ought to be," with a strong sense of respect and unquestioning obedience to their father. When family clashes did develop, Trudy tended to step into the background and let her husband take the lead. Later she might comfort and counsel her sons, but not in the presence of their father.

When the boys reached adolescence and began to participate in athletics, scouting, and other school programs, a number of battles developed between father and sons. Leonard expected his sons to continue to bow to his authority with respect to their activities, choice of friends, and weekend and vacation schedules. His sons, observing the greater freedom enjoyed by their peers, resented their father's dominance and sought ways to assert their independence. The mother, having accepted her husband's dominant role earlier in the marriage, felt unequal to the task of reconciling the divided family.

In many families the problems of juvenile delinquency are often linked to a low level of parental supervision and authority. Sometimes a son or a daughter becomes an "emancipated minor," living outside the parental home and completely free of parents' control. Thomas Smith has attempted to measure and identify the varying determinants of parental authority. Questionnaires were distributed to 3,641 city and suburban sixth-, eighth-, tenth-, and twelfth-grade students in two southern states. Through the questionnaires, Smith attempted to discover what factors had the greatest influence on the teenagers' perception of their parents' authority and their own willingness to accept this authority. The only significant results had to do with the children's perception of the "parent as an individual person." If the young person saw their parents as strong people, worthy of their admiration, then they would resist pressure from their peers to disobey them.[2]

R. W. White has pointed out that the widespread acceptance of peer interaction and influence is a relatively recent development in children. A century ago no literature of advice to parents recommended that children should be kept in each other's company. There were no Boy Scouts, Girl Scouts, YMCAs, or Little Leagues. "Unless strictly supervised by adults or responsible older children, the effect of age-equals on one another was merely to stimulate excitement, mischief, or riotous lack of control."[3] Children were little adults, and needed to learn adult ways and behavior. The scene has changed drastically now, White says, but social interaction with one's peers should not be thought of as a solution for all of an individual's problems.

It is clear that the roles carried out by father and mother today are markedly different from those of past generations. We need to gain a perspective on parenthood, to see these changes as a part of many related changes in contemporary society, rather than to cling to past role patterns that no longer function adequately.

> Current trends clearly favor sexual equality. Father's authority in the household has been reduced along with general changes in the pattern of work and social power in the modern community. Father's domestic power declines relative to mother's, but both parents have relatively less control over their children as outside authorities are allowed a larger role in the care and training of youth. Nevertheless, traces of patriarchy are retained in the form of the "sturdy-oak syndrome," and fathers, more often than mothers, are still dominating figures in the home. In the ideal case, father is self-confident and directive, yet protective of those weaker

[2]Thomas Edwin Smith, "An Empirical Comparison of Potential Determinants of Parental Authority," *Journal of Marriage and the Family*, 39, no. 1 (Feb. 1977), 153–64.
[3]See R. W. White, *The Enterprise of Living: A View of Personal Growth* (New York: Holt, Rinehart & Winston, 1976), pp. 294–95.

Drawing by Opie
©1978 The New York Magazine, Inc.

than himself, and better able than mother to cope with the more difficult family crises caused by unexpected events originating outside the family. [4]

The family should seek to continue its role as an educational institution that prepares the child to take his place as an adult in the larger society. In earlier times, a son was largely confined to his own farm or home and neighborhood and entered the adult world only when he was ready to take full-time employment or to leave school in order to work with his father in the shop or on the farm. Similarly, a girl assumed adult responsibilities when she was ready to leave her parental home and begin a family of her own.

Today, children begin interaction with the larger society very early. Television, newspapers, books, magazines, and other printed materials expose a child to the world before he ever thinks of leaving home. He becomes aware of a bloody war in the Near East or the center of Africa; he is confronted with social changes in New York, Moscow, or Sao Paulo; he observes sports contests in London, Atlanta, or Tokyo; and he becomes acquainted with Americans of differing interests and philosophies in Alaska, Alabama, or Arizona. He must grow up at home, or he will be unable to function successfully when the time finally comes for him to take his place in the com-

[4]Leonard Benson, *Fatherhood: A Sociological Perspective* (New York: Random House, 1968), pp. 109–10.

plicated adult world. (On the other hand, if his family becomes only a stopping-off place between his outside activities, its crucial integrative and interpretative value will be lost.)

Contemporary parents who are trying to meet their responsibilities in preparing their children to live in the modern world must therefore be continually revising and changing the ground rules at home. The freedom and responsibility given to the child of six differs markedly from that given to the same child at three. There will be further changes when he is nine, twelve, fifteen, and eighteen. If the parents do not change their expectations for him and do not place him increasingly on his own, they will fail to prepare him for adult life. When we evaluate the maturity of a college student, for example, or of a couple about to be married, we are actually asking whether the process of socialization has been accomplished. How well did his parents prepare him for this new role? Did he have enough practice in making decisions at home and in choosing his own course in life to do the same thing successfully here in college or in his new home? If his parents' backgrounds are dissimilar and their ideas about raising children are at variance, there will be numerous conflicts. The only solution to such problems lies in compromise. Both husband and wife must discuss their ideals of family life honestly and seek to blend their two viewpoints as harmoniously as possible.

Defining Family Standards and Values

What do we expect from family life? What are the values and standards that motivate family members and the family as a unit to move toward certain particular objectives? Virginia Satir has suggested that each family ought to draw a "family map" to chart the various relationships within the family and the way in which the family works together.[5] Although the family members may seem to be moving in many different directions at first, patterns can be discovered when family relationships are carefully examined.

The need to define family standards does not seem so pressing in the early years of marriage. The first year of a baby's life brings many exciting hours for new parents. They are fascinated as the baby learns to eat, crawl, talk, and deal with the outer world. All of this may take place fairly naturally and easily under the direction of the mother; the father needs only to step in at various times to lend a helping hand and to enjoy his new responsibilities.

But even during the first year, and increasingly in the years that follow, the father and mother must come to share together the responsibility of guiding and encouraging their children. If the children learn that they can sidestep the mother's direction and discipline by appealing to their father (or vice versa), they will quickly form the habit of doing so. If they discover that family discipline is quite different when their father is at home, they will soon learn to exploit the situation to their own advantage. And as they move into later childhood and adolescence, they will begin to measure their parents against the standards they see in the larger society. If they fall far short of the patterns they observe in other people in school, church, or the community, they will have difficulty stabilizing their own concepts of the parental role.

The move toward marriage growth and enrichment during all stages of the marriage is a very positive one in this regard. It has encouraged couples and families to reexamine their commitment to each other, and to seek ways to grow and expand the strength of their family life. Ted Bowman, in discussing three weekend experiences for entire family units sponsored by a family service agency, a school of pastoral care, and a Protestant church regional group, sees this trend as a promising new approach to building more cohesive and satisfying family living. It is an emphasis on healthy families, and stimulates the realization of greater potentials in all of the family units involved.[6]

[5] See Virginia Satir, *Peoplemaking* (Palo Alto, Calif.: Science and Behavior Books, 1972), pp. 141–53.

[6] Ted Bowman, "Developing Strength in Families," *The Family Coordinator*, 25, no. 2 (April 1976), 169–74.

Marshall L. Hamilton has discussed a number of important influences of the father on the development of his children. Parent studies often focus on the mother because she spends more time at home with the children, is readily accessible for school interviews, and is more likely to be able to volunteer to work in youth activities. But the influence of the father on achievement, independence training, aggression, competence, creativity, social conscience, and many other important personality characteristics cannot be ignored. Leadership is needed from both parents. Hamilton concludes:

> A cluster of very desirable and somewhat overlapping behaviors, including competence, high achievement motivation, self-esteem, successfulness, internal control, and to a lesser extent, creativity, seem closely related to behavior patterns in the parents including high but reasonable expectations and demands of the child, consistent but rationally explained discipline, less punitive disciplinary techniques, clear and mutual communication with the child, and desirable models in the parents' own behavior.[7]

Each child in the family needs to build a balanced view of both masculine and feminine roles. A boy needs to know the love and affection of his mother and to be able to sense the feminine way of doing things and the feminine outlook on life before he takes the important step of beginning a family of his own. He gains these insights primarily from his mother. And a girl most easily learns to play the feminine role by imitating her mother.

The father has an equally important relationship to both his daughter and his son. He is the natural person to teach them what a man is like and to show them by his example the way in which a husband should love and respect his wife in their day-by-day relationships. If he fails to provide this example, his son cannot identify with him and his daughter cannot respect his portrayal of the masculine role; a vital and central aspect of their growth toward maturity is lost. Both husband and wife must work together to achieve this goal of true sharing in love, responsibility, and discipline.

It is interesting to note social class differences here, which begin to affect boys and girls even before their teen years. If mother and father come from different social classes, defining family values will be especially difficult. As we saw in Chapter 6, social class level is a major influence on a family's mode of living and its value structure. If a family is of the lower-middle class or working class, they probably will adopt certain viewpoints and living patterns as their own. They may not be aware of those choices, but they do exist, and they are difficult to change in later life. If a woman has been raised

[7]Marshall L. Hamilton, *Father's Influence on Children* (Chicago: Nelson Hall, 1977), p. 140.

in an upper-middle-class family, for example, and has been provided with a great deal of security and material comfort during her childhood and adolescence, she may find adapting to the family life of an industrious working-class husband very difficult. Or, if the husband has been raised in a home with strict standards of discipline, he may be upset when he finds his wife tends to follow a permissive pattern that was the norm in her parental family.

Melvin Kohn has conducted a number of interesting studies of behavioral and attitudinal differences between middle-class and working-class parents.[8] Kohn has proposed the hypothesis that middle-class parents encourage more independence for their children, while working-class parents are more strict with discipline, and less flexible in their direction. Gecas and Nye have examined these differences in socialization with a sample of 210 couples in the state of Washington. They found support for Kohn's theory in sample questions asking for the expected parental response to a child accidentally breaking something or intentionally disobeying. There were differences between the answers of fathers and mothers, and the most significant class differences were between white-collar and blue-collar men.[9] The authors state that their findings give modest support to the Kohn hypothesis. In Kohn's earlier study, the variations were more significant. Perhaps the changes occurring in the family over the past twenty years have blurred some of the class distinctions in our society, and with these changes, our values and standards have changed as well.

Kohn feels that too often sociologists have difficulty in truly understanding the working-class group. They should not simply run a survey and

[8]Melvin L. Kohn, *Class and Conformity: A Study in Values* (Homewood, Ill.: Dorsey Press, 1969).
[9]Viktor Gecas and F. Ivan Nye, "Sex and Class Differences in Parent-Child Interaction: A Test of Kohn's Hypothesis," *Journal of Marriage and the Family*, 36, no. 4 (1974) 742–49.

print the results, since their middle-class values may distort the findings. He writes:

> Since social scientists understand (and largely share) middle-class values, we find middle-class parental behavior self-evidently reasonable. But, because many of us have not had an adequate grasp of working-class values, it has been less apparent that working-class parental behavior is also reasonable. Some have asserted, for example, that working-class parents are oriented only to the present and give little thought to the effects of their actions on their children's futures. We contend, instead, that working-class parents are as concerned as are middle-class parents about their children's futures, but that social scientists have not sufficiently understood working-class goals. Parental actions that seem, from the middle-class perspective, to be oblivious to the children's needs are, from the working-class perspective, altogether appropriate to parental goals in childrearing.[10]

The family's social class also influences to a certain extent the moral and religious teaching parents give to their children. Douglas Graham feels that social classes do not differ greatly in the basic moral values they hold; but that the middle and upper classes may be more influenced by their parents in making moral judgments, and that their superior education and greater verbal fluency may give people the impression that they are more respectable.[11] (Of course, common sense tells us that wealth, power, and intelligence are not necessarily equivalent to truth, honesty, and compassion.) We need to give still more thought to the ways in which moral standards and values are nurtured by the family.

The Democratic Family

Our culture places increasing emphasis on some form of family democracy. The precise form this democracy takes is not fixed, but it will be seen in the attitudes and behavior of the parents, in the opportunities afforded to the children to participate in family decisions, and in the genuine give-and-take evidenced in the family's life together. There are several important basic considerations in making the family operate democratically. The parents must recognize that they cannot maintain the same kind of power in the family that they enjoyed when their children were very young. They must realize the advantages of sharing their authority with the children, so that all family members sense their worth as individuals. Family decision-making should

[10]Kohn, p. 187.

[11]Douglas Graham, *Moral Learning and Development* (New York: Wiley-Interscience, 1972), p. 261.

gradually be shared as the children grow older, so that they will be prepared to assume responsibility for their own lives.

Dr. Rudolf Dreikers has suggested that a careful preparation for family sharing can be achieved through a family council, in which family members enjoy one another and achieve mutual equality and respect. He defines the family council in this way:

> [The family council] is a group of people who live together, whether or not they are related by blood or marriage. The group shall have regularly scheduled meetings and operate under rules agreed upon in advance. The meeting shall be an open forum at which all family members can speak without interruption, with freedom of expression, without fear of consequences, and without regard for age or status. Its deliberations result in decision only when all members present agree—that is, come to a common understanding.[12]

The ideal of the American educational and political systems is to prepare children to take part in the decision-making processes of our society when they are adults. It is difficult to realize this ideal if there is no sense of democracy in a child's home. Family democracy must be expanded to meet the specific needs of family members at each stage. For instance, Evelyn M. Duvall lists eight "developmental tasks" for the family with children in their teens: providing facilities for the teenagers' educational and recreational needs; working out money matters; sharing the responsibilities of family living; defining the nature of the marriage relationship; bridging the communication gap; keeping in touch with relatives; widening horizons; and reworking and maintaining a coherent philosophy of life.[13]

The Family and the Community

Another important part of the development of a family's life is family interaction with the community—neighborhood, school, church, shopping area, and volunteer organizations. In the old-fashioned rural economy, the influence of the community was stabilizing, but indirectly so. When father and sons were busy harvesting a crop, they knew that other farmers nearby were doing the same thing at about the same time. But there would not necessarily be much contact between families until the work was done. There was no teenage culture in which children could compare notes on the day's happenings and share a great deal of leisure time, nor were there playgrounds and other recreational facilities open to younger children. They might create

[12]Rudolf Dreikers, Shirley Gould, and Raymond J. Corsini, *Family Council: The Dreikers Technique* (Chicago: Henry Regnery, 1974), p. 7.

[13]See Evelyn M. Duvall, *Family Development*, 4th ed. (Philadelphia: Lippincott, 1971), pp. 338–50.

their own recreation, Huckleberry Finn style, but only after the work at home was completed.

Today, because of urbanization, in most cases we are in much closer contact with the outside community than people were in previous generations. The school, the church, the Little League team, the Campfire Girls, and many other groups are constantly impinging on the private life of the family. Even if parents attempt to keep their children at home as much as possible when school hours are over, the omnipresent television screen and the other mass media invade their sanctuary and bring the impact of the culture into the home. The family that can live in isolation from these social and cultural phenomena is rare.

Under such conditions, it is imperative that the family take an intelligent stance with respect to the influence of the community. It cannot be ignored; it must be recognized, evaluated, and interpreted to the children so that they can have some freedom of action and choice within it instead of being overwhelmed by a need to conform to all its pressures. It is for this reason that the much-maligned suburban mother and father, rushing from meeting to meeting, cannot be condemned blindly. If parents did not take an interest in the schools, the YMCA, the playgrounds, or the teen center, the gap between family and community would be wider than it is today. Parents may decide that their children should not participate in these activities, or even that they should move the family home to a community more in accord with their own goals and values. However, intelligent leadership is the best way of understanding and interpreting the complex society in which our children grow up and should help to make the internal functioning of the family much smoother. This is an important aspect of socialization.[14]

The family and the various social agencies should be looked on as partners, not as competitors, in the life of the child. Hawkes has suggested that such a partnership can be built up, even though social agencies may often seem to be huge bureaucracies difficult to reconcile with the personal style of family life. However, the increase of two-career families makes this a necessity. Such partnership begins early in the family life cycle, and should be a normal and expected part of the life of the children. Hawkes writes:

> Shared function not only has strong implication for the way in which families and bureaucracies interface but also describes the interface between mother and father roles. In view of emergent life styles and dual-career families, shared parenting is becoming an important dimension

[14]See Edward Z. Dager, "Socialization and Personality Development in the Child," *Handbook of Marriage and the Family*, ed. Harold T. Christensen (Skokie, Ill.: Rand McNally, 1964), pp. 740–81.

in the present alteration of family structure and the articulation of social policy. . . . [15]

The Sex Education of Children

What about the sex education of children? This is an important aspect of family life, and one which should receive special attention in the teenage years. Children need to be given accurate information on sex. One purpose of marriage and family courses in high school and college is to develop wholesome attitudes toward sex so that students may be well prepared for their sexual relationship in marriage. But the question arises: are the late teenage years the best time for sex education? Isn't it far better for children to receive sex education at home, with the values of the parents included in the teaching?

There is some ambivalence about this among family educators. Should family-life education be stressed, or sex education? Can you prepare for effective family living simply by becoming knowledgeable about sexual func-

[15]Glenn R. Hawkes, "Who Will Rear Our Children?" *The Family Coordinator*, 27, no. 2 (April 1978), 165.

"My daughter Patience."

Drawing by Drucker
© 1978 The New York Magazine, Inc.

tioning and experience, without considering other areas of life? On the other hand, what is the good of a family-life course without full and adequate treatment of the sexual side of marriage?

There is no doubt that the physiological and medical aspects of sex can be best dealt with in a classroom situation, where instructional motion pictures, lectures, and visits by obstetricians and other professionals can be taken advantage of. However, the basic attitude of the child toward this information will come from his home environment. Attitudes toward sex are developed not only in adolescence but from the earliest years of life. If the parents have not given the child an understanding of normal sexual functioning and helped him to develop wholesome attitudes toward his sexual makeup, the acquisition of factual material alone will not automatically overcome the deficiency.

Educators have been attempting to develop the kind of insight on the part of parents that will make family life and sex education a highly desirable part of the school curriculum. Critics of sex education courses in the schools have been relentless in attacking sex education programs. But attitudes are changing, and there are signs that parents and community groups are beginning to take a more intelligent view of the need for such programs.[16]

Why do some parents oppose sex education in the schools? Their concern seems to center around three issues. The first is the invasion of privacy. The pressures of the society around us have sharply reduced the scope of our private lives. We are photographed, fingerprinted, lettered, numbered, and filed by a bewildering number of government agencies, offices, bureaus, and organizations. Can't we at least protect the privacy of the home and family? Parents often do not want their family life, their children's sexual development, and their interpersonal relationships to be examined in the classroom.

A second problem is parental embarrassment and even ignorance. Many parents (some of them not yet in the over-thirty generation) find it hard to talk to their children about sex. The subject was never discussed when they were growing up; they find it difficult now that they are in the parental role to be open and frank in talking about sex with their children. It is easier to say nothing. Many an intended heart-to-heart talk about the facts of life boils down to cultural ritual, with nothing of real significance discussed. "Bill, if there's anything you want to know, you can always ask your Dad." "Thanks, Dad." And that's it. We still have hang-ups that carry over from the prejudices of past generations. It is hoped that we will move step by step past ignorance and prejudice.

[16]See Jacqueline Carton and John Carton, "Evaluation of a Sex Education Program for Children and Their Parents: Attitude and Interactional Changes," *The Family Coordinator*, 20, no. 4 (Oct. 1971), 377–86.

Susie, a young bride of nineteen, went to her physician in February to confirm her pregnancy and to prepare for the baby's arrival. The child was due in July, and the expectant mother had many questions to ask as her examination was completed. The doctor talked to her for almost an hour and was able to answer most of her questions.

When she returned the next month, and on subsequent visits, there was always a flood of questions, apparently arising from conversations with her mother. "Will the baby be deformed if I drink too much coffee?" "Do those pains in my left side mean that the baby will be born prematurely?" And so on. No matter how carefully the doctor assured her, she always had a new query.

Finally the day came. Her husband rushed her to the hospital just after 10 in the evening, and before 1 A.M. a strong, healthy baby boy was born. The physician went home for some sleep and then called on his patient the next morning.

"Well, it wasn't so bad after all, was it?" the doctor asked Susie. "The baby came quickly and naturally, and none of those things you were worrying about caused any trouble at all. How do you feel about everything now?"

The young mother had only one brief comment to summarize her reaction to the whole experience. "Wait until I see my mother!" she exclaimed.

Some parents also express concern that sex education will stimulate their children sexually without giving them any sense of personal or moral judgment in sexual relationships. The quality of sex education does vary, it is true. Unfortunately, some teachers of family life and sex education have not majored in sociology, psychology, or some related field, and they are not able to present an objective, thoughtful, and integrated view of the subject. But the vast majority of teachers are highly qualified, and the educational materials available for such courses, from the elementary and secondary levels to the college level, are of very high quality.

In reality, the hypothetical ideal situation of no premarital sexual activity suggested by the vocal opponents of sex education in the public schools does not exist. Every child in every family is constantly bombarded by sex education through the mass media, advertising, peers, friends, and neighbors. No boy or girl can ever grow up in isolation from these influences. The rising rates of venereal disease, teenage abortion, illegitimacy, and teenage marriage remind us of the high level of sexual activity of adolescents—if such a reminder is needed. The only logical response to these conditions, which are often the result of simple ignorance, is a more effective program of family-life and sex education.

Enlarging Family Life

Family living should be expanding constantly as the family enters new experiences and new stages in the life cycle. No two families are identical, and no two patterns of family growth and development will be the same. The important thing is for the family to build its own life consciously, with certain goals and values in view, and then to be certain that each individual member of the family, young or old, has a chance to be himself and to express himself within the love and security of the family circle.

Family living is not divided neatly into economic, educational, religious, psychological, and other kinds of behavior. It is an organic whole. Strengths in some areas will be counterbalanced by weaknesses in others. Parents must

keep the total picture in view and be neither overly optimistic about their achievements nor too discouraged because every phase of their life together does not reach the highest standards. As in all things, a note of realism is needed.

The best way to assess family growth and development is to take inventory at regular intervals. Has the family maintained its physical and emotional health? Are the children able to function independently? Does the family have a sense of unity and teamwork because of shared tasks and shared goals? Is the family's religious faith meaningful and related to their day-by-day experiences as well as to the religious community? Is there a unified sense of purpose in family life and activity or merely a succession of duties and activities, pleasant and unpleasant, that are carried out without any real meaning? By asking these and similar questions, parents and children together may gain a clearer view of the family's present life and its expectations for the future.

The progressive and creative American family will not reach high standards of achievement without toil and struggle. Because of the pressures of high-tension modern living and the many conflicting basic philosophies of life found in our pluralistic society, parents and children must work together to convert their ideals into reality. Only concerted thought and effort will make it possible for the family to achieve its highest purposes.

SUMMARY

The family with older children experiences a change in the relationship between parents and children in the middle years. The family atmosphere should become more open and democratic; children need to find freedom and independence within the family in order to develop the same patterns outside the home. Parents must also redefine their roles in relation to each other as well as to their children.

It is important for parents to define family standards and values. The movement toward marriage enrichment and family growth makes this process easier. Mother and father should share the task of giving guidance to the children. The importance of the role of the father to a child's development has been receiving increasing attention from researchers, since fatherless homes and homes in which the father is absent include a sizable number of American families. The development of a child's values is also influenced by the socioeconomic class of his parents.

The democratic process should be utilized within the family unit. Children should be allowed to participate in family decisions. The school, the playground, the church, and youth groups are now major influences in the lives of most children. The choice of the community in which a family lives is thus of major importance. The family's interpretation of the community is also important to a child's growth.

The sex education of the children should be still another concern of parents in the middle years. Sex education should begin at home, but many parents have difficulty in talking to their children about sex. And some communities face crises in developing adequate sex-education courses in the public schools because of parental objections to sex education outside the home. As a result, too often a child receives no guidance at all on sex. Family-life and sex-education courses that are of high quality can, however, provide an excellent supplement to parental guidance.

There is no simple formula for meeting the constantly changing and expanding needs of the family. But intelligent thinking and planning are basic to the continued stability of a family's life.

SUGGESTED READINGS

Allred, G. Hugh. *How to Strengthen Your Marriage and Family.* Provo, Utah: Brigham Young Univ. Press, 1976. Practical advice for family life; includes case studies and a communication training program.

Hamilton, Marshall L. *Father's Influence on Children.* Chicago: Nelson-Hall, 1977. Emphasizes the importance of the father's role in the family.

Hawkes, Glenn R. "Who Will Rear Our Children?" *The Family Coordinator,* 27, no. 2 (April 1978), 159–66. Examines the results of sharing functions of childrearing.

Kohn, Melvin L. *Class and Conformity: A Study in Values.* Homewood, Ill.: Dorsey Press, 1969. Examines the differences in values and discipline between middle-class and working-class families.

Satir, Virginia. *Peoplemaking.* Palo Alto, Calif.: Science and Behavior Books, 1972. Provides new insights into the development of people within the context of the family circle.

White, R. W. *The Enterprise of Living: A View of Personal Growth.* New York: Holt, Rinehart & Winston, 1976. Study of personality development; special emphasis on family's influence on personality.

21 Separation, Divorce, Remarriage

- What is the present rate of divorce in the United States?
- What factors have been important in the increased number of divorces in the last two decades?
- What are the most common reasons cited for divorce?
- How many married people are separated from their spouses? Is a separation parallel to a divorce?
- How do people face the crisis of divorce?
- What are the special needs of a divorced person who is entering another marriage?
- How does divorce affect the children of the divorcing couple?
- How helpful is counseling for couples who are considering divorce or separation?
- How should people choose a marriage counselor?

Divorce Statistics

Many marriages do not last through the lifetimes of both partners. They can be dissolved in three ways: by death, separation, and divorce. The increasing life expectancy of both men and women means that in the future fewer marriages will end in the death of one partner during the early years of marriage. (There are still a high number of widows and widowers in the population, but they have on the average completed a much longer period of marriage than widows and widowers fifty years ago.)

The overall trend in our society is toward a decreasing marriage rate and a slightly increasing divorce rate. Figure 21–1 reflects this trend as it shows the rates of first marriage, divorce, and remarriage for American women from 1921 to 1977.

Another way of viewing this trend is to compare the marriage and divorce rates for married and unmarried women. The marriage rate for unmarried women has varied during the past fifty-five years from a peak of 92 per 1,000 in 1920 to a low of 66.9 per 1,000 in 1975. In contrast, the divorce rate reached a low point in the Depression and in the years between 1955 and 1960, but, in 1975, climbed to an all-time high of 20.3 per 1,000. (See Table 21–1.) We can also measure the rise in the divorce rate by looking at the absolute number of divorces granted. In 1960 the number of divorces was estimated

Figure 21–1 Rates of First Marriage, Divorce, and Remarriage for U.S. Women: 1921–1977

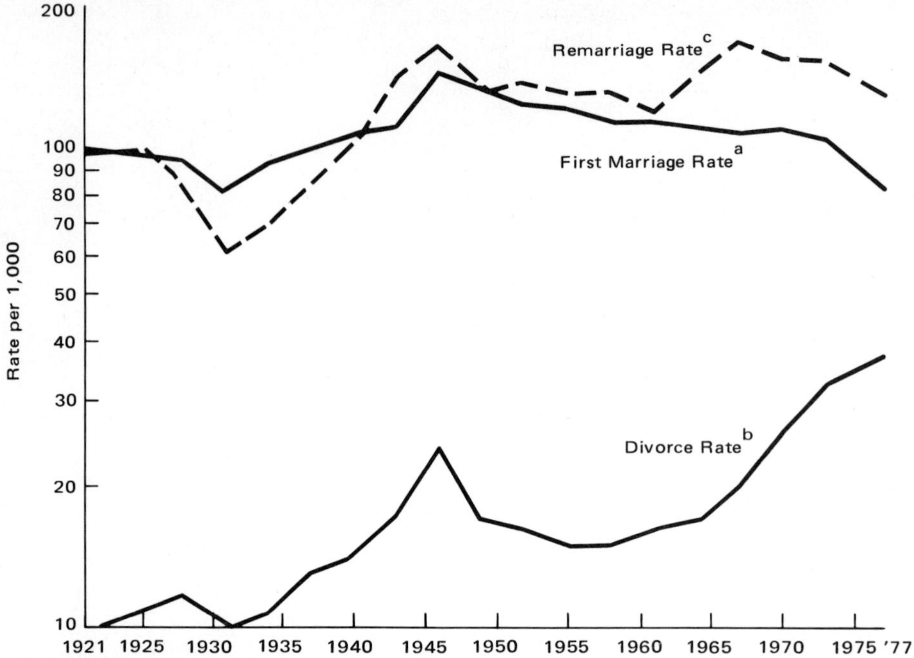

[a]First marriages per 1,000 single women 14 to 44 years old.
[b]Divorces per 1,000 married women 14 to 44 years old.
[c]Remarriages per 1,000 widowed and divorced women 14 to 54 years old.
SOURCES: Adapted with permission from Hugh Carter and Paul C. Glick, *Marriage and Divorce: A Social and Economic Study*, rev. ed. (Cambridge, Mass.: Harvard University Press, 1976), Figure 13.1, p. 394; with computations added for 1975–1977. Reprinted from Paul C. Glick and Arthur J. Norton, "Marrying, Divorcing, and Living Together in the U.S. Today," *Population Bulletin*, 32, no. 5 (Population Reference Bureau, Inc., 1977), 5.

at 393,000, at 915,000 in 1973, and at 1,036,000 in 1975.[1] In addition, the average length of a marriage before divorce, which increased from 1946 to 1962, is now decreasing (see Table 21–2).

There are several factors that affect the marriage and divorce rates. Many young adults are postponing marriage because of education, careers, fewer eligible partners, or disinterest in formalizing a living-together relationship. When divorced people remarry, they add to the marriage rate. The first-marriage rate, however, has dropped sharply from 70 to 56 per thousand men, 20 to 26 years of age. A similar drop was recorded for women.[2]

The recent report cited by Paul Glick and Arthur Norton also gives us

[1]U.S. Bureau of the Census, *Statistical Abstract of the United States, 1977* (Washington, D.C.: U.S. Government Printing Office, 1977), p. 75.

[2]Paul C. Glick and Arthur J. Norton, "Marrying, Divorcing, and Living Together in the U.S. Today," *Population Bulletin*, 32, no. 5 (Washington, D.C.: Population Reference Bureau, Inc., 1977), p. 6.

Table 21–1 Marriage and Divorce Rates: 1920–1975

Year	*Marriages per 1,000 Unmarried Females**	*Divorces per 1,000 Married Females*
1920	92.0	8.0
1930	67.6	7.5
1940	82.8	8.8
1945	83.6	14.4
1950	90.2	10.3
1955	80.9	9.3
1960	73.5	9.2
1964	74.7	10.0
1965	75.0	10.6
1968	79.1	12.4
1972	77.9	17.0
1975	66.9	20.3

*Over fifteen years of age.

SOURCE: U.S. Bureau of the Census, *Statistical Abstract of the United States, 1967* (Washington, D.C.: U.S. Government Printing Office, 1967), p. 62; U.S. Bureau of the Census, *Statistical Abstract of the United States, 1972* (Washington, D.C.: U.S. Government Printing Office, 1972), p. 62; and U.S. Bureau of the Census, *Statistical Abstract of the United States, 1977* (Washington, D.C.: U.S. Government Printing Office, 1977), p. 74.

information about other aspects of divorce and separation. They discovered that the number of "separated" persons in the United States in 1976 was only about "half as large as the number of divorced persons (3.8 million versus 7.2 million). A million more women than men report themselves as separated (2.4 million versus 1.4 million), evidently because many never-married mothers claim to be separated or because some separated men living with nonrelatives were reported as single in the Current Population Survey for March of that year."[3] The largest group of men in the currently separated or divorced category were those from 40 to 44 years old; for women the corresponding peak was age 35 to 39.

Concentrating only on divorce and separation statistics will give us a distorted picture of the state of marriage in our society today. Actually, the majority of men and women remain married to their first partner. Table 21–3

[3]Glick and Norton, p. 15.

Table 21–2 Median Length of Marriages Ending in Divorce or Annulment (by Reporting States): 1950–1975

Year	*Median Length of Marriage*
1950	5.3 years
1955	6.2
1957	6.6
1960	7.1
1962	7.3
1966	7.1
1969	6.9
1973	6.6
1975	6.5

SOURCE: U.S. Bureau of the Census, *Statistical Abstract of the United States, 1966* (Washington, D.C.: U.S. Government Printing Office, 1966), p. 64; U.S. Bureau of the Census, *Statistical Abstract of the United States, 1972* (Washington, D.C.: U.S. Government Printing Office, 1972); and *Statistical Abstract of the United States, 1977* (Washington, D.C.: U.S. Government Printing Office, 1977), p. 75.

shows the marital status of men and women who were born between 1900 and 1959. These figures show that the number of once-married persons is three to five times greater than the number of persons married more than once. However, the percentage of divorced persons increases every year, so these people may become a minority by the end of this century.

A person's age at marriage is apparently the one factor that seems to clearly predict the chance of divorce. Robert Schoen made a careful analysis of the 1969 registration of divorces and annulments in the state of California. The original data showed 77,491 divorces-annulments recorded, with 54,025 males and 51,983 females terminating their first marriage. The age limits were set at 18–29 for men, and at 16–27 for women. The results (see Table 21–4) showed that persons who marry at a young age are much more likely to divorce. Only 338 women who married at age 16 will remain married to the same partner thirty-five years later. In contrast, 726 of the women who married at age 27 will remain with the same partner. Men who married at 18 will have only 363 intact marriages after thirty-five years, against 713 for the group who married at 29. It is also interesting to note that women had a better chance of stability in the marriage at each identical age reported. This reflects their maturity and the older age of their husbands.

Table 21–3 Marital Status of Men and Women Born 1900–1959, as of 1975

Group	Single	Married Once	Married Twice or More
All Men, 16–75	26.1%	62.5%	11.3%
Older Men, 61–75	4.9%	73.9%	21.2%
All Women, 16–75	20.6%	67.0%	12.4%
Older Women, 61–75	6.3%	73.9%	19.7%

SOURCE: U.S. Bureau of the Census, *Statistical Abstract of the United States, 1977* (Washington, D.C.: U.S. Government Printing Office, 1977), p. 75.

Table 21–4 Expected Number of Intact Marriages of California Males and Females, 1969 (of 1,000 Marriages at Each Age of Marriage)

Age at First Marriage	Completed Years of Marriage 1	5	10	20	30	35
			Males			
18	994	844	653	444	375	363
20	995	864	682	534	468	452
23	993	900	785	656	594	581
26	994	928	830	723	672	660
29	992	924	848	772	720	713
			Females			
16	991	804	587	407	348	338
18	993	821	641	497	439	427
20	995	893	771	647	586	574
23	993	923	849	740	690	680
26	992	929	865	775	732	725
27	997	930	851	770	737	726

SOURCE: Adapted from Robert Schoen, "California Divorce Rates by Age at First Marriage and Duration of First Marriages," *Journal of Marriage and the Family,* 37, no. 3 (Aug. 1975), 553–54. Copyrighted 1975 by the National Council on Family Relations. Reprinted by permission.

Divorce as a Social Problem

Divorce constitutes a social problem of major importance for a number of reasons. The stress we put on romantic motivation in courtship and the premium we place on love and fidelity are major aspects of the problem. If we are encouraged in our dating years to search for a special partner who will match our personal dreams and expectations, will we not experience a great deal of frustration and disappointment if we discover that our love has vanished a few years after marriage? The search for a true lover seems doomed to disappointment in one out of every four or five cases.

Economic difficulties also plague many divorced couples, although the divorce settlement is supposed to make equitable distribution of the family's assets. In most cases, the family's money is limited and may be exceeded by its debts. When husband and wife dissolve their partnership and try to create two households where there has been one, the result is often catastrophic.

Moreover, children are often the unwilling pawns in divorce actions. They are either too young to understand the breakup of the family, or they are too emotionally involved in the dispute between their parents to accept the final decisions without bitterness and resentment. We will discuss the effect of divorce on children more fully later in this chapter.

One ethical question keeps intruding into most discussions of divorce. Is it right? Should two people have the freedom to divorce for any cause suitable to themselves, or is it morally and religiously wrong to do so? The answer to this question colors any discussion of divorce in our society. Religious teaching and social custom were strongly against divorce until only

Drawing by Koren
© 1977 The New Yorker Magazine, Inc.

a few years ago. Now we frequently hear divorce spoken of leniently. For example, a thrice-married professor at a large state college writes:

> Parents, teachers, and concerned adults all counsel against premature marriage. But they rarely speak the truth about marriage as it really is in modern middle-class America. The truth as I see it is that contemporary marriage is a wretched institution. It spells the end of voluntary affection, of love freely given and joyously received. Beautiful romances are transmitted into dull marriages, and eventually the relationship becomes constricting, corrosive, grinding, and destructive. The beautiful love affair becomes a bitter contract.
>
> The basic reason for this sad state of affairs is that marriage was not designed to bear the burdens now being asked of it by the urban American middle class.
>
> Marriage was not designed as a mechanism for providing friendship, erotic experience, romantic love, personal fulfillment, continuous lay psychotherapy, or recreation. The Western European family was not designed to carry a lifelong load of highly emotional romantic freight. Given its present structure, it simply has to fail when asked to do so.
>
> . . . Now, the absurdity of much of this lies in the fact that we pretend that marriages of short duration must be contracted for life. Why not permit a flexible contract perhaps for one to two or more years, with periodic options to renew? If a couple felt disenchanted with their life together, they would not feel trapped for life. They would not have to anticipate and then go through the destructive agonies of divorce. . . . Instead of a declaration of war, they could simply let their contract lapse. . . .[4]

Other sociologists are just as vehement in emphasizing the goal of a stable, permanent marriage relationship. Perhaps the strongest argument here is that the advocates of a series of marriages are often arguing from limited personal experience in favor of an individual's right to have freedom from an unsatisfactory marriage. They may not consider the broader social implications of unstable marital relationships. Can we be certain that both the personal and developmental needs of husband, wife, and children are as fully satisfied in two or three marriage partnerships as in one? It is true that we see many examples of couples who are happier, better adjusted, and better able to impart a normal and healthy view of life to their children in a second marriage than in a first. However, we must also observe carefully the large numbers of children who grow up happily with both their natural

[4]Marvyn Cadwallader, "Marriage as a Wretched Institution," *The Atlantic,* 218, no. 5 (Nov. 1966), 62–65.

"Dear Harold, by the time you play this videotape cassette, I will be far away."
Drawing by Levin
© 1978 The New Yorker Magazine, Inc.

parents. Should their chances of happiness with a second or third set of parents be taken lightly?

The Causes of Divorce

It is often difficult to isolate the specific factors that cause marital separation and divorce. There are problems that seem to be universal in happy and unhappy marriages, such as money, sex, in-laws, dominance, and marital roles. The legal complaints filed do not necessarily reflect the actual conditions that existed in the marriage. And the passage of no-fault divorce laws in many states makes it even more difficult to identify the causes of divorce.

However, William J. Goode's study of a sample of divorced women in the Detroit area revealed a multitude of reasons for divorce. Many women gave more than one reason for the breakdown of their marriages (see Table 21–5). Goode notes that the reasons given were related to many variables: rural or urban background; duration of the marriage; whether the wife married upward or downward socially and educationally; and, to some extent, racial differences. There seemed to be few complaints related to religious preference.

Other specific problems may be related to divorce. Child abuse has recently begun to receive public attention; we have learned that family violence is common in many homes on all social levels. Often the innocent child becomes a victim of parental conflict, and the very fact that hostility is vented within the family circle may prevent the real problems involved from being considered in an objective manner and treated professionally. Alcoholism and drug addiction are probably also divorce-related.

The wide range of causes being given for divorce today tells us quite a lot about contemporary society. Whereas the grounds for divorce in earlier generations, it may be generalized, had to be of an extremely serious nature, the basic cause for divorce today seems to be that a couple no longer wish to live together. In other words, we are approaching the logical conclusion of the romantic ideal of marriage. When you fall in love, you should marry the person you love; when you fall out of love, you should dissolve the marriage. This attitude, which influences so many divorces, might be summarized in these terms:

> My partner has not willfully wronged me or deserted me and left me with sole responsibility for the care of the children. He has not deliberately broken with the customs of our community or neighborhood so that he is considered an unfit or unfaithful husband. However, we no longer enjoy each other's company and face conflicts in our marriage at a number

Table 21–5 Main Causes for Divorce Cited by Divorced Women

Theme of Complaint	*Percentage of Responses*	*Percentage of Respondents*
Nonsupport	13%	33%
Authority	12	32
Complex of reasons	12	31
Drinking	12	30
Personality	11	29
Home life	9	25
Values	8	21
Money	8	20
Love triangle	6	16
Miscellaneous	4	12
Desertion	3	8
Relatives	2	4

NOTE: Number of women responding was 425.

SOURCE: Reprinted with permission of Macmillan Publishing Co., Inc., from *After Divorce* by William J. Goode. Copyright © 1956 by The Free Press.

> of points. We are no longer in love as we once were. So we prefer to divorce rather than to try to make the best of a bad situation.

This approach to divorce, now widely accepted in our society, runs counter to the traditional religious view of divorce as valid for only limited and specific reasons, such as desertion or adultery (although those causes are still given by a number of divorced persons).

There are many possible interpersonal combinations of stress and conflict that lead to divorce. The wife may be domineering and may have expected to attain control over her husband after marriage. The husband in turn may be quiet but determined; the more she struggles for dominance, the more strongly he resists. Or the husband may be irresponsible and unable to keep a steady job. At the time of marriage, his wife may have hoped to instill some determination and stability into him, but after eight years she recognizes that that task is impossible. When two individuals do not have compatible personality traits, their marriage can be a very difficult one.

Another basic problem may be a person's failure to meet his spouse's expectations of him. Every person marries with definite expectations. With these expectations, each partner builds up an ideal image of a spouse, an image that is then tested and modified during marriage. If the image and the actuality are too different—if the spouse, through infidelity, laziness, antagonism, or any one of a dozen other ways, consistently violates that image—divorce will appear more and more the logical escape to the other partner.

Still another problem could be the failure of one or both partners to gain ego satisfaction in marriage. Ego satisfaction comes to husband and wife in different ways. It may be the pride of sharing in a spouse's promotion or raise or the pride of seeing one's partner recognized at the P.T.A. or in a neighborhood group. It may come through sharing many tasks and experiences over the years or from a satisfying sexual relationship. It may be the feeling of accomplishment that comes when the children mature and are able to make their own contributions to family and community life. The happily married couple find that each partner obtains a great deal of ego satisfaction through their relationship. When such satisfaction is missing and each day is filled only with boring jobs or family problems that have no solution, a couple may be on the road to divorce. "Why should I stay married," one partner may think, "when I really don't look forward to going home at night?"

One more problem that can lead to a divorce is failure to make satisfactory marital adjustment. When a couple cannot agree on family planning, how to spend their income, which friends to cultivate, or how to express their religious convictions, their marriage will be in danger. The subject has been discussed, the problems have been brought to the surface, but no action is taken. When this happens, the couple are destroying their chances for future happiness; unresolved issues may return to haunt them.

No-Fault Divorce

There are a great many different marriage and divorce laws in the United States, although there are trends toward uniformity. There is a growing agreement on the age for marriage without parental consent and on the need for a medical certificate or affidavit as a protection against the spread of venereal disease. There is no uniform waiting period, however; some states require a waiting period of five days before the ceremony, while others require none. There is also a fairly wide consensus on grounds for annulment, which include fraud, force or duress, marriage between relatives, insanity or feeblemindedness, unrecognized divorce of a previous marriage, and impotence or physical incapacity to consummate the marriage.

A major trend in the last ten years has been toward inclusion of no-fault provisions in the divorce statutes. Under this new law, when a marriage breaks down the courts are instructed to grant a divorce upon proof that the

"Linda and I are getting a divorce, and we divided up our friends. I got you."

separation is permanent. This law has been endorsed by the Family Law Section of the American Bar Association. It focuses on the failure of the relationship between husband and wife. It does not attempt to prove who is at fault for the breakdown of the marriage. In some states the new law has been added to those already in effect; in other states, the principle of fault has been removed.[5] Other states still hold to the traditional grounds for divorce, which cover a wide range of complaints: adultery, desertion, cruelty, felony conviction, drunkenness, and drug addiction among the most common. Less frequent legal grounds include venereal disease, public defamation, and incompatibility. Less than one-third of the states allow divorce on all these common grounds.

Table 21–6 indicates the states in which divorce laws include "no-fault breakdown" reforms up to 1974. It seems certain that similar reforms will be proposed in the next decade in a majority of the "no-reform" states. Wright and Stetson have attempted to analyze the impact of these legal changes on divorce rates. They conclude that the major impact has come from general social conditions and the desire of many couples to divorce (for their own reasons). "Thus, the recent liberalization of divorce statutes may represent an adjustment in American family law narrowing the gap between the law on the books and the law in action."[6]

The Effects of Divorce on Children

As the number of divorces continues to rise, an increasing number of children will be affected by marital dissolution. What is the effect of divorce on children? One study by Janice Loeb and John R. Price of children who were being treated at a child guidance clinic compared the children of 44 mothers from two-parent homes with the children of 44 divorced mothers. It was discovered that:

> The first hypothesis, that children of divorced and separated parents would more frequently have problems including aggressive or acting out behavior, was supported. Twenty-eight (64 percent) of the children from disrupted homes were rated aggressive, whereas 10 (23 percent) of the children of continuously married women were rated aggressive. . . . A particularly striking difference occurred in the girls; 10 out of 15 daughters of divorced and separated women were rated aggressive, whereas

[5]Gerald C. Wright, Jr., and Dorothy M. Stetson, "The Impact of No-Fault Divorce Law Reform on Divorce in American States," *Journal of Marriage and the Family*, 40, no. 3 (Aug. 1978), 575.
[6]Wright and Stetson, p. 580.

Table 21–6 Divorce Law in the States According to No-Fault Breakdown Reforms

No-Reform States	*Breakdown States by Year*	
Alaska	1969	1973
Arkansas	California	Arizona
Illinois		Connecticut
Maryland	1970	Georgia
Massachusetts	Kansas	Iowa
Mississippi	Texas	Maine
North Carolina		Missouri
Pennsylvania	1971	Montana
Rhode Island	Alabama	Oklahoma
South Carolina	Florida	Washington
South Dakota	Oregon	
Tennessee	New Hampshire	1974
Utah	North Dakota	Ohio
Vermont		Minnesota
Virginia	1972	
West Virginia	Colorado	
Wisconsin	Hawaii	
Wyoming	Idaho	
	Kentucky	
	Michigan	
	Nebraska	

SOURCE: Gerald C. Wright, Jr., and Dorothy M. Stetson, "The Impact of No-Fault Divorce Law Reform on Divorce in American States," *Journal of Marriage and the Family*, 40, no. 3 (Aug. 1978), 576. Copyrighted 1978 by the National Council on Family Relations. Reprinted by permission.

only 1 out of 15 daughters of continuously married women was rated aggressive.[7]

A survey of a large statewide population was done by Roland Chilton and Gerald Markle. Their survey indicates that family disruption is significantly related to child referral to juvenile court in the state of Florida.[8] An analysis of the reports on 5,376 juveniles showed that children from broken homes were more than twice as likely to be charged with offenses than would be expected from their number in the general population. "Mother only," "father only," and "neither parent present" homes totaled only 17 percent

[7]Janice Loeb and John R. Price, "Mother and Child Personality Characteristics," *Journal of Consulting Psychology*, 30, no. 2 (April 1966), 112–17.
[8]Roland J. Chilton and Gerald E. Markle, "Family Disruption, Delinquent Conduct and the Effect of Subclassification," *American Sociological Review*, 37, no. 1 (Feb. 1972), 93–99.

of the general population but provided 39.3 percent of the children charged with juvenile crimes and 40 percent of those children charged with offenses that would be considered crimes for adults. Chilton and Markle conclude:

> Our study provides added empirical support for the conclusions of earlier investigators who have suggested that proportionately more children who come into contact with police agencies and with juvenile courts on delinquency charges live in disrupted families than do children in the general population. In addition, the study suggests that children charged with more serious misconduct more often come from incomplete families than children charged with less serious delinquency.[9]

One might ask, however, what role socioeconomic status, ethnicity, religion, family size, and other factors might play, and what kind of record is found for children of divorced parents who remarry?

It may be that the difference in viewpoint of counselors and sociologists is a factor in the differing conclusions of studies on the effect of divorce. Do psychologists look for certain behavioral problems and find them, whereas the sociologist may look at some broader measure of the effects? Since the evidence at this point is contradictory, it is apparent that further research is needed. Most school counselors and psychotherapists would probably agree that it is not always possible to evaluate parental influence on a child's behavior immediately or even at the start of a later period of study, counseling, or treatment. The impact of important events, viewpoints, and experiences may not be fully known until some future date. New in-depth studies are needed to ascertain the long-term effects of parental divorce on young people and young adults, who could be compared with a matched control group from unbroken homes. Answers might then be found to such important questions as: "Is your present life affected in any way by the divorce of your parents?" "Is your attitude toward courtship and marriage affected by the divorce of your parents?" "Are your expectations for the future any different because you have observed the marital failure of your parents?" The high frequency of divorce today means that these questions are relevant to many children. Let us hope that when they are old enough to respond they will not reveal serious scars.

Bernard Steinzor suggests four positive advantages of divorce that may aid the family members to grow and develop in the new situation. He suggests that:

> 1. The emotional smog smothering the whole family in an early spiritual death is cleared away. . . .

[9]Chilton and Markle, p. 98.

2. The broken home makes it possible for the child to form his own views on each parent unobstructed by the smoke screen thrown up by each in front of the other. . . .
3. The divorce is an honest and above-board admission that the adults cannot get along and there is no use pretending that they can provide children with a model of a loving relationship. . . .
4. The child's belief that he is guilty of causing his parents to fight and that only he can save them from hurting each other will be laid to rest by divorce.[10]

Building a New Life

The basic task for any separated or divorced person is to build a new life. One cannot live in the past or expect, in some magical way, to carry over the best of the past and forget completely the hurt, anger, and disappointment of the marriage relationship. Robert Cassidy has tried to guide men into a realistic appraisal of their expectations from a divorce. He recognizes that there are emotional responses that need to be faced. His book is structured to meet the needs of men who are in the process of obtaining a divorce, and gives information about legal procedures, finances, child custody, visitation

[10]Bernard Steinzor, *When Parents Divorce* (New York: Pantheon Books, 1969), pp. 53–57.

rights, and the establishment of a new lifestyle. One must go "beyond survival" and try to create a new life.[11]

Barbara Hirsch has authored a similar book that helps women to know the different grounds for divorce, how to hire a lawyer, where to sue for a divorce, and so forth.[12] Few of these "do it yourself" books on divorce show how to attempt a reconciliation or how to benefit from a trial separation. Perhaps there is an invisible line drawn between marriage and divorce, and when one has crossed that line, the expectation is that one will not turn around and go back.

Again, it is the child who may have the most difficulty in figuring things out in a divorce. Despite all the logical and straightforward adult explanations, it may take some years for a child to understand why his parents are separating.

> My parents divorced when I was eight years old. I considered our home happy. My mother told me they were going to get a divorce and asked me who I wanted to live with. I told her my father and she started to cry.
>
> My father and mother both remarried five years later. The divorce has affected my attitude toward marriage. I'm in no hurry to get married. I want to work and travel before I settle down. I am quite cautious in associating with friends and am careful about the people I meet.[13]

Remarriage

Most divorced persons remarry. This is especially true of younger men and women who divorced in their twenties. Glick and Norton projected that married women who were aged 25 to 29 would have divorces in 38 percent of their original marriages. Three-fourths (29) of them would remarry, but 44 percent, or 13, would become redivorced. In all, the women would be married 129 times, and have 51 divorces. The results for the total group are indicated in Figure 21–2.

How does a divorced person begin again? What new feelings, thoughts, and directions will be necessary? The hurts from the initial experience will heal. In a sense the "goodness" of the divorce must be appreciated, and the value of a new relationship anticipated. We all experience the pain that goes with leaving a familiar neighborhood, a job that we have held for many years, or a high school or college where we have felt comfortable. In the same way, a break must be made with old patterns before successful new ones can begin.

[11]Robert Cassidy, *What Every Man Should Know About Divorce* (Washington, D.C.: New Republic Books, 1977), pp. 35–36, 166–89.
[12]Barbara Hirsch, *Divorce: What a Woman Needs to Know* (Chicago: Henry Regnery, 1973).
[13]Student report.

Mel Krantzler suggests some stages in this process. He suggests that one moves from "remembered pain" to the "questing-experimental stage" and then to "selective distancing" and finally to the "creative-commitment stage." All of this takes time, and a person must deal with each stage of growth and decision one at a time.[14] It is necessary for a person to examine himself or herself, and to make decisions about personal prejudices, habits, and preferences. All this is worthwhile if it will help a person to choose a new partner wisely.

Gillian Dean and Douglas Gurak approach remarriage in sociological terms. They examined the 1970 National Fertility Survey data to see whether women were closer to their second husbands than their first in age, education, and religious identification. The results showed a consistent pattern for women who divorced and remarried. They were more heterogamous (different from their husbands in age, education, and religion) in their first marriages than women who remained married. In their second marriage they married men who were even more different. It is not known whether these women were "divorce-prone" or if they didn't have a wide field of choice in the "marriage market" the second time.[15]

[14]Mel Krantzler, *Learning to Love Again* (New York: Thomas Y. Crowell, 1977), pp. 97–115.
[15]Gillian Dean and Douglas T. Gurak, "Marital Homogamy the Second Time Around," *Journal of Marriage and the Family*, 40, no. 3 (Aug. 1978), 559–70.

Figure 21–2 Marriage and Divorce Projections for Women Aged 25–29: 1975

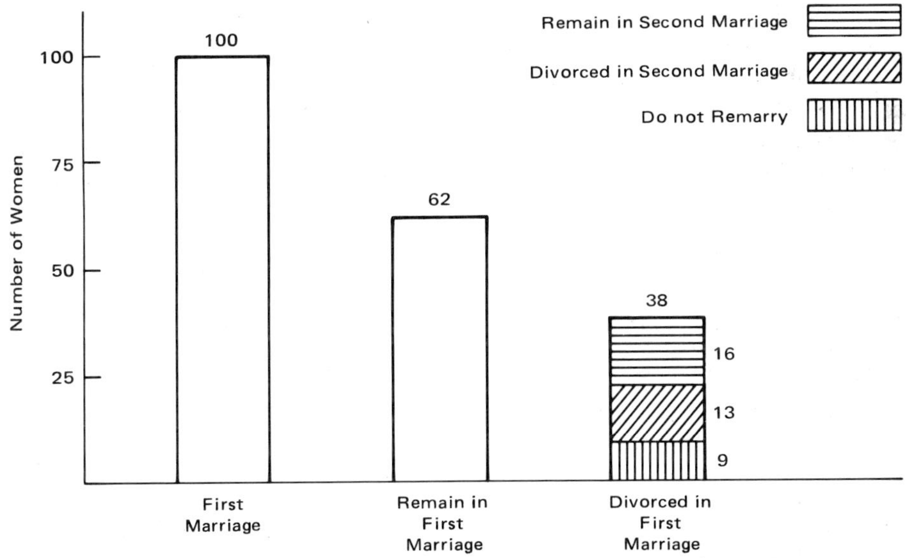

SOURCE: Paul C. Glick and Arthur J. Norton, "Marrying, Divorcing, and Living Together in the U.S. Today," *Population Bulletin*, 32, no. 5 (Population Reference Bureau, Inc., 1977), pp. 36–37.

Lawrence Riley and Elmer Spreitzer made a detailed study of a large number of applicants for Social Security disability benefits in Minnesota, Louisiana, and Ohio, and their findings showed that remarriages were more successful than first marriages.[16] Using a flowchart, they showed that marriage rates were high (89 to 94 percent) for all groups studied. The divorce rates, however, varied widely, with the rate for black females the highest (41.2 percent), followed by the rates for white females (32.8 percent), black males (32 percent), and white males (28.1 percent). About three-fourths of the divorced persons remarried, and except for white females, the remarriages were more stable than the first marriages. Since disability put pressure on many of these marriages, and socioeconomic status was often low, the results of this study are quite surprising.[17]

A further favorable evaluation of remarriage is given in the study by Glenn and Weaver using the General Social Surveys conducted by the National Opinion Research Center in 1973, 1974, and 1975. They found that "there is not a very substantial difference in the reported marital happiness of ever-divorced and never-divorced respondents."[18] In fact, the person who remarries may do about as well as the one in a first marriage. Perhaps social change and the social acceptance of divorce makes this possible.

Stepchildren and Stepparents

One result of divorce is the creation of step-relationships. There are a number of important questions about stepchildren that have been largely neglected by sociologists. Although the classic stories of Cinderella and other folk heroes and heroines are well known, there has been little realistic analysis of the situation of stepchildren in our present cultural environment.

Inquiry might be directed at three particular periods of crisis during the life of the stepchild. First there is the period of family conflict before separation and divorce. At this stage in a family's experience, the child is often the center of marital arguments and even violent physical conflict. In fact, the separation may develop because of the abuse or neglect of the children by the father or mother. The picture is often not a pleasant one. Although both parents may claim to have the best interests of their children at heart and may often cite that as a reason for separation or divorce, few children are fortunate enough to emerge from this period of family tension without definite emotional and psychological scars.

[16]Lawrence E. Riley and Elmer A. Spreitzer, "Lifetime Marital Experience and Remarriage Among the Widowed and the Divorced," paper presented to the annual meeting of the American Sociological Association, Aug. 28–31, 1971.

[17]See Benjamin Schlesinger, "Remarriage: An Inventory of Findings," *Family Coordinator*, 17, no. 4 (Oct. 1968), 248–50.

[18]Norval D. Glenn and Charles N. Weaver, "The Marital Happiness of Remarried Divorced Persons," *Journal of Marriage and the Family*, 39, no. 2 (May 1977), 335.

The period between marriages may bring a second crisis for the stepchild, unless the new partner is immediately chosen or has been related to the family prior to its breakup. The child may suffer because of the problems of the remaining parent, usually the mother. If she is depressed, overworked, plagued by financial problems, or concerned primarily with finding a new husband, the child may bear the brunt of some of her problems and frustrations. There is also a danger of the overdependence of child on mother, or vice versa. Problems are certainly not minimized when all family responsibilities must be carried by the mother.

The final crisis comes when a stepparent enters the home and a whole new set of relationships must be created. Idealization of the missing parent or jealousy of the new partner may cause tension. The stepchild may well be insecure in his relationship with the new parent. In many cases stepparents and stepchildren do work out very satisfactory solutions to their adjustment problems; but a study by Charles E. Bowerman and Donald P. Irish has suggested that "homes involving step-relationships proved more likely to have stress, ambivalence, and low cohesiveness than did normal homes."[19]

Again, evidence on what happens in these new relationships between stepchildren and stepparents is not clear-cut. It is necessary to add the qualification: "It depends on the particular circumstances in the individual family." Wilson and others, in analyzing two national surveys that deal with these relationships, could find no single pattern emerging. The children with stepfathers who were included in the study might have a positive family environment, a negative one, or one with mixed impact on them.[20] Wilson et al. take a more optimistic approach to the growth and development of children in several different home patterns.

Marriage and Family Counseling

In the past twenty years there has been rapid development in the new field of marriage and family counseling. Counselors may be helpful to a couple who are seeking to reconcile their differences and remain married; to those who need to face the realities of separation and divorce; and to men and women who need post-divorce counseling to help them build new life patterns.

Marriage counseling is given by a wide variety of persons; it need not

[19]Charles E. Bowerman and Donald P. Irish, "Some Relationships of Stepchildren to Their Parents," *Marriage and Family Living*, 24, no. 2 (May 1962), 121.

[20]Kenneth L. Wilson, Louis A. Zurcher, Diana Clare McAdamans, and Russell L. Curtis, "Stepfathers and Stepchildren: An Exploratory Analysis from Two National Surveys," *Journal of Marriage and the Family*, 37, no. 3 (Aug. 1975), 526–36.

be done in a formal visit to a marriage counselor's office. Four major groups are involved in rendering this service. One group includes people who counsel as one part of their profession—for instance, members of the clergy, lawyers, physicians, and educators. The increased public awareness of the seriousness of marital problems and the growth of public willingness to seek counsel for those problems have spurred the increase in the number of these counselors.

A second counseling group includes people engaged in marriage counseling per se, either in private practice, in marriage-counseling centers, or in connection with a reconciliation court or other legal service. Professional standards for this work have been rising steadily, and many state and local associations of marriage counselors have been formed in addition to the American Association of Marriage Counselors, which was organized in 1942. These professional marriage counselors offer the benefit of specialized training and experience to couples experiencing marital difficulty.

Marriage counseling services are also rendered through social work agencies, such as the Family Service Association, and through public welfare agencies. There counseling is often done in connection with requests for financial aid, legal aid, or other family needs. This counseling is often extremely helpful because it meets the couple at the particular time and place of their difficulty.

Finally, marriage counseling is done by clinical psychologists and psychiatrists, often in conjunction with mental-health centers. Marital problems are seen by these counselors in the light of the personality needs and development of the individual. They may work with a single individual, couples, or the entire family unit.[21]

Choosing a Counselor

It is important to choose a marriage and family counselor who will be most effective in dealing with our own particular needs and problems. Of course we all receive some kind of advice or counsel from those close to us—families, neighbors, employers, or college professors. But difficult marriage problems require professional help. A counselor who is recommended to us by a friend who has received help from him or her is one starting point. Doctors and many members of the clergy provide some counseling, or will recommend another counselor to you. You may know of an agency that has an excellent counseling service.

An interesting and careful survey of counseling services across the

[21]See Mary Riege Laner, "The Medical Model, Mental Illness, and Metaphoric Mystification Among Marriage and Family Counselors," *The Family Coordinator*, 25, no. 2 (April 1976), 175–81.

country was done by Joanne and Lew Koch.[22] It is possible, of course, to have a bad experience with an individual counselor, especially if he or she is poorly trained, not licensed or supervised by any state or private agency, or does not really have the personal qualities and dedication needed to give effective service. Fortunately, there is a great deal of interdisciplinary work going on in this field, and insights from the varying approaches to counseling are being shared. This is not to say, of course, that there are not counseling programs, particularly in the realm of informal consulting, that are far from adequate. This is a common problem in any rapidly expanding new field.

Every marriage counselor carries on his or her work with a certain value system in mind. Medical doctors may think in terms of sickness and health, clergy in terms of sin and forgiveness, psychologists in terms of behavior modification or nondirective therapy. Many counselors are in their forties and fifties and may have difficulty relating to younger clients with different value systems. Lisa Tsoi-Hosmand discusses this issue in terms of feminist and humanistic values for marriage. When a woman moves her value orientation toward the feminist or humanistic viewpoint, it may affect her marriage relationship. She may then seek counseling from someone who has the same value orientations. On the other hand, a counselor with a different view may be just as effective if acceptable "ground rules" for the ongoing therapy can be worked out.[23]

Specialized Counseling

There are many variations in the way in which counseling is offered. The basic format that places the individual or couple in the counselor's office for a 50-minute counseling session is only the beginning. Some marriage counseling is carried on in connection with a conciliation court. In states that provide such an opportunity for couples, effective counseling may be a means of preventing final marital breakdown and divorce, or settling visitation and custody disputes.[24] Several couples may share counseling together, sometimes with two or more counselors, with a combination of individual and group sessions. Other counselors specialize in working with children, who are especially vulnerable to family tension and conflict.

A number of counselors have begun to specialize in divorce counseling.

[22]Joanne Koch and Lew Koch, *The Marriage Savers* (New York: Coward, McCann, & Geoghegan, 1976), pp. 231–41.

[23]Lisa Tsoi-Hosmand, "Marital Therapy and Changing Values," *The Family Coordinator*, 25, no. 1 (Jan. 1976), 51–56.

[24]See Warren W. Weiss and Henry B. Collada, "Conciliation Counseling: The Court's Effective Mechanism for Resolving Visitation and Custody Disputes," *The Family Coordinator*, 26, no. 4 (Oct. 1977), 444–48.

There has been an additional focus on the needs of widows, who have often been ignored.[25] And finally, many marriage counselors have begun to offer one or more sessions of premarital counseling, thus adding their expertise in this area to the work already done by family-life education and the clergy.

It is becoming easier and more acceptable for couples in all stages of marriage to seek counseling help in solving their particular problems. When we come to the time when such guidance and insight are accepted as naturally as medical treatment for arthritis or the measles, society may be able to salvage many problem marriages that are now beyond the reach of assistance.

Divorce is one of the most perplexing problems facing our society today. In a sense, it stands as a judgment on our culture, on its failure to evolve an educational and courtship system that prepares men and women adequately for stable, mature, and satisfying marriages. The movement toward freedom and equality for women in family life has removed the rigid structure that kept husband and wife fixed within the bonds of marriage whether they liked it or not, and we are not likely to return to that earlier framework. But it may take many generations to develop a society in which men and

[25]See S. Roxanne Hiltz, "Helping Widows: Group Discussion as a Therapeutic Technique," *The Family Coordinator*, 24, no. 3 (July 1975), 331–36.

women are prepared to make their decision for marriage in such a way that it will endure. Until we do, divorce will remain a major social problem.

SUMMARY

Many marriages are ended by death, separation, or divorce. At the present time the marriage rate is decreasing, and the divorce rate increasing. But still the majority of persons remain married to their original partner.

Divorce creates a number of problems. It may seem to be the only way out of a couple's personal frustrations and disappointments, and as such some people are advocating it. But children may be the unfortunate pawns in a divorce action. And social, moral, and religious values and standards are also involved.

There are many reasons for divorce. The number of different reasons given by couples who file for divorce today may indicate that divorce is often mainly a personal decision: husband or wife or both simply choose not to be married any longer. Typical underlying causes of divorce are basic personality clashes, unmet marriage expectations, failure to gain ego satisfaction from marriage, and failure to make satisfactory marital adjustment.

Legal grounds for divorce vary from state to state. It has been suggested that a uniform divorce law for all states would be desirable, but movement toward such a major reform is slow. Significant changes have been made in the divorce laws in many states, however, and all reforms today tend to be toward a more liberal interpretation of the grounds for divorce.

No-fault divorce laws have been adopted by many states. There has been some increase in divorce rates as a result, but, according to research, the new laws are not the only cause.

Divorce has strong effects on children, quite often negative ones. A study of juvenile delinquency in Florida showed that children from broken homes accounted for twice the number of crimes as would be expected from their number. Research does not establish clearly whether in such cases a child's antisocial behavior is the result of the divorce itself or of the unsatisfactory home conditions that caused the divorce. Further study needs to be made of the long-range effects of divorce on children.

The effects on children of a parent's remarriage are also not completely clear. Remarriages are usually less stable than first marriages; each remarriage involves a difficult process of readjustment for parent, children, and stepparent. Different families probably vary widely in their ability to cope with the problems of readjustment.

Marriage counseling can help many families with these problems. A variety of professionals serve in this field and can be of special value to couples and families.

SUGGESTED READINGS

Cassidy, Robert. *What Every Man Should Know About Divorce.* Washington, D.C.: New Republic Books, 1977. Basic information for men about the personal and legal aspects of divorce. Suggestions for post-divorce adjustment.

Eisler, Riane Tennenhaus. *Dissolution—No-Fault Divorce, Marriage and the Future of Women.* New York: McGraw-Hill, 1977. Focuses on the legal changes in divorce and the impact of these changes on women.

Glick, Paul C., and Arthur J. Norton. "Marrying, Divorcing, and Living Together in the U.S. Today." *Population Bulletin,* 32, no. 5 (Washington, D.C.: Population Reference Bureau, Inc., 1977). Summary of recent census data on marriage, divorce, and living together. Valuable resource booklet.

Goode, William J. *After Divorce.* New York: Free Press, 1956. Interviews with divorced women in Detroit, giving their interpretation of causes for family breakup.

Hirsch, Barbara. *Divorce: What a Woman Needs to Know.* Chicago: Henry Regnery, 1973. Practical material for women facing divorce.

Koch, Joanne, and Lew Koch. *The Marriage Savers.* New York: Coward, McCann, and Geoghegan, 1976. Overview of the marriage-counseling field; includes interviews with therapists and clients. Provides helpful resource lists.

Krantzler, Mel. *Creative Divorce.* New York: M. Evans & Co., 1974. Suggestions for beginning again after divorce. Krantzler is a career and family counselor who is divorced.

Peterson, James A. *Marriage and Family Counseling: Perspectives and Prospect.* New York: Association Press, 1968. Historical summary of marriage counseling by a pioneer in the field.

Stenizor, Bernard. *When Parents Divorce.* New York: Pantheon Books, 1969. Discussion of how parents and children can cope with the problems of separation and divorce.

Wilson, Kenneth L., Louis A. Zurcher, Diana Clare McAdamans, and Russell L. Curtis. "Stepfathers and Stepchildren: An Exploratory Analysis from Two National Surveys." *Journal of Marriage and the Family,* 37, no. 3 (Aug. 1975), 526–36. Survey that studied the impact of remarriage on different family members.

Women in Transition, Inc. *Women in Transition: A Feminist Handbook on Separation and Divorce.* New York: Charles Scribner's Sons, 1975. Feminist view of separation, divorce, and child custody. Deals with both the emotional and the legal aspects of divorce.

Wright, Gerald C., Jr., and Dorothy M. Stetson. "The Impact of No-Fault Divorce Law Reform on Divorce in American States," *Journal of Marriage and the Family,* 40, no. 3 (Aug. 1978), 575–80. Indicates that recent changes in divorce laws have not had great impact on divorce rates in most states.

22 Marriage in Maturity

- How can the success of a mature marriage be measured?
- How do parents accept the post-parental stage in their marriage?
- What contributions do programs of marriage enrichment make to the middle-aged couple?
- What has stimulated new interest in family life in the retirement years?
- How would you compare preretirement living with retirement living?
- How can you assess marriage goals over the long term?

Marriage in the Middle Years

A marriage should not be judged prematurely. It has to be experienced and tested over a period of years before it can be evaluated properly. Although most of our discussion has been concerned with the process of courtship and the adjustments of the first years of marriage, we all have more than a passing interest in what happens to marriage in its later years, as children move out into the world and husband and wife look forward to their retirement. College students naturally have the greatest interest in the bright spring of love and romance, and that interest carries them over into the warm summer of early marriage and parenthood. But what will happen when the brisk winds of fall arrive? This is an important question for which we ought to find an honest answer.

There are many ways of considering the later years of marriage. We might ask if couples are as happy at age fifty or fifty-five as they were at age twenty or twenty-five. Or we could attempt to isolate certain early behavior patterns to see if they have changed during marriage. And do couples who are successful in marriage have characteristics different from those of couples who are unsuccessful or divorced? Have they been able to achieve the goals they set for themselves in the beginning years of marriage? All these approaches have been used and will be helpful to us in assessing marriage in maturity.

The most thorough of the early studies of successful marriage—Terman's, Burgess and Cottrell's, and Locke's—found that certain characteristics were evidenced by happily married couples and not by the unhappily married. But all of these studies were made more than thirty years ago. Today, we must consider new evidence and develop new ways of evaluating marital happiness. Indeed, feminists are already complaining of the irrelevance of most of the sociological literature dealing with women. Judith Laws takes the particularly critical stance that today's literature on the family is a suppression of women's goals and aspirations.

> We . . . see evidence that normative definitions of marriage act to suppress female sexuality; that the childbearing complex acts to reduce the wife's feeling of efficacy and even her relative power within the family; that damaging conflicts and powerful sanctions are set up to divorce the wife from the exercise of her talents and assertions of her personhood in the world outside the family, particularly as this takes the form of paid work.
>
> This critique, of course, implicates the whole system of sex role socialization. The family system is not an isolated structure. Indeed, a major fault of the marriage literature (and one source of its conservatism) is the intellectual fallacy of treating the family—particularly the marital dyad—as a closed system.[1]

Richard Kerckhoff, in his 1975 address to the National Council on Family Relations, focused on the problems and possibilities of the middle-aged. He recognizes that there are many pressures and disappointments for them. Men and women fear their inability to succeed in their professional and their personal lives. But this is the negative view. He also notes:

> The middle years can be a time of recognition of our value, not just a time of doubt about our worth. They can be for many a time of reassessment, of withdrawal from energy-consuming activities to which we were never really committed and of focus on those things in life which

[1]Judith Long Laws, "A Feminist Review of Marital Adjustment Literature: The Rape of the Locke," *Journal of Marriage and the Family*, 33, no. 3 (Aug. 1971), 483.

> we now feel sure are worthwhile. There is some room for contemplation and for feelings of satisfaction in the lives of many middle-aged people—time for learning from past experiences, for taking stock and for finding perspective. Middle-aged people, studies indicate, may feel squeezed by being in the middle, but they may, in addition, feel their own importance. They often know that they are the nation's decision-makers; they set the tone for life in this society. Society depends on middle-aged people's leadership and productivity.[2]

Kerckhoff feels that there is always the danger of boredom in marriage when the pressures of the first years of middle age have been surmounted. Just as college students or young adults need to find their sense of selfhood and identity, so do the middle-aged couple have to "enrich" their marriage and their own sense of worth and value.

What is life really like for the couple whose marriage has endured into the middle years? Does their marriage meet their expectations? Or do they find that it falls short of their expectations? John F. Cuber and Peggy B. Haroff report that upper-middle-class mature husbands and wives in the 1960s gave a pessimistic view of their marriages. There were few deeply

[2]Richard K. Kerckhoff, "Marriage and Middle Age," *The Family Coordinator,* 25, no. 1 (Jan. 1976), 5.

structured relationships. The couples stayed together because of convenience, tradition, and social standing, but often had a better relationship outside of marriage with a different partner. Good marriages were the exception rather than the rule.[3]

Why should so many mature people find marriage unsatisfying? If marriage is unsatisfying in the middle years, it may be because of the same underlying factors that lead to divorce: personality clashes; unrealistic expectations; failure to gain ego satisfaction; or unsatisfactory marital adjustment. These underlying causes of divorce may very often be present in a marriage that endures. The fact that the couple remain legally married, however, does not make them happier.

Some marriages do not suffer from the serious problems that lead to divorce. They just seem to fade. The union becomes dull and unexciting; there is really nothing there—no spark of love, interest, or vitality. The children, the job, the in-laws, or other outside persons or things have become of more importance to the partners than their relationship with each other. These are not necessarily marriages that were unsatisfactory at the beginning; husband and wife may have shared a great many things and entered into their normal roles enthusiastically and adequately from the first. But when the needs of two or three children became more insistent, or business demanded more time and energy, or community and recreation interests claimed more attention, the couple slowly but surely moved to meet those outside claims and just as slowly and surely moved away from each other. Such marriages are very common. One day husband and wife wake up to discover that they are no longer in love and wonder why their marriage fell far short of their early hopes and expectations.

Not all evaluations of middle-aged marriage are so negative. Much depends on one's perspective and the sample that you choose to study. We are a very much marriage-oriented society, and, as we noted in Chapter 21, the majority of those who divorce remarry within a few years. Bernice Hunt and Morton Hunt have taken an optimistic view of middle-age marriage. The trends in our society—fewer children, more education, two-career families, extended life expectancy—have changed our expectations of the middle-age years. The Hunts write:

> The first step in realizing the potentialities of middle age is to dispose of certain long-established misconceptions which are still widely held even though they do not stand up under scientific scrutiny, or which may once have been true but no longer are so under contemporary conditions.
>
> Perhaps the most important misconception is the idea that arrival at middle age is a crisis. There may be—and should be—a distinct expe-

[3]John F. Cuber and Peggy B. Haroff, *The Significant Americans* (New York: Appleton-Century-Crofts, 1965).

rience of *transition* in becoming middle-aged, but not every transition is a crisis. Indeed, some recent studies indicate that today for most people the stresses associated with reaching middle age are not critical, and that the transition to certain other stages of life are commonly just as stressful, if not more so. Innumerable people have found it more difficult to become 14 than 40.[4]

Another positive view of the middle-aged couple's married life is emerging from the marriage encounter and marriage enrichment movements. Sponsored by a number of religious and community service movements, these programs help couples in the mature phase of their marriages to find new meaning, growth, and excitement in their life together. Herbert Otto, in reviewing this field, writes:

> Almost unnoticed by the public and large segments of the professional community, a new movement has made its appearance, and has achieved a lusty stature in only a few years. The growth of the marriage and family enrichment movement has been prodigious, and it is still in its infancy. Marriage and family enrichment is based on the growth ethos and the human potentiality hypothesis. These are, briefly, that all persons and all relationships are functioning at a fraction of their potential and that *in every couple or family, there is the potential for growth in the relationship as well as the possibility of personal growth, leading to a more fulfilling togetherness.* It is a further hypothesis that *every union, or family, can be strengthened through the periodic regeneration and renewal offered by marriage and family enrichment programs.*[5]

Is it possible to accurately assess the course of marital adjustment and satisfaction in the middle-age period? Riley and Spreitzer show that a "flow-chart model," frequently used in business, cannot be applied to marriage and the family. It is hard to accumulate data covering a number of years. Using data available through Social Security disability benefits applicants, it was shown that the information submitted did not necessarily verify links between one's childhood family experience, good or bad, and one's later marital history. It could not be proven clearly in this study that a poor childhood environment or the onset of a physical disability had the most disruptive effect on one's marriage.[6]

Another study of married couples living in the states of Iowa, Ohio, and Georgia considered some of the same questions. Does adjustment hit high

[4]Bernice Hunt and Morton Hunt, *Prime Time* (New York: Stein and Day, 1975), pp. 16–17.

[5]Herbert A. Otto, ed, *Marriage and Family Enrichment* (Nashville, Tenn.: Abingdon, 1976), p. 11.

[6]Lawrence E. Riley and Elmer A. Spreitzer, "A Model for Analysis of Lifetime Marriage Patterns," *Journal of Marriage and the Family*, 36, no. 1 (Feb. 1974), 64–70.

spots and low spots during the family life cycle? This seems to be indicated by the Ohio data (see Figure 22–1). Both husbands and wives scored high ratings on the Locke-Wallace Marital Adjustment scales used in the study early in the marriage. But these ratings dropped sharply during the middle stages of the marriage. Then they moved up again toward age fifty.[7]

Changing Roles in the Middle Years

Some couples find it easier to keep their relationship on an even keel when they are under continual pressure to meet the needs of their children. There is always some work to be done, a PTA meeting to attend, a trip with the Scouts to the mountains, a soccer team trip, or the school play to attend.

However, during the second half of married life, when children are grown and the dyadic relationship between husband and wife becomes of central importance again, the roles played by both husband and wife change. A couple's status in the community and in the widened kin-family network is usually strengthened and expanded. The husband may receive positions of greater responsibility and trust in his daily work; his wife may be recognized for her achievement as a mother, for her freer entry into community activities, or for her return to a full- or part-time vocation. They are influential members of society.

Further change in a couple's life pattern comes about because they are able to have a more active life after their youngest child leaves home. Seventy-five years ago, a typical wife raising a family of eight or nine children would always have a child at home during her husband's lifetime, and her own life expectancy would barely extend to the maturity of her youngest children. In our contemporary society, with two or three children born while a typical wife is in her twenties or early thirties, a woman can expect two decades or more of active life after her children are grown.

What should the new goals become for this period beyond parenthood? Howard and Charlotte Clinebell have emphasized the importance of intimacy in marriage. From a background of counseling and teaching, they discuss the many facets of marital intimacy, which can be defined as the "degree of mutual need-satisfaction within the relationship." It involves meaning and trust for the couple—an answer to the crisis of loneliness and alienation and fear. It involves openness, caring, respect, and commitment. It also involves a sense of responsibility. The Clinebells write:

The sense of involvement in humanity and in the sordid problems which

[7]Graham B. Spanier, Robert A. Lewis, and Charles L. Cole, "Marital Adjustment Over the Family Life Cycle: The Issue of Curvilinearity," *Journal of Marriage and the Family*, 37, no. 3 (May 1976), 263–75.

Figure 22–1 Spouses' Mean Scores on the Locke-Wallace Marital Adjustment Scale by Stage in the Family Life Cycle, Newark, Ohio

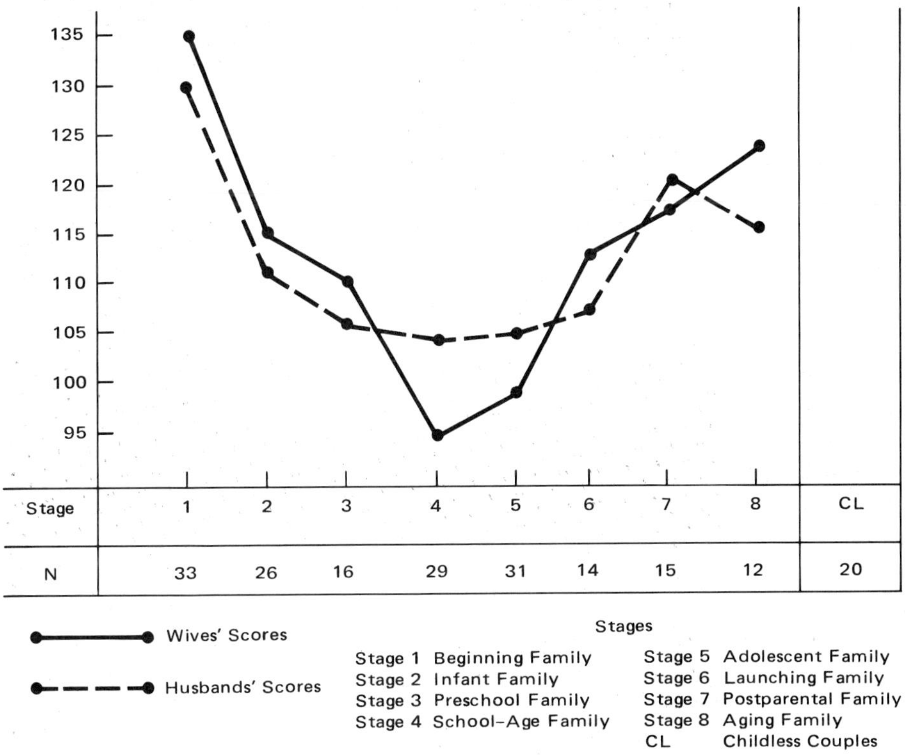

SOURCE: Graham B. Spanier, Robert A. Lewis, and Charles L. Cole, "Marital Adjustment Over the Family Life Cycle: The Issue of Curvilinearity," *Journal of Marriage and the Family,* 37, no. 3 (May 1976), 271. Copyrighted 1976 by the National Council on Family Relations. Reprinted by permission.

perplex our world is particularly needed by children and adults who have lived and matured in suburban islands of privilege and plenty. To break out of the self-congratulatory, comfortable state of mind which characterizes the suburban ghetto is a salutary emancipation for such persons. It is a discovery of the burdened world of which we are all a part and which is a part of all of us. To recognize that man's evolution is unfinished—in terms of both interpersonal relationships and the injustice-breeding structures of society—makes a major contribution to a family's sense of corporate purpose. It does so because it opens the possibility of becoming participants in the process of working to complete creation, to move man's cultural evolution toward the goal of a just, loving society.[8]

[8]Howard J. Clinebell, Jr., and Charlotte H. Clinebell, *The Intimate Marriage* (New York: Harper & Row, 1970), p. 216.

The middle-aged couple should be able to look beyond themselves. There is no question that our society is in the midst of a dramatic change. A combination of factors has turned the middle years of life into a period of high potential for achievement and enjoyment. Smaller family size, improved physical health, more stable economic conditions and provisions for retirement, more leisure time and recreational opportunities, and greater freedom and means of travel are all contributing to change the character of the postparental period. With these significant changes in the social environment, there is also a positive change in the way in which people face physical changes. If one can look forward to a very satisfying life in middle age, such a favorable psychological outlook is bound to have a beneficial impact on the way in which people face growing older.

The marital roles couples play during their middle years will also change. There will be more companionship as the responsibilities of parenthood are lessened and husband and wife have more leisure time to spend with each other. There will be more sharing in daily routines, especially if the wife has returned to full-time employment. There will be lessened authority over the lives of the children, but probably a much closer affectional relationship between husband and wife than when the children were in their turbulent teens. There will be greater interest in recreational activities, and one or both partners may develop hobbies or musical or artistic interests that had been set aside during the busy childrearing years.

This is an entirely new dimension of married life, one of tremendous significance for our society. No longer are aging parents dependent on their children for care and support. There is now a large and influential group of mature couples who are without responsibility for children, in the prime of life, financially well-off, and able to take an active part in business, community, and recreational life.

Another summary of middle-aged responsibilities and opportunities is given by Evelyn Duvall. She notes developmental tasks for both men and women. For the "postparental woman" she lists six major tasks:

> Encouraging young adult sons and daughters to be autonomous. . . .
> Maintaining a healthy sense of well-being. . . .
> Enjoying career and creative accomplishment. . . .
> Relating to aging parents. . . .
> Keeping social life satisfying. . . .
> Assuming civic and community responsibilities.[9]

A person who faces the middle years with such a breadth of interest and concern is bound to find life exciting and worthwhile.

[9]Evelyn Millis Duvall, *Marriage and Family Development*, 5th ed. (Philadelphia: Lippincott, 1977), pp. 357–61.

Retirement: The Senior Years

The final stage in the family life cycle begins with retirement, which occurs on the average at the age of 65. New laws have eliminated mandatory retirement at 65, but on the other hand, there has long been a trend toward early retirement. There are many opportunities to see the senior years in a new perspective. Let us suggest four ways that retired men and women can be brought into the center of community and national life.

First, senior citizens need to be encouraged to deal with the major issues in their lives. Craft classes and pleasure trips are valuable, but there is much more to life than taking up a new hobby. One's adjustment in marriage during the retirement years is a measure of one's adjustment in all areas of life. Morris Medley has defined the dimensions of this adjustment for the retired couple: self-esteem—a positive sense of self-worth is a natural starting point for a satisfying retirement lifestyle; interpersonal commitment—such commitment is just as important now as it is in the earlier stages of the marriage; availability of resources—the couple must be realistic about what they can do with what they have; goal consensus—the couple must team up to work for their shared goals. In all of these ways the couple can enhance the final years of their life together.[10]

Retired men and women have a need to make choices about their living accommodations, their medical care, and their relations with their children and grandchildren. It is often impractical to continue living in a large home. Olga Knopf lists a number of alternatives for such accommodations. Once

[10]Morris L. Medley, "Marital Adjustment in the Post-Retirement Years," *The Family Coordinator*, 26, no. 1 (Jan. 1977), 5–11.

a definite location is chosen, the other matters usually fall into place. Medical care may be offered through a social agency, a convalescent hospital, or by related facilities in some large homes for the elderly.[11] All of these choices, naturally, come more easily to those with the greatest resources. But some help is available through government and private programs.

Loneliness is often a serious problem in the retirement years. It may be due to the loss of a partner, or because a married couple has become isolated from their families and their friends. In a study of 210 persons aged 60 to 94 in Detroit, Jaber F. Gubrium found that "the single and married, the former being isolates but not desolates, both tended to be less negative in their evaluation of everyday life than widowed or divorced persons. Only the latter two would be categorized as desolate. The desolate are also more likely than the nondesolate to say that their personal feelings have changed since age 45."[12] If a person has the support of a partner, or if he or she has developed a satisfying lifestyle as a single person, the retirement years will be less lonely and threatening.

Finally, the retired person needs to continue to build a sense of self-worth

[11]Olga Knopf, *Successful Aging* (New York: Viking Press, 1977), pp. 148–70.

[12]Jaber F. Gubrium, "Marital Desolation and the Evaluation of Everyday Life in Old Age," *Journal of Marriage and the Family*, 36, no. 1 (Feb. 1974), 112.

and dignity. These men and women cannot allow themselves to become "forgotten Americans." Their creativity, their talents, their wisdom, and their achievements should receive recognition. This will come about partly because of the increasing number of retired persons in our society, and partly through retired persons' political activities. There is hope that the future of our senior citizens will continue to improve in the decades ahead.

> Much more, however, needs to be done if the status and image of the older person are to be altered, and his worth and dignity to be considered as important as the worth and dignity of the younger person. In this, as in many other situations, it is difficult to devise a single, clear-cut answer as to how the goal is to be achieved. Here we are confronted with the problem that not only do the needs differ from individual to individual, but they differ also among the age groups within the period designated as "old age." . . .
>
> . . . We must capitalize on our achieved knowledge that the elderly respond positively to any opportunity to utilize their skill and experience, as well as to the prospect of learning and growing.
>
> The achievement of such an important role in life has a bearing not only on the way the older person regards himself, but also on the way in which he is regarded by the younger generation . . . . The appreciation of what the elderly can do makes it possible for the younger to see and admire those qualities which have contributed so much to their own prosperity and the advances enjoyed by them."[13]

It is probable that the extension of the final stage of the life cycle will cause permanent changes in our society. The effects are already visible in many ways—in the increased interest in programs of aid and protection for senior citizens, such as Medicare, Social Security, company pension plans, and union programs; in the political activity of many older citizens; in special retirement communities and other private facilities that cater to older couples; and in facilities for travel and other leisure-time activities for senior citizens. More and more younger couples are making careful and deliberate plans for this period in their lives and are anticipating a fruitful and enjoyable retired life. The transition of the retired from dependence and poverty to independence and activity is not yet complete, nor will the unsatisfactory aspects of their social and psychological environment be quickly eliminated. But there are signs that a change is being effected as more and more retired people become financially secure and as medical science gives people better health in their old age. And there are many ways that society can respond

[13]Minna Field, *The Aged, the Family, and the Community* (New York: Columbia Univ. Press, 1972), pp. 240–41. See also Gary R. Lee, "Marriage and Morale in Later Life," *Journal of Marriage and the Family*, 40, no. 1 (Feb. 1978), 131–39.

to the needs of older families and individuals who are not so fortunate as others. Many retired people find that their leisure time is put to good use doing just that, in fact—working to improve the lot of their fellow senior citizens. Our grandparents' generation is finding a new purpose and a new dignity.

SUMMARY A marriage is best evaluated over a long period of time. We might ask whether a couple are as happy in their middle years as they were in early marriage, or whether they have achieved most of their goals. But in order to do this we need new methods of measuring marital happiness. Early studies of marital adjustment were based on masculine and feminine roles that have changed noticeably over the past few decades.

Marriage in middle age can have many satisfying aspects. As the children grow up and leave home, the husband and wife must reevaluate and revitalize their marital relationship. The relatively short childbearing period in contemporary marriage, and the lengthened life span, place half or more of married life into this postparental period. Here is an opportunity for the middle-aged couple to grow in intimacy, and to seek new purposes and tasks.

Retirement marks the final stage in the marital life cycle. The growing number of senior citizens play an important role in today's society. Retired persons must be realistic about their life and their expectations. Above all, they need to continue to build a sense of self-worth and identity.

SUGGESTED READINGS

Clinebell, Howard J., Jr., and Charlotte H. Clinebell. *The Intimate Marriage.* New York: Harper & Row, 1970. A couple who themselves have a two-career marriage describe the rewards and satisfactions of the intimate marriage.

Cuber, John F., and Peggy B. Haroff. *The Significant Americans.* New York: Appleton-Century-Crofts, 1965. Pessimistic appraisal of upper-middle-class marriages in the 1960s.

Field, Minna. *The Aged, the Family, and the Community.* New York: Columbia Univ.Press, 1972. Discusses the needs of senior citizens in terms of family and community support systems.

Gordon, Michael. *The American Family: Past, Present, and Future.* New York: Random House, 1978. Relates the contemporary family to its historical roots. Note chap. 13—"Family Life in the Later Years."

Hunt, Bernice, and Morton Hunt. *Prime Time.* New York: Stein and Day, 1975. A popular treatment of the new opportunities available to those in the middle years.

Kart, Gary S., and Barbara B. Manare, eds. *Aging in America—Readings in Social Gerontology.* Port Washington, N.Y.: Alfred Publishing Co., 1976. Broad selection of articles on aging.

Laws, Judith Long. "A Feminist Review of Marital Adjustment Literature: The Rape of the Locke." *Journal of Marriage and the Family,* 33, no. 3 (Aug. 1971), 483–516. Feminist critique of the biased, traditional family view of women that limited their goals and aspirations.

Otto, Herbert A., ed. *Marriage and Family Enrichment.* Nashville, Tenn.: Abingdon, 1976. Selections written by leaders in the marriage enrichment field. Summarizes various approaches to family growth.

Peterson, James A. *Married Love in the Middle Years.* New York: Association Press, 1968. Creative approaches to love and satisfaction in the middle years of marriage.

Spanier, Graham B., Robert A. Lewis, and Charles L. Cole. "Marital Adjustment Over the Family Life Cycle: The Issue of Curvilinearity," *Journal of Marriage and the Family,* 37, no. 2 (May 1975), 263–75. Study of couples in three states to ascertain whether marriage satisfaction increases in the later years.

The Future of the Family

Challenges for the Family

What is the mark of the future? Each one of us has his own idea of what future marriage and family life will be like. But whatever changes we may imagine will come with time, we probably can be confident of the family's continuing importance. For we must not forget that the family serves a basic social need—perpetuating human society—that will endure in all future generations.

Mary Jo Bone believes that marriage and family will survive.

> The facts—as opposed to the myths—about marriage, childrearing, and family ties in the United States today provide convincing evidence that family commitments are likely to persist in our society. Family ties, it seems clear, are not archaic remnants of a disappearing traditionalism, but persisting manifestations of human needs for stability, continuity, and nonconditional affection. . . .
>
> . . . Family ties and family feelings are integral to the lives of most Americans. The ethic that governs relationships between people who love and care for each other inevitably intrudes into public life, coloring people's perceptions of what they and others ought to do. Policies that

> ignore this ethic—that imply that public facilities can replace parental care or that the public welfare system is responsible for supporting children—will almost surely be either widely resented or essentially disregarded. . . .[1]

In addition to the discussion taking place between the proponents of a strong and cohesive family unit in a demanding and constricting social environment and those who view the possible demise of the family with little concern, there are new challenges to the nuclear family from a dozen different alternatives to the traditional family patterns (see Chapter 2).

Ira Reiss makes this cautious prediction about the family's future:

> The universal functions of family systems, I think, have been substantiated by the examination undertaken in this book. We have found no societies without family systems that take care of nurturance, legitimation of parenthood, and mate selection. What we are really witnessing in America then is a change in the ways in which these functions are achieved and not any elimination of these functions. . . .
>
> . . . I think the more objective and scientific interpretation of these changes is that there are multiple family systems in America. Life today more often consists of a set of choices among the elements of these family systems, but most all of them fulfill the basic universal functions. . . .
>
> I believe Americans have opened up the range of possibilities but are now entering into an era wherein the rate of change will likely slow down, and we shall come to rank these alternative family forms and learn to choose life styles for ourselves. . . . We are in an era of unprecedented choice—a human experiment not tried by many societies in the entire history of mankind. All of us, young and old, traditional and nontraditional, are on the same voyage.[2]

The Black Family

As we enter the 1980s, there is growing awareness of the roles played by the different family groups in our society. In particular, the black family of the future merits our study and attention. Franklin Frazier's classic study of black families has been challenged on many points, and the search for an accurate appraisal of the contemporary black family continues.[3]

[1]Mary Jo Bone, *Here to Stay: American Families in the Twentieth Century* (New York: Basic Books, 1976), pp. 141–42.

[2]Ira L. Reiss, *Family Systems in America*, 2nd ed. (New York: Holt, Rinehart & Winston, 1976), pp. 439–40.

[3]See E. Franklin Frazier, *The Negro in the United States*, rev. ed. (New York: Macmillan, 1957).

Frazier assumed that black families would gradually be acculturated into the dominant white society, and that any race problems would gradually disappear through the process of assimilation. His conclusions seem to be far out of step with the realities of today's black nationalism. Young black scholars are stressing the changing composition and structure of the black family, and looking toward the future rather than back toward the past.

What is this emerging black family like? First, it is a two-parent family. Although there are still a large number of black families headed by women, the majority of black families have two parents living in the home. This is even more true moving up the social-class scale to the upper-class black family.[4] Second, income levels are rising as more blacks join the ranks of the professional working class. Such changes in employment have not brought the average black person's income up to that of the average white person's income, but a large middle-income group of black families is emerging.

Third, in conjunction with employment, the educational level of both black men and black women is rising. Reiss shows a 100 percent rise in the number of black men, 18 to 24 years of age, enrolled in college during the period from 1965 to 1974 (10 to 20 percent of the total black population in the United States), while the white male enrollment dropped 18 percent (from 34 to 28 percent of all white males). At the same time, black female enrollment jumped by 60 percent (from 10 to 16 percent of all black females).[5]

And finally, although our progress in civil rights and equal opportunity is not all that it should be, step by step the barriers of ignorance and prejudice are being broken down across the country. For example, integration of a school today may have only a limited or even a negative effect on the community. But the leadership of the children from this school thirty or forty years later will have a marked effect on their community.

The Mythology of the Black Family

The summary of the positive elements of the developing black family must be balanced with a recognition of some of the crises these families face. These are not insoluble problems but they are serious. Black scholars suggest that these problems have created the mythology of the black family. According to Marie Peters, when the black family is discussed by white scholars, it is described in terms of "deviancy, pathology, and/or uncontrolled sexuality." The hard-core black poor receive all the attention and emphasis while the majority of black families are ignored.[6] Leonard Lieberman

[4]Ira L. Reiss, *Family Systems in America*, 2nd ed. (Hinsdale, Ill.: Dryden, 1976), pp. 415–23.
[5]Reiss, p. 420.
[6]Marie Ferguson Peters, "The Black Family–Perpetuating the Myths: An Analysis of Family Sociology Textbook Treatment of Black Families," *The Family Coordinator*, 23, no. 4 (Oct. 1974), 349–57.

believes that there must be more studies of the black family, and that scholars of different ethnic backgrounds, especially black scholars, should carry out these studies.[7]

We can identify three major problems that confront a large minority of black families. First, there is the problem of illegitimacy and subsequent one-parent families, usually headed by women. Paul Glick and Arthur Norton report that "in 1976, three times as large a proportion of black women as white women (36 percent versus 11 percent) maintained a family with no husband reported as a member."[8] Yet research by Glick and Norton indicates that only one-third to one-fourth of the difference between the two groups can actually be attributed to the low estimate of black men present in these homes.

The second problem is the misunderstanding of the differences between black sexuality and that of other groups in our society. Robert Staples points out that there are a number of social, cultural, class, and historical influences that affect the black sexual subculture. He writes:

> In essence one might say that the sexual attitudes and experiences of blacks differ from whites, but it is not a difference which confirms the cultural beliefs about black sexuality. The differences are based in part on the different cultural base for black sexual behavior; the legacy of slavery and white racism. Additionally, social class factors need to be considered in any comparison of black and white sexual behavior. Statistically significant differences between blacks and whites in sexual attitudes and behavior should not be allowed to blur the extent to which large numbers in both groups feel and act similarly.[9]

The third problem involves the entire relationship between the varying racial and ethnic groups in our society, and the way in which we build a theoretical framework to study black family life (and that of other minorities) in our society.[10] There is no way of separating black family life, or black economic achievement, or black religious life, or black political programs, from the way in which we seek to bring together and give structure and meaning to a pluralistic society. If economic conditions are especially difficult for black wage earners, this will have an impact on black life. If scholarships and affirmative action programs are cut back in colleges and uni-

[7]Leonard Lieberman, "The Emerging Model of the Black Family," *International Journal of Sociology of the Family*, 3, no. 1 (March 1973), 10–22.

[8]Paul C. Glick and Arthur J. Norton, *Marrying, Divorcing, and Living Together in the U.S. Today* (Washington: Population Reference Bureau, 1977), p. 31.

[9]Robert Staples, "Research on Black Sexuality: Its Implication for Family Life, Sex Education, and Public Policy," *The Family Coordinator*, 21, no. 2 (April 1972), 185.

[10]Walter R. Allen, "The Search for Applicable Theories of Black Family Life," *Journal of Marriage and the Family*, 40, no. 1 (Feb. 1978), 117–29.

versities, this will affect the black family. It is vitally important in studying any one area of black family life to keep the total perspective in view.

A real challenge exists for a black scholar to make a thorough analysis of the black family, considering all of these factors with the sensitivity and understanding of a "participant-observer" in the life of the black family itself.[11] Only by expanding the study of this largest minority group can we develop meaningful and positive public policies and attitudes that will deal realistically with the needs of black families.

Hispanic-Americans

Hispanic-Americans are the second largest minority group in the United States. This group includes the Mexican-Americans, Puerto Ricans, Cubans, and Latin Americans. In most parts of the country, Hispanic-Americans have been isolated from the mainstream of American culture. This isolation has contributed to their continuing problems of poverty, limited education, and lack of employment opportunities. In addition, the growth of ethnic pride and social and political activism has come more slowly to Hispanic-Americans than it did to blacks. Puerto Ricans settled mainly in New York City. Here the opportunities they had come to find were offered in only a limited degree. Overcrowding, illiteracy, poverty, and associated problems were daily facts of life in their new home.

Patricia Cayo Sexton, who has worked in Spanish Harlem, has tried to understand what family means to Puerto Ricans:

> Among Puerto Ricans the family is stressed as the "center of an adult's obligations," while individuality and "doing things just for oneself are discouraged as being of no value."
>
> Success and achievement are encouraged only as ways to help the family. The person who does not succeed can expect help from the family. As one person put it: "A good life is when we work and we have the things we need for all the family." Independence and self-reliance "are not to be encouraged in a child." Good children are defined as "obedient, respectful, and docile."[12]

Sexton indicates the interrelation between the social and economic conditions that affect the Puerto Rican population. Some of their problems are an outgrowth of poverty in Puerto Rico. Others are a reflection of the difficulties in moving from one culture to another.

[11]See Robert Chrisman and Nathan Hare, eds., *Contemporary Black Thought* (Indianapolis: Bobbs-Merrill, 1973).

[12]Patricia Cayo Sexton, *Spanish Harlem* (New York: Harper & Row, 1965), p. 19.

The Mexican-American Family

The largest single group of Hispanics is the Mexican-Americans, who are concentrated in the southwestern United States. Their number has been variously estimated at five to six million, but this may be low considering the large number of uncounted aliens from Mexico.[13] Large families are still very common in this community, and the additional increase of new immigrants from Mexico means that the population in some areas, particularly California, is increasing very rapidly. In California, for example, the Spanish-surname population almost doubled from 1950 to 1960, and the population has continued to increase.[14] Family ties are strong, and family life often follows the more traditional patterns of Mexico, with masculine dominance of many aspects of family life.

Roman Catholicism is still the dominant religion among Mexican-Americans. There is great loyalty to the church among many families, although the activist younger generation is sometimes impatient with the church's response to the social, educational, and economic problems of the Mexican-Americans. Protestant denominations, although a minority, have been active in educational and health programs.[15]

Like blacks, Mexican-Americans are very involved in the social changes of our time. This is expressed in a number of protest and activist movements, and most clearly focused on the rise of "Chicano" consciousness. The Mexican-Americans, or Chicanos, are seeking to build pride and self-awareness of their own cultural heritage.[16] Since they can assimilate more readily than blacks into the dominant culture, a large number of Mexican-Americans will move into the mainstream of American life through intermarriage and adoption of culture and customs from the Anglo majority. However, because so many Mexican-Americans are still concentrated in *barrio* or ghetto areas, and because they have a different language background, a separate cultural life is very important to them.

A number of sociological, psychological, and family studies are being focused on the Mexican-Americans.[17] To attempt to deal with the complex social, political, legal, and economic issues that affect this group without a careful analysis of the life of their families is to ignore a major basis for much of their participation in the community. The Mexican-American subculture

[13]See Leo Grebler, Joan W. Moore, and Ralph C. Guzman, *The Mexican-American People* (New York: Free Press, 1970), p. 106.

[14]Grebler et al., p. 106.

[15]See John H. Burma, ed., *Mexican-Americans in the United States,* Sec. 5, "Family and Religion" (Cambridge, Mass.: Schenkman, 1970), pp. 209–48.

[16]See Tony Castro, *Chicano Power—The Emergence of Mexican-America* (New York: Saturday Review Press, 1974).

[17]See Charles H. Wood and Frank D. Bean, "Offspring Gender and Family Size: Implications from a Comparison of Mexican-Americans and Anglo-Americans," *Journal of Marriage and the Family,* 39, no. 1 (Feb. 1977), 129–39.

is going to play an increasingly important part in the life of our country during the coming years; and it is essential that we understand the importance of their family structure.

What Will the Future Bring?

Some sociologists see the 1970s as a time of crisis for the family and expect to see even more drastic upheavals in the future.

> The traditional monogamous, sexually exclusive marriage will remain for many, but certainly not the majority of people, a desirable and viable pattern despite the increasing tensions of leisure, mobility, women's liberation, our contraceptive technology, negativism of the nuclear family, and an ever increasing life expectancy.
>
> An increasing number of men and women will find an alternative mode of coping with these tensions in a more flexible monogamy allowing for comarital experiences by mutual consent of both parties. . . .
>
> Serial monogamy or consecutive polygamy, which is already commonplace in our patterns of divorce and remarriage, will in the future resolve the patriarchal inequities of alimony, child support, and custody in favor of a "no-fault" dissolution of the marriage. . . .
>
> Unisex marriages of two or more males or females will be accepted. Since we can no longer restrict sexual relations to a procreative function, homosexuality can no longer be condemned as immoral or unnatural merely because it is noncreative.
>
> . . . Couples disillusioned with the institution of marriage may choose unstructured but stable cohabitation.[18]

Robert Francoeur sees this new freedom as part of "the pluralistic culture of the global tribe."[19] Others might see it as an erosion of the stable core—the family—of Western civilization.

Is there a viable substitute for the family as we know it on the horizon? Is it really possible to transmit the social values and customs and traditions that really matter to a new generation without the socializing influences of a stable family? Or is the emphasis we have placed on the nuclear family an unnecessary one?[20] Must we have a new family structure to go along with the changing role behavior that seems to be required in contemporary family relationships? I would predict that the structure of the family of the next

[18]Robert Francoeur, *Eve's New Rib: Twenty Faces of Sex, Marriage and Family* (New York: Harcourt Brace Jovanovich, 1972), pp. 222–23.
[19]Francoeur, p. 224.
[20]See Hazen G. Werner, *Look at the Family Now* (Nashville, Tenn.: Abingdon, 1970), chap. 8.

decades will probably be basically the same as it is now. Men and women will continue to fall in love, marry, and raise children. Most couples will make their monogamous marriages a lifelong commitment. But the functions of the family will continue to change. The changes will be most apparent for women, but men and children will be affected as well. The more successfully we learn to live with these changing functions, the more adequate the structure of the nuclear family will be to meet the challenge of the future.

Our discussion of courtship, marriage, and family life is now complete. For those who have joined in this quest for insight, knowledge, and understanding of this most intimate and personal of all human relationships, we trust that the journey has been a rewarding one. We have tried to move logically from an examination of our lives as individuals through the years of dating and courtship and ahead to married life, with its many immediate adjustments and the myriad subtle changes that come about during the course of adult life.

Two recurrent themes in our discussions are sources of a creative tension in the lives of most husbands and wives. One is the basic need to discover one's self-identity. Unless a person understands himself—his motivations and his goals and values—he will never be able to share fully in the marriage relationship. He will always be missing something, searching for something, until he finds himself.

The second recurrent theme is the need for a real and meaningful partnership between husband and wife. Such a union is perhaps the truest definition of marriage: two become one. Marriage involves a giving up of oneself, in a very real sense, in order to gain another. This kind of giving is an act of love, an act of trust, and an act of faith. We cannot be certain that all our hopes and dreams will be fulfilled. In fact, we are almost positive that marriage, as all of human life, will in some way be fragile, weak, and insecure. But life cannot be changed, nor problems solved, by avoiding challenge and conflict, and we would be none the better if we turned away from a potentially rewarding marriage because of fears and anxieties.

To those whose marriages still lie ahead, let us suggest a few simple guidelines. First, be willing to know yourself. Honest self-examination is indispensable. Second, be willing to look at your family and all your years of development in an objective way. You may wish to change many of your life patterns in the future, but do not fail to take a careful look at the path you have already followed. Third, as you think of entering marriage, be certain to choose your partner well. Utilize the opportunities of courtship before you. If necessary, create new opportunities. However you meet your intended partner, take time to know him, his family, and his background.

Fourth, be willing to evaluate your relationship objectively—with the help of your friends, your parents, your teachers, your minister or priest or rabbi, your physician, or a professional counselor. The choice is too important to be dictated by emotion alone. Finally, decide what kind of life you are going to live in your future marriage. Will it be essentially a selfish one, because all your plans center around yourself, your family, and your friends? Or will yours be a marriage and family life shared with others in the larger community and the world, so that each member of your family will have his chance to make a meaningful contribution to the world in which we live? This is your choice as you plan ahead for your future marriage and family life.

SUGGESTED READINGS

Allen, Walter R. "The Search for Applicable Theories of Black Family Life." *Journal of Marriage and the Family*, 40, no. 1 (Feb. 1978), 117–29. Careful examination of different theories of black families.

Frazier, E. Franklin. *The Negro in the United States*, rev. ed. New York: Macmillan, 1957. Reissue of a classic book on the black family, written prior to the civil rights movement.

Grebler, Leo, Joan W. Moore, and Ralph C. Guzman. *The Mexican-American People.* New York: Free Press, 1970. Comprehensive treatment of the place of Mexican-Americans in our culture.

Lewis, Oscar. *La Vida: A Puerto Rican Family in the Culture of Poverty, San Juan and New York.* New York: Random House, 1966. Good insight into Puerto Rican culture and the life of one family in the two different environments.

Lieberman, Leonard. "The Emerging Model of the Black Family." *International Journal of Sociology of the Family*, 3, no. 1 (March 1973), 10–22. Sees changes in our understanding of the black family, and emergence of new models emphasizing positive elements of Afro-American culture.

Staples, Robert, ed. *The Black Family: Essays and Studies.* Belmont, Calif.: Wadsworth, 1971. Solid readings covering many aspects of black family life patterns.

Appendix
Glossary
Picture Credits
Index

Appendix

Suggested Family Analysis

Your college course in marriage and the family is an introduction to the prospects and problems of married life. Such a course gives you an opportunity to discuss contemporary courtship patterns, alternative lifestyles, and different types of relationships within marriage. It also provides you with a realistic appraisal of the "joys and sorrows" of family life.

In this course you may have had occasion to discuss some of your own family experiences and attitudes, and you will certainly have had the opportunity to think more seriously about your personal development. Unfortunately, however, in the limited time available, you probably have not been able to discuss your particular family in detail. The experiences you have had in your own family, however, may be of major importance to you, not only in interpreting lecture and text material, but in utilizing the knowledge you have gained. This family analysis is intended to help you gain insight into the family environment out of which you emerged. Such insight, coupled with your growing maturity, will give you a strong foundation for marriage.

To many students, this paper will be an introduction to the kind of research carried on in the social sciences. Others will be able to draw on experience and techniques they have gained in comparable courses. Although you will want to use some outside readings and research for the paper, the core of your study should be the familiar daily interaction within your own family, not information gained from academic research. You should know that this paper will be read only by the instructor and that it will be returned to you. You are, of course, perfectly free to withhold any family information you do not wish to include.

The paper is not to be a history of your family—there are too many people and incidents in your life to be included in a brief paper. Rather, you should try to describe how your family functions and how it fits into the larger society. If there have been divorces or remarriages in your family, you may need to sketch the circumstances of each new family unit briefly. Conclude your paper as of the time of your college entrance or high school graduation. (The inclusion of your adult experiences or your own marriage and children may lengthen the report unduly and detract from the discussion of your parental family.)

You will find this paper helpful in direct proportion to: (1) the amount of effort you put into preparation for the paper; (2) the use you make of suitable references (for instance, books in the course bibliography) in analyzing your family and comparing it with other families; and (3) your success in making your family patterns come alive in the pages of your analysis. Every family is different from every other; from reading your analysis, will the instructor feel that he knows your family and can understand the way it functions? Prepare your family analysis carefully, and it will prove to be an extremely valuable project.

Below is a suggested outline for your paper. You may wish to devote equal space to each topic, or you may wish to organize the paper around one or two topics and give only limited treatment to the rest. Perhaps you will even find one dominant theme for the entire family.

A. The family in terms of interpersonal relationships

1. Organization and beginning of the family

Give a very brief introduction to your family. When did your parents meet? What do you know about their courtship, engagement, and marriage? What were their parental families like, and how well-adjusted were they? What were their parents' educational levels and socioeconomic backgrounds? Ask yourself how much you really know or do not know about your grandparents' and your parents' early lives. What were your parents' basic personality patterns when they were young?

2. Marital adjustment

Most studies of American family life suggest that the marital adjustment of the parents is a crucial factor in family life. What has been the course of your parents' marriage? How would you rate their relationship on the five-point scale *Very Poor, Below Average, Average, Above Average, Very Good?* If they are divorced or separated, when did their relationship begin to deteriorate?

3. Role distribution

   Who performs the economic, or breadwinning, role? Is it shared? Who carries out the home management, companionship, kinship, and community relationship roles? Are those roles clearly defined, and do both parents and children understand how they are to be carried out? Do any roles go unfulfilled? Are some members of the family strong in one role and inadequate in others?

4. Power distribution

   Most families may be described as patricentric, matricentric, or egalitarian (democratic). What is the balance of power in your family? Can you see any changes in the pattern of family dominance over the years? What are the strengths and weaknesses in your family power system?

5. Parent-children and sibling relationships

   How many children are there in your family? What relationships exist among them? Are the effects of being the oldest, youngest, or middle child noticeable? Have you had substitute parents (grandparents or other relatives)? Are you an only child? List the basic facts of parent-children and sibling relationships in your family (your age at the birth of your younger brother, the time your father was in the service) even if you cannot see their influence at this point.

6. Effects of parents' employment on the family

   How has your father's occupation affected your family life? What has been the influence of your mother's occupation, if she worked during your childhood or adolescence? Do your parents bring their work home with them? Or, is there a fairly strict division between the office and home? If you grew up in a two-career family, how did this work out? Are your parents happy with the careers they have chosen?

7. Religious patterns

   What importance is attached to religion in your family? Is it a source of unity or conflict? Is the major emphasis on external, or public, religious observance, or on attitudes and beliefs? Would you marry someone of another faith?

8. Courtship and the family

How influential has your family been in your dating and courtship patterns? Are rules set rigidly by your parents, or are you allowed to discuss your privileges and restrictions with them? What family standards have now become internalized for you?

B. The family in social context

1. Geographical location

What area is your home in? Has your family moved from farm to city, or from the city to the suburbs? If so, have those moves affected the family educational level, standard of living, birth rate, or occupations? How does your community affect you? Would you want to raise your children in the same area?

2. Social class

Family life is also influenced by social class. There is a tendency for most families to try to move up on the social scale. (This is often the case with college students whose parents did not attend college.) Try to locate your family on the class scale: upper class, upper-middle class, lower-middle class, or lower class. (In small communities or homogeneous residential suburbs, there may be fewer divisions than this.) How long has your family occupied its present class position? Has it moved up, down, or stayed at the same level? Are there differences in class between different family members?

3. The effects of war, depression, and so on

Has war had an impact on your family? Has your family been forced to move to a new state or a new community because of a recession or because of a military assignment? How has your family reacted to the important world events of the past 50 years?

Glossary[1]

Abortion Expulsion of an embryo or fetus before it is viable (capable of surviving outside the uterus). *Spontaneous abortion* means miscarriage; *induced abortion* means surgical termination of a pregnancy. *Therapeutic abortion* means surgical termination of a pregnancy because it endangers the life of the mother.

Ambivalence A state in which a person experiences contradictory feelings (such as hate and love) toward a given person, thing, or action.

Community A body of persons sharing a common geographical area, common local institutions, and a common daily life.

Conjugal family A family in which the primary emphasis is on the husband-wife relationship rather than on blood relationships.

Courtship The entire process of association of man and woman preparatory to marriage.

Courtship system The organized patterns of interaction between men and women that lead to marriage. Specific expectations, functions, norms, and values are inherent in the system.

Culture A system of behavior shared by members of a society, including language, tools, customs, beliefs, values, and institutions, all of which pattern the social life of a society and are socially transmitted.

Economic functions The functions served by the economic system, consisting primarily of the production, distribution, and consumption of goods and services.

[1] See also Julius Gould and William D. Kolb, eds., *UNESCO Dictionary of the Social Sciences* (New York: Free Press, 1964); Robert F. Winch, *The Modern Family*, 3rd ed. (New York: Holt, Rinehart & Winston, 1971), pp. 3–29; and George A. Theodorson and Achilles G. Theodorson, *A Modern Dictionary of Sociology* (New York: Thomas Y. Crowell, 1969).

Educational functions The functions performed by schools and other educational media, including socialization, the transmission of culture knowledge, and preparation for a particular place in the social structure.

Endogamy The custom requiring marriage within one's own social group and penalizing those who violate that norm.

Engagement The period immediately preceding marriage, initiated by a more or less formal announcement of a couple's intention to marry.

Extended family A family of three or more generations. The extended family is not as significant in contemporary American life as it is in many other nations and cultures.

Familial functions Functions performed by the family, such as reproduction, socialization, and the satisfaction of self, economic, and affectional needs.

Family A group established primarily for the procreation, care, and socialization of children. Some families have only one parent because of death, separation, or divorce. A childless husband and wife may also be considered a family.

Family life cycle The sequence of stages through which a family passes from its beginning to its dissolution.

Family of origin or orientation The family in which one is born, adopted, or raised.

Family of procreation A family formed by the marriage of two persons.

Function A consequence or expectation of a structure. Since persons or things are put together in a certain way, we expect them to operate in a certain way. This expected behavior pattern, or function, usually contributes to the maintenance and survival of the structure.

Group Two or more members or parts existing together and clearly related to each other.

Homogamy The marriage of persons with similar characteristics.

Institution A system of interrelated social roles and norms that satisfy an important social need. Institutions are complex patterns of behavior that are relatively enduring.

Kinship Relationships within the family system, including those based on blood relationships and those based on marriage.

Lesbianism Female homosexuality; sexual attraction between two females. (There is no corresponding technical term for male homosexuality, although "gay" is a term used to describe male homosexuals.)

Marriage The legal partnership of a man and a woman; also the personal relationship between them, including sexual, economic, social, religious, and emotional interaction. In most societies, strong emphasis is placed on the function of procreation of children.

Monogamy The exclusive union of one man and one woman in marriage.

No-fault divorce A divorce granted without cause or fault being established. Replaces system where one partner was "guilty."

Norm A standard shared by members of a social group. Conformity to a norm may be enforced by rewards or punishments.

Nuclear family A family consisting of parents and children, including adopted children. Also termed the conjugal family. In our society, this term also includes childless couples.

Political functions The functions of government, including formalization of laws and norms, protection of society from outside forces, settlement of internal disputes, and enforcement of laws and norms.

Polyandry Marriage of one woman to two or more husbands at the same time.

Polygamy Marriage of one man or woman to two or more spouses at the same time.

Polygyny Marriage of one man to two or more wives at the same time.

Primary group An intimate group stressing face-to-face relationships and involving a high level of shared interests and activities.

Puberty Stage in the life cycle that begins adolescence. Includes maturational and hormonal changes that usually occur between the ages of 11 and 14: rapid physical growth and the development of secondary sex characteristics.

Religious functions Functions providing a social institution and a value system that orient the individual to a concept of ultimate reality.

Role The part of a person's social position that includes the norms and expectations one must meet because of one's status in society.

Sex roles The attitudes and behaviors expected of males and females. Can be stereotyped, so that men are expected to carry out a certain set of roles and women are expected to carry out a different set of roles. These roles are being reexamined and reevaluated in contemporary society.

Social class All those persons who hold a common position in society, particularly on the economic scale.

Socialization The process by which an individual is taught the culture of a social group and learns the roles expected of him; the process by which he is integrated into his society.

Social system A social hierarchy that includes two or more distinct social positions, such as a social class hierarchy or family hierarchy.

Society A number of communities that occupy contiguous territory, are mutually interdependent, and share a common culture.

Status One's relative position, or rank, in society. Closely related to prestige, which depends on personal evaluations of status.

Structure An orderly combination of related parts.

Subculture A unit within the total culture of a society, identifiable by certain differences in values, customs, or norms. Ethnic, occupational, religious, and class subcultures are common in our society.

Picture Credits

page 3: Werner H. Muller, Peter Arnold, Inc.
page 6: Ron Gabel, Guidance Associates
page 8: Andy Corn, Image, Inc.
page 15: Wasyl Szkodzinsky, Guidance Associates
page 22: photo courtesy Johnson Wax Company
page 23: Joe Schuyler, Stock, Boston
page 28: Tim Carlson, Stock, Boston
page 37: Mimi Forsyth, Monkmeyer Press Photo Service
page 46: Mimi Forsyth, Monkmeyer Press Photo Service
page 57: Dave Repp, Image, Inc.
page 63: Paul S. Conklin
page 68: Suzanne Szasz
page 72: Rohn Engh, Sunrise Photos
page 78: Suzanne Szasz
page 102: Hugh Rogers, Monkmeyer Press Photo Service
page 104: John Veltri
page 114: Guidance Associates
page 131: Frank Empson, Image, Inc.
page 137: Michael Hayman, Image, Inc.
page 141: Michael Hayman, Image, Inc.
page 156: Suzanne Szasz
page 163: Billy E. Barnes
page 166: Rohn Engh, Sunrise Photos
page 175: Rohn Engh, Sunrise Photos
page 185: Wolf von dem Bussche, Guidance Associates
page 190: Frank Empson, Image, Inc.
page 194: Ginger Chih
page 198: Sybil Shelton, Monkmeyer Press Photo Service
page 211: HBJ photo
page 217: HBJ photo
page 226: Paul S. Conklin, Monkmeyer Press Photo Service
page 237: Billy E. Barnes
page 241: Steve Perille, Image, Inc.
page 247: Mimi Forsyth, Monkmeyer Press Photo Service
page 255: Foxx, Guidance Associates
page 260: Suzanne Szasz
page 282: Hazel Hankin
page 284: Mimi Forsyth, Monkmeyer Press Photo Service

page 286: Suzanne Szasz
page 289: photo courtesy Cove Haven Resort
page 293: Ira Rosenberg, Image, Inc.
page 299: Peter Vadnai, Guidance Associates
page 302: Sybil Shelton, Monkmeyer Press Photo Service
page 304: Mimi Forsyth, Monkmeyer Press Photo Service
page 309: Peter Kosarin
page 313: Kaplan, HBJ photo
page 319: Suzanne Szasz
page 332: Paul S. Conklin, Monkmeyer Press Photo Service
page 335: Michael Weisbrot
page 339: Ronnie Williams, Image, Inc.
page 354: Theologos, HBJ photo
page 356: Mimi Forsyth, Monkmeyer Press Photo Service
page 362: Mimi Forsyth, Monkmeyer Press Photo Service
page 411: Jerry Spearman, Guidance Associates
page 417: F. Siteman, Stock, Boston
page 423: Billy E. Barnes
page 429: Lew Merrim, Monkmeyer Press Photo Service
page 432: Bohdan Hrynewych, Stock, Boston
page 443: Sybil Shelton, Monkmeyer Press Photo Service
page 460: Les Mahon, Monkmeyer Press Photo Service
page 462: Mimi Forsyth, Monkmeyer Press Photo Service
page 463: Sybil Shelton, Monkmeyer Press Photo Service
page 469: Wasyl Szkodzinsky, Guidance Associates
page 474: Rohn Engh, Sunrise Photos
page 491: Eric Hobbs, Image, Inc.
page 493: E. Alan McGee
page 504: Les Mahon, Monkmeyer Press Photo Service
page 517: Freda Leinwand, Monkmeyer Press Photo Service
page 519: Joe Lippincott, Image, Inc.
page 522: Shostal Associates
page 538: Wasyl Szkodzinsky, Guidance Associates
page 543: Sybil Shelton, Monkmeyer Press Photo Service
page 546: Suzanne Szasz
page 550: Falk, Monkmeyer Press Photo Service
page 566: Ron Tunison, Guidance Associates
page 569: Guidance Associates
page 576: Sallie India Linebaugh, Image, Inc.
page 595: Christy Park, Monkmeyer Press Photo Service
page 602: Suzanne Szasz
page 609: Nancy Hays, Monkmeyer Press Photo Service
page 615: Ginger Chih
page 616: Nancy Hays, Monkmeyer Press Photo Service
page 618: David S. Strickler, Monkmeyer Press Photo Service

Index

A 9
B 0
C 1
D 2
E 3
F 4
G 5
H 6
I 7
J 8